THE
COMMON LAW
LIBRARY

CLERK & LINDSELL

ON

TORTS

Fourth Cumulative Supplement
to the
Seventeenth Edition

Up-to-date until July 1999

LONDON
SWEET & MAXWELL

2000

Published in 1999 by
Sweet & Maxwell Ltd of
100 Avenue Road, London NW3 3PF
(http://www.smlawpub.co.uk)
Computerset by Wyvern 21 Ltd,
Bristol
and Printed in Great Britain by
MPG Books, Bodmin, Cornwall

No natural products were destroyed to make this product;
only farmed timber was used and replanted.

ISBN Main Work 0 421 513 101
ISBN Fourth Cumulative Supplement 0 421 693 002

A catalogue record for this book is available from the British Library.

HOW TO USE THIS SUPPLEMENT

This is the Fourth Cumulative Supplement to the Seventeenth Edition of *Clerk and Lindsell on Torts*, and has been compiled according to the structure of the main volume.

A new **Appendix** has been included at p. 241 *et seq.*, containing the text of the Human Rights Act 1998 and Schedule 1—The Articles of the Convention.

At the beginning of each chapter of this Supplement the mini table of contents from the main volume has been included. Where a heading in this table of contents has been marked by the symbol ■, there is relevant information included in *this* Supplement to which you should refer. Where a heading has been marked by the symbol □, there is information under that heading which has been included in the *previous* Supplement.

Within each chapter, updating information is referenced to the relevant paragraph in the main volume.

Introductory paragraphs containing material pertinent to the chapter as a whole and not to a specific paragraph has been identified as *e.g.* 2a. This enables references contained within these paragraphs to be identified in the tables included in this Supplement.

NOTE

Although the Civil Procedure Rules 1998 introduced major changes in terminology in 1999, the editors have not incorporated these changes in this work, as it supplements the pre-Woolf 17th Edition. Full account will be taken of the new terminology in the 18th Edition, to be published in 2000.

TABLE OF CASES

PARA.

A v. United Kingdom (1999) 27 E.M.R.R. 611 .... 1–05C, 12–74
AB v. South West Water Services; *sub nom.* Gibbons v. South West Water
    Services [1993] Q.B. 507; [1993] 2 W.L.R. 507; [1993] 1 All E.R.
    609; [1993] P.I.Q.R. P167; [1992] N.P.C. 146; (1993) 143 N.L.J. 235;
    The Independent, November 18, 1992; *The Times*, November 26,
    1992, CA 27–69
——— v. Tameside and Glossop Health Authority [1997] P.N.L.R. 147;
    (1997) 35 B.M.L.R. 79; [1997] 8 Med. L.R. 91; (1996) 93 (44) L.S.G.
    30; *The Times*, November 27, 1996, CA . 7–53, 7–127, 7–135, 8–62
ADT v. BDO Binder Hamlyn, unreported, May J., December 6, 1995 8–126
AGDA Systems v. Valcom Ltd (1999) 168 D.L.R. (4th) 351 .... 23–23, 23–83
A.W.A. v. Daniels (1992) 9 A.C.S.R. 383 7–200
Abbott v. Strong [1998] 2 B.C.L.C. 420 8–126
Ahmed v. Saudi Arabia [1996] 2 All E.R. 248; [1996] I.C.R. 25, CA 4–25
Aiken v. Stewart Wrightson Members Agency [1995] 1 W.L.R. 1281;
    (1995) 3 All E.R. 449; [1995] 2 Lloyd's Rep. 618; *The Times*, March
    8, 1995, QBD 7–81, 7–85, 8–13
Airlie v. Edinburgh City D.C. [1996] I.R.L.R. 516, EAT 23–16
Akerhielm v. De Mare [1959] A.C. 789; [1959] 3 W.L.R. 108; 103 S.J.
    527; [1959] 3 All E.R. 485, PC 14–27
Al-Adsani v. Kuwait, *The Times*, March 29, 1996, CA; [1994] P.I.Q.R.
    236, CA 4–21
Al-Nakib Investment (Jersey) v. Longcroft [1990] 3 All E.R. 321; [1990]
    B.C.C. 517; [1991] B.C.L.C. 7; (1990) 140 New L.J. 741; *The Times*,
    May 4, 1990 7–65
Alcock v. Chief Constable of South Yorkshire Police; *sub nom.* Jones v.
    Wright [1992] 1 A.C. 310; [1991] 3 W.L.R. 1057; [1991] 4 All E.R.
    907; [1992] P.I.Q.R. P1; (1992) 136 S.J.L.B. 9; (1991) 141 N.L.J.
    166; [1992] *Gazette*, January 22, 34; *The Times*, November 29, 199;
    The Guardian, December 11, 1991, HL 1–05G, 7–43, 7–52, 7–110, 23–64
Aldred's Case (1610) 9 Co. Rep. 57b 18–10
Ali v. Christian Salvesen Food Services [1997] I.C.R. 25; [1997] I.R.L.R.
    17; (1996) 93(41) L.S.G. 29; (1996) 140 S.J.L.B. 231; *The Times*,
    October 29, 1996; *The Independent*, November 1, 1996, CA   23–16
Allason v. Campbell, *The Times*, May 8, 1996, QBD 21–03, 22–18
——— v. Haines [1996] E.M.L.R. 143; (1995) 145 N.L.J. Rep. 1576; *The
    Times*, July 25, 1995, QBD 21–01, 21–03, 21–97
Alliance & Leicester Building Society v. Edgestop; *sub nom.* Alliance &
    Leicester Building Society v. Hamptons; Same v. Dhanoa; Same v.
    Samva; Mercantile Credit Co. v. Lancaster LTA 94/5856/B, CA;
    affirming [1993] 1 W.L.R. 1462; [1994] 2 All E.R. 38; [1994]
    E.G.L.R. 229; [1993] N.P.C. 79; [1993] E.G.C.S. 93, ChD 23–37
Allied Maples Group v. Simmons & Simmons [1995] 1 W.L.R. 1602;
    [1995] 4 All E.R. 907; [1995] N.P.C. 83; (1995) 145 N.L.J. Rep. 1646,
    CA 2a, 2–09, 8a, 8–92, 27–07
Alphacell v. Woodward [1972] A.C. 824; [1972] 2 W.L.R. 1320; 116 S.J.
    431; [1972] 2 All E.R. 475; 70 L.G.R. 455; [1972] Crim. L.R. 41,
    HL 18–74
Ancell & Ancell v. McDermott [1993] 4 All E.R. 355; [1994] J.P.I.L. 78;
    [1993] R.T.R. 235; (1994) 6 Admin. L.R. 473; (1995) 159 L.G. Rev.
    389; (1993) 90(11) L.S. Gaz. 46; (1993) 143 N.L.J. Rep. 363; (1993)

S.J.L.B. 36; *The Times*, February 4, 1993; *The Independent*, February
18, 1993, CA 7–110
Anderson v. Pringle of Scotland [1998] I.R.L.R. 64, Ct. S 23–16, 23–18
Andrews v. Grand & Toy Alberta (1978) 83 D.L.R. (3d) 452 27–21
Anthony v. Wright [1995] 1 B.C.L.C. 236; [1995] B.C.C. 768; *The Inde-
pendent*, September 27, 1994, Ch.D. 8–12, 8–126
Apotex Fermentation Inc. v. Novopharm (1998) 126 D.L.R. (4th) 111,
Man. CA 23–23, 23–61, 23–70
Appleton v. Garrett [1997] 8 Med. L.R. 75; [1996] P.I.Q.R. P1; (1997) 34
B.M.L.R. 23, QBD 8–28, 27–66
Arab Monetary Fund v. Hashim (No. 11) [1996] 1 Lloyd's Rep. 589 31–03
Arab Republic of Egypt v. Gamal-Eldin [1996] I.C.R. 13, EAT 4–25
Arbuthnot Latham Bank v. Trafalgar Holdings [1998] 2 All E.R. 181, CA 31–32
Armitage v. Nurse [1998] Ch. 241; [1997] 3 W.L.R. 1046; [1997] 2 All
E.R. 705; (1997) 74 P. & C.R. D13; *The Times*, March 31, 1997; *The
Independent*, April 11, 1997, CA; affirming [1995] N.P.C. 110, *The
Independent*, July 3, 1995 (C.S.), ChD 23–62
Armory v. Delamirie 13–134
Armstrong v. British Coal Corporation, *The Times*, December 6, 1996,
CA 7–172
Arthur v. Anker [1997] Q.B. 564; [1996] 2 W.L.R. 602; [1996] 3 All E.R.
783; (1996) 72 P. & C.R. 309; [1996] R.T.R. 308; (1996) 146 N.L.J.
Rep. 86; [1995] N.P.C. 187; *The Times*, December 1, 1995; *The Inde-
pendent*, December 7, 1995, CA 3a, 3–33,
3–34, 10–82, 17a, 17–35, 29–29, 29–33
Askin v. Absa Bank Ltd, *The Times*, February 23, 1999, CA 6–02
Aslan v. Murphy ((No. 1) and (No. 2)); Wynne v. Duke [1990] 1 W.L.R.
766 17–17
Aspro Travel v. Owners Abroad plc [1996] 1 W.L.R. 132; [1995] 4 All
E.R. 728; [1995] E.M.L.R. 501; *The Times*, July 11, 1995; *The Independent*, July 20, 1995, CA 21–14, 21–22, 21–45,
21–50, 21–55, 21–76, 21–117
Associated British Ports v. Transport and General Workers' Union [1989]
1 W.L.R. 939; (1989) 133 S.J. 1200; [1989] 3 All E.R. 822; [1989] 1
C.R. 557; [1989] I.R.L.R. 399, HL 23–04, 23–08, 23–23,
23–41, 23–48, 23–62, 23–66, 23–67, 23–82, 23–83
Associated Provincial Picture Houses v. Wednesbury Corporation [1948]
1 K.B. 223; [1948] L.J.R. 190; 177 L.T. 641; 63 T.L.R. 623; 112 J.P.
55; 92 S.J. 26; [1947] 2 All E.R. 680; 45 L.G.R. 635, CA 7–110
Athey v. Leonati [1997] 1 W.W.R. 97 2–07
Att.-Gen. v. Blake [1997] Ch. 84; [1996] 3 W.L.R. 741; [1996] 3 All E.R.
903; [1996] F.S.R. 727; [1996] E.M.L.R. 382; (1996) 19(7) I.P.D. 13;
The Times, April 23, 1996, ChD 23–44
—— v. Butterworth. *See* Att.-Gen.'s Application, Re
—— v. Guardian Newspapers Ltd (No. 2) [1990] A.C. 109, HL 1–05B
—— v. Prince & Gardner [1998] 1 N.Z.L.R. 262 7–106
Att.-Gen.'s Application, Re, Att.-Gen. v. Butterworth [1963] 1 Q.B. 696;
L.R. 3 R.P. 327; [1962] 3 W.L.R. 879; 106 S.J. 610; [1962] 3 All E.R.
326, CA 23–59
Atwell v. Michael Perry [1998] 4 All E.R. 65; [1998] P.N.L.R. 711; *The
Times*, July 27, 1998 8–69
Autospin (Oil Seals) v. Beehive Spinning [1965] R.P.C. 683; *The Times*,
August 9, 1995, ChD 24–07, 24–12
Awa v. Independent News Auckland [1995] 3 N.Z.L.R. 701 21–13

B v. Arkin (1996) 138 D.L.R. (4th) 309 7–148
B v. Croydon Health Authority; *sub nom.* LB v. Croydon Health Authority
[1995] Fam. 133; [1995] 1 All E.R. 683; [1995] 2 W.L.R. 294; [1995]

1 F.L.R. 470; [1995] 1 F.C.R. 662; [1995] P.I.Q.R. P145; [1995] Fam.
Law 244; (1994) N.L.J. Rep. 1696; *The Times*, December 1, 1994;
The Independent, November 30, 1994, CA; affirming [1995] 1 F.C.R.
332, QBD 8–32
Bank of Credit and Commerce International v. Price Waterhouse (No. 3) *The
Times*, April 2, 1998 .... 7–196, 8–130
BSOIW Local 97 v. Campbell (1997) 152 D.L.R. 4th 547 21–117
Baigent v. McCullough, 1997 Rep. L.R. 107; 1997 G.W.D. 16–73H, OH . 21–117
Baker v. Kaye [1997] I.R.L.R. 219 (1997) 39 B.M.L.R. 12; *The Times*,
December 13, 1996, QBD 8–13
Baltic Shipping Co. v. Translink Shipping [1995] 1 Lloyd's Rep. 673,
QBD .... 28–28—28–34
Banco Exterior Internacional SA v. Thomas [1997] 1 W.L.R. 221; [1997]
1 All E.R. 46; [1997] 1 F.L.R. 703; [1997] 2 F.C.R. 429; [1997] Fam.
Law 326, CA 23–42
Bank of Credit and Commerce International (Overseas) Ltd (in
Liquidation) v. Price Waterhouse (No. 1) [1997] 4 All E.R. 108,
ChD 4–24
Bank of Credit and Commerce International (Overseas) Ltd (in
Liquidation) v. Price Waterhouse (No. 2) [1998] P.N.L.R. 564; *The
Times*, March 4, 1998 .... 6–64, 7–64, 7–66, 8–126
Bank of New Zealand v. Greenwood [1984] 1 N.Z.L.R. 525 18–07
Bank of Scotland v. Edwards (1995) 44 Con.L.R. 77 8–92
Banque Bruxelles Lambert SA v. Eagle Star Insurance Co. [1997] A.C.
191; [1996] 3 W.L.R. 87, HL; [1995] Q.B. 375; [1995] 2 W.L.R. 607;
[1995] 2 All E.R. 769; 73 B.L.R. 47; [1995] 12 E.G. 144; (1995) 145
N.L.J. Rep. 343; (1995) 139 S.J.L.B. 56; (1995) 92 (12) L.S. Gaz. 34;
[1995] N.P.C. 32; [1995] E.G.C.S. 31; *The Times*, February 21, 1995;
The Independent, February 24, 1995; CA; reversing in part 68 B.L.R.
39; [1994] 31 E.G. 68; [1994] 32 E.G. 89; *The Times*, March 7, 1994;
The Independent, April 4, 1994 (C.S.), QBD 1–08, 2a, 2–21, 7–189,
7–196, 8–113, 8–114, 31–09
Banque Bruxelles Lambert v. John D. Wood [1996] P.N.L.R. 380 8–110
Banque Financière de la Cité v. Park (Battersea) [1999] 1 A.C. 221,
HL 23–08
—— v. Westgate Insurance Co. [1998] 2 W.L.R. 475, HL 7–196, 23–08
Banque Keyser Ullmann S.A. v. Skandia (U.K.) Insurance Co. *See* Banque
Financière de la Cité S.A. v. Westgate Insurance Co.
Barclays Bank v. Fairclough Building Co. (No. 2) [1995] I.R.L.R. 605; 44
Con.L.R. 35; [1995] E.G.C.S. 10; *The Times*, February 15, 1995; *The
Independent*, February 20, 1995 (C.S.), CA; 39 Con.L.R. 144; [1994]
E.G.C.S. 141, QBD 1–08, 3–20, 8–117
—— v. RBS Advanta [1996] R.P.C. 307; (1996) 15 Tr.L.R. 262; (1996)
19(3) I.P.D. 18; *The Times*, February 8, 1996, ChD 24–71
—— v. Weeks Legg & Dean; *sub nom.* Barclays Bank plc v. Dean; Barclays Bank plc v. Layton Lougher & Co; Mohamed v. Fahiya; Barclays Bank plc v. NE Hopkin John & Co.; Mohamed v. Farida [1998]
3 W.L.R. 656; [1998] 3 All E.R. 213; [1998] P.N.L.R. 729; [1998] 3
E.G.L.R. 103; [1998] 40 E.G. 182; (1998) 76 P. & C.R. D27; (1998)
95(21) L.S.G. 38; (1998) 95(25) L.S.G. 33; [1998] N.P.C. 89; (1998)
142 S.J.L.B. 180; *The Times*, June 15, 1998; *The Independent*, June 3,
1998, CA 8–84
Barex Brothers v. Morris [1999] P.N.L.R. 344 8–98
Barings plc v. Coopers & Lybrand (A firm); [1997] 1 B.C.L.C. 427; [1997]
B.C.C. 498; [1997] P.N.L.R. 179; *The Times*, December 6, 1996; *The
Independent*, January 13, 1997 (C.S.), CA, affirming (1996) 93(39)
L.S.G. 27; (1996) 140 S.J.L.B. 210; *The Times*, August 13, 1996,
ChD 7a, 7–66, 8–130

Barrett v. Enfield London Borough Council [1998] Q.B. 367; [1997] 3
    W.L.R. 628; [1997] 3 All E.R. 171; [1997] 2 F.L.R. 167; [1997] 3
    F.C.R. 145; (1997) 37 B.M.L.R. 16; [1997] Fam. Law 534; *The Times*,
    April 27, 1997, CA 1–05G, 7A, 7–106, 7–107, 8–61, 11–14
Barrett v. Ministry of Defence [1995] 1 W.L.R. 1217; [1995] 3 All E.R.
    87; *The Times*, January 13, 1995; *The Independent*, January 3, 1995;
    The Guardian, December 24, 1994, CA 3–22, 7–30
Barrow v. Bankside Agency [1996] 1 W.L.R. 257; [1996] 1 All E.R. 981;
    [1996] 1 Lloyd's Rep. 278; [1996] 5 Rep. L.R. 1; [1996] C.L.C. 413;
    The Times, November 10, 1995, CA 30–25
Barrymore v. News Group Newspapers [1997] F.S.R. 600, ChD 26–07
Barton v. Armstrong [1969] 2 N.S.W.R. 451 .... 23–42A
Bateman v. Owen White [1996] P.N.L.R. 1, CA 8–70
Baxter v. Camden London Borough Council [1999] 1 All E.R. 237; [1997]
    E.G.C.S. 102; [1997] N.P.C. 97, CA 18–01, 18–09,
                                                                        18–51, 18–54, 18–67
Bayoumi v. Protim Services (1998) 30 H.L.R. 785; [1997] P.N.L.R. 189;
    [1996] E.G.C.S. 187, CA 8–123
Beaudesert Shire Council v. Smith (1996) 120 C.L.R. 145 .... 23–43, 23–60,
                                                                        23–62, 23–71, 23–81
Belmont Finance Corp. v. Williams Furniture (No. 2) [1980] 1 All E.R.
    393, CA 23–23
Bellefield Computer Services Ltd v. Turner & Sons Ltd, July 22,
    1999 .... 8–117, 9–19
Bennett v. Commissioner of Police of the Metropolis [1995] 1 W.L.R. 488;
    [1995] 2 All E.R. 1; *The Times*, December 28, 1994, *The Times*,
    October 24, 1997, ChD 16–137, 23–08, 23–61
—— v. Greenland Houchen & Co. [1998] P.N.L.R. 458, CA 31–23
—— v. Guardian Newspapers [1997] E.M.L.R. 625; *The Times*, December
    28, 1995, QBD 21–18, 21–182
Berezovsky v. Forbes Inc.; Glouchkov v. Forbes *The Times*, November 27,
    1998, CA 6–02
Berkoff v. Burchill [1996] 4 All E.R. 1008; [1997] E.M.L.R. 139; *The
    Times*, August 9, 1996 .... 21–12, 21–13, 21–14, 21–17, 21–55
Bermuda Cablevision v. Colica Trust [1997] I.R.L.R. 346; [1997] B.C.C.
    982, PC 23–44
Berry Taylor (a firm) v. Coleman & Another [1997] P.N.L.R. 1 7–75
Berryman v. Hounslow London Borough Council [1997] P.I.Q.R. P83; *The
    Times*, December 18, 1996, CA 10–28
Best v. Wellcome Foundation [1994] 5 Med L.R. 81, HC; [1993] 3 I.R.
    421 .... 9–22, 9–26, 9–54
Bestobell Paints v. Bigg (1975) 119 S.J. 678; [1975] F.S.R. 421 22–06
Betts v. Brintel Helicopters [1997] 2 All E.R. 840; [1997] I.C.R. 792;
    [1997] I.R.L.R. 361; (1997) 147 N.L.J. 561; *The Times*, April 1, 1997,
    CA 23–130
Bhatt v. Chelsea and Westminster Health Care Trust [1997] I.R.L.R. 660;
    [1998] C.L.Y. 172; *The Times*, October 24, 1997, EAT 21–131
Biggar v. McLeod [1977] 1 N.Z.L.R. 321 8–69
Biogen Inc. v. Medeva plc [1997] R.P.C. 1; (1997) 38 B.M.L.R. 149;
    (1997) 20(1) I.P.D. 20001; *The Times*, November 1, 1996, HL 24–84
Biotrading & Financing OY v. Biohit Ltd [1998] F.S.R. 109; (1997) 20(12)
    I.P.D. 20125, CA 24–20
Bird v. Hadkinson, *The Times*, April 7, 1999 28–28
Birkett v. James [1978] A.C. 297; [1977] 3 W.L.R. 38; [1977] 121 S.J.
    444; [1977] 2 All E.R. 807, HL 31–32
Birmingham Midshires Building Society v. Phillips [1998] P.N.L.R. 468 .. 8–113
Birse Construction v. Haiste Ltd [1996] 1 W.L.R. 675; [1996] 2 All E.R.
    1; 47 Con.L.R. 162; 76 B.L.R. 31; [1996] P.N.L.R. 8; [1996] C.L.C.

577; (1996) 93(2) L.S.G. 29; (1996) 140 S.J.L.B. 25, *The Times*, December 12, 1995, CA; reversing 44 Con.L.R. 17, QBD 4a, 4–61, 8–117
Blackpool and The Fylde College v. National Association of Teachers in Further and Higher Education [1994] I.C.R. 648; [1994] I.R.L.R. 227; *The Times*, March 23, 1994; *The Independent*, April 18, 1994 (C.S.), CA 23–112
Blackwell v. Barroile (1994) 123 A.L.R. 81 7–81
Blake & Brooks v. Barking & Dagenham L.B. [1999] P.N.L.R. 171 7–105
Blue Circle v. Ministry of Defence [1999] 2 W.L.R. 295; [1998] 3 All E.R. 385; [1998] E.G.C.S. 93; [1998] N.P.C. 100; [1999] Env. L.R. 22; *The Times*, June 16, 1998, CA; [1997] Env.L.R. 341; [1996] E.G.C.S. 190; [1996] N.P.C. 170; (1997) 94(2) L.S.G. 25; (1997) 141 S.J.L.B. 11; *The Times*, December 11, 1996, ChD 9–18, 11–12, 19–93, 23–44, 23–68
Boddington v. British Transport Police [1998] 2 W.L.R. 639; [1998] 2 All E.R. 203; (1998) 162 J.P. 455; (1998) 10 Admin. L.R. 321; (1998) 148 N.L.J. 515; *The Times*, April 3, 1998, HL 23–44, 23–64, 23–71
Bogajewicz v. Sony of Canada (1996) 128 D.L.R. (4th) 530 (Queb. S.C.) . 23–61
Bolam v. Friern Hospital Management Committee [1957] 1 W.L.R. 582; 101 S.J. 357; [1957] 2 All E.R. 118 .... 2–10, 8a, 8–34, 8–73
Boldack v. East Lindsey D.C. (1999) 31 H.L.R. 41 .... 10a, 10–64, 10–66, 10–67
Bolitho v. City and Hackney Health Authority [1997] 3 W.L.R. 1151 [1997] 4 All E.R. 771; (1997) 94 (47) L.S.G. 30; (1997) 141 S.J.L.B. 238; *The Times*, November 27, 1997, HL affirming [1993] P.I.Q.R. P334; [1993] 4 Med.L.R. 381, CA 2–03, 2–10, 7–135, 8a, 8–34, 8–35
Bolkiah (Prince Jefri) v. KPMG [1999] 1 W.L.R. 215; [1999] 1 All E.R. 517; [1999] P.N.L.R. 220; [1999] 2 C.L. 1 8–85
Boma Mfg Co. v. Canadian Imperial Bank of Commerce (1997) 140 D.L.R. (4th) 463 13–156
Bone v. Seale [1975] 1 W.L.R. 797; (1974) 119 S.J. 137; [1975] 1 All E.R. 787, CA 18–19
Bonnard v. Perryman [1891] 2 Ch. 269; [1891–4] All E.R. Rep. 965 21–232
Boulting v. Association of Cinematograph, Television and Allied Technicians [1963] 2 Q.B. 606; [1963] 2 W.L.R. 529; 107 S.J. 133; [1963] 1 All E.R. 716, CA 23–43
Bow Valley Husky v. Saint John Shipbuilding [1997] 3 S.C.R. 1210; (1995) 126 D.L.R. (4th) 1 .... 7–59, 9–18, 9–23
Bradburn v. Gt Western Ry (1874) L.R. 10 Ex. 1 8–92
Bradley v. Eagle Star Insurance Co. [1989] A.C. 957; [1989] 2 W.L.R. 568; [1989] 1 All E.R. 961; [1989] I.C.R. 301; (1989) 133 S.J. 359; [1989] 1 Lloyd's Rep. 465; [1989] B.C.L.C. 469; (1989) 138 New L.J. 330; 1989 Fin.L.R. 253; (1989) L.S.Gaz. May 3, 38, HL; affirming [1988] Fin.L.R. 238; [1988] 2 Lloyd's Rep. 233 4–31
Brain v. Ingledew Brown Bennison & Garrett [1996] F.S.R. 341; (1996) 19(5) I.P.D. 5, CA; [1995] F.S.R. 552; *The Independent*, April 18, 1995 (C.S.), ChD 22–05
—— v. —— (No. 3) [1997] F.S.R. 511; (1997) 20(5) I.P.D. 20047, ChD . 22–05
Brandeis Goldschmidt & Co. v. Western Transport [1981] Q.B. 864; [1987] 3 W.L.R. 187; (1987) 125 S.J. 395; [1982] 1 All E.R. 28; [1980] F.S.R. 487, CA 13–122
Brasserie du Pecheur v. Germany (C-46/93); R. v. Secretary of State for Transport, ex p. Factortame Ltd (No. 4) (C48/93) [1996] Q.B. 404; [1996] 2 W.L.R. 506; [1996] All E.R.(E.C.) 301; [1996] 1 E.C.R. 1029; [1996] 1 C.M.L.R. 889; [1996] I.R.L.R. 267; [1996] C.E.C. 295, ECJ 1–03, 23–71
Brindle v. Commissioner of Police for the Metropolis, June 5, 1998 (unreported) 1–05G

Bridlington Relay v. Yorkshire Electricity Board [1965] Ch. 436; [1965] 2
    W.L.R. 349; [1965] 1 All E.R. 264; 109 S.J. 12 18–10
Brinks v. Abu-Saleh (No. 3); [1996] C.L.C. 133; (1996) 60 Conv. 447; *The
    Times*, October 23, 1995, ChD 23–30, 23–62, 23–80
Briscoe v. Shattock [1999] 1 W.L.R. 432; *The Times*, October 12, 1998 ... 20–09
Bristol Myers Squibb v. Paranova (Cases C–427/93, C–429/93 and C–436/
    93) [1997] F.S.R. 102 24–71
Bristol & West Building Society v. Baden Barnes Groves & Co., Nov-
    ember 22, 1996 (unreported) 8–85
—— v. Fancy & Jackson [1997] 4 All E.R. 582; [1997] N.P.C. 109,
    ChD 8–85
—— v. —— (No. 2) [1997] 3 All E.R. 206; [1996] N.P.C. 31, ChD 8–92, 8–112
—— v. Mothew [1997] 2 W.L.R. 436; [1996] 4 All E.R. 698; [1997]
    P.N.L.R. 11; [1996] E.G.C.S. 136; [1996] N.P.C. 126; (1996) 146
    N.L.J. 1273; (1996) 140 S.J.L.B. 206; *The Times*, August 2, 1996,
    CA 2–21, 8–113
British Columbia v. H.B.T. Agra (1994) 120 D.L.R. (4th) 726 .... 7–66, 7–67
British Data Management plc v. Boxer Commercial Removals plc [1996]
    3 All E.R. 707; [1996] E.M.L.R. 349; *The Times*, February 28, 1996,
    CA 21–232
British Racing Drivers' Club v. Hextall Erskine [1996] 3 All E.R.
    667; [1997] 1 B.C.L.C. 182; [1996] B.C.C. 727; [1996] P.N.L.R. 523,
    ChD 8–92, 27–63
British Railways Board v. Herrington [1972] A.C. 877; [1972] 2 W.L.R.
    537; 116 S.J. 178; [1972] 1 All E.R. 749, HL; affirming *sub nom.*
    Herrington v. British Railways Board [1971] 2 Q.B. 107; [1971] 2
    W.L.R. 477; (1970) 114 S.J. 954; [1971] 1 All E.R. 897, CA; affirming
    (1970) 214 E.G. 561 7–130
—— v. National Union of Railwaymen [1989] I.C.R. 678; [1989] I.R.L.R.
    349, CA 23–114
British Sugar plc v. James Robertson & Son [1966] R.P.C. 281 ...... 24–62, 24–70
British Telecommunications plc v. One in a Million [1998] 4 All E.R. 476;
    [1998] Info. T.L.R. 423; [1998] I.T.C.L.R. 146; [1998] Masons C.L.R. 165;
    (1998) 95(37) L.S.G. 37; (1998) 148 L.N.J. 1179; *The Times*, July 29, 1998;
    The Independent, July 31, 1998, CA 23–04, 23–29, 23–44,
                                      23–79, 23–83, 24–70, 25–09
British Telecommunications plc v. Thomson (James) & Sons [1999] 2 All
    E.R. 241; 1997 S.C. 59; 1997 S.L.T. 767; 1997 S.C.L.R. 228; [1997]
    Re L.R. 325; 82 B.L.R. 1; 54 Con.L.R. 108; 1997 Rep. L.R. 23; (1997)
    13 Const. L.J. 332; 1997; G.W.D. 3–77; *The Times*, January 28, 1997,
    OH 7–87
Brooks v. Lind, *The Times*, March 26, 1997, OH 21–204
Brown v. Bennett, *The Times*, January 3, 1998, ChD 23–03, 23–23, 23–43, 23–62
—— v. British Columbia (1994) 112 D.L.R. (4th) 1 7–100
—— v. Durham Regional Police Force (1996) 134 D.L.R. (4th)
    174 .... 23–59, 23–60
—— v. Gould & Swayne [1996] P.N.L.R. 130, CA 7–135, 8–80
—— v. KMR Services; Sword-Daniels v. Pitel [1995] 4 All E.R. 598;
    [1995] 4 All 2 Lloyd's Rep. 2; Lloyd's Rep. 1, *The Times*, July 26,
    1995; *The Independent*, September 13, 1995; *Lloyd's List*, October 3,
    1995 (I.D.), CA; affirming [1994] 4 All E.R. 385; *The Independent*,
    April 19, 1994; *The Guardian*, April 22, 1994, QBD 7–196
—— v. Merchant Ferries [1998] I.R.L.R. 682, N.I.C.A. 23–34
—— v. University of Alberta Hospital (1997) 145 D.L.R. (4th) 63 ..... 8–12, 8–45
Brownie Wills v. Shrimpton [1999] Lloyd's Rep. P.N. 7–64
Brugger v. Medicaid [1996] F.S.R. 362; [1996] R.P.C. 635; (1996) 19 (4)
    I.P.D. 2, Pat Ct 24–29, 24–90
Bruton v. London & Quadrant Housing Trust [1997] 4 All E.R. 970; [1997]

2 E.G.L.R. 91; [1997] 50 E.G. 87; [1997] N.P.C. 124; (1997) 147
N.L.J. 1385; [1997] E.G.C.S. 125; *The Times*, August 14, 1997, CA .. 17–17
Bryan v. Phillips New Zealand [1995] 1 N.Z.L.R. 632 .... 7–53, 27–22
Buchan and Ivey v. Secretary of State for Employment [1997] I.R.L.R. 80;
    [1997] B.C.C. 145, EAT 5–03
Buckingham v. R.J. Reynolds 731 A 2d 381 (1998) 9–42
Buckley v. Farrow & Buckley [1997] P.I.Q.R. Q78 7–43
Buehler A.G. v. Chrones Richardson Ltd [1998] 2 All E.R. 960, CA 30–25
Bull v. Chief Constable of Sussex (1995) 159 L.G.Rev. 893, CA 12–49
Burgess v. Auger [1998] 2 B.C.L.C. 478 8–133
Burke v. Royal Liverpool University Hospital NHS Trust [1997] I.C.R.
    730 23–16
Burnett v. George [1992] 1 F.L.R. 525; [1992] Fam. Law. 156; [1993] 1
    F.C.R. 1012, CA 23–42A
Burns v. General Accident Fire and Life Assurance Corp. plc, *The Times*,
    January 12, 1999, CA 4–31
Burris v. Azadani [1995] 1 W.L.R. 1372; [1995] 4 All E.R. 802; [1996] 1
    F.L.R. 266; [1996] 1 F.C.R. 618; [1996] Fam. Law 145; (1995) 145
    N.L.J.Rep. 1330; *The Times*, August 9, 1995, CA 1–03, 1–20, 12–16,
                                                23–42A, 28–02, 28–13—28–20
Bussey v. Icon Entertainment plc [1995] E.M.L.R. 596 24–41
Byrne v. Hall Pain & Foster [1999] 2 All E.R. 400; *The Times*, January 8,
    1999 31–09

C (Adult Patient) (Access: Jurisdiction), Re [1994] 1 F.C.R. 705, Fam.
    Div. 1–03, 1–19, 1–24
—— v. Mirror Newspapers [1997] 1 W.L.R. 131; [1996] 4 All E.R. 511;
    [1996] 2 F.L.R. 532; [1997] 1 F.C.R. 556; [1996] E.M.L.R. 518;
    [1996] Fam. Law 671; (1996) 146 N.L.J. Rep. 1093; *The Times*, July
    15, 1996; *The Independent*, July 19, 1996, CA 21–05, 31–43
—— (A Minor) v. Hackney London Borough Council [1996] 1 W.L.R.
    789, CA; [1995] 2 F.L.R. 681; [1995] 2 F.C.R. 306; [1996] Fam. Law.
    23; *The Times*, November 10, 1995; *The Independent*, November 16,
    1995, CA 30–20, 30–25
C.B.C. v. Color Your World Corp., (1998) 156 D.L.R. (4th) 27 21–13
CES v. Superclinics (Aust) pty [1995] 38 N.S.W.L.R. 47 7–20
CUI-Centres for Medical Innovation GmbH v. Phytopharm plc [1999]
    F.S.R. 235 .... 26–10, 26–20
C.P.R. v. Aikins [1998] 6 W.W.R. 351 8–85
Cable and Wireless plc v. British Telecommunications plc [1998] F.S.R.
    383; (1998) 21(4) I.P.D. 21042 .... 22–19, 24–71
Cala Homes (South) v. Alfred McAlpine Homes East [1995] F.S.R. 818,
    Ch.D 24–13
—— v. —— (No. 2) [1996] F.S.R. 36 27–67
Calascoine v. Dixon (1993) 19 B.M.L.R. 97 7–43
Cambridge Water Co. v. Eastern Counties Leather; Same v. Hutchings and
    Harding [1994] 2 A.C. 264; [1994] 2 W.L.R. 53; [1994] 1 All E.R.
    53; [1994] 1 Lloyd's Rep. 261; [1994] Env.L.R. 105; (1994) 138
    S.J.(LB) 24; [1993] E.G.C.S. 211; (1994) 144 N.L.J. 15; *The Times*,
    December 10, 1993; *The Independent*, December 10, 1993, HL 19–16
Camdex International v. Bank of Zambia [1998] Q.B. 22; *The Times*, April
    3, 1996, CA 4–42
—— v. —— (No. 2) [1997] 1 W.L.R. 632; [1997] 1 All E.R. 728; [1996]
    5 Bank. L.R. 336; [1996] C.L.C. 1945, CA .... 28–28 to 28–34
Camelot Group plc v. Centaur Communications [1998] 2 W.L.R. 379;
    [1998] 1 All E.R. 251; [1998] I.R.L.R. 80; [1998] E.M.L.R. 1; (1997)
    147 N.L.J. 1618; (1997) 94(43) L.S.G. 30; (1998) 142 S.J.L.B. 19;

The Times, October 30, 1997; *The Independent*, October 28, 1997,
CA 23–01
Campbell v. NI Housing Executive [1996] 1 B.N.I.L. 99 .... 10a, 10–24
Campbell v. Teachers' Retirement Fund (1993) 110 D.L.R. (4th) 400 7–71
Canada (Human Rights Commission) v. Canadian Liberty Net (1998) 157
D.L.R. (4th) 385, SCC; (1996) 132 D.L.R. (4th) 95, FCA 23–42A
Canadian Egg Marketing Agency v. Richardson (1996) 166 D.L.R. (4th) 1
(SCC) 23–01
Cancer Research Campaign v. Ernest Brown [1997] S.T.C. 1425; [1998]
P.N.L.R. 592 .... 7–82, 8–77
Candler v. Thomas (t/a London Leisure Lines) [1998] R.T.R. 214, CA
Canon Kabushiki Kaisha v. Metro-Goldwyn-Mayer Inc. (C-39/97) [1998]
All E.R. (E.C.) 934; [1998] E.S.R. 332; [1998] C.E.C. 920; *The Times*,
October 10, 1998, ECJ 24–70
Caparo Industries v. Dickman [1990] 2 A.C. 605; [1990] 2 W.L.R. 358;
[1990] 1 All E.R. 568; (1990) 134 S.J. 494; [1990] B.C.C. 164; [1990]
B.C.L.C. 273; [1990] E.C.C. 313; (1990) L.S.Gaz. March 28, 42;
[(1990) L.S.Gaz. September 26, 28; [1991] J.B.L. 36]; (1990) 140
New L.J. 248, HL; reversing [1989] Q.B. 653; [1989] 2 W.L.R. 316;
(1989) 133 S.J. 221; [1989] 1 All E.R. 798; (1989) 5 B.C.C. 105;
[1989] B.C.L.C. 154; 1989 P.C.C. 125, CA; reversing in part 7–63, 7–64,
7–66, 7–96, 8–126
Capital and Counties plc v. Hampshire County Council [1997] Q.B. 1004;
[1997] 3 W.L.R. 331; [1997] 2 All E.R. 865; [1997] 2 Lloyd's Rep.
161; (1997) 147 N.L.J. 599; (1997) 141 S.J.L.B. 92; *The Times*, March
20, 1997; *The Independent*, April 10, 1997, CA; affirming [1996] 1
W.L.R. 1553, [1996] 4 All E.R. 336; (1997) 147 New L.J. 599; *The
Times*, March 20, 1997; *The Times*, April 26, 1996, QBD .. 1–05G, 7a, 7–32,
7–103, 7–109, 7–110, 11–14
Carlile v. Council of Shire of Kilkivian and Briet Kreutz, (1997) 10
A.J.L.L. 229 .... 23–42A
Carlson v. Rio Tinto plc [1999] C.L.C. 551 6–02
Carmichael v. National Power plc [1998] I.R.L.R. 301, CA 5–03
Carr-Glynn v. Frearsons (A firm) [1998] 4 All E.R. 225; [1998] 3 F.C.R.
487; [1998] Fam. Law 739; [1998] N.P.C. 136; [1998] E.G.C.S. 128;
(1998) 148 N.L.J. 1487, CA; [1997] 2 All E.R. 614; [1997] P.N.L.R.
343 .... 7a, 7–82, 8–77, 8–92
Carroll v. Fearon, [1998] P.I.Q.R. P416, *The Times*, January 26, 1998,
CA 7–175, 9a, 9–01, 9–21, 9–23
Carson v. John Fairfax & Sons (1993) 113 A.L.R. 577; (1993) 178 C.L.R.
44 .... 21–203, 27–74
Cassidy v. City of Manchester, July 21, 1995 (unreported), CA 7–149
Cassin v. Bexley London Borough Council, *The Times*, February 15, 1999,
CA 7–147
Cavalier v. Pope [1906] A.C. 428 10–64
Cavendish Funding v. Henry Spencer & Sons [1998] P.N.L.R. 122 8–114
Cavity Trays v. RMC Panel Products [1996] R.P.C. 361; *The Times*, Febru-
ary 10, 1996, CA 24–97
Central London Commercial Estates Ltd [1998] 4 All E.R. 948; [1998] 3
E.G.L.R. 55; [1998] 46 E.G. 185; [1998] E.G.C.S. 117; (1998) 95(37)
L.S.G. 37; (1998) 95(29) L.S.G. 28; (1998) 142 S.J.L.B. 252; [1998]
N.P.C. 125; *The Times*, July 27, 1998 17–81
Chadha v. Dow Jones & Co., *The Times*, May 18, 1999 6–02
Chakravarti v. Advertiser Newspapers (1998) 72 A.L.J.R. 1115–1116 21–42
Chaplin v. Boys [1971] A.C. 356; [1969] 3 W.L.R. 322; 113 s.J. 608;
[1969] 2 All E.R. 1085, HL 6–07
—— v. Hicks [1911] 2 K.B. 786; 80 L.J.K.B. 1292; 105 L.T. 285; 27
T.L.R. 458; 55 S.J. 580, CA 2–09

Chapman v. Barclays Bank [1998] P.N.L.R. 14, CA 7–82
—— v. Barking and Dagenham L.B.C. [1997] 2 E.G.L.R. 141; [1997] 48
E.G. 154; [1997] N.P.C. 82, QBD... 18–60
—— v. Ellesmere (Lord) [1932] 2 K.B. 431 21–119
—— v. Honig [1963] 2 Q.B. 502; [1963] 3 W.L.R. 19; 107 S.J. 374;
[1963] 2 All E.R. 513, CA 23–59
Chappell v. Hart [1998] H.C.A. 55; (1998) 156 A.L.R. 517, H.C. of Aus-
tralia 2–10
Charleston News Group Newspapers [1995] 2 A.C. 65; [1995] 2 W.L.R.
450; [1995] 2 All E.R. 313; [1995] 3 E.M.L.R. 129; (1995) 145
N.L.J.Rep. 490; (1995) 139 S.J.L.B. 100; *The Times*, March 31, 1995;
The Independent, March 31, 1995, HL; affirming [1994] E.M.L.R.
186; *The Times*, January 12, 1994; *The Independent*, January 14, 1994;
The Guardian, February 26, 1994, CA 21–43
Chatterton v. Gerson [1981] Q.B. 432; [1980] 3 W.L.R. 1003; (1980) 124
S.J. 885; [1981] 1 All E.R. 257 8–28
Cheticamp Fisheries Co-op v. Canada (1995) 123 D.L.R. (4th) 121
(NSCA) 23–08, 23–10, 23–38, 23–43, 23–56
Chiron Corp. v. Murex Diagnostics (No. 12) [1996] F.S.R. 153; [1996]
R.P.C. 588; (1997) 37 B.M.L.R. 28; (1996) 19(3) I.P.D. 2, CA 24–83,
24–92
Chocosuisse Union des Fabricants Suisses de Chocolat v. Cadbury Ltd,
The Times, March 15, 1999, CA 25–01
Christensen v. Scott [1996] 1 N.Z.L.R. 273 .... 7–57, 7–65, 7–87, 8–126
Christie v. Wilson [1998] 1 W.L.R. 1694; [1998] P.N.L.R. 748; (1998)
95(30) L.S.G. 25; (1998) 142 S.J.L.B. 205; *The Times*, July 6, 1998,
The Independent, June 22, 1998 (C.S.), CA 8–85
Chung Ping Kwan v. Lam Island Development Co. [1997] A.C. 38; [1996]
3 W.L.R. 448; [1996] N.P.C. 115; (1996) 140 S.J.L.B.; *The Times*,
July 16, 1996, PC 17–74
Ciarlariello v. Schacter [1994] 5 Med.L.R. 213, Sup. Ct. Canada 8–37
Citadel General Assurance v. Lloyds Bank Canada (1998) 152 D.L.R. (4th)
411, SCC 23–23, 23–62, 23–80
Clark v. Associated Newspapers Ltd [1998] 1 W.L.R. 1558; [1998] 1 All
E.R. 959; [1998] R.P.C. 261; [1998] E.C.C. 185; (1998) 21(3) I.P.D.
21025; (1998) 95(7) L.S.G. 31; (1998) 148 N.L.J. 157; *The Times*,
January 28, 1998, *The Independent*, January 23, 1998 24–38
—— v. Chief Constable of Cleveland Police, *The Times*, May 13, 1999 ... 21–209
—— v. MacLennan [1983] 1 All E.R. 416 7–174
—— v. Oxfordshire Health Authority [1998] I.R.L.R. 125, CA 5–03
—— v. Bruce Lance & Co. [1988] 1 W.L.R. 887; (1987) 131 S.J. 1698;
[1988] 1 All E.R. 364; (1988) 7 Tr. L. 200; (1987) 137 New L.J.
1064; (1988) 85 L.S.Gaz. 37, CA 7–82
Clarke v. Chief Constable of Northamptonshire Police, *The Times*, June
14, 1999, CA 11–05, 11–16A, 12–20
Claydon Architectural Metalwork v. Higgins (D.J.) & Sons [1997] F.S.R.
475; (1997) 20(3) I.P.D. 20026, ChD 24–29
Clift v. Welsh Office [1998] 4 All E.R. 852; [1998] 38 R.V.R. 303; (1998)
95(36) L.S.G. 31; (1998) 76 P. & C.R. D46; *The Times*, August 24,
1998; *The Independent*, July 29, 1998, CA 18–12
Clunis v. Camden and Islington Health Authority [1998] 2 W.L.R. 902;
[1998] 3 All E.R. 180; *The Times*, December 27, 1996 .... 1–05F,
2–35, 3a, 3–03,
3–04, 7–22, 8–45,
11–14, 11–21
Coad v. Cornwall Health Authority [1997] 1 W.L.R. 189; [1997] P.I.Q.R.
P92; [1997] 8 Med. L.R. 154; (1997) 33 B.M.L.R. 168; (1996) 93(27)
L.S.G. 28; (1996) 140 S.J.L.B. 168; *The Times*, July 30, 1996, CA 31–23

Coates v. Government Insurance Office of N.S.W. [1995] 36 N.S.W.L.R.
7 .... 7—51
Cobra Gulf v. Rata (No. 2) [1997] 2 W.L.R. 629; [1997] 2 All E.R. 150;
[1997] F.S.R. 317; (1997) 20(2) I.P.D. 20013; *The Times*, October 11,
1996, ChD .... 28–22—28–27
Cocks v. Thanet District Council [1983] 2 A.C. 286; [1982] 3 W.L.R.
1121; (1982) 126 S.J. 820; [1982] 3 All E.R. 1135; (1983) 81 L.G.R.
81; (1984) 24 R.V.R. 31, HL 11–14
Coflexip SA v. Stolt Comex Seaway US Ltd [1999] 2 All E.R. 593; [1999]
F.S.R. 473; (1999) N.L.J. 196; *The Times*, February 4, 1999 .... 24–93, 28–02
Coins Control Ltd v. Suzo International (U.K.) Ltd [1998] 3 W.L.R. 420;
[1997] 3 All E.R. 45; [1997] F.S.R. 660; (1997) 20(8) I.P.D.
20073 6–07
Comdel Commodities v. Siporex Trade S.A. [1997] 1 Lloyd's Rep. 424,
CA .... 28–28—28–34
Comeau Sea Foods v. Canada (1995) 123 D.L.R. (4th) 180 7–100
Comer v. Governors of St Patrick's School, November 13, 1997
(unreported) 10–31
Commission v. France (C–265/95) *The Times*, December 11, 1997, ECJ . 23–42A,
23–71, 23–124
—— v. U.K. (C–300/95) [1997] All E.R. (EC) 48; [1997] 3 C.M.L.R. 923;
The Times, June 23, 1997 .... 9–36, 9–59
Company, A (No. 00679 of 1995), Re [1996] 2 All E.R. 417 8–80
Condon v. Basi [1985] 1 W.L.R. 866; (1985) 129 S.J. 382; [1985] 2 All
E.R. 453; (1985) 135 New L.J. 485, CA 7–120
Connolly v. Dale [1996] Q.B. 120; [1995] 3 W.L.R. 786; [1996] 1 All E.R.
224; [1996] 1 Cr. App. R. 200; *The Times*, July 13, 1995, QBD 23–59
Connelly v. RTZ Corp. Plc [1997] 3 W.L.R. 373; [1997] 4 All E.R. 335;
[1997] C.L.C. 1357; (1997) 94(32) L.S.G. 28; (1997) 147 N.L.J. 1346;
(1997) 141 S.J.L.B. 199; *The Times*, August 4, 1997, HL 6–02
Connex South Eastern Ltd v. NURMT [1999] I.R.L.R. 249, CA 23–112,
23–114
Connolly v. Dale [1996] Q.B. 120; [1995] 3 W.L.R. 786; [1996] 1 All
E.R. 224; [1996] 1 Cr. App. R. 200; *The Times*, July 13, 1995; *The
Independent*, July 27, 1995 23–59
Connolly-Martin v. Davis, May 27, 1999 8–78
Cookson v. Knowles [1979] A.C. 556; [1978] 2 W.L.R. 978; (1978) 122
S.J. 386; [1978] 2 All E.R. 604; [1978] 2 Lloyd's Rep. 315, HL;
affirming [1997] Q.B. 913; [1997] 3 W.L.R. 279; (1977) 121 S.J. 461;
[1977] 2 All E.R. 820; [1997] 2 Lloyd's Rep. 412, CA 27–14
Co-operative Wholesale Society v. British Railways Board [1995] N.P.C.
200; *The Times*, December 20, 1995, CA 29–08
Cornwall County Care v. Brightman [1998] I.R.L.R. 228, EAT 23–130
Corporacion Nacional del Cobre de Chile v. Sogemin Metals [1997] 1
W.L.R. 1396; [1997] 2 All E.R. 917; [1997] C.L.C. 435; (1996) 93
(46) L.S.G. 29; (1997) 167 N.L.J. Rep. 161; *The Times*, December 24,
1996; *The Independent*, December 16, 1996, ChD 23–30, 23–37,
23–82
Costello v. Chief Constable of Northumbria [1999] 1 All E.R. 550; *The
Times*, December 15, 1998, CA 7A, 7–109
Cox v. Hockenhull [1999] 3 All E.R. 582 27–44
Coulthard v. Disco Mix Club [1999] 2 All E.R. 457; *The Times*, March 25,
1999 .... 23–23, 23–43, 23–61
Crawley Borough Council v. Ure [1996] Q.B. 13 CA; [1995] 3 W.L.R. 95;
(1995) 27 H.L.R. 524; [1995] 1 F.L.R. 806; 93 L.G.R. 307; [1995]
Fam. Law 411; [1995] N.P.C. 24; *The Times*, February 23, 1995; *The
Independent*, April 18, 1995 (C.S.), CA 23–23, 23–30,
23–42, 23–62, 23–70, 23–80, 23–82

Creation Records Ltd v. News Group Newspapers Ltd [1997] F.S.R. 444;
    [1997] E.M.L.R. 444; (1997) 20(7) I.P.D. 20070; (1997) 141 S.J.L.B.
    107; (1997) 94(21) L.S.G. 32; *The Times*, April 29, 1997 26–03
Credit Lyonnais Bank Nederland NV (Now Generale Bank Nederland) v.
    Burch [1997] 1 All E.R. 144; (1997) 29 H.L.R. 513; (1997) 74 P. &
    C.R. 384; [1997] 1 F.L.R. 11; [1997] 2 F.C.R. 1; [1996] 5 Bank. L.R.
    233; [1997] C.L.C. 95; [1997] Fam. Law. 168; [1996] N.P.C. 99;
    (1996) 93 (32) L.S.G. 33; (1996) 146 N.L.J. Rep. 1421; (1996) 140
    S.J.L.B. 158; *The Times*, July 1, 1996; *The Independent*, June 27,
    1996, CA 23–42, 23–100
—— v. Export Credit Guarantee Department [1999] 2 W.L.R. 540, HL;
    [1998] 1 Lloyd's Rep. 19; [1997] C.L.Y. 2982, CA 5–38, 23–01, 23–03,
                            23–04, 23–07, 23–08, 23–09, 23–23, 23–28, 23–29,
                            23–30, 23–41, 23–48, 23–62, 23–65, 23–69, 23–70,
                            23–78, 23–79, 23–80, 23–81, 23–83, 23–88, 23–110
Crédit Suisse Fides Trust SA v. Cuoghi [1997] 3 W.L.R. 871; [1997] 3 All
    E.R. 724; [1997] C.L.C. 1, 87; *The Times*, July 3, 1997, CA ... 28–28—28–34
Crocker v. British Coal Corporation (1995) 29 B.M.L.R. 159; *The
    Times*, July 5, 1995, QBD 31–03
Cross v. Kirklees Metropolitan Borough Council [1998] 1 All E.R. 564,
    CA; *The Times*, July 9, 1997 .... 7–146, 11–12, 18–111
Crown River Cruises v. Kimbolton Fireworks [1996] 2 Lloyd's Rep.
    533; [1996] C.L.C. 1214; *The Times*, March 6, 1996, QBD 18a, 18–13,
                                       18–19, 19a, 19–13, 19–18
Cruise v. Express Newspapers [1999] 1 W.L.R. 327, CA; *The Times*, Sep-
    tember 1, 1998 .... 21–49, 21–84
Curmi v. McLennan [1994] 1 V.R. 513 7–148
Curust Financial Services v. Loewe-Lack-Werte Gmbh [1994] 1 I.R. 450 . 23–18
Customs and Excise Commissioners v. Anchor (No. 2) [1999] 3 All E.R.
    268; *The Times*, April 1, 1999 28–28

D & F Estates v. Church Commissioners for England [1988] 3 W.L.R.
    368; (1988) 132 S.J. 1092; [1988] 2 All E.R. 992; (1988) 41 B.L.R.
    1; (1988) 138 New L.J. 210; (1988) L.S.Gaz. September 14, 46, HL;
    affirming [1987] 1 F.T.L.R. 405; (1987) Const.L.J. 110; (1987) 36
    Build.L.R. 72; (1988) 11 Con.L.R. 12, CA; affirming in part (1987) 7
    Con.L.R. 40 7–95
DN Heritage v. Steenson Varning Mulcahy (1998) 60 Con. L.R. 33 8–119
Daishowa v. Friends of the Lubicon (1998) 158 D.L.R. (4th) 699, Ont.
    CA 23–13, 23–83
Daly v. General Steam Navigation Co.; Dragon, The [1981] 1 W.L.R. 120;
    (1980) 125 S.J. 100; [1980] 3 All E.R. 696; [1980] 2 Lloyd's Rep.
    415, CA; affirming [1979] 1 Lloyd's Rep. 257 27–10
D'Amato v. Badger (1996) 137 D.L.R. (4th) 129 7–57
Daniels v. Griffith [1998] E.U.L.R. 489; (1997) 147 N.L.J. 1809; (1997)
    94(48) L.S.G. 29; *The Times*, December 2, 1997, CA 21–91
—— v. Whetstone Entertainments and Allender [1962] 2 Lloyd's Rep. 1 . 5–34
Danns v. Department of Health; [1996] P.I.Q.R. P69; (1995) 25 B.M.L.R.
    121 11–14
Darlington Building Society v. Anor v. O'Rourke James Scourfield &
    McCarthy (a firm) [1999] P.N.L.R. 365 8–85
Das v. Ganju (1998) 42 B.M.L.R. 28; *The Times*, May 4, 1999 31–23
Davey v. Chief Constable of the Royal Ulster Constabulary [1988] N.I.L.R.
    139 .... 23–42A
Davies v. Wyre Forest District Council [1998] P.I.Q.R. P58 7–126
Deeny v. Gooda Walker (No. 2) [1996] 1 W.L.R. 426; [1996] 1 All E.R.
    933; [1996] 1 R.L.R. 109; [1996] S.T.C. 299; [1996] 5 Re L.R. 43;

(1996) 93(15) L.S.G. 32; (1996) 146 N.J.J. Rep. 369; (1996) 140
S.J.L.B. 92; *The Times*, March 8, 1996, HL; affirming 27–16

Defreitas v. O'Brien [1995] 6 Med.L.R. 108; [1995] P.I.Q.R. P281; *The
Times*, February 16, 1995; *The Independent*, April 3, 1995 (C.S.), CA;
affirming [1993] 4 Med.L.R. 281, QBD 7–135, 8–35

Delaney v. Southmead Hospital Authority (1992) 26 B.M.L.R. 111 7–177

Delaware Mansions Ltd v. Westminster City Council, *The Times*, August
25, 1999, (1998) 88 B.L.R. 99 18–19

Department of Social Security v. Butler [1995] 1 W.L.R. 1528; [1995] 4
All E.R. 193; [1995] 1 F.C.R. 63; (1995) 159 J.P.N. 796; *The Times*,
August 11, 1995; *The Independent*, August 14, 1995 (C.S.), CA 28–03,
28–28—28–34

Derbyshire County Council v. Times Newspapers [1993] A.C. 534; [1993]
1 W.L.R. 449; [1993] 1 All E.R. 1011; 91 L.G.R. 179; (1993) 137
S.J. (LB) 52; (1993) 143 N.L.J. 283; *The Times*, February 19, 1993;
The Independent, February 19, 1993; *The Guardian*, February 19,
1993, HL 21–25

Derby & Co. v. Weldon (No. 3 and No. 4) [1990] Ch. 65; [1989] 2 W.L.R.
412; (1989) 133 S.J. 83; (1989) 139 N.L.J. 11, CA .... 28–28—28–34

Derry v. Ministry of Defence, [1999] P.I.Q.R. P204; *The Times*, June 8,
1998 4–10

Desert Sun Loan Corp. v. Hill [1996] 2 All E.R. 847; [1996] 5 Bank L.R.
98; [1996] C.L.C. 1132; (1996) 140 S.J.L.B. 64; *The Times*, February
21, 1996, CA 30–25

Dhaliwal v. Person Representatives of Hunt (dec'd) [1995] P.I.Q.R. Q56,
CA 27–15

Dillenkofer v. Germany (C–178/94); [1997] Q.B. 259; [1997] 2 W.L.R.
253; [1997] All E.R. (EC) 917; [1997] I.R.L.R. 60; *The Times*,
October 14, 1996, ECJ 11–17, 23–01, 23–63, 23–71, 26–63

Dimond v. Lovell [1999] 3 W.L.R. 561, CA 27–11

DPP v. Fidler [1992] 1 W.L.R. 91; (1992) 94 Cr.App.R. 286; [1992]
Crim.L.R. 62; [1992] C.O.D. 104; (1992) 156 J.P.N. 140; *The Times*,
August 27, 1991, *The Independent*, August 30, 1991, DC 23–38, 23–123

—— v. Hancock and Tuttle [1995] Crim.L.R. 139; [1995] C.O.D. 32,
QBD 12–41

—— v. Jones (Margaret) [1999] 2 W.L.R. 625; [1999] 2 All E.R. 257, HL;
[1998] Q.B. 563; [1997] 2 W.L.R. 578; [1997] 2 All E.R. 119; [1997]
2 Cr. App. R. 59; (1997) 161 J.P. 324; [1997] Crim. L.R. 599; (1997)
147 N.L.J. 162; (1997) 94(6) L.S.G. 27; (1997) 161 J.P.N. 434; *The
Times*, January 27, 1999; *The Independent*, January 30, 1997 .... 17a, 1–32,
17–28, 17–41, 23–42A,
23–123, 23–124

—— v. Mills [1997] Q.B. 300; [1996] 3 W.L.R. 1093; [1997] 2 Cr. App.
R. 6; [1996] Crim. L.R. 746; [1996] C.O.D. 352; (1996) 160 J.P.N.
482; *The Times*, April 2, 1996, QBD 23–40, 23–42A

—— v. Mosley (Joanna), *The Times*, June 23, 1999 12–16

Djemal v. Bexley Health Authority [1995] 6 Med.L.R., QBD 8–42

Dobbie v. Medway Health Authority [1994] 1 W.L.R. 1234; [1994] 4 All
E.R. 450; [1994] P.I.Q.R. P353; [1994] 5 Med.L.R. 160; (1994) 144
N.L.J. Rep. 828; *The Times*, May 18, 1994; *The Independent*, June 6,
1994 (C.S.) CA 31–23

Dobson v. Tyneside Area Health Authority [1997] 1 W.L.R. 596; [1996] 4
All E.R. 474; [1997] 1 F.L.R. 598; [1997] 2 F.C.R. 651; [1997] 8
Med. L.R. 357; (1997) 33 B.M.L.R. 146; [1997] Fam. Law 326;
(1996) 93(31) L.S.G. 29; (1996) 146 N.L.J. Rep. 1458; (1996) 140
S.J.L.B. 165; *The Times*, July 15, 1996; *The Independent*, July 18,
1996, ... 13a, 13–50

Docker v. Chief Constable of West Midlands Police, *The Times*, April 29,
1998, CA 15–53, 16–137
Doe v. Toronto Commissioner of Police (1989) 58 D.L.R. (4th) 396 .... 1–05G
Domicrest v. Swiss Bank Corporation [1998] 3 All E.R. 577 6–02
Donnelly v. Joyce [1974] Q.B. 454; [1973] 3 W.L.R. 514; 117 S.J. 488;
[1973] 3 All E.R. 475; [1973] 2 Lloyd's Rep. 130, CA 27–11
Donaghue v. Stevenson [1932] A.C. 532 .... 7–13, 9a, 9–19, 9–21, 9–28
Dooley v. Cammell Laird & Co. and Mersey Insulation Co. [1951] 1
Lloyd's Rep. 271 7–53
Doran v. Delaney [1998] 2 I.L.R.M. 1 8–78
—— v. —— (No. 2) [1999] 1 I.L.R.M. 225 8–93
Double Bar L Ranching v. Baguet Corp'n [1996] 10 W.W.R. 673 9–23
Downs v. Chappell [1997] 1 W.L.R. 426; [1996] 3 All E.R. 344; [1996]
C.L.C. 1492, CA 2–21, 14–34
Downsview Nominees v. First City Corp. [1993] A.C. 295; [1993] 2
W.L.R. 86; [1993] 3 All E.R. 626; [1993] B.C.C. 46; [1994] 2
B.C.L.C. 49; (1992) 136 S.J. (LB) 324; *The Times*, December 15,
1992, PC 8–132, 8–133
Doyle v. Wallace [1998] P.I.Q.R. Q146 .... 2–09, 27–07
Drew v. Abassi and Packer, unreported, May 24, 1995 4–63
D'Souza v. DPP; *sub nom.* R. v. D'Souza (E); Same v. D'Souza (C) [1992]
1 W.L.R. 1073; [1992] 4 All E.R. 545; (1993) 96 Cr.App.R. 279;
(1992) 142 N.L.J. 1540; *The Times*, October 16, 1992, HL 12–62
Dubai Aluminium v. Salaam (1999) 1 Lloyd's Rep. 415 .... 4–53, 23–23, 23–62
Duffy v. Carnabane Holdings [1996] 2 I.L.R.M. 86 10–30
Duncan Investments v. Underwoods (A firm) [1998] P.N.L.R. 754, CA;
[1997] P.N.L.R. 521, ChD 7–70, 8–112
Dunlop v. Customs and Excise Commissioners, *The Times*, March 17,
1998, CA 15–05
Dureau v. Evans [1995] 5 P.I.Q.R. Q18 27–21
Dutton v. Bognor Regis U.D.C. [1972] 1 Q.B. 373; [1972] 2 W.L.R. 299;
(1971) 116 S.J. 16; 70 L.G.R. 57; *sub nom.* Dutton v. Bognor Regis
United Building Co. [1972] 1 All E.R. 462; [1972] 1 Lloyd's Rep.
227, CA; affirming [1971] 2 All E.R. 1003 8–117

E v. Dorset County Council [1994] 4 All E.R. 640 .... 9–96, 11a, 11–14
E.C.M. (Vehicle Delivery Service) v. Cox [1998] I.C.R. 631; *The Times*,
June 10, 1998, EAT 23–130
Ealing L.B.C. v. Metha, April 24, 1997, Trans. Ref. 96/074715, CA 16–137
Earl v. Wilhelm [1998] 2 W.W.R. 522 8–77
Eastcare Inc. v. Bryan Lawrence & Co. [1995] F.S.R. 597 22–06
East Suffolk Rivers Catchment Board v. Kent [1941] A.C. 74; [1940] 2
All E.R. 527, HL 7–103, 17–32
Edinburgh Council v. Brown [1999] I.R.L.R. 208 23–16
Electra Private Equity Partners v. K.P.M.G. Peat Marwick [1998] P.N.L.R.
135, ChD 7–62, 7–70, 8–126
Electronic Techniques (Anglia) v. Critchley Components [1997] F.S.R.
401; (1997) 20(4) I.P.D. 20037, ChD 24–07, 24–20
Elguzouli-Daf v. Commissioner of Police of the Metropolis; McBrearty v.
Ministery of Defence [1995] Q.B. 335; [1995] 2 W.L.R. 173; [1995]
1 All E.R. 833; (1995) 7 Admin.L.R. 421; (1995) 145 N.L.J.Rep. 151;
The Times, November 23, 1994, CA; affirming 15–39
Elliott v. Chief Constable of Wiltshire, *The Times*, December 5, 1996,
ChD 16–137
—— v. Saunders (1994) (unreported) 7–120
Ellison v. Ministry of Defence (1997) 87 B.L.R. 101, QBD 18–29, 19–12,
19–16, 19–27

Emaco Ltd v. Dyson Appliances Ltd, *The Times*, February 8, 1999 22–19
Emeh v. Kensington and Chelsea Area Health Authority [1985] Q.B. 1012;
    [1985] 2 W.L.R. 233; (1984) 128 S.J. 705; [1984] 3 All E.R. 1044;
    (1984) 81 L.S. Gaz. 2856, CA 2–34
Empress Car Co. (Abertillery) v. National Rivers Authority [1998] 1 All
    E.R. 481, HL 18–74
Equipment Supplies Ltd v. ACL Ltd, *The Times*, August 14, 1997, CA 23–62
Ernst and Young v. Butte Mining [1996] 1 W.L.R. 1605; [1996] 2 All E.R.
    623; (1996) N.L.J. Rep. 553; *The Times*, March 22, 1996, ChD 23–61
Esanda Finance Corporation v. Peat Marwick Hungerfords [1997] 188
    C.L.R. 241, HC; (1992) 61 S.A.S.R. 424 .... 7–64, 7–65, 7–66, 8–126
Essex Electric (PTE) v. I.P.C. Computers (U.K.) [1991] F.S.R. 690 23–01
Esterhuizen v. Allied Dunbar, *The Times*, June 10, 1998, QBD 8–77
Europe Mortgage Co. v. Halifax Estate Agencies; [1996] E.G.C.S. 84;
    [1996] N.P.C. 68; *The Times*, May 23, 1996 8–112
European Ltd (The) v. The Economist Newspaper Ltd [1998] F.S.R. 283;
    [1998] E.M.L.R. 536; [1998] E.T.M.R. 307; (1998) 21(3) I.P.D.
    21022, CA 24–70
Express & Echo Publications Ltd v. Tanton [1999] I.R.L.R. 367, CA 5–03

F v. West Berkshire Health Authority [1990] 2 A.C. 1; [1989] 2 W.L.R.
    1025; (1989) 133 S.J. 785; [1989] 2 F.L.R. 376; (1989) 139 N.L.J.
    789, HL 12–66
Fairhurst v. St Helens and Knowsley Health Authority [1995] P.I.Q.R. Q1;
    [1994] 5 Med.L.R. 422, High Ct. 27–11
Fairlie v. Carruthers, S.L.T. 1996 20–16
Family Housing Association v. Jones [1990] 1 W.L.R. 779; [1990] 1 All
    E.R. 385; (1990) 134 S.J. 233; (1990) 22 H.L.R. 45; (1990) 60 P. &
    C.R. 27; [1990] 22 E.G. 118; (1989) 139 N.L.J. 1709; [1990] L.S.Gaz.
    February 21, 33, CA 17–17
Farmers Build Ltd v. Carier Bulk Materials Handling Ltd [1999] R.P.C. 461;
    The Times, December 23, 1998 24–46
Feakins (K.A.) Ltd v. Dover Harbour Board, *The Times*, September 9,
    1998 .... 23–44, 23–69
Feldman (1995) 111 L.Q.R. 562 12–37
Femis-Bank (Anguilla) v. Lazer; Singh (Dinesh Kumar) v. Lazer [1991]
    Ch. 391; [1991] 3 W.L.R. 80; [1991] 2 All E.R. 865; *The Times*,
    February 11, 1991 23–01
First City Corporation v. Downsview Nominees [1989] 3 N.Z.L.R. 710;
    [1990] 2 N.Z.L.R. 426, H.C. 4–42
First Interstate Bank of California v. Cohen Arnold & Co. [1996] P.N.L.R.
    17; [1995] E.G.C.S. 188; *The Times*, December 11, 1995, CA 2–09, 8–92
—— v. Loxleys [1997] P.N.L.R. 211, CA 7–62, 7–74, 8–78
—— v. Taylor [1997] P.N.L.R. 37, CA 8–114
Fitzgerald v. Lane [1988] 3 W.L.R. 356; (1988) 132 S.J. 1064; [1988] 2
    All E.R. 961; (1988) 138 New L.J. 209; (1988) L.S.Gaz. September
    7, 44, HL; affirming [1987] Q.B. 781; [1987] 3 W.L.R. 249; (1987)
    131 S.J. 976; [1987] 2 All E.R. 455; (1987) 84 L.S.Gaz. 1334; (1987)
    137 New L.J. 316, CA 4–63, 7–200
—— v. Lane and Patel [1989] A.C. 328; [1990] R.T.R. 133, HL 7–200
Fleming v. Secretary of State for Trade and Industry [1997] I.R.L.R. 682 . 5–03
Forbes v. Wandsworth Health Authority [1996] 3 W.L.R. 1108; [1996] 4
    All E.R. 881; [1996] 7 Med. L.R. 175; (1997) 36 B.M.L.R. 1; (1996)
    93 (15) L.S.G. 32; (1996) 146 N.L.J. Rep. 477; (1996) 140 S.J.L.B.
    85; *The Times*, March 21, 1996, CA 31–23
Ford Motor Co. and Iveco Fiat SpA's Design Application [1993] R.P.C.
    399; [1995] R.P.C. 167 24–54

Fort Dodge Animal Health Ltd v. Akzo Nobel NV; *sub nom.* Akzo Nobel
  NV's European Patent (No. 189958) [1998] F.S.R. 222; [1998] I.L.Pr.
  732; (1998) 21(1) I.P.D. 21003, CA; (1997) 20(12) I.P.D. 20120, *The
  Times*, October 24, 1997 24–01
Forward v. Hendricks [1997] 2 All E.R. 395, CA 31–33
Foskett v. McClymont, 1998 S.C. 96; 1998 S.L.T. 892, OH 20–03
—— v. McKeown [1998] 2 W.L.R. 298; [1998] Ch. 265, CA 23–23
Foss v. Harbottle (1843) 2 Hare 461 8–130
Foulkes v. Chief Constable of Merseyside Police [1998] 3 All E.R. 705;
  The Times, June 16, 1998, CA 12–37
Fowles v. Bedfordshire County Council [1995] P.I.Q.R. P380; [1996]
  Ed.L.R. 51; *The Times*, May 22, 1995, CA 7–149, 10–03
Fox, Re (1996) 112 L.Q.R. 186 .... 4–24, 4–25
Francis v. Brown (1998) 30 H.L.R. 143, CA 27–69, 27–71
Frankling v. BPS Public Sector [1999] I.R.L.R. 212; [1999] I.C.R. 347 23–130
Fraser v. Winchester Health Authority, The Times, July 12, 1999, CA 3–48
Freeman v. Sutter [1996] 4 W.W.R. 749 8–57
French v. Mason (No. 2), *The Times*, November 13, 1998 .... 23–23, 23–43,
                                                                               23–62, 23–80
Friend v. Civil Aviation Authority [1998] I.R.L.R. 253; *The Times*, February 5,
  1998, CA 21–119
—— v. Institution of Professional Managers & Specialists [1999] I.R.L.R.
  173 4–52
Friends Provident Life Office v. Hillier Parker May & Roden Estates and
  General Plc [1997] Q.B. 85; [1996] 2 W.L.R. 123; [1996] 4 All E.R.
  260; (1996) 71 P. & C.R. 286; [1995] E.G.C.S. 64; [1995] N.P.C. 63;
  The Times, April 15, 1995, CA 4a, 4–61
Frost v. Chief Constable of South Yorkshire Police [1997] 3 W.L.R. 1194;
  [1997] 1 All E.R. 540; [1997] I.R.L.R. 173; (1997) 33 B.M.L.R. 108;
  (1996) 146 N.L.J. Rep. 1651; *The Times*, November 6, 1996; CA;
  reversing, *The Times*, July 3, 1995, QBD 7–25, 7–50, 7–110
Fujitsu Application [1997] R.P.C. 610 24–83
Fulton v. Globe & Mail (1997) 152 D.L.R. (4th) 377 21–07
Fylde Microsystems v. Key Radio Systems, *The Times*, February 18,
  1998, ChD 24–13

Gable House Estates v. Halpern Partnership (1995) 48 Const.L.R. 1 8–121
Galaske v. O'Donnell (1994) 112 D.L.R. (4th) 109 7–148
Gapper v. Chief Constable of Avon and Somerset Constabulary [1998] 4
  All E.R. 248, CA 12–51, 16–105
Gardner v. Davis [1999] E.H.L.R. 13 18–113
Gartner v. Kidman (1962) 36 A.L.J.R. 43 19–27
Geenty v. Channel Four T.V. Corp. [1998] E.M.L.R. 524; *The Times*, February 11,
  1998, CA 21–49
Generale Bank Nederland NV v. Export Credits Guarantee Dept. *See* Credit
  Lyonnais Bank Nederland NV v. Export Credits Guarantee Department
Gerber Garment Technology Inc. v. Lectra Systems [1995] R.P.C. 383;
  The Independent, January 30, 1995 (C.S.), CA; [1994] F.S.R. 471, Pat
  Ct 24–93
Gerrard v. Staffordshire Potteries [1995] I.C.R. 502; [1995] P.I.Q.R. P169,
  CA 11–11, 11–25
Gibbs v. Rea [1998] A.C. 786; [1998] 3 W.L.R. 72; (1998) 142 S.J.L.B.
  98; *The Times*, February 4, 1998, PC 15–02,
                                                                       15–08, 15–20, 23–08
Gibson v. British Rail Maintenance, 1995 S.L.T. 953 7–173
Gilberthorpe v. Hawkins, *The Times*, April 3, 1995; *The Independent*, May
  1, 1995 (C.S.), CA 21–03

Gillick v. British Broadcasting Corp. [1996] E.M.L.R. 267; *The Times*,
    October 20, 1995; *The Independent*, October 31, 1995, CA 21–12,
                                                                        21–13, 21–14
Gillon v. Chief Constable of Strathclyde, *The Times*, November 22, 1996 .   7–127
Gizzonio v. Chief Constable of Derbyshire, *The Times*, April 29, 1998,
    CA 15–02, 15–53, 16–137
Glass v. Cambridge Health Authority [1995] Med. L.R. 91   7–180
Gloag (Matthew) & Sons v. Welsh Distilleries, *The Times*, February 27,
    1998 25–01
Goddard (Theodore) v. Fletcher-King [1997] 2 E.G.L.R. 131; [1997] 32
    E.G. 90, QBD 8–105
Godfrey v. Demon Internet Ltd [1999] 4 All E.R. 342 .... 21–03, 21–61
Godwin v. Uzoigwe (1992) 137 S.J. (LB) 205; [1993] Fam.Law. 65; *The
    Times*, June 18, 1992; *The Independent*, August 27, 1992, CA 23–42A
Gold Coin Joqilliers S.A. v. United Bank of Kuwait [1997] 6 Bank L.R.
    60; [1997] P.N.L.R. 217; *The Times*, November 4, 1996, CA   7–65
Goldsmith v. Bhoyrul [1997] 4 All E.R. 268; [1997] E.M.L.R. 407; (1997)
    94 (28) L.S.G. 26; (1997) S.J.L.B. 151; *The Times*, June 20, 1997 21–25
Goodes v. East Sussex County Council, *The Times*, January 7, 1999,
    CA 7–146, 11–12
Goodwill v. British Pregnancy Advisory Service [1996] 1 W.L.R. 1397;
    [1996] 2 All E.R. 161; [1996] 2 F.L.R. 56; [1996] 2 F.C.R. 680;
    [1996] P.I.Q.R. P197; [1996] 7 Med. L.R. 129; (1996) 31 B.M.L.R.
    83; (1996) 93(5) L.S.G. 31; (1996) 146 N.L.J. Rep. 173; (1996) 140
    S.J.L.B. 37; *The Times*, January 29, 1996, CA 7a, 7–63, 7–82, 8–25
Goold Estate v. Stoddart Publishing Co. (1998) 161 D.L.R. (4th) 321, Ont.
    CA 23–04, 23–61
Gotha City v. Sotheby's (No. 2), *The Times*, October 10, 1998 13–157
Gran Gelato v. Richcliff (Group) [1992] Ch. 560; [1992] 2 W.L.R. 867;
    [1992] 1 All E.R. 865; [1992] 1 E.G.L.R. 297; [1991] E.G.C.S. 136;
    (1992) 142 N.L.J. 51; *The Independent*, December 18, 1991; *The
    Times*, December 19, 1991   8–78
Grant v. Norway (1851) 10 C.B. 665   5–42
Gray v. Motor Accident Commission (1998) 73 A.L.J.R. 45 27–70
—— v. Taylor [1998] 1 W.L.R. 1093; [1998] 4 All E.R. 17; (1998) 95(20)
    L.S.G. 34; [1998] N.P.C. 60; [1998] E.G.C.S. 62; (1998) 142 S.J.L.B.
    141; *The Times*, April 24, 1998, CA 17–17
Great House at Sonning v. Berkshire C.C. [1996] R.T.R. 407; [1996]
    E.G.C.S. 54; (1996) 93(14) L.S.G. 30; (1996) 140 S.J.L.B. 123; *The
    Times*, March 25, 1996, CA 18–93, 23–44, 23–64, 23–71
Green v. Chenoweth [1998] 2 Qd. R. 572   8–66
—— v. Cunningham (John) (1995) 46 Con.L.R. 62, CA   8–96
Gregory v. Portsmouth City Council (1997) 94(46) L.S.G. 29; *The Times*,
    November 26, 1997, CA 15–02
—— v. Shepherds, *The Times*, February 18, 1999   8–75
Grice v. Stourport Tennis, Hockey and Squash Club February 28, 1997,
    (unreported), CA 4–50, 10–06
Griffin v. Kingsmill, February 20, 1998, CA; [1998] P.N.L.R. 157; [1998]
    P.I.Q.R. P24   8–69
—— v. Mersey Regional Ambulance [1998] P.I.Q.R. P34, CA 7–132, 7–141
Griffiths v. Brown, *The Times*, October 23, 1998 7–142
Grovit v. Doctor [1997] 1 W.L.R. 640; [1997] 2 All E.R. 417; [1997]
    C.L.C. 1038; (1997) 147 N.L.J. 633; (1997) 141 S.J.L.B. 107; (1997)
    94(20) L.S.G. 37; *The Times*, April 25, 1997; *The Independent*, May
    1, 1997, HL 31–32
Gulf Oil (Great Britain) v. Page [1987] Ch. 327; [1987] 3 W.L.R. 166;
    [1987] 131 S.J. 695; [1987] 3 All E.R. 14; (1987) 137 New L.J. 408;
    (1987) 84 L.S. Gaz. 1968, CA 23–01

Gustafsson v. Sweden (1997) 26 I.L.J. 79; (1996) 22 E.H.R.R. 409,
ECHR 23–01

H.F. Pension Scheme Trustee Ltd v. Ellison (1999) 149 N.L.J. Digest
249 .... 4–53, 31–38
H.G. & R. Nominees v. Fava [1997] 2 V.R. 368 8–92
HIV Haemophiliac Litigation, Re [1996] P.N.L.R. 290; [1996] P.I.Q.R.
P220; (1990) 140 N.L.J. Rep. 1349; *The Guardian*, September 28,
1990; *The Independent*, October 2, 1990; *Daily Telegraph*, October
11, 1990, CA 7–99
Habinteg Housing Association v. James (1995) 27 H.L.R. 299; [1994]
E.G.C.S. 166; [1994] N.P.C. 132, CA 18–51
Hague v. Deputy Govenor of Parkhurst Prison [1992] 1 A.C. 58; [1991] 3
W.L.R. 340; [1991] 3 All E.R. 733; (1991) 135 S.J.L.B. 102; [1992]
C.O.D. 69; (1993) 5 Admin. L.R. 425; *The Times*, July 25, 1991; *The
Guardian*, July 31, 1991; *The Independent*, September 4, 1992,
HL 1–05C, 7–53
Haigh v. Wright Hassell & Co. [1994] E.G.C.S. 54, CA 8–90
Hale v. Guildarch Ltd [1999] P.N.L.R. 44 7–69
Halifax Mortgage Services (Formerly BNP Mortgages) v. Stepsky (1995)
N.P.C. 184; *The Times*, December 1, 1995, CA; affirming [1995] Ch.
1; [1995] 3 W.L.R. 701; [1995] 4 All E.R. 656; (1995) 92 (27)
L.S.Gaz. 31; *The Times*, June 27, 1995; *The Independent*, July 24,
1995 (C.S.), ChD 8–85
Hall v. Dart Valley Light Railway 1998 C.L.Y. 3933 20–16
—— v. Foong (1996) 65 S.A.S.R. 281 8–88
—— v. Simons [1999] Lloyd's Rep. PN 47; [1999] P.N.L.R. 374 ..... 1–05G, 7A,
7–111, 8–01, 8–69, 8–70
Hamble Fisheries Ltd v. Gardner and Sons Ltd [1999] 1 Lloyd's Rep.
1 .... 7–90, 9–01, 9–18, 9–23
Hamilton v. Al-Fayed (No. 1) [1999] 1 W.L.R. 1569; *The Times*, March
30, 1999 21–96
—— v. —— (No. 2), *The Times*, March 30, 1999 21–96
—— v. Guardian, *The Times*, July 22, 1995 .... 21–01, 21–96, 21–97
Hamlin v. Edwin Evans; [1996] P.N.L.R. 398; (1997) 29 H.L.R. 414; 80
B.L.R. 85; 52 Con. L.R. 106; [1996] 47 E.G. 141; [1996] 2 E.G.L.R.
106; [1996] N.P.C. 110; [1996] E.G.C.S. 120; (1996) 93(27) L.S.G.
29; (1996) 140 S.J.L.B. 167; *The Times*, July 15, 1996, CA .... 31–38—31–39
Harris v. Evans [1998] 1 W.L.R. 1285; [1998] 3 All E.R. 522; [1998]
E.H.L.R. 142; *The Times*, May 5, 1998, CA 1–05G, 7–102, 7–106
Harrison v. Duke of Rutland [1893] 1 Q.B. 142 17–41
—— v. Michelin Tyre Co. [1985] I.C.R. 696; [1985] 1 All E.R. 918, DC . 5–34
—— v. Thanet D.C., September 10, 1997 (unreported) 10–31
Harrods v. Harrodian School; [1996] R.P.C. 697; (1996) 19(10) I.P.D. 4;
The Times, April 3, 1996, CA 23–61, 25–14
Harrow London Borough Council v. Johnstone [1997] 1 W.L.R. 459;
[1997] 1 All E.R. 929; (1997) 29 H.L.R. 475; [1997] 1 F.L.R. 887;
[1997] 2 F.C.R. 225; [1997] Fam. Law 478; (1997) 61 Conv. 288;
(1997) 161 J.P. Rep. 580; (1997) 147 N.L.J. 413; [1997] E.G.C.S. 41;
(1997) 94(15) L.S.G. 26; [1997] N.P.C. 40; *The Times*, March 14,
1997, HL 23–42A, 23–59
Hassall v. Secretary of State for Social Security [1995] 1 W.L.R. 812;
[1995] 3 All E.R. 909; [1995] P.I.Q.R. P292; [1995] R.T.R. 316;
(1995) 139 S.J.L.B. 57; (1995) 92 (08) L.S.Gaz. 41; *The Independent*,
December 16, 1994; *The Times*, December 26, 1994, CA 27–17
Hay v. Grampian Health Board [1995] 6 Med.L.R. 128 .... 7–23, 7–179

Hayden v. Hayden [1992] 1 W.L.R. 986; [1992] P.I.Q.R. Q111; [1993] 2
F.L.R. 16; [1993] Fam. Law 466; *The Times*, April 8, 1992, CA 27–50
Haydon v. Kent County Council [1978] Q.B. 343; [1978] 2 W.L.R. 485;
121 S.J. 894; [1978] 2 All E.R. 97; (1977) 76 L.G.R. 270; [1978]
J.P.L. 174, CA 11–12, 18–111
Hayes v. Leo Scaffolding, December 1996 (unreported), CA 9a, 9–28
Haywood v. Somerfield Stores, *The Times*, July 9, 1997 12–17
Hedley Byrne & Co. v. Heller & Partners [1964] A.C. 465; [1963] 2
W.L.R. 101; 107 S.J. 454; [1963] 2 All E.R. 575; [1963] 1 Lloyd's
Rep. 485, HL 7–62, 7–74, 7–76
Hellewell v. Chief Constable of Derbyshire [1995] 1 W.L.R. 804; [1995]
4 All E.R. 473; (1995) 92 (07) L.S. Gaz. 35; (1995) 139 S.J.L.B. 49;
The Times, January 13, 1995, QBD 23–62, 26–08, 26–19
Henderson v. Henderson (1843) 67 E.R. 313; (1843) 3 Hare 100 4–55
—— v. Merrett Syndicates; Hallam-Eames v. Same; Hughes v. Same;
Arbuthnott v. Feltrim Underwriting Agencies; Deeny v. Gooda Walker
(In Liquidation) [1995] 2 A.C. 145; [1994] 3 W.L.R. 761; [1994] 3
All E.R. 506; [1994] 2 Lloyd's Rep. 468; (1994) N.L.J.Rep. 1204; *The
Times*, July 26, 1994; *The Independent*, August 3, 1994, HL; affirming
The Times, December 30, 1993; *The Independent*, December 14, 1993,
CA; affirming *The Times*, October 20, 1993   4–58, 7–62, 7–74, 7–75, 8–13
Henry Ansbacher and Coln v. Binks Stern (1997) 94(27) L.S.G. 22; (1997)
141 S.J.L.B. 151; *The Times*, June 26, 1997, CA 14–27
Hercules Management v. Ernst & Young [1997] 2 S.C.R. 115; (1995) 125
D.L.R. (4th) 353 .... 7–66, 8–126
Herd v. Clyde Helicopter *sub nom*. Fellowes v. Clyde Helicopters [1997]
A.C. 534; [1997] 2 W.L.R. 380; [1997] 1 All E.R. 775; 1997 S.C.
(HL) 86; 1997 S.L.T. 672; 1997 S.C.L.R. 308; (1997) 94(12) L.S.G.
22; (1997) 141 S.J.L.B. 64; *The Times*, March 7, 1997, HL 27–53
Hickman v. Maisey [1900] 1 Q.B. 752 17–41
Higham v. Stena Sealink [1996] 1 W.L.R. 1107; [1996] 3 All E.R. 660;
[1996] 2 Lloyd's Rep. 26; [1996] C.L.C. 1193; [1996] P.I.Q.R. P351;
The Times, February 26, 1996, CA 31–42
Hill v. Baxter [1958] 1 Q.B. 277; [1958] 2 W.L.R. 76; 122 J.P. 134; 102
S.J. 53; [1958] 1 All E.R. 193; 56 L.G.R. 117; 42 Cr. App. R. 51 4–39
—— v. Chief Constable of West Yorkshire [1989] A.C. 53, HL   1–05G
—— v. General Accident Fire & Life Assurance Corp. plc 1998 S.C.L.R.
1031; [1998] I.R.L.R. 641 23–34
—— v. Van Erp [1997] 188 C.L.R. 159 .... 7–81, 7–110
Hill Samuel v. Brand (1995) 4 Con.L.R. 141 8–117
Hinduja v. Asian T.V. [1998] E.M.L.R. 524, *The Times*, December 12,
1997, CA 21–49
Hodge Clemco v. Airblast [1995] F.S.R. 806, ChD .... 28–13—28–20
Hogan v. Newfoundland (1997) 149 D.L.R. (4th) 468, SC 23–95
Holbeck Hall Hotel v. Scarborough Borough Council; [1997] 2 E.G.L.R.
213; 57 Con. L.R. 113; [1997] N.P.C. 141; *The Times*, October 15,
1997 .... 7–33, 18–17
Holland v. Lampen-Wolfe [1999] 1 W.L.R. 188; (1998) 95(36) L.S.G. 32;
(1998) 142 S.J.L.B. 227; *The Times*, August 29, 1998, CA 4–23, 4–27
Holley v. Smyth [1998] Q.B. 726; [1998] 2 W.L.R. 742; [1998] 1 All E.R.
853; [1998] E.M.L.R. 133; (1998) 95(2) L.S.G. 23; (1998) 142
S.J.L.B. 35; *The Times*, December 20, 1997, CA 21–232, 23–01
Hollis v. Dow Corning (1996) 129 D.L.R. (4th) 609 .... 9–23, 9–24, 9–25
Holt v. Payne Skillington [1996] P.N.L.R. 179; 77 B.L.R. 51; 49 Con. L.R.
99; [1995] E.G.C.S. 201; (1996) 93(2) L.S.G. 29; (1996) 140 S.J.L.B.
30; [1995] N.P.C. 202; *The Times*, December 22, 1995, CA 1–08, 7a,
7–75, 8–10, 8–89, 8–109, 8–119
Home Office v. Dorset Yacht Co. [1970] A.C. 1004 7–99

Horsfall v. Heywoods, *The Times*, March 11, 1999 8–77
Horsley v. MacLaren; Ogopogo, The [1971] 2 Lloyd's Rep. 410, Canada-
  Supreme Ct 7–32
Hotson v. East Berkshire Health Authority *sub nom.* Hotson v. Fitzgerald
  [1987] A.C. 750; [1987] 3 W.L.R. 232; (1987) 131 S.J. 975; [1987] 2
  All E.R. 909; (1987) 84 L.S.Gaz. 2365, HL; reversing [1987] 2 W.L.R.
  287; [1987] 1 All E.R. 210; (1986) 130 S.J. 925; (1986) 136 New L.J.
  1163; (1987) 84 L.S.Gaz. 37, CA; affirming [1985] 1 W.L.R. 1036;
  (1985) 129 S.J. 558; [1985] 3 All E.R. 167; (1985) 82 L.S.Gaz. 2818 .. 8–66
Hounslow London Borough Council v. Michinton [1977] N.P.C. 44, CA 17–77
Howard v. Wessex Regional Health Authority [1994] 5 Med. L.R. 57,
  QBD 7–177
Howarth v. Adey [1996] 2 V.R. 535 8–40
Hughes v. Lloyds Bank plc [1998] P.I.Q.R. P98, CA 7–109, 7–110
—— v. United Kingdom, Application No. 11590195 .... 1–05G
Humber Oil Terminal Ltd v. Owners of the Ship Sivand; The Sivand
  [1998] 2 Lloyd's Rep. 97; [1998] C.L.C. 751, CA 2–25
Hunt v. Severs [1994] 2 A.C. 350; [1994] 2 W.L.R. 602; [1994] 2 All E.R.
  385; (1994) 138 S.J.L.B. 104; (1994) 144 N.L.J. 603; *The Times*, May
  2, 1994; *The Independent*, May 5, 1994, HL 27–11
Hunter v. Butler [1996] R.T.R. 396; *The Times*, December 28, 1995,
  CA 27–17, 27–44
—— v. British Coal Corporation [1998] 2 All E.R. 97, CA 7A, 7–44, 7–47,
                                                                  7–52, 7–53, 7–189
—— v. Canary Wharf; Hunter v. London Docklands Development Corp
  [1997] A.C. 655; [1997] 2 W.L.R. 684, HL; [1996] 1 All E.R. 482;
  (1995) 139 S.J.L.B. 214; (1995) 92 (39) L.S. Gaz. 28; [1995] N.P.C.
  155; (1995) 145 N.L.J.Rep. 1645; [1995] E.G.C.S. 153; *The Times*,
  October 13, 1995; *The Independent*, October 19, 1995, CA; affirming
  in part, *The Independent*, December 20, 1994, QBD 18a, 18–10, 18–11,
                                                           18–39, 18–92, 18–121,
                                                                  23–42A, 23–61
—— v. West Midlands Chief Constable [1982] A.C. 529; [1980] Q.B. 283;
  [1980] 2 W.L.R. 689; (1980) 124 S.J. 83; [1980] 2 All E.R. 227,
  CA 8–70
Huntingdon Life Sciences v. Curtin, *The Times*, December 11, 1997,
  QBD 23–42A
Hurlingham Estate v. Wilde [1997] 1 Lloyd's Rep. 525; [1997] S.T.C. 627;
  [1997] B.T.C. 240; (1997) 147 N.L.J. 453; *The Times*, January 3,
  1997, *The Independent*, February 17, 1997 8–89
Hurst v. Hampshire C.C. (1997) 96 L.G.R. 27 18–60
Hussain v. Lancaster City Council [1999] 4 All E.R. 125, ... 7–103, 18–54
Hyde Park Residence Ltd v. Yelland [1999] R.P.C. 655; *The Times*, March
  24, 1999 24–24

I Congreso del Partido, The [1993] 1 A.C. 4–23
Impress (Worcester) v. Rees [1971] 2 All E.R. 357; 115 S.J. 245; 69 L.G.R.
  305, DC 18–74
Indata Equipment Supplies v. A.C.L., (1997) [1998] F.S.R. 248; [1998] 1
  B.C.L.C. 412; (1997) 141 S.J.L.B. 216; *The Times*, August 14, 1997,
  CA 23–01, 23–23, 23–30, 23–32, 23–42,
                                              23–43, 23–70, 23–80, 23–82, 26–01
Indian Herbs (UK) Ltd v. Hadley & Ottoway Ltd, January 21, 1999
  (unreported) 13–51, 13–147
Intelsec v. Grech-Cini [1999] 4 App. E.R. 11 23–15
Intercity West Coast v. NURMT [1996] I.R.L.R. 583, CA 23–115
International Bulk Shipping and Services v. Minerals and Metals Trading

Corp. of India [1996] 1 All E.R. 1017; [1996] 2 Lloyd's Rep. 474;
  The Independent, December 11, 1995, CA 31–07
Invarcargill City Council v. Hamlin [1996] 1 All E.R. 756; [1996] 2
  W.L.R. 367; (1995) 72 B.L.R. 39; (1995) 11 Const.L.J. 285, CA;
  [1994] 3 N.Z.L.R. 513 .... 7–95, 8–117, 31–09
Inverugie Investments v. Hackett [1995] 1 W.L.R. 713; [1995] 3 All E.R.
  841; [1995] N.P.C. 36; [1995] E.G.C.S. 37, PC 13–138, 17–73, 27–73
Irving v. Keen, March 3, 1995 (unreported) 13a, 13–121, 13–151
—— v. Post Office, The [1987] I.R.L.R. 289, CA 5–20
Island Records v. Tring International plc [1995] 3 All E.R. 444; [1995]
  F.S.R. 560; *The Times*, April 28, 1995, ChD .... 24–29, 30–03 to 30–04
Issa v. Hackney Borough Council [1997] 1 W.L.R. 956; [1997] 1 All E.R.
  999; (1997) 29 H.L.R. 640; [1997] Env. L.R. 157; [1996] N.P.C. 167;
  [1996] E.G.C.S. 184; (1997) 94(1) L.S.G. 24; (1996) 140 S.J.L.B. 262;
  The Times, November 26, 1996, CA 11a, 11–03,
                                                                 11–18, 18–03, 23–44

JEB Fasteners Ltd v. Marks Bloom & Co. [1983] 1 All E.R. 583, CA 2–10
J.F.S. (UK) Ltd v. Dwr Cymru Cyf [1999] 1 W.L.R. 231, CA 31–01
Jacobs v. Moreton [1994] 72 B.L.R. 92, QBD 8–117, 9–19
Jaconelli v. Jaconelli (1998) 20 J. Soc. Wel. & Fam. Law 151 12–74
James v. Commonwealth The (1938) 62 C.L.R. 364 23–42
—— v. London Borough of Havering (1992) 15 B.M.L.R. 1, CA 4–39
—— v. Williams, *The Times*, April 13, 1999 23–23
Jameson v. Central Electricity Generating Board [1999] 2 W.L.R. 141;
  [1999] 1 All E.R. 193; [1999] I.C.L. 171, HL; [1998] Q.B. 323; [1997]
  3 W.L.R. 151; [1997] 4 All E.R. 38; [1997] P.I.Q.R. Q89; (1997) 141 S.J.L.B.
  55; *The Times*, February 25, 1997, CA 4–01, 4–55, 4–60,
                                                                   4–61, 27–41, 27–50
Janvier v. Sweeney [1919] 2 K.B. 316, CA 23–42A
Jaundrill v. Gillett, *The Times*, January 30, 1996 .... 20–01, 20–03, 20–05, 20–14
Jayes v. I.M.I. (Kynoch) [1985] I.C.R. 155; (1984) 81 L.S. Gaz. 3180,
  CA 7–198
Jeffrey v. Commodore Cabaret (1996) 13 B.C.L.R. (3d) 149; (1995) 128
  D.L.R. (4th) 535 .... 7–25, 10–30
Jerry Juhan Developments v. Arco Tyres, *The Times*, January 15, 1999 13–34
Jobson v. Record (1997) 74 P. & C.R. D16; [1997] N.P.C. 56, CA 17–39
John v. MGN [1997] Q.B. 586; [1996] 3 W.L.R. 593; [1996] 2 All E.R.
  35; [1996] E.M.L.R. 229; (1996) 146 N.L.J. Rep. 13; *The Times*,
  December 14, 1995, CA 21–05, 21–203, 21–204, 21–209, 21–225,
                                         21–228, 21–229, 27–09, 27–66, 27–68, 27–70, 27–74
Johnson v. Bingley [1997] P.N.L.R. 392; [1995] N.P.C. 27; *The Times*,
  February 28, 1995, QBD 7–136, 8–86
—— v. British Midland Airways [1996] 5 P.I.Q.R. Q8 27–45
—— v. Gore Wood & Co. [1999] Lloyd's Rep. P.N. 91; [1999] C.P.L.R.
  155; [1999] P.N.L.R. 426, CA 7–81, 8–130
—— v. Unisys [1999] I.R.L.R. 90, CA 23–34
—— v. Walton [1990] 1 F.L.R. 350; [1990] Fam. Law 260; [1990] F.C.R.
  568; (1990) 154 J.P.N. 506, CA 23–42A
Jolley v. London Borough of Sutton [1998] 3 All E.R. 559; (1998) New
  L.J. 1014; *The Times*, June 23, 1998, CA 7–190, 10–31
Jones v. Pollard [1997] E.M.L.R. 233, CA 21–204
—— v. Skelton [1963] 1 W.L.R. 1362; 107 S.J. 870; [1963] 3 All E.R.
  952, PC 21–51
—— v. Tower Boot Co. [1997] 2 All E.R. 406; [1997] I.C.R. 254; [1997]
  I.R.L.R. 168; (1997) 147 N.L.J. Rep. 60; *The Times*, December 16,
  1996; *The Independent*, January 16, 1997, CA 5–20

Joyce v. Sengupta [1993] 1 W.L.R. 337; [1993] 1 All E.R. 897; (1992)
   136 S.J.L.B. 274; (1992) 142 N.L.J. 1306; *The Independent*, August
   11, 1992; *The Guardian*, August 12, 1992, CA 21–03, 23–34
Joyce v. Wandsworth Health Authority [1996] 7 Med L.R. 1; [1996]
   P.I.Q.R. P121; 2–10, 8–47
Jules Dethier Equipement SA v. Dassy (C319/94) [1998] All E.R. (E.C.)
   346; [1998] I.C.R. 541; [1998] I.R.L.R. 266; [1998] C.E.C. 295; *The
   Times*, March 18, 1998, ECU 23–130

K Mart (1997) 149 D.L.R. (4th) 1 B.C.C.A. 23–01
Kamloops v. Nielsen, Hughes and Hughes [1984] 5 W.W.R. 1; (1984) 1
   Const.L.J. 207, Supreme Ct. of Canada 7–95
Kapfunde v. Abbey National plc [1999] Lloyd's Rep. (Med.) 48 [1999]
   I.C.R. 1a; [1998] I.R.L.R. 583; [1998] E.C.C. 440; *The Times*, April
   6, 1998; *The Independent*, April 1, 1998, CA 5–09, 7–82
Kastner v. Rizla [1995] R.P.C. 585; *The Times*, June 23, 1995, CA   24–82, 24–90
Kaye v. Robertson [1991] F.S.R. 62; *The Times*, March 21, 1990, CA 1–05E
Kelley v. Corston [1998] Q.B. 686; [1998] 3 W.L.R. 246; [1997] 4 All
   E.R. 466; [1997] N.P.C. 111; (1997) 94(32) L.S.G. 28; (1997) 147
   N.L.J. 1276; (1997) 141 S.J.L.B. 206; *The Times*, August 20, 1997,
   CA 1–05G, 8a, 8–69, 8–70
Kennedy v. Van Emden & Co. (1997) 74 P. & C.R. 19; [1996] P.N.L.R.
   409; [1997] 2 E.G.L.R. 137; [1997] 44 E.G. 201; [1996] N.P.C. 56;
   (1996) 93(16) L.S.G. 31; (1996) 140 S.J.L.B. 99; *The Times*, April 5,
   1996, CA 8–92
Kent v. British Railways Board [1995] P.I.Q.R. Q42, CA 27–12
Kerr v. DPP [1994] 158 J.P. 1048; [1995] Crim.L.R. 394; (1994) 158
   J.P.N. 653; *The Times*, August 5, 1994, QBD 16–124
Khazanchi v. Faircharm Investments Ltd; McLeod v. Butterwick [1998] 2
   All E.R. 901 .... 16–26, 16–37
Khorasandjian v. Bush [1993] Q.B. 727; [1993] 3 W.L.R. 476; [1993] 3
   All E.R. 669; (1993) 25 H.L.R. 392; (1993) 137 S.J.L.B. 88; [1993] 2
   F.L.R. 66; [1995] Fam. Law 679; *The Times*, February 18, 1993; *The
   Independent*, March 16, 1993, CA 1–28, 18–29, 18–39, 23–42A
King v. Smith (t/a Clean Glo) [1995] I.C.R. 339; [1995] P.I.Q.R. P48; *The
   Times*, November 3, 1994, CA 3–22, 7–172
Kirby-Hains v. Baxter [1995] E.M.L.R. 516; *The Times*, June 15, 1995,
   CA 21–41, 21–42, 21–183
Kirkham v. Chief Constable of Greater Manchester Police [1990] 2 Q.B.
   283; [1990] 2 W.L.R. 987; (1990) 134 S.J. 758; [1990] 3 All E.R.
   246; (1990) 140 N.L.J. 209; *The Independent*, February 10, 1989,
   CA 3–05, 7–23
Kitano v. Commonwealth, The (1974) 129 C.L.R. 151 23–43
Kitchen v. Royal Air Force Association [1958] 1 W.L.R. 563; 102 S.J.
   363; [1958] 3 All E.R. 241 .... 2–09, 8–96
Kitechnology BV v. Unicor GmbH Plastmaschinen [1995] F.S.R. 765,
   CA 24–01, 26–01
Kleinwort Benson v. Glasgow City Council [1999] 1 A.C. 153; [1997] 3
   W.L.R. 923, HL; [1997] 4 All E.R. 641; [1997] C.L.C. 1609; (1997)
   9 Admin.L.R. 721; (1997) 147 N.L.J. 1617; (1997) 141 S.J.L.B. 237;
   (1997) 94(44) L.S.G. 36; *The Times*, October 31, 1997 23–08
Knightly v. Johns [1982] 1 W.L.R. 349; [1982] 1 All E.R. 851; [1982]
   R.T.R. 182; 126 S.J. 101, CA 7–110
Knowles v. Fire Brigades Union [1996] 4 All E.R. 653; [1997] I.C.R. 595;
   [1996] I.R.L.R. 617 (1996) 93(34) L.S.G. 34; (1996) 140 S.J.L.B. 206;
   The Times, August 15, 1996, CA 23–37
Kroeker v. Jansen (1995) 123 D.L.R. (4th) 652 27–10

Kuwait Airways Corp. v. Iraqi Airways [1995] 1 W.L.R. 1147; [1995] 3
All E.R. 694; [1995] 2 Lloyd's Rep. 317; (1995) 139 S.J.L.B. 176;
(1995) 92 (28) L.S.Gaz. 28; *The Times*, July 25, 1995; *The Independent*, August 15, 1995, HL; affirming in part [1994] 1 Lloyd's Rep.
276; [1995] 1 Lloyd's Rep. 251; (1993) 90 (45) L.S.Gaz. 39; *The
Times*, October 27, 1993, CA; reversing, *Financial Times*, July 17,
1992, QBD 4–16, 4–24, 4–25

L, Re [1998] 3 W.L.R. 107; [1998] 3 All E.R. 289; [1998] 2 F.L.R. 550;
[1998] 2 F.C.R. 501; (1998) 44 B.M.L.R. 1; (1998) 1 C.C.L. Rep.
390; [1998] C.O.D. 312; [1998] Fam. Law 592; (1998) 148 N.L.J.
1014; (1998) 142 S.J.L.B. 195; (1998) 95(29) L.S.G. 27; *The Times*,
June 30, 1998; *The Independent*, June 30, 1998, HL 8–29
Lac Minerals v. International Corona [1990] F.S.R. 441, SCC 23–01, 23–23,
23–32, 23–42, 23–70, 23–82
Lam v. Brennan and Borough of Torbay [1997] P.I.Q.R. P488; [1997]
N.P.C. 135, CA 11–14
Lambert v. West Devon District Council [1997] J.P.L. 735; (1997) 94(11)
L.S.G. 35; (1997) 141 S.J.L.B. 66; *The Times*, March 27, 1997 . 7–71, 7–108
Lancashire County Council v. Municipal Mutual Insurance [1997] Q.B.
897; [1996] 3 W.L.R. 493; [1996] 3 All E.R. 545; [1996] C.L.C. 1459;
(1996) 160 L.G. Rev. 612; (1996) 93(21) L.S.G. 27; (1996) 140
S.J.L.B. 108; *The Times*, April 8, 1996, CA 27–70
Landall v. Dennis Faulkner & Alsop [1994] 5 Med.L.R. 268, QBD 8–70
Lane v. Shire Roofing Co. (Oxford) [1995] I.R.L.R. 493; [1995] P.I.Q.R.
P417; *The Times*, February 22, 1995, CA 5–03, 7–166
Lange v. Atkinson Australia Consolidated Press [1997] 2 N.Z.L.R. 22,
NZCA 21–05, 21–135
—— v. Australian Broadcasting Corp. (1997) 145 A.L.R. 91 .... 21–05, 21–135
Langley v. Dray and M.T. Motor Policies at Lloyds [1998] P.I.Q.R. P314,
CA 7–13, 7–141
Laurentide Motels v. Beauport [1989] 1 S.C.R. 705 7–99
Law Debenture Trust Corpn v. Ural Caspian Oil Corpn [1995] Ch. 152;
[1994] 3 W.L.R. 1221; [1995] 1 All E.R. 157; *The Independent*, March
10, 1994, CA; reversing [1993] 1 W.L.R. 138; [1993] 2 All E.R. 355;
The Independent, March 12, 1992; *Financial Times*, March 20,
1992 .... 8–114, 23–02, 23–03, 23–04, 23–08, 23–09, 23–10
23–11, 23–13, 23–15, 23–19, 23–23, 23–29, 23–31,
23–32, 23–43, 23–46, 23–50, 23–59, 23–62, 23–69, 23–82
Law Society of England and Wales v. Society of Lawyers [1996] F.S.R.
701 25–06
Leach v. Chief Constable of Gloucestershire Constabulary [1999] 1 All
E.R. 215, CA 7A, 7–53, 7–109
Leakey v. National Trust for Places of Historic Interest and Natural Beauty
[1980] Q.B. 485; [1980] 2 W.L.R. 65; (1979) 123 S.J. 606; [1980] 1
All E.R. 17; (1979) 78 L.G.R. 100, CA 18–17
Lee Ting Sang v. Chung Chi-Keing [1990] 2 A.C. 374; [1990] 2 W.L.R.
1173; (1990) 134 S.J. 909; [1990] I.C.R. 409; [1990] I.R.L.R. 236;
[1990] L.S. Gaz. April 4, 43, PC 5–09
Leech v. National, Bank of N.Z. [1996] 3 N.Z.L.R. 707 8–132
Legal & General Mortgage Services v. Underwoods [1997] P.N.L.R.
567 .... 8–106, 8–112
Lewis v. Daily Telegraph (1963). *See* Rubber Improvement v. Daily Tele-
graph
Liddell v. Middleton [1996] 5 P.I.Q.R. P36; *The Times*, July 17, 1995,
CA 7–140, 7–142

Lippiatt v. South Gloucestershire Council [1999] 4 All E.R. 149, CA 18–46, 18–54, 19–07

Littlejohn v. Wood and Davidson [1997] S.L.T. 1353, CS (OH) 23–64

Littrell v. Government of the United States of America (No. 2) [1995] 1 W.L.R. 82; [1994] 4 All E.R. 203; [1994] P.I.Q.R. P141; (1993) 137 S.J. (L.B.) 278; *The Times*, November 24, 1993; *The Independent*, December 2, 1993, CA 4–23

London v. British Coal Corpn [1995] I.C.R. 565; [1995] 4 P.I.Q.R. Q48 ... 27–20

London and South of England Building Society v. Stone [1983] 1 W.L.R. 1242; (1983) 127 S.J. 446; [1983] 3 All E.R. 105; (1983) 267 E.G. 69; (1983) L.S.Gaz. 3048, CA 8–113

London Underground v. National Union of Railwaymen, Maritime and Transport Staff [1995] I.R.L.R. 636; (1995) 139 S.J.L.B. 211; [1995] E.G.C.S. 636; *The Times*, October 9, 1995; *The Independent*, October 30, 1995 (C.S.), CA 23–91, 23–96, 23–112, 23–114

Lone Star Toys v. J.M. Enterprises of Wetherby [1996] F.S.R. 857; (1996) 19(7) I.P.D. 11, Pat Ct 24–56

Longden v. British Coal Corp. [1997] 3 W.L.R. 1336; (1997) 147 N.L.J. 1774; *The Times*, November 28, 1997, HL 27–12, 27–20

Lonrho v. Fayed [1992] 1 A.C. 448; [1991] 3 W.L.R. 188; [1991] 3 All E.R. 303; (1991) 135 S.J.L.B. 68; [1991] B.C.C. 641; [1991] B.C.L.C. 779; (1991) 141 N.L.J. 927; *The Guardian*, June 28, 1991; *The Times*, July 3, 1991; *The Independent*, July 3, 1991; *Financial Times*, July 3, 1991, HL 23–23

—— v. —— (No. 5) [1993] 1 W.L.R. 1489; [1994] 1 All E.R. 188; (1993) 137 S.J.L.B. 189; (1993) 143 N.L.J. 1571; *The Times*, July 27, 1993; *The Guardian*, July 24, 1993; *The Independent*, July 27, 1993, CA 23–34

—— v. —— [1981] 3 W.L.R. 33; (1981) 125 S.J. 429; [1981] 2 All E.R. 456, HL 11–20

—— v. Shell Petroleum Co. (No. 2) [1982] A.C. 173; [1980] 1 W.L.R. 627; (1980) 124 S.J. 412, HL 23–64

Loveless v. Earl, *The Times*, November 11, 1998, CA 21–76, 21–183

Lowe v. AGC [1992] 2 V.R. 671 8–126

Lubrizol Corporation v. Esso Petroleum Corporation Co. [1997] R.P.C. 195, Pat Ct 24–92

Lumley v. Gye (1853) 2 E. & B. 216 .... 23–11, 23–23

Lybert v. Warrington Health Authority [1996] P.I.Q.R. P45; [1996] 7 Med.L.R. 71 (1995) 92 (20) L.S.G. 40; *The Times*, May 17, 1995, CA 2–10, 8–57

M v. Calderdale Health Authority [1998] Lloyd's Rep. (Med.) 157 8–63

M v. Newham London Borough Council; X (Minors) v. Bedfordshire County Council [1995] 2 A.C. 633; [1995] 3 All E.R. 353, HL; [1994] 2 W.L.R. 554; [1994] 4 All E.R. 602; [1994] 1 F.L.R. 431; 92 L.G.R. 427; (1994) 144 New L.J. 357; *The Times*, March 3, 1994; *The Independent*, February 24, 1994; *The Guardian*, February 28, 1994, CA; affirming [1993] 2 F.L.R. 575; [1993] Fam. Law 575 ... 1–05G, 1–15, 1–106, 7–103, 7a, 7–96, 7–99, 8–61, 11a, 11–03, 11–13, 11–14, 11–15, 11–19, 11–21, 11–25, 23–44, 23–45 23–62, 23–66

M (a minor) v. Newham London Borough Council [1994] 2 W.L.R. 554; [1994] 4 All E.R. 602; [1994] 1 F.L.R. 431; 92 L.G.R. 427; (1994) 144 N.L.J. 357; *The Times*, March 3, 1994, CA 7–53

M.B. (Caesarian Section), Re [1997] 2 F.L.R. 426; [1997] 2 F.C.R. 541; [1997] 8 Med.L.R. 217; (1997) 38 B.M.L.R. 175; [1997] Fam. Law 542; (1997) 147 N.L.J. 600; *The Times*, April 18, 1997; *The Independent*, April 8, 1997, CA 3–62, 8a, 8–26, 8–27

MCC Proceeds Inc. v. Lehman Bros. [1998] 4 All E.R. 675; *The Times*,
January 14, 1998, CA 13a, 13–01, 13–80
M.T.M. Construction v. William Reid Engineering 1997 S.C.L.R. 778;
1997 Rep. L.R. 27; *The Times*, April 22, 1997, QBD 5–57
McAllister v. Lewisham and North Southwark Health Authority [1994] 5
Med. L.R. 343 2–10
McCann v. Wright [1995] 1 W.L.R. 1556; [1995] 2 F.L.R. 579; (1995)
139 S.J.L.B. 166; (1995) 92 (28) L.S.Gaz. 41; *The Times*, July 10,
1995; *The Independent*, July 17, 1995 (C.S.) CA 23–42A
McCausland v. Duncan Lawrie [1997] 1 W.L.R. 38; [1996] 4 All E.R. 995;
(1997) 74 P. & C.R. 343; (1996) 60 Conv. 366; [1996] N.P.C. 94;
[1996] E.G.C.S. 103; (1996) 93(26) L.S.G. 19; (1996) 146 N.L.J. Rep.
1387; *The Times*, June 18, 1996, *The Independent*, June 11, 1996,
CA 23–09
McCartan Turkington & Breen v. Times Newspapers [1998] N.I. 358; *The
Times*, November 4, 1998, CA, H.L. 21–180
McCord v. Swansea City F.C., *The Times*, February 11, 1997, QBD 7–120
McCullagh v. Lane Fox and Partners [1995] E.G.C.S. 195; [1996] P.N.L.R.
205, CA; affirming 38 Con.L.R. 14; [1994] 08 E.G. 118; (1994) 138
S.J.L.B. 54; [1994] E.G.C.S. 2; [1994] N.P.C. 4; *The Times*, January
25, 1994, QBD 7a, 7–62, 7–70, 7–74, 8–14, 8–15, 8–78
McDermid v. Nash Dredging and Reclamation Co. [1987] A.C. 906; [1987]
3 W.L.R. 212; [1987] I.C.R. 917; (1987) 131 S.J. 973; [1987] 2 All
E.R. 878; [1987] 2 F.T.L.R. 357; [1987] I.R.L.R. 334; [1987] 2
Lloyd's Rep. 201; (1987) 84 L.S. Gaz. 2458, HL 8–63
McDonald's Corp. v. Steel [1995] 3 All E.R. 615; [1995] E.M.L.R. 527;
The Times, April 14, 1994; *The Independent*, April 22, 1994, CA 21–01,
21–02, 21–76
McElroy Milne v. Commercial Electronics [1993] 1 N.Z.L.R. 39 8–93
McFarlane v. Tayside H.B., 1998 S.C. 389; 1998 S.L.T. 307; 1998
S.C.L.R. 126; (1998) 44 B.M.L.R. 140; *The Times*, May 8, 1998 2–34,
8–57
—— v. Wilkinson, [1997] 2 Lloyds Rep. 259; [1997] P.N.L.R. 578; *The
Times*, February 13, 1997, CA 8–70, 8–73, 8–96, 11–04
McGeown v. NI Housing Executive [1995] 1 A.C. 233; [1994] 3 W.L.R.
187; (1994) 138 S.J.L.B. 156; [1994] N.P.C. 95; (1994) 144 N.L.J.
901; *The Times*, June 24, 1994; *The Independent*, June 28, 1994,
HL(N.I.) 10–24
McGirney v. Golderslea, November 6, 1997 (unreported) CA 10–32
McHale v. Watson (1966) 115 C.L.R. 199 4–32
McLeod v. Butterwick *sub nom.* Khazanchi v. Faircharm Investments Ltd
[1996] 1 W.L.R. 995; [1996] 3 All E.R. 236; *The Times*, March 12,
1996, ChD 16–26, 16–33, 16–37, 16–67
—— v. Metropolitan Police Commissioner [1994] 4 All E.R. 553; *The
Independent*, February 21, 1994 (C.S.), CA 12–37, 16–107
—— v. United Kingdom (1999) 27 E.H.R.R. 493 .... 1–05C, 12–37, 16–107
McLelland v. Greater Glasgow H.B. 1998 S.C.L.R. 1081; *The Times*,
October 14, 1998 8–57
McLoughlin v. O'Brian [1983] A.C. 410; [1982] 2 W.L.R. 982; (1982)
126 S.J. 347; [1982] 2 All E.R. 398; [1982] R.T.R. 209; (1982) 79
L.S.Gaz. 922, HL 7–43
McMeechan v. Secretary of State for Employment [1997] I.C.R. 549;
[1997] I.R.L.R. 353, CA 5–02, 5–03
MacMillan Bloedel v. Simpson (1997) 137 D.L.R. (4th) 637 (SCC); (1995)
118 D.L.R. (4th) 1 (BBCA) 23–35, 23–44, 23–47, 23–52, 23–66, 23–68
Macmillan Magazines v. R.C.N. Publishing Co. [1998] F.S.R. 9; (1997) 20(9) I.P.D.
20089 .... 22–06, 22–19, 24–71

McPhilemy v. Times Newspapers Ltd [1999] 3 All E.R. 775; *The Times*,
May 26, 1999 .... 21–03, 21–51, 21–55
Macarthur v. Meuser (1997) 146 D.L.R. (4th) 125 21–189
Machin v. Adams (1997) 84 B.L.R. 79; [1997] E.G.C.S. 74; [1997] N.P.C.
73, CA 8–13, 8–116, 8–117
Mahmood v. Siggins [1996] 7 Med.L.R. 76 8–45
Mahon v. Rahn [1997] 3 W.L.R. 1230; [1997] 3 All E.R. 687 [1997]
E.M.L.R. 558; *The Times*, June 12, 1997, CA 21–61
Mahoney v. Kruschich (1984) 156 C.L.R. 522 23–79
—— v. Purnell [1996] 3 All E.R. 61; [1997] 1 F.L.R. 612; [1997] Fam.
Law 169, QBD 23–23, 27–64
Mahmud v. Bank of Credit and Commerce International SA [1998] A.C.
20; [1997] 3 W.L.R. 95; [1997] 3 All E.R. 1; [1997] I.C.R. 606; [1997]
I.R.L.R. 462; (1997) 94(25) L.S.G. 33; (1997) 147 N.L.J. 917; *The
Times*, June 13, 1997; *The Independent*, June 20, 1997, HL 23–34
Malaysian Industrial Development Authority v. Jeyasingham [1998] I.C.R.
307, EAT 4–25
Malone v. Lasky [1907] 2 K.B. 141 .... 18–19, 23–42A
Manchester Airport plc v. Dutton [1999] 2 All E.R. 675; *The Times*, March
5, 1999 17–18
Mansfield v. Weetabix [1998] 1 W.L.R. 1263; [1998] R.T.R. 390; [1997]
P.I.Q.R. P526, CA 4–39
Mapp v. News Group, [1997] E.M.L.R. 397; (1997) 147 N.L.J. 562; *The
Times*, March 10, 1997, CA 21–18, 21–50, 21–51
Marc Rich & Co. AG v. Bishop Rock Marine Co. Bethmarine Co. and
Nippon Kaiji Kyokai; Nicholas H, The [1996] 1 A.C. 211; [1995] 3
W.L.R. 227; [1995] 3 All E.R. 307; [1995] 2 Lloyd's Rep. 299; (1995)
145 N.L.J. Rep. 1033; (1995) 139 S.J.L.B. 165; *The Times*, July 7,
1995; *The Independent*, August 18, 1995; *Lloyd's List*, July 19, 1995
(I.D.), HL; affirming [1994] 1 W.L.R. 1071; [1994] 3 All E.R. 686;
[1994] 1 Lloyd's Rep. 492; *The Times*, February 23, 1994; *The Inde-
pendent*, March 2, 1994, CA; reversing [1992] 2 Lloyd's Rep. 481,
Financial Times, July 15, 1992 .... 7a, 7–13
Margereson v. Roberts (J.W.) [1996] P.I.Q.R. P154, QBD 7–184, 7–189
Marinari v. Lloyds Bank [1996] 2 W.L.R. 159; [1996] All E.R. (EC) 84;
[1996] 5 Bank L.R. 84; [1996] C.E.C. 14; *The Times*, October 19,
1995, ECJ 6–02
Mark Wilkinson Furniture v. Woodcraft Designs (Radcliffe) [1998] F.S.R.
63; *The Times*, October 13, 1997, ChD 24–47
Market Investigations v. Minister of Social Security [1969] Q.B. 173;
[1969] 2 W.L.R. 1; (1968) 112 S.J. 905; [1968] 3 All E.R. 732 5–03
Marks & Spencer v. Granada Television, *The Guardian*, March 4, 1998 ... 21–14
Marshall v. Osmond [1983] Q.B. 1034; [1983] 3 W.L.R. 13; (1983) 127
S.J. 301; [1983] 2 All E.R. 225; [1983] R.T.R. 475, CA 7–110
—— v. Rubypoint Ltd (1997) 29 H.L.R. 850; [1997] 1 E.G.L.R. 69; [1997]
25 E.G. 142; [1997] E.G.C.S. 12, CA 2–28
Martin v. Watson [1996] 1 A.C. 74; [1995] 3 W.L.R. 318; [1995] 3 All
E.R. 559; (1995) 145 N.L.J.Rep. 1093; (1995) 139 S.J.L.B. 190; *The
Times*, July 14, 1995; *The Independent*, July 19, 1995, HL; reversing
[1994] Q.B. 425; [1994] 2 W.L.R. 500; [1994] 2 All E.R. 606; (1994)
91 (12) L.S.Gaz. 39; (1994) 138 S.J.L.B. 55; *The Times*, January 27,
1994; *The Independent*, January 26, 1994; *The Guardian*, January 31,
1994, CA 12–24, 12–63, 15a, 15–10,
15–14, 15–38, 15–53, 23–05
Martin Boston & Co. v. Roberts & Others [1996] P.N.L.R. 45; [1995]
N.P.C. 28; *The Times*, March 17, 1995, CA 8–82, 8–91, 8–92
Martindale Estates v. Martindale (1998) 163 D.L.R. (4th) 475, B.C. CA ... 23–23
Mason v. Westside Cemeteries (1996) 135 D.L.R. (4th) 361 13–50

Masters v. Brent London Borough Council [1978] Q.B. 841; [1978] 2
    W.L.R. 768; (1977) 122 S.J. 300; [1978] 2 All E.R. 664; (1977) 76
    L.G.R. 379; (1977) 245 E.G. 483 18–19
Matrix Securities v. Theodore Goddard [1998] S.T.C. 1; [1998] P.N.L.R.
    290 .... 8–73, 8–87
Maudsley v. Palumbo, *The Times*, December 19, 1995, ChD 23–62, 23–82
May v. Woollcombe Beer & Watts (a firm) [1999] P.N.L.R. 283 7–135
Mayfield Investments v. Stewart (1995) 121 D.L.R. (4th) 7–41
Meah v. McCreamer [1985] 1 All E.R. 367; (1985) 135 New L.J. 80 2–35
Mecklermedia Corporation v. D.C. Congress GmbH [1997] 3 W.L.R. 479;
    [1997] F.S.R. 627; [1997] Info T.L.R. 132; [1997] Masons C.L.R. 20;
    (1997) 20(4) I.P.D. 20042; *The Times*, March 27, 1997, ChD 6–02
Meehan v. Tremblett (1996) 133 D.L.R. (4th) 738 23–82
Mehta v. Royal Bank of Scotland plc, *The Times*, January 25, 1999 17–18
Melhuish v. Clifford, August 18, 1998, (unreported), QBD 4–50, 10–06
Mennell v. Newell and Wright [1997] I.C.R. 1039; [1997] I.R.L.R. 519;
    (1997) 94(33) L.S.G. 26; (1997) 141 S.J.L.B. 185; *The Times*, July
    18, 1997, reversing CA; [1996] I.C.R. 607; [1996] I.R.L.R. 384; *The
    Times*, May 2, 1996, EAT 23–39, 23–41
Mercedes Benz v. Clydesdale Bank, 1997 S.L.T. 905; 1996 S.C.L.R. 1005;
    [1997] C.L.C. 81; *The Times*, September 16, 1996 OH 23–11, 23–12
—— v. Leiduck [1996] 1 A.C. 284; [1995] 3 W.L.R. 718; [1995] 3 All
    E.R. 929; [1995] 2 Lloyd's Rep. 417; (1995) 145 L.J. Rep. 1329;
    (1995) 139 S.J.L.B. 195; (1995) 92(28) L.S.G. 28; *The Times*, August
    11, 1995, PC .... 28–28—28–34
Merck & Co. Inc. v. Primecrown (Cases C–267/95 and C–268/95) [1997]
    F.S.R. 237, ECJ 24–92
Meridian Global Funds Management Asia v. Securities Commission [1995]
    2 A.C. 500; [1995] 3 W.L.R. 413; [1995] 3 All E.R. 918; [1995] 2
    B.C.L.C. 116; [1995] B.C.C. 942; (1995) 139 S.J.L.B. 152; (1995) 92
    (28) L.S.Gaz. 39; *The Times*, June 29, 1995, PC 23–10, 23–26, 23–78
Merlin v. British Nuclear Fuels [1990] 2 Q.B. 557; [1990] 3 W.L.R. 383;
    [1990] 3 All E.R. 711 .... 11–12, 19–93
Merrell Dow Pharmaceuticals Inc. v. H.N. Norton & Co. [1996] R.P.C. 76;
    (1997) 33 B.M.L.R. 201; (1996) 19(1) I.P.D. 7; (1995) 139 S.J.L.B.
    245; (1995) 92 (45) L.S.Gaz. 31; *The Times*, October 27, 1995, HL;
    affirming *The Independent*, February 28, 1994 (C.S.); [1994] 2 *Legal
    Times* 12, CA; [1994] R.P.C. 1, ChD 24–83
Metall und Rochstoff AG v. Donaldson Lufkin and Jenrette Inc. [1990] 1
    Q.B. 391; [1989] 3 W.L.R. 563; (1989) 133 S.J. 1200; [1989] 3 All
    E.R. 14, CA; reversing in part 23–23, 23–62
Metropolitan Properties v. Jones [1939] 2 All E.R. 202 18–19
Microdata Information Services v. Rivendale and Clyne [1991] F.S.R. 681,
    CA 23–01
Mid Kent Holdings plc v. General Utilities plc [1997] W.L.R. 14; [1996]
    3 All E.R. 132; (1996) 93(19) L.S.G. 28; (1996) 140 S.J.L.B. 119;
    The Times, May 6, 1996, ChD 23–43, 23–63, 23–64, 23–66,
                                                            23–68, 23–82, 23–86
Middle Temple v. Lloyds Bank plc [1999] 1 All E.R. Comm. 193 13–114
Midland Bank v. Cox McQueen, *The Times*, February 2, 1999 8–75
Millar v. Bassey [1994] E.M.L.R. 44; *The Independent*, August 26, 1993,
    CA 23–11
Minchillo v. Ford [1995] 2 V.R. 594 9–18
Ministry of Defence v. Ashman (1993) 66 P. & C.R. 195; [1993] 40 E.G.
    144; [1993] N.P.C. 70, CA 13–138
Mitchell v. Faber & Faber [1998] E.M.L.R. 807 21–13
Modus Vivendi v. British Products Sanmex [1996] F.S.R. 790; (1996)
    19(10) I.P.D. 2, ChD 6–02

Mölnlycke AB v. Procter and Gamble (No. 5) [1994] R.P.C. 49, CA 24–84
Monarch Airlines v. Luton Airport [1998] 1 Lloyd's Rep. 403 .... 10–06, 10–57
Mond v. Hyde [1998] 3 All E.R. 833, CA 15–53, 21–91
Monk v. Warbey [1935] 1 K.B. 75; 104 L.J.K.B. 153; 152 L.T. 194; 51
 T.L.R. 77; 78 S.J. 783; 50 L1.L.Rep. 33 11–20
Morgan v. Oldhams Press [1971] 1 W.L.R. 1239; 115 S.J. 587; [1971] 2
 All E.R. 1156, HL 21–51
Morris v. Martin (C. W.) and Sons Ltd [1966] 1 Q.B. 716; [1965] 3 W.L.R.
 276; 109 S.J. 451; [1965] 2 All E.R. 725; [1965] 2 Lloyd's Rep. 63,
 CA 5–35
—— v. Murjani; [1996] 1 W.L.R. 848; [1996] 2 All E.R. 384; [196]
 B.P.I.R. 458; *The Times*, December 27, 1995, CA .... 28–28—28–34
Morris v. Wentworth-Stanley [1999] 2 W.L.R. 470, CA 4–55
Morrison v. Forsyth [1995] 6 Med. L.R. 6 8–25
Mortgage Express v. Bowerman & Partners (No. 2) [1996] 2 All E.R. 836;
 [1996] 1 P.N.L.R. 62; [1996] 1 E.G.L.R. 126; [1996] 04 E.G. 126;
 (1996) 60 Conv. 204; [1995] N.P.C. 129; [1995] E.G.C.S. 129; *The
 Times*, August 1, 1995, CA 8a, 8–85
Mortgage Express v. Newman [1996] P.N.L.R. 603, ChD 8–114
Mount v. Barker Austin [1998] P.N.L.R. 493 8–96
Mulcahy v. Ministry of Defence; [1996] Q.B. 732; [1996] 2 W.L.R. 474;
 [1996] 2 All E.R. 758; [1996] P.I.Q.R. P276; (1996) 146 N.L.J. Rep.
 334; *The Times*, February 27, 1996; *The Independent*, February 29,
 1996, CA 4–10, 7a, 7–13, 7–109
Mullady v. DPP [1997] C.O.D. 422, QBD 16–104
Mullin v. Richards [1998] 1 W.L.R. 1304; [1998] 1 All E.R. 920; [1998]
 P.I.Q.R. P276, CA 3–24, 4–32, 7–122, 7–149
Multigroup Bulgaria Holdings v. Oxford Analytica 1995–M–2141, QBD .. 21–119
Murdoch v. Glacier Metal Co., *The Times*, January 21, 1998, CA 18–09
Murphy v. Brentwood District Council [1991] 1 A.C. 398; [1990] 3 W.L.R.
 414; [1990] 2 All E.R. 908; (1990) 22 H.L.R. 502; (1990) 134 S.J.
 1076; 21 Con.L.R. 1; 89 L.G.R. 24; (1990) 6 Const.L.J. 304; (1990)
 154 L.G.Rev. 1010; (1990) L.S.Gaz., August 29, 15; (1990) 134 S.J.
 1058; (1990) 134 S.J. 1974; [1990] L.G.C., September 14, 14; 50
 B.L.R. 1; (1991) 3 Admin.L.R. 37; (1990) 6 P.N. 158; (1990) 6 P.N.
 150; (1990) 134 S.J. 1256, HL; reversing [1990] 2 W.L.R. 944; [1990]
 2 All E.R. 269; 88 L.G.R. 333; (1990) 134 S.J. 458; (1990) L.S.Gaz.,
 February 7, 42, CA; affirming 13 Con.L.R. 96 .... 7–90, 7–95,
 7–103, 8–117
Murray v. Bitango [1996] 7 W.W.R. 163 10–44
—— v. Hibernian Dance Club [1997] P.I.Q.R. 46; *The Times*, August 12,
 1996, CA 4–50
—— v. Ministry of Defence [1998] 1 W.L.R. 692, HL 1–05E
—— v. Yorkshire Fund Managers [1998] 1 W.L.R. 951; [1998] 2 All E.R.
 1015; [1998] F.S.R. 372; (1998) 95(3) L.S.G. 24; (1998) 95(4) L.S.G.
 33; (1998) 142 S.J.L.B. 45; *The Times*, December 18, 1997, CA 23–23,
 23–42, 23–62,
 23–80, 26–01

N v. C [1998] 1 F.L.R. 63; *The Independent*, April 28, 1997, CA 8–20
N.T.S.U. v. Att.-Gen. Nova Scotia (1993) 102 D.L.R. (4th) 267, NSSC 23–01
N.Z. Jet Boat River Racing v. N.Z. Seamen's Union [1990] 1 N.Z.I.L.R.
 529 23–81
Nadezhda Krupskaya, The [1997] 2 Lloyd's Rep. 35 .... 23–11, 23–27, 23–31
Nagle v. Rottnest Island Authority (1992) 177 C.L.R. 423 7–149
National Hockey League v. Pepsi Cola Canada (1995) 122 D.L.R. (4th)
 412 B.C.C.A. 23–09, 23–13, 23–21, 23–28, 23–32

National Home Loan Corp. v. Giffen, Couch and Archer [1998] 1 W.L.R.
207; [1997] 3 All E.R. 808; [1998] P.N.L.R. 111; [1997] N.P.C. 100;
The Times, October 9, 1997, CA; reversing (1997) 94(2) L.S.G. 24;
(1997) 141 S.J.L.B. 29; *The Times*, December 31, 1996; *The Inde-
pendent*, January 27, 1997 (C.S.) 8–85
Nationwide Building Society v. Balmer Radmore (a firm). *See* Nationwide
Building Society v. Various Solicitors (No. 3)
—— v. Lewis [1998] Ch. 482; [1998] 2 W.L.R. 915; [1998] 3 All E.R.
143; *The Times*, March 6, 1998; *The Independent*, March 9, 1998
(C.S.), CA; reversing [1997] 1 W.L.R. 1181; [1997] 3 All E.R. 498;
The Times, June 16, 1997 4–53
—— v. Thumbleby & Co. [1999] Lloyd's Rep. P.N. 359 .... 3–19, 14–36
—— v. Various Solicitors (No. 3), *The Times*, March 1, 1999 ... 8–01, 8–85, 23–01,
23–08, 23–23, 23–37,
23–62, 23–80, 23–82
Navaei v. Navaei, January 6, 1995; Deputy District Judge Radcliffe;
Eastbourne County Ct. [Ex rel. Russell Pyne, Barrister] 27–43
Neal v. Bingle [1998] 2 W.L.R. 57, CA 27–17
Nelhams v. Sandells Maintenance [1996] 5 P.I.Q.R. P52; 46 Con. L.R. 40;
The Times, June 15, 1995, CA 7–164
Nelson v. Nelson; [1997] 1 W.L.R. 233; [1997] 1 All E.R. 970; [1997]
P.N.L.R. 413; [1997] B.P.I.R. 702; (1997) 94(2) L.S.G. 26; (1997)
147 N.L.J. Rep. 126; (1997) 141 S.J.L.B. 30; *The Times*, January 8,
1997, CA 8–80
Neutrogena Corporation v. Golden [1996] R.P.C. 473; (1996) 19(4) I.P.D.
5, CA 25–14
New York Times v. Sullivan (1964) 376 U.S. 254 21–182
New Zealand Guardian Trust Co. v. Brooks [1995] 1 W.L.R. 96; [1995] 2
B.C.L.C. 242; [1995] B.C.C. 407; (1994) 138 S.J.L.B. 240; (1995) 92
(01) L.S.Gaz. 36, PC 7–81
Newell & Newell v. Goldenberg [1995] 6 Med.L.R. 371, QBD 8–25, 8–35
News Group Newspapers v. Society of Graphical and Allied Trades '82
(No. 2) [1987] 1 C.R. 187 .... 23–42A
Nicholas H, The. *See* Marc Rich & Co. AGV. Bishop Rock Marine Co.
Bethmarine Co. and Nippon Kaiji Kyokai
Nicholls v. Nicholls [1997] 1 W.L.R. 314; [1997] All E.R. 97; [1997] 1
F.L.R. 649; [1997] 3 F.C.R. 14; [1997] Fam.Law 321; (1997) 147
N.L.J. Rep. 61; *The Times*, January 21, 1997 CA 23–42A
Nicol and Selvanayagam v. DPP (1996) 160 J.P. 155; [1996] Crim. L.R.
318; (1996) 160 J.P.N. 14; *The Times*, November 22, 1995 12–39
Nigel Upchurch Associates v. The Aldridge Estates Investment Co. [1993]
1 Lloyd's Rep. 535, DC 4–31
Nifsson v. Redditch Borough Council [1995] P.I.Q.R. P199, CA [Ex rel.
David Platt, Barrister] 7–129
Noble v. Harrison [1926] 2 K.B. 332 18–60
Norglen Ltd (in liquidation) v. Reeds Rains Prudential Ltd; Circuit Systems
Ltd (in liquidation) v. Zuken-Redac (UK) Ltd [1997] 3 W.L.R. 1177;
[1998] 1 All E.R. 218; [1998] 1 B.C.L.C. 176; [1998] B.C.C. 44; 87
B.L.R. 1; (1998) 75 P. & C.R.D. 21; (1997) 147 N.L.J. 1773; (1997)
94(48) L.S.G. 29; (1998) 142 S.J.L.B. 26; *The Times*, December 1,
1997, HL 4–42
Norman v. Future Publishing, February 1999 C.L. 175 21–17
Normart Management v. West Hill Redevelopment Co. (1998) 155 D.L.R.
(4th) 627, Ont. CA 23–07, 23–82
Norowzian v. Arks Ltd [1999] F.S.R. 79 24–07
Northern Territory v. Mengel (1995) 185 C.L.R. 307 .... 23–08, 23–42,
23–60, 23–62, 23–63, 23–71, 23–81, 23–82

Norweb v. Dixon [1995] 1 W.L.R. 636; [1995] 3 All E.R. 952; *The Times*,
  February 24, 1995, QBD 16–81
Norwich City Council v. Harvey (Paul Clarke) (1988) 39 B.C.R. 75; (1988)
  4 Const. L.J. 217 7–87
Nwabudike v. London Borough of Southwark, May 8, 1996 (unreported) . 7–149
Nykredit v. Edward Erdman & Co. (No. 2) [1997] 1 W.L.R. 1627; [1998]
  1 All E.R. 305; [1998] Lloyd's Rep. Bank 39; [1998] P.N.L.R. 197;
  [1998] 1 E.G.L.R. 99; [1998] 05 E.G. 150; [1998] C.L.C. 116; (1998)
  75 P. & C.R. D28; [1997] N.P.C. 165; (1998) 95(1) L.S.G. 24; (1998)
  142 S.J.L.B. 29; *The Times*, December 3, 1997, HL 3–22, 8–112, 31–09

OLL Ltd v. Secretary of State for Transport [1997] 3 All E.R. 897; (1997)
  147 N.L.J. 1099; *The Times*, July 22, 1997, Q.B.D. 7–32, 7–103, 7–109
Oak Tree Leisure v. RA Fisk and Associates, *The Times*, January 1, 1997,
  CA 4–63
Oates v. Pitman (1998) 76 P. & C.R. 496 .... 8–91, 8–112
Ocular Sciences Ltd v. Aspect Vision Care Ltd (No. 2) [1997] R.P.C. 289;
  (1997) 20 (3) I.P.D. 20022, Pat Ct 24–46, 26–20
Olinski v. Johnson [1997] 32 O.R. (3d) 653 10–11
Oliver v. McKenna & Co., *The Times*, December 20, 1995, ChD 8–84
O'Loughlin v. Chief Constable of Essex [1998] 1 W.L.R. 374, CA 16–95,
                                                                    16–107
Olotu v. Home Office [1997] 1 W.L.R. 328; [1997] 1 All E.R. 385; (1997)
  94(1) L.S.G. 24; (1997) 147 S.J.L.B. 14; *The Times*, December 11,
  1996; *The Independent*, December 5, 1996, CA 1–05C, 11–03,
                            11–05, 11–16a, 12–20, 16–119, 23–68, 23–82
Omega Trust v. Wright, Son & Pepper (1997) 73 P. & C.R. D39; [1997]
  P.N.L.R. 425; [1997] 1 E.G.L.R. 120; [1997] 18 E.G. 120; [1996]
  N.P.C. 189, CA 7–74, 8–14
—— v. —— (No. 2) [1998] P.N.L.R. 337 .... 8–98, 8–114
Ontario v. Barleven Town Centre Inc. (1995) 121 D.L.R. (4th) 748 (Ont.)   23–08
Ontario Att.-Gen. v. Dielman (1994) 117 D.L.R. (4th) 449, Ont. 23–123
Orient Express Trade Mark [1996] R.P.C. 25, ChD 24–68
Orjula, The [1995] 2 Lloyd's Rep. 395 .... 9A, 9–18, 9–19
Ormrod v. Crosville Motor Services Ltd [1953] 1 W.L.R. 1120; 97 S.J.
  570; [1953] 2 All E.R. 753, CA; affirming [1953] 1 W.L.R. 409; 97
  S.J. 154; [1953] 1 All E.R. 711 5–66
O'Rourke v. Camden London Borough Council [1997] 3 W.L.R. 86;
  [1998] A.C. 188; [1997] 3 All E.R. 23; (1997) 29 H.L.R. 793; (1997)
  6 Admin.L.R. 649; (1997) 161 J.P.N. 1038; (1997) 94(26) L.S.G. 30;
  (1997) 141 S.J.L.B. 139; [1997] N.P.C. 93; *The Times*, June 21, 1997;
  The Independent, June 17, 1997, HL 11–14, 11–15, 23–44, 23–66
O'Shea v. Royal Borough of Kingston on Thames [1995] P.I.Q.R. 208,
  CA 7–149
Osman v. Ferguson [1993] 4 All E.R. 344 .... 1–05G
—— v. United Kingdom (1998) 5 B.H.R.C. 293; [1998] H.R.C.D. 966;
  The Times, November 5, 1998, ECHR 1–05G
Oswald v. Countryside Surveyors (1996) 50 Con.L.R. 1; [1996] 37 E.G.
  140 [1996] 2 E.G.L.R. 104; [1996] E.G.C.S. 100, CA 8–112
Oyston v. Blaker [1996] 1 W.L.R. 1326; [1996] 2 All E.R. 106; [1996]
  E.M.L.R. 125; *The Times*, November 15, 1995, CA 31–43

P v. T [1997] 1 W.L.R. 1309; [1997] 4 All E.R. 200; [1997] I.C.R. 887;
  [1997] I.R.L.R. 405; *The Times*, May 7, 1997, ChD 21–61
PCR Ltd v. Dow Jones Telerate Ltd [1998] F.S.R. 170 26–04
Page v. Sheerness Steel plc. *See* Wells v. Wells 27–14, 27–20

—— v. Smith [1996] 1 A.C. 190; [1995] 2 W.L.R. 644; [1995] 2 All E.R. 736; [1995] 2 Lloyd's Rep. 95; [1995] P.I.Q.R. P329; [1995] R.T.R. 210; (1995) 145 N.L.J.Rep. 723; (1995) 95 (23) L.S.Gaz. 33 (1995) 139 S.J.L.B. 173; *The Times*, May 12, 1995; *The Independent*, May 12, 1995; Lloyd's List, May 25, 1995 (I.D.), HL; reversing [1994] 4 All E.R. 522; [1994] R.T.R. 293; [1995] P.I.Q.R. P58; (1994) 144 N.L.J. Rep. 756; *The Times*, May 4, 1994, CA; reversing [1993] P.I.Q.R. Q55 .... 1–21, 7–45, 7–52, 7–184
—— v. —— (No. 2) [1996] 1 W.L.R. 855; [p1996] 3 All E.R. 272; [1996] P.I.Q.R. P364, CA 2–06
Palmer v. Tees Health Authority [1998] Lloyd's Rep. (Med.) 447; *The Times*, June 1, 1998 7–47
Parry (1995) 15 L.S. 335 10–01
Paragon Finance plc v. Thakerar [1999] 1 All E.R. 400 23–77
Parfums Christian Dior SA v. Evora BV (C337/95) [1998] R.P.C. 166; [1998] E.T.M.R. 26, ECJ 24–71
—— v. Cleaver [1970] A.C. 1; [1969] 2 W.L.R. 821; 113 S.J. 147; [1969] 1 All E.R. 555; 6 K.I.R. 265; [1969] 1 Lloyd's Rep. 183, HL 27–20
—— v. Clwyd Health Authority [1997] P.I.Q.R. P1; [1997] 8 Med.L.R. 243 .... 31–03, 31–23
Partizan v. Kilkenny (O.J.) & Co. [1998] 1 B.C.L.C. 157 15–42
Patel v. Patel [1988] 2 F.L.R. 179; (1988) 18 Fam. Law 213 .... 23–42A
Paterson v. Humberside County Council, *The Times*, April 19, 1995, QBD; [1995] E.G.C.S. 39; [1995] N.P.C. 37 7–33
Paton Calvert Cordon Bleu Trade Mark [1996] R.P.C. 94, TMR 24–65
Patrick Stovedoves Operations v. ITWF [1998] 2 Lloyd's Rep. 523; [1998] C.L.C. 1022 23–18
Peach Publishing v. Slater & Co. [1998] P.N.L.R. 364, CA 7–62
Pearce v. Ove Arup Partnership [1999] 1 All E.R. 769; [1999] F.S.R. 525, CA; [1997] Ch. 293; [1997] 2 W.L.R. 799; [1997] 3 All E.R. 31; [1997] F.S.R. 641; (1997) 20(8) I.P.D. 20081; (1997) 94(15) L.S.G. 27; (1997) 141 S.J.L.B. 73; *The Times*, March 17, 1997 .... 6–03, 6–06, 6–07, 6–09,

24–01
—— v. Secretary of State for Defence [1988] A.C. 755; [1988] 2 W.L.R. 1027; (1988) 132 S.J. 699; [1988] 2 All E.R. 348, HL 4–10
—— v. United Bristol Healthcare Trust [1999] P.I.Q.R. P53, CA 7–137, 8–46
Pearson v. Lightning (1998) 95(20) L.S.G. 33; (1998) 142 S.J.L.B. 143; *The Times*, April 30, 1998, CA 7–127
Penn v. Bristol and West Building Society [1995] 2 F.L.R. 938; (1995) 139 S.J.L.B. 164; (1995) 92 (27) L.S. Gaz. 31; *The Times*, June 19, 1995, ChD 1–05G, 7A, 7–13, 7–102, 8–77, 9–15
Percy v. Hall [1997] Q.B. 924; [1997] 3 W.L.R. 573; [1996] 4 All E.R. 523; (1996) 160 J.P. Rep. 788; [1996] N.P.C. 74; (1996) 93(23) L.S.G. 36; (1996) 140 S.J.L.B. 130; *The Times*, May 31, 1996, CA   12–17
Perrett v. Collins [1998] 2 Lloyd's Rep. 225; *The Times*, June 23, 1998, CA 9–15
Perry v. DPP [1995] 3 All E.R. 124, DC 12–39
Peters-Brown v. Regina District Health Board [1997] 1 W.W.R. 638 8–23
Phelps v. Hillingdon London Borough Council; [1999] 1 W.L.R. 500; [1999] 1 All E.R. 421; [1998] C.L.Y. 3945, CA; [1997] 3. F.C.R. 621; (1997) 9 Admin. L.R. 657; [1997] New L.J. 1421; (1997) 39 B.M.L.R. 51; (1997) 94(39) L.S.G. 39; (1997) 141 S.J.L.B. 214; *The Times*, October 10, 1997, QBD 7A, 7–106
Philips v. Ward [1956] 1 W.L.R. 471; 100 S.J. 317; [1956] 1 All E.R. 874, CA 8–112
Philips Electronics NV v. Ingman Ltd [1999] F.S.R. 112 24–92

Phillips v. Britannia Hygienic Laundry Co. [1923] 2 K.B. 832; 93 L.J.K.B.
    5; 129 L.T. 777; 39 T.L.R. 530; 68 S.J. 102; 21 L.G.R. 709; [1923]
    All E.R. Rep. 127; affirming [1923] 1 K.B. 539 11–19
—— v. Eyre (1870) L.R. 6 Q.B. 1 6–07
—— v. Perry & Dalgety Agriculture, March 6, 1997 (unreported) 10a, 10–37
Pickett v. British Rail Engineering Ltd [1980] A.C. 136; [1978] 3 W.L.R.
    955; [1979] 1 All E.R. 774; [1979] 1 Lloyd's Rep. 519; (1978) 122
    S.J. 778, HL 4–55
Pickford v. Imperial Chemical Industries plc [1998] 1 W.L.R. 1189; [1998]
    3 All E.R. 462; [1998] I.C.R. 673; [1998] I.R.L.R. 435; (1998) 43
    B.M.L.R. 1; (1998) 95(31) L.S.G. 36; (1998) 148 N.L.J. 978; (1998)
    142 S.J.L.B. 198; The Times, June 30, 1998; The Independent, July 1,
    1998, HL 2–04, 7–174
Pigliavento v. Tyler 669 N.Y.S. 2d (1998) 9–42
Pioneer Electronics Capital Inc. and Another v. Warner Music Manufactur-
    ing Europe GmbH and Another [1995] R.P.C. 487 24–88
Pirelli General Cable Works v. Faber (Oscar) and Partners [1983] 2 A.C.
    1; [1983] 2 W.L.R. 6; (1983) 127 S.J. 16; [1983] 1 All E.R. 65; (1983)
    265 E.G. 979; (1983) 133 New L.J. 63, HL; reversing (1982) 263 E.G.
    879, CA 31–09
Platform Home Loans v. Oyston Shipways [1999] 1 All E.R. 833; [1999]
    P.N.L.R. 469, HL; [1998] Ch. 466; [1998] 3 W.L.R. 94; [1998] 4 All
    E.R. 252; [1998] 1 E.G.L.R. 108; [1998] 13 E.G. 148; [1998] P.N.L.R.
    512; [1997] E.G.C.S. 184; (1998) 95(1) L.S.G. 26; (1998) 142 S.J.L.B.
    46; [1997] N.P.C. 185; The Times, January 15, 1998, CA 3–22, 8a,
                                                                                    8–01, 8–114
Pollard v. Chief Constable of West Yorkshire, Trans. Ref. CCTRF 97/1396
    CMS2 April 28, 1998, CA 12–36
Polly Peck International plc, Re [1997] 2 B.C.L. C.630; [1996] N.P.C. 176;
    (1997) 94(1) L.S.G. 23; (1997) 141 S.J.L.B. 21; The Times, December
    27, 1996, ChD 6–06
—— (No. 4), Re, The Times, May 18, 1998, CA 23–43, 23–62, 23–80
Possfund Custodian Trustee v. Diamond and Others; [1996] 1 W.L.R.
    1351; [1996] 2 All E.R. 774; [1996] B.C.L.C. 665; The Times, April
    18, 1996, ChD 7–64, 7–65, 14–31
Post Office v. Union of Communication Workers [1990] 1 W.L.R. 981;
    [1990] 3 All E.R. 199; [1990] I.C.R. 258; [1990] I.R.L.R. 143, CA ... 23–114
Pounder v. London Underground [1995] P.I.Q.R. P217, QBD 27–40
Powell v. Boldaz (1997) 39 B.M.L.R. 35; [1998] Lloyd's Rep. (Med.) 117,
    CA 8–12
Powney v. Coxage, The Times, March 8, 1988 27–27
Prince v. Att.-Gen. [1996] 3 N.Z.L.R. 733 .... 7–148, 8–61
Prince plc v. Prince Sports Group Inc. [1998] F.S.R. 21 [1998] Info. T.L.R. 329;
    [1998] Masons C.L.R. 139 .... 22–05, 24–75
Pro Sieben Media AG v. Carlton UK Television Ltd [1999] 1 W.L.R. 605;
    The Times, January 7, 1999 24–24
Probert v. Society for the Welfare of Horses, Daily Telegraph, February 7,
    1997 13–110
Prole v. Allen [1950] 1 All E.R. 476; [1950] 209 L.T. 183 4–50
Prosser v. Edmonds (1835) 1 Y. & C. 481; 160 E.R. 196 4–42
Prudential Assurance Co. v. Lorenz (1971) 11 K.I.R. 78 23–23
—— v. Waterloo Real Estate Inc., The Times, February 8, 1999 17–77
Public Service Employees Relations Act, Re (1987) 38 D.L.R. (4th) 161,
    SCC 23–01
Punford v. Gilberts (a firm) [1998] P.N.L.R. 763, CA 8–77

Q's Estate, Re (1999) N.L.J. 442; The Independent, March 19, 1999 28–28

Quilty v. Windsor 1999 S.L.T. 346 21–14
Quinn v. McGinty 1998 Rep. L.R. 107 .... 4–49, 11–20
—— v. Ministry of Defence, P.I.Q.R. P387, CA 4–10
—— v. TVN2 [1995] 3 N.Z.L.R. 216 21–204

R. v. BHB Community Healthcare NHS Trust, *ex p.* Barker, *The Times*,
    October 14, 1998, CA .... 12–66—12–68
—— v. Basra [1998] P.N.L.R. 535 8–80
—— v. Blake [1997] 1 W.L.R. 1167; [1997] 1 All E.R. 963; [1997] 1 Cr.
    App. R. 209; [1997] Crim. L.R. 207; *The Times*, August 17, 1996,
    CA 23–59
—— v. Bournewood Community and Mental Health Services Trust, ex p.
    L [1998] 3 W.L.R. 107; [1998] 1 All E.R. 289, HL 3–62, 8–32, 12–11,
                                                                        12–17, 12–66
——v. Bow Street Metropolitan Stipendiary Magistrate, *ex p.* Pinochet
    Ugarte (No. 3) [1999] 2 W.L.R. 827, HL 4–21
—— v. Bowden [1996] 1 W.L.R. 98; [1995] 4 All E.R. 505; [1996] 1 Cr.
    App. R. 104; 94 L.G.R. 137; (1995) 159 J.P. 502; (1995) 159 J.P. 502;
    (1995) 159 L.G. Rev. 649; (1995) 159 J.P.N. 370; *The Times*, March
    6, 1995; *The Independent*, April 5, 1995, CA 16–138
—— v. Brown (Anthony); R. v. Laskey (Colin); R. v. Jaggard; R. v. Lucas
    (Saxon); R. v. Carter; R. v. Cadman [1994] 1 A.C. 212; [1993] 2
    W.L.R. 556; [1993] 2 All E.R. 75; (1993) 97 Cr.App.R. 44; (1993)
    157 J.P. 337; (1993) 143 N.L.J. 399; (1993) 151 J.P.N. 233; *The
    Times*, March 12, 1993; *The Independent*, March 12, 1993, HL;
    affirming [1992] Q.B. 491; [1992] 2 W.L.R. 441; [1992] 2 All E.R.
    552; (1992) 136 S.J.L.B. 90; (1992) 94 Cr.App.R. 302; (1992) 142
    N.L.J. 275; (1992) 156 J.P.N. 396; *The Independent*, February 20,
    1992; *The Times*, February 21, 1992; *The Guardian*, March 4, 1992,
    CA 3–36, 12–08
—— v. Burstow [1997] 1 Cr.App.R. 20 12–12
—— v. Chalkley [1998] 2 All E.R. 155 .... 12–54, 16–06
—— v. Chief Constable of North Wales Police, ex p A.B. [1998] 3 W.L.R.
    57; [1998] 3 W.L.R. 57; [1998] 3 All E.R. 310; [1998] 2 F.L.R. 571;
    [1998] 3 F.C.R. 371; [1998] Fam. Law 529; (1998) 95(17) L.S.G. 29;
    The Times, March 23, 1998; *The Independent*, March 26, 1998,
    CA 1–05a, 1–05B, 1–23, 1–05E
—— v. Chief Constable of Sussex, ex p. International Trader's Ferry;
    [1998] 3 W.L.R. 1260; (1998) N.L.J. 1750; (1998) 142 S.J.L.B. 286;
    (1998) 95(47) L.S.G. 29; *The Times*, November 16, 1998, HL;
    affirming [1998] Q.B. 477; [1997] 3 W.L.R. 132; [1997] 2 All E.R.
    65; [1997] C.O.D. 311; *The Times*, February 12, 1997; *The Independ-
    ent*, January 31, 1997, CA 23–71, 23–124
—— v. Chief Constable of the Warwickshire Constabulary, ex p. F [1999]
    1 W.L.R. 564 16–129
—— v. City of London Corpn., ex p. Mystery of the Barbers of London
    (1997) 73 P. & C.R. 59; [1996] 2 E.G.L.R. 128; [1996] 42 E.G. 156;
    [1996] J.P.L. B125; [1996] N.P.C. 91; [1996] E.G.C.S. 101, *The
    Times*, June 28, 1996, QBD 23–37
—— v. Constanza [1997] 2 Cr. App.R. 492; [1997] Crim. L.R. 576; *The
    Times*, March 31, 1997, CA 12–12
—— v. Criminal Injuries Compensation Board, ex p. K [1999] 2 W.L.R.
    948 27–50
—— v. Croydon Health Authority [1998] P.I.Q.R. Q26; [1998] 1 Lloyd's
    Rep. (Med.) 44, CA 7–189, 8–45
—— v. Gateway Foodmarkets [1997] 3 All E.R. 78; [1997] 2 Cr. App. R.
    40; [1997] I.C.R. 382; [1997] I.R.L.R. 189; [1997] Crim. L.R. 512;

(1997) 94(3) L.S.G. 28; (1997) 141 S.J.L.B. 28; *The Times*, January 2, 1997; *The Independent*, February 10, 1997, CA 23–26, 23–78
—— v. Governor of Brockhill Prison, ex p. Evans [1997] Q.B. 443; [1997] 2 W.L.R. 236; [1997] 1 All E.R. 439; [1997] 1 Cr.App.R. 282; [1997] Crim. L.R. 148; [1997] C.O.D. 242; (1996) 146 N.L.J. Rep. 1721; (1996) 93(46) L.S.G. 28; *The Times*, November 20, 1996; *The Independent*, November 22, 1996, QBD 12–17, 12–20
——v. —— (No. 2) [1998] 4 All E.R. 993; [1998] C.O.D. 378; (1998) 95(33) L.S.G. 35; (1998) 142 S.J.L.B. 196; *The Times*, July 6, 1998; *The Independent*, June 24, 1998, CA 12–17, 12–20, 27–68
—— v. Ireland [1998] A.C. 147; [1997] 3 W.L.R. 534; [1997] 4 All E.R. 225; [1998] 1 Cr. App. R. 177; [1998] 1 F.L.R. 105; (1997) 161 J.P. 569; [1998] Fam. Law 137; [1997] Crim. L.R. 810; (1997) 161 J.P.N. 816; (1997) 147 N.L.J. 1273; (1997) 141 S.J.L.B. 205; *The Times*, July 25, 1997; *The Independent*, July 30, 1997, HL; affirming [1997] Q.B. 114; [1996] 3 W.L.R. 650; [1997] 1 All E.R. 112; [1996] 2 Cr. App. R. 426; [1997] 1 F.L.R. 687; (1996) 160 J.P. 597; [1997] Crim. L.R. 434; [1997] Fam. Law 323; (1996) 93(23) L.S.G. 35; (1996) 160 J.P.N. 448; (1996) 140 S.J.L.B. 148; *The Times*, May 22, 1996; *The Independent*, July 15, 1996, CA 12–12, 23–40, 23–42A, 23–123
—— v. Johnson [1997] 1 W.L.R. 367; [1996] 2 Cr.App.R. 434; (1996) 160 J.P. 605; [1996] Crim. L.R. 828; (1996) 93(22) L.S.G. 26; (1996) 160 J.P.N. 696; (1996) 140 S.J.L.B. 183; *The Times*, May 22, 1996, CA 23–42A, 23–123
—— v. Kelly, [1998] 3 All E.R. 741; *The Times*, May 21, 1998; *The Independent*, June 4, 1998, CA 13–50
—— v. Lambeth Borough Council ex p. Wilson (1997) 29 H.L.R. 104; (1996) 3 F.C.R. 146; (1996) 8 Admin.L.R. 376; (1996) 160 L.G.Rev. 484; [1996] C.O.D. 281; *The Times*, March 21, 1996, QBD 8–80
—— v. Linekar (Gareth) [1995] Q.B. 250; [1995] 2 W.L.R. 237; [1995] 3 All E.R. 69; [1995] 2 Cr.App.R. 49; [1995] Crim.L.R. 320; (1994) 138 S.J.L.B. 227; (1995) 92 (02) L.S.Gaz. 35; *The Times*, October 26, 1994; *The Independent*, December 19, 1994 (C.S.), CA 12–09
—— v. Lord Chancellor's Department ex p. Nangle [1992] 1 All E.r. 897; [1991] I.C.R. 743; [1991] I.R.L.R. 3443; [1991] C.O.D. 484 4–10
—— v. Luton J.J., ex p. R January 27, 1998 (unreported) CA 8–80
—— v. Macklin (1838) 168 E.R. 1136 23–88
—— v. Ministry of Agriculture, Fisheries and Food, ex p. Monsanto plc, *The Times*, October 12, 1998 28–13
—— v. Ministry of Defence, ex p. Walker [1999] P.I.Q.R. Q168 4–10
—— v. Northavon District Council ex p. Palmer (1995) 27 H.L.R. 576; [1995] N.P.C. 125; *The Times*, August 1, 1995; *The Independent*, August 9, 1995, CA 23–44, 23–64
—— v. Owino (Nimrod) [1995] Crim.L.R. 743, CA 12–36
—— v. Portsmouth City Council, ex p. Bonaco Builders, June 6, 1995 (unreported) 23–44, 23–64
—— v. Richardson (Diana) [1998] 2 Cr.App.R. 200; *The Times*, April 6, 1998 12–09
—— v. St George's Healthcare Trust (No. 2), *The Times*, August 3, 1998 8–26
—— v. Secretary of State for Home Department, ex p. Gilmore [1998] 2 W.L.R. 618; [1998] 1 All E.R. 264; [1997] 2 Cr. App. R. 374; [1997] C.O.D. 365; *The Times*, July 4, 1997 23–76
—— v. Secretary of State for Transport, ex p. Factortame (No. 5) [1999] 2 All E.R. 640, CA 1–04, 27–69
—— v. South Western Magistrates' Court, ex p. Cofie [1997] 1 W.L.R. 885; (1997) 161 J.P. 69; (1996) 160 J.P.N. 1046; *The Times*, August 15, 1996, DC 16–129
—— v. TNT Canada Inc. (1996) 131 D.L.R. (4th) 289 23–18

—— v. Wilson (Alan Thomas) [1997] Q.B. 47; [1996] 3 W.L.R. 125;
  [1996] 2 Cr.App.R. 241; [1996] Crim.L.R. 573; (1996) 140 S.J.L.B.
  93; *The Times*, March 5, 1996, CA 3–36, 12–08
—— v. Wilson, ex p. Williamson, *The Independent*, April 19, 1995,
  QBD 12–66, 12–67, 12–68
RCA Corp. v. Pollard [1983] Ch. 135; [1982] 3 W.L.R. 1007; [1982] 3 All
  E.R. 771; [1983] F.S.R. 9, CA; reversing [1982] 1 W.L.R. 979; (1982)
  126 S.J. 379; [1982] 2 All E.R. 468; [1982] F.S.R. 369 23–21
RJB Mining (UK) v. National Union of Mineworkers [1997] I.R.L.R. 621
  CA; [1995] I.R.L.R. 556 .... 23–112, 23–114, 23–115, 23–118, 23–121
R (L) v. Witherspoon [1999] P.N.L.R. 766 8–70
RWDSO v. Pepsi (1999) 167 D.L.R. (4th) 412 (Sask. CA) 23–71
Raflatac Ltd v. Eade [1999] 1 Lloyd's Rep. 506 3–20
Ranger Uranium Mines v. Fedn. Miscellaneous Workers Union [1987] 54
  N.T.R. 6; (1988) 8 I.L.L.R. 429 23–55
Rantzen v. Mirror Newspapers [1994] Q.B. 670; [1993] 3 W.L.R. 953;
  [1993] 4 All E.R. 975; (1993) 143 N.L.J. 507; *The Independent*, April
  1, 1993; *The Times*, April 6, 1993, CA 21–203, 21–229
Ratcliff v. McConnell [1999] 1 W.L.R. 670; *The Times*, December 16,
  1998, CA 3–48, 10–80, 10–85
Ratcliffe v. Plymouth Health Authority [1998] P.I.Q.R. P170; [1998]
  Lloyd's Rep. Med. 162; (1998) 42 B.M.L.R. 64, CA 8–50
Ray v. Classic FM plc [1998] E.S.R. 622; [1998] E.C.C. 488; (1998) 21(5)
  I.P.D. 21047; (1998) 148 N.L.J. 445; (1998) 95(17) L.S.G. 32; *The
  Times*, April 8, 1998 24–13
Reaveley v. Safeway Stores plc [1998] P.N.L.R. 526 8–80
Redrow Homes v. Bett Brothers plc [1998] F.S.R. 345; 1997 S.C. 142; *The
  Times*, May 2, 1997, HL.. 24–29, 27–67
Reeman v. Department of Transport [1997] 2 Lloyd's Rep. 648; [1997]
  P.N.L.R. 618, CA 7–63, 7–64, 7–102
Reeves v. Commissioner of Police for the Metropolis [1999] 3 W.L.R. 363;
  [1999] 3 All E.R. 897, HL 2–24, 2–35, 3a, 3–04, 3–05, 3–08,
                             3–09, 3–22, 3–47, 3–61, 7–23, 11–25
—— v. Thrings & Long (A Firm) [1996] P.N.L.R. 265; [1995] 11 P.N.
  32; [1993] E.G.C.S. 196; [1993] N.P.C. 159, CA 8–88
Reibl v. Hughes (1980) 114 D.L.R. (3d) 1 8–41
Reilly v. Merseyside Regional Health Authority [1995] 6 Med. L.R. 246;
  The Independent, April 29, 1994, CA 7–43
Revill v. Newberry; [1996] Q.B. 567; [1996] 2 W.L.R. 239; [1996] 1 All
  E.R. 291; (1996) 146 N.L.J. Rep. 49; (1995) 139 S.J.L.B. 244; (1995)
  92 (44) L.S.Gaz. 31; *The Times*, November 3, 1995; *The Independent*,
  November 10, 1995, CA 3–02, 3–03, 3–05,
                     3–07, 3–08, 7–22, 10a, 10–03, 10–76, 12–03, 29–02, 29–06
Reynolds v. Times Newspapers; [1998] 3 All E.R. 961; *The Times*, July 9,
  1998 .... 21–01, 21–04, 21–117, 21–119, 21–120
Rhodes v. Spokes [1996] 7 Med. L.R.135, QBD 8–46
Richardson v. Kitching [1995] 6 Med.L.R. 257, QBD 8–66
—— v. Pitt-Stanley [1995] Q.B. 123; [1995] 2 W.L.R. 26; [1995] 1 All
  E.R. 460; [1995] I.C.R. 303; [1994] P.I.Q.R. 496; *The Times*, August
  11, 1994; *The Independent*, September 6, 1994, CA 4–49, 11–12,
                                             11–20, 11–23
Richardson-Vicks Inc's Patent [1995] R.P.C. 568 24–84
Riches v. News Group Newspapers [1986] Q.B. 256; [1985] 3 W.L.R. 43;
  (1985) 129 S.J. 401; [1985] 2 All E.R. 345; (1985) 135 New L.J. 391;
  (1985) 82 L.S. Gaz. 2088, CA 21–209
Rigby v. Chief Constable of Northamptonshire [1985] 1 W.L.R. 1242;
  [1985] 2 All E.R. 985; (1986) 83 L.S. Gaz. 46 .... 7–110, 19–18
Rivtow Marine v. Washington Iron Works (1973) 40 D.L.R. (3d) 530 7–90

Robbins v. Jones (1863) 15 C.B.N.S. 221 18–51
Robert Marley Foundation v. Dino Michelle, May 12, 1994 (unreported) .. 23–61
Roberts v. Chief Constable of Cheshire [1999] 2 All E.R. 326; *The Times*,
    January 27, 1999, CA 12–17, 12–20, 16–119
—— v. Ramsbottom [1980] 1 W.L.R. 823; [1980] 1 All E.R. 7; [1980]
    R.T.R. 261; (1980) 124 S.J. 313 4–39
Robertson v. Forth Road Bridge Joint Board 1995 S.L.T. 263, Ct of Sess . 7–53
—— v. Nottingham Area Health Authority [1997] 8 Med.L.R. 113, CA ... 8–63
—— v. Ridley [1989] 1 W.L.R. 872; (1989) 133 S.J. 1170; [1989] 2 All
    E.R. 474, CA 4–50, 10–06
Roe v. Minister of Health; Woolley v. Same [1954] 2 Q.B. 66; [1954] 2
    W.L.R. 915; 98 S.T. 319; [1954] 2 All E.R. 131, CA 7–189
Rogerson, Re (1995) 44 I.C.L.Q. 650 6–09
Rondel v. Worsley [1969] 1 A.C. 191; [1967] 3 W.L.R. 1666; 111 S.J. 927;
    [1967] 3 All E.R. 993, HL 1–05G, 8–69
Rookes v. Barnard [1964] A.C. 1129; [1964] 2 W.L.R. 269; 108 S.J. 93;
    [1964] 1 All E.R. 367; [1964] 1 Lloyd's Rep. 28, HL ... 23–18, 23–50, 23–62
Rosser v. Lindsay, *The Times*, February 25, 1999, CA 7–140
Roussel Uclaf S.A. v. Hockley International [1996] R.P.C. 441, Pat Ct 24–92
Rowe v. Herman [1997] 1 W.L.R. 1390; *The Times*, June 9, 1997,
    CA 5–52, 7–161
—— v. McCartney [1976] 2 N.S.W.L.R. 72 7–189
Royal Brunei Airlines Sdn Bhd v. Tan (Philip Kok Ming) [1995] 2 A.C.
    378; [1995] 3 W.L.R. 64; [1995] 3 All E.R. 97; [1995] B.C.C. 899;
    (1995) 145 N.L.J. Rep. 888; (1995) 139 S.J.L.B. 146; (1995) 92 (27)
    L.S.Gaz. 33; *The Times*, May 29, 1995; *The Independent*, June 22,
    1995, PC 23–03, 23–23, 23–30, 23–43, 23–62, 23–80
Rozario v. Post Office [1997] P.I.Q.R. P15, CA 7–173
Rubber Improvement v. Daily Telegraph; Same v. Associated Newspapers
    [1964] A.C. 234; [1963] 2 W.L.R. 1063; 107 S.J. 356; *sub nom.* Lewis
    v. Daily Telegraph; Same v. Associated Newspapers [1963] 2 All E.R.
    151, HL 21–18, 21–45, 21–51
Ruxley Electronics and Construction v. Forsyth [1996] A.C. 344; [1995] 3
    W.L.R. 118; [1995] 3 All E.R. 268; 73 B.L.R. 1, 45 Con.L.R. 61;
    (1995) 14 Tr.L.R. 541; [1995] E.G.C.S. 11; (1995) 11 Const.L.J. 381;
    (1995) 145 N.L.J.Rep. 996; (1995) 139 S.J.L.B. 163; *The Times*, July
    3, 1995; *The Independent*, July 12, 1995, HL 18–23
Rylands v. Fletcher (1868) L.R. 3 H.L. 330 .... 19a, 19–07, 19–12,
    19–13, 19–15, 19–18

S (Adult: Refusal of Treatment), Re [1993] Fam. 123; [1992] W.L.R. 806;
    [1992] 4 All E.R. 671; [1993] 1 F.L.R. 26; [1993] 4 Med.L.R. 28;
    (1992) 136 S.J. L.B. 299; (1992) 142 N.L.J. 1450; [1992] 2 F.C.R.
    893; [1993] Fam. Law 221; *The Independent*, October 14, 1992; *The
    Times*, October 16, 1992 .... 3–62, 8–27
S-C (Mental Patient: Habeas Corpus), Re; *sub nom.* Simpson-Cleghorn Re
    [1996] Q.B. 599; [1996] 2 W.L.R. 146; [1996] 1 All E.R. 532; [1996]
    1 F.L.R. 548; [1996] 2 F.C.R. 692; (1996) 29 B.M.L.R. 138; [1996]
    Fam. Law 210; *The Times*, December 4, 1995, CA 12–66, 12–67, 12–68
S v. London Borough of Newham, [1998] 1 F.L.R. 1061; [1998] 3 F.C.R.
    277; [1998] E.M.L.R. 583; [1998] Fam. Law 387; (1998) 95(11)
    L.S.G. 35; (1998) 142 S.J.L.B. 102; *The Times*, March 5, 1998; *The
    Independent*, February 26, 1998, CA 21–91
—— v. M (Wasted Costs Order), *The Times*, March 26, 1998 8–80
—— v W [1995] 1 F.L.R. 862 31–23
S.G.E.U. v. Saskatchewan (1997) 149 D.L.R. 109, Sask. CA 23–01

S.O.S. Kinderdorf International v. Bittaye [1996] 1 W.L.R. 987; (1996)
    93(24) L.S.G. 26; (1996) 140 S.J.L.B. 175, PC 23–37
Sabel BV v. Puma AG (C-251/95) [1998] R.P.C. 199; [1998] E.T.M.R. 1,
    ECJ 24–70
Sabrini-Tabrizi v. Lothian H.B., 1998 S.L.T. 608 8–57
Sabri-Tabrizi v. Lothian Health Board 1998 S.C. 373; 1998 S.L.T. 607;
    (1998) 43 B.M.L.R. 190; 1998 Rep. L.R. 37 2–34
Sachs v. Miklos [1948] 2 K.B. 23; [1948] L.J.R. 1012; 64 T.L.R. 181;
    [1948] 1 All E.R. 67, CA 13–121
Saif Ali v. Mitchell (Sydney) & Co. [1980] A.C. 198; [1978] 3 W.L.R.
    849; [1978] 122 S.J. 761; [1978] 3 All E.R. 1033, HL 8–69
Saigol v. Cranley Mansions [1996] E.G.C.S. 81, July 6, 1995, CA 8–117
Sainsbury (J.) plc v. Broadway Maylan (a firm) (Ernest Green Partnership
    Ltd Third Party) [1999] P.N.L.R. 286; 61 Con. L.R. 31 .... 2–09, 4–60
St Albans City and District Council v. International Computers Ltd [1996]
    All E.R. 481; [1997] Info T.L.R. 58; (1996) 15 Tr.L.R. 444; (1997)
    20(2) I.P.D. 20020; [1996] Masons C.L.R. 13; The Times, August 14,
    1996, CA; reversing in part [1995] F.S.R. 686; [1997] Info T.L.R. 25;
    [1994] Masons C.L.R. 14; The Times, November 11, 1994, QBD 9–38
St George's Healthcare NHS Trust v. S [1998] 3 All E.R. 673; The Times,
    May 8, 1998, CA 3–62, 8a, 8–26, 12–66, 12–69
Saleslease Ltd v. Davis, The Times, April 15, 1999 13–136
Salsbury v. Woodland [1970] 1 Q.B. 324 5–52
Sampson v. Hodson-Pressinger (1981) 125 S.J. 623; [1981] 3 All E.R. 710;
    (1984) 12 H.L.R. 40; (1982) 261 E.G. 891, CA 18–51
Samuels v. Coole & Haddock CCRTI 96/1182/G, CA 22–02
Sanders v. Snell (1998) 72 A.L.J.R. 1507 23–63
Sandman (Aubrey Max) v. Panasonic U.K. Ltd [1998] F.S.R. 651; [1998]
    Masons C.L.R. 220; (1998) 21(4) I.P.D. 21038 24–07
Saratoga Fishing Co. v. Martinac [1997] A.M.C. 2113 9–20
Sasea v. KPMG, The Times, August 25, 1998 .... 8–127, 8–130
Satnam Investments Ltd v. Dunlop Heywood Ltd [1999] 3 All E.R. 652
    [1998] N.P.C. 169; [1998] E.G.C.S. 190; The Times, December 31,
    1998, CA 23–23, 23–62, 23–70, 23–80
Saunders v. Edwards [1987] 1 W.L.R. 1116; (1987) 131 S.J. 1039; [1987]
    2 All E.R. 651; (1987) 84 L.S. Gaz. 2193; (1987) 137 New L.J. 389;
    (1987) 84 L.S.Gaz. 2535, CA 14–03
Saxby v. Morgan [1997] P.I.Q.R. P531; [1997] 8 Med.L.R. 293; (1997) 38
    B.M.L.R. 126; The Times, May 2, 1997, CA 31–23
Scandecor Development AB v. Scandecor Marketing AB [1999] F.S.R. 26,
    CA 24–75
Schofield v. Chief Constable of West Yorkshire (1998) 43 B.M.L.R. 28;
    The Times, May 15, 1998, CA 7–52
Schulke & Mayr U.K. Ltd v. Alkapharm U.K. Ltd [1999] F.S.R. 161 22–10
Scotlife Homeloans (No. 2) v. Kenneth James & Co. [1995] E.G.C.S. 70,
    QBD 8–106
Scott v. Sampson (1882) 8 QBD 491; 51 L.J.Q.B. 380; 46 L.T. 412 21–219
Secretary of Defence v. Percy [1999] 1 All E.R. 732; The Times, May 11,
    1998 .... 17–41, 23–64, 23–71
Secretary of State for Employment v. Mann [1997] I.C.R. 209; [1997]
    I.R.L.R. 21, CA 23–01
Secretary of State for Trade and Industry v. Bottrill [1999] I.R.L.R. 326;
    [1998] I.C.R. 564; [1998] I.R.L.R. 120, EAT 5–03
Series 5 Software v. Philip Clarke; [1996] 1 All E.R. 853; [1996] F.S.R.
    225; [1996] C.L.C. 631; (1996) 19(3) I.P.D. 16; The Times, January
    19, 1996, ChD .... 24–71, 24–93, 28–13—28–20
Shah v. Standard Chartered Bank [1998] 3 W.L.R. 592; [1998] 4 All E.R.

155; [1998] E.M.L.R. 597; (1998) 142 S.J.L.B. 164; *The Times*, May
13, 1998, CA 21–14, 21–45,
21–49, 21–76
Shah & Shah v. Singh [1996] P.N.L.R. 83, QBD 8–80
Shanson v. Howard [1997] Q.B.E.N.F., January 30, 1997 (Lexis) 21–02,
21–13, 21–39
Sharp v. Pereira [1999] 1 W.L.R. 195 27–27
Sharpe v. Southend Health Authority [1997] 8 Med. L.R. 299; *The Times*,
May 9, 1997, QBD 8–35
Shaw v. Halifax (South West) Ltd [1996] P.N.L.R. 451; (1997) 13
Const.L.J. 127, CA 8–112
Shelley Films Ltd v. Rex Features Ltd [1994] E.M.L.R. 134 26–03
Shepherd v. The Post Office, *The Times*, June 15, 1995; *The Independent*,
July 31, 1995 (C.S.), CA 27–40
Shevill v. Presse-Alliance S.A. [1995] 2 A.C. 18; [1995] 2 W.L.R. 499;
[1995] All E.R. (E.C.) 289; [1995] E.M.L.R. 543; *The Times*, April 6,
1995; *Financial Times*, March 21, 1995, ECJ; [1992] 2 W.L.R. 1;
[1992] 1 All E.R. 409; *The Times*, March 13, 1991; *The Independent*,
March 13, 1991; *Financial Times*, March 20, 1991, CA 6–02
Siddell v. Smith Cooper & Partners (a firm) [1999] Lloyd's Rep. P.N. 79,
CA 7–64
Silcott v. Commissioner of Police of the Metropolis (1996) 8 Admin.L.R.
633; *The Times*, July 9, 1996, CA 15–53, 16–137, 23–80
Silhouette International Schmied GmbH & Co. K.G. v. Hartlauer Hand-
elsgesellschaft mbH (Case C–355/96), [1998] 3 W.L.R. 1218; [1998]
All E.R. (E.C.) 769; [1998] F.S.R. 729; [1998] E.T.M.R. 539; [1998]
C.E.C. 676; (1998) 21(10) I.P.D. 21110; *The Times*, July 22, 1998,
ECJ 24–71
Sion v. Hampstead Health Authority [1994] P.I.Q.R. P329, CA; [1994] 5
Med. L.R. 170; [1994] J.P.I.L. 241; [1994] J.P.I.L. 250; *The Times*,
June 10, 1994, CA 7–44, 7–51
Sirros v. Moore [1975] Q.B. 118; [1974] 3 W.L.R. 459; 118 S.J. 661;
[1974] 3 All E.R. 776, CA 16–03
Saskina, The [1979] A.C. 210; [1977] 3 W.L.R. 818; 121 S.J. 744; [1977]
3 All E.R. 803; [1978] 1 C.M.L.R. 190; *sub nom.* Siskina (Owners of
Cargo Lately on Board) v. Distos Compania Naviera (1977) 121 S.J.
744; [1977] 3 All E.R. 803; [1978] 1 Lloyd's Rep. 7, HL .... 28–28—28–34
Silva v. Toronto Star Newspapers Ltd (1999) 167 D.L.R. (4th) 554 21–135
Singh v. Aitkin [1998] P.I.Q.R. Q37 7–192
Skuse v. Granada Television, *The Independent*, April 2, 1992, CA 21–13
Slater v. Metropolitan Police Commissioner, *The Times*, January 23, 1996,
QBD 13–55
Slim v. Daily Telegraph [1968] 2 Q.B. 157; [1968] 2 W.L.R. 599; 112 S.J.
97; [1968] 1 All E.R. 497, CA 21–51
Smith v. Arnolt (1997) 148 D.L.R. (4th) 488, SCCD 8–41
—— v. Barking, Havering and Brentwood Health Authority [1994] 5 Med.
L.R. 285 2–10
—— v. Bush (Eric S.); Harris v. Wyre Forest District Council [1990] 1
A.C. 831; [1989] 2 W.L.R. 790; (1989) 133 S.J. 597; (1990) 9 Tr.L.R.
1; 87 L.G.R. 685; (1989) 21 H.L.R. 424; [1989] 2 All E.R. 514; [1989]
17 E.G. 68; [1981] 18 E.G. 99; (1989) 139 N.L.J. 576; (1989) 153
L.G. Rev. 984, HL; affirming 7–64
—— v. Chief Superintendent Working Police (1983) 76 Cr.App.R. 234 ... 23–42A
—— v. Lawson (1998) 75 P. & C.R. 466; [1997] E.G.C.S. 85; [1997]
N.P.C. 87, CA 17–75
—— v. Leurs (1970) C.L.R. 256 7–148
—— v. New Brunswick (Human Rights Commission) (1996) 137 D.L.R.
(4th) 7686–9, N.B. QB 23–06

—— v. Scott [1973] Ch. 314; [1972] 3 W.L.R. 783; 116 S.J. 785; [1972]
3 All E.R. 645 18–54
Smith New Court Securities v. Scrimgeour Vickers (Asset Management);
Smith New Court Securities v. Citibank NA [1997] A.C. 254; [1996]
3 W.L.R. 1051; [1996] 4 All E.R. 769; [1997] 1 B.C.L.C. 350; [1996]
146 N.L.J. Rep. 1722; [1996] 93 (46) L.S.G. 28; (1997) 141 S.J.L.B.
5; *The Times*, November 22, 1996; *The Independent*, November 27,
1996, HL 23–08
Smoldon v. Whitworth & Nolan [1997] P.I.Q.R. P133; [1997] E.L.R. 249;
The Times, December 18, 1996, CA 7–120, 7–149
Soulos v. Korkontzilas, 1997 S.C.R. 217 .... 23–23, 23–43, 23–62, 23–80
South Australian Asset Management Corp. v. York Montague [1997] A.C.
191; [1996] 3 W.L.R. 87; [1996] 3 All E.R. 365; [1996] P.N.L.R. 455;
[1996] 5 Bank. L.R. 211; 50 Con.L.R. 153; 80 B.L.R. 1; [1996] 27
E.G. 125; [1996] 2 E.G.L.R. 93; [1996] C.L.C. 1179; [1996] N.P.C.
100; [1996] E.G.C.S. 107; (1996) 93(22) L.S.G. 33; (1996) 146 N.L.J.
Rep. 956; (1996) 140 S.J.L.B. 156; *The Times*, June 24, 1996; *The
Independent*, July 2, 1996, HL, CA; [1995] N.P.C. 66; [1995] E.G.C.S.
71, QBD 3–22, 7a, 7–196, 8a,8–92, 8–93, 8–106,
8–110, 8–113, 8–114, 8–130
South West Hertfordshire Health Authority v. KB [1994] 2 F.C.R. 1051,
Fam. Div. 12–69
Spargo v. North East District Health Authority [1997] P.I.Q.R. P235;
[1997] 8 Med. L.R. 125; (1997) 37 B.M.L.R. 99; (1997) 94(15) L.S.G.
26; (1997) 141 S.J.L.B. 90; *The Times*, March 21, 1997, CA 31–23
Spectrum Investment Co. v. Holmes [1981] 1 W.L.R. 221; [1981] 1 All
E.R. 6; (1981) 41 P. & C.R. 133; 125 S.J. 47 17–81
Spring v. Guardian Assurance [1995] 2 A.C. 296; [1994] 3 W.L.R. 354;
[1994] 3 All E.R. 129; [1994] I.C.R. 596; [1994] I.R.L.R. 460; (1994)
138 S.J. (L.B.) 183; (1994) 144 New L.J. 971; *The Times*, July 8,
1994; *The Independent*, July 12, 1994, HL; reversing [1993] 2 All E.R.
273; 1993] I.C.R. 412; [1993] I.R.L.R. 122; (1993) 137 S.J. (L.B.) 47;
(1993) 12 Tr.L.R. 33; (1993) 143 New L.J. 365; *The Times*, December
22, 1992; *The Independent*, January 26, 1993, CA; reversing
[1992] I.R.L.R. 173; (1992) 11 Tr.L.R. 100; *The Times*, February 10,
1992 .... 2–09, 4–58
Springhead Spinning Co. v. Riley (1868) L.R. 6 Eq. 551 23–44
Standard Chartered Bank v. Walker [1982] 1 W.L.R. 1410; (1982) 126 S.J.
479; [1982] 3 All E.R. 938; (1982) 264 E.G. 345; [1982] Con. L.R.
223; (1982) 79 L.S. Gaz. 1137, CA 8–133
Stanley v. Saddique [1992] Q.B. 1; [1991] 2 W.L.R. 459; [1991] 1 All
E.R. 529; *The Times*, May 24, 1990, CA 27–50
Stansbie v. Troman [1948] 2 K.B. 48; [1948] L.J.R. 1206; 64 T.L.R. 226;
92 S.J. 167; [1948] 1 All E.R. 599; 46 L.G.R. 349, CA 2–28
Stanton v. Callaghan [1998] 4 All E.R. 961; [1998] 3 E.G.L.R. 165; [1998]
E.G.C.S. 115; (1998) 95(33) L.S.G. 33; (1998) 95(28) L.S.G. 32;
(1998) 148 N.L.J. 1355; (1998) 142 S.J.L.B. 220; [1998] N.P.C. 113;
The Times, July 25, 1998; *The Independent*, July 16, 1998, CA 1–05G,
7A, 7–111
Staples v. West Dorset District Council [1995] P.I.Q.R. P439; (1995) 92
(18) L.S.Gaz. 36; (1995) 139 S.J.L.B. 117; *The Times*, April 28, 1995,
CA 10–31
Stein v. Blake [1998] 1 All E.R. 724, CA 23–23, 23–43, 23–62
—— v. —— [1995] 2 W.L.R. 710; [1995] 2 All E.R. 961; [1995] 2
B.C.L.C. 94; [1995] B.C.C. 543; (1995) 145 N.L.J.Rep. 760; *The
Times*, May 19, 1995; *The Independent*, May 19, 1995, HL; affirming
[1994] Ch. 16; [1993] 3 W.L.R. 718; [1993] 4 All E.R. 225; [1993]

B.C.C. 587; [1993] B.C.L.C. 1478; *The Times*, May 13, 1993; *The
Independent*, June 14, 1993 (C.S.), CA 4–42
—— v. —— (No. 2) [1998] 1 All E.R. 724; [1998] 1 B.C.L.C. 593; [1998]
B.C.C. 316, CA 23–23, 23–43, 23–61, 23–62, 23–80
Stern v. Piper [1997] Q.B. 123; [1996] 3 W.L.R. 715; [1996] 3 All E.R.
385; [1996] E.M.L.R. 413; (1996) 93 (22) L.S.G. 27; (1996) 140
S.J.L.B. 175; *The Times*, May 30, 1996; *The Independent*, June 17,
1996 (C.S.), CA 21–45, 21–76
Stieller v. Porirua City Council [1986] 1 N.Z.L.R. 84; (1987) 3 Const.L.J.
312, N.Z.C.A. 7–95
Stovin v. Wise (Norfolk County Council, third party) [1996] A.C. 923;
[1996] 3 W.L.R. 388; [1996] 3 All E.R. 801; [1996] R.T.R. 354;
(1996) 146 N.L.J.Rep. 1185; (1996) 93(35) L.S.G. 33; (1996) 140
S.J.L.B. 201; *The Times*, July 26, 1996; *The Independent*, July 31,
1996, HL; reversing [1994] 1 W.L.R. 1124; [1994] 3 All E.R. 467; 92
L.G.R. 577; [1994] R.T.R. 225; (1994) 91(14) L.S.G. 48; (1995) 159
J.P.N. 722; (1994) 138 S.J. (L.B.) 60; *The Times*, March 8, 1994,
CA 1–05G, 7–28, 7–99, 7–100, 7–103, 11–07, 18–102, 23–10, 23–64
Stovold v. Barlows [1996] 1 P.N.L.R. 91; (1996) 71 P. & C.R. 03; [1996]
C.L.C. 228; [1995] N.P.C. 154; [1995] E.G.C.S. 155; (1995) 92 (40)
L.S.Gaz. 82; *The Times*, October 30, 1995, CA 2–09, 8–92, 27–07
Strand Electric and Engineering Co. v. Brisford Entertainments [1952] 2
Q.B. 246; [1952] 1 T.L.R. 939; 96 S.J. 260; [1952] 1 All E.R. 796,
CA 13–138
Strathford East Kilbride v. Film Design 1999 S.L.T. 121; 1997 S.C.L.R.
877; 1997 Rep.L.R. 112; *The Times*, December 1, 1997 .... 7–90, 8–119
Street v. Mountford [1985] A.C. 809; [1985] 2 W.L.R. 877; [1985] 2 All
E.R. 289; (1985) 17 H.L.R. 402; (1985) 50 P. & C.R. 258; [1985] 1
E.G.L.R. 128; (1985) 274 E.G. 821; (1985) 135 N.L.J. 460; (1985)
129 S.J. 348; (1985) 82 L.S.G. 2087, HL 17–17
Stubbings v. United Kingdom (Case 36–37/1996) [1997] 1 F.L.R. 105;
[1997] 3 F.C.R. 157; (1997) 23 E.H.R.R. 213; (1997) 1 B.H.R.C. 316;
[1997] Fam. Law 241; *The Times*, October 24, 1996; *The Independent*,
October 24, 1996, ECHR 31–23
—— v. Webb [1993] A.C. 498; [1993] 2 W.L.R. 1210; [1993] 1 All E.R.
322; [1993] P.I.Q.R. P86; [1993] 1 F.L.R. 714; (1993) 137 S.J. (L.B.)
32; *The Times*, December 17, 1992, HL; reversing [1992] Q.B. 197;
[1991] 3 W.L.R. 383; [1991] 3 All E.R. 949; [1992] 1 F.L.R. 296;
[1992] Fam. Law 61; *The Times*, April 3, 1991; *The Daily Telegraph*,
May 14, 1991, CA 31–23
Supply of Ready Mixed Concrete (No. 2), (Re) *sub nom.* Director General
of Fair Trading v. Pioneer Concrete (U.K.) [1995] 1 A.C. 456; [1994]
3 W.L.R. 1249; [1995] 1 All E.R. 135; [1995] I.C.R. 25; (1995) 139
S.J.L.B. 14; (1995) 145 N.L.J.Rep. 17; (1995) 92(01) L.S. Gaz 37;
The Times, November 25, 1994; *The Independent*, November 30,
1994, HL 23–59
Sutcliffe v. Thackrah [1974] A.C. 727; [1994] 2 W.L.R. 295; 118 S.J. 148;
[1974] 1 All E.R. 859; [1974] 1 Lloyd's Rep. 318, HL 1–05G
Sutherland Shire Council v. Heyman (1985) 157 C.L.C. 424 7–103
Süzen v. Zehnacker Gebäudereinigung GmbH (13/95) [1997] All E.R. (EC)
289; [1997] I.C.R. 255; (1997) Tr.L.R. 365; [1997] I.R.L.R. 225; *The
Times*, March 26, 1997, ECJ 23–130
Swain v. Puri [1996] P.I.Q.R. P442, CA 10a, 10–74, 10–76
Swanson Estate v. Canada (1991) 80 D.L.R. (4th) 741 7–102
Swinamer v. Nova Scotia (1994) 112 D.L.R. (4th) 18 7–100
Swindle v. Harrison [1997] 4 All E.R. 705; [1997] P.N.L.R. 641; [1997]
N.P.C. 50; *The Times*, April 17, 1997, CA 23–23
Swinney v. Chief Constable of Northumbria [1997] Q.B. 464; [1997] A.C.

464; [1996] 3 W.L.R. 968; [1996] 3 All E.R. 449; [1996] P.N.L.R.
473; (1996) 146 N.L.J.Rep. 878; *The Times*, March 28, 1996 ...... 7A, 7–109,
7–110, 7–111

T, Re [1998] 1 F.L.R. 48 8–33
T (A Minor) (Wardship: Medical Treatment), Re; *sub nom.* T (A Minor)
(Liver transplant: Consent), Re; C (A Minor) (Medical Treatment:
Refusal of Parental Consent), Re [1997] 1 W.L.R. 242; [1997] 1 All
E.R. 906; [1997] 1 F.L.R. 502; [1997] 2 F.C.R. 363; (1997) 35
B.M.L.R. 63; [1997] 8 Med.L.R. 166; (1996) 146 N.L.J.Rep. 1577;
(1996) 93(42) L.S.G. 28; (1996) 140 S.J.L.B. 237; *The Times*, October
28, 1996; *The Independent*, October 29, 1996, CA 3–62, 8–31
T v. North Yorkshire County Council, [1999] I.R.L.R. 98; (1998) 10
Admin. L.R. 573; [1998] E.L.R. (1998) 95(32) L.S.G. 29; (1998) 142
S.J.L.B. 218; *The Times*, September 10, 1998; *The Independent*, July
27, 1998 (C.S.), CA 5–20, 5–35
TNT Express (U.K.) v. Downes [1994] I.C.R. 1; [1993] I.R.L.R. 432,
EAT 23–105
TVN2 v. Prebble [1994] 3 All E.R. 407 .... 21–03, 21–96
Talbot v. Berkshire County Council [1994] Q.B. 290; [1993] 3 W.L.R.
708; [1993] 4 All E.R. 9; [1993] R.T.R. 406; [1993] P.I.Q.R. P319;
(1993) 143 New L.J. 402; (1993) 157 L.G.Rev. 1004; *The Times*,
March 23, 1993, CA 30–20
Tameside and Glossop Acute Services Trust v. CH (A Patient) [1996] 1
F.L.R. 762; [1996] 1 F.C.R. 753; (1996) 31 B.M.L.R. 93; [1996] Fam.
Law 353; *The Independent*, February 26, 1996, Fam. Div. 12–69
Taylor v. S.F.O. [1997] 4 All E.R. 887; (1997) 94(36) L.S.G. 44; (1997)
147 N.L.J. 1309; (1997) 141 S.J.L.B. 216; *The Times*, August 27,
1997; *The Independent*, July 24, 1997, CA 21–61
—— v. Serviceteam Ltd [1998] P.I.Q.R. P201 4–42
Taylorson v. Shieldness Produce [1994] P.I.Q.R. P329, CA 7–44, 7–51
Ter Neuzen v. Korn (1995) 127 D.L.R. (4th) 577 .... 7–135, 9–38, 8–03
Tertiary Institutes Allied Staff Association v. Tahana [1998] 1 N.Z.L.R.
41 21–91
Tettenborn, Re [1996] C.L.J. 36 13–80
Thacker v. Crown Prosecution Service, *The Times*, December 9, 1997,
CA 15–39
Thomas v. Brighton Health Authority [1996] 5 P.I.Q.R. Q44; [1996] 7
Med.L.R. 21; (1996) 32 B.M.L.R. 179; *The Times*, November 10,
1995, QBD 27–14
—— v. National Union of Mineworkers (South Wales) Area [1986] Ch.
20; [1985] 2 W.L.R. 1081; [1985] I.C.R. 886; (1985) 129 S.J. 416;
[1985] 2 All E.R. 1; [1985] I.R.L.R. 157; (1985) 82 L.S.Gaz.
1938 .... 18–95, 23–42A
—— v. Sawkins [1935] 2 K.B. 249; 104 L.J.K.B. 572; 51 T.L.R. 514 12–37
Thompson v. Blake-James [1998] Lloyd's Rep. (Med) 187; (1998) 41
B.M.L.R. 144; [1998] P.I.Q.R. P286, CA 2–10
—— v. Commissioner of Police for the Metropolis [1997] 3 W.L.R. 403;
[1997] 2 All E.R. 762; (1997) 147 N.L.J. 341; *The Times*, February
20, 1997; *The Independent*, February 28, 1997, CA 12–80, 21–209,
27–09, 27–66, 27–68, 27–74
Thompson-Schwab v. Costaki [1956] 1 W.L.R. 335; 100 S.J. 246; [1956]
1 All E.R. 652, CA 18–07
Thornton v. Kirklees Metropolitan Borough Council [1979] Q.B. 626, CA;
[1979] 3 W.L.R. 1; (1979) 77 L.G.R. 417; *sub nom.* Thornton v.
Kirklees Metropolitan District Council (1979) 123 S.J. 285; [1979] 2
All E.R. 349; [1979] J.P.L. 459, CA 11–14

Three Rivers District Council v. Bank of England (No. 3) [1996] 3 All
    E.R. 558; *The Times*, April 22, 1996, QBD 16–137, 23–08, 23–43
—— v. —— (No. 4), *The Times*, December 10, 1998 .... 16–137, 23–01,
    23–08, 23–43
Tidman v. Reading Borough Council [1994] N.P.C. 136; *The Times*, Nov-
    ember 10, 1994 .... 7–70, 7–72
Timeplan Education Group v. NUT [1997] I.R.L.R. 457, CA 23–10,
    23–11, 23–37
Tinsley v. Milligan [1994] 1 A.C. 340; [1993] 3 W.L.R. 126; [1993] 2 All
    E.R. 65; (1993) 68 P. & C.R. 412; [1993] F.L.R. 963; [1993] N.P.C.
    97; [1993] E.G.C.S. 118; *The Times*, June 28, 1993; *The Independent*,
    July 6, 1993, HL; affirming [1992] Ch. 310; [1992] 2 W.L.R. 508;
    [1992] 2 All E.R. 391; (1991) 63 P. & C.R. 152; (1991) 135 S.J.
    (L.B.) 108; [1991] N.P.C. 100; *The Times*, August 22, 1991, CA 3–03,
    3–04, 14–03
Tolstoy Miloslavsky v. Lord Aldington [1996] 1 W.L.R. 736; [1996] 2 All
    E.R. 556; [1996] P.N.L.R. 335; (1996) 93(1) L.S.G. 22; (1996) 140
    S.J.L.B. 26; *The Times*, December 27, 1995; *The Independent*, January
    3, 1996, CA 8–80, 21–227
—— v. United Kingdom (1995) 20 E.H.R.R. 442; [1996] E.M.L.R. 152;
    The Times, July 19, 1995; *The Independent*, September 22, 1995,
    ECHR 21–04, 21–05, 21–227
Toronto-Dominion Bank v. Carotenuto (1998) 154 D.L.R. (4th) 627 13–14,
    23–62
Torquay Hotel v. Cousins [1969] 2 Ch. 106; [1969] 2 W.L.R. 289; (1968)
    113 S.J. 52; [1969] 1 All E.R. 522; 6 K.I.R. 15, CA 23–18, 23–62
Toumia v. Evans, *The Times*, April 1, 1999, CA 12–21, 16–137, 23–01
Tracey v. Crosville Wales; [1997] 3 W.L.R. 800; [1997] 4 All E.R. 449;
    [1997] I.C.R. 862; [1997] I.R.L.R. 691; (1997) 94(41) L.S.G. 28;
    (1997) 147 L.S.G. 28; (1997) 147 N.L.J. 1582; *The Times*, October
    20, 1997, HL 23–105
Trachuk v. Olinek [1996] 4 W.W.R. 137 13–63
Trailways Transport v. Thomas [1996] 2 N.Z.L.R. 443 13–122
Tredget v. Bexley Health Authority [1994] 5 Med. L.R. 178, County Ct. .. 7–44
Trendtex Trading Corp. v. Credit Suisse [1982] A.C. 679; [1981] 3 W.L.R.
    766; (1981) 125 S.J. 761; [1981] 3 All E.R. 520; [1981] Com.L.R.
    262, HL; affirming [1980] Q.B. 629; [1980] 3 W.L.R. 367; (1980) 124
    S.J. 396; [1980] 3 All E.R. 721, CA 4–42
Trust Co. of Australia v. Perpetual Trustee Co. (1997) 42 N.S.W.L.R.
    237 8–92
Tsikata v. Newspaper Publishing plc [1997] 1 All E.R. 655; [1997]
    E.M.L.R. 117; (1996) 146 N.L.J.Rep. 1686; *The Independent*, October
    15, 1996, CA 21–178, 21–179
Tyburn Productions v. Conan Doyle [1991] Ch. 75; [1990] 3 W.L.R. 167;
    [1990] 1 All E.R. 909; [1990] R.P.C. 185 6–07

UFCW Local 1518 v. K. Mart (1997) 149 D.L.R. (4th) 7, BCCA 23–71
Union Carbide Group v. BP Chemicals Ltd [1998] F.S.R. 1; [1998] R.P.C.
    1; (1998) 21(8) I.P.D. 21083; (1997) 20 (8) I.P.D. 20077 24–93
United Mizrahi Bank v. Doherty [1998] 1 W.L.R. 435; [1998] 2 All E.R.
    230; *The Times*, December 15, 1997 .... 23–23, 23–80
United States of America v. Silk (1946) 331 U.S. 704 5–03
University College London Hospitals NHS Trust v. Unison [1999] I.C.R.
    204, CA 23–130, 23–132
University of Glasgow v. Economist [1997] E.M.L.R. 495, QBD 6–03

Valeo Vision S.A. v. Flexible Lamps [1995] R.P.C. 205, Pat Ct 24–51
Van Camp Chocolates v. Aulsebrooks [1984] 1 N.Z.L.R. 354 23–81
Vasey v. Surrey Free Inns [1996] P.I.Q.R. P373, CA 5–34
Vaswani v. Italian Motors [1996] 1 W.L.R. 270; [1996] R.T.R. 115; (1996)
    93(2) L.S.G. 27; (1996) 140 S.J.L.B. 27; *The Times*, December 15,
    1995, PC 23–51
Veasey v. Millfeed Co. [1997] P.N.L.R. 100, CA 8–80
Veracruz Transportation Inc. v. V.C. Shipping Co. Inc. and Den Norske
    Bank A/S (The Veracruz) [1992] 1 Lloyd's Rep. 353; *The Times*,
    November 14, 1991; *Financial Times*, November 19, 1991,
    CA .... 28–28—28–34
Vernon v. Bloomsbury Health Authority [1995] 6 Med. L.R. 297,
    QBD 7–174, 8–42
—— v. Bosely [1996] 1 All E.R. 577; [1997] P.I.Q.R. P255; (1997) 35
    B.M.L.R. 135; [1997] R.T.R. 1; [1997] Fam. Law 476; (1996) 146
    N.L.J.Rep. 589; *The Times*, April 3, 1996, CA 1–21, 2–06, 7a,
                                             7–43, 7–47, 7–51
Virgin Management v. De Morgan Group & Another [1996] E.G.C.S. 16;
    [1996] N.P.C. 8, CA 8–89

W v. Essex County Council [1998] 3 W.L.R. 534; [1998] 3 All E.R. 111;
    [1998] 2 F.L.R. 278; [1998] 2 F.C.R. 269; [1998] P.I.Q.R. P346;
    [1998] Fam. Law 455; (1998) 95(20) L.S.G. 33; *The Times*, April 9,
    1998, CA 1–05G, 7A, 7–44, 7–106, 8–61
—— v. Home Office [1997] Imm.A.R. 302; *The Times*, March 14, 1997;
    The Independent, March 19, 1997, CA 7–105
W.B.S. v. Fineberg [1998] P.N.L.R. 216 8–80
Wadey v. Surrey County Council [1999] 2 All E.R. 334; *The Times*, Janu-
    ary 8, 1999 27–17
Wagamama v. City Centre Restaurants plc [1995] F.S.R. 713; [1997]
    Eu.L.R. 313, ChD 24–62
Walker v. Medlicott & Son [1999] 1 All E.R. 685; [1998] C.L.Y. 4584 .... 7A,
                                                7–81, 8–77
—— v. Northumberland County Council [1995] 1 All E.R. 737; [1995]
    I.R.L.R. 35; [1995] I.C.R. 702; [1995] P.I.Q.R. P521; (1994) 144
    N.L.J.Rep. 1659; *The Times*, November 24, 1994; *The Independent*,
    November 18, 1994, QBD 7–53, 7–130, 7–131, 7–172
Walkin v. South Manchester Health Authority [1995] 4 All E.R. 132;
    [1995] 1 W.L.R. 1543; *The Times*, July 3, 1995, CA 31–23
Walpole v. Partridge & Wilson (A Firm) [1994] Q.B. 106; [1993] 3 W.L.R.
    1093; [1994] 1 All E.R. 385; *The Times*, July 8, 1993; *The Indepen-
    dent*, September 23, 1993, CA 8–84
Wandsworth London Borough Council v. D'Silva [1998] I.R.L.R. 193,
    CA 23–16
Wapshot v. Davies Donovan; (1996) 72 P. & C.R. 244; [1996] P.N.L.R.
    361; [1995] E.G.C.S. 199; [1995] N.P.C. 197, CA 8–112
Ward v. Chief Constable of West Midlands Police, *The Times*, December
    15, 1997, CA 12–49, 15–21
—— v. Newalls Insulation Co. [1998] 2 All E.R. 690 27–12
Warren v. Warren [1997] Q.B. 488; [1996] 3 W.L.R. 1129; [1996] 4 All
    E.R. 664; [1996] 2 F.L.R. 777; [1997] 1 F.C.R. 237; [1996] Fam. Law
    720, CA 16–03, 16–07
Waterford Wedgewood plc v. David Nagli Ltd [1998] F.S.R. 92; [1998]
    C.L.C. 1011; *The Times*, May 13, 1998 25–06
Waters v. Commissioner of Police of the Metropolis [1997] I.C.R. 1073;
    [1997] I.R.L.R. 589; *The Times*, July 21, 1997, CA 7–53, 7–109
Watson v. Gray, *The Times*, November 26, 1998 7–120

Watts v. Times Newspapers [1997] Q.B. 650; [1996] 1 All E.R. 152; *The
Times*, September 22, 1995, CA 21–112, 21–131, 21–218
Waugh v. James K. Allan Ltd [1964] 2 Lloyd's Rep. 1; 1964 S.C. (H.L.)
162; 1964 S.L.T. 269, HL 4–39
Waverley Borough Council v. Fletcher [1995] 3 W.L.R. 772; [1995] 4 All
E.R. 756; (1995) 70 P. & C.R. D47; (1995) 159 L.G. Rev. 789; [1995]
N.P.C. 122; (1995) 145 N.L.J.Rep. 1365; *The Times*, July 14, 1995;
The Independent, July 14, 1995, CA 13–62
Wells v. First National Bank [1998] P.N.L.R. 552, CA 7–82
—— v. Wells; Thomas v. Brighton Health Authority; Page v. Sheerness
Steel Co. plc [1998] 3 W.L.R. 329, HL; [1997] 1 W.L.R. 652; [1997]
1 All E.R. 673; [1997] P.I.Q.R. Q1; (1997) 37 B.M.L.R. 111; (1996)
93(40) L.S.G. 25; (1996) 140 S.J.L.B. 239; *The Times*, October 24,
1996; *The Independent*, November 13, 1996, CA; reversing [1996]
P.I.Q.R. Q62, QBD 27–10, 27–12, 27–14, 27–20, 27–25
Welton v. North Cornwall District Council [1997] W.L.R. 570; [1997]
P.N.L.R. 108; (1997) 9 Admin.L.R. 45; (1997) 161 J.P.Rep. 114;
(1996) 93(34) L.S.G. 34; (1996) 140 S.J.L.B. 186; *The Times*, July
19, 1996, CA 7a, 7–62, 7–102
Wessex Regional Health Authority v. HLM Design (1994) 71 B.L.R. 32;
(1994) 10 Const.L.J. 165, QBD 1–08, 8–115
West v. Versil, *The Times*, August 31, 1996, CA 27–12, 27–20
West Wiltshire District Council v. Garland [1995] Ch. 297; [1995] 2
W.L.R. 439; [1995] 2 All E.R. 17; 93 L.G.R. 235; [1995] R.V.R. 97;
(1995) 159 L.G.Rev. 529; (1994) 144 N.L.J.Rep. 1733; (1995) 92 (03)
L.S.Gaz. 38; (1995) 139 S.J.L.B. 18; *The Times*, December 5, 1994;
The Independent, December 7, 1994, CA; affirming [1993] Ch. 409;
[1993] 3 W.L.R. 626; [1993] 4 All E.R. 246; *The Times*, March 4,
1993, ChD 23–63, 23–65
Western Trust and Savings Ltd. v. Travers (Clive) & Co. [1997] P.N.L.R.
295 8–113
Westminster City Council v. Clarke [1992] 2 A.C. 288; [1992] 2 W.L.R.
229; [1992] 1 All E.R. 695; (1992) 136 S.J.L.B. 82; 90 L.G.R. 210;
(1992) 24 H.L.R. 360; [1992] E.G.C.S. 13; [1992] N.P.C. 18; (1992)
142 N.L.T. 196; (1992) 156 L.G.Rev. 681; *The Independent*, February
7, 1992; *The Guardian*, February 12, 1992; *The Times*, February 13,
1992, HL 17–17
Wheeldon v. Wheeldon [1997] 3 F.C.R. 769; Fam. Law 602, CA 12–59
Whent v. T. Cartledge [1997] I.R.L.R. 153 23–16
Whitbread v. Kingston and District NHS Trust, *sub nom.* Whitbread
(Mental Patient: Habeas Corpus), Re (1997) 94(27) L.S.G. 23; (1997)
141 S.J.L.B. 152; *The Times*, July 14, 1997, CA 12–68
White v. Chief Constable of South Yorkshire Police [1998] 3 W.L.R. 1509;
[1999] 1 All E.R. 1, HL 1–21, 7A, 7–52, 7–53, 7–110
—— v. Jones [1995] 2 A.C. 207; [1995] 2 W.L.R. 187; [1995] 1 All E.R.
691; [1995] 3 F.C.R. 51; (1995) 139 S.J.L.B. 83; (1995) 145
N.L.J.Rep. 251; [1995] N.P.C. 31; *The Times*, February 17, 1995; *The
Independent*, February 17, 1995, HL; affirming [1993] 3 W.L.R. 730;
[1993] 3 All E.R. 481; [1993] N.P.C. 37; (1993) 143 N.L.J.Rep. 473;
(1993) 90 (23) L.S.Gaz. 43; *The Times*, March 9, 1993; *The Indepen-
dent*, March 5, 1993, CA 4–58, 7–82, 8–77
Widdowson v. Newgate Meat Corporation [1998] P.I.Q.R. P138,
CA 7–142, 7–180
Wilkinson v. Downton [1897] 2 Q.B. 57 .... 23–42A
Williams v. Natural Life Health Foods [1998] 1 W.L.R. 830; [1998] 2 All
E.R. 577, HL; *The Times*, January 9, 1997; [1996] 1 B.C.L.C. 131,
CA 1–08, 4–49, 7a, 7–62, 7–69, 7–75, 23–78, 23–83

Williamson v. East London & City Health Authority [1998] 1 Lloyd's Rep.
(Med) 6 8–37
Williamson v. Phillips, Son & Neale, July 29, 1998, (unreported) 13–134
Wilson v Housing Corporation [1997] I.R.L.R. 346; *The Times*, December
18, 1996, QBD 23–44, 23–69
—— v. The Governors of the Sacred Heart Roman Catholic School [1998]
P.I.Q.R. P145, CA 7–149
Wilson & Horton v. Att.-Gen. [1997] 2 N.Z.L.R. 513 7–133
Wince v. Ball (1996) 136 D.L.R. 104 .... 7–41, 7–148
Winnipeg Child & Family Services v. G (1997) 152 D.L.R. (4th) 193 8–26
Winnipeg Condominium No. 36 v. Bird Construction Co. (1995) 121
D.L.R. (4th) 513 8–117
Wisely v. John Fulton (Plumbers) Ltd 1998 S.L.T. 1026 27–17
Wisniewski v. Central Manchester Health Authority [1998] P.I.Q.R. P324;
[1998] Lloyd's Rep. Med. 223, CA 2–22, 7–175, 7–189
Wood v. Law Society [1995] N.P.C. 39; *The Times*, March 2, 1995; *The
Independent*, March 1, 1995, CA; affirming (1993) 143 N.L.J.Rep.
1475; *The Times*, July 30, 1993; *The Independent*, July 29, 1993 7–43
Heavy Industrial Turbines Ltd Wood Group v. Crossan [1998] I.R.L.R.
680 23–34
Woods v. Lowns [1995] 36 N.S.W.L.R. 344 7–30
Woodward v. Wolferstans [1997] N.P.C. 51; *The Times*, April 8, 1997,
ChD 8–79
Woolwich Building Society v. Taylor [1995] 1 B.C.L.C. 132; *The Times*,
May 17, 1994, ChD 4–31
Wynbergen v. Hoyts Corporation Pty Ltd [1998] 72 A.L.J.R. 65 7–198

X v. Y and Y Establishment [1990] 1 Q.B. 220; [1989] 3 W.L.R. 910;
[1989] 3 All E.R. 689; (1989) 133 S.J. 945; [1989] 2 Lloyd's Rep.
561 .... 28–28—28–34
—— (Minors) v. Bedfordshire County Council. *See* M v. Newham London
Borough Council; X (Minors) v. Bedfordshire County Council

Yamada v. Mock (1996) 29 O.R. (3d) 53 8–90
Young v. Charles Church (Southern) Ltd (1998) 39 B.M.L.R. 146; *The
Times*, May 1, 1997, CA 11–10, 23–64
Yorkshire Regional Health Authority v. Fairclough Building [1996] 1
W.L.R. 210; [1996] 1 All E.R. 519; 78 B.L.R. 59; 47 Con.L.R.
120; [1996] C.L.C. 366; (1995) 139 S.J.L.B. 247; *The Times*,
November 16, 1995; *The Independent*, November 27, 1995, (C.S.),
CA 31–07
Young v. Charles Church (Southern) Ltd, *The Times*, May 1, 1997,
CA 23–64
Yuen (Cheng) v. Royal Hong Kong Golf Club [1998] I.C.R. 131, PC 5–03
Yukong Line Ltd of Korea v. Rendsberg Investments Corpn. of Liberia
(No. 2) (The Rialto) [1999] 2 W.L.R. 540, HL; [1998] 1 W.L.R. 294;
(1997) 94(39) L.S.G. 39; (1997) 141 S.J.L.B. 212; *The Times*, October
30, 1997, QBD (Comm Ct) 23–04, 23–08, 23–23, 23–26,
23–41, 23–43, 23–48, 23–61, 23–62, 23–65,
23–69, 23–78, 23–80, 23–81, 23–82, 23–83

Zino Davidoff SA v. A & G Imports Ltd [1999] R.P.C. 631; *The Times*,
May 24, 1999 24–71
Zumpano v. Montagnese [1997] 2 V.R. 525 8–117
Zwebner v. Mortgage Corporation [1998] P.N.L.R. 769; [1998] E.G.C.S.
104, CA 8–75, 8–90

TABLE OF STATUTES

1689 Bill of Rights Act (2
    Will & Mar., c. 2)—
    Art. 9 ... 21–01, 21–03, 21–96
1888 Law of Libel Amend-
    ment Act (51 & 52
    Vict., c. 64)—
    s. 3 .... 21–95, 21–167
1824 Vagrancy Act (5 Geo. 4,
    c. 83)
    s. 6 .... 12–51, 16–105
1897 Police (Property) Act
    (60 & 61 Vict., c.
    30) 13–60
1906 Trade Disputes Act (6
    Edw. 7, c. 47)—
    s. 2 23–123
1925 Law of Property Act
    (15 & 16 Geo. 5, c.
    20) 23–09
    s. 2 23–09
1930 Third Parties (Rights
    against Insurers)
    Act (20 & 21 Geo.
    5, c. 35) 4–31
1935 Law Reform (Married
    Women and
    Tortfeasors) Act
    (25 & 26 Geo. 5, c. 30)
    s. 6(1)(a) 4–55
1936 Public Health Act (26
    Geo. 5 & 1 Edw. 8,
    c. 49)—
    Pt. III 11–18
    s. 94(2) 11–03
1945 Law Reform (Contribu-
    tory Negligence)
    Act (8 & 9 Geo. 6,
    c. 28) 8–114,
    23–01
1947 Crown Proceedings Act
    (10 & 11 Geo. 6, c.
    44)—
    s. 10 4–10
    (1) 4–10
    (2) 4–10
    s. 29 4–09
1948 Law Reform (Personal
    Injuries) Act (11 &
    12 Geo. 6, c. 41)—
    s. 2(1) 27–17
    (1A) 22–17
    (3) 27–17
    (6) 27–17

1952 Defamation Act (15 &
    16 Geo. 6 & 1 Eliz.
    2, c. 66) 21–95
    s. 4 .... 21–03, 21–09,
    21–59, 21–75
    (3) 21–59
    s. 7 .... 21–177, 21–178
    (1) 21–179
    (3) 21–178
    s. 8 21–167
    s. 9(2) 21–167
    Sched. 1 para. 5 21–179
1957 Occupiers' Liability Act
    (c. 31) 10–03, 10–06
    s. 2 10–28
    (3)(b) 10–37
1960 Public Bodies
    (Admission to
    Meetings) Act (8 &
    9 Eliz. 2, c.
    67) 21–180
1961 Factories Act (9 & 10
    Eliz. 2, c. 34) 11–10
1965 Compulsory Purchase
    Act (c. 56)
    s. 10 18–08
    Nuclear Installations Act
    (c. 57) 9–18
1967 Criminal Law Act (c. 58)
    s. 3 .... 1–05C
1968 Civil Evidence Act (c.
    64)—
    s.2A 21–79
    s. 13 21–79
1969 Children and Young
    Persons Act (c.
    54) 16–107
    Employers' Liability
    (Compulsory
    Insurance) Act (c.
    57) 11a, 11–20
    s. 1 .... 4–49, 11–20
1971 Animals Act (c. 22) 20–01
    s. 2 20–03
    (2) 20–03
    (b) 20–05
    s. 8 20–14
1972 Defective Premises Act
    (c. 35) 8–123
    Local Government Act
    (c. 70) 21–180
    ss. 100A–100D 21–180
    s. 100E 21–180

li

1972 Local   Government
        Act—*cont.*
    s. 100J 21–180
        (1) 21–180
1973 Fair Trading Act (c. 41)—
    s. 93 23–43
    Local   Government
        (Scotland) Act (c.
        65)—
    ss. 50A–50D 21–180
    s. 50E 21–180
1974 Merchant Shipping Act
        (c. 43) 19–85
1975 Sexual   Discrimination
        Act (c. 65)—
    s. 41 5–20
1976 Congenital   Disabilities
        (Civil Liability) Act
        (c. 28)—
    s. 1 4–38
        (4) 4–38
    s. 1A 4–38
1976 Fatal Accidents Act (c.
        30) 1–05F, 4–55,
                    27–17, 27–41
    s. 3 4–55
    s. 4 .... 4–55, 27–50
    Race Relations Act (c.
        74)—
    s. 32 5–20
        (1) 5–20
1977 Torts (Interference with
        Goods) Act (c. 32) . 13–86
    s. 8 13–103
    Patents Act (c. 37) 24–82
    s. 60(1)(c) 24–88
    s. 70(4) 24–97
        (2) 22–05
1978 State Immunity Act (c.
        33)—
    s. 12(1) 4–24
    s. 16(2) 4–23
    Civil Liability (Con-
        tribution) Act (c.
        47)— 4a, 4–21,
                4–55, 8–117, 13–114
    s. 1 .... 4–21, 4–60, 4–61
        (1) 4a, 4–61, 13–114
    s. 1(3) 4–61
    s. 2(1) 4–61
    s. 6(1) 4a, 4–61
    s. 14(2) 4–24
1979 Sale of Goods Act (c.
        54)—
    s. 20A 13a, 13–86A
    s. 20B 13a, 13–86A
        (1)(a) 13–86A
        (3)(a) 13–86A

1979 Sale of Goods Act—*cont.*
        (b) 13–86A
        (4) 13–86A
1980 Limitation Act (c. 58)—
    s. 4A 31–43
    s. 11 31–23
    s. 32A 21–05, 31–43
        (2)(a)–(c) 31–43
    s. 33 31–43
        (3) 31–43
        (a)–(f) 31–43
    Local Government Plan-
        ning and Land Act
        (c. 65) 23–44, 23–64
    Highways Act (c. 66)
    s. 41 11–12
    s. 96 18–60
    s. 152 18–111
1981 Contempt of Court Act
        (c. 49) 21–95, 21–167
    Supreme Court Act (c.
        54)
    s. 33(2) 4–31
1982 Civil   Jurisdiction   and
        Judgments Act (c.
        27)—
    s. 25 .... 28–28—28–34
    s. 30 6–06
1983 Matrimonial Homes Act
        (c. 19) 18–19
    Mental Health Act (c.
        20) 2–35, 8–26,12–66,
                    12–67, 12–68
    Pt. IV 12–69
    ss. 2–5 12–66
    s. 25D .. 12–66, 12–67, 12–68
        (4) 12–66, 12–67, 12–68
    s. 26 ..... 12–66, 12–67, 12–68
    s. 63 8–32
    s. 117 .... 3–03, 11a,
                    11–14, 11–21
    s. 131(1) 12–17, 12–66
1984 Occupiers' Liability Act
        (c. 3) 10a, 10–03,
                    10–24, 10–74
    s. 1 7–22
        (3)(b) 10–74
    Trade Union Act (c. 49)   21–114
    Police   and   Criminal
        Evidence Act (c.
        60) 1–05A, 16–105, 16–119
    s. 8 16–129
    s. 17 .... 16–95, 16–107
        (1)(b) 12–37, 16–107
    s. 25 16–104
    s. 26 .... 12–51, 16–105
    s. 117 16–95
    Sched. 2 12–51

1985 Companies Act (c. 6)—
  s. 1(3) 21–180
  Prosecution of Offences
    Act (c. 23) 11–05, 23–68
  s. 19A 8–80
  Administration of Justice
    Act (c. 61)—
  s. 57 31–43
  Housing Act (c. 68)
  s. 63(1) 11–14
  Pt. III 11–14
1986 Latent Damage Act (c.
    37)—
  s. 1–2 .... 31–38 to 31–39
  Insolvency Act (c. 45)—
  s. 323 4–42
  s. 333 .... 26–28 to 28–34
  Wages Act (c. 48) 23–41
  Public   Order   Act
    (c. 64) 12–41
  s. 4A 23–42A
  s. 5(4) 12–41
  ss. 14A–14C 17–41
  s. 14A 17a, 17–41,
    23–42A, 23–123, 23–124
  s. 14B 23–42A
1987 Consumer   Protection
    Act (c. 43)—
  Pt. 1 .... 9—38
  s. 1(2) 9–40
  s. 4(1)(e) 9–36, 9–59
  s. 41 11–12
1988 Employment Act (c. 19)—
  s. 17 23–114
  Sched. 3, para. 5 23–114
  Copyright, Designs and
    Patents Act (c. 48)—
  Pt. I 21–61
  s. 5A 24–09
  s. 5B 24–09
  s. 10 24–13
  s. 12 24–07
  s. 13A 24–09
  s. 13B 24–09
  s. 51(3) 24–47
  s. 66A 24–09
  s. 97(2) 24–29, 27–67
  s. 191 24–41
  s. 213(2)(c) 24–47
  s. 226 24–47
  Housing Act (c. 50)
  ss. 27–28 27–69
1989 Companies Act (c. 40)—
  s. 141(3) 4–31
1990 Human Fertilisation and
    Embryology Act (c.
    37)—
  s. 44 4–38

Employment Act (c. 38)—
  s. 7 23–114
  Sched. 2 23–114
  Courts and Legal Ser-
    vices Act (c. 41)—
  s. 8 21–203
  Broadcasting Act (c. 42)—
  s. 166(3) 21–167
1991 Water Resources Act (c.
    57)
  s. 85(1) 2–28
1992 Social Security Adminis-
    tration Act (c. 5)—
  Pt. IV 27–17
  Carriage of Goods by
    Sea Act (c. 50)—
  s. 4 5–42
  s. 5(5) 5–42
  Trade Union and Labour
    Relations (Consoli-
    dation) Act (c. 52) ... 23–91,
                              23–114
  s. 31A 23–114
  s. 62 .... 23–91, 23–114
    (2)(a)(ii) 23–114
  s. 179 23–18
  s. 219 23–114
    (1) 23–114
  s. 220 23–114
  ss. 226–235 23–114
  s. 226(2) 23–115
  s. 226(2)(a)(ii) .23–114, 23–120
  s. 226A 23–91, 23–112,
                              23–114
    (2) ... 23–112, 23–115
    (3) ... 23–112, 23–115
  s. 226 (3A) 23–114
  s. 227 23–115
  s. 228(3) 23–115
  s. 229 23–115
    (2) 23–112
    (4) 23–112
  s. 230(1)(a) 23–118
  s. 231 .... 23–91, 23–112
    A 23–112, 23–115
  s. 232A 23–114
  s. 232B 23–114
  s. 234 23–115
  s. 234A 23–91, 23–112,
                      23–114, 23–115
    (3)(a) 23–112
  s. 236 23–121
  s. 238 .... 23–105, 23–115
  s. 238A 23–112
    (3) 23–115
  s. 241 23–123
  s. 244 .23–18, 23–114, 23–130
    (1)(a)–(e) 23–115

1992 Trade Union and Labour
Relations (Con-
solidation) Act—*cont.*
Sched. A1 23–18
Sched. 1, para. 31(6) .. 23–18
Part IV 23–18
1993 Trade Union Reform and
Employment Rights
Act (c. 19)—
ss. 17–21 23–114
s. 33 23–130
1994 Trade Marks Act (c.
26)—
s. 10(2) 24–70
(3) 24–70
(6) 22–19,
24–71
s. 12 24–71
s. 21(1) 24–75
Criminal Justice and
Public Order Act (c.
33) 12–41,
12–42
s. 51 .... 23–42A
s. 70 23–123,
23–124
s. 154 .... 23–42A
Local Government etc.
(Scotland) Act (c.
39)—
s. 2 21–180
1995 Finance Act (c. 4)—
s. 142 27–29
Prisoners (Return to
Custody) Act (c.
16) 12–62, 16–107
Merchant Shipping Act
(c. 21) 4–09
ss. 172–182 19–85
s. 183 31–42
s. 192 4–09
s. 230 4–09
Sched. 6 31–42
Sale of Goods
(Amendment) Act
(c. 28) 13a, 13–86A
Private International
Law (Miscellaneous
Provisions) Act (c.
42) 6a, 6–07,
6–09
Pt. III 6–09
ss. 9–15 23–34
Mental Health (Patients
in the Community)
Act (c. 52) ... 12–66, 12–67,
12–68, 12–69

1996 Prevention of Terrorism
(Additional Powers)
Act (c. 7) 12–42, 16–98,
16–110, 16–129
1996 Law Reform (Year and a
Day Rule) Act (c.
19) 19–05
Defamation Act (c.
31) 21–01, 21–02,
21–03, 21–41, 21–59,
21–61, 21–69, 21–95,
21–164, 21–166, 21–167,
21–175, 21–177,
21–178, 31–43
s. 1 .... 21–59, 21–61, 21–66
(1)(b) 21–61
(c) 21–61
(3)(d) 21–61
(3)(e) 21–61
(4) 21–65
(5) 21–66
ss. 2–4 21–59
s. 4 21–01
s. 5 21–05
s. 6 21–05
s. 7 .... 21–14, 21–49, 21–51
ss. 8–10 21–03
s. 12 21–79
(1) 21–79
s. 13 ..... 21–01, 21–03, 21–96
(5) 21–96
s. 14 .... 21–95, 21–164,
21–166, 21–167
(3) 21–166
s. 15 .... 21–177, 21–178
(4) 21–178
Sched. 1 21–167
Pt. I 21–177, 21–179
Pt. II 21–177, 21–180
Sched. 2 21–75
Damages Act (c. 48)—
s.1(1) 27–14
s. 3 .... 27–28, 27–29, 27–41
s. 4 27–29
s. 6 27–29
Employment Rights Act
(c. 18) 23–104
s. 13 .... 23–39, 23–41
s. 44 23–131
(1)(d)–(e) 23–105
s. 100 23–131
(1)(d)–(e) 23–105
s. 104 .... 23–39, 23–41
s. 122(2) 23–105
s. 123(6) 23–105
s. 166(7) 5–03
s. 216 23–112
s. 230 5–03

Treasure Act (c. 24)   13a, 13–65
  s. 1 13–65
  s. 2 13–65
  s. 4(1) 13–65
    (2) 13–65
    (4)(a) 13–65
      (b) 13–65
  s. 10 13–65
    (6) 13–65
  s. 11 13–65
Noise Act (c. 37)   18–03, 18–07
Party Wall etc Act (c.
  40) 17–23
  s. 8 17–34
Public Order (Amend-
  ment) Act (c. 59) 12–41
1997 Civil Procedure Act (c. 12)—
  s. 7 .... 28–22 to 28–27
Social   Security
  (Recovery   of
  Benefits) Act (c. 27) . 27–17
  s. 8 27–17
  Sched. 1,
  Pt. II 27–17
  Sched. 2 27–17
Police (Property) Act (c.
  30) 13–60
Protection from Harass-
  ment Act (c. 40) 1–20,
           11–12, 12–12,
           18–39, 18–95,
          23–40, 23–123,
                23–124
  s. 1 12–16,
                23–42A
    (1) 12–16
    (2) 12–16
    (3) 12–16
      (c) 12–16
  s. 2 .... 23–42A
  s. 3 12–16
    (1) 23–42A
    (2) 12–16,
                23–42A
    (6) 23–42A
    (7) 23–42A
  s. 4 .... 23–42A
  s. 5 .... 23–42A

1997 Protection from Harass-
    ment Act—*cont.*
  ss. 7–11 .... 23–42A
Police Act (c. 50)
  s. 86 5–14
Public Interest Disclos-
  ure Act (c. 23) 23–01
Competition Act (c. 41) .. 23–43,
                23–86
1998 Human Rights Act (c. 42)   1–05,
         1–05B, 1–05G, 8–69,
      21–01, 21–05, 21–228,
            23–01, 23–17
               Appendix
  s. 1 .... 1–05A
  s. 3 .... 1–05A
  ss. 6–8 .... 1–05A
  s. 6 .... 1–05A
    (3)(a) 1–05A
      (b) 1–05A, 1–05G
  s. 7 .... 1–05a, 1–05E,
                21–04
  s. 8 .... 1–05a, 21–04
    (4) 1–05a
  s. 9 21–04
1999 Employment   Relations
    Act (c. 26) .. 23–18, 23–91,
           23–112, 23–114,
                23–115
  Sched. 1 23–18
    para. 31(3) 23–18
        (4) 23–18
        (6) 23–18
    para. 63(3) 23–18
        (4) 23–18
        (5) 23–18
  Sched. 3, para. 2 23–120
        (2) 23–120
    para. 3 23–114
    para. 3(2) 23–112
        (3) 23–112
    para. 4 .... 23–114, 23–120
    para. 5 .... 23–112, 23–115
    para. 6 .... 23–114, 23–120
      (2) 23–112
    para. 7 .... 23–114, 23–120
    para. 11 .. 23–112, 23–114
  Sched. 5, para. 3 23–112

TABLE OF STATUTORY INSTRUMENTS

1961 Construction (General Provisions) Regulations (S.I. 1961 No. 1580)
reg. 44(2) 11–10

1974 Protection of Eyes Regulations (S.I. 1974 No. 1681) 11–11, 11–25

1981 Transfer of Undertakings (Protection of Employment) Regulations (S.I. 1981 No. 1794) 4–42

1986 Companies (Northern Ireland) Order (S.I. 1986 No. 1032) 21–180

1989 Limitation (Northern Ireland) Order (S.I. 1989 No. 1339) 21–05

1991 Public Works Contracts Regulations (S.I. 1991 No. 2680) 23–44

1995 Duration of Copyright and Rights in Performances Regulations (S.I. No. 3297)—
reg. 5 24–07
reg. 6(1) 24–09
    (2) 24–09
reg. 7(1) 24–10
reg. 9(1) 24–09
reg. 10 24–41
regs. 18–20 24–14
reg. 20 24–15
reg. 21 24–40

1995 Duration of Copyright and Rights in Performances Regulations—*cont.*
reg. 22 24–35
reg. 23 24–17
reg. 24 24–40
reg. 25 24–40

1996 Health and Safety (Consultation with Employees) Regulations (S.I. 1996 No. 1513) 23–103

1997 Civil Jurisdiction and Judgments Act 1982 (Interim Relief) Order (S.I. 1997 No. 302) 28–28–28–34

Treasure Act 1996 (Commencement No. 1) Order (S.I. 1997 No. 760) 13–65

Treasure Act 1996 (Commencement No. 2) Order (S.I. 1997 No. 1977) 13–65

Protection from Harassment (Northern Ireland) Order (S.I. 1997 No. 1180) (N.I. 9) 23–42A

Visiting Forces (Designation) Order (S.I. 1997 No. 1779) 4–27

1998 Visiting Forces (Resignation) Order (S.I. 1998 No. 1268) 4–27

RULES OF THE SUPREME COURT

Ord. 2 31–43

Ord. 11

  r. 1(1) .... 28–28 to 28–34

      (f) 23–23

Ord. 13

  r. 3 .... 13–109, 13–111

Ord. 14A 8–78

Ord. 15,

  r. 7 31–01

  r. 10A 13–103, 13–142, 13–165

Ord. 18,

  r. 19 21–51

r. 4 13–109

Ord. 29,

  r. 2 13–113

Ord. 32

  rr. 9–10 31–43

Ord. 42,

  r. 1A 13–109, 13–141

Ord. 53 11–14

Ord. 59,

  r. 11(4) 21–203

Ord. 82,

  r. 3A 21–49, 21–51, 21–55

TABLE OF CIVIL PROCEDURE RULES

Civil Procedure Rules 1998 13–103,
21–03, 21–49,
21–51, 21–55
   Part 12, r. 4(1) 13–109,
13–111
Part 16
Practice Direction
   para. 8 .... 21–03, 21–55
      (2) 21–42
   para. 9 21–55
Part 25 .... 28–22, 28–28
   r. 1(1)(c) 13–113

      (e) 13–113
      (f) 28–28
      (h) 28–22
   r. 2 4–31
Part 40
   r. 14 .... 13–109, 13–141
   Sched. 1 .... 21–03, 21–49,
21–55
Ord. 42
   r. 1A 13–109
Ord. 82 .... 21–03, 21–55
   r. 3A 21–49

CHAPTER 1.—PRINCIPLES OF LIABILITY IN TORT

		PARA.
■1.	Defining tortious liability	1–01
□2.	Boundaries of torts	1–06
■3.	Interests protected by the law of torts	1–16
4.	Common elements of wrongdoing	1–36
5.	Damage	1–54

1.—DEFINING TORTIOUS LIABILITY

Functions of the law of torts   1–03

In *Burris v. Azadani* [1995] 1 W.L.R. 1372, CA and *Re C (Adult Patient) (Access: Jurisdiction)* [1994] 1 F.C.R. 705 the role of tort in protecting fundamental human rights and interests has been re-affirmed vigorously.

European Community law   1–04

See now *Brasserie du Pecheur v. Germany* [1996] 1 C.M.L.R. 889; *Dillenkofer v. Federal Republic of Germany* [1997] 2 W.L.R. 253, ECJ; *R v. Secretary of State for Transport, ex p. Factortame Ltd (No. 5)* [1999] 2 All E.R. 640 CA. And see *Downes* (1997) 17 L.S. 286.

The Human Rights Act 1998   1–05A

The development of the law of torts in the next century will potentially be pro-foundly affected by the Human Rights Act 1998 which is expected to come into force in the latter part of 2000. Subsequent sections of this Supplement briefly map out some of the issues arising from the Act which will be fully dealt with in the forthcoming eighteenth edition of this work.

The Human Rights Act does *not* incorporate the European Convention on Human Rights into English law. The Act provides that, wherever possible, primary and subordinate legislation must be interpreted in a way which is compatible with "Convention Rights" (section 3), and that it is unlawful for any *public authority* to act in a way which is incompatible with "Convention Rights" (sections 6–8). "Convention Rights" mean those fundamental rights and freedoms set out in Articles 2–12 of the European Convention on Human Rights, Articles 1–3 of the First Protocol (relating to rights of property, education and free elections) and Articles 1 and 2 of the Sixth Protocol (abolishing the death penalty) (section 1); (see *post,* Supplement, Appendix I) "Convention Rights" are without prejudice to, and in addition to common law rights (section 11).

The Human Rights Act will affect the development of torts in three principal ways:

(1) Legislation, relevant to a claim in tort, will be scrutinised to assess its compatibility with "Convention Rights". For example, legislation such as the Police and Criminal Evidence Act 1984, relating to police powers of arrest, search and entry will have to be examined. The Human Rights Act does not enable judges to strike down primary legislation. In the case of conflict between *unambiguous* statutory provisions and "Convention Rights", all the court can do is issue a declaration of incompatibility, requiring the government to take the requisite action to remedy any breach of the Convention.

(2) Where a claim is brought against a public authority, violation of a "Convention Right" could give rise to an action under section 7 of the Act. Section 8 provides that when the relevant court has power to award damages, it may do so subject to the following conditions. The court must take

into account all the circumstances of the case, including any other relief or remedy granted, and the consequences of any decision to order compensation. The court must be satisfied that the award of damages is necessary to afford just satisfaction to the person in whose favour it is made. In deciding whether to award damages and determining the *quantum* of such damages, courts must be guided by principles developed by the European Court of Human Rights (section 8(4)). Public authority is broadly defined to embrace "*any person certain of whose functions are of a public nature*" (section 6(3)(b)). Institutions such as state schools and universities clearly fall within the definition of public authorities, but so may parts of the media, and "public" charities such as the RSPCA and the NSPCC. It should be noted that the creation of an action for breach of statutory duty by section 7 of the 1998 Act does not necessarily mean that all (or even many) claims against a public authority which in substance allege violation of a "Convention Right" will be brought under the Act. For example, an action against the police for unlawful arrest could in certain circumstances create a claim for violation of Article 5 of the Convention. However the well-established tort of false imprisonment protects the same substantive interest in liberty. Within a claim for false imprisonment, it is the boundaries of that tort which will need to be reviewed in the light of the provisions of the Convention. Only if no existing tort extends to offer adequate protection of the "Convention Right" in question will direct resort to an action under section 7 be essential.

(3) Where the defendant is not a public authority, nonetheless the Act will still have an impact on claims in tort. While no express provision of the Act directs judges to develop the common law in conformity with "Convention Rights", at least two factors will result in their so doing. First, for a number of years now English judges have sought, whenever possible, to ensure that the common law is consistent with the provisions of the Convention (see *post*, Supplement § 1–05B). Second, section 6 of the Human Rights Act, making it unlawful for public authorities to act in a manner incompatible with the Convention expressly declares that courts are classified as public authorities (section 6(3)(a)). A judge ruling on a claim in tort must therefore attempt to develop and interpret the law to ensure consistency between the common law and "Convention Rights", otherwise the court itself acts unlawfully. So, for example, while the common law has not expressly recognised any tort of breach of privacy, in developing torts with the potential to protect privacy, such as harassment and breach of confidence, courts will have to regard to Article 8 of the Convention requiring respect for "private and family life", and to Article 6 requiring access to justice.

1–05B The European Convention and the common law

Even before the Human Rights Act enters into force, "Convention Rights" have begun to have an effect on the law of torts. The courts have on several occasions expressed a clear intent to seek to develop the common law in conformity with the Convention. In *Att.-Gen. v. Guardian Newspapers Ltd* [1990] A.C. 109 at 283 Lord Goff declared ". . . [I] conceive it to be my duty, when I am free to do so, to interpret the law in accordance with the obligations of the Crown under [the ECHR]".

Where primary or secondary legislation is ambiguous, Neill L.J. ruled that the convention should ". . . be deployed for the purpose of the resolution of an ambiguity": *Rantzen v. Mirror Group Newspapers* [1994] Q.B. 670 at 691.

Lord Woolf M.R. said in *R. v. Chief Constable of North Wales Police, ex p. AB* [1998] 3 All E.R. 310 at 321, "The Convention is not yet part of our domestic law, but all parties were agreed that the actions of the [defendants] had to be judged against the background of the requirements of Article 8."

1–05C Trespass to the person

The "Convention Rights" set out in Articles 2–5 of the Convention address the

2

same groups of interest, in bodily integrity, freedom from international injury, and liberty, as does trespass to the person. Issues which may arise in determining whether the common law is consistent with the Convention include the following. The common law recognises a right of self-defence and section 3 of the Criminal Law Act 1967 authorises the reasonable use of force to prevent crime or effect an arrest. Article 2(2) provides that deadly force is justifiable only if "absolutely necessary". Will Article 2(2) place further limits on what constitutes reasonable force? Article 3 prohibiting inhuman or degrading treatment or punishment will undoubtedly result in further restrictions on the defence of parental chastisement. The European Court of Human Rights has already held that beating a child with an implement contravenes Article 3 (*A v. United Kingdom* (1999) 27 E.H.R.R. 611). Articles 3 and 5 may in concert force a review of case law relating to false imprisonment. The House of Lords in *Hague v. Deputy Governor of Parkhurst Prison* [1992] 1 A.C. 58 ruled that detention in intolerable conditions did not constitute false imprisonment. Yet grossly unsatisfactory conditions of detention are likely to contravene Article 3. In many claims relating to police powers of arrest and detention, and detention in custody more generally, Article 5 must be seen to be complied with (see *Olutu v. Home Office* [1997] 1 W.L.R. 328, CA).

The European Court in *McLeod v. United Kingdom* (1999) 27 E.H.R.R. 493 reviewed common law powers relating to prevention of breaches of the peace and, while acknowledging that such powers were not in principle contrary to "Convention Rights", stressed the requirement that the exercise of such powers must be *proportionate* to the threat posed to public order. In claims for trespass to the person generally it may well be the scope of defences allowed at common law which will need to be revisited in addressing "Convention Rights". The extent and nature of powers granted to detain and treat mentally incapacitated individuals both under the Mental Health Acts and at common law may be questioned. The case law relating to parental powers to consent to treatment on behalf of their children may be scrutinised in the light of Article 8.

Trespass to goods and land   1–05D
Note that the First Protocol to the Convention in Article 1 provides for a right to ". . . the peaceful enjoyment of his possessions" albeit permitting limited State intervention "in the public interest".

Privacy   1–05E
It is the absence of a remedy for breach of privacy at common law which may pose the most significant challenge to the English courts in developing the law of torts in conformity to "Convention Rights". Conduct such as photographing a person without consent, which has been held not to constitute assault (*Murray v. Ministry of Defence* [1998] 1 W.L.R. 692, HL and see *Kaye v. Robertson* [1991] F.S.R 62), almost certainly violates Article 8 (respect for private and family life). Where an infringement of privacy is committed by a public authority resort may be had to claim under section 7 of the Human Rights Act. Where a claim is brought against a private individual, two possibilities present themselves to develop the common law to allow an effective remedy for violation of Article 8. *Either* a claim might be brought within a common law expansion of harassment (see *Khorasandjian v. Bush* [1993] Q.B. 727, CA) *or* an extended obligation of confidentiality (*R. v. Chief Constable of North Wales, ex p. AB* [1998] 3 All E.R. 310 at 321–323).

Defences   1–05F
Just as defences to claims in trespass may need to be scrutinised for consistency with "Convention Rights" so may general defences in tort. Where a defence operates to exclude the plaintiff from a remedy completely, conformity with "Convention Rights" may be questionable. The judgment of the Court of Appeal in *Clunis v. Camden and Islington Health Authority* [1998] 2 W.L.R. 902, CA on the defence of *ex turpi causa* is vulnerable to attack. The Court of Appeal ruled that where a claim in tort arises from the plaintiff's participation in criminal conduct no cause of action

could arise, and that no issue of the proportionality of the wrong done by the plaintiff and the harm done to him could ameliorate the absolute bar on redress the criminality of his conduct demands. On the facts of *Clunis* (see *post*, Supplement § 3–03), the mental impairment suffered by the plaintiff was effectively disregarded. The rejection in *Clunis* of any discretionary element in the defence of *ex turpi* may violate Article 6 of the Convention, and in claims brought under the Fatal Accidents Act 1976 by dependants, Article 2 may also be invoked. Is criminal conduct *per se* always a sufficient justification to exclude a claimant's entitlement to access to justice and in extreme cases his very right to life?

1–05G Negligence

The marked trend of recent years to limit the scope of the duty of care is likely to come under scrutiny. The entitlement to a hearing under Article 6 may deter courts from striking out claims on the grounds of public interest immunity. The right to life under Article 2 may have implications for the liability of the police, rescue and safety services. The right to respect for private and family life under Article 8 may be relevant in cases as diverse as those concerning child care, psychiatric damage and bereavement. Finally, section 6 of the Human Rights Act, which gives the Convention direct effect against public authorities, may have an indirect effect upon the development of negligence liability.

Article 6

Article 6.1 provides that "In the determination of his civil rights and obligations everyone . . . is entitled to a . . . hearing." It seems from the European Court of Human Rights (ECHR) decision in *Osman v. United Kingdom* (1998) 5 B.H.R.C. 293, that where an immunity flows from the application of the normal test of fairness, justice and reasonableness, Article 6 may require the courts to consider the competing public policy considerations before concluding that an immunity applies. The *Osman* ruling stemmed from the Court Appeal decision in *Osman v. Ferguson* [1993] 4 All E.R. 344, in which McCowan L.J., giving the judgment of the Court of Appeal, held that although there was an arguable case that there was sufficient proximity between the police and the plaintiffs to give rise to a duty, the claim had to be struck out as it was "doomed to failure" by the immunity of the police in relation to the investigation of crime established by the House of Lords in *Hill v. Chief Constable of West Yorkshire* [1989] A.C. 53, H.L. Before the E.C.H.R., the United Kingdom Government defended the police immunity as flowing from an application of the general test of fairness, justice and reasonableness, which was justified by the need to maintain the effectiveness of the police service. Whilst accepting that this was a legitimate justification for an immunity, the court ruled that: "it must be open to a domestic court to have regard to the presence of other public interest considerations which pull in the opposite direction to the application of the rule. Failing this, there will be no distinction made between degrees of negligence of harm suffered or any consideration of the justice of a particular case." The *Osman* case involved allegations of failure to protect the life of a child, grave negligence and an assumption of responsibility by the police for the plaintiff's safety. These considerations had to "be examined on the merits and not automatically excluded by the application of a rule which amounts to the grant of an immunity to the police". Such a refusal to consider competing public interest considerations was a disproportionate response to the aim of maintaining police effectiveness and deprived the plaintiffs of their right to a hearing under Article 6.

The implication of Article 6 as applied in the *Osman* case was considered in *Barrett v. Enfield London B.C.* [1999] 3 W.L.R. 628, HL. The plaintiff's claim against the authority for negligence in respect of placements with foster parents, had been struck out by the Court of Appeal on the ground that it would be contrary to the public interest to impose a duty of care. The House of Lords held that the claim should proceed to trial as only an investigation of the facts could substantiate the public interest argument. Whilst the other Law Lords considered the issue solely on the basis of common law principles, Lord Browne-Wilkinson also considered the impact of *Osman*, commenting that:

> "In view of the decision in *Osman's* case it is now difficult to foretell what would be the result in the present case if we were to uphold the striking out order. It seems to me that it is as least probable that the matter would then be taken to Strasbourg. That court, applying its decision in *Osman's* case if it considers it be correct, would say that we had deprived the plaintiff of his right to have the balance struck between the hardship suffered by him and the damage to be done to the public interest in the present case if an order were to be made against the defendant council. In the present very unsatisfactory state of affairs, and bearing in mind that under the Human Rights Act Art 6 will shortly become part of English law, in such cases as these it is difficult to say that it is a clear and obvious case calling for striking out."

In addition to the implications for police and public service liability, Article 6 may require reconsideration of the immunity for participants in legal proceedings. This immunity applies to advocates, witnesses, judges and in some circumstances, private arbitrators. (For the detail, see §§ 7–111 and 8–69 *et seq.*) The immunity is well established. Courts consider whether particular facts come within the defined scope of the immunity but do not normally consider the policy merits of applying the immunity to the facts. Where a claimant's case falls squarely within the scope of the immunity, it could be said that the blanket application of the immunity deprives him of the hearing to which he is entitled under Article 6. The counter-argument would be that the existence of the blanket immunity means that the claimant has no civil right, e.g. to sue a barrister in respect of court room negligence, in respect of which Article 6 can "bite". Although this issue did not arise in *Osman v. United Kingdom*, two of the judges suggested that the Court should meet the argument by adopting a broad definition of civil rights as being "all those rights which are individual rights under the national legal system and fall within the sphere of general individual freedom" (Judge Jambrek) or those rights which were protected by the Convention (Judge Foighel). Arguably either definition would enable a claimant to question the imposition of a blanket immunity under Article 6. It is noticeable that the Court of Appeal has recently moved from taking a definitional approach to the "intimate connection" immunity under which all "door of court" settlements would be protected (*Kelley v. Corston* [1998] Q.B. 686, CA), to a merits approach. Thus, in *Hall v. Simons* [1999] Lloyd's Rep. P.N. 47, Lord Bingham said "Save where a claim relates to the acts or omissions of an advocate conducting a case in open court, forensic immunity is not to be recognised on the application of any blanket rule. It is always necessary to look with care at the specific complaint of negligence made against the lawyer in the context of the particular case." A similar merits approach was taken to witness immunity by Otton L.J. in *Stanton v. Callaghan* [1998] 4 All E.R. 961, CA, when stating that in each case it was a question of whether "it would serve the interests of justice to grant immunity". It is suggested that Article 6 may similarly require the courtroom immunity of advocates established by *Rondel v. Worsley* [1969] 1 A.C. 191, HL, to be considered on the merits rather than applied as a blanket rule. The immunity for private arbitrators recognised in *Sutcliffe v. Thackrah* [1974] A.C. 727, might similarly require reconsideration.

Article 2
The ECHR in *Osman* considered the application of Article 2 to the failures of the police. The court held that the Right to Life implied "in certain well defined circumstances a positive obligation to take protective operational measures to protect an individual whose life is at risk from the criminal acts of another individual." To establish breach of this obligation it had to be shown that "the authorities knew or ought to have known at the time of the existence of a real and immediate risk to the life of an identified individual from the criminal acts of a third party and failed to take measures within the scope of their powers which, judged reasonably, might

have been expected to avoid that risk". On the facts "it could not be said that the police ought to have known that the lives of [the applicants' family] were at real and immediate risk" and that having regard to the presumption of innocence, the police "reasonably held the view that they lacked the required standard of suspicion to use [their] powers". Hence, the conduct of the police did not violate Article 2. The facts of *Brindle v. Commissioner of Police for the Metropolis* (unreported, 5 June 1998) might well fall on the other side of the line. There the police knew of the immediate threat of the plaintiff's assassination but preferred to set a trap rather than warning him. Whilst that may have been a reasonable approach to catching the assassin, it may not be regarded as reasonable from the perspective of the plaintiff who was wounded in the process.

Article 2 may also be of significance in relation to rescue services. The ECHR in *Osman* held that the Article required a State to "take appropriate steps to safeguard the lives of those within its jurisdiction". The positive obligation of the State to protect an individual whose life is at risk from criminal acts of another must surely extend to protecting an individual whose life is at risk from fire or accident. Indeed, in *Hughes v. United Kingdom* (Application No. 11590195) the European Human Rights Commission suggested that the common law was defective in failing to recognise a duty to rescue. What constitutes "appropriate steps" may be debated, but the negligent failure of a rescue service to respond to an emergency call when resources are available would seem to be a prima facie breach of Article 2. Yet, as the common law stands such a failure would not give rise to liability in negligence. In *Stovin v. Wise* [1996] A.C. 923, HL, Lord Hoffman held a highway authority to be under no common law duty to remove road hazards adjacent to the highway despite the foreseeable danger to motorist, and in *Capital and Counties plc v. Hampshire County Council* [1997] Q.B. 1004 Stuart-Smith L.J. followed that lead stating *obiter*, that "the fire brigade are not under a common law duty to answer the call for help and are not under a duty to take care to do so". The justification is doctrinal, that the common law does not recognise a general duty to act positively to protect or rescue others. It is not based on the policy merits. Indeed, Stuart-Smith L.J. thought that policy arguments for immunity such as the undesirability of litigation and the adverse impact on rescue services in terms of defense attitudes, to be unpersuasive. Once again, it is suggested that viewed from the perspective of the Right to Life, a court might have difficulty in regarding the present blanket approach of the common law as being a proportionate response to the issue. Whilst it might well be acceptable for highway authorities to owe no duty to protect the general road user from roadside hazards given the need to prioritise work in the light of the resources available, where a fire creates an immediate danger to individuals and the authority has the resources to respond, it might be difficult to deny a duty other than on doctrinal grounds. If the fire merely threatened property, as was the case in *Capital and Counties*, then the position would be different. Article 2 would not be relevant and as Lord Hoffman suggested in *Stovin*, "individuals can and do protect themselves by insurance against the risk of fire".

Article 2 may also be of relevance to the question whether those responsible for enforcing safety legislation should owe a duty to those whose lives have been endangered by a negligent failure to inspect and apply the legislation. (See further § 7–102 and annotation.) In *Harris v. Evans* [1998] 1 W.L.R. 1285, CA, a Court of Appeal led by Sir Richard Scott V.-C. held that no duty was owed by an inspector whose alleged negligence had led to the plaintiff suffering financial loss. The decision was justified on the policy ground that any duty would cut across the statutory system of safety regulation and might lead to a "defensive" approach being taken by those charged with enforcement. However, a month later in *Perrett v. Collins* [1999] 1 P.N.L.R. 77, CA, a differently constituted Court of Appeal led by Hobhouse L.J., held that an inspector charged with inspecting the construction of light aircraft did owe a duty of care to those injured in a crash caused by the defective construction of the aircraft. *Harris* was not cited to the court, but Hobhouse L.J. distinguished previous cases denying a duty on the ground that they were concerned with financial loss and not personal injury. The inspector in *Perrett* worked for a private inspection services and it might be argued that a public authority inspector would not owe a duty on the basis of the arguments invoked in *Harris*. It is suggested that the influence of Article 2 is likely to lead the courts to extend the approach taken in *Perrett* rather than that taken in *Harris*.

Article 8
Article 8 was considered by the ECHR in *Osman*. The applicants argued that the failure of the police to bring to an end the campaign of harassment waged by the suspect constituted a breach of Article 8. This claim was rejected on the factual ground that for most of the period the police had insufficient evidence against the suspect and that as soon as they had sufficient evidence, they did unsuccessfully attempt to arrest. If the police had failed to take any action once there was sufficient evidence against the suspect, a further issue would have arisen, that is whether the availability to the applicants of the civil remedy of an injunction against the suspect provided sufficient protection of the Article 8 right for the State to be exonerated of breach. The European Human Rights Commission took the view that the availability of the injunction meant that the failure of the police did not give rise to a breach of the Article. The ECHR did not comment on the issue. Clearly, the potential protection available through both civil and criminal process must be considered together in determining whether the State has provided adequate protection for the Right to Respect. Much will depend on the particular facts. In cases of minor harassment, it may be acceptable for the police to take the view on resource grounds, that the matter should be left to the civil law. Wright ("Local Authorities, the Duty of Care and the European Convention on Human Rights" (1998) 18 O.J.L.S. 1) suggested that the reluctance of the court to interfere where resources are concerned would similarly be the main impediment to a finding of breach in a case such as *Bedfordshire* where the authorities failed to take adequate action to protect a child from abuse. However, she pointed out that the *Newham* case which was considered in the same House of Lords appeal as *Bedfordshire*, raised a different issue for in that case the authority had removed the child from its family in the mistaken belief that a member of the family was responsible for abuse. The decision to remove the child was taken on expert advice and could be justified under the defence in Article 8.2 as action taken for the protection of health. But she argued that the failure to return the child to its mother for a year after the mother had undertaken to exclude the suspected abuser from her home, amounted to a disproportionate action, taking the authority outside the scope of Article 8.2. Thus, there may be situations in which the negligence of a social work authority may involve a breach of Article 8.

A clearer example of a possible breach may be provided by *W v. Essex County Council* [1998] 3 W.L.R. 534, where the authority had failed to warn a fostering family that the foster child being placed with them had a record of being an abuser. The Court of Appeal refused to strike out a negligence claim by the natural children of the fostering family who suffered psychiatric injury as a result of abuse by the foster child. To that extent the right to respect for family life was protected. However, the court struck out the claim of the parents in respect of the psychiatric shock they suffered on the ground that "shock involves the sudden appreciation by sight or sound of a horrifying event" and "does not include psychiatric illness caused by the accumulation over a period of time of more gradual attacks of the nervous system" (see further § 7–44 and annotation). This is a general restriction on the right to claim in respect of psychiatric illness but its effect in the context of the *Essex* case may be regarded as depriving the parties of full respect for their family life. The restriction would be all the more difficult to justify as the Law Commission has recommended reform of the law to allow such "accumulation" claims to succeed. The rejection of psychiatric claims by siblings under the present *Alcock* criteria (see § 7–49) might similarly be regarded as a denial of respect for family life and has also been criticised by the Law Commission. The limitations on bereavement damages might also be regarded as a breach of Article 8.)

Human Rights Act 1998, s. 6
Section 6 gives the Convention direct effect against public authorities. An individual

may bring a claim against an authority for breach of Article 2 or Article 8. Thus, a court faced with the failure of the police to protect in a situation such as that in *Brindle* or a failure to rescue as envisaged in *Capital and Counties*, could provide the claimant with a remedy under the provisions of the Human Rights Act. But the availability of the Convention remedy may also lead the court to develop an alternative common law remedy in negligence. It may be noted that in *Doe v. Toronto Commission of Police* (1989) 58 D.L.R. (4th) 396, a Canadian court faced with facts similar to those in *Brindle*, held the police liable under the Right to Life provision in the Canadian Charter of Rights but also developed the common law sufficiently to impose liability under that head as well.

2.—BOUNDARIES OF TORT

1–08   Concurrent liability

In *Holt v. Payne Skillington (a firm), The Times*, December 22, 1995 the Court of Appeal held that where a duty of care arose concurrently in contract and tort the scope of the tortious duty was not necessarily co-extensive with the duty arising under contract. Providing that nothing in the contract between the parties excluded such a duty in tort, a Hedley Byrne duty of care wider than any contractual duty can arise from the particular circumstances of the parties' relationship.

> "... there is no reason in principle why a Hedley Byrne type duty of care cannot arise in an overall set of circumstances where, by reference to certain limited aspects of those circumstances, the same parties enter into a contractual relationship involving more limited obligations than those imposed by the duty of care in tort. In such circumstances, the duty of care in tort and the duties imposed by the contract will be concurrent but not co-extensive. The difference in scope between the two will reflect the more limited factual basis which gave rise to the contract and the absence of any term in that contract which precludes or restricts the wider duty of care in tort" *per* Hirst L.J.

cf. Conway v. Crowe Kelsey & Partners 39 Con.L.R. 1. And see also *Wessex Regional Health Authority v. HLM Design* (1994) 10 Const.L.J. 165; *Barclays Bank plc v. Fairclough Building Ltd (No. 2)* [1995] I.R.L.R. 605, CA; *Williams v. Natural Life Ltd* [1998] 1 W.L.R. 830, HL.
And see *Banque Bruxelles Lambert SA v. Eagle Star Insurance Co. Ltd* [1996] 3 W.L.R. 87, 93, HL.

1–15   Tort and public law

Note *X v. Bedfordshire County Council* [1995] 2 A.C. 633, HL, *post*, at Chap. 11

3.—INTERESTS PROTECTED BY THE LAW OF TORTS

1–19   Personal freedom

In *Re C (Adult Patient) (Access: Jurisdiction)* [1994] 1 F.C.R. 705, Eastham J. asserted that denying an adult mentally handicapped daughter access to her mother, where such an act was contrary to the daughter's will or against her best interests, could itself be a tortious act. Her "freedom" was interfered with. The judge acknowledged that he was treading on "unbroken new ground" and did not expand on the limits of tort's role in enforcing a larger right to personal freedom. Perhaps the crucial issue is whether an act such as preventing family access to an individual is calculated to cause her harm, so falling within the lively development or the tort established in *Wilkinson v. Downton*; see *post*, § 1–20.

1–20   Physical safety and freedom from harm

In *Burris v. Azadani* [1995] 1 W.L.R. 1372, CA the Court of Appeal upheld the legality of an "exclusion one" order to prevent repetition of a tortious campaign of harassment on the part of the defendant.

Note that the Protection from Harassment Act 1997 creates a civil remedy in respect of the newly created crime of harassment: see *post*, Supplement § 12–16.

Psychiatric harm   1–21

Note *Page v. Smith* [1995] 2 W.L.R. 644, HL; *White v. Chief Constable of South Yorkshire* [1999] 3 W.L.R. 1509, HL.

Note too *Vernon v. Bosley (No. 1)* 1 All E.R. 577, CA where the plaintiff recovered for pathological grief disorder triggered by witnessing the horrific deaths of his daughters: see *post*, Supplement § 7–43.

Privacy   1–23

See *R. v. Chief Constable of North Wales Police, ex p. AB* [1998] 3 W.L.R. 57, CA.

Family interests   1–24

Might it be argued that *Re C (Adult Patient) (Access: Jurisdiction), supra*, recognises access to family as an interest now (slightly) protected by the law of torts?

Enjoyment of property   1–28

In *Hunter v. Canary Wharf* [1977] 2 W.L.R. 684, the House of Lords restated the fundamental principle that only persons with an interest in the affected property could sue in nuisance, overruling the majority judgment of the Court of Appeal in *Khorasandjian v. Bush*; see *post*, Chap. 18.

Public rights   1–32

Note that in *DPP v. Jones* [1999] 2 W.L.R. 625, the House of Lords, held that a "peaceful demonstration" constituted a reasonable use of the highway.

9

CHAPTER 2.—CAUSATION IN TORT: GENERAL PRINCIPLES

		PARA.
1.	Introduction	2–01
■2.	Factual causation	2–03
■3.	Remoteness of damage	2–18
■4.	*Novus actus interveniens*	2–24

2–01   Two recent judgments address the thorny issue of economic loss. *Allied Maples Group Ltd v. Simmons & Simmons (a firm)* [1995] 1 W.L.R. 1602, CA addresses liability in respect of loss of a chance to avoid such loss. *Banque Bruxelles Lambert SA v. Eagle Star Insurance Co. Ltd* [1996] 3 W.L.R. 87, HL illustrates the uncertain boundary between the scope of duty of care and principles of causation.

2.—Factual Causation

2–03   **Establishing a causal link**
Note the judgment of the House of Lords in *Bolitho v. City and Hackney Health Authority* [1997] 3 W.L.R. 1151; see further *post*, Supplement § 2–10 and § 8–34.

2–04   In *Pickford v. Imperial Chemical Industries plc* [1998] 3 All E.R. 462 the plaintiff alleged that she had developed a prescribed disease, PDA4 (cramp of the hand or forearm due to repetitive movements), in the course of her employment as a secretary. There was conflicting medical evidence as to whether the plaintiff's condition was organic in nature, as a result of physical injury, or whether it was psychogenic (as the defendants contended). The trial judge dismissed the action, holding that the plaintiff had failed to establish that her condition was organic in nature or that it had been caused by her typing work. The Court of Appeal reversed the trial judge on the basis that he had misdirected himself that the onus was on the plaintiff to establish that the cause was organic and that ICI did not have to satisfy him that the cause was psychogenic. On appeal by ICI, the House of Lords held that the burden of proof was on the plaintiff to show that her condition had an organic cause, and ICI's failure to prove that the condition was psychogenic was simply one relevant factor in the decision as to whether the plaintiff's explanation of the cause should be accepted. Thus, the judge was correct to consider evidence other than the medical evidence and was entitled to conclude that the plaintiff had not satisfied the burden of proof.

2–06   **Cause or material contribution**
In *Page v. Smith (No. 2)* [1996] 1 W.L.R. 855, CA the plaintiff had suffered for several years from chronic fatigue syndrome. At a time when the disease appeared to be in remission he was involved in a collision with a motor vehicle negligently driven by the defendant and, soon afterwards, the plaintiff suffered an acute recrudescence of chronic fatigue syndrome. Evidence that stress materially contributed to that disease, together with the juxtaposition of the accident and the plaintiff's renewed illness, were held to be sufficient to establish that the defendant's negligence materially contributed to the plaintiff's illness, notwithstanding that the plaintiff's reaction to the accident was "not necessarily proportional to the trauma". See also *Vernon v. Bosley (No. 1)* [1997] 1 All E.R. 577 applying this approach to psychiatric damage.

2–07   In *Athey v. Leonati* [1997] 1 W.W.R. 97 the Supreme Court of Canada held that the defendant's negligence, which the trial judge had concluded was no more than a 25 per cent contributory factor to the plaintiff's injury, constituted a material contribution to the damage and held the defendant liable for the full loss.

Loss of a chance   **2–09**

In *Allied Maples Group Ltd v. Simmons & Simmons (a firm)* [1995] 1 W.L.R. 1602 the Court of Appeal held that where the plaintiff's loss depends on the hypothetical action of a third party, either in addition to action by the plaintiff or independently of such action, the plaintiff need only prove that there was a substantial chance that that third party would have so acted to eliminate any loss to the plaintiff. He is not obliged to establish that it is more than not (51:49 likely) that the third party would have acted to avoid the risk of loss to the plaintiff. Evaluation of the value of the chance lost to the plaintiff is then a matter of quantification of damages (at 914–17).

Following *Chaplin v. Hicks* and *Kitchen v. Royal Air Force Association* the Court of Appeal awarded damages in negligence to the plaintiffs on the following facts. The plaintiffs had been engaged in the acquisition of certain businesses from another furnishing group Gillow. They were advised by the defendant solicitors. Their original intention had been to "cherry pick" portions of Gillow's businesses. Difficulties with planning permission forced them to adopt a different strategy and acquire a whole group of businesses, divesting themselves of those which they did not want at a later date. The original draft agreement with Gillow contained a warranty, whereby Gillow undertook that there were no existing or contingent liabilities in respect of properties previously owned, etc., by that group. In the course of negotiations that warranty was deleted. The plaintiffs ultimately found themselves liable for substantial sums under certain leases previously held by the Gillow group. They alleged negligence by the defendants in failing to advise them of the effect of deleting that warranty. On the issue of causation, the question arose of what action the plaintiff would have taken if properly advised, and, whether, if approached, Gillow would have agreed to offer the plaintiff the protection requested against the liabilities which ultimately ensued. The Court of Appeal found that whilst the plaintiffs had to prove on the balance of probability that they would have sought protection from Gillow, they need only prove a substantial chance that Gillow would have agreed to provide them with total or at least partial protection from open-ended liability. Quantification of that chance was remitted to the trial judge in the light of further evidence of Gillow's likely response to a request for protection from liability.

The tenor of the judgment is that such a loss of a chance, a loss dependent on the putative conduct of a third party, is indeed recoverable in tort. See also *Spring v. Guardian Assurance plc* [1995] 2 A.C. 296 at 327.

The approach in *Allied Maples* has been followed in two subsequent Court of Appeal cases. In *Stovold v. Barlows* [1996] 1 P.N.L.R. 91, the sale of the plaintiff's property fell through because of the negligence of his solicitors. The trial judge had assessed damages on the basis that if the plaintiff succeeded in demonstrating on the balance of probabilities that but for the negligence the sale would have proceeded he was entitled to the difference between what the prospective purchaser would have paid and what he eventually received for the property when it was sold later. The Court of Appeal held that this was the wrong approach to causation, where the loss depended upon the action of an independent third party in circumstances which *ex hypothesi* did not arise. The correct approach was to evaluate the loss of the plaintiff's chance that but for the defendant's negligence the sale would have gone ahead, applying *Allied Maples*. If the plaintiff proved that he had lost a real or substantial chance as opposed to a speculative one the evaluation of that chance was part of the assessment of the *quantum* of damage. In *First Interstate Bank of California v. Cohen Arnold & Co.* [1996] 1 P.N.L.R. 17 the plaintiffs had lent money to X, a client of the defendants, who were accountants. The defendants negligently told the plaintiffs that X was much wealthier than in fact he was. As a consequence of this misrepresentation the plaintiffs delayed calling in the loan. During the period of the delay the value of the property upon which the loan was secured fell and was therefore insufficient to cover the plaintiffs' loss when X defaulted on the loan. The Court of Appeal held that the proper basis for dealing with these facts was to assess of the chance of selling at the full price before the delay, which was estimated at two to one (i.e. a two-thirds chance). Although *Stovold v. Barlows* involved a claim

11

against solicitors and is therefore analogous to *Kitchen v. RAF Association* (which it could be argued is simply a case based in contract), *First Interstate Bank of California* was undoubtedly a claim based in the tort of negligent misrepresentation.

See also *J. Sainsbury plc v. Broadway Maylan (a firm) (Ernest Green Partnership Ltd, Third Party)* [1999] P.N.L.R. 286 at 322–329; and *Doyle v. Wallace* [1998] P.I.Q.R. Q146.

2–10   Add to paragraph: This type of causation problem arises whenever the plaintiff's loss depends upon what the plaintiff would have done, hypothetically, if there had been no breach of duty by the defendant. Typically this will occur in "advice" cases, where it is alleged that had the defendant not been negligent in the advice or information given (or not given) the plaintiff would have done something different, thereby avoiding the loss that has materialised. Thus, where an accountant supplies negligently audited accounts in reliance upon which the plaintiff purchases a company which proves to be worth less than anticipated, then even if the plaintiff is able to establish that the accountants owed him a duty of care, he must also prove that had the accounts been accurate he would not have proceeded with the purchase: see *JEB Fasteners Ltd v. Marks Bloom & Co.* [1983] 1 All E.R. 583, 589. Similarly, a patient who alleges that a doctor negligently failed to advise her about the risks of an operative procedure must prove that had she been informed about the risks she would have declined the treatment, thereby avoiding the risk that has now materialised: see *Smith v. Barking, Havering and Brentwood Health Authority* (1988) [1994] 5 Med. L.R. 285; *McAllister v. Lewisham and North Southwark Health Authority* [1994] 5 Med. L.R. 343; *Lybert v. Warrington Health Authority* [1996] 7 Med. L.R. 71, CA; *Thompson v. Blake-James* [1998] Lloyd's Rep. Med. 187, CA. See also *Chappell v. Hart* [1998] H.C.A. 55, (1998) 156 A.L.R. 517, HCt of Australia.

This problem is not limited to circumstances where the question is what would the plaintiff have done, in hypothetical circumstances, but also arises when there is a question as to what, hypothetically, the *defendant* would have done had she not been negligent. This is illustrated by *Bolitho v. City and Hackney Health Authority* [1997] 3 W.L.R. 1151, HL, in which the plaintiff, who was in hospital, suffered brain damage as a result of a cardiac arrest caused by an obstruction of the bronchial air passages. The defendants admitted negligence because a doctor had not attended to the plaintiff in response to calls for assistance. The damage could have been avoided if the plaintiff had been seen by a doctor and "intubated", clearing the obstruction. The doctor who failed to respond said that had she attended she would not have intubated, and therefore the cardiac arrest and subsequent brain damage would have occurred in any event. There was evidence that a responsible body of professional opinion would have supported a decision not to intubate, although five medical experts for the plaintiff said that he should have been intubated, and it was agreed that this was the only course of action that would have prevented the damage.

Lord Browne-Wilkinson said that in all cases the primary question is one of fact: did the wrongful act cause the injury? In cases where the breach of duty consists of an omission to do an act which ought to have been done (such as the failure of a doctor to attend the patient) the factual inquiry is necessarily hypothetical. The question is what would have happened if an event, which by definition did not occur, had occurred? The first question is: what would have happened – either the doctor would have intubated, had she attended, or she would not. The *Bolam* test, by which standards of professional negligence are measured by reference to a "responsible body of professional opinion", was not, and could not, be relevant to that question (see *Bolam v. Friern Hospital Management Committee* [1957] 1 W.L.R. 582, see § 8–34). The defendant doctor said that she would not have intubated, and therefore the plaintiff would in any event have sustained the brain damage. But she could not escape liability by proving that she would have failed to act as any reasonably competent doctor would have acted in the circumstances: "A defendant cannot escape liability by saying that the damage would have occurred in any event because he would have committed some other breach of duty thereafter." *per* Lord Browne-Wilkinson [1997] 3 W.L.R. 1151 at 1156–57. Applying *Joyce v. Wandsworth Health*

Authority [1996] P.I.Q.R. P121 Lord Browne-Wilkinson, concluded that there were
two questions for the judge to decide on causation:
  (1) what would the doctor have done, or authorised to be done, if she had
      attended the plaintiff? and
  (2) if she would not have intubated, would that have been negligent?
The *Bolam* test had no relevance to first question, but was central to the second.

3.—REMOTENESS OF DAMAGE

Unintended consequences   2–21

> "Rules which make the wrongdoer liable for all the consequences of his wrong-
> ful conduct are exceptional and need to be justified by some special policy.
> Normally the law limits liability to those consequences which are attributable
> to that which made the act wrongful"; *Banque Bruxelles Lambert S.A. v. Eagle
> Star Insurance Co Ltd* [1996] 3 W.L.R. 87, HL, *per* Lord Hoffmann at 94.

In *Banque Bruxelles Lambert SA v. Eagle Star Insurance Co. Ltd* the House of
Lords held that valuers who negligently provided the plaintiffs with incorrect
information (an inaccurate valuation) on the basis of which the plaintiffs lent money
on property were responsible only for the foreseeable consequences of that information being wrong. The measure of damages therefore should be quantified by reference to the difference between the correct valuation and the negligent valuation
proffered by the defendants, *i.e.* the loss attributable to the plaintiff having less
security than they believed. The defendants were not liable for the entire financial
loss ensuing to the plaintiffs from making the relevant loans on the basis of incorrect
valuations, where that loss resulted in part from falls in the market. Their Lordships
thus overturned the judgment of the Court of Appeal that the defendants valuers
"should bear all the risks of the transaction". The language of Lord Hoffmann's
sole judgment resonates with the language of causation. It is submitted, however,
that the substance of his findings on the limits of the valuers' duty relates rather to
the limits of the valuers' duty of care, on which see, *post*, § 7–196.
  NOTE 81. Add: In *Downs v. Chappell* [1996] 3 All E.R. 344 at 351 the Court of
Appeal held that in an action for deceit once it is proved that the plaintiff was in
fact induced to act to his detriment by a material misrepresentation, the question of
what the plaintiff would have done but for the representation becomes irrelevant.
"The judge was wrong to ask how [the plaintiffs] would have acted if they had been
told the truth. They were never told the truth. They were told lies in order to induce
them to enter into the contract. The lies were material and successful." This appears
to run counter to the normal rules on causation in tort, where, if the plaintiff would
in any event have acted in the same way and suffered the same damage even if the
wrong had not been committed, the action will fail on causation on the basis that
the wrong did cause the plaintiff's loss. Although there is clearly an element of
policy in this approach in the context of an action for deceit (where, by definition,
the defendant has been fraudulent) the same "test" on causation was applied in that
case to the second defendants who were guilty only of negligence. Nonetheless, in
Bristol and West Building Society v. Mothew [1996] 4 All E.R. 698 at 705–706 the
Court of Appeal confirmed that *Downs v. Chappell* applies to actions in negligence.

  At the end of paragraph add: Of course, it is not necessary that the precise events   2–22
be foreseeable provided that they fell within the scope of the risk created by the
defendant's breach of duty. In *Wisniewski v. Central Manchester Health Authority*
[1998] Lloyd's Rep. Med. 223, CA, the defendants were held liable in respect of
hypoxia suffered by the plaintiff infant during the course of his birth when the
defendants' negligence created a risk of oxygen starvation in the womb, though the
actual mechanism by which the plaintiff sustained the hypoxia was by strangulation
because the umbilical cord was looped round his neck and had a knot in it which

gradually tightened. The evidence was that a "true knot" in the umbilical cord is very rare, and could not have been foreseen, although a cord being looped around the neck is much more common. The Court of Appeal held that as the damage was of a foreseeable kind, it was irrelevant that the precise mechanism by which the hypoxia occurred was unforseeable: ". . . it would in my judgment be regarded as an affront to common sense, and the law would look an ass, if we reached any different conclusion," *per* Brooke L.J. at 245.

4.—Novus Actus Interveniens

2–24   **Novus actus interveniens**
     The suicide of the deceased, where it resulted from the defendants' negligence in failing to act to minimise the known risk of such self-harm, does not constitute a *novus actus*. The harm arises from breach of a duty to prevent just such an act and so does not obliterate the defendants' wrongdoing. It is not a new act. It is the very harm the defendant were under a duty to try to prevent: *Reeves v. Commissioner of Police for the Metropolis* [1999] 3 All E.R. 897, HL: see *post*, Supplement § 2–35.

2–25   Add: In *Humber Oil Terminal Trustee Ltd v. Owners of the Ship "Sivand"; The Sivand* [1998] 2 Lloyd's Rep. 97, CA the Sivand negligently damaged the plaintiff's harbour installations. The plaintiffs engaged contractors to carry out the repairs on standard terms, ICE conditions, which provided for additional payment to the contractor if physical conditions were encountered which could not have been reasonably foreseen by an experienced contractor, adding to the cost of carrying out the repairs. The contractors lost a barge when the sea bed under one of the barge's legs collapsed. The contractors were successful in recovering this additional cost from the plaintiffs under the terms of the contract, and the plaintiffs then sought to recover that cost from the owners of the Sivand. The defendants argued that the unforeseen condition of the sea bed constituted an intervening event that broke the chain of causation between their admitted negligence and the additional loss sustained by the plaintiffs. The Court of Appeal held that the defendants were liable for the additional sum. Although the collapse of the sea bed was unforeseeable it did not have the effect of breaking the chain of causation, unless it affected the plaintiffs's duty to mitigate the loss. Since the plaintiffs had acted entirely reasonably in engaging the contractors on standard terms they had not failed to mitigate their loss:

> "This is a claim for damages for the negligent damaging of the plaintiffs's property. Once the causation of physical damage to the plaintiffs' property is complete, the only remaining question is the assessment of that damage in monetary terms, prima facie the difference between the value of the undamaged property and the value of the damaged property quantified as the cost of repair or reinstatement. Where the plaintiff acts in mitigation of his loss the sole relevant criterion is the reasonableness of the steps which he took in mitigation. Provided he has acted reasonably, he is entitled to recover the cost of that mitigation (even if unsuccessful) as the correct measure of his loss. Questions of foreseeability are not relevant, save so far as they may enter into the question of the reasonableness of what the plaintiff did in mitigation." (*per* Hobhouse L.J.)

2–28   Add to paragraph: Even a criminal act by a third party will not necessarily constitute an intervening act (see *Marshall v. Rubypoint Ltd* (1997) 29 H.L.R. 850, CA – landlord liable to tenant in respect of burglary, resulting in personal injuries and stolen property, since the state of the front door to the premises was found to be a substantial cause of the burglary), though in these circumstances the issue will tend to shade into a question of the nature of the defendant's duty (see § 2–30). In *Empress Car Co. (Abertillery) Ltd v. National Rivers Authority* [1998] 1 All E.R. 481, HL, a case concerning criminal liability for the act of an unknown person, who had opened the tap of a diesel oil tank, for "causing" polluting matter to enter controlled waters contrary to the Water Resources Act 1991, s.85(1), Lord Hoffman commented (at 488–489) that:

"These examples show that one cannot give a commonsense answer to a question of causation for the purpose of attributing responsibility under some rule without knowing the purpose and scope of the rule. Does the rule impose a duty which requires one to guard against, or makes one responsible for, the deliberate acts of third persons? If so, it will be correct to say, when loss is caused by the act of such a third person, that it was caused by the breach of duty. . . . Before answering questions about causation, it is therefore first necessary to identify the scope of the relevant rule. This is not a question of common sense fact; it is a question of law. In *Stansbie v. Troman* [1948] 2 K.B. 48, [see § 7–37], the law imposed a duty which included having to take precautions against burglars. Therefore breach of that duty caused the loss of the property stolen."

At the end of paragraph add: *Emeh v. Kensington and Chelsea Area Health Authority* was applied by the Court of Session (Inner House) in *McFarlane v. Tayside Health Board* (1998) 44 B.M.L.R. 140, where it was held that the decision of a plaintiff not to undergo an abortion, having conceived following an allegedly negligently performed sterilisation operation, does not break the chain of causation between the negligence and the birth of the child. On the other hand, where following a failed sterilisation operation, a plaintiff knew that she was not sterile, and decided nonetheless to proceed to have sexual intercourse without taking contraceptive measures, this breaks the chain of causation between the negligent performance of the surgery and the subsequent birth of a child. Although the defence of *volenti non fit injuria* did not apply in these circumstances because the plaintiff's acceptance of the risk must occur either before or at the same time as the negligent act or omission, the plaintiff's decision constituted a *novus actus interveniens*: see *Sabri-Tabrizi v. Lothian Health Board* 1998 S.C. 373, (1998) 43 B.M.L.R. 190.

2–34

Suicide

2–35

In *Reeves v. Commissioner of Police for the Metropolis, supra,* the deceased hanged himself in a police cell. The defendants were aware that he was a suicide risk. *Inter alia*, the flap on the cell door had been left down allowing the deceased to tie his shirt through the spy hole in the door and so hang himself with his shirt. There was no evidence that the deceased had been diagnosed as suffering from any specific mental disorder. Nonetheless, the House of Lords found that the evidence available to the defendants about his disturbed state and suicidal tendencies imposed on them a duty of care to protect the plaintiff, effectively from himself. His suicide did not break the causal link with their negligence. Suicide was what the defendant should have foreseen, not a new intervening act.

NOTE 40: It may be that *Meah v. McCreamer* would not now be followed in the light of the decision of the Court of Appeal in *Clunis v. Camden & Islington Health Authority* [1998] 2 W.L.R. 902 where the plaintiff, a man with a history of mental disorder and seriously violent behaviour, sued his health authority for negligence in failing to provide after care, following his discharge from hospital where he had been detained under the Mental Health Act 1983. Three months after his discharge the plaintiff killed a stranger in a sudden and completely unprovoked attack. He was charged with murder, but a plea of manslaughter on the ground of diminished responsibility was accepted by the prosecution and he was detained in a special hospital. He alleged that with proper treatment he would not have committed the crime and therefore would not have been convicted and detained following a conviction. The action was struck out as disclosing no reasonable cause of action. Although it was accepted that the plaintiff's mental responsibility was substantially impaired, nonetheless a plea of diminished responsibility did not remove liability for his criminal act. He had to be taken to have known what he was doing and that it was wrong: "public policy would preclude the court from entertaining the plaintiff's claim unless it could be said that he did not know the nature and quality of his act or that what he was doing was wrong" (at 188). In passing, the court commented that *Meah v. McCreamer* could no longer be regarded as authoritative on this issue.

CHAPTER 3.—GENERAL DEFENCES

		PARA.
■1.	Introduction	3–01
■2.	Conduct of the plaintiff	
	(a) Plaintiff's wrongdoing	3–02
	(b) Contributory negligence	3–09
■3.	Assumption of risk and exclusion of liability	
	(a) Consent	3–33
	(b) Exclusion of liability	3–38
	(c) *Volenti non fit injuria*	3–43
■4.	Miscellaneous defences	
	(a) Necessity and private defence	3–57
	(b) Authorisation	3–64
	(c) Mistake	3–69
	(d) Inevitable accident	3–70
	(e) Limitation	3–71
	(f) Personal immunity	3–72

3a   In *Clunis v. Camden and Islington Health Authority* [1998] 2 W.L.R. 902, the Court of Appeal unequivocally confirmed the applicability of a defence of *ex turpi causa* in tort. Their Lordships rejected public conscience as a proper test for the applicability of *ex turpi*. In *Reeves v. Commissioner of Police for the Metropolis* [1998] 2 W.L.R. 401, a differently constituted appeal court had expressly invoked public conscience to find that the suicide of the deceased did not bar his dependants from successful pursuit of a claim under the Fatal Accidents Act. The limits and content of a defence of *ex turpi* remain confused and confusing. On appeal to the House of Lords, the issues of *ex turpi causa* were not pursued. However, their Lordships held that suicide was not necessarily a *novus actus* breaking the chain of causation where self-harm was the very harm which the defendants owed a duty to guard against. In appropriate circumstances, where the suicide victim was of sound mind, his conduct could nonetheless constitute contributory negligence; *Reeves v. Commissioner of Police for the Metropolis* [1999] 3 W.L.R. 363, HL. *Arthur v. Anker* [1996] 2 W.L.R. 602, CA upheld, subject to strict conditions, the legality of wheel-clamping.

2.—CONDUCT OF THE PLAINTIFF

(a) *Plaintiff's Wrongdoing*

3–02   Plaintiff's wrongdoing not a defence per se
Note *Revill v. Newberry* [1996] 2 W.L.R. 239, 249, CA, *per* Evans L.J.

3–03   Ex turpi causa non oritur actio
The Court of Appeal has made it crystal clear that a defence of *ex turpi* (whether rendered in Latin or otherwise) does apply in tort. In *Clunis v. Camden and Islington Health Authority* [1998] 2 W.L.R. 902, the plaintiff had been discharged from a mental hospital and was supposed to be receiving after-care services in the community as provided for by section 117 of the Mental Health Act 1993. In December 1992, his mental condition deteriorated and he stabbed and killed a stranger. The plaintiff was convicted of manslaughter on the grounds of diminished responsibility and ordered to be detained indefinitely in a special hospital. He sued the health authority for negligence and breach of statutory duty. Finding that his claim was defeated because it was based on his own illegal act, the court held:

"We do not consider that the public policy that the court will not lend its aid to a litigant who relies on his own criminal or immoral act is confined to particular causes of action."

Their Lordships rejected argument by counsel for the plaintiff that in the very special circumstances of the plaintiff's crime, and given his reduced responsibility for that crime, the public conscience would not be affronted by affording him a remedy. Save where insanity deprived the plaintiff of any knowledge of his act or its nature, public policy must not allow the law of tort to be an "... instrument to enforce obligations alleged to arise out of the plaintiff's own criminal act". Public conscience as a test for *ex turpi causa* is roundly condemned. *Ex turpi* is presented in *Clunis* as an absolute bar on any claim arising out of criminal conduct. Such an approach applied uniformly would cast doubt on earlier authorities such as in *Revill v. Newberry* (see *post*, Supplement § 3–05).

NOTE 4. Add: See now *Tinsley v. Milligan* [1994] 1 A.C. 340, HL.

Ex turpi and public policy   3–04

In *Clunis v. Camden and Islington Health Authority, supra*, both theories of *ex turpi* described in the main text appear to be discarded. The rule is presented as very simply an absolute bar on any claim in tort arising out of a criminal *or immoral* act. Appeal to public conscience is rejected. However, no guidance given as to how immoral (but non-criminal) conduct sufficient to give rise to a defence of *ex turpi* will be defined. By contrast in *Reeves v. Commissioner of Police for the Metropolis* (*post*, Supplement § 3–05) public conscience seems to be the basis on which it is re-affirmed that suicide, or attempted suicide, is not conduct barring a claim in tort.

For criticism of the "public conscience" test in contract and in relation to propriet-ary interests see *Tinsley v. Milligan* [1994] 1 A.C. 390 at 363–64, *per* Lord Goff.

Application of ex turpi   3–05

In *Reeves v. Commissioner of Police for the Metropolis* [1998] 2 W.L.R. 401, CA, the Court of Appeal held that when the deceased had committed suicide in circumstances where the defendant was in breach of his duty of care to prevent such self-harm, his suicide did not give rise to a defence of *ex turpi* against his estate or his dependants. The judgment in *Kirkham v. Chief Constable of Greater Manchester Police* did not limit the principle that suicide resulting from a third party's negli-gence was no bar to a claim in tort to persons of unsound mind. Public attitudes to suicide today were such that it would be no moral affront to public conscience to allow a claim based on suicide where the defendant was a breach of a duty to protect the deceased from harming himself. Suicide is, of course, no longer a criminal act. (Note that no further appeal on questions of *ex turpi causa* was pursued on appeal to the House of Lords: [1999] 3 W.L.R. 363). Nonetheless some difficulty may be found in reconciling the underlying reasons of the different courts in *Reeves* and *Clunis*.

Firing a shotgun to deter a burglar, careless of whether or not the pellets injured him and so shooting a burglar who was intent on stealing from an allotment shed but was "not displaying any intention of resorting to violence" was found to be disproportionate to the threat to the plaintiff, so ruling out any defence of *ex turpi*; *Revill v. Newberry* [1996] 2 W.L.R. 239, CA.

If the reasoning in *Clunis*, were applied to *Revill v. Newberry*, could the burglar plaintiff now succeed? He suffered injury only because of his criminal act of entering the plaintiff's property.

Plaintiff a trespasser   3–07

The judgment of the Court of Appeal in *Revill v. Newberry* [1996] 2 W.L.R. 239 makes it clear that evidence that the plaintiff was a trespasser, albeit a trespasser intent on burglary will never *of itself* give rise to a complete defence of *ex turpi causa*. Trespassers are owed either a duty of care under the 1984 Act or a "common duty of humanity" (as stated in the main text). However, it may well be that there could be aggravated features of the trespass which would allow *Revill v. Newberry* to be distinguished clearly. Were there an immediate threat of significant violence to the defendant or his household, a complete defence of self-defence might arise. *Quaere* if the burglar was well within the house and wrecking the defendant's property, whether *ex turpi* might be relevant? The plaintiff burglar in *Revill v. Newberry* was found to be two-thirds contributory negligent in respect of his injuries. See also *post*, §§ 29–06, 29–05.

3–08   **Ex turpi, volenti and contributory negligence**
   NOTE 36. Add: *Revill v. Newberry, supra*; *Reeves v. Commissioner of Police for the Metropolis, supra*.

(b) *Contributory Negligence*

3–09   **Fault of the plaintiff**
Fault within the Law Reform (Contributors Negligence) Act 1945 extends to cover intentional acts on the part of the plaintiff in those rare cases where the defendant has a duty to prevent deliberate self-harm by the plaintiff. So in *Reeves v. Commissioner of Police for the Metropolis* [1999] 3 W.L.R. 363 the House of Lords held that the suicide of the deceased could give rise to a defence of contributory negligence in a claim by his defendants under the Fatal Accidents Act. The deceased killed himself while in police custody after having been identified as a "suicide risk". Their Lordships held that suicide did not constitute a *novus actus* where self-harm was the very kind of harm which the defendants owed a duty to prevent. As Lord Jauncey put it "The deceased's suicide was the precise kind of event to which the duty was directed . . ." (at 375 and see *per* Lord Hoffmann at 367–369). However, where the deceased was of sound mind at the time he killed himself he bore at least partial responsibility for his death. His death resulted from the combination of the failure of the police to protect him from himself and his own deliberate decision to end his life and accordingly damages were reduced by 50 per cent (see *per* Lord Hoffmann at 370–372 and *per* Lord Jauncey at 375). It must be noted that in *Reeves* the defendant's duty to protect the deceased could be discharged without invasive measures violating his autonomy. Simply removing the means by which the deceased hanged himself would have sufficed. Given the findings, somewhat reluctantly accepted, at least by Lord Hope at 380, that the deceased was *not* mentally disturbed, no measures such as force-feeding or physically restraining the deceased could have been justified by the defendants or required of them (*per* Lord Hoffmann at 367–365). See also *ante*, Supplement at 2–35.

3–19   **Contributory negligence excluded**
   NOTE 88. Add: *Nationwide Building Society v. Thimbleby & Co.* [1999] Lloyd's Rep. P.N. 359.

3–20   **Contributory negligence and contract**
   NOTE 90. Add: *Barclays Bank plc v. Fairclough Building Ltd (No. 2)* [1995] I.R.L.R. 605; *Raflatac Ltd v. Eade* [1999] 1 Lloyd's Rep. 506.

3–22   **The standard of care**
   In a series of claims relating to negligent over-valuations, defendant valuers have sought to reduce the damages awarded against them by pleading contributory negligence; see *post*, Supplement § 8–114. In *Platform Home Loans Ltd v. Oyston Shipways* [1999] 1 All E.R. 833 the House of Lords held that imprudent lending policies could constitute contributory negligence. The plaintiffs had failed to check information provided by the borrower and incautiously lent 70% of the value of the property without ensuring adequate security for the loan. The complex principles developed by the House of Lords in the *SAAMCO* litigation (*South Australia Asset Management Corporation v. York Montague Ltd* [1997] A.C. 191) and *Nycredit Mortgage Bank*

plc v. Edward Erdman Group (No. 2) [1997] 1 W.L.R. 1627 provide that where a
lender suffers loss as a result of a negligent overvaluation, damages are to be calculated in two stages:

(1) The loss suffered by the plaintiff as a result of having entered into the
transaction must be assessed. The principal component of this loss will be
the difference between the amount of the loan and the sum realised by
enforcing the security. This sum constitutes the plaintiff's *basic loss.*

(2) In order to ascertain the loss falling within the valuer's duty of care, the
amount constituting the difference between the negligent valuation and the
true value of the property at the date of valuation is estimated. The plaintiff's damages are limited to the lesser of the two sums.

In *Platform Home Loans,* it was held that deductions for contributory negligence
should in general be made to the plaintiff's basic loss and, not until that figure has
been arrived at, should any further deduction be made to limit the damages to the
extent of the over-valuation. Lord Millett (at 853) suggested that if the plaintiff's
contributory negligence contributed directly to the over-valuation then in such a case
the deduction for contributory negligence might be applied to the amount of the
over-valuation; see *post,* Supplement § 7–198, § 8–113.

Note *Barrett v. Ministry of Defence* [1995] 1 W.L.R. 1217, CA and *King v. Smith*
[1995] I.C.R. 339.

NOTE 4. Add: And see *Reeves v. Commissioner for Police for the Metropolis,*
supra.

Contributory negligence of children   3–24
NOTE 17 Add: *Mullin v. Richards* [1998] 1 W.L.R. 1304.

3.—ASSUMPTION OF RISK AND EXCLUSION OF LIABILITY

(a) *Consent*

Consent and liability   3–33
On the difficulties, or perhaps irrelevance of attempting to draw any distinction
between consent and *volenti,* see *Arthur v. Anker* [1996] 2 W.L.R. 602, 607, CA,
per Sir Thomas Bingham M.R.

Consent and the intentional torts   3–34
In *Arthur v. Anker, supra,* the Court of Appeal held that the trespass to goods
inherent in wheelclamping could, in appropriate conditions, be justified by a defence
of consent/*volenti.* Where a motorist parked his vehicle on clearly marked private
land in defiance of a notice indicating that unauthorised vehicles would be clamped,
he was found voluntarily to have accepted both the risk that his vehicle would be
clamped and the risk that it would not be released unless he paid a reasonable
charge. Any exorbitant charge or delay in releasing the vehicle after the motorist
had indicated a willingness to pay would exceed the boundaries of any implied
consent and render further detention of the vehicle tortious.

Consent and crime   3–36
NOTE 65. Add: *R. v. Brown* was distinguished in *R. v. Wilson (Alan Thomas), The*
Times, March 5, 1996. See also Law Commission Consultation Paper No. 139 *Con-*
sent in the Criminal Law.

Freely and voluntarily   3–47
A prisoner who committed suicide in circumstances where the defendant was in
breach of his duty to guard against just that act of self-destruction could not be said

to be *volenti* to the defendant's lack of care. Even though the deceased was of sound mind, he in no sense assumed the risk of the defendant's lack of care or his failure to fulfil the responsibilities owed to the plaintiff in his distressed and suicidal state: *Reeves v. Commissioner of Police for the Metropolis* [1998] 2 W.L.R. 401, CA; [1999] 3 W.L.R. 363, HL.

3–48   Knowledge of danger
   Note *Ratcliff v. McConnell* [1999] 1 W.L.R. 670, CA (no liability to adult trespasser who dived into the shallow end of a swimming pool at night); *cf. Fraser v. Winchester Health Authority, The Times,* July 12, 1999, CA.

4.—MISCELLANEOUS DEFENCES

(a) *Necessity and Private Defence*

3–57   Necessity
   Just as providing treatment or physical care to a mentally incapacitated person may be justified on the basis of necessity, rendering lawful conduct which might otherwise constitute trespass to the person, so may detaining such a person for his own safety and welfare: *R. v. Bournewood Community and Mental Health Services Trust, ex p. L* [1998] 3 W.L.R., HL; See *post,* Supplement § 12–66.

3–61   Acting in the plaintiff's interest
   Note 83a. Add: *Reeves v. Commissioner of Police for the Metropolis* [1999] 3 W.L.R. 363, HL.

3–62   Protecting the foetus
   The Court of Appeal in *In re MB (Caesarian Section)* [1997] 8 Med. L.R. 217, and again in *St George's Healthcare NHS Trust v. S* [1998] 3 All E.R. 673, held that there was no jurisdiction to compel a competent woman to undergo medical treatment without her consent to protect the interests of the foetus. Until birth the foetus had no interests which could be asserted against its mother. The dicta of Lord Donaldson in *Re T* relating to the "necessity" of saving a viable foetus were rejected by the Court of Appeal, and in so far as the judgment derived from those dicta, the judgment in *Re S* is overruled: see *post,* Supplement § 8–27.

CHAPTER 4.—CAPACITY AND PARTIES

		PARA.
■1.	Introduction	4–01
■2.	The Crown	4–02
	(a) Crown Proceedings Act 1947	4–03
	(b) Other Acts	4–17
3.	The Post Office	4–18
■4.	Foreign states and ambassadors	4–21
■5.	Visiting forces	4–27
■6.	Bankrupts	4–28
□7.	Minors	4–32
■8.	Persons of unsound mind	4–39
9.	Husband and wife	4–40
■10.	Assignees	4–42
■11.	Corporations	4–43
■12.	Unincorporated associations and trade unions	4–50
■13.	Partners	4–53
■14.	Joint and several torts	4–54
15.	Joint plaintiffs	4–68

4–01 Two important decisions of the Court of Appeal concerning the question of from whom contribution is recoverable under the Civil Liability (Contribution) Act 1978 are noted in this Supplement. The broad formulation of the 1978 Act is stressed in *Friends' Provident Life Office v. Hillier Parker* [1997] Q.B. 85: holding that claims for restitution and for damages could be claims for compensation in respect of the same damage under section 1(1) and section 6(1). Conversely, *Birse Construction v. Haiste Ltd* [1996] 1 W.L.R. 675 underlines the fact that for there to be an entitlement to claim contribution the two parties had to be liable in respect of the same damage suffered by a third party.

The House of Lords in *Jameson v. Central Electricity Generating Board* [1999] 2 W.L.R. 141 held that a "full and final" settlement by a plaintiff with a tortfeasor in a personal injuries action prevented a dependency claim after his death against a concurrent tortfeasor. In relation to joint and several torts, this case includes a useful review of the present law on the defence of accord and satisfaction and the separate defence of satisfaction.

2.—THE CROWN

(a) *Crown Proceedings Act 1947*

Ships and harbours   **4–09**
The Merchant Shipping Acts have been consolidated in the Merchant Shipping Act 1995. On the liability of shipowners and the application to the Crown and its ships now see section 192 of the Merchant Shipping Act 1995; salvage claims are dealt with in section 230 (subject to section 29 of the Crown Proceedings Act 1947) and see Schedule 11 to Part I of Article 25.

Armed forces   **4–10**
In *Mulcahy v. Ministry of Defence* [1996] 2 W.L.R. 474, CA a soldier was injured by a fellow soldier when engaging the enemy in battle conditions. The plaintiff alleged that the Ministry of Defence was vicariously liable for negligence. The Secretary of State had not acted to reintroduce the immunity contained in section 10 of the Crown Proceedings Act 1947, hence the court had to consider whether there was

a duty of care owed. The Court of Appeal held no duty of care was owed as between active soldiers; nor indeed was there an obligation on the Ministry to maintain a safe system of work in battle situations.

NOTE: *R. v. Ministry of Defence, ex p. Walker* [1999] P.I.Q.R. Q168—the Criminal Injuries (Overseas) Scheme, which provides compensation for members of the armed forces who are the victims of crimes of violence abroad, does not apply where the act of violence which causes the injury is committed by an enemy where a state of war exists. The applicant was injured by a tank shell fired by a Serbian tank in Bosnia, at a time when he was on UN peacekeeping duties, and was held not to be entitled to compensation under the scheme.

In *Quinn v. Ministry of Defence* [1998] P.I.Q.R. P387, CA, the plaintiff, during his service in the Royal Navy, had stripped asbestos insulation from boilers and pipes, which had caused or exacerbated both pleural thickening and mesothelioma. He argued that the removal of the asbestos had been done under an unsafe system of work, and that the Crown was in breach of a duty in tort to provide a safe system of work. Alternatively, he alleged that he had been employed under a contract of service and that the Crown, as employer, was in breach of its obligation to provide a safe system of work. The Court of Appeal, applying *Pearce v. Secretary of State for Defence*, held that the Crown had immunity by virtue of section 10(2) of the Crown Proceedings Act 1947. The plaintiff's injuries were a consequence of "the nature or condition" of the ships on which he served, not of an unsafe system of work. Moreover, it was impossible to accept that Parliament intended that the Crown should be immune from claims in respect of death or personal injury suffered by a member of the armed forces in consequence of the nature or condition of the land, premises, ship, aircraft or vehicles, but should not be immune if the cause of the injury was an act or omission on the part of Crown servants which caused the land or equipment to be dangerous or resulted in the injured member of the armed forces not being protected from the danger. In addition, the court concluded, both on existing authority and as a matter of public policy, that no contract of employment exists between members of the armed forces and the Crown (though the position may be different in the case of a civil servant: see *R. v. Lord Chancellor's Department, ex p. Nangle* [1991] I.C.R. 743).

In *Derry v. Ministry of Defence* [1999] P.I.Q.R. P204, CA, the plaintiff, a soldier, alleged that a military doctor had been negligent in failing to diagnose cancer. He brought an action against the Ministry of Defence for personal injury and loss of life expectancy, arguing that the Ministry could not rely on the immunity contained in the Crown Proceedings Act 1947, s.10 where there was a negligent failure to diagnose a pre-existing medical condition. The Court of Appeal held that the immunity in section 10 applied. The "thing suffered" for the purpose of section 10(1) was the misdiagnosis, which occurred on each occasion that he was examined at the military hospital, where he was on Crown land, and therefore fell within section 10(1). Chadwick L.J. commented:

"I reach that conclusion with regret. It is easy to see why, in 1947, s.10(1) should have been thought necessary in order to protect the Crown from claims to common law damages arising out of incidents during military training under simulated warlike conditions – including mistakes made by doctors operating in field hospitals under such conditions. It is more difficult to see why it was thought necessary to extend that protection to doctors (and others) exercising professional skill under conditions which were indistinguishable from those applicable to their civilian counterparts. The anomaly was recognised by the repeal of s.10 of the 1947 Act in 1987 ... But, sadly for Sergeant Derry, the change in the law came too late. We must apply the law as it was at the relevant time."

4–16   Act of State

On the relationship of the plea of Act of State and justiciability to state immunity see *Kuwait v. Iraqi Airways Co.* [1995] 1 W.L.R. 1147, HL.

4.—FOREIGN STATES AND AMBASSADORS

State Immunity Act 1978   4–21
Note *Al-Adsani v. Kuwait, The Times*, March 29, 1996, CA. The government of
Kuwait entitled to state immunity under section 1 of the 1978 Act re alleged acts of
torture that had taken place in Kuwait. The 1978 Act was a comprehensive code and
not subject to overriding considerations of international agreements against torture.
    See now *R. v. Bow Street Metropolitan Stipendiary Magistrate, ex p. Pinochet
Ugarte (No. 3)* [1999] 2 W.L.R. 827, HL, on the immunity of an ex-Head of State
for acts of torture.

Immunity in tort   4–23
NOTE 88. Add: Proceedings in relation to armed forces of a state while present in
the UK are excluded from the ambit of the 1978 Act by section 16(2). For immunity
under the common law, see *Littrell v. Government of the United States of America
(No. 2)* [1995] 1 W.L.R. 82, CA.
    In *Holland v. Lampen-Wolfe* [1999] 1 W.L.R. 188, CA, the plaintiff was a U.S.
citizen who undertook some teaching at a military base in the United Kingdom
operated by the U.S. government. She brought a defamation action against an educational services officer at the base, also a U.S. citizen, who was employed by the
U.S. Department of Defense. The Court of Appeal held that state immunity did not
arise under the State Immunity Act 1978, because s.16(2) excluded from the Act
things done by or in relation to the armed forces of a foreign state while present in
the United Kingdom, and although the plaintiff was not a member of the armed
forces the defendant's conduct was clearly something done by the armed forces.
Immunity at common law applied, however, since the provision of education to
armed forces posted away from their own country was a normal and necessary part
of the overall activity of maintaining those forces in a foreign country (applying
Littrell v. United States (No. 2)).   .
    NOTE 92. Add: The Court of Appeal applied *I Congreso del Partido* [1993] 1
A.C. in *Littrell v. Government of the United States of America (No. 2)* [1995] 1
W.L.R. 82: in determining whether the defendant's conduct giving rise to the plaintiff's claim should be characterised as involving acts *jure imperii* (in respect of which
a foreign sovereign was entitled to immunity from suit), or acts *jure gestionis* (in
respect of which he was not), no one factor would be determinative in itself. It was
necessary to look at the nature of the activity, the identity of those who deal with it
and the place where it took place.

Immunities and privileges of foreign states   4–24
Note the judgment in *Kuwait v. Iraqi Airways Co.* [1995] 1 W.L.R. 1147, HL.
The main issue for the House of Lords was whether the seizure and subsequent use
of Kuwaiti aircraft by Iraqi Airways Company (a separate entity distinct from the
organs of government of the State of Iraq) was covered by immunity from jurisdiction by section 14(2) of the 1978 Act. To show this, the IAC had to prove that the
proceedings against it related to something done by it in the exercise of sovereign
authority and that the circumstances were such that a state would have been immune.
The court held that the seizure was covered by immunity under section 14(2) of the
1978 Act, as acts done by a separate entity but in the exercise of sovereign authority.
However, the subsequent retention and use was commercial (and therefore not subject to immunity), though done on the direction of Iraq, acting *in jure imperii* (Lord
Mustill and Lord Slynn dissented on this point). The reason for this distinction was
the coming into effect of Iraqi expropriatory legislation so that the use of the aircraft
"were acts done by it in consequence of the vesting or purported vesting of the
aircraft by legislative decree" (at 1163). Fox (1996) 112 L.Q.R. 186 is critical of
the decision, arguing that it breaks down the commercial/immune distinction, simply
because the acts are done on authorisation of legislation.
    Note that service of proceedings on a State under the State Immunity Act 1978

section 12(1) can only be served at the Ministry of Foreign Affairs in the country concerned.

Bank of Credit and Commerce International (Overseas) Ltd (In Liquidation) v. Price Waterhouse (No. 1) [1997] 4 All E.R. 108, Laddie J., ChD. Liquidators started actions against the defendants, former auditors of BCCI. Price Waterhouse sought to bring into the proceedings Abu Dhabi, a constituent territory of the United Arab Emirates (a recognised state). They issued a third party notice against Z, the ruler of Abu Dhabi and the president of the United Arab Emirates. The defendants claimed that the proceedings were against Z in his public capacity as ruler of Abu Dhabi and that, as the territory was not immune from suit, neither should Z be. Held, the proceedings against Z should be struck out. Z, as sovereign/head of a recognised state was immune from suit, when acting in a public capacity, under the State Immunity Act 1978. In all other circumstances, the Diplomatic Privileges Act 1964 provided him with immunity.

4–25   Submission to the jurisdiction

NOTE 6. Add: *Arab Republic of Egypt v. Gamal-Eldin* [1996] I.C.R. 13, EAT, Mummery J.; *Ahmed v. Saudi Arabia* [1996] I.C.R. 25, CA.

NOTE 8. Add: *Kuwait v. Iraqi Airways* now decided by the House of Lords, see [1995] 1 W.L.R. 1147, HL and see note by Fox (1996) 112 L.Q.R. 186. On the issue of submission to jurisdiction, as no argument was addressed on this point, the House of Lords was not prepared to depart from the decision of the Court of Appeal that there had been no submission to the jurisdiction.

NOTE 10. Add: Re who can waive immunity under section 2(7) of the State Immunity Act 1978 see *Malaysian Industrial Development Authority v. Jeyasingham* [1998] I.C.R. 307, EAT, Judge Hull Q.C.

5.—VISITING FORCES

4–27   Visiting forces

Visiting Forces (Designation) Order 1997, S.I. 1997, No. 1779. Designates as countries to which the provisions of the 1952 Act apply: Albania, Bulgaria, Czech Republic, Estonia, Hungary, Latvia, Lithuania, Poland, Romania, Slovak Republic and Sweden. In force July 22, 1997.

Visiting Forces (Designation) Order 1998, S.I. 1998, No. 1268. Designates as countries to which the provisions of the 1952 Act apply: Armenia, Austria, Azerbaijan, Belarus, Finland, Georgia, Kazakhstan, Kyrgyzstan, the Former Yugoslav Republic of Macedonia, Moldova, Russia, Switzerland, Turkmenistan, Ukraine and Uzbekistan.

See *Holland v. Lampen-Wolfe* [1999] 1 W.L.R. 188, CA (see *supra*, Supplement § 4–23, n. 88).

6.—BANKRUPTS

4–31   Liability insurance

NOTE 57. Add: Third Parties (Rights against Insurers) Act 1930, *Woolwich BS v. Taylor* now reported [1995] 1 B.C.L.C. 132, Lindsay J. and see *Nigel Upchurch Associates v. Aldridge Estates Investment Co. Ltd* [1993] 1 Lloyd's Rep. 535, Barbara Dohmann, Q.C., sitting as an Official Referee. Note that the actual decision in *Bradley v. Eagle Star Insurance Co. Ltd* [1989] 2 W.L.R. 568 would now be subject to the court's power to set aside the winding up at any time in a case of personal injuries, section 141(3) of the Companies Act 1989.

A claim against insurers under the Third Parties (Rights against Insurers) Act 1930 is not a claim for personal injuries and therefore the plaintiff cannot seek an order for pre-action discovery under the Supreme Court Act 1981, s. 33(2) and RSC, Ord. 24, r.7A: *Burns v. Shuttlehurst* [1999] P.I.Q.R. P229, CA.

Add: In *Mullin v. Richards* [1998] 1 W.L.R. 1304 two 15-year-old schoolgirls **4–32** were playing at fencing with plastic rules when one of the rulers broke and a piece of plastic entered the plaintiff's eye. The trial judge took the view that they were equally to blame and held the defendant liable, with 50% contributory negligence. The Court of Appeal held that given the history of events at the school, the risk of injury was not reasonably foreseeable by a 15-year-old schoolgirl (though it might conceivably be foreseeable as a remote risk) and accordingly there was no negligence. The test, said Hutchison L.J., was not whether the actions of the defendant were such as an ordinarily prudent and reasonable adult in the defendant's situation would have realised created a risk of injury, but whether an ordinarily prudent and reasonable 15-year-old schoolgirl in the defendant's situation would have realised the risk. Allowance has to be made for the age of the child (applying the decision of the High Court of Australia in *McHale v. Watson* (1966) 115 C.L.R. 199).

7.—Minors

Pre-natal injuries **4–38**
Note that section 44 of the Human Fertilisation and Embryology Act 1990 inserted section 1A into the Congenital Disabilities (Civil Liability) Act 1976 to extend section 1 of the 1976 Act to cover infertility treatments. The new subsection mirrors section 1(4) of the 1976 Act.

8.—Persons of Unsound Mind

Add: In *Mansfield v. Weetabix Ltd* [1997] P.I.Q.R. P526 the Court of Appeal held **4–39** that a driver who becomes unable to control a vehicle will not be liable for damage caused by his loss of control if he is unaware of the disabling condition from which he is suffering, whether the disabling event is sudden or gradual. On this point, *Roberts v. Ramsbottom* had been wrongly decided, though the decision in *Roberts* could be supported on the alternative ground that the defendant continued to drive when he was unfit to do so, and when he should have been aware of his unfitness. The defendant will be liable if he knew that he was susceptible to periods of unfitness to drive (*Hill v. Baxter* [1958] 1 Q.B. 277) or if he ought to have known that he was subject to a condition rendering him unfit to drive (*Waugh v. James K. Allan Ltd* [1964] 2 Lloyd's Rep. 1).
NOTE 10. At the end of the note add: cf. *James v. London Borough of Havering* (1992) 15 B.M.L.R. 1, CA.

10.—Assignees

Assignees **4–42**
Although it is still true that an assignment of the "bare right to litigate" in tort (or, indeed, in contract) is not permitted, on the basis that the transaction smacks of maintenance or champerty (see *Prosser v. Edmonds* (1835) 1 Y. & C. Ex. 481), where the assignee has an appropriate interest in the litigation the same public policy considerations may not apply. Generally, there appears to have been a change in judicial policy concerning maintenance and champerty: in considering the principle of policy that renders maintenance and champerty illegal, *Camdex International Ltd v. Bank of Zambia* [1998] Q.B. 22, CA, a case concerning the assignment of a debt, Hobhouse L.J. noted that what was objectionable was trafficking in litigation. Maintenance and champerty involved the support of litigation by a party who could show no legitimate interest in the action. However, he noted that the modern tendency was to recognise less specific interests as justifying the support of the litigation of another.
Indeed, in *Trendtex Trading Corp. v. Credit Suisse*, Lord Roskill stated ([1982]

A.C. 679 at 703) that though it was still a fundamental principle of our law that you cannot assign a "bare right to litigate", "an assignee who can show that he has a genuine commercial interest in the enforcement of the claim of another and to that extent takes an assignment of that claim to himself is entitled to enforce that assignment unless by the terms of that assignment he falls foul of our law of champerty . . .". Thus he stated that the court should look at the "totality of the transaction": if the assignment is of a property right or interest and the cause of action is ancillary to that right or interest or if the assignee has a genuine commercial interest in taking and enforcing it for his own benefit, there seems to be no policy reason to prevent such an assignment. Although *Trendtex* was an assignment of an action arising out of contract, Professor Rogers (in *Winfield and Jolowicz on Tort*, 14th ed., 1994) argues that unless an arbitrary line is to be drawn between tort and contract, the notion of "genuine commercial interest" could be carried over into assignments of tort actions so that, for example an assignment to a bank of the assignor's claim for damages for negligent misstatement inducing a contract which the bank has financed would be valid. On this basis, presumably, the assignment of causes of action essentially personal in nature such as claims for defamation, false imprisonment or personal injuries would still not be permitted. Indeed, Lord Denning, in the *Trendtex* case at Court of Appeal level [1980] Q.B. 629, although favouring the abandonment of the rule against "bare right to litigate" would still have supported a rule against the assignment of "personal tort" claims. Gault J. reviewed this area in *First City Corporation Ltd v. Downsview Nominees Ltd* [1989] 3 N.Z.L.R. 710 (reversed on other grounds by the N.Z. CA, [1990] 2 N.Z.L.R. 265).

Add to paragraph: An assignment by a limited company to a majority shareholder of the right to pursue an action in the name of the company is not invalid as contrary to public policy on the basis that it was made with the intention of enabling the assignee to obtain legal aid or avoid an order for security for costs in the litigation, at least where the assignor has a continued interest in the fruits of the litigation; nor does it make any difference that the assignee has the right to pursue the action in the name of the assignor: see *Norglen Ltd v. Reeds Rains Prudential Ltd*; *Circuit Systems Ltd (in liq.) v. Zuken-Redac (UK) Ltd* [1997] 3 W.L.R. 1177.

In *Taylor v. Serviceteam Ltd* [1998] P.I.Q.R. P201 it was held that on the transfer of an employee's contract of employment as part of the transfer of an undertaking within the meaning of the Acquired Rights Directive 77/187 and the Transfer of Undertakings (Protection of Employment) Regulations 1981, liability to pay the employee compensation for personal injuries sustained as a result of the transferor's negligence or breach of statutory duty passes to the new employer, notwithstanding the fact that the new employer was not the plaintiff's employer at the time of the accident.

NOTE 33. Add: *Stein v. Blake* [1995] 2 W.L.R. 710, HL A and B had mutual claims against each other. When A became bankrupt the question arose whether his claim against B continued to exist, so that A's trustee could assign it to a third party or whether the effect of section 323 of the Insolvency Act 1986 extinguished the claims of A and B and substituted a claim for the net balance owing after setting off one against the other. Held, the bankruptcy extinguished the claims as separate choses in action (section 323 of the Insolvency Act 1986) and replaced them by a claim for the net balance owing after setting one off against the other. If the set-off was in the bankrupt's favour, this could be assigned to the bankrupt before the net balance had been ascertained by the taking of an account between himself and the other party.

11.—CORPORATIONS

4–49 Liability of directors of limited company

On the question of personal liability see *Williams v. Natural Life Health Foods Ltd* [1998] 1 W.L.R. 830, HL. The director of a company was not held personally liable for negligent misstatements. The court noted that in order to fix a director with personal liability it had to be shown that he assumed personal responsibility for the negligent misstatements made on behalf of the company. The test is objective. The fact that the director owned and controlled the company and that the plaintiffs were given a brochure linking the performance of the company with that of the director were not sufficient to constitute an assumption of personal responsibility by the director to the plaintiffs for misleading advice given by the company. There had been no personal dealings between the plaintiffs and the director which might have indicated an assumption of personal liability.

In *Richardson v. Pitt-Stanley* [1995] 2 W.L.R. 26 the Court of Appeal held that a director was not liable for breach of statutory duty in failing to see that the company complied with its obligation under the Employers' Liability (Compulsory Insurance) Act 1969, s.1, to arrange insurance against the company's potential liability as an employer to its employees in respect of personal injury or death; *cf. Quinn v. McGinty* 1998 Rep. L.R. 107. For discussion see *post*, Supplement, § 11–20.

12.—UNINCORPORATED ASSOCIATIONS AND TRADE UNIONS

Unincorporated associations   4–50
Grice v. Stourport Tennis, Hockey and Squash Club [1997] 9 C.L. 592, CA.

Personal injuries claim brought against club and its officers by one of its members, alleging negligence and breach of statutory duty. Plaintiff allowed to amend statement of claim outside the limitation period as proceedings had been issued against the club, an unincorporated association, in its own name, rather than against named representative members of the club. *Murray v. Hibernian Dance Club* [1997] P.I.Q.R. 46, CA, referred to (consideration of the principle which allows amendment of the name of a party). In deciding on potential liability of the club officers, membership of the club, though not itself giving rise to a duty of care, does not provide immunity where a duty otherwise arises. In deciding whether a duty of care arose, the court may look to the rules of the club: *Prole v. Allen* [1950] 209 L.T. 183; *Robertson v. Ridley* [1989] 1 W.L.R. 872, considered. Note: in *Melhuish v. Clifford*, unreported, August 18, 1998, (QBD) Hooper J. asserted that *Robertson v. Ridley* would probably be decided differently now, on the basis of the Court of Appeal decision in *Grice v. Stowport Tennis, Hockey and Squash Club*.

Add: A trade union has a duty of care in the tort of negligence to use reasonable   4–52
skill and care in advising or acting for a member in an employment dispute, though once the union engages solicitors to act on behalf of the member that duty ceases and any failings in the advice rendered is the responsibility of the solicitors: see *Friend v. Institution of Professional Managers & Specialists* [1999] I.R.L.R. 173.

13.—PARTNERS

Partners   4–53
In *Nationwide Building Society v. Lewis* [1998] Ch. 482 W was employed as a "salaried partner" in a firm of solicitors, of which L was the sole equity partner. W's name appeared on the firm's headed paper. The firm acted for the plaintiff building society in a mortgage transaction, which was dealt with entirely by L. A report on title was sent to the plaintiff together with a letter on the firm's notepaper which included W's name. The plaintiff suffered a loss due to the firm's negligence and claimed that W was liable on the basis that he was held out as a partner of the firm. The Court of Appeal held that a plaintiff who claimed that he had acted in reliance on a person holding himself out as a partner in a firm had to prove actual reliance in fact; there was no presumption of reliance in favour of the plaintiff. Although the plaintiff had relied on the report of title, there was no evidence that the plaintiff had even noticed W's name on the notepaper and no evidence that it

had actually relied on a representation that W was a partner giving his authority to the report.

NOTE 86. It is possible for a partner to commit a fraud in the ordinary course of business. This will be treated as a question of fact: *Dubai Aluminium Co. Ltd v. Salaam, The Times,* September 4, 1998, QBD. An incoming partner cannot be liable as a principal for the earlier negligent acts of a co-partner: *H.F. Pension Scheme Trustee Ltd v. Ellison* (1999) 149 N.L.J. Digest 249.

14.—JOINT AND SEVERAL TORTS

4–55   The freedom for plaintiffs to bring successive actions in respect of the same damage against different defendants appears now to be in the process of being curtailed by the courts. Multiplicity of actions is being discouraged and plaintiffs would be well-advised to sue all potential defendants in a single action. Thus, in *Morris v. Wentworth-Stanley* [1999] 2 W.L.R. 470, CA, M entered into a contract with a farming partnership consisting of O, his brother C, and C's wife S. M sued the partnership for £60,000 for breach of the contract. C died and M then agreed to remove the names of both C and S from the action. At trial a consent order was made that O should pay M £60,000, but subsequently, because of O's financial problems, the judgment debt was compromised by O's payment of £45,000 in full and final settlement. M then sued S and C's executors for the balance, relying on section 3 of the Civil Liability (Contribution) Act 1978 that judgment against a person jointly liable for any debt or damage is not a bar to an action against any other person jointly liable with him for the same debt or damage. S claimed that discharge of one joint debtor discharged all other joint debtors under the principle of accord and satisfaction. The action was struck out as an abuse of process; M appealed. The Court of Appeal dismissed the appeal. The purpose of section of 3 of the 1978 Act, said the court, was to extend the provisions of section 6(1)(a) of the Law Reform (Married Women and Tortfeasors) Act 1935 in respect of joint tortfeasors by removing the common law defence of "release by judgment" in its entirety, so that judgment against one of two or more persons jointly liable for the same debt or damage should not in itself be a bar to an action against those others who were liable but not party to the judgment. It was not intended to remove the rule that release of one person jointly liable for the debt operated to release all others jointly liable by accord and satisfaction (in the absence of a reservation by the plaintiff of a right to maintain the claim against the other joint debtors). Thus, the compromise of the action through the consent order and the plaintiff's acceptance of the payment in "full and final settlement" released S from liability. The action could also be considered to be an abuse of process. Section 3 did not detract from the general proposition that it was plainly desirable that all persons who are to be sued should, as a general rule, be sued at the same time and in the same proceedings where such a course is reasonably practicable. If this was not done, then the rule in *Henderson v. Henderson* (1843) 3 Hare 100 (see § 30–25) could apply to render a second action an abuse of process.

Morris v. Wentworth-Stanley concerned defendants who were jointly liable. A similar principle has been established by the House of Lords in relation to concurrent tortfeasors. In *Jameson v. Central Electricity Generating Board* [1999] 2 W.L.R. 141, J brought a claim against his former employer (BE) for personal injuries (malignant mesothelioma) due to exposure to asbestos. He reached a settlement with BE "in full and final settlement and satisfaction" of his claim. J died before the money was paid over, and therefore it fell into his estate and was inherited by his widow. After his death, his executors brought an action under the Fatal Accidents Act 1976 on behalf of his widow for her loss of dependency against the CEGB, at whose premises J had carried out work for BE. The basis of the claim for damages was the same exposure of J to asbestos, with similar allegations of negligence and breach of statutory duty. CEGB then joined BE as third party. The Court of Appeal

held that the plaintiffs were entitled to maintain the action under the Fatal Accidents
Act 1976, and that CEGB were entitled to contribution from BE under the Civil
Liability (Contribution) Act 1978 on the basis that their respective liabilities were
"in respect of the same damage", namely the alleged wrong that caused injury and
death to J (see §§ 4–58 and 4–59 for the meaning of "the same damage"). On
appeal to the House of Lords, the question of whether CEGB were entitled to claim
contribution against BE was not pursued, but was assumed to be correct by Lord
Hope (at 201). The issue was whether the plaintiffs were entitled to maintain the
Fatal Accidents Act claim against CEGB, the answer to which depended upon
whether the liability of concurrent tortfeasors for the same harm is discharged by a
settlement which has been entered into with one of them. (It was not a case of
accord and satisfaction which would extinguish the liability of joint tortfeasors. The
normal rule has been that a release from liability granted to a joint tortfeasor will
release the others, whereas a release of one of several concurrent tortfeasors will
not – CEGB and BE were concurrent, rather than joint, tortfeasors.) In order for the
plaintiffs to succeed under the Fatal Accidents Act the deceased must have been
entitled to maintain an action in respect of the wrong causing the death immediately
before his death (Fatal Accidents Act 1976, s.3; in *Pickett v. British Rail Engineering
Ltd* [1980] A.C. 136 the House of Lords assumed that where the deceased had sued
the defendant to a judgment or settled his claim while still alive, the dependants
could not sue under the 1976 Act). The difficulty which the majority of the House
of Lords (Lord Lloyd dissenting) sought to address was that J's widow had inherited
the £80,000 paid by BE to J's estate under the settlement. She had also been awarded
£142,000 against CEGB as the agreed sum for the loss of her dependency under the
Fatal Accidents Act, but section 4 of that Act provides that any benefits accruing to
the dependant from the estate of the deceased, including sums received as compensation for the injuries, are to be disregarded. Thus, if the Court of Appeal's decision
stood, she would receive "double" compensation, whereas BE would be liable to a
claim for contribution under the Civil Liability (Contribution) Act 1978 from CEGB,
notwithstanding the settlement reached with J before his death. On the other hand,
the plaintiff contended that the settlement that J reached with BE was less than the
full value of the claim, and the plaintiff should be able to make up the shortfall by
claiming against the other joint tortfeasor.

Lord Hope said that the basic rule is that damages are compensatory, and that a
plaintiff cannot recover more than the amount of his loss:

> "The liability which is in issue in this case is that of concurrent tortfeasors,
> because the acts of negligence and breach of statutory duty which are alleged
> against Babcock and the defendant respectively are not the same. So the plaint-
> iff has a separate cause of action against each of them for the same loss. But
> the existence of damage is an essential part of the cause of action in any claim
> for damages. It would seem to follow, as a matter of principle, that once the
> plaintiff's claim has been satisfied by any one of several tortfeasors, his cause
> of action for damages is extinguished against all of them." (*per* Lord Hope at
> 202)

The question then was whether the agreement between the plaintiff and one concurrent tortfeasor had "satisfied" his claim for damages, because if it had not then it
would not extinguish the plaintiff's claim against the other concurrent tortfeasor.
This was to be tested by looking at the terms of the agreement and comparing it
with what had been claimed. The intention of the parties is to be found in the
wording of the settlement. If it is not expressed to be in full and final satisfaction,
or if the plaintiff specifically reserves the right to maintain a claim against other
concurrent tortfeasors, it should not have the effect of extinguishing those claims.
The question, said Lord Hope, is not whether the plaintiff has received the full value
of his claim but whether the sum which he has received in settlement of it was
intended to be in full satisfaction of the tort. This takes effect from the date of the

settlement, not from the date when payment is made under the settlement (subject to the proviso that if payment is not made the agreement becomes void *ab initio*).

The consequence of the majority ruling of the House of Lords in *Jameson* is that plaintiffs should be advised when accepting a settlement expressly to reserve their rights to maintain an action against any other concurrent tortfeasors. If this had been done in *Jameson* then the element of "double recovery" that their Lordships were anxious to avoid would still have occurred. This, as Lord Lloyd pointed out in his strong dissenting speech, is a consequence of the effect of section 4 of the Fatal Accidents Act 1976, which provides that in claim under the Act for loss of dependency any benefit accruing to the dependants from the deceased's estate is to be ignored. Thus, this is an explicit result of a deliberate policy choice taken by Parliament. Similarly, the fact that BE might have been subject to a claim for contribution by CEGB, notwithstanding that BE had already made a "full and final settlement" with J is also the result of the wording of the Civil Liability (Contribution) Act 1978 as interpreted by the courts, a view upheld by the Court of Appeal in *Jameson* and not appealed to their Lordships' House (see paragraph 4–61). As Lord Lloyd commented in his dissenting speech:

> "On the face of it, it would seem strange and unjust that a plaintiff who settles a claim against A in respect of one cause of action should be unable to pursue a claim in respect of a separate cause of action against B. Of course if the plaintiff recovers the whole of his loss from A, then he will have nothing left to recover against B. The payment received from A will have 'satisfied' his loss, though I would for my part prefer not to use the term 'satisfy' in this context, in order to avoid confusion with the quite different concept of accord and satisfaction. In the present case Mr Jameson agreed to accept £80,000 plus costs in settlement of his claim against Babcock. If during his lifetime he had started a fresh action against Babcock he would have been met with the defence of accord and satisfaction, the satisfaction being the £80,000 which he agreed to accept in settlement of his claim against Babcock. But there would have been nothing whatever to stop him claiming against the CEGB during his lifetime, unless, of course, £80,000 had been the full amount of his loss. But it was not. On the agreed facts it was less than two-thirds of his loss." (at 197)

4–58   NOTE 24. Note that in *Henderson v. Merrett Syndicates Ltd* [1995] 2 A.C. 145 the House of Lords placed liability for negligent statements firmly within the concept of a voluntary undertaking of responsibility by the defendant; see also *White v. Jones* [1995] 2 A.C. 207 and *Spring v. Guardian Assurance plc* [1995] 2 A.C. 296.

4–60   Section 1 of the Civil Liability (Contribution) Act 1978 is concerned with liability not *quantum*, so a person from whom contribution is sought is entitled to argue that certain heads of loss were irrecoverable in law by the plaintiff from the defendant (notwithstanding that such heads of loss were included as part of a settlement between plaintiff and defendant), and therefore could not form part of the sum in respect of which the defendant was entitled to claim contribution: *J. Sainsbury plc v. Broadway Maylan (a firm) (Ernest Green Partnership Ltd, Third Party)* [1999] P.N.L.R. 286, where the court accepted that the settlement with the plaintiff by D1 should have been on the basis of the loss of a chance of avoiding the damage that the plaintiff suffered, rather than for the full reinstatement value of the claim. Similarly, D1 is not entitled to claim contribution from D2 in respect of parts of a settlement which are excessive, because they have been overstated by the plaintiff, again on the basis that contribution is only available in respect of sums which the plaintiff was entitled to claim from the D1 in law. Sums paid to the plaintiff in a settlement for the plaintiff's costs cannot be recovered in contribution proceedings, because legal costs are not "the same damage" within the meaning of section 1 of the Act: *ibid.*

NOTE also the statement in the text: "But if a person settles the matter of his liability with the plaintiff by means of a release or otherwise, can he then be sued for contribution by some other person liable, jointly or otherwise, in respect of the same damage? The Act provides no express answer but case law appears to hold that he can still be liable for contribution" must now be considered in the light of *Jameson v. Central Electricity Generating Board* [1999] 2 W.L.R. 141. Although the Court of Appeal in *Jameson* held that the answer was yes, the matter was not appealed to the House of Lords, and Lord Hope assumed the proposition to be correct, the decision of their Lordships in *Jameson* means that where there is a settlement in full and final satisfaction of P's claim against D1 (irrespective of whether this is discounted from its full "value" for litigation risk or otherwise) this operates as a bar to a claim by P against D2, at least for concurrent tortfeasors liable for the same damage, so that D2 will have no liability to pay damages to P for which he is likely to seek contribution from D1. On the other hand, if the settlement is not in full and final satisfaction or P reserves his right to claim against other tortfeasors, D1 remains open to a contribution claim from D2 when P either sues D2 to judgment or settles his claim with D2.

From whom may contribution be claimed 4–61

By section 1(1) of the Civil Liability (Contribution) Act 1978 contribution is recoverable from any person liable in respect of the same damage as the party seeking contribution. The issue of "liability in respect of the same damage" has been raised in recent decisions of the Court of Appeal. In *Friends' Provident Life Office v. Hillier Parker* [1997] Q.B. 85, CA in a development agreement, the plaintiff agreed to share the development costs with the developer. The plaintiff engaged the defendant firm of chartered surveyors as consultants in connection with the development, part of the defendants' responsibilities being to check and authorise payment of the developers' claims for the plaintiffs' share of the costs. The defendant had advised the plaintiff to pay sums including notional interest where the agreement with the developer did not entitle them to such sums. The plaintiff sued the defendant for negligence and breach of contract and the defendant brought third party proceedings claiming contribution from the developer. The defendant claimed that the third party was liable to the plaintiff in restitution for money paid under a mistake of fact or for no consideration or was liable as trustees of the interest. The judge had struck out the third party claims as disclosing no reasonable cause of action, holding, *inter alia*, that the restitutionary claim did not fall within section 1(1). However, the Court of Appeal set that order aside. The court drew attention to the "broad formulation" of the 1978 Act, in particular the wide language of section 6(1) and held that claims for restitution and for damages could be a claim for compensation in respect of the same damage under section 1(1) and section 6(1). It was noted that the 1978 Act was "clearly intended" to be given a wide interpretation. The word "damage" did not limit the provision to compensatory damages. The claim in restitution by the plaintiff against the developers for repayment of the notional interest was a claim in respect of the same damage alleged by the plaintiff against the defendant under section (1) of the 1978 Act. Auld L.J. (at 272):

> "the difference between asking for a particular sum of money back or for an equivalent sum of money for the damage suffered because of the withholding of it is immaterial in this statutory context, which is concerned with 'compensation' for 'damage' ".

The use of the word "responsibility" in section 2(1) (dealing with apportionment of damages) was not intended to confine the operation of section 1(1) to liability arising from breach of duty or default.

It is worth noting that the plaintiffs had settled their contractual claim against the third party but this did not prevent the defendants from continuing with their third party claim: section 1(3).

In *Birse Construction v. Haiste Ltd* [1996] 1 W.L.R. 675, CA, the plaintiffs designed and constructed a reservoir for Anglian Water Authority, retaining the defendants as consulting engineers. Anglian Water Authority employed N as their construction engineer, to issue all necessary certificates. The reservoir was defective; under the settlement of the claim brought by Anglian Water Authority against the plaintiffs the plaintiffs agreed to build a new reservoir at their own expense. The plaintiffs brought a claim to recover this financial loss against the defendants and the defendants claimed contribution from N. The issue was whether the liability of N to Anglian Water Authority was liability in respect of the same damage as the defendants to the plaintiffs, within section 1(1) of the 1978 Act. The Court of Appeal found that the appeal raised a novel point under that subsection. It was not the right approach to hold that the damage was in substance the defective reservoir and the need to repair it. Section 1(1) of the 1978 Act provides "... any person liable in respect of any damage suffered by another person may recover contribution from any other person liable in respect of the same damage". This should be construed directly and simply as it stood: "the same damage" could only refer to the damage spoken of some dozen or so words earlier in the subsection and to damage suffered by the same person. The loss suffered by Anglian Water Authority in not having a properly working reservoir at the time that they had expected, the loss sustained by the plaintiffs in having to construct another reservoir at their own expense or the damages the defendant might have to pay to the plaintiffs or for which N might be liable to Anglian Water Authority were not "the same damage" within the meaning of section 1(1).

NOTE also *Jameson v. Central Electricity Generating Board* [1999] 2 W.L.R. 141, discussed *supra*, Supplement § 4–55 and § 4–60.

4–63   Apportionment of damages

Fitzgerald v. Lane applied by the Court of Appeal in *Drew v. Abassi and Packer* (unreported, May 24, 1995).

Oak Tree Leisure Ltd v. RA Fisk and Associates, The Times, January 1, 1997, CA. Concurrent and several claims. The plaintiff accepted a payment into court by one defendant. In relation to the case against the second defendant, in the absence of apportionment and no material provided by the plaintiff to prove its claim, it was for the court to consider and assess the value of the claim itself.

CHAPTER 5.—VICARIOUS LIABILITY

		PARA.
1.	Introduction	5–01
■2.	Employer and employee	5–03
■3.	Liability of the employer	5–20
□4.	Independent contractors	5–46
□5.	Loan of chattel	5–65
6.	Principal and agent	5–69
7.	Ratification of torts	5–70

The vexed question of the employment status of temporary or casual workers is addressed by the Court of Appeal in *McMeechan v. Secretary of State for Employment* [1997] I.R.L.R. 353. The court distinguishes between specific assignments undertaken by the worker and the general terms of engagement with the employment agency.

2.—EMPLOYER AND EMPLOYEE

Relationship of employer and employee   5–03

In *Lane v. Shire Roofing* [1995] I.R.L.R. 493, CA, the plaintiff traded as a one-man firm and was categorised as self-employed for tax purposes. He was injured while working, after he had been hired by the defendant roofing contractor. The court decided that he was an employee and therefore was owed a duty of care by the defendant on that basis. The court asked whose business was it: was the workman carrying on his own business or was he carrying on that of his employers. Reference was made to the test of the United States Supreme Court in *United States of America v. Silk* 331 U.S. 704 (1946), which sought the "economic reality" of the situation. In particular, the issue of financial risk and the opportunity of profiting from sound management in the performance of the task were important (as noted in *Market Investigations Ltd v. Minister of Social Security* [1969] Q.B. 173). Interestingly, Henry L.J. noted that there are good policy reasons in the safety at work field "to ensure that the law properly categorises between employee and independent contractor", given the incentives to independent contractor status on both sides.

The courts have had to address the status of a worker where that worker has performed temporary tasks, pursuant to a general engagement. *McMeechan v. Secretary of State for Employment* [1997] I.R.L.R. 353, CA. The employment status of temporary or casual workers was discussed by the Court of Appeal. Held, that a temporary worker can be an employee of an employment agency in respect of a particular assignment, even if not an employee under their general terms of engagement. Waite L.J.: "there is nothing inherently repugnant, whether to good relations in the workplace or in law about a state of affairs under which, in an employment agency case, the status of employee of the agency is allocated to a temporary worker in respect of each assignment actually worked notwithstanding that the same worker may not be entitled to employee status under his general terms of engagement" (p. 359). The converse situation arose for decision in *Clark v. Oxfordshire Health Authority* [1998] I.R.L.R. 125, CA. In *McMeechan* the issue became (at Court of Appeal level) whether an individual engagement could be a contract of employment; in *Clark* the issue was whether the general engagement constituted a continuing overriding engagement, amounting to a "global" or "umbrella" contract of employment. Here Clark worked for a nursing bank on a casual basis. She was offered work as and when an appropriate temporary vacancy occurred. The Court of Appeal held that without "mutuality of obligation" no contract of employment could arise. However, the court did not discuss whether each specific contract could have amounted to a contract of employment. Mutuality of obligation was also lacking in *Cheng Yuen v. Royal Hong Kong Golf Club* [1998] I.C.R. 131, PC, and led to a finding that the worker was not an employee of the Golf Club. However, there was a strong dissenting judgment from Lord Hoffmann who found him to be an employee of the Club when he offered his services, though continuity might have been lacking. It must be stressed, however, that the presence of otherwise of mutuality is difficult to predict. In *Carmichael v. National Power plc* [1998] I.R.L.R. 301, CA, guides employed by the respondents on an "as required" basis were held to be employees. The Court of Appeal (Kennedy L.J., dissenting) held there to be an implied term in the contract that the respondents would provide a reasonable amount of work and that the guides would perform a reasonable amount of work offered.

The need for personal service was stressed in *Express & Echo Publications Ltd v. Tanton,* [1999] I.R.L.R. 367. The issue concerned whether the driver was an employee within section 230 of the Employment Rights Act 1996. The driver's contract allowed him to arrange at his own expense for another suitable person to perform the services. It was also the common intention of the parties that the worker should be a self-employed contractor. *Clark v. Oxfordshire HA* [1998] I.R.L.R. 125 referred to.

In *Secretary of State for Trade and Industry v. Bottrill,* [1999] I.R.L.R. 326, the Court of Appeal held that a controlling shareholder of a company can be an employee of that company (the issue was the recovery from the Secretary of Statue of money owed by the company when it became insolvent: an employee is so entitled under the Employment Rights Act 1996, s. 166(7)). Of the conflicting previous decisions on this point – *Buchan v. Secretary of State for Employment* [1997] I.R.L.R. 80, EAT and *Fleming v. Secretary of State for Trade and Industry* [1997] I.R.L.R. 682, Inner House of Court of Session – the Court of Appeal preferred *Fleming* which held that such a shareholder could be an employee. The Court of Appeal offered guidance on this issue. Regard had to be had to all the facts, there was no simple test that would determine whether a shareholder or director was an employee. The fact that he was a controlling shareholder, though significant was only one factor. The tribunal should consider how and for what reasons the contract had come into existence (was it a "sham"); the degree of control exercised by the company over the shareholder (*e.g.* did the company's constitution give the share-holder rights so that he was in reality answerable only to himself and incapable of being dismissed). If he were a director it might be relevant to consider whether he could vote, under the articles of association, on matters in which he was personally interested (such as the termination of his employment).

5–09   The "multiple" test
Kapfunde v. Abbey National plc [1999] I.C.R. 1 a GP was retained by the defendant employer as an occupational health adviser, to provide, at the request of the defend-ant, medical examinations of staff; pre-employment medical examinations for job applications and general medical/health advice to the defendants. She could appoint a locum to fulfil these obligations. The GP used her own equipment and premises and negotiated a higher fee as costs rose. She paid her own National Insurance and tax. The issue concerned potential vicarious liability. The Court of Appeal applied the *Ready Mixed* test, as refined by the Privy Council decision in *Lee Ting Sang v. Chung Chi-Keing* [1990] I.C.R. 409. The issue was one of fact and the finding of the judge, who had directed himself clearly on the law and all the relevant facts, that the GP was self-employed would not be interfered with (though there were points in favour of her being an employee).

5–14   *Police*
By section 86 of the Police Act 1997, the Director General of the National Crime Squad is vicariously liable for torts committed by members of the NCS, "in like manner as a master is liable in respect of torts committed by his servants in the course of their employment".

3.—LIABILITY OF THE EMPLOYER

Liability of employer for torts of employee   5–20

The vicarious liability of employers for acts of sex or race discrimination under
the relevant statutes may be wider than under the common law. In *Jones v. Tower
Boot Co Ltd* [1997] I.C.R. 254, the Court of Appeal held that, given the importance
and purposes of the Race Relations Act 1976 (and the Sex Discrimination Act 1975)
the provisions governing vicarious liability should be given a broad interpretation.
The case involved physical assaults (motivated by race) on the employee by colleagues: the employer was found liable for the actions of his employees under section 32 of the Race Relations Act 1976 (the corresponding section in the Sex Discrimination Act 1975 is section 41). Section 32(1) states: "Anything done by a
person in the course of his employment shall be treated for the purposes of this Act
. . . as done by the employer as well as by him, whether or not it was done with the
employer's knowledge or approval". There is a "reasonable steps" defence. The
Court of Appeal held that the reading of the phrase "course of his employment"
was not subject to the gloss imposed on it in the common law context of vicarious
liability; rather tribunals should interpret that phrase in the sense in which every
layman would understand them. The earlier Court of Appeal decision in *Irving v.
The Post Office* [1987] I.R.L.R. 289 which used the common law test of vicarious
liability in a case brought under the Race Relations Act 1976 was not binding on
this point because section 32 was never referred to. See also *T v. N. Yorkshire
County Council* [1999] I.R.L.R. 98, CA.

The statutory anti-discrimination laws and vicarious liability are discussed in
Monaghan and Javaid, "No laughing matter" (1997) N.L.J. 147, 350–352.

Assault by employee   5–34

Note *Vasey v. Surrey Free Inns*, unreported May 5, 1995, CA, [1995] 10 C.L.
641. Club doormen reacted with excessive violence when the plaintiff damaged their
employer's property. Held that the reaction of the employees was not a private
quarrel but was due to the damage to their employer's property, which it was their
duty to protect. Although unlawful, this was not a frolic of their own but an unauthorised act within the province of their duty. The employer was therefore vicariously liable: *Harrison v. Michelin Tyre Co.* [1985] 1 All E.R. 918 applied; *Daniels
v. Whetstone Entertainments and Allender* [1962] 2 Lloyd's Rep. 1 distinguished.

Damage to goods bailed to the employer in *T v. North Yorkshire County Council*   5–35
[1999] I.R.L.R. 98, CA, a mentally disabled schoolboy was sexually abused by the
teacher into whose care he had been placed during a school trip. The Court of
Appeal held that the local authority was not vicariously liable as the teacher had
acted outside the scope of his employment. The plaintiff had sought to rely, *inter
alia*, on bailment cases, such as *Morris v. C. W. Martin & Sons Ltd* [1966] 1 Q.B.
716, to argue that the conduct of the teacher was a perverted form of his duty of
care. The Court of Appeal held that the bailment cases were either a category on
their own or were limited to fraudulent performance of an authorised act.

Fraud of employee   5–38

*Credit Lyonnais Nederland N.V. (now known as Generale Bank Nederland N.V.)
v. Export Credits Guarantee Department,* [1999] 2 W.L.R. 540, HL. A fraud by a
third party on the plaintiff bank, involving the participation of one of the defendant's
employees. However, though the employee was clearly involved in that fraud as a
conspirator and joint tortfeasor, the activities which constituted such liability were
not within his actual or ostensible authority. Though within his employment, mere
assistance, not itself the deceit, did not constitute a tort and could not render the
employer vicariously liable.

Exceptions   5–42

Section 4 Carriage of Goods by Sea Act 1992 abolished the rule in *Grant v.*

Norway (1851) 10 C.B. 665 [note 70] which stated that a ship's master had no authority to sign bills of lading for goods not put on board. Under section 4 a bill of lading which represents goods to have been shipped on board a vessel (or to have been received for shipment on board a vessel) and which has been signed by the master of the vessel is conclusive evidence of the shipment or receipt against the carrier in favour of the lawful holder of the bill. The bill will also be conclusive evidence against the carrier where it was signed not by the master but by a person who had "the express, implied or apparent authority" of the carrier to sign bills of lading. Note, however, that section 4 is subject to the Hague-Visby Rules (see section 5(5)) and only applies to bills of lading.

5–52 **Operations on the highway**
See *Rowe v. Herman* [1997] 1 W.L.R. 1390, CA; *Salsbury v. Woodland* [1970] 1 Q.B. 324, applied.

4.—INDEPENDENT CONTRACTORS

5–57 **Extra-hazardous acts**
MTM Construction Ltd v. William Reid Engineering Ltd, The Times, April 22, 1997, Outer House of the Court of Session. A contractor engaged a subcontractor to undertake an inherently dangerous operation. The subcontractor engaged a sub-subcontractor to undertake this dangerous work. Held that the subcontractor was not liable to the principal contractor for the negligence of the sub-subcontractor. The court had not been referred to any authority in which intermediate employers were liable for the negligence of subcontractors and were of the opinion that only the ultimate employer had a co-existent liability, together with the party who carried out the work, for the negligent performance of the inherently dangerous work.

5.—LOAN OF CHATTEL

5–66 Essentials of liability. *Re Ormrod v. Crosville Motor Services Ltd* [1953] 1 W.L.R. 1120, add *Candler v. Thomas (T/A London Leisure Lines)* [1998] R.T.R. 214, CA.

CHAPTER 6.—FOREIGN TORTS

The Private International Law (Miscellaneous Provisions) Act 1995 introducing **6–01**
new statutory rules for choice of law in tort entered into force on May 1, 1996.

Jurisdiction   **6–02**
See *Shevill v. Presse Alliance SA* [1995] 2 A.C. 18, ECJ wherein the European
Court of Justice confirmed that the courts of every jurisdiction where a libel is
disseminated enjoy jurisdiction over the tort under Article 5(3) of the Civil Jurisdic-
tion and Judgment Conventions. That jurisdiction is limited, however, to harm actu-
ally caused in the state of that court. Note too the subsequent judgments in *Shevill
v. Presse Alliance S.A.* [1996] 3 W.L.R. 420, HL, and *Berezovsky v. Forbes Inc.,
The Times*, November 27, 1998, CA; *cf. Chadha v. Dow Jones & Co., The Times*,
May 18, 1999. See also *Marinari v. Lloyds Bank* [1996] 2 W.L.R. 159, ECJ; *Modus
Vivendi Ltd v. British Products Sanmex Ltd* [1996] F.S.R. 790 and *Mecklermedia
Corporation v. D.C. Congress GmbH* [1997] 3 W.L.R. 479 (applying Article 5(3)
to the tort of passing off).

The availability of legal and (or some other form of financial assistance) may
exceptionally be a factor in determining issues of *forum non conveniens*. Lord Goff
suggested that a court might properly consider ". . . whether the plaintiff can establish that substantial justice will not in the particular case be done if the plaintiff has
to proceed in the appropriate forum where no financial assistance is available".
Connelly v. RTZ Corporation plc [1997] 3 W.L.R. 373 at 385, HL. And see *Askin
v. Absa Bank Ltd, The Times*, February 23, 1999, CA; *Carlson v. Rio Tinto plc*
[1999] C.L.C. 551.

NOTE 5. Add: *Domicrest v. Swiss Bank Corporation* [1998] 3 All E.R. 577.

Choice of law at common law   **6–03**
If evidence as to foreign law is insufficient or non-existent, the courts will apply
the presumption that the foreign law is the same as English law. In tort, at common
law, all that the plaintiff need do is assert that the tort is actionable in the foreign
jurisdiction. It is for the defendant to show that the law in that jurisdiction differs
from English law: *University of Glasgow v. Economist Ltd* [1997] E.M.L.R. 495.

NOTE 30. Add: *Pearce v. Ove Arup Partnership Ltd.* [1999] 1 All E.R. 769, at
801–804.

Torts relating to land abroad   **6–06**
The Court of Appeal in *Pearce v. Ove Arup Partnership Ltd* [1999] 1 All E.R.
769 at 793 has made it clear that in relation to land situated within a state party to
either the Brussels or Lugano Conventions there is no longer any basis for the rule
in the *Mocambique* case.

As to the interpretation of section 30 of the Civil Jurisdiction and Judgments Act
1982 see *Re Polly Peck International plc* [1996] N.P.C. 176.

Intellectual property   **6–07**
The Court of Appeal in *Pearce v. Ove Arup Partnership Ltd, supra,* has cast
doubt on the judgment of Vinelott J. in *Tyburn Productions Ltd v. Conan Doyle*
extending the application of the *Mocambique* rule to actions relating to foreign intellectual property rights. Their Lordships refused to strike out a claim for breach of a
Dutch copyright. The judgment in *Pearce* makes it absolutely clear that where an
action for infringement of copyright is brought against a defendant domiciled in
England, the English courts have jurisdiction to hear the plaintiff's claim by virtue
of Article 2 of the Brussels and Lugano Conventions. The jurisdiction of the English
courts falls within the ambit of the Conventions, and Article 6(1) allows related
claims against defendants domiciled in the Netherlands also to be brought in Eng-

land. The local rule advanced in the judgment in *Tyburn Productions* applied (if at all) only to oust jurisdiction against defendants domiciled in, and intellectual property rights arising or granted under, the laws of non-Convention states. Nor would the "double actionability" rule necessarily prevent the plaintiff's claim for breach of a Dutch copyright from succeeding, for the exception to the rule in *Phillips v. Eyre* established in *Chaplin v. Boys* allowed the English court to apply Dutch law.

Albeit not cited in the judgments in *Pearce*, the first instance judgment in *Coins Control Ltd v. Suzo International (U.K.) Ltd* [1997] 3 W.L.R. 420 must now be open to doubt. In *Coins Control* the judge described the "rule" that an English court should not entertain an action for breach of foreign intellectual property rights as a fundamental rule of public policy based on the undesirability of the English courts adjudicating on issues which were essentially foreign and local. The rule had nothing to do with "double actionability" and thus survived the Private International Law (Miscellaneous Provisions) Act 1995. Yet in *Pearce* the Court of Appeal appeared to commend the application of just that "double actionability" rule, albeit, on the facts of the case, invoking the exception to the rule. *Tyburn Productions* in so far as it remains good law, may well be limited to its special facts and rest on the evidence before the judge that any order he might have made would be unenforceable in the United States of America and thus an "exercise in futility" (see *Pearce v. Ove Arup Partnership Ltd, supra* at 799).

6–09   **Private International Law Bill**
The Bill has been enacted as the Private International Law (Miscellaneous Provisions) Act 1995. Part III relating to choice of law in tort follows the provisions of the Bill described in the main text. Part III of the Act came into force on May 1, 1996. See *Rogerson* (1995) 44 I.C.L.Q. 650; *Morse* (1996) 45 I.C.L.Q. 888.

NOTE 47. Add: see *University of Glasgow v. Economist Ltd, supra*; and note *Pearce v. Ove Arup Partnership Ltd* and *Coins Control Ltd v. Suzo International (U.K.) Ltd, supra*.

CHAPTER 7.—NEGLIGENCE

		PARA.
■1.	The tort of negligence	7–01
■2.	Duty of care: the general criteria	7–05
■3.	Duty of care: problem areas	7–18
	(a) The status of the parties	7–19
	(b) Omissions and affirmative duties	7–28
	(c) Distress and shock	7–43
	(d) Pure economic loss	7–54
	(e) Public service liability	7–96
■4.	Breach of duty	7–112
	(a) Introduction	7–112
	(b) The criteria of reasonableness	7–115
	(c) Particular situations	7–138
	(d) Proof of carelessness	7–174
5.	Causation	7–181
■6.	Foreseeability and actionability	7–182
	(a) Factual duty: foreseeability of damage to the plaintiff	7–184
	(b) Remoteness: foreseeability of the kind of damage	7–186
■7.	The extent of responsibility apportioned to the defendant	7–197
8.	General reflections	7–201

In the period since publication of the Seventeenth Edition there have been six **7a** significant decisions of the House of Lords. *Marc Rich & Co. v. Bishop Rock Marine Co. Ltd* is an important illustration of the three-stage approach to duty being applied to physical damage rather than economic loss. *White v. Chief Constable of South Yorkshire Police* clarifies the basis of the duty of care in relation to psychiatric injury. *X (minors) v. Bedfordshire County Council, Barrett v. Enfield London Borough Council* and *Stovin v. Wise* consider the scope of the duty of care in relation to public authorities. *Williams v. Natural Life Health Foods* has clarified the basis of liability for economic loss and *South Australia Asset Management Corp. v. York Montague Ltd* introduces a new approach to remoteness of damage based upon the purpose of the duty of care.

The Court of Appeal has also been active. *Vernon v. Bosley (No. 1)* and *Hunter v. British Coal Corp* examined the extent of liability for psychiatric injury. In *Welton & Anor v. North Cornwall DC, Harris v. Evans* and *Perrett v. Collins*, the court considered the extent of the duty owned by safety regulators. In *W. v. Essex County Council* and *Phelps v. Hillingdon London BC* it considered the extent of the duty owed by welfare and education authorities. *Capital and Counties plc v. Hampshire County Council* examined the liability of the rescue services. In *Swinney v. Chief Constable of Northumbria, Costello v. Chief Constable of Northumbria* and *Leach v. Chief Constable of Gloucestershire Constabulary* the extent of police immunity was considered. In *Stanton v. Callaghan* and *Hall v. Simons* the court considered the extent of immunity for expert witnesses and advocates respectively. In the context of pure economic loss, *Barings plc v. Coopers & Lybrand* applied the *Caparo* test to hold an auditor under a duty to the parent company of the client whilst *Goodwill v. British Pregnancy Advisory Service* applied the test to deny a duty in relation to advice about the success of a vasectomy. *McCullagh v. Lane Fox and Partners Ltd* both upheld the validity of an estate agent's disclaimer of liability and contained an extensive consideration by Hobhouse L.J. of the basis of liability for economic loss. *Holt v. Payne Skivington* has established that a tortious duty may be more extensive than any contractual duty between the parties. In *Carr-Glynn v.*

Frearsons (a firm) and *Walker v. Medlicott & Son* the extent of a solicitor's duty to a beneficiary has been further considered.

2.—Duty of Care: The General Criteria

7-13 **Three-stage approach**

In *Marc Rich & Co. v. Bishop Rock Marine Co. Ltd* [1996] 1 A.C. 211, the House of Lords affirmed the decision of the Court of Appeal that no duty was owed by the defendant. The case concerned a cargo ship which developed a crack in the hull whilst on a voyage. At its next stop in port, it was inspected by a marine surveyor employed by the defendant who inspected the safety of ships on behalf of an association of shipowners. The surveyor approved a temporary repair and allowed the ship to continue its voyage but the repair failed and it sank with loss of cargo worth $6 million. The plaintiff was the owner of the cargo and alleged that through its surveyor, the defendant had been negligent. The issue in the case was whether the defendant owed the plaintiff a duty of care.

Giving the judgment of the majority of the House of Lords, Lord Steyn held that no duty was owed. He confirmed the view of the Court of Appeal that "the elements of foreseeability and proximity as well as considerations of fairness, justice and reasonableness are relevant to all cases whatever the nature of the loss". That the loss was foreseeable as a result of the defendant's negligence was not disputed and Lord Steyn was also prepared to assume (without deciding) that there was a sufficient degree of proximity. But he held that the imposition of a duty would not be fair, just and reasonable for three reasons: First, it would undermine the limits to shipowners' liability established by contract with the cargo owners and by the Hague Rules. The insurance of international trade depends upon these limits and yet they would be outflanked because classification societies such as the defendant were owned by shipowners and would simply pass any liability to the cargo owner back to the shipowners. Secondly, potential liability might lead the classification societies to adopt a more defensive position and be less effective in their primary role of promoting the safety of lives and ships at sea. For example, they might be unwilling to survey the very vessels which most urgently required independent examination for fear of liability. Thirdly, liability would lead to an increase in litigation against societies, an expensive complex settlement process and the diversion of men and resources to this process and from that of saving lives and ships.

Dissenting, Lord Lloyd commented that the requirements of proximity and fairness had been developed as a means of containing liability for pure economic loss. He argued that in physical damage cases "proximity very often goes without saying" and that "where the facts cry out for the imposition of a duty of care, as they do here, it would require an exceptional case to refuse to impose a duty on the ground that it would not be fair, just and reasonable." He concluded that no difficulties arose in the case: "We are not here asked to extend the law of negligence into a new field. We are not even asked to make an incremental advance. All that is required is a straightforward application of *Donoghue v. Stevenson*." On the points that swayed Lord Steyn, he was wary of the insurance argument in absence of any evidence on the point, and considered that liability would be welcomed by the shipping community "who are increasingly concerned by the proliferation of substandard classification societies."

In *Mulcahy v. Ministry of Defence* [1996] 2 W.L.R. 474, Neill L.J. considered that two points were clear from the decision of the House of Lords in the *Marc Rich* case: first, that the elements of foreseeability, proximity and fairness were relevant to "all cases of alleged negligence whatever the nature of the harm", and secondly, that in deciding whether it is fair, just and reasonable to impose a duty "one must consider all the circumstances including the position and role of the alleged tortfeasor and any relevant policy considerations." In *Mulcahy* the Court of Appeal held that a serviceman owed no duty of care to his fellow servicemen in battle conditions since as matter of common sense and policy it would not be fair, just and reasonable to impose such a duty even if proximity and foreseeability were established. Both Neill L.J. and Sir Iain Glidewell cited the analogous immunity of the police in battle conditions'. See further § 7–109.

The speech of Lord Steyn and the role of the three-stage test in the context of physical damage was extensively considered by the Court of Appeal in *Perrett v. Collins* [1999] P.N.L.R. 77, CA, where it was held that the defendants, who were responsible for inspecting the airworthiness of a light aircraft, owed a duty of care to the plaintiff who was injured when the aircraft crashed allegedly due to lack of airworthiness. Hobhouse L.J. noted that, having presented the three-stage test as an over-arching formula, Lord Steyn had recognised that "for some categories of conduct, as for example where it creates a risk of harm (by which I take him to be referring to personal injury), 'it is obvious that as a matter of common sense and justice a duty should be imposed"'. Hobhouse L.J. commented:

> "If this understanding is correct, and it ties with what Lord Bridge said about attaching greater importance to the more traditional categorisation of established situations of liability ... no problem arises. The over-arching formula does not affect the outcome. Established categories, with or without the assistance of 'common sense and justice', provide the answer. The certainty provided by the previous authorities is not undermined. Indeed, it would be surprising if Lord Steyn had, by his decision of what he described as a *novel* question relating to property or economic interests, intended to depart from or call in question established decisions or principles relating to personal injury."

Swinton Thomas L.J. considered that in context of the particular case, the questions of proximity and fairness could "conveniently be considered together". Buxton L.J. commented that "when one turns to the judgmental issues of justice, fairness and reasonableness the importance of the fact that what is put at risk is the plaintiff's body, and not just his goods, is ... deeply embedded in the law of negligence".

See also *Langley v. Dray and M.T. Motor Policies at Lloyds* [1998] P.I.Q.R. P314, CA, where Stuart-Smith L.J., leading the Court of Appeal, considered the three-stage test in holding that the plaintiff, a police officer injured in a car crash when in pursuit of a speeding driver, was owed a duty of care by that driver.

3.—DUTY OF CARE: PROBLEM AREAS

(a) *The Status of the Parties*

Wrongful life or birth   **7–20**
NOTE 99. Add: See also *CES v. Superclinics (Aust) Pty* [1995] 38 N.S.W.L.R. 47, in which the New South Wales Court of Appeal divided on the policy issue.

(3) *Wrongdoers*

Add to end of paragraph: In *Revill v. Newberry*[21a] Neill L.J. held that in the case   **7–22**
of a burglar shot by an occupier, there was no need to consider the "joint criminal enterprise cases or the application of the doctrine of ex turpi causa" as by section 1 of the Occupiers' Liability Act 1984 "Parliament has decided that an occupier cannot treat a burglar as an outlaw and has defined the scope of the duty owed to him." The burglar's claim succeeded with his damages being reduced by two thirds for contributory negligence.

NOTE 21a. [1996] 2 W.L.R. 239.

NOTE 12. Add: See also *Clunis v. Camden and Islington Health Authority* [1998] 2 W.L.R. 902, CA, where it was held on grounds of *ex turpe causa* that a plaintiff who had been convicted of a serious criminal offence could not sue a health authority for negligently failing to treat him properly so as to prevent the commission of the offence, unless it could be shown that he did not know the nature or quality of his act.

7-23 **Suicide**

NOTE 24: Add: *Kirkham* has been applied where the prisoner was of sound mind in *Reeves v. Commissioner of Police of the Metropolis* [1998] 2 All E.R. 381, CA. Buxton L.J. held that the claim was not barred by the principles of *volenti*, causation or public policy and that no reduction of damages for contributory negligence was appropriate. Morritt L.J. agreed that *volenti* and public policy were inapplicable but dismissed the claim on the ground that the deliberate suicide of a sane individual broke the chain of causation and in the alternative regarded the trial judge as being correct in applying a 100 per cent reduction for contributory negligence. Lord Bingham C.J. agreed with Buxton L.J. in rejecting the *volenti*, causation and public policy defences but, if sitting alone would have reduced damages by 50 per cent. The House of Lords has ruled in favour of Lord Bingham's approach and reduced damages by 50 per cent: [1999] 3 All E.R. 897.

See also *Hay v. Grampian Health Board* [1995] 6 Med. L.R. 128: liability for allowing a depressed patient to go unaccompanied to the bathroom where he attempted suicide suffering brain damage as a result.

(4) Rescuers

7-25 **Reasonably foreseeable rescues**

NOTE 49. Add: In *Jeffrey v. Commodore Cabaret Ltd* (1995) 128 D.L.R. (4th) 535, the Canadian Supreme Court held that the plaintiff who attempted to stop a fight in a bar following the failure of the defendant owner to intervene, should recover damages but subject to a reduction of 50 per cent for contributory negligence.

(b) Omissions and Affirmative Duties

7-28 **No liability for pure omissions**

NOTE 69: Add: In *Stovin v. Wise* [1996] 3 All E.R. 801 at 819, HL, Lord Hoffmann, after citing the passage from Lord Diplock's speech, said: "There are sound reasons why omissions require different treatment from positive conduct. . . . One can put the matter in political, moral or economic terms. In political terms it is less of an invasion of an individual's freedom for the law to require him to consider the safety of others in his actions than to impose upon him a duty to rescue or protect. A moral version of this point may be called the 'Why pick on me?' argument. A duty to prevent harm to others or to render assistance to a person in danger or distress may apply to a large and indeterminate class of people who happen to be able to do something. Why should one be held liable rather than another? In economic terms, the efficient allocation of resources usually requires an activity should bear its own costs. If it benefits from being able to impose some of its costs on other people the market is distorted because the activity appears cheaper than it really is. So liability to pay compensation for loss caused by negligent conduct acts as a deterrent against increasing the cost of the activity to the community . . . But there is no similar justification for requiring a person who is not doing anything to spend money on behalf of someone else. Except in special cases . . . English law does not reward someone who voluntarily confers a benefit on another. So there must be some special reason why he should have to put his hand in his pocket."

(1) Responsibility for a person

7-30 **Protective relationships**

NOTE 85. Add: *Barrett v. Ministry of Defence* is now reported at [1995] 1 W.L.R. 1217, [1995] 3 All E.R. 87.

NOTE 81. Add: See now *Woods v. Lowns* [1995] 36 N.S.W.L.R. 344, in which it was held that in the light of a failure to treat an emergency being regarded as professional misconduct, a doctor could owe a duty of care to respond properly to a request to provide medical assistance. On the facts, the doctor had refused to treat the plaintiff who had collapsed with an epileptic fit 300 metres from the doctor's surgery. The judge stressed the relevance of physical proximity and the fact that the request was made in a professional context, *i.e.* when the doctor was at his place of practice.

Reliance and entitlement 7–31
NOTE 92. Add: See further the annotation to supplement § 7–103, *post.*

Ineffective intervention 7–32
NOTE 95. Add: In *Capital and Counties plc v. Hampshire County Council* [1997] 2 All E.R. 865 at 885 and 883, CA, Stuart-Smith L.J. approved *Horsley v. MacLaren* as being "consistent with the *East Suffolk* case" and said of a rescuer: "If he volunteers his assistance, his only duty as a matter of law is not to make the victim's condition worse." A fire authority which made the fire damage worse by switching off the plaintiff's sprinkler system, was held liable for the damage but authorities which merely failed to detect the fire or fight it effectively were held not liable.

NOTE 96. Add: The proposition that it may be possible to show that the victim is worse off because others have been deterred from making an effective rescue by seeing the defendant commencing his (ineffective) intervention must now be doubted in the light of the decision in *OLL Ltd v. Secretary of State for Transport* [1997] 3 All E.R. 897. In that case, May J. held that the coastguard service could not be held liable for allegedly misdirecting Royal Navy helicopters with the result that rescue of the plaintiffs was delayed. May J. regarded the turning off of the sprinkler system in *Capital and Counties* as giving rise to liability because it directly inflicted physical injury. Deterring third parties from attempting rescue may make the victim worse off but does not directly inflict injury.

(2) *Responsibility for property*

Occupiers of land 7–33
NOTE 98. Add: See also *Paterson v. Humberside County Council, The Times,* April 19, 1995, in which a local council responsible for trees was held liable in negligence and nuisance for foreseeable subsidence damage resulting from the drying out of soil due to the tree roots, and *Holbeck Hall Hotel Ltd v. Scarborough Borough Council* [1997] 2 E.G.L.R. 213, where a downhill neighbour was held liable in negligence and nuisance to an uphill plaintiff for failing to prevent a landslip on the downhill land which led to the collapse of a building on the uphill land. The judge considered that it would be irrational for the duty applied to uphill owners in *Leakey*, not to apply to downhill owners.

(3) *Responsibility for third party's action*

Control over third party 7–38
NOTE 30. Add: In *Laplante v. Laplante* (1995) 126 D.L.R. (4th) 569, a father was held liable to passengers in his car for allowing his qualified but inexperienced son to drive in dangerous icy conditions which led to an accident. Somewhat inconsistently, the court held that the father himself could recover against the son without any reduction for contributory negligence. The court clearly considered that a higher standard of care is required when considering liability than when considering the defence of contributory negligence.

Responsibility for danger 7–41
NOTE 65. Add: See also *Mayfield Investments Ltd v. Stewart* (1995) 121 D.L.R. (4th), in which the Supreme Court of Canada held that the defendant restaurant owner who served drinks to a group of four customers did owe a duty of care to the

plaintiff who was subsequently injured on the highway as a result of drunken driving of one of the group. However, the defendant was not liable as it was reasonable for him to assume that one of the two non-drinkers in the group would have driven the group's car.

In *Wince v. Ball* (1996) 136 D.L.R. 104, it was held that a social host would only be liable if it could be shown that he had contributed in some way to the drunk driving by a guest. Simply allowing a teenage drinking party would not result in liability being imposed on the parents for any resultant drunk driving accidents.

(c) *Distress and Shock*

7–43   Distress and derivative claims

NOTE 74. Add: In *Wood v. Law Society, The Times*, March 2, 1995, the Court of Appeal held that the plaintiff could not recover for her distress at the Law Society's alleged negligent failure to investigate complaints against her solicitor as, even if the Society owed a duty of care in relation to the investigation, it was not a duty to give peace of mind or freedom from distress. See also *Reilly and Reilly v. Merseyside R.H.A.* [1995] 6 Med. L.R. 246, CA, in which it was held by the Court of Appeal that the plaintiffs who had suffered panic and worry when trapped in a hospital lift for 20 minutes, could not recover because there was no evidence of psychiatric damage or physical injury to them. Mann L.J. cited *Hicks* and stated that fear was a normal human emotion for which there was no recovery.

NOTE 81. Add: See also *Buckley v. Farrow & Buckley* [1997] P.I.Q.R. Q78, CA, where Simon Brown L.J. stated that it was "plain beyond argument that an infant child, deprived of his mother's care as a result of her being tortiously injured, cannot recover damages against the tortfeasor."

Add to end of paragraph in main text: In *Vernon v. Bosley (No. 1)*[82a] the Court of Appeal held that damages for mental illness caused by grief (referred to as pathological grief disorder or PGD) are recoverable where that illness was caused or contributed to by the shock of witnessing the horrific events resulting from the defendant's negligence. The plaintiff had witnessed the unsuccessful attempts to rescue his daughters from a submerged car which the defendant had negligently driven into a river. The defendant's expert witnesses suggested that the plaintiff's mental illness was caused by grief (PGD) rather than shock (referred to as post-traumatic stress disorder or PTSD). The defendant argued that the plaintiff had to prove his illness was due to PTSD rather than PGD in order to recover. Stuart-Smith L.J., dissenting, accepted the defendant's argument and held that the plaintiff had failed to establish on the balance of probabilities that his illness was caused by PTSD rather than PGD. Thorpe and Evans L.JJ. held for the plaintiff on the ground that the trial judge had found that the mental illness had been contributed to by the shock of witnessing the events. Thorpe L.J. stated that "if a plaintiff proves PGD as well as all the necessary features of success as cited by Lord Oliver [in *Alcock v. Chief Constable of South Yorkshire*] . . . he is entitled to succeed."[82b] Evans L.J. endorsed the view that no distinction should be drawn between PGD and PTSD, noting both the practical difficulty of distinguishing between the symptoms of the two forms of mental illness and the fact that as medical science developed "these or different categories may come and go". Evans L.J. also noted that the reason for denying compensation for the normal grief following bereavement was "not the policy induced rule, recognised in *McLoughlin v. O'Brian*, which limits the scope of the duty of care, but rather a restriction on the heads of damage which may be recoverable by a successful plaintiff." Consequently, he considered that there was "no policy reason for limiting the damages" by discovering "what part of the plaintiff's illness should be ascribed to the bereavement rather than to the traumatic experience of witnessing the accident." He concluded that "even if the illness is partly attributable to the pathological consequences of grief and bereavement, it was nevertheless caused by the defendant's negligent act, and the policy reasons which limit the scope and number of those to whom a duty is owed do not provide equal justification for limiting the damages recoverable by those who can sue."[82c]

NOTE 82a [1997] 1 All E.R. 577.

NOTE 82b. Thorpe L.J. cited with approval the statement of Neill L.J. in *Calascoine v. Dixon* (1993) 19 B.M.L.R. 97, that the "crucial question . . . is whether the sights and sounds which [the plaintiff] experienced caused or contributed to her PGD".

NOTE 82c. Evans L.J. cited *Clerk and Lindsell on Torts* § 7–51 "Policy and flexibility" in support of this proposition.

Shock 7–44

NOTE 83. Add: In *W v. Essex County Council* [1998] 3 W.L.R. 534, CA, it was held that parents could not recover for psychiatric illness suffered as a result of learning that the defendant's negligence had led to their children being abused. Their illness was not caused by shock in the sense of a "sudden appreciation by sight or sound of a horrifying event which violently agitates the mind". In *Hunter v. British Coal Corporation* [1998] 2 All E.R. 97, CA, it was held that a plaintiff could not recover for psychiatric illness caused by a mistaken feeling of guilt for an accident caused by the defendant's negligence, unless he had been present at the scene of the accident and could be classed as a primary victim. In *Sion v. Hampstead Health Authority* [1994] 5 Med L.R. 170, CA and *Taylorson v. Shieldness Produce Ltd* [1994] P.I.Q.R. P329, CA, the Court of Appeal held that a parent could not recover where psychiatric illness resulted from the prolonged experience of watching a child die in hospital. Contrast *Tredget v. Bexley Health Authority* [1994] 5 Med. L.R. 178, CC, in which Judge White considered that the shock requirement was satisfied because although the child died two days after negligent treatment during childbirth, the process was "effectively one event". The Law Commission Report on Liability for Psychiatric Illness (1998, Law Com. No. 249) recommends statutory abolition of the shock requirement. See further the annotation to Supplement § 7–51.

Reasonable foreseeability of injury and illness 7–45

NOTE 88. Add: The Law Commission Report on Liability for Psychiatric Illness (1998, Law Com. No. 249) recommended that "in establishing a duty of care it should be a requirement that, at least where the plaintiff is outside the area of reasonably foreseeable physical injury, it was reasonably foreseeable that the plaintiff might suffer psychiatric illness". Where physical injury was reasonably foreseeable, the Report recommended no change to the rule in *Page v. Smith* that additional foreseeability of psychiatric illness was not required. It rejected calls for the reversal of *Page* on the grounds that there was no strong support for reversal among legal practitioners or judges and that insufficient time had passed to assess the impact of the decision.

Closeness to the accident 7–47

NOTE 98. Add: See also *Hunter v. British Coal Corp* [1998] 2 All E.R. 97, CA, where the plaintiff was unable to recover because he had not witnessed the incident and had been prevented from seeing the aftermath, and *Palmer v. Tees Health Authority* [1998] Lloyd's Rep. (Med.) 447, where a mother was unable to recover for psychiatric illness suffered as a result of seeing the mutilated body of her child three days after she had been murdered by a patient for whom the defendant was responsible. For an example of sufficient closeness in time to the accident, see *Vernon v. Bosley (No. 1)* [1997] 1 All E.R. 577, CA, in which the plaintiff watched the police attempts to recover from a river, the car in which his daughters had drowned.

Policy and flexibility 7–51

Add NOTE 12a to title of paragraph.

NOTE 12a. This paragraph was cited by Evans L.J. in *Vernon v. Bosley (No. 1)* [1997] 1 All E.R. 577, CA, in support of the proposition that "the policy reasons which limit the scope and number of those to whom a duty is owed do not provide equal justification for limiting the damages recoverable by those who can sue." In § 7–51 it was argued that the policy underlying the proximity requirement was to ensure that the "illness was linked to the shocking nature of the incident rather than mere bereavement" and that once this is established, courts should not limit recovery by the use of arbitrary criteria. It should be noted that a similar approach has been taken by Kirby P. in a powerful dissenting judgment in *Coates v. Govt Insurance Office of N.S.W.* [1995] 36 N.S.W.L.R. 1. The children of a man killed by the negligence of the defendant, claimed for shock suffered as a result of being informed of the death but without having seen the accident or body. Kirby P. said that ". . . the law should recognise that it is as much the direct emotional involvement of a person in an accident, as his or her physical presence at or near the scene or directly in its aftermath, that is pertinent to nature of the injury suffered." He concluded that adhering to the stereotypes derived from England might result in injustice, given the different cultural approach to grief in Australia.

NOTE 14. Add: The Law Commission Report on Liability for Psychiatric Damage (1998, Law Com. No. 249) recommended that "restrictions based on the plaintiff's physical and temporal proximity to the accident and the means by which he or she learned of it should be removed; but that the first control—the need for a close tie of love and affection should be retained". It also recommended "the removal of two further restrictions that appear to apply generally to liability for negligently inflicted psychiatric illness: first, that the illness must be caused by a 'shock' and, secondly, that the illness must not result from the death, injury or imperilment of the defendant him or herself". It proposed that these recommendations should be implemented by legislation imposing a statutory duty of care to avoid causing another person to suffer psychiatric illness as a result of the death, injury or illness of someone (whether third party or defendant) with whom he or she had a close tie of love and affection. In relation to other categories of plaintiff such as rescuers, involuntary participants and employees, the common law would continue to determine whether a duty was owed but the legislation would remove the need to show that the plaintiff's illness was induced by shock.

The Report (para. 2.63) described as "harsh and seemingly arbitrary" the decisions in *Sion v. Hampstead Health Authority* [1994] 5 Med. L.R. 170, CA, and *Taylorson v. Shieldness Produce Ltd* [1994] P.I.Q.R. P329, CA, in which the Court of Appeal held that lack of shock precluded liability to parents who suffered psychiatric illness as a result of witnessing their child's slow death in hospital.

7–52 Participation in the event

The nature of Lord Oliver's "participation" category and its relationship to the category of "primary victims" identified by Lord Lloyd in *Page v. Smith* was considered by the House of Lords in *White v. Chief Constable of South Yorkshire Police* [1998] 3 W.L.R. 1509, [1999] 1 All E.R. 1, HL. The majority view, as expressed in the speech of Lord Steyn, was that all victims of psychiatric injury other than those within the range of potential physical injury, "are secondary victims and must satisfy the control mechanisms laid down in the *Alcock* case". As the rescuing police officers who suffered psychiatric injury had not thought that they were exposed to personal danger and did not satisfy the control mechanisms, their claim failed. To the argument that Lord Oliver had treated rescuers as an example of "participants", Lord Steyn responded: "None of the other Law Lords in the *Alcock* case discussed this category. Moreover, the issue of rescuers' entitlement to recover for psychiatric harm was not before the House on that occasion and Lord Oliver was not considering the competing arguments presently before the House." Lord Steyn explained *Chadwick* as a case where "the rescuer had passed the threshold of being in personal danger" and concluded:

> "In order to recover compensation for pure psychiatric harm as a rescuer it is not necessary to establish that [the] psychiatric condition was *caused* by the perception of personal danger . . . [b]ut in order to contain the concept of res-

cuer in reasonable bounds for the purposes of the recovery of compensation for pure psychiatric harm the plaintiff must at least satisfy the threshold requirement that he objectively exposed himself to danger or reasonably believed that he was doing so. Without such limitation one would have the unedifying spectacle that, while bereaved relatives are not allowed to recover as in the *Alcock* case, ghoulishly curious spectators, who assisted in some peripheral way in the aftermath of a disaster, might recover."

See also *Hunter v. British Coal Corp.* [1998] 2 All E.R. 97, CA, the majority of the Court of Appeal held that an employee who suffered psychiatric illness as a result of blaming himself for the incident causing the death of a fellow employee could not recover against the employer whose negligence was truly responsible for the death because he had not witnessed the incident and was prevented from attempting rescue. Contrast *Schofield v. Chief Constable of West Yorkshire, The Times,* May 15, 1998, CA, where it was held that a police woman suffering psychiatric illness as a result of a colleague negligently discharging a pistol in her presence, was entitled to recover as that conduct exposed her to a risk of injury.

Responsibility for psychiatric well-being   7–53
    In AB & Others v. Tameside and Glossop Health Authority [1997] P.N.L.R. 140, CA, Brooke L.J. was prepared to impose liability on a health authority for communicating accurate but distressing information in a careless manner resulting in psychiatric illness to the recipient of the information. The plaintiffs alleged they suffered psychiatric illness as a result of receiving a letter from the authority informing them that they had been treated by someone subsequently discovered to have been HIV positive. They claimed that the authority should have arranged for their GPs to tell them face to face and the failure to do this had increased their shock and distress. The Court of Appeal found that the use of the letter was not unreasonable or negligent. However, in *White v. Chief Constable of South Yorkshire Police* [1998] 3 W.L.R. 1509, [1999] 1 All E.R. 1, HL, the House of Lords held that the employment relationship did not impose on the employer a special duty of care not to cause the employee psychiatric injury. Lord Steyn said:

> "It is a non sequitur to say that because an employer is under a duty to an employee not to cause him physical injury, the employer should as a necessary consequence of that duty (of which there is no breach) be under a duty not to cause the employee psychiatric injury. ... The rules to be applied when an employee brings an action against his employer for harm suffered at his work place are the rules of tort. One is therefore thrown back to the ordinary rules of the law of tort which contain restrictions on the recovery of compensation for psychiatric harm."

Lord Goff agreed with Lord Steyn, commenting that he was putting "on one side those cases in which an employee is seeking damages from his employer in respect of stress at work, as to which see ... *Walker v. Northumberland CC* [1995] 1 All E.R. 737". Lord Hoffmann distinguished *Walker* as a case where the employee "was in no sense a secondary victim. His mental breakdown was caused by the strain of doing the work which his employer had required him to do." Negligent failure to prevent bullying or harassment of an employee resulting in psychiatric illness might fall in the same category, but see *Waters v. Commissioner of Police of the Metropolis* [1997] I.C.R. 1073, CA. In *Leach v. Chief Constable of Gloucestershire Constabulary* [1999] 1 All E.R. 215, CA, the Court of Appeal held that the police owed no duty of care to protect those volunteering to sit in on interviews from psychiatric injury suffered as a result of the traumatic nature of the interviews, although it held that the failure to provide adequate counselling services for the volunteer might give rise to liability. Brooke L.J. commented that the Law Commission had:

"identified a miscellaneous group of cases in which recovery may be available for a negligently inflicted psychiatric illness . . . These include a case where a patient suffers a psychiatric illness because of negligent treatment by his/her psychiatrist (cf *M (a minor) v. Newham London BC* [1995] 3 All E.R. 353); where a prisoner foreseeably suffers a psychiatric illness as a result of ill-treatment by prison officers (cf *Hague v. Deputy Governor of Parkhurst Prison* [1991] 3 All E.R. 733 at 745–746, [1992] 1 AC 58 at 165–166); and where recipients of distressing news suffer reasonably foreseeable psychiatric illness as a result of the news being broken in an insensitive manner (*AB v. Tameside and Glossop Health Authority* (1996) 35 B.M.L.R. 79). These are useful illustrations, but there is not yet any English case of the types described in which it has not been comparatively easy to establish that the requisite duty of care exists."

In the absence of grounds for holding that the police had assumed a responsibility to the volunteer, Brooke L.J. refused to extend this category of case, commenting that it was for "the House of Lords to take any new policy decisions in this field, if it is considered to be an appropriate subject for judicial law-making at all".

(d) *Pure Economic Loss*

(1) *Relational economic loss*

7–57 The rationale of the no-recovery rule

NOTE 38. Add: The recent decision of the Supreme Court of Canada in *D'Amato v. Badger* (1996) 137 D.L.R. (4th) 129, exemplifies both the no recovery rule and its rationale. The defendant negligently injured one of the key employees of the plaintiff company which claimed to have suffered a $73,000 loss as a result. The Supreme Court held that no duty was owed to the plaintiff company. Imposing such a duty would result in indeterminacy with potential duties rippling out to other individuals and corporations affected by the injury. It would also remove the incentive to companies to plan for such events by insurance or contracts allocating risk. Contrast *Christensen v. Scott* [1996] 1 N.Z.L.R. 273, where the New Zealand Court of Appeal held that it was arguable that solicitors acting for a company also owed a direct duty to the sole shareholder in the company who suffered a diminution in the value of his shares as a consequence of the solicitor's alleged negligence.

7–59 A "joint venture" exception?

NOTE 45. Add: The "joint venture" exception has subsequently been considered in *Bow Valley Husky Ltd v. Saint John Shipbuilding* (1995) 126 D.L.R. (4th) 1. The defendants' negligence led to a fire on a third party's oil rig which the plaintiff was using for drilling. The plaintiff was contractually bound to pay rental to the third party during the period whilst the rig was out of action due to the fire damage. The plaintiff argued that it was engaged in a joint venture with the rig owner and was entitled to recover under the principle in *Norsk*. The NewFoundland Court of Appeal held that the joint venture exception was inapplicable. The plaintiff's relationship with the owner of the damaged property had only lasted four years as compared with the 70 years in *Norsk*. Furthermore, the plaintiff could have protected its interest in the contract negotiated with the owner and the parties having determined the contractual position, tort should not interfere.

(2) *Reliance on statements*

7–62 The criteria of liability

NOTE 57b. Add: Lord Goff's speech in *Henderson* identifying assumption of responsibility as the key criterion of duty in relation to economic loss, has been endorsed by Lord Steyn giving the only speech in *Williams v. Natural Life Health Foods Ltd* [1998] 1 W.L.R. 830, HL. Lord Steyn stated that once a case was identified as falling within the assumption of responsibility principle enunciated in *Hedley Byrne*, "there is no need to embark on any further inquiry whether it is fair just and reasonable to impose liability for economic loss". He considered academic criticism of the criterion to be overstated, arguing that "the restricted conception of contract in English law" meant that "the law of tort, as the general law, has an essential gap-filling role" and that "[i]n these circumstances there was, and is, no better rationalisation for the relevant head of tort liability than assumption of responsibility". Explaining the objective nature of the criterion, he said: "The touchstone of liability is not the state of mind of the defendant. An objective test means that the primary focus must be on things said or done by the defendant or on his behalf in dealings with the plaintiff. Obviously, the impact of what the defendant says or does must be judged in the light of the relevant contextual scene. Subject to this qualification, the primary focus must be on exchanges . . . which cross the line between the defendant and the plaintiff." At Court of Appeal level, Lord Goff's speech has been cited with approval by Hobhouse L.J. in *McCullagh v. Lane Fox & Partners* [1996] P.N.L.R. 205, 225, CA; Nourse L.J. in *First National Commercial Bank v. Loxleys* [1997] P.N.L.R. 211, CA; Rose L.J. in *Welton & Anor v. North Cornwall D.C.* [1997] P.N.L.R. 108, 117, CA; and Morritt L.J. in *Peach Publishing Ltd v. Slater & Co.* [1998] P.N.L.R. 364, CA. See also the test of "conscious assumption of responsibility" adopted by Carnwath J. in *Electra Private Equity Partners v. KPMG Peat Marwick* [1998] P.N.L.R. 135.

NOTE 67: Add: See also *Goodwill v. British Pregnancy Advisory Service* [1996]   **7–63**
2 All E.R. 161, where the Court of Appeal considered the application of the *Caparo* principle to the unusual circumstance of allegedly negligent advice that a vasectomy had been successful. It was alleged that having been given this advice, the man in question communicated it to a subsequent partner, who relied upon it and became pregnant as a result of not using any other form of contraceptive. She claimed the cost of bringing up the child from the defendant who gave the original advice. Peter Gibson L.J. doubted whether the case met the second requirement enunciated by Lord Oliver in *Caparo*, namely that the adviser knows actually or inferentially that "his advice will be communicated to the advisee, either specifically or as a member of an ascertainable class" and was clear that the third requirement, namely that it was known that the advice would be acted on without independent inquiry, had not been met: "The defendants could know nothing about the likely course of action of future sexual partners of [the man]". See also *Reeman v. Department of Transport* [1997] P.N.L.R. 618, CA, in which the Court of Appeal applied the *Caparo* test to conclude that the Department did not owe a duty of care to potential purchasers of a fishing vessel when issuing a seaworthiness certificate for that vessel.

NOTE 71: Add: In *Bank of Credit and Commerce International (Overseas) Ltd v.*   **7–64**
Price Waterhouse (No. 2) [1998] P.N.L.R. 564 at 588, CA, Sir Brian Neill commented that "[T]he general trend of the authorities makes it clear that liability will depend not on intention but on the actual or presumed knowledge of the adviser and on the circumstances of the particular case." On this view, it is knowledge of the purpose of the information which is the key factor in establishing a duty. This differs from the view taken by Lightman J. in *Possfund v. Diamond* [1996] 1 W.L.R. 1351 at 786, that "For the purpose of the torts of deceit and negligent misrepresentation, it is necessary to establish a material misrepresentation intended to influence the mind of the represented". However, as he went on to explain that "the intention must be objectively established", there may be little practical difference between the two approaches.
Add to end of paragraph: The relationship between the principles governing liability for pure economic loss have been reviewed by Sir Brian Neill giving the judgment of the Court of Appeal in *Bank of Credit and Commerce International (Overseas) Ltd v. Price Waterhouse (No. 2)* [1998] P.N.L.R. 564 at 583–587, CA.[71a] After explaining that "the search for a principle or test has followed three separate but parallel paths" (the "threefold" test stated by Lord Griffiths in *Smith v. Bush*;

the "assumption of responsibility" test; and the incremental approach recognised by Lord Bridge in *Caparo*), he commented that: "The fact that all these approaches have been used and approved by the House of Lords in recent years suggests: (a) that it may be useful to look at any new set of facts by using each of the three approaches in turn . . . (b) that if the facts are properly analysed and the policy considerations correctly evaluated the several approaches will yield the same result." He considered that the following factors would be relevant in deciding whether the criteria for either the threefold test or assumption of responsibility had been met:

"(a) the precise relationship between the adviser and the advisee . . . (b) the precise circumstances in which the advice or information or other material came into existence. Any contract or relationship with a third party will be relevant. (c) the precise circumstances in which the advice or information or other material was communicated to the advisee, and for what purpose . . . and whether the communication was made by the advisee or by a third party. It will be necessary to consider the purpose . . . of the communication as seen by the adviser and as seen by the advisee, and the degree of reliance which the adviser . . . should reasonably have anticipated would be placed on its accuracy by the advisee . . . (d) the presence or absence of other advisers on whom the advisee would or could rely . . . (e) the opportunity, if any, given to the adviser to issue a disclaimer."

Note that in *Siddell v. Smith Cooper & Partners (a firm)* [1999] Lloyd's Rep. P.N. 79, CA, Clarke L.J. followed a similar approach citing the judgement of Sir Brian Neill. However, in *Reeman v. Department of Transport* [1997] P.N.L.R. 618, CA, Peter Gibson L.J. commented that he had "some difficulty seeing how that [the test of assumption of responsibility] can be the appropriate test in a case such as the present where there is no contract between [the parties], nor a situation the equivalent of contract." See also the review of the basis of liability by the High Court of Australia in *Esanda Finance Corporation Ltd v. Peat Marwick Hungerfords* [1997] 188 C.L.R. 241, and the New Zealand Court of Appeal in *Brownie Wills v. Shrimpton* [1999] Lloyd's Rep. P.N. 39, where Blanchard J. commented that whether there was reasonable reliance by the plaintiff "in turn depends upon whether the reliance was induced by the conduct of the defendant in assuming or appearing to assume responsibility for advising the plaintiff".

NOTE 71a. Note that in *Reeman v. Department of Transport* [1997] P.N.L.R. 618, CA, Peter Gibson L.J. commented that he had "some difficult seeing how that [the test of assumption of responsibility] can be the appropriate test in a case such as the present where there is not contract between [the parties], nor a situation the equivalent of contract". See also the review of the basis of liability by the High Court of Australia in *Esanda Finance Corp Ltd v. Peat Marwick Hungerfords* [1997] 188 C.L.R. 241.

7–65   The primary purpose

Add NOTE 73a to the fourth sentence in § 7–65 concerning the purpose of a bank providing a reference.

NOTE 73a. Note that in *Gold Coin Joailliers S.A. v. United Bank of Kuwait* [1997] P.N.L.R. 217, CA, the Court of Appeal held that the purpose of a bank credit reference was limited to the customer's credit and did not concern the identity of the person seeking the credit.

NOTE 74. Add: See the similar conclusion reached by the High Court of Australia in *Esanda Finance Corporation Ltd v. Peat Marwick Hungerfords* [1997] 188 C.L.R. 241.

NOTE 76. Add: But see the judgment of Lightman J. in *Possfund v. Diamond* [1996] 1 W.L.R. 1351. The defendant company issued a prospectus alleged to contain negligent misrepresentations. The prospectus stated that, as part of the same exercise as the allotment, the facility would be available for the shares to be traded on the unlisted securities market. The plaintiffs purchased shares in the unlisted market (known as after-market purchases) and sued the defendant when it subsequently went into receivership. The defendant moved to strike out the plaintiffs' claims. Lightman J. held that a duty could be owed by those responsible for the prospectus if it was established that an after-market purchaser was intended to rely on the prospectus for this purpose and the necessary proximity existed between the parties. He argued that although the starting point for determining the ambit of the duty of care in respect of a prospectus was its statutory purpose, that was not necessarily the end point as it did not preclude a "super-added" purpose if such could positively be shown to exist. [see *post*, § 7–66] He considered that if the plaintiffs could establish that "there has been developed and generally recognised an additional purpose, an additional perceived intention on the part of the issuer and other parties to a prospectus, namely to inform and encourage after-market purchasers", then it was arguable that a duty of care was owed to the investors. In adopting this analysis, Lightman J. seemed to be endorsing the view of *Gower on Company Law* (5th ed., 1992), p.498, that the decision in *Al-Nakib Investments* should be reviewed.

(3) *The defendant's intention*

Secondary purposes   7–66
NOTE 78. Add: See also *Barings plc v. Coopers & Lybrand (a firm)* [1997] P.N.L.R. 179, CA, where Leggatt L.J. held that the auditors of a Barings subsubsidiary owed a duty of care to Barings because they knew that their audit was required so that "the directors of Barings could comply with their obligation to provide accounts which showed a true and fair view of the financial affairs of the group"; and *Bank of Credit and Commerce International (Overseas) v. Price Waterhouse* [1998] P.N.L.R. 564, CA, where Sir Brian Neill held that Ernst Whinney who audited the accounts of B.C.C.I. Holdings could owe a duty of care to the associated B.C.C.I. Overseas despite the fact that Overseas accounts were separately audited by Price Waterhouse because the business of the two banks, Holdings and Overseas, intermingled and Ernst Whinney was in effect the supervising firm with responsibilities extending to Overseas and Price Waterhouse.

NOTE 81. Add: *Columbia* has been overruled by the decision of the High Court in *Esanda Finance Corporation Ltd v. Peat Marwick Hungerfords* [1997] 188 C.L.R. 241, in which Brennan C.J. delivered a judgment similar in tenor to that in *Caparo*. See also *Hercules Managements Ltd v. Ernst & Young* (1995) 125 D.L.R. (4th) 353, where the Manitoba Court of Appeal followed *Caparo* and held that the defendant's audit manual, which acknowledged a responsibility to the investing public, did not justify the imposition of a duty to care to that public.

Widening the purpose   7–67
NOTE 86. Add: In *British Columbia Ltd v. HBT Agra Ltd* (1994) 120 D.L.R. (4th) 726, the British Columbia Court of Appeal followed *Caparo* in holding that an engineer providing a soil report for a property owner, owed no duty of care to a subsequent purchaser to whom the engineer was not aware that his report would be shown.

(4) *The plaintiff's reasonable reliance*

The nature of the relationship   7–69
NOTE 90. Add: In *Williams v. Natural Life Health Foods Ltd* [1998] 1 W.L.R. 830, HL, Lord Steyn regarded the view of La Forest J. in *Edgeworth* as being "consistent with English law" and adopting his emphasis on the need for *reasonable* reliance rather than merely reliance in fact, held that the plaintiffs who were customers of a company could not have reasonably looked to the defendant director of the company for indemnification against loss. Lord Steyn also considered that the lack of personal dealings between the director and the customers meant that there "were not exchanges which could have conveyed to the plaintiffs that [the defendant director] was willing to assume a personal responsibility to them". In *Hale v.*

Guildarch Ltd [1999] P.N.L.R. 44, *Williams* was applied to deny the personal liability of financial advisers working for an accountancy practice.

7–70   Verification of information

Add to end of paragraph: In *Tidman v. Reading Borough Council, The Times*[98a] Buxton J. held that a local authority answering the plaintiff's inquiry on a planning matter, did not owe a duty of care. In part, this was because it was reasonable to assume that as the matter was of crucial importance, the plaintiff would not rely on the authority's view but would seek independent advice. In *Electra Private Equity Partners v. KPMG Peat Marwick*[98b] Carnwath J. followed *McNaughton* in denying a duty partly on the ground that the plaintiff had its own advisers employed to investigate its proposed purchase of the company alleged to have been negligently audited by the defendants. Again, in *McCullagh v. Lane Fox & Partners*[98c] it was held that an estate agent owed no duty of care to a prospective purchaser of a property in respect of a statement about the area of the plot, where he was entitled to assume that his statements would be independently checked by the purchaser or his advisers. Note that in *Duncan Investments Ltd v. Underwoods (a firm)*[98d] *McNaughton* and *McCullagh* were distinguished on the ground that the estate agent advising the purchaser as to the resale price of the property, knew it was unlikely the purchaser would obtain independent advice and, hence, owed a duty.

NOTE 98a *The Times*, November 10, 1994.
NOTE 98b [1998] P.N.L.R. 135.
NOTE 98c [1996] P.N.L.R. 205, CA.
NOTE 98d [1997] P.N.L.R. 521.

7–71   Advice given informally

Add to end of paragraph: However, the fact that the information was provided in a telephone call does not necessarily mean that the occasion can be classed as informal or social.[4a]

NOTE 4a. *Campbell v. Teachers' Retirement Fund* (1993) 110 D.L.R. (4th) 400. The plaintiff was given negligent advice about his pension by an employee of the fund in a telephone call. The court held that a duty was owed. See also *Lambert v. West Devon Borough Council, The Times*, March 27, 1997, in which it was held that local authority was liable for negligent oral advice given by a building control officer.

7–72   The content of the statement

NOTE 11. Add: *Tidman v. Reading Borough Council, The Times*, November 10, 1994, in which it was held that a planning department did not owe a duty of care, partly because the plaintiff should have verified the advice and partly because the department's duty to the general public was inconsistent with any duty to an individual.

7–74   Exclusion of liability

NOTE 26. Add: But see the view of Nourse L.J. in *First National Commercial Bank plc v. Loxleys* [1997] P.N.L.R. 211, CA, that since the observations of Lord Griffiths in *Smith*: "the law has moved on, or perhaps back, in particular through the decision of the House of Lords in *Henderson v. Merrett Syndicates* ... which has rehabilitated the 'assumption of responsibility' concept." He concluded: "In this uncertain state of the law I cannot be confident that the duty of care issue can be decided as a discrete point. It is at least possible that the existence or not of such a duty will be held to depend partly on the effect of the disclaimer."

After the sentence which reads: "Clearly, the more commercial the relationship between the parties, the more likely it is that any disclaimer will be regarded as reasonable". Add: Thus in *McCullagh v. Lane Fox and Partners Ltd*[27a] the Court of Appeal held an estate agent's disclaimer of liability for errors in the description of the property, to be reasonable in the context of a property marketed at £850,000 and a sophisticated purchaser. Similarly, in *Omega Trust Co. Ltd v. Wright Son & Pepper (a firm)*[27b] it was held to be reasonable for a valuer valuing commercial properties for a commercial client to disclaim any additional responsibility to any unknown third parties who might lend relying on the valuation.

NOTE 27a. [1996] P.N.L.R. 205, CA, Hobhouse L.J. also criticised the approach of the trial judge in treating the disclaimer in the written particulars as a contractual exclusion and construing it narrowly so as not to apply to the oral misrepresentation of the agent. He commented: "The right approach, as is made clear in *Hedley Byrne*, is to treat the existence of the disclaimer as one of the facts relevant to answering the question whether there had been an assumption of responsibility by the defendants for the relevant statement. This questions must be answered objectively by reference to what a reasonable person in the position of [the purchaser] would have understood at the time he finally relied on the representation."

NOTE 27b. [1997] P.N.L.R. 424, CA.

Inconsistency   7–75

NOTE 36. Add: Note also that in *Berry Taylor (a firm) v. Coleman & Anor* [1997] P.N.L.R. 1, the Court of Appeal held the fact that an accountant had a conflict of interest when advising the plaintiff to invest in another client's business, did not prevent there being a duty to the plaintiff.

Add to end of paragraph: In *Williams v. Natural Life Health Foods Ltd*[36a] the Court of Appeal held that it would be inconsistent with the purpose of incorporation with limited liability if a director of a company was held to owe a duty in respect of advice given on behalf of the company. Only where there were special circumstances amounting to a personal assumption of responsibility, would a duty be owed by the director.

NOTE 36a. [1991] 1 B.C.L.C. 131.

Statements going beyond the scope of the contract   7–76

Add to end of paragraph: In *Holt v. Payne Skivington (a firm)*[39a] Hirst L.J. clarified the position as follows: "In our opinion, there is no reason in principle why a *Hedley Byrne* type duty of care cannot arise in an overall set of circumstances where, by reference to certain limited aspects of those circumstances, the same parties enter into a contractual relationship involving more limited obligations than those imposed by the duty of care in tort. In such circumstances the duty of care in tort and the duties imposed by the contract will be concurrent but not coextensive." On the facts, no more extensive duty in tort was found to exist.

NOTE 39a. [1996] P.N.L.R. 179, 195, CA.

(5) Negligent services

Services to a third party for the benefit of the plaintiff   7–81

NOTE 65. Add: In *Hill v. Van Erp* [1997] 188 C.L.R. 159, the Australian High Court upheld a duty in a *Ross* situation.

NOTE 66. Add: Note that in *Walker v. Medlicott & Son* [1999] 1 All E.R. 685, CA, where it was conceded that a duty to follow the testator's instructions with reasonable care was owed to a intended beneficiary, the Court of Appeal considered that the beneficiary must first mitigate by seeking rectification of the will. The costs of rectification could then be recovered from the defendant solicitor. On the facts, there was no evidence that the solicitor had been negligent in following instructions.

NOTE 68. Add: See *Blackwell v. Barroile* (1994) 123 A.L.R. 81, in which it was held that a solicitor owed a duty not to mislead to the trustee in bankruptcy of his client; and *Christensen v. Scott* [1996] 1 N.Z.L.R. 273, in which it was held that a solicitor acting for a company might also owe a direct duty of care to the sole shareholder in the company. See the consideration of *Christensen* in *Johnson v. Gore Wood & Co* [1999] Lloyd's Rep. P.N. 91, CA.

NOTE 69. Add: *Aiken v. Stewart Wrightson Agency Ltd* has now been fully reported: [1995] 1 W.L.R. 1281, [1995] 3 All E.R. 449. NOTE 71. Add: See also *New Zealand Guardian Trust Co. v. Brooks* [1995] 1 W.L.R. 96, in which the Privy

Council held that directors of a company when preparing a certificate for trustees under a debenture trust deed, owed a duty of care to the debenture holders.

7–82 NOTE 70: Add: in *Chapman v. Barclays Bank* [1998] P.N.L.R. 14, CA, it was held that a bank providing services for a company did not owe a duty of care to a director of the company in relation to its decision to cancel the overdraft facilities of the company. The bank had not assumed a responsibility to the director and such a duty of care would have led to a conflict of interest with the bank's duty to its own shareholders as a commercial lender.

NOTE 71: Add: in *Wells v First National Bank* [1998] P.N.L.R. 552, CA, it was held that where a customer had issued an irrevocable instruction to a bank to pay a third party, the bank did not owe a duty of care to the third party in relation to the payment. Such a duty would have revolutionised Banking Law and its imposition could not be regarded as incremental. *White* was distinguished on the basis of the non-availability of any effective remedy and the peculiar status of the solicitor when preparing a will.

In *Carr-Glynn v. Freasons (a firm)* [1998] 4 All E.R. 225, CA, the Court of Appeal distinguished *Clarke v. Bruce Lance* when holding that a solicitor owed a duty to an intended beneficiary disappointed by the fact that he had failed to take steps to ensure that the testatrix severed her joint tenancy in the bequeathed property. As a result, the property passed to the remaining joint tenant by survivorship. Contrast *Cancer Research Campaign v. Ernest Brown* [1998] P.N.L.R. 592, where Harman J. held that a solicitor was under no duty to a beneficiary to draft the will to minimise its tax liability as this was not within the terms of the retainer from the testator.

Add to end of paragraph: In *Goodwill v. British Pregnancy Advisory Service*[72a] it was held that the *White v. Jones* principle could not be applied by analogy to the case where the defendant was alleged to have negligently advised a man that his vasectomy operation was successful with the result that he had unprotected intercourse with the plaintiff who became pregnant and sued for the financial cost of bringing up the child. Peter Gibson L.J. considered that the doctor who performs the vasectomy "cannot realistically be described as employed to confer a benefit on the man's sexual partners in the form of avoiding pregnancy". He also stated that since the complaint was not about the service itself, that is the vasectomy, but rather about the advice, he could not "accept that the present is a *White v. Jones* type of case at all."

NOTE 72a. [1996] 2 All E.R. 161. See also *Kapfunde v. Abbey National plc, The Times,* April 6, 1998, CA, in which the Court of Appeal held that a doctor engaged by an employer to assess the suitability of potential employees, did not owe a duty of care to the potential employee when reporting to the company. Kennedy L.J. considered that the doctor's position was analogous to that of a doctor examining an applicant for life insurance cover.

7–85 NOTE 92. Add: *Aiken v. Stewart Wrightson Agency Ltd* has now been fully reported: [1995] 1 W.L.R. 1281, [1995] 3 All E.R. 449.

7–87 **Exclusion of liability**

NOTE 9. Add: *Norwich CC v. Harvey* was distinguished by the House of Lords in *British Telecommunications plc v. James Thomson & Sons (Engineers) Ltd* [1999] 2 All E.R. 241, HL, where it was held that a domestic subcontractor did owe a duty of care in respect of physical damage to the employer as the main contract only required the employer to insure against damage by nominated subcontractors and not domestic subcontractors.

(6) Negligent provision of products or buildings

7–89 **Dangerous defects and economic loss**

7–90 NOTE 19. Add: In *Strathford East Kilbride Ltd v. Film Design Ltd, The Times,*

December 1, 1997, the Outer House of the Court of Session held that *Murphy* applied to preclude a duty being owed by an architect to a client's tenants.

NOTE 23. Add: In *Hamble Fisheries Ltd v. Gardner and Sons Ltd, The Times,* January 5, 1991, CA, the Court of Appeal held that the majority view in *Rivtow* was not recognised in English law and, hence, a shipowner could not recover loss of profit during the period of repairs to the ship's engine which were necessitated by its negligent design for which the defendant was responsible.

Economic loss overview   7–95

NOTE 62. Add: For recent Commonwealth authority rejecting the "no recovery bright line" see: *Invercargill City Council v. Hamlin* [1996] 2 W.L.R. 367, [1996] 1 All E.R. 756, in which the Privy Council confirmed that the New Zealand Court of Appeal was entitled to develop the common law according to local policy considerations and was free to reject the approach taken by the House of Lords in *D & F Estates* and *Murphy* in favour of that taken by itself in *Stieller* and the Canadian Supreme Court in *Kamloops*; and *Bryan v. Maloney* (1995) 128 A.L.R. 163, in which the Australian High Court held a builder liable to a subsequent purchaser.

(e) *Public Service Liability*

The leading analysis of public service liability is now to be found in the speech   7–96
of Lord Browne-Wilkinson in *X (minors) v. Bedfordshire County Council* [1995] 2 A.C. 633. This case grouped together the appeals from the Court of Appeal decisions in *M v. Newham London Borough Council* and *E v. Dorset County Council* discussed in §§ 7–107 and 7–108. The issue was whether local authorities owed duties of care in relation to child care services and educational services. In the child care litigation, it was claimed in one case that the social workers had negligently intervened to remove a suspected victim of child abuse from its home in the mistaken belief that the mother's partner was the abuser, and in the other case that they had negligently failed to intervene and remove the child from its home. In the education litigation, it was claimed in one case that the authority had negligently failed to identify the child's special needs and provide the required special schooling, and in another case that it had negligently determined that the child had special needs and placed him in a special school when he was of normal ability and should have remained in a normal school.

Lord Browne-Wilkinson classified private law claims for damages against public authorities into four different categories:

> "(A) actions for breach of statutory duty simpliciter (*i.e.* irrespective of negligence); (B) actions based solely on the careless performance of a statutory duty in the absence of any other common law right of action; (C) actions based on a common law duty of care arising from the imposition of the statutory duty or from the performance of it; (D) misfeasance in public office, *i.e.* the exercise of statutory powers with the intention to injure the plaintiff or in the knowledge that the conduct is unlawful."

As misfeasance was not in issue, Lord Browne-Wilkinson discussed it no further. He considered the requirements for breach of statutory duty simpliciter, *i.e.* that "as a matter of construction of the statute, the statute was imposed for the protection of a limited class of the public and that Parliament intended to confer on members of that class a private law right of action for breach of the duty". Nothing that there seemed to be no case in which "statutory provisions establishing a regulatory system or a scheme of social welfare for the benefit of the public at large had been held to give rise to a private right of action", he concluded that no such right arose in relation to the child protection and education schemes in issue. After analysing the leading authorities, he concluded that the second category of claim (B) could never succeed, stating that "careless performance of a statutory duty does not in itself give rise to any cause of action in the absence of a statutory right of action (category A) or a common law duty of care (category C)". He devoted the major part of his speech to an analysis of this latter category, the common law duty of care. Within this category he considered both the possibility of a direct common law duty owed by the authority and its vicarious liability for the breach of duty by its servants.

Policy and discretion

7–97   Lord Browne-Wilkinson drew a distinction between cases in which the alleged duty concerned the exercise of a statutory discretion, for example, a decision to close a school, and those in which it concerned the implementation of a statutory duty or decision, for example, taking care for the safety of pupils within a school. In the "implementation" category of case, the usual *Caparo* principles of foreseeability, proximity and reasonableness would determined duty but their application would be "profoundly influenced by the statutory framework" within which the service was provided. In the "discretion" category of case a duty could only be owed if the decision complained of was "so unreasonable that it fell outside the ambit of the discretion conferred on the . . . authority". In deciding whether this was the case, the court could assess the factors taken into account by the authority save for those involving policy matters, for example, the allocation of resources or the balancing of social objectives. Courts cannot adjudicate on such matters and cannot reach the conclusion that a decision was outside the ambit of the discretion on the basis of the policy involved. As a result, "a common law duty of care in relation to the taking of decisions involving policy matters cannot exist". Summarising the analysis, Lord Browne-Wilkinson put forward a three stage test for determining whether an authority owed a direct duty of care:

> "(a) Is the negligence relied upon negligence in the exercise of a statutory discretion involving policy considerations: if so the claim will pro tanto fail as being non-justiciable; (b) were the acts alleged to give rise to the cause of action within the ambit of the discretion conferred on the local authority; if not, (c) is it appropriate to impose on the local authority a common law duty of care."

This three stage test applies where the authority is exercising a statutory discretion. Where it is simply providing a service or conducting an activity not involving the exercise of such discretion, it is solely the third stage, the appropriateness of the duty, that the courts must consider.

Applying the first stage of this test, Lord Browne-Wilkinson considered that the claims did not necessarily involve questions of resourcing or policy which would be non-justiciable. Moving to the second stage, he considered it likely that the decisions would fall within the ambit of the discretion conferred on the authority but refused to strike out the claims on this ground as it was "possible that the plaintiffs might be able to demonstrate at trial that the decisions of the local authority were so unreasonable that no reasonable authority could have reached them and therefore . . . f[e]ll outside the ambit of the discretion conferred by Parliament." It was at the third stage, the appropriateness of the duty of care, that the child abuse and education claims based on the allegedly negligent decisions of the authorities failed. In the abuse cases it was considered that the imposition of a duty would undermine the statutory system for the protection of children and impinge on the delicate decision-making process. In the education cases it was considered that the administrative failures were best dealt with by the statutory appeals procedure rather than by litigation. However, in one of the education cases it was also alleged that the authority had provided negligently wrong psychological advice to parents and pupils. Lord Browne-Wilkinson considered that the position was entirely different in relation to this claim, stating that:

> "True it is that, in the absence of a statutory power or duty, the authority could not offer such a service. But once the decision is taken to offer such a service, a statutory body is in general in the same position as any private individual or

organisation holding itself out as offering such a service. By opening its doors to others to take advantage of the service offered, it comes under a duty of care to those using the service to exercise care in its conduct. The position is directly analogous with a hospital conducted by a health authority in the exercise of its statutory powers. In such a case the authority running the hospital is under a duty to those whom it admits to exercise reasonable care in the way it runs it."

Hence, the negligent advice claim against the education authority was not struck out.

Vicarious liability

See § 7–107. Lord Browne-Wilkinson stated that the vicarious liability of an authority depended upon whether the duty of care alleged to be owed by its professional as "consistent with the proper performance of his duties to the local authority" and was such that it was appropriate to impose on the professional. In relation to the vicarious liability claim against the authorities employing the social workers and psychiatrists in the child abuse cases, he found that the professionals "were employed retained to advise the authority in relation to the well-being of the plaintiffs but not to advise or treat the plaintiffs." Their report would not be relied upon by the plaintiffs but would influence the way in which the authority acted. Hence, the professionals had not "assumed any general professional duty of care to the plaintiff children" and there could be no vicarious liability. However, in the education cases he held that the professionals could owe a duty of care in the assessment and determination of a child's educational needs. He distinguished the education context from that of child abuse on the ground that the advice of the education professionals was relied upon by the parents and that there was "no potential conflict of duty between the professional's duties to the plaintiff and the education authority." Consequently, the vicarious liability claim in the education cases was not struck out. The approach taken by Lord Browne-Wilkinson appears contrary to the view in § 7–108 that public authority professionals should not be held personally liable for their advice as a "backdoor route" to establishing the liability of the authority.

Policy

NOTE 81, Add: See also *Re HIV Haemophiliac Litigation* [1996] P.N.L.R. 290, [1996] P.I.Q.R. P220, CA in which the Court of Appeal rejected the defendant's contention that the plaintiffs had no arguable case and hence, their application for production of documents should be refused. Bingham L.J. was not persuaded that the plaintiff was wrong in asserting that the complaint "relate[d] not to any policy decision taken by the Secretary of State but to the Department's [of Health] failure to implement the policy decision taken, that is, to the implementation not the formulation of policy."   **7–99**

(1) Policy

Add to end of paragraph: Two further decisions of the Supreme Court of Canada in *Brown v. British Columbia*[83a] and *Swinamer v. Nova Scotia*[83b] have now added to the guidance. In *Brown* the issue was whether the decision of a highway authority to run on to November with a summer schedule of road maintenance using fewer men than the winter schedule, was a policy rather than an operational decision. Cory J., giving the judgment of the majority, described the policy/operational distinction as follows: **7–100**

"True policy decisions involve social, political and economic factors. In such decisions, the authority attempts to strike a balance between efficiency and thrift, in the context of planning and predetermining the boundaries of its undertakings and their actual performance. True policy decisions will usually be dictated by financial, economic, social and political factors or constraints. The operational area is concerned with the practical implementation of the formulated policies; it mainly covers the performance or carrying out of a policy. Operational decisions will usually be made on the basis of administrative direction, expert or professional opinion, technical standards or general standards of reasonableness."

He rejected the argument that "policy decisions must be limited to threshold decisions, *i.e.* broad initial decisions as to whether something will or will not be done", holding instead that they can be "made by persons at all levels of authority" and that it was the "nature of the decision itself that must be scrutinised rather than the position of the person who makes it." Applying these principles to the issue, he concluded that the decision "was clearly one of policy" and could "not be reviewed on a private standard of reasonableness". In *Swinamer* the Court held that a highway authority's decision to conduct a survey to identify dead and dangerous trees along the roadside rather than immediately adopting a policy of removing such trees, was a policy decision as "it was a preliminary step in what would eventually become a policy decision involving the expenditure and allocation of funds". Cory J. added that "the fact the budgetary considerations are questions of policy is not changed by the fact that the cost of the measures sought may be small". In *Stovin v. Wise*[83c] Lord Hoffmann commented that the Canadian decisions illustrated "the inadequacy of the concepts of policy and operations to provide a convincing criteria for deciding when a duty of care should exist". However, this comment was made in the context of the suggestion in *Anns* that the distinction could provide the sole criterion for deciding whether a duty was owed in respect of an omission. The analysis of Lord Browne-Wilkinson does not rest the existence of a duty on the distinction, rather it requires the plaintiff to establish the absence of a non-justiciable policy issue as one of the conditions for establishing a duty. In this context, it is suggested that the Canadian authorities may still provide helpful guidance on the question of justiciability.

NOTE 83. Add: In *Comeau Sea Foods Ltd v. Canada* (1995) 123 D.L.R. (4th) 180, Robertson J.A. held that revocation of an off-shore fishing licence was a non-justiciable policy decision. Linden J.A. disagreed and also argued that even if it was, there could still be liability if the decision was so unreasonable as not to be a proper exercise of discretion. Stone J.A. held that there was no duty as the administrative law remedies were sufficient. Linden J.A. rejected this argument, commenting that "administrative law does not trump tort law".

NOTE 83a. (1994) 112 D.L.R. (4th) 1.

NOTE 83b. (1994) 112 D.L.R. (4th) 18.

NOTE 83c. [1996] 3 All E.R. 801 at 830, HL.

7–102   Proximity and regulatory functions

NOTE 91. Add: In *Reeman v. Department of Transport* [1997] P.N.L.R. 619, CA, it was held that the Department owed no duty of care to subsequent purchasers of vessels when certifying their seaworthiness. This was because the purpose of the certification scheme was to promote the public interest safety at sea rather than to protect the private interest of purchasers, and because potential purchasers did not form a sufficiently limited class of plaintiffs in either time or geography. See also *Harris v. Evans* [1998] 1 W.L.R. 1285, CA, where it was held that a safety inspector owed no duty of care to a business suffering loss as a result of the inspector's decision to close its operation on safety grounds. But contrast *Welton & Anor v. North Cornwall District Council* [1997] P.N.L.R. 108, CA, where the Court held that an environmental health officer who negligently required the plaintiff to undertake unnecessary work on his guest house, did owe the plaintiff a duty of care; and *Perrett v. Collins* [1999] P.N.L.R. 77, CA, where it was held that the defendants, who were responsible for inspecting the airworthiness of a light aircraft, owed a duty of care to the plaintiff who was injured when the aircraft crashed allegedly due to lack of airworthiness.

NOTE 92. Add: *Swanson Estate v. Canada* (1991) 80 D.L.R. (4th) 741, has been followed in *Perrett v. Collins* [1999] P.N.L.R. 77, CA, where it was held that the defendants, who were responsible for inspecting the airworthiness of a light aircraft, owed a duty of care to the plaintiff who was injured when the aircraft crashed allegedly due to lack of airworthiness.

The basis on which a public body may owe a duty in respect of omissions has **7–103** been fully considered by Lord Hoffmann giving the majority judgment in *Stovin v. Wise*.[8a] He took as his starting point the principle stated by Lord Romer in *East Suffolk Rivers Catchment Board v. Kent*[8b] that: "Where a statutory authority is entrusted with a mere power, it cannot be made liable for any damage sustained by a member of the public by reason of a failure to exercise that power." Lord Hoffmann was critical of both the basis on which Lord Wilberforce distinguished the *East Suffolk* case and the adequacy of his distinction between policy and operational decisions as a basis for defining when a duty was owed. However, he concluded by preferring to "leave open the question whether *Anns*' case was wrong to create any exception to Lord Romer's statement of principle in the *East Suffolk* case" and went on to consider the minimum conditions for justifying such a duty. These were

> "first, that it would in the circumstances have been irrational not to have exercised the power, so that there was in effect a public law duty to act, and secondly, that there are exceptional grounds for holding that the policy of the statute requires compensation to be paid to persons who suffer loss because the power was not exercised."[8c]

Lord Hoffmann suggested that failure to exercise a power would be irrational where it was exercised to provide a service as a matter of routine but arbitrarily withheld on the occasion in question. The routine exercise may have created a general expectation in the community that the power would continue to be exercised and a realisation by the authority that there was a general reliance on its exercise. He cited the examples of general reliance given by Mason J. in *Sutherland Shire Council v. Heyman*[8d]: the control of air traffic, the safety inspection of aircraft and the fighting of a fire. Lord Hoffmann considered that the exceptional grounds for holding that the policy of the statute requires compensation might include situations where the power was intended to protect members of the public from risks against which they could not guard themselves, or it might be found in the general patterns of socio-economic behaviour.[8e] Where there is a failure to perform a statutory duty, the courts will be concerned solely with the question of whether the policy of the statute requires compensation to be paid for loss caused by the failure. It should be noted that where a public body has represented that it will act in such a way as to create particular reliance by the plaintiff or a class of plaintiffs, then a duty of care may arise. Lord Hoffmann commented "This form of liability, based on representation and reliance, does not depend upon the public nature of the authority's powers and causes no problems".

In *Stovin v. Wise* the defendant highway authority having taken an internal decision to remove an earth bank adjacent to a road and which was impeding drivers' vision of the road, failed to implement the decision. The plaintiff was subsequently injured in a road accident caused in part by the impaired visibility resulting from the bank. By a majority, the House of Lords held that the authority owed no duty of care to the plaintiff to take positive steps to remove the earth bank. Applying the requirements of irrationality and exceptional grounds, Lord Hoffmann held that the highway authority had not acted irrationally as there could be no general reliance on road hazards being routinely removed and the plaintiff had not been arbitrarily deprived of a benefit provided to others. Furthermore, there was no legislative intent to impose a duty and any such duty would distort the budgetary priorities of local authorities. The tenor of Lord Hoffmann's judgment suggests that authorities will rarely, if ever, be liable for omissions. Whilst conceding that there might be general reliance on an authority exercising its inspection powers and that might justify a view that an arbitrary failure to inspect in a case such as *Anns* would be irrational, he argued that an exceptional ground was still required to support a duty. He noted that in *Murphy v. Brentwood DC*[8f] their Lordships not only held that an authority in an *Anns* situation would owe no duty in respect of the economic loss resulting from the need to repair the property, but were also "somewhat sceptical" of whether there could be any duty in respect of physical injury, for example, caused to the occupier by a dangerous defect. Even in the case of a fire service with the authority to fight a fire, Lord Hoffmann doubted whether a duty of care in respect of omissions would be justified.[8g]

NOTE 8a. [1996] 3 All E.R. 801, HL.

NOTE 8b. [1941] A.C. 74 at 102, [1940] 4 All E.R. 527 at 543, HL.

NOTE 8c. [1996] 3 All E.R. 801 at 828, HL.

NOTE 8d. (1985) 157 C.L.R. 424 at 464.

NOTE 8e. As exemplified by the Privy Council decision in *Invercargill City Council v. Hamlin* [1996] 1 All E.R. 756, [1996] 2 W.L.R. 367, PC.

NOTE 8f. [1991] 1 A.C. 398, [1990] 2 All E.R. 908, HL.

NOTE 8g. [1996] 3 All E.R. 801 at 829/830, HL. He cited the view of Mason J. in *Sutherland Shire Council v. Heyman* (1985) 157 C.L.R. 424 at 464, that a duty could be justified on the ground that "the power was intended to protect members of the public from risks against which they could not guard themselves". But he questioned whether this analysis was adequate when the public do protect themselves by insurance against the risk of fire and the consequence of a duty in respect of a negligent failure to respond to a fire might simply be to transfer funds from the fire service to the insurance companies with which people had insured.

NOTE 8g. Add: In *Capital and Counties plc v. Hampshire County Council* [1997] 2 All E.R. 865 at 876–877, CA, Stuart-Smith L.J. noting Lord Hoffmann's view that "there is not a general expectation that fires will necessarily be extinguished by the fire brigade", concluded that the appeared to be "no case, except *Anns* itself, which could be said to be an example of its [the doctrine of general reliance] application". In *OLL v. Secretary of State for Transport* [1997] 3 All E.R. 897 at 906, May J. read this passage in *Capital* as "in effect saying that in English Law no duty of care arises in cases such as this from a general expectation". He distinguished from the general duty to search and rescue, cases where there was a particular duty "derived from a specific expectation publicly induced and relied on," for example "that a lighthouse authority will not withdraw and existing light without giving due notice. See also *Hussain v. Lancaster City Council* [1999] 4 All E.R. 125, CA, where the Court of Appeal held that a local authority was under no duty to prevent council tenants from harassing nearby property owners. Hirst L.J. held that the facts did not fall within any of the special categories of duty identified by Lord Hoffman in *Stovin*, and following *Bedfordshire*, it would not be fair just and reasonable to impose a duty.

(3) *Justice and reasonableness*

7–104   The statutory scheme

7–105   NOTE 14. add: See also *W v. Home Office, The Times*, March 14, 1997, in which it was held that an immigration officer taking a decision whether to detain a person under the relevant legislation, did not owe a duty of care as the plaintiff had other remedies and imposition of a duty might lead to defensive decision making. Similarly, in *Blake & Brooks v. Barking & Dagenham L.B.* [1999] P.N.L.R. 171, it was held that the defendant authority owed no duty of care to the plaintiff tenant when valuing his flat for the purpose of fixing the price for its sale to the tenant, as the tenant had the right to seek an independent valuation from the district valuer if he was dissatisfied.

7–106   The public interest

In the *Newham* appeal, *X (minors) v. Bedfordshire County Council* [1995] 2 A.C. 633, HL, Lord Browne-Wilkinson held that imposition of a duty would not be fair, just and reasonable as it would encourage both undesirable, defensive practice by the authority and hopeless, costly litigation by plaintiffs. Similar reasoning was employed by the Court of Appeal in *Phelps v. Hillingdon London Borough Council* [1999] 1 W.L.R. 500, CA, to hold that an education authority owed no duty of care to pupil in relation to the diagnosis of dyslexia; and in *Harris v. Evans* [1998] 1 W.L.R. 1285, CA, to hold that a safety inspector owed no duty of care to a business suffering loss as a result of the inspector's closure of its operation. However, in *W v. Essex County Council* [1998] 3 W.L.R. 354, CA, the court held, Stuart-Smith L.J. dissenting, that an authority could owe a duty to warn a fostering family of a particular risk with regard to a child being placed with them as the policy arguments against imposing a duty were outweighed by the counter-argument that foster parents would be discouraged from coming forward if they believed that authorities might keep them ignorant of such risks. In *Barrett v. Enfield London Borough Council* [1999] 3 W.L.R. 628, the House of Lords refused to strike out a claim by a foster child in relation to allegedly negligent foster placements by the authority, on the ground that the public interest arguments had to be considered in the light of an investigation of the facts (see further *supra*, supplement § 1.05G). Note also that in *Att.-Gen. v. Prince & Gardner* [1998] 1 N.Z.L.R. 262, the New Zealand Court of Appeal whilst denying a duty in relation to adoption decisions, held that a duty of care could be owed in relation to the investigation of complaints about the conduct of adoptive or fostering parents.

The liability of the individual public servant   7–107
NOTE 26. Add: See also *Barrett v. Enfield London Borough Council* [1997] 3 W.L.R. 628, CA, in which Lord Woolf M.R. stated that "If it is not fair or just to make the authority liable for the way in which it exercised its discretion when caring for the plaintiff [a child alleged to have been placed by the authority with a series of inappropriate foster parents], then equally there would be no justification for placing the social workers who in practice would exercise the discretion on behalf of the local authority in any different position". However, Lord Woolf went on to suggest that "[s]ocial workers and other members of the staff could be negligent in an operational manner. They could ... be careless in ... reporting what they had observed for the purposes of an inter-disciplinary assessment of what action should be taken in relation to a child. They could also be negligent in failing to carry out instructions properly." The claim was struck out as there was no prospect of the evidence establishing that any such operational negligence had made any substantial contribution to the psychiatric injury in respect of which the plaintiff claimed.

NOTE 31. Add: See also *Lambert v. West Devon District Council, The Times,*   7–108
March 27, 1997, in which a local authority was held vicariously liable for negligent advice given by an employee.
NOTE 32. Add: Contrast *Phelps v. Hillingdon London Borough Council* [1999] 1 W.L.R. 500, CA, where the Court of Appeal classified the damage suffered by a plaintiff, whose dyslexia had not been diagnosed by an educational psychologist employed by the defendant education authority, as economic loss. Consequently, a duty could only be owed by the employee if she had assumed a personal responsibility to the plaintiff. Leading the Court of Appeal, Stuart-Smith L.J. concluded that: "her duty was to advise the school and the LEA. Merely because the plaintiff was the object of her advice and the parents were told in effect what the advice was, does not ... amount to such an assumption of responsibility." He noted that it was conceivable that if the plaintiff had approached the psychologist for private advice there might have been a sufficient assumption of responsibility but in such circumstances, the psychologist would have been acting outside the course of her employment and the defendant authority would not have been vicariously liable. Stuart-Smith L.J. also noted that policy grounds on which similar "educational malpractice" claims had been struck out in the United States, but commented that "in our jurisprudence" such arguments should be not treated as establishing an immunity, but rather as grounds for holding that there was no assumption of respons-

ibility or alternatively, that it would not be fair, just and reasonable to impose a duty in the absence of a clear assumption of responsibility.

(4) *Public service immunities*

7-109   Police immunity

The "police immunity" was applied in *OLL Ltd v. Secretary of State for Transport* [1997] 3 All E.R. 897 to cover the conduct of the coastguard in responding to distress signals on the ground that the situation was analogous to the police immunity in responding to 999 calls, and, in *Mulcahy v. Ministry of Defence* [1996] 2 W.L.R. 474, to servicemen operating in "battle conditions" by analogy with the *Hughes* decision. However, in *Capital and Counties plc v. Hampshire County Council* [1997] Q.B. 1004, CA, Stuart-Smith L.J. suggested that the immunity should not apply to the fire service. After considering criticisms of the immunity, he concluded:

> "In our judgment there is considerable force in the criticisms made. If we had found a sufficient relationship of proximity . . . we do not think that we would have found the arguments for excluding a duty of care on the grounds that it would not be just fair and reasonable. The analogy with the police exercising their functions of investigating or suppressing crime is not close. The floodgates argument is not persuasive; nor is that based on insurance. Many of the other arguments are equally applicable to other public services for example the National Health Service. We do not think that the principles which underlie those decisions where immunity has been granted can be sufficiently identified in the case of fire brigades."

In three recent decisions the Court of Appeal has held that exceptionally a duty may be owed in respect of matters related to the investigation of crime. In *Swinney v. Chief Constable of Northumbria* [1997] Q.B. 464, CA, it refused to strike out a claim by a person who had supplied information in confidence to the police and was then threatened following a leak of the information allegedly as a result of police negligence. It was considered arguable that the police had assumed a responsibility to the informant and that the policy arguments for immunity were outweighed by policy interest in encouraging informers to come forward without undue fear that their identity would be disclosed to others. In *Costello v. Chief Constable of Northumbria* [1999] 1 All E.R. 556, CA, the court followed *Swinney* when holding that a police officer who failed to go to the assistance of a colleague who was being attacked by a suspect, owed a duty of care as he had assumed a responsibility to his colleague. May L.J. considered that the policy supporting immunity was outweighed by the consideration that "the law should accord with common sense and public perception" and that "the public would be greatly disturbed if the law held there was no duty of care in this case". He distinguished *Waters v. Commissioner of Police of the Metropolis* [1997] I.C.R. 1073, CA, in which the court had rejected a female police officer's claim that her superiors owed her a duty of care to prevent harassment by colleagues, as not being concerned with operational circumstances. In the third decision, *Leach v. Chief Constable of Gloucestershire Constabulary* [1999] 1 All E.R. 215, CA, the court refused to strike out a claim by a lay person who had volunteered to sit in on the interviewing of a suspect, that the police authority owed her a duty of care in respect of offering post-interview counselling, given the horrific nature of the details disclosed in the interviews. The majority of the court considered that the duty did not extend to taking care in vetting volunteers or protecting them during the interview process as there was no assumption of such a responsibility and it would hinder the process of investigation.

7-110   In *Frost v. Chief Constable of South Yorkshire Police* [1997] 3 W.L.R. 1194, CA, Henry L.J. explained the relationship of *Hill, Hughes, Rigby,* and *Knightly* in the following terms: "I find no difficulty in the result reached in any of those four decisions. In *Hill* and *Hughes* it was for the police to decide on the priorities which dictated the scale of the response, and absent grounds for a *Wednesbury*-type challenge . . . the decision was one for the exercise of their discretion. But in *Rigby* and . . . the police (by their negligence) were creating the very danger they were engaged to prevent. Public policy does not render the force immune in such circumstances." Applying this reasoning to the facts in *Frost*, Henry L.J. said: "When planning for and dealing with crowd control on what should be a peaceful recreational occasion, I see no public policy justification for exempting chief constables . . . from the consequences of antecedent operational negligence which inevitably created one of the very dangers that the police presence was designed to prevent—namely fatal overcrowding." The issue was not considered by the other member of the Court of Appeal nor by the House of Lords which denied a duty on the basis of policy factors relating to the psychiatric nature of the police injuries: *White v. Chief Constable of South Yorkshire Police* [1999] 3 W.L.R. 1509, HL. A distinction similar to that drawn by Henry L.J. has emerged in the fire service case, *Capital and Counties plc v. Hampshire County Council* [1997] Q.B. 1004, CA, where, after noting the immunity cases of *Hill, Hughes* and *Ancell*, Stuart-Smith L.J. said that: "On the other hand liability has been imposed when, in the course of carrying out their duties, the police have themselves created the danger (see *Rigby v. Chief Constable of Northamptonshire, Knightly v. Jones, Alcock v. Chief Constable of South Yorkshire* and *Marshall v. Osmond*)."

Immunity for participants in legal proceedings   7–111
The extent of the advocate's immunity has been reviewed by the Court of Appeal in *Hall v. Simons* [1997] P.N.L.R. 374, CA. Giving the judgment of the court, Lord Bingham C.J. held that the first question was whether a claim against an advocate should be struck out as being an abusive collateral challenge to an earlier judgment of a court and if the claims were not struck out on that ground, then the court should consider secondly, whether the claim should be struck out on the grounds of the advocates' immunity. In applying the "abusive challenge" test, the court had to consider the nature and effect of the earlier judgment, the nature of the claim made in the later proceedings, and the grounds relied on to justify the collateral challenge. Lord Bingham noted that under this approach, greater weight would be "accorded to a criminal conviction than to a final judgment in a contested civil trial, and greater weight to the judgment in a contested civil trial than to an interlocutory judgment or consent order". Applying that test, he held that none of the claims in question should have been struck out on the abuse ground. Turning to the immunity ground, he stated that: "Save where a claim relates to the acts or omission of an advocate conducting a case in open court, forensic immunity is not to be recognised on the application of any blanket rule. It is always necessary to look with care at the specific complaint of negligence made against the lawyer in the context of the particular case." Once again, that immunity was not justified in respect of any of the claims. See further *post*, Supplement, § 8.69.

The extent of expert witness immunity has been reviewed by the Court of Appeal in *Stanton v. Callaghan* [1998] 4 All E.R. 961, CA. Chadwick L.J. held that the immunity extended to an expert agreeing a joint report with the other side's expert prior to a civil trial as it was necessary "in order to avoid the tension between the desire to assist the court and fear of the consequences of a departure from previous advice". Otton L.J. seemed to take a more pragmatic approach, holding that in each case it was a question whether "it would serve the interests of justice to grant immunity". Thus, a large firm of accountants providing expert advice on the basis of letters of engagement which provide an opportunity for excluding liability are in an entirely different position from a doctor providing an expert opinion with the minimum of legal formality or protection. On the particular facts, he agreed with Chadwick L.J. that "the duty to the court must override the fear of suit" and that the immunity was justified.

The extent of both advocate's and witness immunity may require reconsideration in the light of Article 6 of the European Convention on Human Rights which provides that "in the determination of his civil rights . . . everyone . . . is entitled to a fair hearing". See further *supra*, Supplement §§ 1–05A–1–05G.

4.—BREACH OF DUTY

(b) *The Criteria of Reasonableness*

(1) *Objectivity*

7–120   Sporting activity

NOTE 95. Add: In *Smoldon v. Whitworth & Nolan* [1997] P.I.Q.R. P133, CA, a rugby referee was held in breach of his duty to control the match so as to ensure that the players were not exposed to unnecessary risk of injury and to have particular regard to the fact that some of the players (including the injured plaintiff) were under the age of eighteen. Lord Bingham C.J. held that the plaintiff was not *volens* to the risk of injury, having consented to the ordinary incidents of the game and not to a breach of duty by the official whose duty it was to apply the rules of the game. See *Elliott v. Saunders* (1994) unreported, in which Drake J. doubted the suggestion in *Condon* that a higher degree of care was required in a first division match than in a local league match. The case concerned a Premiership match and on the evidence no negligence was established. In *McCord v. Swansea City FC, The Times,* February 11, 1997, it was held that a serious mistake by a football player which fell short of recklessness, was capable of giving rise to negligence liability. In *Watson v. Gray, The Times,* November 26, 1998, one professional footballer was held liable in negligence to another on the ground that a reasonable professional player would have known that the conduct created a significant risk of serious injury to the other.

7–122   Age

NOTE 4. Add: The approach taken in *McHale* was followed by the Court of Appeal in *Mullin v. Richards* [1998] 1 W.L.R. 1304, CA, where Hutchison L.J. stated that the test was "not whether the actions of the defendant were such as an ordinarily prudent and reasonable adult in the defendant's situation would have realised gave rise to a risk of injury" but "whether an ordinarily prudent and reasonable 15 year-old schoolgirl in the defendant's position would have realised as much".

(2) *Balancing cost and benefit*

7–126   Known abnormality of plaintiff

NOTE 16. Add: In *Davies v. Wyre Forest District Council* [1998] P.I.Q.R. P58, Alton J. in holding the design and supervision of a leisure pool to be negligent, commented: "There was some discussion as to whether that duty of care [for the plaintiff's safety when using the pool] is variable, and it must be right that how one performs a particular duty must depend upon the class of persons, for example, young, old, fit, disabled and the like, who one might reasonably anticipate will use the facility. If one anticipates a range of persons would use that facility then . . . surely the defendant must design to accommodate the safety of the broadest class of anticipated visitor. That is not, however, to say that if a fit, able person should have been in a position to safely negotiate a particular feature, he is entitled to succeed because an unfit or disabled person would not. In such circumstances a plaintiff would not be able to prove negligence as causative of his injury."

7–127   Degree of likelihood of harm

NOTE 23. Add: In *Gillon v. Chief Constable of Strathclyde, The Times,* November 22, 1996, it was held that the foreseeable risk of a police constable watching spectators at a football match would be injured by a player impelled off the pitch was so small that a reasonable man would not guard against it. In *AB v. Tameside & Glossop Health Authority* [1997] P.N.L.R. 147, CA, it was held that the decision to warn patients of the risk of HIV infection by letter rather than by a personal meeting with their GPs, was reasonable given the large number of patients to be contacted and the lack of evidence to show that any serious psychiatric injury would be likely to result from the postal communication.

NOTE 24. Add: In *Pearson v. Lighting, The Times,* April 30, 1998, CA, a golfer was held liable in negligence when his shot bounced off a tree and hit another player. He was playing a difficult shot and, although the risk of injury was small, it was foreseeable that someone might be injured if the shot went wrong.

Cost of precautions   7–129
NOTE 31. Add: See also *Nilsson v. Redditch Borough Council* [1995] P.I.Q.R. 199, in which an appeal against liability was allowed because the trial judge had failed to consider the issues of practicability and cost.

Lack of resources   7–130
Add to end of paragraph: But note that in *Walker v. Northumberland County Council*[42a] in the context of a local authority's duty to protect an employed social worker from work stress, Colman J. cited *Herrington* and stated that: "The practicability of remedial measures must clearly take into account the resources and facilities at the disposal of the person or body owing the duty of care and the purpose of the activity giving rise to the risk of injury".
NOTE 42a. [1995] I.C.R. 702, [1995] 1 All E.R. 737.

Public authorities and resource constraints   7–131
Add to end of paragraph: In *Walker v. Northumberland County Council*[53a] in the context of the duty of an employer public body to provide a safe system of work, Colman J. said of the resources issue: "there can be no basis for treating the public body differently *in principle* from any other commercial employer, although there would have to be taken into account considerations such as budgetary constraints and perhaps lack of flexibility of decision-taking which might not arise with a commercial employer."
NOTE 53a. [1995] I.C.R. 702, [1995] 1 All E.R. 737.

The utility of the activity   7–132
NOTE 54: Add: for a recent example of the liability of an emergency service crossing junction lights at red, see *Griffin v. Mersey Regional Ambulance* [1998] P.I.Q.R. P34, CA.

Cost/benefit analysis   7–133
NOTE 63. Add: The Learned Hand formulation was applied by the New Zealand Court of Appeal in *Wilson v. Horton v. Att.-Gen.* [1997] 2 N.Z.L.R. 513.

(3) *Community values*

Common practice   7–135
Add to end of paragraph: In *Ter Neuzen v. Korn*[78a] the Canadian Supreme Court held that whilst it was open to a jury to consider whether a common practice on a matter of ordinary common sense was consistent with what would be expected of the hypothetical reasonable man, this was not the case where the common practice was based on specialised and technical expertise. This could not be questioned.

NOTE 71. Add: Where there is no accepted standard of practice sanctioned by common usage, the court will view the matter as one to be determined by the general test of reasonableness applied to the totality of the evidence and not by expert evidence as to professional practice. See *AB and others v. Thameside & Glossop Health Authority* [1997] P.N.L.R. 140, CA (procedure for notifying former patients of a health worker found to be HIV positive); and *Brown v. Gould & Swayne* [1996] P.N.L.R. 130, CA (procedure for establishing client's right of way). But contrast *May v. Woollcombe Beer & Watts (a firm)* [1999] P.N.L.R. 283, where it was said that *Brown* required the court to be satisfied that evidence of practice was necessary. On the facts expert evidence was allowed as there was no guidance from text books or the Law Society.

NOTE 72. Add: In *Defreitas v. O'Brien* (1995) 6 Med. L.R. 108, the Court of Appeal stressed that in the professional context the question was whether there was a "responsible body of opinion" supporting the particular practice and that this was not to be measured in purely quantitative terms.

NOTE 77. Add: In *Bolitho v. City & Hackney H.A.* [1997] 4 All E.R. 771 at 779, HL, Lord Browne-Wilkinson, after citing *Edward Wong*, stated that: "if in a rare case, it can be demonstrated that the professional opinion is not capable of with-standing logical analysis, the judge is entitled to hold that the body of opinion is not reasonable or responsible".

NOTE 78a. (1995) 127 D.L.R. (4th) 577.

7–136 Safety codes
Add note 81a to end of paragraph.
NOTE 81a. In *Johnson v. Bingley* [1997] P.N.L.R. 392 the court held that a solicitor's breach of the Guide to Professional Conduct was not *ipso facto* negligence as the Guide was not mandatory.

7–137 Reasonable expectations
NOTE 87. Add: See the approach of Lord Woolf M.R. in *Pearce v. United Bristol Healthcare Trust* [1999] P.I.Q.R. P53, CA.

(c) *Particular Situations*

7–140 Carelessness on the highway
Add to end of paragraph: In *Liddell v. Middleton*[95a] the Court of Appeal commented that in road traffic cases it was the exception rather than the rule that expert witnesses were required. Expert evidence should be confined to matters outside the knowledge and experience of the layperson.
NOTE 95a. [1996] 5 P.I.Q.R. P36, CA.
NOTE 93. Add: In *Rosser v. Lindsay, The Times,* February 25, 1999, CA, it was held that the Highway Code requirement for frequent use of mirrors was not a prescriptive rule for drivers on a construction site but merely a useful guide and hence, the trial judge was entitled the treat the plaintiff's argument based on the Highway Code as a "counsel of perfection" and not an application of reasonable care.

7–141 Traffic accidents
NOTE 8. Add: a driver of an emergency vehicle may treat a red signal as a "Give Way" sign but may be liable for not proceeding with care, whilst a driver crossing on green and colliding with such an emergency vehicle may be held contributory negligent: *Griffin v. Mersey Regional Ambulance* [1998] P.I.Q.R. P34, CA.
NOTE 96. Add: In *Langley v. Dray and M.T. Motor Policies at Lloyds* [1998] P.I.Q.R. P314, CA, it was held that a joyrider, speeding to escape a pursuing police car, was liable for the personal injuries suffered by the police driver when the police car skidded and crashed. Stuart-Smith L.J. considered that the joyrider's failure to stop when required was not the cause of the accident but "merely gave occasion for the careless and dangerous driving which was the cause of the accident".

7–142 Pedestrian accidents
Add to end of paragraph: In *Griffiths v. Brown, The Times,* October 23 1998, it was held that a taxi driver setting down a drunk passenger, close to but on the other side of the road from his stated destination and near a pedestrian crossing, was not liable for his injuries sustained when crossing the road.
NOTE 25. Add: See also *Liddell v. Middleton* [1996] 5 P.I.Q.R. P36, CA.

Note 31. Add: Contrast *Widdowson v. Newgate Meat Corporation* [1998] P.I.Q.R. P138, CA, where the Court of Appeal based liability on the maxim *Res Ipsa Loquitur* in circumstances in which the defendant driver provided no explanation for having collided with the plaintiff pedestrian.

Highway authority liability 7–146
Note 57. Add: In *Cross v. Kirklees Metropolitan Council* [1998] 1 All E.R. 564, CA, it was held that the duty under section 41 was limited to taking reasonable steps to prevent the formation of ice or deal with it promptly after it had formed. On the facts, there was no liability to the plaintiff who had slipped on ice. See also *Goodes v. East Sussex County Council, The Times,* January 7, 1999.

Note 61. Add: See also *Cassin v. Besley London Borough Council, The Times,* February 15, 1999, CA, where an authority was held liable for removing keep left bollards without giving any motorists any warning of the resulting hazard.

(3) The standard of care of persons in charge of children

Parent and child 7–148
Note 68. Add: See also *Prince v. Attorney General* [1996] 3 N.Z.L.R. 733, where in the context of an action by a child alleging that the welfare authority had negligently allowed it to be adopted by inadequate parents, the court commented that an action by a child against its own parents for negligently inadequate parenting would be inimical to family relationships.

Note 69. Add: See also *Galaske v. O'Donnell* (1994) 112 D.L.R. (4th) 109, in which the Canadian Supreme Court held that a car driver must take reasonable steps to see that child passengers wear seat belts.

Note 70. Add: See also *B v. Arkin* (1996) 138 D.L.R. (4th) 309. No vicarious liability for child shoplifting. Liability only for negligent failure to control child.

Note 71. Add: See also *Curmi v. McLennan* [1994]1 V.R. 513, in which the Appeal Division of Victoria followed *Smith v. Leurs* in holding a father liable in circumstances where he had allowed his sixteen year old son and similar age friends to use a house boat for a week without removing an air gun from the boat. One of the boys accidently shot another with the gun: *Laplante v. Laplante* (1995)126 D.L.R. (4th) 569, see *supra*, § 7–38: and *Wince v. Ball* [1996] 136 D.L.R. (4th) 104, in which it was held that simply allowing a teenage drinking party would not result in liability being imposed on the parents for any resultant drink driving accidents. The parents would only be liable if it could be shown that they had contributed in some way to the drunk driving by a guest. See *ante*, § 7–41.

Teacher and pupil 7–149
Add to end of paragraph: Similar principles apply to those who offer sporting facilities to members of the public. Thus a local authority providing gymnastic activities at a youth centre must ensure that there is a proper system of instruction[88a] and those responsible for swimming pools must provide a safe system of supervision involving, if necessary, the prohibition of diving.[88b]

Note 79. Add: See now *Mullin v. Richards* [1998] 1 W.L.R. 1304, CA, where the teacher was held not liable at first instance for failing to prevent the classroom "ruler fencing" which led to injury to one of the schoolgirls involved.

Note 80. Add: In *Wilson v. The Governors of the Sacred Heart Roman Catholic School* [1998] P.I.Q.R. P145, CA, it was held that the school was not negligent in failing to supervise the departure of pupils to the school gate at the end of the day in the same way as the dinner break would have been supervised. Hirst L.J. said: "the very short period in which the pupils moved from the school building to the gate at the other end of the playground is quite different [from the dinner break period in the playground]. Moreover, and to my mind most importantly, there was no evidence that supervision at that juncture, as contrasted with the lunch break, is standard procedure, as it surely would be if it was a reasonable requirement."

Note 86. Add: But contrast *Nwabudike v. London Borough of Southwark* (unreported, May 8, 1996) where an authority was held not liable for injuries resulting from the "escape" of a child. The judge commented: "a balance had to be struck between security and preventing a school being turned into a fortress" and that "whatever precautions are taken there is always a risk particularly if a child is determined to act in a way which breaks the rules designed to protect him or her".

NOTE 88a. *Fowles v. Bedfordshire County Council* [1995] P.I.Q.R. P380. See also *Smoldon v. Whitworth & Nolan* [1997] P.I.Q.R. P133, CA, liability for failure to take adequate care in refereeing a rugby game and *Cassidy v. City of Manchester* (unreported, July 21, 1995, CA) liability for conduct of gymnasium game.

NOTE 88b. *O'Shea v. Royal Borough of Kingston on Thames* [1995] P.I.Q.R. P208, where prohibition of diving was the only safe system. See also *Nagle v. Rottnest Island Authority* (1992) 177 C.L.R. 423, where the High Court of Australia held that a warning sign would have been sufficient.

7–161   Liability to persons on the highway

NOTE 74. Add: See also *Rowe v. Herman, The Times*, June 9, 1997, CA, where Simon Brown L.J. explained that the liability for the work of an independent contractor arose where the work was being carried out under statutory powers and obstruction of the highway arose directly from the work and was integral to it. The rule did not apply where the occupier had a garage built by a contractor who covered the pavement with protective plates over which the plaintiff tripped.

(8) The standard of care in the employment relationship

7–164   The non-delegable nature of the duty

NOTE 1. Add: See also *Nelhams v. Sandells Maintenance Ltd* [1996] 5 P.I.Q.R. P52, CA.

7–166   Scope of the duty

NOTE 13. Add: Note that in *Lane v. Shire Roofing Co. (Oxford) Ltd, The Times*, February 22, 1995, the Court of Appeal commented that because of the importance of safety at work, it was in the public interest to recognise an employer-employee relationship where it existed. Applying this policy, the Court held that those hired "on the lump" to undertake roofing work were employees and were owed a duty of care by the employer.

7–172   Safe system of work

NOTE 64. Add: In *Armstrong v. British Coal Corporation, The Times*, December 6, 1996, CA, liability was based on the fact that by 1973 the employer should have realised that the system of working with vibratory tools gave rise to a reasonably foreseeable risk of the condition known as vibratory white finger. See also *King v. Smith, The Times*, November 3, 1994, in which it was held that a particular window cleaning operation was so inherently dangerous it should not have been performed at all. No system of work could have made it reasonably safe to undertake the operation.

Add to end of paragraph: In *Walker v. Northumberland County Council*[73a] Colman J. considered the standard of care required in providing a system of work which protected employees from the risk of psychiatric illness resulting from work stress and pressures. On the facts, it was held that the employer was not liable for the employee's first breakdown because the risk of such breakdown was not sufficiently high to justify precautions. However, the employer was liable for the employee's second breakdown suffered after he returned to work and came under the same level of stress. The court held that knowing of the real risk of further breakdown, the employer ought to have provided additional assistance to reduce the plaintiff's workload and in choosing to continue to employ the plaintiff without providing effective help, it had acted unreasonably and in breach of its duty of care.

NOTE 73a [1995] I.C.R. 702, [1996] 1 All E.R. 737.

68

Supervision   7–173
NOTE 76. Add: But see *Gibson v. British Rail Maintenance Ltd*, 1995 S.L.T. 953,
in which the Inner House of the Court of Session held that the trial judge was
entitled to find that the absence of a foreman from a workshop and the consequent
playing of a game of football by the employees which led to injury, amounted to a
negligent failure to provide adequate supervision.
Add: See also *Rozario v. Post Office* [1997] P.I.Q.R. P15, CA, in which an
employer was held not to be in breach in failing to supervise the lifting technique
of an employee. Stuart-Smith L.J. commented that it was a perfectly simple task
which the employee had been doing for many years.

(d) *Proof of carelessness*

Burden of proof   7–174
NOTE 86. Add: In *Pickford v. Imperial Chemical Industries plc* [1998] 1 W.L.R.
1189, HL, the plaintiff's claim in respect of repetitive strain injury failed. It was
held that the onus was on the plaintiff to prove that her condition had been caused
by repetitive movements whilst typing. Whilst the defendant employer's failure to
prove an alternative explanation was a factor to be taken into account in deciding
whether the plaintiff had discharged the onus, but it was not decisive as it still left
open the question of what caused the injury.
NOTE 93. Add: In *Vernon v. Bloomsbury Health Authority* [1995] 6 Med. L.R.
297, Tucker J. refused to reverse the burden of proof on the basis of *Clark v.
MacLennan.*

Inference of carelessness   7–175
NOTE 97. Add: In *Carroll v. Fearon* [1998] P.I.Q.R. P416, CA, it was held that negligence on the part of a manufacturer of a tyre having a lethal defect which led to tread
strip and an accident, was established by evidence of a defective manufacturing process
without any requirement to identify a responsible individual or act of negligence. It
followed from the fact that if the process had worked as intended, the defect should not
have been present. See also *Wisniewski v. Central Manchester Health Authority* [1998]
P.I.Q.R. P324, CA, where Brooke L.J. held that the trial judge was entitled to treat the
doctor's failure to give evidence "in the face of a charge that his negligence had been
causative, as strengthening the plaintiff's case on causation".

Occurrence cannot normally happen without negligence   7–177
Add to end of paragraph: In *Delaney v. Southmead Hospital Authority*[19a] the Court
of Appeal in holding that the application of *res ipsa loquitur* to a anaesthesia incident
was rebutted by evidence that common practice had been followed, commented that
it was doubtful if the maxim was of much help in medical negligence cases as
medical science was not so precise as to anticipate the precise risk of carrying out
routine procedures. There was always room for the wholly unexpected result to
occur even when the correct procedure was followed.
NOTE 19a. (1992) 26 B.M.L.R. 111, [1995] 6 Med. L.R. 355, CA. See also
Howard v. Wessex R.H.A. [1994] 5 Med. L.R. 56.

Cause of occurrence unknown to plaintiff   7–179
NOTE 27. Add; See also *Hay v. Grampian Health Board* [1995] 6 Med. L.R. 128,
where it was held that the maxim had no application to a suicide attempt by a
depressed patient as the circumstances were fully known.

Procedural effect of doctrine   7–180
NOTE 32. Add: See also *Glass v. Cambridge H.A.* [1995] 6 Med. L.R. 91, where
it seems to have been assumed that the maxim shifted the burden of proof.
NOTE 34. Add: This passage was cited and applied in *Widdowson v. Newgate
Meat Corporation* [1998] P.I.Q.R. P138, CA, where the Court of Appeal applied the
maxim to driver who provided no explanation for having collided with a pedestrian.

6.—FORESEEABILITY AND ACTIONABILTY

(a) *Factual Duty: Foreseeability of Damage to the Plaintiff*

7–184   NOTE 44. Add: *In Margereson v. JW Roberts Limited* [1996] P.I.Q.R. P154, Holland J. rejected a two stage approach consisting of "First, . . . a finding as to whether any risk of personal injury to anyone was foreseeable; and second, if the answer be 'yes' then [a] further finding as to whether [the plaintiffs] were within the ambit of such foreseeability." Rather, there was a single issue: ". . . ought the defendants at any material time have reasonably foreseen that their conduct would expose [the plaintiff] to the risk of personal injury so as to come under a duty of care to him." As authority Holland J. cited Lord Lloyd in *Page v. Smith* [1996] 1 A.C. 190; "The test in every case ought to be whether the defendant can reasonably foresee that his conduct will expose the plaintiff to risk of personal injury. If so, then he comes under a duty of care to that plaintiff." Russell L.J., giving the judgment of the Court of Appeal, [1996] P.I.Q.R. P358, also cited Lord Lloyd when affirming the decision of Holland J. that a manufacturer responsible for the escape of asbestos dust from its premises owed a duty of care to children living in the vicinity who had played with the dust and susbequently contracted the lung disease mesothelioma.

(b) *Remoteness: Foreseeability of the Kind of Damage*

7–189   NOTE 76. Add: In the asbestos pollution case, *Margereson v. JW Roberts Limited* [1996] P.I.Q.R. P358, Russell L.J., giving the judgment of the Court of Appeal, said: ". . . we take the view that liability only attaches to these defendants if the evidence demonstrates that they should reasonably have foreseen a risk of some pulmonary injury, not necessarily mesothelioma."

7–189   **Categorisation of kind of damage**
        Add to end of paragraph: In *R.v. Croydon Health Authority*[79a] the Court of Appeal applied the dictum of Lord Denning in *Roe v. Minister of Health* [1954] 2 Q.B. 56 at 85, that the consequence had "fairly to be regarded as withing the risk created by the negligence", to hold that the cost of bringing up a child did not fall within the risk created by a radiologist's negligent failure to diagnose a heart defect in the plaintiff who would not have become pregnant had she known of the defect. The plaintiff was awarded compensation for medical complications which would not have arise but for the negligent delay in diagnosing the defect. Kennedy L.J. cited the speech of Lord Hoffmann in *Banque Bruxelles SA v. Eagle Star* (see annotation to paragraph 7–196) as further authority for the proposition that the kind of damage must fall within the scope of the duty broken to be recoverable.[79b]
        But contrast *Wisniewski v. Central Manchester Health Authority*[79c] where Brooke L.J. considered Lord Hoffmann's speech but rejected the defendant's argument that "the harm which befell [the plaintiff] during his passage down his mother's birth canal (in effect, strangulation because the umbilical cord was looped around his neck . . .) was quite different from the harm to which the health authority's breach of duty had wrongfully exposed him (the risk of damage by oxygen starvation within the womb)". Such a distinction would have been "an affront to common sense, and the law would look an ass, if we reached any different conclusion". He confirmed the view of the trial judge that "it makes no difference, in these circumstances that the precise mechanism by which the later, much more serious hypoxia arose, was not foreseeable".
        NOTE 79a. [1998] P.I.Q.R. Q26, CA.
        NOTE 79b. See also *Hunter v. British Coal Corp.* [1998] 2 All E.R. 97 at 122, CA, where Hobhouse L.J., dissenting, explained the Australian decision in *Rowe v. McCartney* [1976] 2 N.S.W.L.R. 72, on the ground that the guilt induced psychiatric illness suffered by the plaintiff was outside the scope of any duty of care owed by the defendant who was injured as a result of negligently driving the plaintiff's car.

Brooke L.J. accepted the view that the the illness was not a foreseeable consequence of the events.
NOTE 79c. [1998] P.I.Q.R. P324, CA.

Manner of causation   7–190
NOTE 83. Add: In *Jolley v. London Borough of Sutton* [1998] 3 All E.R. 559, the defendant was held to be in breach of its duty of care in failing to remove from its land an abandonned boat which was a reasonably foreseeable cause of injury to children because of its allurement and dangerous condition. However, it was held not liable for the injury sustained when the boat fell on a child who was attempting to raise it with a car jack in order to attempt repairs. The injury was not caused by the allurement or dangerous condition of the boat but by an unforeseeable conduct on the part of the boy.
NOTE 96. Add: For a recent example of the egg-shell skull rule, see *Singh v.*   7–192
Aitken [1998] P.I.Q.R. Q37.

(2) Economic loss

Pure economic loss   7–196
Add to end of paragraph: In three appeals from the *Banque Bruxelles* litigation going under the name of *South Australia Asset Management Corp. v. York Montague Ltd*,[27a] the House of Lords reversed the ruling of the Court of Appeal. Giving the unanimous opinion of the House of Lords, Lord Hoffmann held that the plaintiff must show that he was owed "a duty in respect of the kind of loss which he has suffered". In the case of a valuer whose only duty is to supply information as opposed to providing investment advice, "he must take reasonable care to insure that the information is correct and if he is negligent, will be responsible for all the foreseeable consequences of the information being wrong." This meant that he could not be responsible for much of the loss due to the market fall, for such loss would have occurred even if the information had been correct. Although in *South Australia* the valuer was sued on contract, Lord Hoffmann held that the same principle was applicable to tort actions and had been implicit in the decision in *Banque Keyser Ullman SA v. Skandia (U.K.) Insurance Co.* In *Brown v. KMR Services Ltd*[27b] the Court of Appeal cited the judgment of Sir Thomas Bingham in *Banque Bruxelles* for the proposition that "if the kind of damage was reasonably foreseeable it is immaterial that the extent of the damage is not". Consequently, the court in *Brown* held that a members' agent was liable to a Lloyd's name for underwriting loss even though the extent of such loss was unprecedented. The loss was of the kind that was foreseeable. Although *Brown* was a contract decision, the same principle would apply to a tort action and, it is submitted, that it remains unaffected by the *South Australia* decision. Provided the loss is reasonably foreseeable and falls within the scope of the duty of care owed by the defendant, the fact that the extent of the loss was unforeseeable should remain immaterial.
NOTE 27a. [1996] 3 W.L.R. 87; [1996] 3 All E.R. 365, HL. The principle has been applied by Laddie J. in *BCCI v. Price, Waterhouse (No. 3), The Times*, April 2, 1998, in holding that auditors were not liable to clients in relation to trading losses as the duty of care was limited to informing shareholders whether the accounts gave a true and fair view of the client's financial position and did not extend to protecting the client from future trading losses.
NOTE 27b. [1995] 4 All E.R. 598.

7.—EXTENT OF RESPONSIBILITY APPORTIONED TO THE DEFENDANT

The principles of apportionment   7–198
NOTE 36. Add: In *Reeves v. Commissioner of Police of the Metropolis* [1998] 2 All E.R. 381, CA, Morritt L.J., dissenting, preferred the prior Court of Appeal decision in *Jayes v. IMI (Kynoch) Ltd* [1985] I.C.R. 155, CA, to which the court in

Pitts was not referred and which upheld an apportionment of 100 per cent. Of the majority judges, Bingham C.J. suggested that *Jayes* should be "properly understood as based on causation", and Buxton L.J., whilst accepting on the basis of *Jayes* that there was no rule of law against a 100 per cent deduction, held that it would be inappropriate where the plaintiff's fault [in committing suicide] was the very thing "that the defendant had a duty to take steps to prevent". See also *Wynbergen v. Hoyts Corporation Pty Ltd* [1998] 72 A.L.J.R. 65, in which the High Court of Australia approved the view taken in *Pitts*.

7–200 **Overlap of contributory negligence and contribution**
NOTE 44. Add: The approach taken in *Fitzgerald* was applied to economic loss by the Supreme Court of New South Wales in *A.W.A. Ltd v. Daniels* (1992) 9 A.C.S.R. 383.

NOTE 45. Add: The Law Commission consultative document *Feasibility Investigation of Joint and Several Liability* (1996) rejected the proportionate recover principle as unworkable, not least because of its incompatibility with the decision in *Fitzgerald v. Lane and Patel.*

CHAPTER 8.—PROFESSIONAL LIABILITY

PARA.

■1. General considerations 8–01
■2. Medicine and allied professions 8–25
    (a) Consent to treatment 8–26
    (b) Medical negligence 8–34
■3. Law
    (a) Barristers 8–69
    (b) Solicitors 8–75
■4. Surveyors 8–97
■5. Architects and consulting engineers 8–115
■6. Finance 8–125

Noteworthy developments since the last edition include (1) the decisions in *Re*   **8–01**
M.B. [1997] 2 F.L.R. 837, and *St George's Hospital Trust v. S* [1998] 3 All E.R.
673, dealing with the right unreasonably to refuse treatment; (2) *Bolitho v. Hackney*
H.A. [1997] 3 W.L.R. 1151 [1997] 4 All E.R. 771 HL, dealing with the application
of the *Bolam* test in medical negligence cases; (3) *Kelley v. Corston* [1998] 3 W.L.R.
246, [1997] 4 All E.R. 466 and *Hall v. Simons* [1999] P.N.L.R. 374, on the extent
of legal advisers' immunity in respect of mismanagement of court proceedings; (4)
South Australia Asset Management v. York Montague [1996] 3 W.L.R. 87 [1996] 3
All E.R. 365 and *Platform Home Loans v. Oyston Shipways* [1999] P.N.L.R. 469 on
the measure of damages for misvaluation by a mortgagee's surveyor; (5) a recent
string of authority about what may amount to contributory negligence in a mortgagee
who relies on such a negligent valuation (see *post*, Supplement § 8–114); (6) *Mort-*
gage Express Ltd v. Bowerman & Partners (No. 2) [1996] 1 P.N.L.R. 62 and
Nationwide Building Society v. Balmen Radmore [1999] P.N.L.R. 606 dealing with
the position of a solicitor acting for both mortgagor and mortgagee; and (7) *Allied*
Maples v. Simmons & Simmons [1995] 1 W.L.R. 1602; [1995] 4 All E.R. 907 and
subsequent decisions on recovery for loss of a chance.

1.—General Considerations

NOTE 9: Add: See the informative borderline case of *Ter Neuzen v. Korn* (1995)   **8–03**
127 D.L.R. (4th) 577 (arranging supply of semen does not count as supplying goods
so as to attract strict liability).

Duties in tort and contract: concurrent liability   **8–10**
In *Powell v. Baldaz* (1997) 39 B.M.L.R. 35; [1998] Lloyd's Rep. (Med.) 117, a
boy died: his parents alleged that the cause of death had been concealed by the
doctors who had treated him and they had suffered psychological illness. The doctors
were held to owe no duty to the parents in the circumstances.
    On concurrent liability, see too *Holt v. Payne Skillington* [1996] P.N.L.R. 179,
where the Court of Appeal observed that there was no inherent impossibility (as
against unlikelihood) of a tort duty being wider than a contractual one. Thus where
surveyors who had not been retained to advise purchasers on planning matters nevertheless chose to do so, it was held that they owed a duty of care in respect of the
advice provided (though in the event the claim failed on the facts).

Duties to third parties   **8–12**
On duties to third parties, note too *Anthony v. Wright* [1995] 1 B.C.L.C. 237

(where trustees engaged auditor to supervise trust investments, auditor's duty owed to them alone and not direct to beneficiaries of trust).

See too *Palmer v. Tees N.H.S. Trust* [1998] Lloyd's Rep. (Med) 447 (mental hospital not liable for failing to take steps to supervise or control unstable out-patient who brutalised and murdered little girl).

NOTE 51. Add: See too the Canadian decision in *Brown v. University of Alberta Hospital* (1997) 145 D.L.R. (4th) 63.

8–13   On third party liability, see generally Hedley [1995] CLJ 27 and Haydon [1996] CLJ 238. It is now clear that a doctor instructed by an employer to examine a prospective employee to determine his suitability for the post owes no duty of care to that employee. The doctor acts on behalf of the employer, not the candidate, and is under no duty to the latter: see *Kapfunde v. Abbey National plc,* [1999] Lloyd's Rep. (Med.) 48, overruling *Baker v. Kaye* (1997) 39 B.M.L.R. 12.

On architects' duties to third parties, see *Machin v. Adams* (1997) 84 B.L.R. 79 (architect employed by building owner to inspect building for faults owes no duty to prospective purchaser).

NOTE 52. Add: On *Henderson v. Merrett Syndicates Ltd*, see too *Aiken v. Stewart Wrightson* [1995] 1 W.L.R. 1281 (Lloyd's sub-agent owes duty to future Names likely to be affected by present incompetent underwriting).

8–14 **Excluding a duty of care**
On exclusion of liability, see too *McCullagh v. Lane Fox & Partners Ltd* [1996] P.N.L.R. 205 (presence of an exclusion clause in particulars of sale held to negative any *Hedley Byrne* duty to purchaser by making it unforeseeable that purchaser would rely on it) and also *Omega Trust v. Wright, Son & Pepper* [1997] P.N.L.R. 424.

8–15   See too *McCullagh v. Lane Fox & Partners Ltd* [1996] P.N.L.R. 205 (sophisticated purchaser of very expensive London house unable to invoke Unfair Contract Terms Act to invalidate exemption clause in particulars of sale). There are also suggestions in Hobhouse L.J.'s judgment that this may apply to particulars of sale generally in view of the universal assumption that "the intending purchaser, before he exchanges contracts, is able through his own solicitor to interrogate the proposed vendor and is entitled to rely upon the answers to such enquiries as representations which have induced the contract with all the legal consequences that flow from that situation".

Immunities from suit
8–20   In *N v. C* [1998] 1 F.L.R. 63, a valuer appointed by a court to appraise property the subject of a financial provision order was held not to be covered by arbitrator's immunity (though the action failed on other grounds).

8–23 **Equitable obligations: confidential information**
On confidentiality, see too the Canadian decision in *Peters-Brown v. Regina District Health Board* [1997] 1 W.W.R. 638 (liability for nervous shock when hospital negligently lost plaintiff's embarrassing medical records).

2.—MEDICINE AND ALLIED PROFESSIONS

8–25 **Liability of medical practitioners**
Two cases concern the liability of a medical practitioner to third parties. In *Newell & Newell v. Goldenberg* [1995] 6 Med. L.R. 371 a doctor carrying out a vasectomy which failed was accepted to owe a duty not only to the patient but to his wife. But in *Goodwill v. British Pregnancy Advisory Service* [1996] 1 W.L.R. 1397 the Court of Appeal declined to hold that any such duty was owed to the client's future mistress, of whom the doctor had no knowledge, but who later became pregnant by him. Compare, too, *Palmer v. Tees NHS Trust* [1998] Lloyd's Rep.

(Med) 447 (hospital not liable for failure to take steps to supervise demented out-patient who killed and mutilated little girl).

NOTE 17. Add: In *Morrison v. Forsyth* [1995] 6 Med. L.R. 6 it seems to have been accepted that a doctor could be under a duty to visit (though the claim failed for lack of proof that no reasonable doctor would have refused in the circumstances).

(a) *Consent to Treatment*

Adults   8–26

In *St George's Hospital Trust v. S* [1998] 3 All E.R. 673, the Court of Appeal trenchantly reaffirmed the right of an individual to refuse treatment, however unreasonably. A pregnant mother refused medical attention, knowing that if she had her child at home she and it would probably die. Forcible treatment was ordered. She sued the hospital authority, and (save for where the hospital was protected from liability by the provisions of the Mental Health Act 1983) was held to be entitled to damages. On what will vitiate refusal to submit to treatment so as to justify court intervention, see now *Re MB* [1997] 8 Med. L.R. 217, [1997] 2 F.L.R. 837 (patient had no objection to treatment as such, but prior injection necessary to carry out treatment and patient had morbid phobia of needles: Court of Appeal upheld order for treatment despite refusal).

See generally Skene, *When can doctors treat patients who cannot or will not consent?* (1997) 23 Monash L.R. 77.

For some practical guidance to doctors faced with such situations, see *R. v. St George's Healthcare Trust (No. 2), The Times,* August 3, 1998.

The viable foetus   8–27

On the relevance of the interests of a possible unborn child, see now *Re MB* [1997] 2 F.L.R. 837. There the Court of Appeal expressed the view adumbrated in the text: an unborn child not being a legal person, its best interests did not fall to be considered at all. It followed that they could not be invoked to override a clear refusal of treatment by the prospective mother. *Re S* [1992] W.L.R. 806 must presumably now be regarded as discredited. See too the decision of the Court of Appeal in *St George's Hospital Trust v. S* [1998] 3 All E.R. 673 (no right forcibly to perform Caesarian operation on mother even though without it both mother and child liable to die). And similarly in Canada: *Winnipeg Child & Family Services v. G* (1997) 152 D.L.R. (4th) 193.

See too *Appleton v. Garrett* [1997] 8 Med.L.R. 75. A dishonest dentist massively   8–28
overtreated his patients in order to defraud the NHS and increase his own income. He was held liable to the patients for assault, apparently on the basis that their acquiescence had been obtained by fraud and was ineffective. *Sed quaere*: it is very hard to reconcile this with the reasoning in *Chatterton v. Gerson* [1981] Q.B. 432, or with the very similar criminal case of *R. v. Richardson* [1998] 2 Cr.App.R. 200, where in almost identical circumstances a conviction for assault was quashed.

On when a child is "*Gillick* competent", see too *Re L* [1998] 2 F.L.R. 810.   8–29

Younger children   8–31

NOTE 48. See too *Re T (a minor)* [1997] 1 All E.R. 906.

Mentally incapacitated patients   8–32

Note that "treatment" under section 63 of the 1983 Act includes force-feeding: *B v. Croydon Health Authority* [1995] 1 F.L.R. 470. And in *R. v. Bournewood NHS Trust, ex p. L* [1998] 3 W.L.R. 107, the House of Lords held that an informal patient who, owing to autism, was incapable of expressing assent or dissent could lawfully be treated at common law under the doctrine of necessity, provided such treatment was in his own best interests.

See too *Re T* [1998] 1 F.L.R. 48 (disturbed, but not incapacitated, 25-year-old   8–33
refuses kidney dialysis: held, competent to do so, and no jurisdiction to intervene).

8–34   In *Bolitho v. Hackney Health Authority* [1997] 3 W.L.R. 1151, the House of Lords held that the *Bolam* principle applied to hypothetical as well as to actual treatment. A hospital doctor negligently failed to attend a child, who later died. The authority resisted the estate's claim on the basis that even if she had attended, the doctor would have recommended no treatment and hence the child would have died anyway. The patient countered by alleging such a recommendation would itself have been negligent. Held: in considering the latter question, *Bolam* should be applied.

8–35   On the *Bolam* test, it was held in *De Freitas v. O'Brien* [1995] 6 Med. L.R. 108, that the existence of even a relatively small body of opinion (a mere 11 spinal surgeons) could suffice to acquit the defendant of negligence. However, in the significant decision in *Bolitho v. Hackney Health Authority* [1997] 3 W.L.R. 1151, the House of Lords emphasised that the *Bolam* test should be applied cautiously and realistically. Lord Browne-Wilkinson emphasised that the mere presence of a supportive body of opinion would not of itself exonerate the defendant: the opinion concerned had in addition to be "responsible" and "reasonable". It had to have a logical basis, and where the weighing of comparative risks was in account, it had to be shown that those advancing the opinion had directed their minds to the matter and reached a defensible conclusion about it. (See [1997] 4 All E.R. 771, 778, *eq seq.*). See too *Newell v. Goldberg* [1995] 6 Med.L.R. 371, *per* Mantell J. (holding that in the circumstances the view advanced on the defendant doctor's behalf was neither responsible nor reasonable, and declining to take account of it).

Note also *Sharpe v. Southend Health Authority* [1997] 8 Med. L.R. 299, where Cresswell J. emphasised that a medical expert testifying as to the correct method of treatment should state whether in his opinion there was a responsible body of practitioners who might disagree with him.

On *Bolam* generally, see Davies [1996] 12 P.N. 120.

8–37   **Failure to warn: negligence**

On the duty to warn, see too the Canadian Supreme Court decision in *Ciarlariello v. Schacter* [1995] 6 Med. L.R. 213 (once effect of operation properly explained, no duty to do so again when operation temporarily halted, even though patient conscious).

Note that the duty to warn may apply even where the treatment proposed is clinically impeccable, but for cosmetic or other reasons the patient may reasonably want to know of the alternatives. See *Williamson v. East London & City Health Authority* [1998] 1 Lloyd's Rep. (Med.) 6, (failure to tell patient that alternative to mastectomy possible: patient recovers £20,000 for trauma over lost breast).

8–40   See also *Howarth v. Adey* [1996] 2 V.R. 535 (Supreme Court of Victoria), holding that a gynaecologist's duty to warn of the risks inherent in a risky obstetric procedure is owed not only to the mother but to the child as well. Hence where a child was born with cerebral palsy as a result of failure to warn, the child could sue.

8–41   **Failure to warn: causation**

NOTE 2. But a different result has been reached in Canada: *Reibl v. Hughes* (1980) 114 D.L.R. (3d) 1 (Supreme Court), and *cf. Smith v. Arndt* (1997) 148 D.L.R. (4th) 488, SCC.

8–42   **Breach of duty: general**

Note also *Vernon v. Bloomsbury Health Authority* [1995] 6 Med. L.R. 297 (where the condition is life-threatening and immediate measures are required, doctor is to be leniently judged: it is not negligent in the circumstances considerably to exceed the recommended dose of gentamicin for endocarditis).

NOTE 4. Add: See too *Djemal v. Bexley Health Authority* [1995] 6 Med. L.R. 269.

8–45   **Breach of duty: diagnosis**

See also the fairly significant decision in *Mahmood v. Siggins* [1996] 7 Med. L.R.

76 (doctor should have realised patient was manic depressive, but took no steps to refer to community mental health team: liable when patient killed himself). And see too *Clunis v. Camden Health Authority*, [1998] 2 W.L.R. 902.

A doctor's liability for failing to diagnose an ailment and bring it to his patient's attention may on occasion be limited by the purpose for which the examination is carried out. In *R. v. Croydon Health Authority*. [1998] P.I.Q.R. 626; [1998] 1 Lloyd's Rep. (Med.) 44 a doctor examining a patient on behalf of a prospective employer failed to notice pulmonary hypertension. As a result the patient later went on to have a child, which she would not have done had she been informed that she had the disease. Her action for the costs of bringing up the child failed. Although the defendants admitted liability for the suffering caused by complications in pregnancy, the Court of Appeal left it open whether that admission had been rightly made, since the purpose of the examination had not been to appraise the plaintiff's fitness for childbirth.

Conversely, there is Canadian authority that where in the course of examining a child or vulnerable patient a practitioner discovers evidence of cruelty, he may be negligent in not passing it on to others involved. See *Brown v. University of Alberta Hospital* (1997) 145 D.L.R. (4th) 63.

Breach of duty: planning treatment and prescribing 8–46
A doctor may disregard a very slight risk without fear of an action for negligence: see, e.g. *Pearce v. United Bristol Healthcare* [1999] P.I.Q.R. P53 (doctor entitled to disregard a 0.1–0.2% risk of stillbirth in pregnant woman).

Note that a doctor is entitled to refuse to prescribe treatment which he reasonably considers unnecessary, even where such treatment is otherwise harmless and the patient is prepared to pay for it. See *Rhodes v. Spokes* [1996] 7 Med. L.R. 135 (doctor not negligent in refusing to order CT scan despite patient's offer to bear cost, even though in the event this might have revealed undetected illness and enabled earlier treatment of it).

Breach of duty: errors in treatment 8–47
When discharging a hospital patient, a doctor may be negligent if he does not warn the patient to contact him if disquieting symptoms recur: *Joyce v. Wandsworth Health Authority* [1996] 7 Med. L.R. 1 (in fact the claim failed on causation grounds).

On *res ipsa loquitur* in medial negligence cases, see now *Ratcliffe v. Plymouth* 8–50
Health Authority [1998] Lloyd's Rep. (Med.) 162, where Brooke L.J. at 172 limited the application of the maxim to cases of straightforward medical foolishness and declined to apply it to a case where a spinal injection had engendered a neurological complaint.

Failed sterilisation 8–57
Note *Crouchman v. Cleveland Medical Laboratories* (unreported, July 9, 1997) (person performing sterilisation has duty to check if patient already pregnant; liable for failure to do so with result that unplanned child born).

In *Sabrini-Tabrizi v. Lothian H.B.* 1998 S.L.T. 608, the Court of Session held, not surprisingly, that where the plaintiff continued to indulge in unprotected sexual intercourse after discovering that her sterilisation surgery might have failed, this broke the chain of causation and she could not recover in respect of a subsequent pregnancy.

NOTE 80. Add: Similar doubts were expressed in Scotland, but the Inner House of the Court of Session has now followed the *Emeh* line: *McFarlane v. Tayside H.B.* 1998 S.L.T. 308. For the measure of damages in such a case, see *McLelland v. Greater Glasgow H.B.* 1998 S.C.L.R. 1081 (whole costs of bringing up mongol child recoverable, with no deduction for putative costs of healthy child).

NOTE 81. In Canada it has been held that the duty to carry out the abortion with reasonable care is owed only to the mother, at least where she is not living with the father. Thus the father could not sue for the extra expense he had to incur by way of maintenance for an unplanned bastard child: see *Freeman v. Sutter* [1996] 4 W.W.R. 749.

NOTE 83. See too *Lybert v. Warrington Health Authority* [1996] 7 Med. L.R. 71.

8–61   Liability of other allied professions

On allied professions see too *X v. Bedfordshire County Council* [1995] 3 All E.R. 353 (local authority psychiatrist advising on possible child abuse owes no duty to parents or child because of public policy, but does owe a duty in advising on a child's educational needs), and *Barrett v. Enfield* [1999] 3 W.L.R. 79.

NOTE 9. Add: And *cf. Prince v. Att.-Gen.* [1996] 3 N.Z.L.R. 783 (social workers reporting on potential adopters owe no duty to adoptee who alleged adoptive parents entirely unsuitable). But in *W v. Essex County Council* [1998] 3 W.L.R. 534, the Court of Appeal refused to strike out a claim against a social worker for failure to inform prospective foster-parents about the rampant sexual demands of a child placed with them, who proceeded to brutalise another child within the same family. See too *Phelps v. Hillingdon Borough Council* [1999] 1 W.L.R. 500 (council educational psychologist undertakes, and owes, no duty of care re diagnosis of dyslexia in individual child).

8–62   Liability of hospitals and health authorities

In *AB & Others v. Tameside & Glossop Health Authority* [1997] P.N.L.R. 140 ex-patients at a number of hospitals, informed (correctly) by the defendant health authority that someone who had treated them was HIV positive, alleged nervous shock resulting from the defendants' insensitive method of communicating this information to them. It was conceded by counsel for the defendants, but pointedly not decided by the CA, that a duty of care was owed in these circumstances. In the event the plaintiffs failed to show negligence and hence their action failed. See (1997) 13 P.N. 70.

8–63   Health authorities and professionals not employed by them

On the liability of health authorities, see now *Robertson v. Nottingham AHA* [1997] 8 Med. L.R. 113, where Brooke L.J. in the CA stated that health authorities were under a personal, non-delegable, duty to see that care was taken in providing treatment. His Lordship specifically invoked the analogy of the employer's non-delegable duty as exemplified in cases such as *McDermid v. Nash Dredging* [1987] A.C. 906. See too the similar result reached in the county court case of *M v. Calderdale Health Authority* [1998] Lloyd's Rep. (Med.) 157 (health authority contracted out treatment to private hospital: liable for shortcomings of that hospital's employees).

8–66   Causation: loss of a chance of recovery

On *Hotson v. East Berkshire AHA* [1987] A.C. 750 see too *Richardson v. Kitching* [1995] 6 Med. L.R. 257, another case of culpable non-diagnosis. Also *Green v. Chenoweth* [1998] 2 Qd.R. 572 (*Hotson* applied to doctor's failure to warn of consequences).

3.—LAW

(a) *Barristers*

8–69   Immunity from suit

In *Griffin v. Kingsmill & Ors* (unreported, February 20, 1998), the Court of Appeal held that forensic immunity could not apply to advice as to settlement before proceedings had been begun. (However, it struck out the plaintiff's claim on the basis that the settlement had been on behalf of an infant which required the approval of the court, and that the present action amounted to a collateral risk on the court's order: on which, see below).

The advocate's immunity in respect of settlement of proceedings which have been commenced has now been thrown into some confusion as a result of two decisions in the Court of Appeal.

In *Kelley v. Corston* [1998] Q.B. 686; [1998] P.N.L.R. 37, Pill and Butler-Sloss L.J. accorded forensic immunity to a barrister who settled on ancillary relief claim at the door of the court, on the basis that the settlement negotiations were intimately connected with the hearing of the cause (following *Biggar v. McLeod* [1997] 1 N.Z.L.R. 321). Judge L.J. disagreed on this point (but he held that the claim against the advocate fell to be struck out as a collateral attack on the judge's consent order, a conclusion with which the other members of the court agreed *obiter*: on this point see below).

In *Hall v. Simons* [1999] P.N.L.R. 374, however, a differently constituted Court of Appeal refused to strike out claims against solicitors for alleged negligence in settling ancillary relief claims, including one case where the settlement had been made at the door of the court. Lord Bingham C.J., having referred to *Kelley* as a "very difficult case to follow and apply", and where "the ratio of the majority is somewhat elusive", said that a lawyer was entitled to forensic immunity only when acting "as advocate". The fact that the settlement might have been made at the door of the court was, he said, of little weight in answering this question: more important was the nature of the alleged negligence. A mistake as to the strength of a party's case was more likely to attract immunity than failure to pay heed to a relevant statute or other authority. On this basis, alleged negligence relating to the valuation of the matrimonial home (in two cases) and briefing incompetent counsel (in one) was held not to attract forensic immunity.

The result of *Hall v. Symons* seems to be to reduce forensic immunity in respect of settlement of court proceedings almost to vanishing point, since while a mistake as to the strength of a party's case may be negligent, it is unlikely in practice to be shown to be so. A number of earlier decisions holding that immunity applied must now be regarded as doubtful (*e.g. Atwell v. Michael Perry* [1998] 4 All E.R. 65, [1998] P.N.L.R. 711 (counsel in boundary dispute immune despite failure to take account of obvious Ordnance Survey evidence).

Indeed, the case exhibits a distinct tendency to limit immunity generally: significantly, Lord Bingham C.J., while accepting the decisions in *Rondel v. Worsley* [1969] 1 A.C. 191 and *Saif Ali v. Sydney Mitchell & Co.* [1980] A.C. 198, suggested that they might be open to reconsideration in the light of the Human Rights Act 1998 when that was in force. See further *supra,* Supplement §§ 1–05A–1–05G.

NOTE 50. The rule that a judicial decision cannot be impugned by subsequent **8–70** proceedings against legal representatives has undergone clarification. In *Kelley v. Corston* [1997] 4 All E.R. 466, a barrister was accused of negligence in drawing up a "door-of-court" settlement in matrimonial proceedings. The Court of Appeal held that the advocate's immunity applied; it also expressed the view, *obiter*, that in any case where (as here) a settlement required the approval of the court and had received that approval, an action for negligence against legal representatives should be struck out as an abuse of process. However, the scope of the collateral attack rule has now been drastically reduced since *Hall v. Simons* [1999] P.N.L.R. 374. Like *Kelley,* three of these consolidated cases concerned actions for negligence against solicitors in settling ancillary proceedings where the settlements had to be approved by the court. Although Lord Bingham C.J. accepted that proceedings against legal advisers which amounted to a challenge to a final decision on the merits should remain severely restricted (see *Hunter v. West Midlands Chief Constable* [1982] A.C. 529), there was less need to protect the integrity of consent orders under the Matrimonial Proceedings Act 1973. Hence while a collateral challenge to such an order would normally be an abuse of process, it would nevertheless be permitted if the plaintiff had either been deprived of the opportunity of appreciating that better terms might have been obtained, or been bound to a settlement significantly less advantageous than should have been available. As a result of this, said his Lordship, earlier decisions such as *Bateman v. Owen White* [1996] 1 P.N.L.R. 1, *Landall v. Dennis Faulkner & Alsop* [1994] 5 Med. L.R. 268 and *McFarlane v. Wilkinson* [1996] 1 Lloyd's Rep. 406 should now be regarded as of doubtful authority.

The effect of this judgment seems to be that, as regards consent orders on ancillary relief applications and other settlements requiring court approval (*e.g.* on behalf of infants and those under disability), the collateral attack point is now virtually a dead letter. Unless the plaintiff is complaining that the settlement was overly disadvantageous to him, he would be unlikely to bring proceedings against his advisers in the first place.

As regards settlements which were not required to be approved by the court, but in respect of which consent orders were made simply by agreement of the parties, Lord Bingham C.J. in *Hall v. Simons* doubted whether a collateral attack on them would ever be objectionable as an abuse of process.

On collateral attack, see too *R (L) v. Witherspoon* [1999] P.N.L.R. 766. Solicitors delayed in bringing contact proceedings: by the time proceedings were brought, they were dismissed on the basis that because of the passage of time arrangements should not be disturbed. No doubt because there was no chance of a successful appeal against that order, an action for negligence against the solicitors was held not to be an abuse of process.

8–72   Supreme Court Act 1981, s.51
See too *R. v. Rodney* [1997] P.N.L.R. 489 (barrister liable for clerk's inadvertence, even if not personally at fault).

8–73   See too *Matrix Securities Ltd v. Theodore Goddard* [1998] P.N.L.R. 290, holding that a barrister is to be judged according to the standard of the reasonable barrister of his standing (there, a senior tax silk).

NOTE 65. Add: See too *Matrix Securities Ltd v. Theodore Goddard* [1998] P.N.L.R. 290, (wrong advice re effectiveness of tax avoidance scheme: barrister not negligent in cicumstances).

NOTE 66. Add: See now *McFarlane v. Wilkinson* [1997] P.N.L.R. 578 and *Matrix Securities Ltd v. Theodore Goddard* [1998] P.N.L.R. 337, confirming that the *Bolam* test applies to barristers.

8–75   A solicitor can, of course, undertake a stricter duty by contract, as in *Zwebner v. Mortgage Corporation* [1998] P.N.L.R. 769 (solicitor processing forged mortgage deed held to have warranted genuineness of signature). But this is not readily inferred: *cf. Midland Bank v. Cox McQueen, The Times,* February 2, 1999 (rather similar facts, but no such warranty found).

See too *Gregory v. Shepherds, The Times,* February 18, 1999 (although country solicitors liable for fault of London agents, no liability in English solicitors for fault of foreign lawyers employed by them).

(b) *Solicitors*

8–77   Duties to third parties
In *Esterhuizen v. Allied Dunbar, The Times,* June 10, 1998, it was held that *White v. Jones* applied not only to solicitors as such, but to other organisations such as insurance companies employing professional will-drafters. See too *Punsford v. Gilberts* [1998] P.N.L.R. 763. And in *Carr-Glyn v. Frearsons* [1998] 4 All E.R. 225; [1999] P.N.L.R. 13 the *White v. Jones* duty was extended to matters ancillary to the actual drafting of the will (solicitors liable to beneficiary when they correctly drafted will leaving testatrix's share of house to her, but carelessly omitted to remind testatrix to sever the joint tenancy before she died so as to bar *ius accrescendi*). But *cf. Cancer Research Campaign v. Ernest Brown* [1998] P.N.L.R. 592 (no *White v. Jones* duty to protect legatee's interest from depredations of the Inland Revenue).

80

In *Carr-Glyn v. Frearsons* it was also made clear that *White v. Jones* would not apply where it could create a double liability. The Court of Appeal emphasised that had the estate there had a claim in its own right against the solicitors for the diminution in its own value (which in the event was held not to be the case), it would not have been just and equitable to allow the plaintiff to sue in addition.

In a suitable case a *White v. Jones* plaintiff may be under a duty to mitigate his loss: see, *e.g., Walker v. Medlicott* [1999] 1 All E.R. 685, [1999] P.N.L.R. 532 (legatee could obtain rectification of will: duty to exhaust this remedy before suing solicitor). However, this is a somewhat exceptional result. The plaintiff is only bound to do what is reasonable, and in most cases it is not reasonable to expect a plaintiff to engage in litigation which he may not win: see *Horsfall v. Heywoods, The Times,* March 11, 1999, a similar case going the other way. It is respectfully suggested that for the future *Horsfall* is likely to represent the norm and *Walker* the exception.

See also *Penn v. Bristol & West Building Society, The Times,* May 22, 1995 (husband forged wife's signature on conveyance of matrimonial home: husband's solicitor liable to wife for not checking authenticity).

NOTE 90. Add: In the Canadian case of *Earl v. Wilhelm* [1998] 2 W.W.R. 522, a solicitor adjudged liable to beneficiaries under the principle in *White v. Jones* was allowed to claim contribution from the testator himself, on the ground that the latter had failed to instruct him properly and could thus have been sued by the would-be beneficiaries. With respect, this must be wrong. A testator can owe no conceivable duty to potential legatees to take care in disposing of his own property.

Extent of liability to third parties   8–78
NOTE 92: See, too, *Connolly-Martin v. Davis* (unreported, May 27, 1999) (defendant to plaintiff's claim undertakes to pay money into account controlled by parties' solicitors jointly: defendant's barrister wrongly advises his client that undertaking not binding: money withdrawn and lost: CA strike out plaintiff's claim in negligence against barrister).

NOTE 93. Add: In *McCullagh v. Lane Fox & Partners Ltd* [1996] P.N.L.R. 205, Hobhouse L.J. regarded *Gran Gelato v. Richcliff Group* [1992] Ch. 560 with some scepticism as turning very much on its facts. Subsequently the Irish Supreme Court has regarded *Gran Gelato* as overruled by *McCullagh*: see *Doran v. Delaney* [1998] 2 I.L.R.M. 1.

And in *First National Commercial Bank plc v. Loxleys* [1997] P.N.L.R. 211, where the facts were very similar to those in *Gran Gelato,* the CA pointedly refused to halt the plaintiff's claim under RSC, Ord. 14A.

See too *Woodward v. Wolferstans, The Times,* April 8, 1997. A father guaranteed   8–79
his daughter's mortgage payments. The solicitor acting for the father was held to owe at least a potential duty to the daughter, but a duty limited to what he was instructed to do by the father. Hence in the circumstances his duty did not extend to ensuring the daughter knew what commitments she was undertaking.

Liability under the Supreme Court Act 1981, s.51   8–80
In *R. v. Lambeth Borough Council, ex p. Wilson, The Times,* March 21, 1996 it was held that officers of a council in charge of litigation could be made liable for wasted costs under section 51(3) of the 1981 Act on principles analogous to those obtaining under section 51(6).

NOTE 6. Add: And see *S v. M, The Times,* March 26, 1998.

NOTE 7. Add: "Improper" action includes making an application on behalf of a penniless litigant for the purpose of harassing another party to the litigation: *Tolstoy (Count) v. Lord Aldington* [1996] 1 W.L.R. 736, and making hopeless applications in a housing case in order to put off the day when possession has to be surrendered (*W.B.S. v. Fineberg* [1998] P.N.L.R. 216). It may also include the premature and over-enthusiastic presentation of an insolvency petition in order to pressurise a company into paying a disputed debt: *Re a Company (No 00679 of 1995)* [1996] 2 All E.R. 417. In the same case it was not surprisingly held that the swearing of a false

affidavit in support of the petition was equally improper. And *cf. R. v. Basra* [1998]
P.N.L.R. 535 (misuse of witness summons procedure penalised under section 19A
of the Prosecution of Offences Act 1985).

NOTE 9. Add: See too *Shah & Shah v. Singh* [1996] P.N.L.R. 83 (sending unquali-
fied clerk to appear on application and failing to tell her what to say characterised
as "negligent" and visited with wasted costs order). In *Veasey v. Millfeed Co* [1997]
P.N.L.R. 100 a solicitor was similarly treated who allowed an action to proceed
with his clients misdesignated, causing the necessity of an expensive interlocutory
application to the Court of Appeal to put the matter right.

NOTE 10. Add: See too *Tolstoy (Count) v. Lord Aldington* [1996] 2 All E.R. 556,
above.

NOTE 12. See too *Nelson v. Nelson* [1997] 1 All E.R. 970, refusing a wasted costs
order against a solicitor starting proceedings on behalf of a client who, unknown to
him, was bankrupt and had no *locus standi* to bring them. (The solicitor equally
escaped liability for breach of warranty of authority on the basis that he did not
warrant that his client had a good cause of action). See too *R. v. Luton JJ., ex p. R*
(unreported, January 27, 1998, CA) and *Reaveley v. Safeway Stores plc* [1998]
P.N.L.R. 526 (wasted costs order will not normally be made against solicitor relying
in good faith on counsel's advice).

NOTE 13. Add: Note that in *Tolstoy (Count) v. Lord Aldington* [1996] 2 All E.R.
556, above, the solicitor was held liable despite the signature of both leading and
junior counsel on the application.

NOTE 20. Add: But see now the important judgment in *Brown v. Gould & Swayne*
[1996] P.N.L.R. 130, where Millet L.J. suggested that questions of acceptable conveyancing practice should now be regarded as questions of law.

8–82 NOTE 22. Add: See too *Martin Boston & Co. v. Roberts & Ors* [1996] P.N.L.R.
45 (failure to demand real rather than personal security for costs negligent in the
circumstances, even though common practice not to do so).

It is, of course, always possible for a solicitor expressly to undertake a higher
duty, or even a strict liability. But clear evidence of such intention to do so is
generally required. *cf. Barclays Bank v. Weeks Legg & Dean* [1998] 3 W.L.R. 656,
[1998] P.N.L.R. 729 (solicitor put in funds by mortgage lender undertakes to part
with money in exchange for "good and marketable title": disburses loan against
cleverly forged documents: held, undertaking does not raise duty above duty to take
care, and hence solicitor escapes).

8–84 NOTE 35. Add: The solicitor's immunity from suit, while it extends to matters
such as failure to collect relevant evidence for use by counsel in court as much as
to actual advocacy (see *Walpole v. Partridge & Wilson* [1994] Q.B. 106), may be
overridden if new and compelling evidence of negligence on his part subsequently
becomes available. See *Smith v. Linskills* [1995] 3 All E.R. 482 (where, however, it
was not found to be present). See too *Oliver v. McKenna & Co., The Times*,
December 20, 1995 (allegation that solicitors negligently applied for appointment of
incompetent receiver relates to conduct of court proceedings and is inadmissible).

8–85 Conflicts of interest

The solicitor's duty not to subject himself to a conflict of interest has been clarified by the decision of the House of Lords, in *Prince Jefri Bolkiah v. KPMG* [1999]
1 W.L.R. 215, [1999] 1 All E.R. 517, [1999] P.N.L.R. 220. Forensic accountants
acted for the plaintiff in the course of protracted litigation and obtained much confidential information. They then sought to act against the plaintiff in other litigation
by erecting a "Chinese Wall" information barrier within the firm. The House of
Lords held that they could not do so: the only way they could justify their activity
was by proving that there was no prospect of leakage or misuse of information, and
this they had failed to do. Although the decision concerned accountants, it is clearly
applicable *a fortiori* to solicitors.

Conversely, where a solicitor has advised a party but has had no access to any confidential information, then there is objection on principle to his acting against that party in future litigation: see *Christie v. Wilson* [1998] P.N.L.R. 748 (solicitor can represent plaintiff in libel proceedings despite having read relevant newspaper for libel at time of publication). And *cf. C.P.R. v. Aikins* [1998] 6 W.W.R. 351.

The position of a solicitor acting for both mortgagor and mortgagee has been clarified in a number of recent cases brought by mortgage lenders. Despite his dual capacity, he continues to owe the mortgagees the same duty of care (and fiduciary duty) as if he were instructed by them alone: see *Bristol & West Building Society v. Baden Barnes Groves & Co.* (unreported, November 22, 1996) and *Nationwide Building Society v. Balmore Radmore* [1999] P.N.L.R. 606, *per* Blackburne J. As such, and subject to anything to the contrary in his instructions (see *National Home Loans Corporation plc v. Giffen Couch & Archer* [1997] 3 All E.R. 808), his position is as follows:

(1) He must report to the mortgagees any matters he discovers in the course of acting for them which would be likely to affect their decision to lend on that security. Such matters include a recent sale at substantially below the valuation (*Mortgage Express v. Bowerman* [1996] 2 All E.R. 836; *Bristol & West Building Society v. Fancy & Jackson* 1997] 4 All E.R. 582 at 605–606; *Nationwide Building Society v. Balmer Radmore* [1999] P.N.L.R. 000); moneys purportedly paid to the vendor other than through the solicitors (*Bristol & West Building Society v. Fancy & Jackson,* above; *Nationwide Building Society v. Balmer Radmore* [1999] P.N.L.R. 606 and hidden reductions in the price, *e.g.* payments by vendors to cover purchasers' legal and conveyancing costs (*Nationwide Building Society v. Balmer Radmore* [1999] P.N.L.R. 606 at 646 *et seq, per* Blackburne J).

(2) In the event that such matters, although discovered in the course of acting for the mortgagees, are covered by an obligation of confidence *vis-à-vis* the borrower, he is bound to ask the borrower for consent to disclose them to the mortgagees; and if such consent is unforthcoming, he must cease acting for the borrower (see *Halifax Mortgage Services v. Strepsky* [1995] 4 All E.R. 656; *Omega Trust v. Wright, Son & Pepper (No. 2)* [1998] P.N.L.R. 337; *Nationwide Building Society v. Balmer Radmore* [1999] P.N.L.R. 606 at 638 *et seq.*

(3) However, prima facie matters going simply to the borrower's personal ability to repay, such as arrears on a previous mortgage, need not be reported: see *National Home Loans Corporation plc v. Giffin Couch & Archer* [1997] 3 All E.R. 808, as interpreted by Blackburne J. in *Nationwide Building Society v. Balmer Radmore* [1999] P.N.L.R. 606.

(4) Prima facie he need not report to the mortgagees matters of which he is aware other than through acting for them, even if these would be likely to influence a lender's judgment (*Bristol & West Building Society v. Baden Barnes Groves & Co* (unreported, November 22, 1996); *Nationwide Building Society v. Balmer Radmore* [1999] P.N.L.R. 606 at 625 *et seq.*

(5) However, where matters come to his attention which suggest that the borrower is involved in fraud, then whatever the source of his information he is bound to pass it on (see *Darlington Building Society & Anor v. O'Rourke James Scourfield & McCarthy (a firm)* [1999] P.N.L.R. 365 at 371–372).

Proving negligence

On proof of negligence, see too *Johnson v. Bingley, Dyson & Finney* [1997] P.N.L.R. 392 (mere fact that defendant followed guide to professional conduct not enough *per se* to absolve him).

8–87   Acting on counsel's advice

NOTE 48. Add: And see also *Matrix Securities Ltd v. Theodore Goddard* [1998] P.N.L.R. 290.

8–88   Duty to advise

NOTE 62. Add: In *Reeves v. Thrings & Long* [1996] P.N.L.R. 265, CA, it was held sufficient for solicitors for a hotel purchaser to go over a licence agreement concerning parking rights without any extended explanation of its importance.

Note also *Hall v. Foong* (1996) 65 S.A.S.R. 281, holding that even where a solicitor has not been negligent in initially providing advice, he owes a duty to the client to correct that advice if he receives subsequent information indicating that it was wrong.

8–89   See too *Virgin Management v. De Morgan Group & Anor* (unreported, January 24, 1996, CA (solicitors carrying out sale and leaseback arrangement for large and sophisticated company not liable for failing to draw its attention to potential VAT trap). It was also held in the same case that solicitors drafting a contract were not liable for expenses incurred by the client in refuting an erroneous interpretation of it put forward by the other side.

Compare, however, *Hurlingham Estate v. Wilde* [1997] 1 Lloyd's Rep. 525, where on this occasion a solicitor was held to owe a duty to spot, and warn about, a potential tax trap. Lightman J. stressed that in this case the solicitor had no reason to think that the client possessed expertise, or would have recourse to other professional advice, on the tax matters concerned.

Note also *Holt v. Payne Skillington* [1996] P.N.L.R. 179, a case concerning surveyors. Surveyors had been retained by purchasers to find a property, but not to advise on planning matters. They neverthelss chose to do so, and were held to owe a duty of care in respect of the advice provided (in the event, however, the claim failed on the facts).

8–90   In *Zwebner v. Mortgage Corporation*, {1998] P.N.L.R. 769, a husband forged his wife's signature on a mortgage deed, with consequent loss to the mortgagee. The mortgagee's solicitors were held to have been negligent in omitting to take steps to send correspondence to both potential mortgagors separately or otherwise to guard against such imposture (*cf.*, in Canada, *Yamada v. Mock* (1996) 29 O.R. (3d) 53, holding a solicitor liable in just such a situation and also *Johnson v. Bingley, Dyson & Finney* [1997] P.N.L.R. 392).

See too *Haigh v. Wright Hassall & Co.* [1994] E.G.C.S. 54 (client failed to produce deposit on disadvantageous property transaction: solicitor lent him the money: solicitor not negligent in doing this rather than advising him not to proceed).

8–91   Conduct of litigation

See too *Martin Boston & Co. v. Roberts & Ors* [1996] P.N.L.R. 45 (failure to demand real rather than personal security for costs negligent in the circumstances).

In *Oates v. Pitman* (1998) 76 P. & C.R. 490, solicitors acting for Purchasers of holiday falts failed to notice that no planning permission existed for this use. They were held liable for the difference between the price paid and the actual value, and for the cost of obtaining the necessary permission, but not for any lost profits.

Damages

8–92   In *Allied Maples v. Simmons & Simmons* [1995] 1 W.L.R. 500 the Court of Appeal decided that where the chance of avoiding a loss depended on the hypothetical actions of a third party, a *pro rata* award for "loss of chance" was appropriate. Hence where solicitors negligently drafted a takeover agreement which inadequately protected their clients against liabilities of the company absorbed, the clients recovered the amount of these liabilities discounted by the probability that, if asked, the vendors would have refused to provide extended protection. See too *Stovold v. Barlows* [1996] P.N.L.R. 91 (solicitors negligently caused sale of house to be aborted:

liable for loss of chance of successful sale had they not been negligent), and *First Interstate Bank of California v. Cohen Arnold* [1996] P.N.L.R. 17. It is submitted that the contrary result reached in *Martin Boston & Co. v. Roberts & Ors* [1996] P.N.L.R. 45 can no longer be supported.

On the relevant date for assessing damages, see *Kennedy v. Van Emden* [1996] P.N.L.R. 409.

Where a plaintiff's damages include professional fees he has had to pay to other solicitors, or legal costs awarded against him in favour of a third party, the plaintiff is under a duty to mitigate where appropriate by demanding a taxation of the costs or fees concerned. The defendant is thus entitled to limit his liability to such sum as would have been payable had there been such a taxation. See *British Racing Drivers' Club v. Hextall Erskine* [1996] 3 All E.R. 667.

As a general rule insurance recoveries are out of account in assessing damages (see *post*, § 27–20 and *Bradburn v. Gt Western Ry* (1874) L.R. 10 Ex. 1). On this basis, a mortgage lender was held to have retained its right of recovery against negligent solicitors, even though it had already collected on a mortgage indemnity policy and despite the fact that the underwriters had waived any right of recoupment (see *Bristol & West Building Society v. May, May & Merriman (No. 2)* [1997] 3 All E.R. 206).

NOTE 90. Add: This must now be qualified in the light of the House of Lords' decision in *South Australia Asset Management v. York Montague* [1997] A.C. 191, which means that a defendant who has provided erroneous advice will only be liable for the consequences of that advice being erroneous. It seems that for this reason the solicitor will now not be liable in respect of the decline in property values. Such has indeed been decided in Australia: *Trust Co. of Australia v. Perpetual Trustee Co.* (1997) 42 N.S.W.L.R. 237 (see too *H. G. & R. Nominees v. Fava* [1997] 2 V.R. 368). And *cf. Carr-Glyn v. Frearsons* [1998] 4 All E.R. 25 [1999] P.N.L.R. 13 (solicitors instructed by testatrix to leave share in house to X negligently fail to remind testatrix to sever joint tenancy: no liability to estate, since object of instructions was to benefit X, not to preserve value of estate *in abstracto*).

See too *Bank of Scotland v. Edwards* (1995) 44 Con.L.R. 77.

Remoteness of damage 8–93

On how far a plaintiff can claim loss due to his own impecuniosity, see *Doran v. Delaney (No. 2)* [1999] 1 I.L.R.M. 225 (solicitors failed to notice boundary dispute preventing plaintiffs using building-plot: plaintiffs too poor to sort matters out, and forced to sell at a loss: solicitors liable for all wasted expenditure).

On remoteness of damage, note the House of Lords' decision in *South Australia Asset Management v. York Montague*, [1996] 3 W.L.R. 87, holding that a surveyor valuing property for a mortgagee could not be liable, even if negligent, for loss caused by a subsequent general drop in property prices. The limitations of that decision must, however, be realised. The reason for limiting the surveyor's liability is that a surveyor is generally called on to value a property at a given time, not to advise on future trends or the wisdom of a particular loan. This is not true of a solicitor employed, for instance, to ensure that his client gets a good title to property he is buying: Lord Hoffmann accepted that in such a case the solicitor would be liable for the full extent of his client's loss on the transaction even if partly due to depreciation of property generally (*cf. McElroy Milne v. Commercial Electronics* [1993] 1 N.Z.L.R. 39, approved by his Lordship in the course of his judgment).

Bungled litigation: measure of damages 8–96

In order to attract "loss of chance" damages under *Kitchen v. RAFA* [1958] 1 W.L.R. 563, the action must, it seems, have had a chance on the merits. The mere "nuisance value" inherent in a demonstrably bad claim will not do: see dicta in *Kitchen* itself, and now *McFarlane v. Wilkinson* [1997] P.N.L.R. 578. On the burden of proof where the defendant solicitor alleges that the plaintiff's action would have failed anyway, see *Mount v. Barker Austin* [1998] P.N.L.R. 493.

See too *Green v. Cunningham John* (1995) 46 Con.L.R. 62 (litigation settled on defendant's behalf without authority, but for sum which would have been recovered anyway: nominal damages only).

8–98   Duties to third parties

In *Omega Trust v. Wright, Son & Pepper* [1997] P.N.L.R. 424 a mortgage valuation was commissioned by a lender, both on its own behalf and also as undisclosed agent for another financier which was putting up part of the money. Henry L.J. at 427–428 left it open whether the latter would generally be owed a duty of care by the valuer (in the event the matter was pre-empted by an exemption clause). His Lordship's doubts, it is suggested, are well-founded. It is hard to argue convincingly that there should be "proximity" in tort between a professional and a person he does not know and of whose very existence he is unaware. And see too *Barex Brokers v. Morris* [1999] P.N.L.R. 344 (valuer owes no duty in tort to client's assignee).

8–101   Exclusion of duty

See too *Omega Trust v. Wright, Son & Pepper* [1997] P.N.L.R. 424 (surveyors held validly to have excluded liability towards third parties to whom valuation passed on).

8–105   Standard of care

NOTE 39. Add: And see *Theodore Goddard v. Fletcher-King* [1997] 2 E.G.L.R. 131.

4.—SURVEYORS

8–106   Breach of duty: valuation

NOTE 48. Add: Note, however, that the margin of permissible error plays no part in the assessment of damages: once liability is established, these are calculated from the court's estimate of actual value, without reference to any hypothetically permissible overvaluation. See *Scotlife Homeloans v. Kenneth James & Co.* [1995] E.G.C.S. 70 and *South Australia Asset Management v. York Montague*, [1997] A.C. 191, *per* Lord Hoffmann. Conversely, it seems a valuation which is within the permissible margin of error cannot give rise to recovery, even if the plaintiff is prepared to allege and prove specific instances of negligence: *Legal & General Mortgage Services v. Underwoods* [1997] P.N.L.R. 567. A number of cases on the allowable margin of error are discussed by Wilkinson at (1995) 145 New L.J. 1267.

8–109   Breach of duty: advice and representation

Note too, on duties arising in respect of advice on matters outside the surveyor's retainer, *Holt v. Payne Skillington* [1996] P.N.L.R. 179, see *supra*, Supplement § 8–89.

8–110   Surveyors' negligence: causation

On causation, see too *South Australia Asset Management v. York Montague*, [1996] 3 W.L.R. 87 and *Banque Bruxelles Lambert v. John D. Wood* [1996] P.N.L.R. 380.

8–112   Surveyors' negligence: damages

With *Philips v. Ward*, compare *Oates to Pitman* (1998) 76 P. & C.R. 490 (solicitors acting for purchasers of holiday flats fail to notice lack of planning permission: no liability for lost profits on use).

Although the measure of damages against a surveyor who fails to spot a defect is prima facie the difference in value and not the cost of correcting the defect, in cases of difficulty the latter may be taken as some evidence of the former. Thus in *Oswald v. Countrywide Surveyors* (1996) 50 Const. L.R. 1, the Court of Appeal refused to interfere with a rough and ready computation by the trial judge based on the cost of repairs less a discount for estimated betterment. Note also that, at least in certain cases, the plaintiff's intentions relating to the property bought may affect the damages he is entitled to: *Duncan Investments v. Underwood* [1998] P.N.L.R. 754.

The fact that a plaintiff has recovered compensation from a third party for defects a surveyor negligently failed to spot will not (it has been held by the Court of Appeal) reduce his recovery. See *Gardner v. Marsh & Parsons (a firm) & Another* [1997] 3 All E.R. 871 (defects in leasehold flat missed by surveyor but later repaired by landlord at his expense under terms of lease: purchaser nevertheless recovered difference between price paid and value at time of purchase). *A fortiori*, where a lender complains that his security has been over-valued, it is irrelevant for the defendant valuer to allege that the lender was never ultimately at risk because the funds he advanced in fact came from elsewhere. See *Legal & General Mortgage Services v. Underwoods* [1997] P.N.L.R. 567.

On the effect of insurance on damages in cases of this sort, see *Europe Mortgage Co. v. Halifax Estate Agencies, The Times*, May 23, 1996 (in action by mortgagee against surveyor for overvaluation, no account taken of recovery under mortgage indemnity policy). And *cf. Bristol & West Building Society v. May, May & Merriman (No. 2)* [1997] 3 All E.R. 206 (similar result in case of a negligent solicitor).

On the date at which damages are reckoned, see the solicitors' case of *Wapshot v. Davies Donovan* [1996] P.N.L.R. 361. Where solicitors culpably failed to spot a fatal defect in title, damages were reckoned as at the date of purchase, not as at the later date when the plaintiff tried unsuccessfully to sell. Presumably similar reasoning would apply to surveyors who failed to notice a damning defect which would have caused the purchaser to abandon the transaction. See too *Shaw v. Halifax (South West) Ltd* [1996] P.N.L.R. 451, and (generally) *Nykredit v. Edward Erdman & Co. (No. 2)* [1998] 1 All E.R. 305, [1998] P.N.L.R. 197.

See also a useful article by Wilkinson at (1995) 145 New L.J. 1267.

NOTE 90. Add: Compare *Wapshot v. Davies Donovan* [1996] P.N.L.R. 361 (damages of £3,000 against solicitor whose negligence compelled growing family to continue living in unsaleable—and very cramped—flat).

The text at Note 46 is no longer accurate since the overruling of *Banque Bruxelles Lambert v. Eagle Star Insurance* [1995] 3 W.L.R. 87 by the House of Lords in *South Australia Asset Management v. York Montague* [1997] A.C. 191. That case held that a surveyor who negligently over-valued property for a mortgagee could not be liable for losses suffered by the latter due solely to a general decline in property prices. The surveyor was employed to value the property at a given date, not to advise on future trends or on the wisdom of making the loan at all; hence he owed no duty of care in respect of losses due to these latter features. The prima facie measure of the surveyor's liability was therefore the amount lost by the mortgagee, but limited to the amount by which he had overvalued the property at the time of the valuation, plus any other losses foreseeably flowing from such over-valuation. Presumably similar principles will apply to advice given to a potential purchaser of property. **8–113**

The *South Australia* case was followed and elucidated by the Court of Appeal in *Bristol & West Building Society v. Mothew* [1997] 2 W.L.R. 436. Solicitors retained by mortgagees informed the latter, incorrectly, that the mortgagors had no plans to grant a second charge. On the faith of this statement the mortgage funds were advanced against a first charge; a second charge was then executed in favour of a third party. The mortgagor defaulted and the mortgagees suffered loss when they sold the property. In an action against the solicitors, the Court of Appeal refused to award the mortgagees their whole loss, however, foreseeable it might have been: their claim was limited to such loss (if any) as resulted from the falsity of the information provided by the solicitors.

On the *South Australia* case generally, see Stapleton (1997) 113 L.Q.R. 1, and O'Sullivan [1997] C.L.J. 19.

On recovery of interest charges incurred by way of special damages, see *Birmingham Midshires Building Society v. Phillips* [1998] P.N.L.R. 468.

NOTE 94. On the duty to mitigate, see too *Western Trust & Savings v. Clive*

Travers & Co [1997] P.N.L.R. 295. Mortgage lenders alleged negligence against their solicitors in failing to inform them of possible defects in the title to the mortgaged property, but made no serious effort to obtain possession or sell when the borrower defaulted, seeking instead to recover the whole of the amount of their loan from the defendant's solicitors. The CA refused to allow this. Distinguishing *London & South of England Building Society v. Stone* [1983] 1 W.L.R. 1242, they held that in failing to proceed against the actual security itself (as opposed to suing on the borrower's personal covenant) the plaintiffs had unreasonably failed to mitigate their loss.

8-114   In an increasing number of misvaluation cases, defendants have attempted to reduce potentially huge recoveries by pleading contributory negligence on the part of the plaintiff. This tactic has met with some success. For instance, in *Platform Home Loans v. Oyston Shipways & Others* [1998] Ch. 466, [1998] P.N.L.R. 512, mortgagees who advanced 70% of £1 million plus on a property on the basis of only two opinions and without even bothering to ask the purchase price were held 20% contributorily negligent in a later action against their surveyors for negligent overvaluation. For other cases on what amounts to contributory negligence in this connection, see *Cavendish Funding v. Henry Spencer* [1998] P.N.L.R. 123, *Mortgage Express v. Newman* [1996] P.N.L.R. 603, *First National Commercial Bank v. Taylor* [1997] P.N.L.R. 37, and *Omega Trust v. Wright, Son & Pepper (No. 2)* [1998] P.N.L.R. 337.

Assuming a plaintiff is held to have been contributorily negligent in lending money in reliance on a valuation, a further awkward issue arises. Suppose (a) the principle in *South Australia Asset Management v. York Montague* [1997] A.C. 191 applies, and has the effect of limiting the recoverable loss to the consequences of the valuation being wrong, but (b) although the plaintiff was negligent, his contributory negligence was unconnected with that misvaluation (for example, where he lent without properly checking the borrower's credit history). Logically, there is much to be said for leaving such contributory fault out of account, on the basis that it has nothing to do with the recoverable loss (a point made by Phillips J. at first instance in *Banque Bruxelles Lambert v. Eagle Star* [1995] 3 W.L.R. 87). But such a rule would engender considerable complexity, and in *Platform Home Loans v. Oyston Shipways* [1998] Ch. 466, [1998] P.N.L.R. 512 the Court of Appeal, after an exhaustive survey of the authorities, declined to apply it. It was decided that, on a proper construction of the Law Reform (Contributory Negligence) Act 1945, account should be taken of all contributory negligence, whatever its nature, and a deduction made accordingly. An appeal by the plaintiffs to the House of Lords against this holding was dismissed: see [1999] 1 All E.R. 833.

There is a further, related, point. In the *Platform* case the plaintiffs' actual loss was £600,000 but, owing to the effect of *South Australia Asset Management*, their recoverable loss was limited to £500,000. In addition, the plaintiffs had been 20 per cent contributory negligent. Did this mean they actually recovered £480,000 (£600,000 less 20 per cent) or £400,000 (£500,000 less 20 per cent)? The House of Lords at [1999] 1 All E.R. 833 held that the former figure was correct. This is, with respect, a little odd: despite having been 20 per cent responsible for their own misfortune, the plaintiffs ended up with only 4 per cent less than they would have got had they been entirely blameless.

South Australia Asset Management caused yet another complication in *Law Debenture Trust Corp. plc v. Hereward Phillips* [1999] P.N.L.R. 725. A pension fund bought an ailing company in circumstances amounting to a breach of trust by its trustees. Its total loss recoverable from the trustees was £4.07m: of this £2.5m (the over-valuation) was held also recoverable from the fund's accountants, who had been negligent in valuing the concern. The trustees had, however, settled the claim against them for £1.5m. Held: the fund could appropriate the £1.5m to that part of its loss which was irrecoverable from its accountants, and hence no deduction fell to be made from its recovery of £2.5m from the latter.

5.—ARCHITECTS AND CONSULTING ENGINEERS

Duties to clients   **8–115**
Wessex Regional HA v. HLM Design (1994) 40 Con. L.R. 1 confirms the possibility of a concurrent duty in tort being placed on an architect.

Duties to third parties   **8–116**
On architects' duties to third parties, see also *Machin v. Adams* (1997) 84 B.L.R.
79, (architect employed by building owner to inspect premises owes no duty to
prospective purchaser).

See too *Barclays Bank v. Fairclough Construction (No. 2)* (1995) 76 B.L.R. 6   **8–117**
(sub-subcontractor in building works creates asbestos hazard which subcontractor
has to pay to remove: held to owe duty of care in tort to subcontractor). In *Birse
Construction v. Haiste Ltd* [1996] 1 W.L.R. 675, a case on the Civil Liability
(Contribution) Act 1978, it was held that a consulting engineer employed by a building owner arguably owed a duty to the constructor to take care to point out to him
defects in the works. *Sed quaere*: it is difficult to see why the constructor should be
in any better position than, say, a subsequent purchaser. It should be noted that
Birse's case merely involved a refusal to strike out such a claim as unarguable, and
it is respectfully suggested that the point must continue to be regarded as doubtful.
cf. Saigol v. Cranley Mansions (unreported July 6, 1995, CA) (architect supervising
works in common parts of mansion block owes no tort duty in respect of economic
loss to flat owner).
See too *Jacobs v. Moreton* (1994) 72 B.L.R. 105, holding that a repairer of a
building (and, inferentially, an architect supervising the repair) did owe a duty to a
subsequent purchaser of it. *Sed quaere; cf. Bellefield Computer Services Ltd v.
Turner & Sons Ltd* (unreported, July 22, 1999).
The status of a "duty of care letter", sometimes issued by a professional to a
purchaser in order to get round the rule in *Murphy v. Brentwood District Council*
[1991] 1 A.C. 398, is discussed in *Hill Samuel v. Brand* (1995) 4 Con. L.R. 141.
NOTE 14. Add: Note that Commonwealth positions now vary on this point. Australian courts have decisively rejected the builder's (and by implication the
architect's) immunity from suit in respect of economic loss, and have returned to
Dutton v. Bognor Regis UDC [1972] 1 Q.B. 373—see *Bryan v. Moloney* (1994) 128
A.L.R. 163 (though *cf. Zumpano v. Montagnese* [1997] 2 V.R. 525). The New Zealand courts have done the same: see *Invercargill County Council v. Hamlin* [1994]
3 N.Z.L.R. 513, approved by the PC at [1996] 1 All E.R. 756. The Canadian courts
have taken an intermediate position, holding the builder liable where the defect
threatens health or safety but not otherwise: *Winnipeg Condominium No. 36 v. Bird
Construction Co.* (1995) 121 D.L.R. (4th) 513. See too *327973 British Columbia
Ltd v. HBT Agra* (1995) 120 D.L.R. (4th) 726.
In *Machin v. Adams* (1997) 84 B.L.R. 79, it was held that an architect employed
by a building owner to inspect the premises owed no duty to a prospective purchaser
of them.

Breach of duty: design and supervision   **8–119**
Consulting engineers are generally entitled to assume that other professionals on
the project will do a proper job: see *DN Heritage v. Steenson Varning Mulcahy*
(1998) 60 Con. L.R. 33 (engineers on British Library project could assume Balfour
Beatty would install cabling properly).
Note too, on duties arising in respect of advice on matters outside the contractual
retainer, *Holt v. Payne Skillington* [1996] P.N.L.R. 179, *supra* § 8–89.
NOTE 16. But see now *Strathford East Kilbride v. Film Design* 1999 S.L.T. 121
(architects employed by parent company to design garage owe no duty to subsidiary,
company suffering loss due to garage being unusable).

8–121 Breach of duty: advice
See too *Gable House Estates v. Halpern Partnership* (1995) 48 Const. L.R. 1 (architect engaged to advise on how to maximise profit on speculative commercial development liable for loss caused by his misestimating floor area by 500 sq. ft.: statement that "all measurements approximate" was not sufficient warning to clients in the circumstances).

8–123 On the measure of damages under the Defective Premises Act 1972, see now *Bayoumi v. Protim Services* (1998) 30 H.L.R. 785.

6.—FINANCE

8–126 Accountants and auditors: duties to third parties
Caparo v. Dickman has been followed in two Australian cases (*Lowe v. AGC* [1992] 2 V.R. 671, and *Esanda v. Peat Marwick* (1992) 61 SASR 424, upheld in High Court at (1997) 15 A.C.L.C. 483), and in Canada (*Hercules Management v. Ernst & Young* [1997] 2 S.C.R. 115).

Note too *Anthony v. Wright* [1995] 1 BCLC 236 (auditor engaged by trustee company owed no direct duty to beneficiaries of trust), and *Electra Private Equity Partners v. KPMG Peat Marwick* [1998] P.N.L.R. 135, (auditors provided information on company but recipients relied primarily on warranties given by others: in circumstances no assumption of responsibility and no duty of care). But contrast *Coulthard v. Neville Russell* [1998] P.N.L.R. 276 (auditors advised transaction between directors and company which was in fact illegal: directors disqualified as a result: the Court of Appeal refuse to strike out negligence claim by directors personally).

NOTE 62. Add: See too *ADT Ltd v. BDO Binder Hamlyn* (unreported, December 6, 1995, May J.) (where predator set up specific meeting to take advice from auditors of target company, duty of care owed), and *Christensen v. Scott* [1996] 1 N.Z.L.R. 273 (accountants to small family company owed independent duty of care to family members as guarantors of its liabilities). In *BCCI v. Price Waterhouse & Anor* [1998] P.N.L.R. 564, the auditors of one company in the BCCI group who had failed to spot sizeable irregularities in its operations were sued for negligence by another company in the same group. It was held that they owed a duty of care to the latter, on the basis that since the group had been run (and robbed) as one unit, insistence on the separate legal personality of the different companies within it would be excessively artificial.

However, all cases depend on their facts, and even where advice is directly requested by a person seeking to take over a company, this does not necessarily give rise to a duty of care. See *Peach Publishing Ltd v. Slater & Co* [1998] P.N.L.R. 364 (requested accounts specifically not guaranteed; refusal by accountant to provide further legally binding assurances; recipient of advice very experienced business operator; CA hold no duty owed in circumstances). A case with some similarity to *Peach Publishing* is *Abbott v. Strong* [1998] 2 B.C.L.C. 420 (accountants advise directors of company what to say to the shareholders; directors follow that advice; no direct duty of care owed by accountants to shareholders, who relied solely on the directors).

8–127 See *Sasea v. KPMG, The Times,* August 5, 1998, see *post*, Supplement § 8–130.

8–130 Causation and damages
In *Sansea v. KPMG, The Times,* August 5, 1998, auditors allegedly failed to spot that a company was insolvent because of frauds practised on it, as a result of which the company paid a dividend it would not otherwise have paid. The court refused to strike out an action by the company for damages against the auditors.

See too *Barings plc v. Coopers & Lybrand* [1997] P.N.L.R. 179, where accountants engaged by a holding company to audit its subsidiary failed to spot massive unauthorised trading by an employee of the subsidiary. The Court of Appeal confirmed that despite the rule in *Foss v. Harbottle* (1843) 2 Hare 461 there was no reason why the holding company should not recover damages based on the depreciation of the value of its own shares in its subsidiary. And see *Johnson v. Gore Wood* [1999] P.N.L.R. 426.

Note that, just as valuers are only liable for the consequences of their advice being wrong and not for all losses suffered as a result of reliance on that advice (*South Australia Asset Management v. York Montague* [1997] 3 A.C. 191), negligent auditors similarly escape liability for losses which were not within the scope of the duty broken. See *BCCI v. Price Waterhouse (No. 3), The Times*, April 2, 1998 (auditors of BCCI subsidiary negligently failed to detect huge losses: no liability for loss suffered by parent company in lending to, and guaranteeing debts of, that subsidiary. The object of the audit requirement was not to protect against ordinary business risks).

Receivers
8–132

NOTE 86. In *Leech v. National Bank of N.Z.* [1996] 3 N.Z.L.R. 707 it was confirmed that in applying the *Downsview* case referred to in the text, no distinction was to be drawn between legal and equitable mortgagees.

In *Burgess v. Auger* [1998] B.C.L.C. 478 Lightman J held, following *Downsview Nominees v. First City Corporation* [1993] 2 W.L.R. 86, that a receiver owed no duty to the sole shareholder of the company concerned. He also expressed some doubts as to whether *Standard Chartered Bank v. Walker* [1982] 1 W.L.R. 1410, which held that a receiver could be liable to a guarantor, was reconcilable with *Downsview*.

8–133

CHAPTER 9.—PRODUCT LIABILITY AND CONSUMER PROTECTION

		PARA.
■1.	Product liability in general	9–01
□2.	Contract	9–04
■3.	Negligence	
	(a) Generally	9–09
	(b) Qualification of negligence liability	9–27
■4.	The Consumer Protection Act 1987, Pt I	
	(a) Generally	9–34
	(b) The statutory scheme	
	(1) What is a "product"?	9–38
	(2) When is a product "defective"?	9–41
	(3) Who can be sued?	9–46
	(4) Who can sue?	9–53
	(5) What defences are available?	9–54
	(6) What damage is recoverable?	9–60
	(c) Limitation	9–62
	(d) Miscellaneous matters	9–65
5.	Breach of statutory duty: the Consumer Protection Act 1987, Pt II	9–68

9–01   Recent developments of note include (1) *The Orjula* [1995] 2 Lloyd's Rep. 395 on recovery for physical and economic loss; (2) the *C.J.D. Litigation* [1996] 7 Med. L.R. 309, on the liability of the Medical Research Council and others for failing to advert to possible dangers in drugs developed under their auspices; (3) *Carroll v. Fearon & Others* concerning *res ipsa loquitur* in the context of products liability; (4) the unfortunately unreported decision in *Hayes v. Leo Scaffolding*, December 3, 1996, CA, on the relevance of intermediate inspection to *Donoghue v. Stevenson* liability; and (5) *Hamble Fisheries Ltd v. Gardner* [1999] 1 Lloyd's Rep. 1, on the duty to warn.

2.—CONTRACT

9–05   **(a) Compliance with description: section 13**
The example of petrol sold as diesel fuel was prophetic. A claim of precisely this type was settled in November 1995 for £400 by Asda Supermarkets: see the *Daily Mail*, November 27, 1995, p. 26.

3.—NEGLIGENCE

(a) *Generally*

9–15   **Quality control and certification**
NOTE 74. On the liability of those involved in the checking and certification of drugs, compare the *CJD Litigation* [1996] 7 Med. L.R. 309. Here Morland J. was prepared to hold that the Medical Research Council could be liable in negligence if they were proved to have continued to promote research into, and consequent production of, Human Growth Hormone after its ingestion had been shown to carry risks of infection with Creuzfeld-Jacob disease. As regards certification generally, see too *Perrett v. Collins*, [1999] P.N.L.R. 77, CA (defendant certified aeroplane fit

92

to fly for purposes of Civil Aviation Act 1982; aeroplane crashed: held that defendant owed duty of care to member of crew injured in crash).

For what damage?   9–18
See too *Minchillo v. Ford* [1995] 2 V.R. 594. But note *The Orjula* [1995] 2 Lloyd's Rep. 395. Where a stow of containerised drums of acid collapsed because of incompetent staging erected round it by the suppliers, Mance J. refused to strike out a claim by carriers for the cost of decontaminating the drums, even though this loss was purely economic. The normal rule, he thought, might not apply where (as here) the possessor of dangerously defective goods had no realistic option of abandoning or otherwise disposing of them.

Furthermore, it seems that for these purposes "damage" may include contamination, even in the absence of other physical impairment: *cf. Blue Circle v. Ministry of Defence* [1997] Env. L.R. 22 (radioactive contamination of land owing to activities of A.W.R.E. at Aldermaston is "damage" within meaning of Nuclear Installations Act 1965).

In *Bow Valley Husky v. St John Shipbuilding Co.* [1997] 3 S.C.R. 1210, it was held that a defendant guilty of failure to warn about defects in his products (see *post*, Supplement, § 9–23) would not be liable for purely economic damage. It seems to follow that the requirement of damage to other property applies to the manufacturer who fails to warn about defects as much as to the manufacturer guilty of negligent fabrication. That that is indeed the case has now been confirmed by the Court of Appeal in *Hamble Fisheries v. Gardner* [1999] 1 Lloyd's Rep. 1 (marine engine manufacturer fails to warn boat owners of indications that pistons unusually brittle: pistons failed causing damage to engine and towage expenses: held, manufacturer owed no duty to owner.)

Damage to "other property"; definition   9–19
See too *The Orjula* [1995] 2 Lloyd's Rep. 395. Suppliers of drums of acid stuffed a container provided by the carrier; owing to defective staging erected in the container, the stow collapsed and both drums and container were damaged. Mance J. held that the damage to the container counted as physical damage to other property, actionable under *Donoghue v. Stevenson*, but not the damage to the drums themselves.

NOTE 85. Add: In the building case of *Jacobs v. Moreton* (1994) 72 B.L.R. 92, an attempt was apparently made to resurrect the "complex structure" theory so as to make a repairer of one part of a building liable to a subsequent purchaser for damage to the rest of it. Although if correct this might well have implications for product liability, it is respectfully suggested that the decision is highly doubtful on this point. It is worth noting that in *The Orjula*, above, Mance J., in denying that the contamination of the drums counted as physical damage to other property, specifically rejected the "complex structure" argument *cf. Bellefield Computer Services Ltd v. Turner & Sons Ltd* (unreported, July 22, 1999).

On liability for components fitted by a predecessor in title of the plaintiff, the   9–20
U.S. Supreme Court has now held that the component manufacturer does owe a duty of care to the plaintiff: see *Saratoga Fishing Co. v. Martinac* [1997] A.M.C. 2113. It remains to be seen whether this view will be accepted in England.

Donoghue v. Stevenson: proof of negligence   9–21
On *res ipsa loquitur* in the products liability context, see now *Carroll v. Fearon & Others* [1998] P.I.Q.R. P146, where the Court of Appeal discountenanced suggestions that *res ipsa loquitur* could not apply to *Donoghue v. Stevenson* liability in a suitable case. It accordingly held the manufacturers of a defective Dunlop tyre liable when it exploded and caused a serious accident, despite the lack of specific evidence as to how the fault got there.

Manufacturing and design defects   9–22
In connection with design defects, note that the mere fact that the defendant has

complied with any relevant regulations about testing, etc., will not as such suffice
to absolve him: *Best v. Wellcome Foundation* [1993] 3 I.R. 421 (testing of DTP
vaccine).

9–23   **Failure to warn**
On failure to warn, see too *Carroll v. Fearon & Others* [1998] P.I.Q.R. P416
(failure to warn of potentially lethal defect in tyre), *Hollis v. Dow Corning* (1996)
129 D.L.R. (4th) 609 (failure to warn re breast implants' disconcerting tendency to
break up after installation), and *Bow Valley Husky v. St John Shipbuilding Co.*
[1997] 3 S.C.R. 1210 (duty to warn that pipe cladding for use on oil-rigs unusually
flammable). In *Hamble Fisheries v. Gardner* [1999] 1 Lloyd's Rep. 1, an issue arose
as to whether a separate legal entity that had bought and carried on a manufacturer's
business could itself come under a duty to warn of defects coming to its attention.
Tuckey L.J. expressed the view that the answer was "Yes" (though in the event the
question did not fall to be answered).
In *Bow Valley Husky v. St John Shipbuilding Co.* [1997] 3 S.C.R. 1210, the
Supreme Court of Canada held that a the plaintiff's knowledge of the risk would
not as such negative a duty to warn: the defendant had to go further, and show that
the plaintiff was *volens* in that he had knowingly agreed to accept the risk. *Sed
quaere*. Why should a defendant be under a duty to warn the plaintiff about something he knows of already?
NOTE 15. Add: See too *Double Bar L Ranching v. Bayvet Corporation* [1996] 10
W.W.R. 673, (veterinary preparation had 1:50,000 chance of killing cattle: no duty
to warn in circumstances).
NOTE 18. Add: In *Bow Valley Husky v. St John Shipbuilding Co.* [1997] 3 S.C.R.
1210, the Supreme Court of Canada suggested that warning someone other than the
consumer would suffice only in two situations: (a) where the product was a technical
one only to be used under expert supervision (*e.g.* prescription drugs), and (b) where
it was unrealistic or impracticable to warn all consumers.

9–24   **Failure to warn: subsequent dangers**
See too *Hollis v. Dow Corning* (1996) 129 D.L.R. (4th) 609 (liability for failure
to warn re breast implant likely to rupture).
On the American jurisprudence concerning subsequent duties to warn (which in
the absence of much home-grown authority may well be relevant in England), see
Matula (1996) 32 Tort & Ins L.J. 87.

9–25   **Effect of warning**
In *Hollis v. Dow Corning* (1996) 129 D.L.R. (4th) 609 (concerning manufacturers
who neglected to warn doctors about potentially unstable breast implants) La Forest
J. in the Supreme Court of Canada suggested that in "learned intermediary" cases
of this sort, the plaintiff did not have to prove that the intermediary would have
acted on a warning if given. In his view either the burden was on the defendant to
prove that a warning would have made no difference, or possibly (and even more
radically) the defendant would remain liable whatever evidence he produced as to
the hypothetical effect of a warning. With respect, it is very doubtful whether an
English court would accept either proposition.

        Causation
9–26   NOTE 26. Add: See too *Best v. Wellcome Foundation* [1993] 3 I.R. 421 (where
on the facts the burden was found to have been discharged). This is one of the very
few cases in which an action against the manufacturer of a drug has succeeded.
See too Goldberg [1996] *Anglo-American Law Rev.* 286; Goldberg [1996] Med.
Law. Rev. 32.

9–28   **Intermediate examination: "probability" or "possibility"?**
On intermediate examination, note the troublesome decision in *Hayes v. Leo Scaffolding* (unreported, December 3, 1996, CA). A defective scaffolding plank broke,

depositing the plaintiff on the ground 17 feet below. Despite clear evidence of negligence, the plaintiff's claim against the producer of the plank failed on grounds of the likelihood of an intermediate examination by the plaintiff's employers. Simon Brown L.J. suggested, indeed, that a *Donoghue v. Stevenson* claimant could not succeed unless he proved a *probability* that there would be *no* intermediate examination. *Sed quaere*. This is, with respect, a very restrictive formulation of the liability concerned, and arguably out of line with much of the other authority cited in the text.

4.—THE CONSUMER PROTECTION ACT 1987, PT I

(a) *Generally*

Interpretation

On the possible discrepancy between the provisions of the Directive and those of the Act, see now the ECJ's decision in case C-300/95 *Commission v. United Kingdom* [1997] All E.R. (E.C.) 481. In proceedings brought against the for failing properly to implement Article 7 of the Directive, the ECJ declined to find any conflict between it and section 4(1)(e) of the Act. The ECJ evidently thought section 4(1)(e) on its proper interpretation did enact Article 7: but, with the greatest respect, it remains to be seen whether an English court faced with the necessity of interpreting section 4(1)(e) would necessarily reach the same conclusion.

9–36

(b) *The Statutory Scheme*

(1) *What is a "product"?*

NOTE 64. Add: *Ter Neuzen v. Korn* has now been affirmed by the Supreme Court of Canada: see (1995) 127 D.L.R. (4th) 577.

The decision in *St Albans City Council v. ICL*, now reported at [1995] F.S.R. 686, has been upheld on appeal: [1996] All E.R. 481.

NOTE 65. Add: *St Albans City Council v. ICL* is now reported at [1995] F.S.R. 686.

9–38

Primary agricultural and fishery produce

See too McLeish (1997) 147 New L.J. 682, dealing with the position of a "cloned" animal grown in a laboratory. He suggests that such a beast would not be "produce of the soil, of stock farming or of fisheries" within section 1(2) of the Act, and that the producer of it would therefore fall outside the protection given to producers of primary agricultural produce. *Sed quaere*. This seems, with respect, to depend on an excessively restricted definition of "stock farming".

9–40

On strict liability and inevitable dangers, compare the warning in the recent American cigarette case of *Buckingham v. R.J. Reynolds* 731 A 2d 381 (1998): "strict liability should not be used as a tool of social engineering to mandate that manufacturers bear the entire risk and costs of injuries caused by their products".

On design defects, see the instructive decision in *Pigliavento v. Tyler* 669 N.Y.S. 2d (1998) (safety rail supplied as optional extra with cement mixer: mixer not defective within American strict liability regime simple because purchaser chose not to buy or fit rail, with result that employee injured).

9–42

(5) *What defences are available?*

Compliance with a legal requirement

NOTE 9. Add: See too the product liability negligence case of *Best v. Wellcome Foundation* [1993] 3 I.R. 421.

9–54

9–59 **Development risks**

NOTE 21. Note that the Commission's proceedings against the United Kingdom alleging non-implementation of Art. 7 have now failed: *Commission v. United Kingdom* [1997] 3 C.M.L.R. 923. The ECJ seems to have opined that despite its wording, 4(1)(e) would be interpreted to conform with the narrow scope of the defence as provided in Art. 7; hence the lack of proved conflict. It remains to be seen whether the ECJ's confidence is well-founded.

CHAPTER 10.—OCCUPIERS' LIABILITY AND DEFECTIVE PREMISES

		PARA.
■1.	Liability of occupiers to visitors for conditions of premises	10–01
□2.	The Occupiers' Liability Act 1957	10–02
□3.	Liability of landlord	10–63
■4.	Liability to trespassers	10–69
5.	Liability to persons not on the premises	10–86

Note in particular since the last edition (1) *Revill v. Newberry* [1996] 2 W.L.R. 239, on liability to trespassers; (2) *Campbell v. Housing Executive* [1996] 1 B.N.I.L. 99, on the duty owed to highway users; (3) *Swain v. Puri* [1996] P.I.Q.R. P442 and *Ratcliff v. McConnell* [1999] 1 W.L.R. 670 (rare cases on the Occupiers' Liability Act 1984); (4) the decision of the Court of Appeal in *Phillips v. Perry & Dalgety Agriculture Ltd*, unreported, 6 March 1997, concerning dangers incidental to a visitor's trade or calling; and (5) *Boldack v. East Lindsey District Council* (1999) 31 H.L.R. 41, on the liability of landlords for dangers in the property let.

1.—LIABILITY OF OCCUPIERS TO VISITORS FOR CONDITION OF PREMISES

Common law 10–01
See generally Parry (1995) 15 L.S. 335.

2.—THE OCCUPIERS' LIABILITY ACT 1957

"Occupancy duty" and "activity due" 10–03
In *Revill v. Newberry* [1996] 2 W.L.R. 239, Neill L.J. expressed the view at 297–298 that the Occupiers' Liability Act 1984 was limited in its ambit to "occupancy duties": by parity of reasoning, presumably the same applies to the 1957 Act (as suggested in the text).

A similar view appears in the decision of the Court of Appeal in *Fowles v. Bedfordshire County Council* [1995] P.I.Q.R. P380; [1996] Ed. L.R. 51 (failure by those in charge of gymnasium to teach somersaulting properly, resulting in injury from fall, a matter for general law and not the 1957 Act).

Premises 10–06
On the definition of "premises", note too *Monarch Airlines v. Luton Airport Ltd* [1998] 1 Lloyd's Rep. 403, Clarke J. where it was accepted that the 1957 Act covered an airport runway (which disintegrated in use, causing alarming damage to an aeroplane traversing it at the time). *Robertson v. Ridley*, holding that officers of a club could not be sued in respect of the condition of the club premises, has now been thrown into some doubt. See *Melhuish v. Clifford & Others* (unreported, August 18, 1998, Hooper J.) and *cf. Grice v. Stourport Tennis Club* (unreported, CA, February 28, 1997).

See too *Olinski v. Johnson* (1997) 32 O.R. (3d) 653 (sports team who took over 10–11
a stadium and agreed to provide security for the evening held to be occupiers for purpose of Ontario occupiers' liability law).

Highway users 10–24
Note the Northern Ireland Court of Appeal's decision in *Campbell v. NI Housing Executive* [1996] 1 B.N.I.L. 99 (plaintiff exercising public right of way *en route* to

shop unprotected by Occupiers' Liability Act). The case is important in rejecting suggestions made—*obiter*—by Lord Browne-Wilkinson in *McGeown v. NI Housing Executive* [1995] 1 A.C. 233 at 247–248 that an invitee, as against a licensee, might exceptionally come within the Act even though passing over the highway. It is now clear that all those using the highway are to be treated similarly.

10–28 The common duty of care

Note *Berryman v. Hounslow LBC* (unreported November 20, 1996, CA). There, Stuart-Smith L.J. observed that, however widely drafted, the common duty of care was not apt to cover all defects in premises. A resident in a block of council flats, finding the lift inoperative, slipped a disc in carrying quantities of shopping up the stairs. His Lordship opined—rightly, it is suggested—that the lack of a working lift could not amount to a breach of section 2 of the 1957 Act so as to afford a right of action in tort against the landlords. The proper and only cause of action was in contract, for breach of the covenant in the lease to keep the lift in good repair.

10–30 Examples

See too *Jeffrey v. Commodore Cabaret* (1996) 13 B.C.L.R. (3d) 149 (occupiers of night-club liable for not having sufficient precautions in force to stop fight once it had started). And in another night-club case, *Duffy v. Carnabane Holdings* [1996] 2 I.L.R.M. 86, the Irish Supreme Court held the proprietors liable for allowing a dance floor to become strewn with spilt liquor and broken glass.

10–31 See too *Staples v. West Dorset District Council* (1995) 93 L.G.R. 536, (no duty to warn users of the Cobb at Lyme Regis that it might be slippery). But *cf. Harrison v. Thanet D.C.*, unreported, September 10, 1997, (where inviting but shallow water next to promenade, negligent not to have notice to warn against diving).

In *Jolley v. L.B. of Sutton* [1998] 3 All E.R. 559, CA, a small boy was badly injured when a boat abandoned next to a block of council flats fell on him while he was trying to jack it up in order to restore it. The Court of Appeal, reversing [1998] 1 Lloyds Rep. 433, exonerated the council as occupiers. Although the council had been negligent in leaving the boat there and it was foreseeable that the plaintiff might be hurt while playing on it, the actual accident that occurred was outside the range of foreseeability. In addition Woolf and Roch L.JJ. opined that in any case the unpredictable nature of the plaintiff's activities would have broken the chain of causation.

NOTE 18. Add: See too *Comer v. Governors of St Patrick's School* (unreported, November 13. 1997, CA) (school not liable to participant in sports day fathers' race who injudiciously collided with playground wall just beyond finishing line).

10–32 Where the plaintiff complains of the dangerous construction of premises, the standard of safety demanded is normally reckoned according to the standards prevailing at the time of construction. An occupier cannot be expected constantly to refit his premises to keep up with advances in technology or building regulations. See *McGivney v. Golderslea* (unreported, November 6, 1997, CA) (ordinary glass in door shattered on impact and cut visitor: use of such glass standard practice when premises built, though at time of accident building regulations stipulated toughened glass: no liability for failing subsequently to reglaze pane with toughened glass). *Quaere*, however, whether this would obtain in all cases, or where the risks involved were very serious. Could an industrialist escape liability to his employees under the 1957 Act if he continued to operate an elderly factory replete with blue asbestos, merely because when the premises were built such standards were regarded as acceptable? It seems unlikely.

10–37 Visitors entering premises

On risks incidental to a visitor's calling, *cf.* too *Phillips v. Perry & Dalgety Agriculture Ltd* (unreported, March 6, 1997, CA) (farmer asked for animal feed to be delivered onto trailer: configuration of trailer made transfer of bags from delivery vehicle hazardous; deliveryman injured when he fell off trailer). The Court of Appeal exonerated the farmer, using precisely the reasoning inherent in section 2(3)(b) (though oddly without citing the section itself). They stressed that there was nothing dangerous about the trailer as such: the danger lay in the process of delivering the feed, and this was a risk incidental to the deliveryman calling which should be borne by him.

Volent non fit injuria   10–44
NOTE 68. See too *Murray v. Bitango* [1996] 7 W.W.R. 163, where it was stated that awareness of a risk will only give rise to a defence of *volenti* if the risk is "virtually certain".

The statutory "requirement of reasonableness"   10–57
On the reasonableness of exclusion clauses in connection with occupiers' liability, see *Monarch Airlines v. Luton Airport Ltd* [1998] 1 Lloyd's Rep. 403 (badly-maintained runway disintegrated, showering aircraft with debris: term excluding liability save in the case of deliberate wrongdoing or reckless conduct knowing damage likely to ensue: clause upheld as reasonable).

3.—LIABILITY OF LANDLORD

NOTE 41. Add: In *Boldack v. East Lindsey District Council* (1999) 31 H.L.R. 41),   **10–64**
the Court of Appeal held that *Cavalier v. Pope* remained good law in the case of pure non-feasance. Hence a small boy was held to have no possible common law claim against the council when a large paving slab left against the wall of his council house fell down and injured him.

NOTE 49. Add: It also seems that "construction, repair or maintenance" is limited   **10–66**
to work on the premises themselves, and hence s.3 does not apply to failure to deal with extraneous dangers. See *Boldack v. East Lindsey District Council* (1999) 31 H.L.R. 41) (failure to remove paving-slab leaning dangerously against wall of council house not covered by s.3 when slab fell on small boy).

NOTE 56. Add: However, it must be noted that s.4(4) only protects the landlord   **10–67**
against claims *by the tenant*. It has no effect where the claimant is a third party: see *Boldack v. East Lindsey District Council*, unreported, February 2, 1998, CA).

4.—LIABILITY TO TRESPASSERS

Brief history of the law   10–70
This test of deliberate harm or reckless disregard has now been adopted by statute in Ireland: see the (Irish) Occupiers' Liability Act 1995, s.4(1).

Occupiers' Liability Act 1984   10–74
In *Swain v. Puri* [1996] P.I.Q.R. P442, the Court of Appeal held that the words "has reasonable grounds to believe" in section 1(3)(b) of the 1984 Act required actual knowledge of facts that would lead a reasonable man to expect the presence of the trespasser: mere culpable ignorance, or constructive knowledge, would not do. The words "knows or ought to know" on page 552, line 2, must therefore now be read in this light. On the facts, the owner of an empty warehouse abutting a council estate did not have the necessary knowledge to put him under a duty of care to an agile but mischievous small boy who climbed on the roof and fell through a skylight.

The standard of care   10–76
See too *Swain v. Puri* [1996] P.I.Q.R. P442, where the Court of Appeal by a

majority held that surrounding an empty warehouse with a seven-foot fence topped with barbed wire amounted to adequate precautions, even though some of the wire was missing.

NOTE 88. Add: That this is indeed the case was confirmed by Neill L.J. in *Revill v. Newberry* [1996] 2 W.L.R. 239, [1996] 1 All E.R. 291, 297–298, who specifically approved the statement in the text. Hence the Act had no relevance to the case of an occupier who shot a burglar.

10–80   In *Ratcliff v. McConnell* [1999] 1 W.L.R. 670 (16-year-old, who surreptitiously entered a swimming-bath after hours, dived in the pool and was crippled when he hit the bottom, failed in his action against the occupiers for not warning him of the dangers. Stuart-Smith L.J. expressed the view that where adults or near-adults were concerned, an occupier who had taken reasonable steps to exluce them would not normally be required to do more.

10–82   **Exclusion of the duty owed under the Occupiers' Liability Act 1984**

NOTE 17. Add: But *cf. Arthur v. Anker* [1996] 2 W.L.R. 602 (right to wheelclamp trespassing car may be afforded by suitably-worded notice). Similar reasoning could be applied to a notice excluding liability for injury.

See too on this case Weir [1996] C.L.J. 423.

10–83   NOTE 29. This point has been taken account of in Ireland. There, even *vis-à-vis* a lawful entrant it is enacted that the occupier cannot reduce his duty below that of avoiding deliberate harm or reckless disregard. See the (Irish) Occupiers' Liability Act 1995, s.5(3).

10–85   See too *Ratcliff v. McConnell, The Times* [1999] 1 W.L.R. 670 (16-year-old who entered a swimming-bath after hours, dived in the poll and was crippled when he hit the bottom held *volens* within section 1(16) as regards the risk).

CHAPTER 11.—BREACH OF STATUTORY DUTY

		PARA.
■1.	Requisites for liability	11–01
	(a) Injury within the ambit of the statute	11–07
	(b) Liability to action	11–12
	(c) Non-fulfilment of statutory duty	11–25
	(d) Injury caused by breach of duty	11–27
■2.	Defences to an action on statutory duty	11–29

The House of Lords in *X v. Bedfordshire County Council* [1995] 3 All E.R. 353 **11–01** upheld the judgment of the Court of Appeal in *M v. Newham L.B.C.* and *E v. Dorset County Council* striking out claims for breach of statutory duty arising out of alleged failures by local authorities to enforce child protection legislation and to implement the Education Acts. In the course of his judgment Lord Browne-Wilkinson re-stated the classic principles limiting the ambit of any tort of breach of statutory duty. He further cast doubt on the availability of a claim in breach of statutory duty arising out of any regulatory system of scheme or social welfare enacted for the benefit of society at large. See, *post*, Supplement, §§ 11–03, 11–14—11–15, 11–20—11–21.

The judgment of the Court of Appeal in *Richardson v. Pitt-Stanley* [1995] Q.B. 123, CA is also noteworthy both because of its finding that no civil cause of action lies for breach of the Employers' Liability (Compulsory Insurance) Act 1969 and the utilisation of the relatively new judicial freedom to refer to *Hansard* to assist in the interpretation of statutory provisions.

Two further judgments illustrate the difficulties in establishing that Parliament may be found to have intended to create a right of action for breach of statutory duty. It is insufficient simply to establish that the relevant statutory provision was designed to protect the interests of the plaintiff. In *Issa v. Hackney Borough Council* no civil claim was found to lie in respect of the commission of a statutory nuisance. In *Olotu v. Home Office* the Court of Appeal held that violation of the custody time limits prescribed in the Prosecution of Offences (Custody Time Limits) Regulations did not give rise to any civil claim for damages. And in *Clunis v. Camden and Islington Health Authority* it was held that no action lay in respect of breach of section 117 of the Mental Health Act 1983, imposing obligations in relation to mental patients in receipt of community care.

1.—REQUISITES FOR LIABILITY

Private law right
11–03

In *X v. Bedfordshire County Council* [1995] 3 All E.R. 353, Lord Browne-Wilkinson re-affirmed that for an action for breach of statutory duty to lie the plaintiff must establish that statutory duty was "imposed for the protection of a limited class of the public and that Parliament intended to confer on members of that class a private right of action for breach of the duty" (at 364). Where the statute provides some alternative remedy to enforce the relevant duty that will *normally* indicate that the statutory right was designed to be enforceable by those means and not by private right of action. However the ". . . mere existence of some other statutory remedy is not necessarily decisive". It may still be possible to show that on the true construction of the Act ". . . the protected class was intended by Parliament to have a private remedy" (at 364).

The Court of Appeal reinforced the need to establish that Parliament intended that a private law right of action should be created by the relevant statutory provision in *Issa v. Hackney London Borough Council* [1997] 1 W.L.R. 956. Their Lordships held that breach of section 94(2) of the Public Health Act 1936 making it a criminal

101

offence to commit a statutory nuisance did not give rise to a civil remedy for breach of statutory duty. The defendant local authority was convicted for its failure as landlord to abate conditions in their property injuring the child plaintiffs' health. In construing the statute, the Court of Appeal held that the vast majority of victims of a statutory nuisance under the Act would enjoy alternative civil remedies against their private sector landlords. The Court of Appeal found that Parliament would not have intended to create a civil remedy, which would necessarily have been available to all victims of statutory nuisance solely to assist the small minority who lack such alternative remedies. See also *Olotu v. Home Office* [1997] 1 W.L.R. 328, CA; see post, § 11–16A.

11–04 Kind of damage
See *McFarlane v. Wilson* [1997] 2 Lloyd's Rep. 259, CA (psychiatric harm).

11–05 Secondary legislation
Note also *Olotu v. Home Office* [1997] 1 W.L.R. 328, 339 where Mummery L.J. doubts that Parliament intended to authorise the Secretary of State to confer a private law right of action when making regulations as to custody time limits under the Prosecution of Offences Act 1985. *cf. Clarke v. Chief Constable of Northamptonshire Police, The Times*, June 14, 1999, CA—duty of care in negligence in respect of custody time limits.

(a) *Injury Within the Ambit of the Statute*

11–07 Injury not contemplated by statute
NOTE 27. Add: *Stovin v. Wise* [1994] 1 W.L.R. 1124, 1129–1130, CA. As to liability in negligence, see [1996] A.C. 923, HL and see *supra*, Supplement, § 7–103.

Type of damage outside the scope of the Act
11–10 NOTE 45. Add: In *Young v. Charles Church (Southern) Ltd* (1998) 39 B.M.L.R. 146 the Court of Appeal held that breach of the Construction (General Provisions) Regulations 1961, reg. 44(2) applied to an employee who suffered psychiatric damage as a result of witnessing the electrocution of a fellow worker, at least where he was working very close to the danger—the regulation was not limited to physical electrocution.

11–11 In *Gerrard v. Staffordshire Potteries* [1995] I.C.R. 502, CA the plaintiff was injured at work when a foreign body flew out of the earthenware jar she was spraying with glaze. The Protection of Eyes Regulations 1974 required that eye protection be provided wherever there arose a "reasonably foreseeable risk engaged in the work from particles or fragments thrown off ". The Court of Appeal held that the relevant statutory duty was not limited to protection from particles dislodged from the object being worked on but to any object dislodged by the worker in the course of his own work.

(b) *Liability to Action*

11–12 Liability to action
Note that in *Richardson v. Pitt-Stanley* [1995] Q.B. 123, CA reference was made to debate in *Hansard* utilising the new freedom to refer to *Hansard* created by *Pepper v. Hart*.
The Protection from Harassment Act 1997 expressly creates a civil remedy in respect of violation of the Act: see *post*, Supplement § 12–16.
Note too the judgment in *Blue Circle Industries plc v. Ministry of Defence* [1999] 2 W.L.R. 295 distinguishing *Merlin v. British Nuclear Fuels plc* and defining physical damage within the Nuclear Installations Acts. Evidence that radioactive contamination of the plaintiffs' land necessitated an extensive cleansing operation and

resulted in restrictions on the use of the land was sufficient to demonstrate physical damage and thus enable the plaintiffs to recover for the consequent diminution in the value of their property.

NOTE 59. After "Consumer Protection Act 1987, s. 41" add: Highways Act 1980, s.41 — duty of highway authority to maintain the highway (subject to the defence in s.58 for the highway authority to prove that it exercised reasonable care), on which see *Haydon v. Kent County Council* [1978] Q.B. 343, CA; *Cross v. Kirklees Metropolitan Borough Council* [1998] 1 All E.R. 564, CA; *Goodes v. East Sussex County Council, The Times,* January 7, 1999, CA.

Where no sanction is prescribed   11–13

In *X v. Bedfordshire County Council* [1995] 3 All E.R. 353, HL. Lord Browne-Wilkinson at 364 re-asserted that if ". . . the statute provides no other remedy for its breach and the Parliamentary intention to protect a limited class is shown, that indicates that there may be a private right of action since otherwise there is no method of securing the protection the statute was intended to confer".

In the last sentence of the paragraph, delete from: "and a homeless person was entitled . . ." to the end of the sentence, including Note 70.

Action against public authorities   11–14

Upholding the judgments of the Court of Appeal in *M v. Newham London Borough Council* and *E v. Dorset County Council*, the House of Lords in *X v. Bedfordshire County Council, supra*, suggested that only exceptionally will ". . . an administrative system designed to promote the social welfare of the community" give rise to private rights enforceable by an action for breach of statutory duty.

Dismissing claims for breach of statutory duty arising out of the child abuse cases, Lord Browne-Wilkinson found that the only factor imputing any Parliamentary intention to create a private law right of action was that the legislation was primarily designed to protect a limited class of persons, children at risk of abuse. However the language and structure of the legislation was equally clearly inconsistent with any intention to create private law rights. The judgments to be made were of "peculiar sensitivity" involving striking the difficult balance between a child risking harm from its parents and harm in being removed from its parents.

Decisions often had to be taken on inadequate and disputed facts. Lord Browne-Wilkinson said that:

> ". . . in such a context it would require exceptionally clear statutory language to show a parliamentary intention that those responsible for carrying out these difficult functions should be liable in damages if, on subsequent investigation with the benefit of hindsight, it was shown that they had reached an erroneous conclusion and therefore failed to discharge their statutory duties" (at 378)

He further cast doubt on whether a claim for breach of statutory duty could ever arise where the relevant duty was dependent on the defendant first having formed a subjective belief. He suggested that the decision in *Thornton v. Kirklees Metropolitan B.C.* [1979] Q.B. 626, CA was "puzzling" and might need to be re-considered at a later date.

Subsequently in *O'Rourke v. Camden L.B.C.* [1997] 3 W.L.R. 86 the House of Lords overruled *Thornton v. Kirklees Metropolitan Borough Council*, holding that a housing authority's duty to provide temporary accommodation under section 63(1) of the Housing Act 1985, although framed in objective terms, does not confer any private law right to sue for damages. Part III of the Housing Act 1985 was part of scheme of social welfare providing housing assistance to individuals for the benefit of society in general which required in its implementation an element of subjective judgment on the part of the housing authority indicative of a public law function, and had been intended by Parliament to be enforceable solely by way of judicial review. Applying *Cocks v. Thanet District Council* [1983] 2 A.C. 286 (see § 11–15) their Lordships considered that challenges to administrative decisions made by public authorities must be made by an application for judicial review, under RSC, Ord. 53, not an action for breach of statutory duty. Similarly, in *Lam v. Brennan and Borough of Torbay* [1997] P.I.Q.R. P488 the Court of Appeal held that the power to grant or refuse planning permission under the Town and Country Planning Act 1971, s.29 did not give rise to a common law duty of care because it was inevitable in granting planning permission that some members of the public might be adversely affected, whereas a planning authority has to consider a range of other factors in reaching its decision in the public interest. These types of challenge to the exercise of administrative discretion will tend to run into the same sort of problems as those raised by an action in negligence in respect of the exercise of statutory powers (see §§ 7–96 *et seq.*).

Note that the policy considerations which might point against finding that a social services authority should not be held liable for breach of statutory duty, nor be held to owe a duty of care in negligence, in respect of the manner in which it discharged its statutory child protection functions will not, in all circumstances, provide an authority with immunity. See *W v. Essex County Council* [1998] 3 W.L.R. 534 where, by a majority, the Court of Appeal held that the local authority could owe a duty of care in negligence to children (the plaintiffs) who were not in its care when making decisions about a foster placement of a child with the plaintiffs' family, when that child was known to have committed sexual abuse on younger children in the past.

Note also that in *Barrett v. Enfield London Borough Council* [1999] 3 W.L.R. 628 the House of Lords refused to strike out the plaintiff's claim in negligence against the local authority in respect of decisions taken about his upbringing after he had been taken into care. Although the decision to take a child into care in the exercise of a statutory power was not justiciable, it did not follow that having taken the child into care the authority could not owe a duty of care in respect of what was or was not done in relation to the child, once in care.

In *X. v. Bedfordshire County Council, supra,* in the education cases once again their Lordships accepted that children having special educational needs formed a class of persons for whose benefit the relevant legislation was enacted. However, nothing in the legislation demonstrated a parliamentary intention to give that class a right of action in damages for breach of statutory duty. As was the case in the child abuse claims, no duty could arise unless a series of judgments were first made by the education authority. Moreover, an elaborate system for consultation and appeals clearly indicated that system adequately provided remedies for any grievance on the part of the parents. "To suggest that Parliament intended, in addition, to confer a right to sue for damages is impossible" (at 399).

In *Clunis v. Camden and Islington Health Authority* [1998] 2 W.L.R. 902, the Court of Appeal ruled than no right of action for damages arose from breach of section 117 of the Mental Health Act 1983. While section 117, which imposes duties to provide after-care services for patients discharged from mental hospitals, was undoubtedly designed to promote the social welfare of such individuals, the wording of the section was ". . . not apposite to create a private law cause of action for failure to carry out the duties under the statute" (at 912). The language used fell short of the "exceptionally clear statutory language" which Lord Browne-Wilkinson had ruled in *X v. Bedfordshire County Council,* was necessary to create a claim for breach of statutory duty arising out of social welfare legislation.

See also *Capital and Counties plc v. Hampshire County Council* [1997] 3 W.L.R. 331, CA.

NOTE 78. *Hincks* was affirmed at (1980) 1 B.M.L.R. 93, CA. And see *Danns v. Department of Health* [1998] P.I.Q.R. P226, CA.

11–15 Public/private law remedies?
See generally *X v. Bedfordshire County Council, supra.*
NOTE 81: Add: applied in *O'Rourke v. Camden L.B.C.* [1997] 3 W.L.R. 86, HL.

11–16A Breach of the Prosecution of Offences (Custody Time Limits) Regulations
Failure on the part of the Crown Prosecution Service to comply with the pre-

scribed time limit for remand in custody laid down in the Prosecution of Offences (Custody Time Limits) Regulations did not give rise to an action for breach of statutory duty on the part of the plaintiff who remained in custody for 81 days beyond the 112 days maximum period allowed by the Regulations. The intention of the Regulations was to achieve greater expedition in the prosecution of offences and to ensure that accused persons did ". . . not languish in prison for excessive periods awaiting trial". The protection of accused persons, the class of which the plaintiff was a member, was quite clearly an object of the providing of those Regulations. However, the Court of Appeal found that neither Parliament nor the Secretary of State would have envisaged circumstances where *both* the Crown Prosecution Service failed to comply with its duty under the Regulations *and* the person on remand failed to apply for immediate bail as she was entitled to do on the expiry of the 112 days. Thus there would be no consideration of, or intention to create, a private law right to claim for damages in such a case: *Olotu v. Home Office* [1997] 1 W.L.R. 328, CA.

See, however, *Clarke v. Chief Constable of Northamptonshire Police, The Times,* June 14, 1999, where the Court of Appeal considered that the police could owe a duty of care in negligence to pass on accurate information to the prison service about a prisoner's period of detention, and that therefore there could be liability in negligence for misinforming the prison service as to the date of the prisoner's arrest, as a result of which the prisoner was detained beyond the proper term stipulated by the court. Similarly, the prison authorities could be liable for their own negligence in detaining a prisoner beyond the period authorised by the court.

European legislation

NOTE 99. Add: *Dillenkofer v. Federal Republic of Germany* [1997] 2 W.L.R. 253, ECJ.

11–17

Where some other sanction is prescribed

Note the importance in determining the impact of other sanctions for an alleged breach of statutory duty of looking at the statute as a whole. In finding that no claim for breach of statutory duty arose in respect of a statutory nuisance committed under the Public Health Act 1936, the Court of Appeal stressed that Part III of the Act must be read as a whole and construed as at the date of its enactment: *Issa v. Hackney London Borough Council* [1997] 1 W.L.R. 956, [1997] 1 All E.R. 999, 1064.

11–18

General public as a particular class

Lord Browne-Wilkinson in *X v. Bedfordshire County Council, supra* (at 364) appears to endorse the view that only a "limited class of the public" can benefit from a private law right of action for breach of statutory duty. He does not however consider the judgment of Atkin L.J. in *Phillips v. Britannia Hygienic Laundry* or the argument discussed in the main text.

11–19

Alternative remedies

In *Richardson v. Pitt-Stanley* [1995] Q.B. 123 the Court of Appeal held that no action in damages for breach of statutory duty lay for breach of section 1 of the Employers' Liability (Compulsory Insurance) Act 1969 against either the employer-company or any director who in breach of section 1 connived at or facilitated a failure to insure under the Act. The plaintiff had been awarded damages in respect of an accident at work against the defendants, his employers. The defendant company however had gone into liquidation and failed to insure against liability to the plaintiff as required by the 1969 Act. Distinguishing *Monk v. Warbey* (where an action was held to lie for breach of the duty to insure imposed by the Road Traffic Act), the Court of Appeal (Sir John Megaw dissenting) found that no civil cause of action for breach of the analogous provisions of the 1969 Act arose, largely because alternative remedies available to the plaintiff at common law and the imposition of

11–20

substantial criminal penalties militated against the imposition of civil liability under the Act.

(1) In relation to any private law right against the company, their Lordships held that, unlike the Road Traffic Act, the 1969 Act created no new liability against the defendant. The plaintiff already enjoyed common law remedies against his employer in respect of his injuries. He could enforce any judgment in negligence, or for breach of statutory duty under the Factories Act, against company assets. If there were no such assets and no insurance against liability, an additional cause of action for breach of statutory duty under the 1969 Act would be of no avail against the employer company.

(2) The imposition under the Act of very substantial criminal penalties and the language of the Act militated against any inference that Parliament intended that the Act be enforced by civil action for breach of statutory duty.

(3) Some slight evidence could be found by reference to *Hansard* that no new civil liability on employers was intended to be created by the Act.

(4) If no civil liability was imposed on the company, no civil liability was likely to be intended to be imposed on individual directors.

This decision appears to run contrary to the policy of the Employers' Liability (Compulsory Insurance) Act 1969, which is to protect the financial position of injured employees bringing actions against their employers. The majority of the Court of Appeal considered that the Act was not exclusively for the protection of employees but also for the protection of employers, particularly the small employer who might be bankrupted by a claim unless insured against it, though if this were the case it is not clear why the employer should be protected from the financial consequences of his own errors in failing to insure by substantial criminal penalties. Sir John Megaw, in his dissenting judgment, considered that the facts fell within Lord Diplock's exception in *Lonrho Ltd v. Shell Petroleum Co. Ltd* [1981] 2 All E.R. 456, namely that the obligation was imposed for the protection of a particular class of individuals, but this was not employers: "The obligation to insure against bodily injury or disease sustained by employees was imposed by Parliament for one purpose, and one purpose only. The purpose was to give protection to a particular class of individuals, the employees, to eliminate, or at least reduce, the risk to an injured employee of finding that he was deprived of his lawful compensation because of the financial position of the employer." (at 315) An action in tort for breach of statutory duty against those responsible for the fact that there is no insurance cover clearly supplements both the underlying policy of the Act and the common law rule which provides that the injured employee is entitled to compensation.

For cogent criticism of *Richardson v. Pitt-Stanley*, see O'Sullivan [1995] C.L.J. 241.

In *Quinn v. McGinty* 1998 Rep. L.R. 107 (Sheriff Court) Judge E.F. Bowen Q.C., Sheriff Principal, declined to follow *Richardson v. Pitt-Stanley* on identical facts, on the basis that the Act was intended to protect a distinct class of persons, namely employees, and any incidental benefit to employers was irrelevant. Although section 1 created an obligation on the part of the company to insure, section 5 also required the officers of the company to see that section 1 was complied with, and therefore an action for breach of statutory duty could lie.

11–21 Administrative "remedies"

In *Clunis v. Camden and Islington Health Authority, supra*, it was said that the primary means of enforcing section 117 of the Mental Health Act 1983 was by way of complaint to the Secretary of State.

NOTE 26. Add: *X v. Bedfordshire County Council, supra*.

Other factors
Note that in *Richardson v. Pitt-Stanley (supra)* Stuart Smith L.J. declared (at 132) "In my opinion, the court will more readily construe a statutory provision so as to provide a civil cause of action where the provision relates to the safety and health of a class of a persons rather than where they have merely suffered economic loss".

Proposals for reform
See *Bennion* (1996) 17 Stat. L.R. 192.

(c) *Non-Fulfilment of Statutory Duty*

The nature of the duty
In *X v. Bedfordshire County Council* [1995] 3 All E.R. 353 at 365–367, Lord Browne-Wilkinson makes it clear that careless performance of a statutory duty does not of itself give rise to an action in tort. The plaintiff must either establish that Parliament intended to confer on him a private law right of action for breach of statutory duty *simpliciter* or that the circumstances are such as to raise a duty of care at common law.

Where the Protection of Eyes Regulations 1974 required that eye protection be provided where there was a "reasonably foreseeable risk of injury to the eyes of any person engaged in the work from particles or fragments thrown off", once there was *objective* evidence such a risk existed, the employer was subject to an absolute duty to provide such protection; *Gerrard v. Staffordshire Potteries* [1995] I.C.R. 502, CA.

2.—Defences to an Action on Statutory Duty

Contributory negligence
See *Reeves v. Commissioner of Police for the Metropolis* [1999] 3 All E.R. 897, HL.

CHAPTER 12.—TRESPASS TO THE PERSON

		PARA.
□1.	Introduction	12–01
□2.	Battery	12–05
■3.	Assault	12–12
■4.	False imprisonment	
	(a) What constitutes a false imprisonment	12–17
	(b) Responsibility for imprisonment committed through the instrumentality of officers of justice	12–23
■5.	Justification of trespass to the person	12–33
	(a) Self-defence	12–35
	(b) Preventing breach of the peace, or making lawful arrest	12–36
	(c) Assisting officers of the law	12–63
	(d) Confinement of mentally disordered persons	12–65
	(e) Parental or other authority	12–76
	(f) Authority of shipmaster	12–79
■6.	Damages	12–80

The judgment of the House of Lords in *O'Hara v. Chief Constable of the Royal Ulster Constabulary* reviews the principles determining what constitutes reasonable grounds for suspicion. The decision of the House of Lords in *R. v. Bournewood Community and Mental Health Services Trust, ex p. L* is crucial both to the definition of the tort of false imprisonment and to the extent of powers to treat patients informally in mental hospitals. The Court of Appeal in *R. v. Governor of Brockhill Prison, ex p. Evans (No. 2)* re-affirmed that liability for false imprisonment does not require that the defendant is aware that his detention of the plaintiff is unlawful.

1.—INTRODUCTION

12–03 **Trespass: intention and negligence**
NOTE 9. Add: See also *Revill v. Newberry* [1996] 2 W.L.R. 239 at 243, CA.

2.—BATTERY

12–08 **How far consent a defence**
The European Court of Human Rights ruled that the judgment in *R. v. Brown* did not constitute a violation of Article 8 of the Convention (respect for private life): *Brown v. United Kingdom, The Times,* February 20, 1997.

NOTE 31. Add: *R. v. Brown* was distinguished in *R. v. Wilson (Alan Thomas),* [1996] 3 W.L.R. 125, CA. See generally Law Commission Consultation Paper No. 139 *Consent in the Criminal Law.*

12–09 **Consent induced by fraud**
See now *Appleton v. Garrett* [1996] P.I.Q.R. P1 (dentist liable in battery when he deliberately misled patients into believing treatment was necessary, when in fact that treatment was both unnecessary, and grossly inappropriate). However, in *R. v. Richardson (Diana), The Times,* April 6, 1998, it was held that failure by a dentist to tell patients that she had been struck off the dental register did not vitiate the patient's consent so as to render the accused criminally liable for assault.

NOTE 49. Add: See now *R. v. Linekar* [1995] 2 W.L.R. 237 at 241–246, CA.

Consent or lawful excuse

In *R. v. Bournewood Community and Mental Health Sources Trust, ex p. L* [1998]
3 W.L.R. 107, the House of Lords confirmed that restraining or detaining a mentally
incapacitated person for his own immediate safety and welfare can be justified by a
defence of necessity; see *post*, Supplement § 12–66.

3.—ASSAULT

Assault

Note developments in the criminal law relating to assault. Conduct designed to   **12–12**
cause psychiatric harm has been found to constitute assault albeit there was no direct
attack on the victim nor any immediate threat of violence: see *R. v. Ireland* [1997]
3 W.L.R. 534, HL; *R. v. Constanza, The Times*, March 31, 1997.

It *may* be however that the common law relating to assault will be rendered
somewhat irrelevant by the civil action now created by the Protection from Harassment Act 1997: see *post*, Supplement, § 12–16.

Harassment causing injury to health   **12–16**

In *Burris v. Azadani* [1995] 1 W.L.R. 1372, CA the Court of Appeal refused to
question the legality of an "exclusion zone" order imposed to prevent repetition of
gross harassment and persecution of the plaintiff constituting clearly tortious conduct
in infringement of her rights.

The Protection from Harassment Act 1997 creates a civil remedy in respect of a
breach or threatened breach of the Act. Section 1 of the Act provides that:

"(1)–(1) A person must not pursue a course of conduct—

   (a) which amounts to harassment of another, and
   (b) which he knows or ought to know amounts to harassment of the other

(2) For the purposes of this section the person whose course of conduct is in
question ought to know that it amounts to harassment of another if a reasonable
person in possession of the same information would think that the course of
conduct amounted to harassment of the other."

Sub-section 3 of section 1 establishes defences relating to the prevention or detection of crime, statutory authority and a broad defence in section 1(3)(c) "... *that in
the particular circumstances the pursuit of the course of conduct was reasonable*"

Section 3 of the Act grants victims of harassment a civil claim in respect of both
an actual or apprehended breach of section 1. Section 3(2) provides that:

"... damages may be awarded for (*among other things*) any anxiety caused by
the harassment and any financial loss resulting from the harassment".

The impact of the Act would seem to turn very much on judicial interpretation of
its rather broad and vague terms. Three questions appear open to debate.

   (1) What constitutes harassment? (See *DPP v. Mesley (Joanna) The Times*,
       June 23, 1999)

   (2) What circumstances render harassment "reasonable" within section
       1(3)(c)?

   (3) What other kinds (other than anxiety and financial loss) fall within section
       3(2)?

Section 3 of the Act will come into force on a day to be appointed by the Lord
Chancellor.

4.—FALSE IMPRISONMENT

(a) *What Constitutes a False Imprisonment*

12–17   False imprisonment defined

The tort of false imprisonment is established on proof of (1) the fact of imprisonment and (2) absence of lawful authority to justify that imprisonment. It is irrelevant whether or not the defendant honestly and reasonably believed that he had the necessary authority to detain the plaintiff, if, in fact, no such authority existed. Thus where a judgment of the Court of Appeal (*R. v. Governor of Brockhill Prison, ex p. Evans* [1997] 2 W.L.R. 236) held that miscalculation of the formula used to determine the plaintiff's date of release from gaol resulted in her remaining in prison for an additional 59 days the governor of the prison was found liable in false imprisonment. The effect of the judgment of the Court of Appeal was that the earlier judgments affirming the mistaken basis for calculating length of sentence should be treated as if they did not exist: *R. v. Governor of Brockhill Prison, ex p Evans (No. 2)* [1998] 4 All E.R. 993, CA. *ex p Evans* is to be contrasted with *Percy v. Hall* [1996] 4 All E.R. 523, CA, where the Court of Appeal said (*obiter*) that constables arresting the plaintiff under byelaws subsequently found to be invalid would not be liable in false imprisonment. There was authority for regarding a byelaw, albeit one later found invalid, as entitled to some recognition at least to the extent of providing a defence to an action in false imprisonment. As Lord Woolf M.R. declared in *Ex p. Evans* (at 1002).

"There is no similar authority for regarding a decision authoritatively overruled as still for some purpose correctly setting out the law"

To be liable in false imprisonment, it must be demonstrated that the defendant had the necessary intention, as well as the ability, to detain the plaintiff. It must be shown that had the plaintiff attempted to leave premises controlled by the defendant, the defendant would have taken steps to stop him. In *R. v. Bournewood Community and Mental Health Services Trust, ex p. L* [1998] 3 W.L.R. 107, HL, a mentally incapacitated patient was admitted to a mental hospital as an informal patient under section 131(1) of the Mental Health Act 1983. The patient very clearly lacked any independent capacity to consent to his admission to hospital or to his medical care, and his carers objected to his remaining in hospital. The patient was housed in an unlocked ward, however, and evinced no desire to leave the hospital. The issue arose before the House of Lords of whether L was in fact detained, "imprisoned", in the hospital. While their Lordships unanimously agreed that any detention of the patient was lawful by virtue of the common law principles of necessity, the House divided on whether L was in fact "imprisoned" during his residence in the hospital. Lord Goff (giving the judgment of the majority) found that while L was an informal patient in the hospital, he was *not* detained there. He was free to leave and not restrained by any physical barriers from choosing to do so. The fact that had he shown any desire to leave, doctors would have moved to take powers to detain him compulsorily, Lord Goff considered irrelevant. Lords Nolan and Steyn dissented. Lord Steyn considered that the sedation administered to L, the constant monitoring of his movements by staff, and the veto on contact with his carers rendered any suggestion that L was free to leave ". . . a fairy tale". (See, further, *post*, Supplement § 12–66).

NOTE 80. Add: *Haywood v. Somerfield Stores Ltd, The Times*, July 9, 1997.

NOTE 87. Add: *Roberts v. Chief Constable of Cheshire* [1999] 2 All E.R. 326 at 333, CA.

12–20   Continuance of imprisonment

In *R. v. Governor of Brockhill Prison, ex p. Evans* [1997] 2 W.L.R. 236, the Court of Appeal rejected the formula on the basis of which the plaintiff's release date had been calculated to allow for time spent in custody on remand. Earlier judgments setting out how time spent on remand should be set off against concurrent sentences were overruled. Consequently the plaintiff spent an additional period in custody subsequent to the date on which she was lawfully entitled to be released. Her claim for false imprisonment against the prison governor succeeded. Albeit he was not at fault, and honestly believed that on the authority of the earlier judgments he was entitled to continue to detain the plaintiff, her detention was not lawful. Blameworthiness plays no part in false imprisonment. The sole issue is whether the plaintiff's detention is justified in law; *R. v. Governor of Brockhill Prison, ex p. Evans (No. 2)* [1998] 4 All E.R. 993, CA; see also *Roberts v. Chief Constable of Cheshire* [1999] 2 All E.R. 326, CA; *Clarke v. Chief Constable of Northamptonshire, The Times,* June 14, 1999, CA; and see, *Post,* Supplement § 16–119.

However, failure on the part of the Crown Prosecution Service to comply with the Prosecution of Offences (Custody Time Limits) Regulations 1987 resulting in the plaintiff's detention on remand beyond the 112 day limit imposed by those Regulations did not render her continued detention unlawful and a false imprisonment. The plaintiff had been lawfully committed into the custody of the prison governor and his duty was to detain her until ordered to deliver her to the Crown Court. He never received such an order and had no independent authority to release her. A claim for breach of statutory duty against the Crown Prosecution Service also failed: *Olutu v. Home Office* [1997] 1 W.L.R. 328 CA (see also *supra,* § 11–16A and *post,* § 16–119. Unlike the plaintiff in *Ex p. Evans, supra,* the plaintiff in *Olutu* had no *right* to be released, save by order by order of the court.

Imprisonment in authorised places or conditions 12–21
In *Toumia v. Evans, The Times,* April 1, 1999, the Court of Appeal refused to strike out a claim in false imprisonment by a prisoner against police officers who refused to unlock cells at the usual times in the course of an illegal industrial dispute.

(b) *Responsibility for Imprisonment Committed through the Instrumentality of Officers of Justice*

Ministerial and judicial proceedings 12–24
NOTE 12. Add: The Court of Appeal judgment in *Martin v. Watson* was overruled by the House of Lords [1995] 3 All E.R. 559; see, *post,* Supplement, § 15–10.

5.—JUSTIFICATION OF TRESPASS TO THE PERSON

Preventing crime 12–36
In appropriate circumstances the use of a properly trained police dog does not constitute an unreasonable use of force in effecting an arrest. The question of what constitutes unreasonable force in making an arrest is a mixed question of fact and law and should generally be left to the jury: *Pollard v. Chief Constable of West Yorkshire,* Trans. Ref. CCTRF/97/1396 CMS2, April 28, 1998, CA.
NOTE 52. Add: *R. v. Owino* [1996] 2 Cr.App.R. 128.

In cases of breaches of the peace 12–37
Note that *McLeod v. Commissioner of Police of the Metropolis* [1994] 4 All E.R. 552, CA confirms that at common law, police have the power to enter private premises to prevent a reasonably anticipated breach of the peace. That common law power is expressly preserved by section 17(b) of the Police and Criminal Evidence Act 1984. The power of entry is *not* limited to places where public meetings are taking place and, despite criticism of *Thomas v. Sawkins* [1935] 2 K.B. 249, that authority remains good law. The police exercising such a power of entry into private premises must however have a genuine apprehension of a breach of the peace in the near future and any power to enter private premises against the will of the occupier must be exercised with "great care and discretion" In *McLeod v. United Kingdom* (1999) 27 E.H.R.R. 493 the European Court of Human Rights held that the common

law concept of breach of the peace and the powers granted to constables to prevent breaches of the peace and to enter property to do so did not in principle violate Article 8 of the European Convention on Human Rights. Nonetheless in the particular circumstances of the case the constable's action was disproportionate to the threat posed to public order and the applicant's claim for violation of Article 8 succeeded. See, *post*, Supplement § 16–107. And see Feldman (1995) 111 L.Q.R. 562; Nicolson and Reid [1996] Crim.L.R. 764.

However, where no actual breach of the peace has taken place in the presence of the arrestor, a power of arrest to prevent an imminent breach of the peace must be based on evidence of a real and present threat that a breach of the peace is about to occur. Refusal to accept a constable's advice to leave the vicinity of an earlier disturbance did not of itself amount to sufficient evidence that the arrested person was about to commit a breach of the peace. The "extreme" step of depriving a person of his liberty for something which he might be about to do must be justified; *Foulkes v. Chief Constable of Merseyside Police* [1998] 3 All E.R. 705, CA.

12–39   What is a breach of the peace

A civil trespass alone will not constitute a breach of the peace. There must be evidence that violence might reasonably be expected to result from that trespass; *Perry v. DPP* [1995] 3 All E.R. 124, D.C. See also *Nicol v. DPP, The Times*, November 22, 1995.

12–41   Public Order Act 1986

Section 5(4) of the Public Order Act 1986 has been amended by the Public Order (Amendment) Act 1996 to read:

"A constable may arrest a person without warrant if he engages in offensive conduct which *a* [formerly '*the*'] constable warns him to stop"

The effect of the amendment is to reverse the effect of *DPP v. Hancock and Tuttle* [1996] Crim.L.R. 139 DC which held that under the original section 5(4) only the actual constable who personally issued the warning to stop the relevant offensive conduct could arrest a person continuing to engage in offensive conduct contrary to his prior warning.

12–42   Criminal Justice and Public Order Act 1994

Note that yet further powers to stop and search pedestrians, to search goods and to impose police cordons are conferred by the Prevention of Terrorism (Additional Powers) Act 1996.

12–49   Reasonable cause for suspicion

In *O'Hara v. Chief Constable of the Royal Ulster Constabulary* [1997] 2 W.L.R. 1 the House of Lords revisited the interpretation of statutory provisions requiring that a constable has reasonable grounds for suspicion to carry out a lawful arrest. Their Lordships held that a *mere* order from a superior officer to arrest a suspect is not capable of amounting to reasonable grounds for suspicion. The arresting officer himself must be in possession of information capable of creating reasonable suspicion in his own mind. The test is partly subjective and partly objective. The arresting officer must both himself have grounds for suspicion, and, those grounds must be objectively reasonable. However where, as in *O'Hara*, the arresting constable had been present at a briefing where superior officers informed him that the plaintiff had been involved in a murder, that briefing sufficed to create reasonable grounds for suspicion entitling the constable to arrest the plaintiff. In order to have reasonable suspicion, a constable need not have evidence amounting to a *prima facie* case. Hearsay information, including information from other officers, may properly suffice to create reasonable grounds to arrest. But that information must be within the knowledge of the arresting officer. The discretion to arrest vests in the constable, not his superior officers.

NOTE 5. Add: *Ward v. Chief Constable of West Midland Police, The Times,*
December 15, 1997, CA.

Other statutory powers of summary arrest

Section 26 of the Police and Criminal Evidence Act 1984, which repeals all prior
statutory provisions conferring summary powers of arrest expressly on constables
(save for those statutory powers saved by Schedule 2 to the Act), relates only to
powers of arrest granted *exclusively* to constables. Where a statute, prior to 1984,
conferred a power of arrest exercisable by constables or private citizens, section 26
is inapplicable and a constable, as much as any private individual, can exercise the
relevant general power of arrest ". . . otherwise the absurd position would arise that
a citizen would be entitled to arrest a person under the provision of section 6 of the
1824 [Vagrancy] Act whereas a constable would not": *Gapper v. Chief Constable
of Avon and Somerset Constabulary* [1998] 4 All E.R. 248, CA.

The grounds for arrest

In *R. v. Chalkley* [1998] 2 All E.R. 155, the Court of Appeal held that where an
arrested person had been told a true ground for his arrest, that arrest did not become
unlawful because police also wished to investigate another more serious offence.

Constables and private persons

Note that specific statutory powers of arrest may prescribe a time period within
which the arrested person must be brought before a magistrate: *Wheeldon v. Wheeldon* [1997] 3 F.C.R. 769.

NOTE 5. Add: *Bull v. Chief Constable of Sussex* (1995) 159 L.G.Rev. 893, CA.

Escape from custody

The Prisoners (Return to Custody) Act 1995 amends section 17 of the Police and
Criminal Evidence Act to allow police to enter to recapture escaping or absconding
prisoners without the limitation of the requirement of hot pursuit imposed by
D'Souza v. DPP. That Act does not apply to absconding mental patients.

(c) *Assisting Officers of the Law*

Assisting officers of the law

Note that the Court of Appeal judgment in *Martin v. Watson* has been overruled
by the House of Lords [1995] 3 All E.R. 559; see, *post,* Supplement § 15–10.

(d) *Confinement of Mentally Disordered Persons*

Detention under the Mental Health Act 1983

The House of Lords held in *R. v. Bournewood Community and Mental Health
Services Trust, ex p. L* [1998] 3 W.L.R. 107, that common law powers to detain
mentally incapacitated patients on grounds of the necessity to safeguard their welfare
survive, and exist in parallel with, the Mental Health Act 1983. In a landmark judgment the Law Lords overturned the judgment of the Court of Appeal that the Bournewood Trust had falsely imprisoned L. L was 48 years old, autistic and severely
mentally retarded. He was unable to speak, and had very limited understanding. He
clearly lacked any independent capacity to consent to medical care and treatment. L
had spent 30 years in hospital until in 1994 he went to live with paid carers. In
1997, he became agitated at a day centre and his carers could not be contacted. He
was taken by ambulance first to the emergency ward at Bournewood hospital and
later admitted as an informal patient to the psychiatric unit. He remained there for
several months albeit his carers wanted him to return to them. L was in an unlocked
ward and did not attempt to leave. Two issues arose before their Lordships (1) Was
L in fact imprisoned, detained, against his will? (2) If he was so detained, did the
hospital have lawful authority to justify that detention? On the issue of L's detention,
their Lordships all agreed that there were periods when L was undoubtedly detained,

notably when he was first brought by ambulance to the hospital. On his admission to the psychiatric unit, Lord Goff for the majority held that, given that L was kept in an unlocked ward and not ever physically restrained from leaving, he was not then detained. Lords Nolan and Steyn dissented (see *supra*, Supplement § 12–17). The Law Lords nonetheless unanimously agreed that given his profound mental incapacity any detention of L was lawful under the common law principles of necessity developed in *F v. Berkshire Health Authority*. Such common law powers to provide mental health care to persons unable to consent to treatment survive, and are inherent to, section 131(1) of the Mental Health Act. No patient with the requisite capacity to determine his own medical care may be admitted to hospital save by virtue of sections 2–5 of the Mental Health Act. Section 131(1) permits competent patients to consent to informal admission and allows informal admission of patients lacking mental capacity where such a mode of treatment is necessary for their welfare.

In *Re S-C (mental patient: habeas corpus)* [1996] 1 All E.R. 532 the Court of Appeal re-affirmed that compliance with the provisions of the Mental Health Act 1983 governing the detention of patients in hospital will be strictly enforced. "[N]o adult citizen of the United Kingdom is liable to be confined in any institution against his will, save by the authority of law" (*per* Sir Thomas Bingham M.R. at 534).

It followed that when a social worker obtained the patient's admission to hospital relying on the patient's mother's "consent" as nearest relative, when she was well aware that it was the father who was the nearest relative as defined by section 26 of the Act (and that the father objected to the application), the patient's admission to hospital was unlawful.

Unusual or irrational thinking, or the maintenance of a judgment many people might find shocking, are not evidence of mental disorder. Detaining a pregnant woman with pre-eclampsia who refused to comply with medical advice to consent to admission to hospital and declared that she was prepared to see her baby die rather than give up her plans for a totally natural birth was unlawful (*St George's Healthcare NHS Trust v. S* [1998] 3 All E.R. 673, CA).

The Mental Health (Patients in the Community) Act 1995 amends the 1983 Act to provide for a new regime of supervised discharge and after-care for certain patients released from detention in hospital. A person subject to a supervision order on his release from hospital will have his liberty curtailed by the provisions of the newly inserted section 25D of the Mental Health Act 1983. He will *inter alia* be obliged to reside at a specific place, to attend for treatment and training, and to allow his supervisor access to him. Most importantly section 25(D)(4) provides that a recalcitrant patient may be "taken and conveyed" by his supervisor or any person authorised by him "to any place where the patient is required to reside or attend for the purpose of medical treatment, occupation, education or training".

Criteria governing imposition of such a supervision order are broadly similar to criteria governing involuntary admission to hospital. See generally *Parkin* (1996) 59 M.L.R. 414.

See also: *R. v. Wilson, ex p. Williamson, The Independent*, April 19, 1995.

NOTE 2. Add: *R. v. BHB Community Healthcare NHS Trust, ex p. Barker, The Times*, October 14, 1998, CA.

NOTE 5. Add: *Whitbread v. Kingston and District NHS Trust, The Times*, July 14, 1997.

12–69   Consent to treatment

Note that nothing in the Mental Health (Patients in the Community) Act 1995 authorises non-consensual treatment of patients subject to a supervision order. Presumably however a patient "taken and conveyed" to a specific place for medical treatment who persists in refusing psychiatric treatment or medication may simply be re-detained in hospital where the provisions of Part IV of the Mental Health Act 1983 would once again apply to him.

NOTE 13a. Add: *South West Hertfordshire Health Authority v. KB* [1994] 2 F.C.R. 1051. And see also *Tameside and Glossop Acute Services Trust v. CH (A Patient)*

[1996] 1 F.C.R. 753, where Wall J. held that a caesarean section could be authorised under section 63 as the birth of a live child was in the interests of the patient and a successful pregnancy was a necessary part of the treatment for the patient's psychiatric disorder. However, note that the Mental Health Act cannot be used to compel a woman, who retains mental capacity and is not suffering from mental disorder, to undergo a Caesarian section; *St George's Hospital NHS Trust v. S, supra.*

Protection against civil or criminal proceedings　　　　　　　　　**12–74**
　　NOTE 29. Add: see J Jaconelli and A. Jaconelli (1998) 20 J.Soc.Wel.&Fam.L. 151.

(e) *Parental or other Authority*

Note that the European Court of Human Rights has now held that beating a child with a cane constitutes inhuman or degrading punishment contrary to Article 3 of the European Convention on Human Rights: *A v. United Kingdom* (1999) 27 E.H.R.R. 611.

6.—DAMAGES

Damages　　　　　　　　　**12–80**
　　Note that in *Thompson v. Commissioner of Police for the Metropolis* [1997] 3 W.L.R. 403, the Court of Appeal set out guidelines for juries on awards of damages in false imprisonment and malicious prosecution; see *post*, Supplement § 27–68. And see *Clark v. Chief Constable of Cleveland, The Times*, May 13, 1999, CA.

CHAPTER 13.—WRONGFUL INTERFERENCE WITH GOODS

		PARA.
□1.	General	13–01
■2.	Modes of conversion	13–12
	(a) Conversion by taking or receiving property	13–14
	(b) Conversion by transfer	13–20
	(c) Conversion by wrongful but effective sale	13–27
	(d) Conversion by keeping	13–28
	(e) Conversion by destruction or misuse	13–38
	(f) Conversion by denial of right	13–40
■3.	Subject-matter of conversion	13–42
■4.	Person entitled to sue	
	(a) Generally	13–51
	(b) Title by mere possession	13–58
	(c) Title to sue by virtue of immediate right to possession	13–77
■5.	Position of defendant	
	(a) Co-owners	13–83
	(b) Defendant ignorant of plaintiff's title	13–87
6.	Multiple claims: *jus tertii*, estoppel and double liability	13–99
	(a) *Jus tertii*: joinder of competing claimants	13–102
	(b) Joinder of concurrent actions	13–105
	(c) Double liability	13–106
7.	Forms of relief generally	13–108
■8.	Orders for delivery	
	(a) Judgment for specific delivery	13–110
	(b) Judgment for delivery or damages	13–112
	(c) Interlocutory orders for delivery	13–113
■9.	Damages	
	(a) General rule: value of the good	13–114
	(b) Damages beyond value of goods: special damages	13–135
	(c) Nature of plaintiff's interest	13–141
	(d) Return of chattel	13–151
	(e) Successive conversions and satisfaction	13–154
	(f) Contributory negligence	13–156
	(g) Limitation of actions	13–157
10.	Trespass	13–158
■11.	Negligence resulting in damage to goods	13–163
12.	Reversionary injury	13–166
13.	Wrongful interference by other torts	
	(a) Other torts generally	13–168
	(b) Rescous and pound breach	13–169
■14.	Replevin	13–170

13–01   New developments since the last edition include (1) the unfortunately unreported case of *Irving v. Keen*, March 3, 1995 on the measure of damages in conversion; (2) the provisions of sections 20A and 20B of the Sale of Goods Act 1979 inserted by the Sale of Goods (Amendment) Act 1995 to deal with sales of part of a bulk; (3) the Treasure Act 1996, replacing the ancient rules relating to treasure trove; (4) the macabre decision in *Dobson v. Tyneside A.H.A.* [1997] 1 W.L.R. 596, concerning the proprietary status of human remains; and (5) *MCC Proceeds Inc. v. Lehman Bros* [1998] 4 All E.R. 675 on the right of an equitable owner to sue in conversion.

2.—MODES OF CONVERSION

(a) *Conversion by Taking or Receiving Property*

Intention to excercise dominion   **13–14**

In order to amount to a conversion, the dealing must of course be inconsistent with the plaintiff's proprietary rights. Hence where A defrauds B into providing C with a bank draft made out in C's name, which C cashes, there is no conversion by C. The bank intended the draft to go to him all along, albeit as a result of a mistake. See *Toronto-Dominion Bank v. Carotenuto* (1998) 154 D.L.R. (4th) 627.

On the burden of proof in bailment cases, see too *Jerry Juhan Developments v.*   **13–34**
Arco Tyres, The Times, January 15, 1999. Bailors wrongfully failed to collect tyre moulds from bailees at the appointed time. When the bailees did arrive, the moulds had inexplicably disappeared. It was unclear whether they had vanished before the bailors' failure to collect (when the bailees would have to disprove negligence) or afterwards (in which case the bailors would have to prove fault). Held: in order to invoke the presumption of negligence against the bailees, the bailors had to prove the time of disappearance. Since they could not, their action failed.

3.—SUBJECT-MATTER OF CONVERSION

Dead bodies and human tissue   **13–50**

Add at end: It seems, however, that preservation of body parts for purely investigative or administrative purposes will not suffice to turn them into ownable property. Nor, even if body parts do count as property, do the next-of-kin have any automatic right to them. See *Dobson v. North Tyneside AHA* [1997] 1 W.L.R. 596 (person died in hospital: brain preserved in paraffin for inquest, used as evidence and later disposed of by health authority; action in conversion so by next-of-kin failed).

By contrast, it has been held in Canada that the ashes of a deceased person can be the subject matter of conversion: see *Mason v. Westside Cemeteries* (1996) 135 D.L.R. (4th) 361 (ashes deposited in cemetery vault; next-of-kin successfully sued cemetery as bailee when it lost them).

NOTE 61. The statement in the text gains support from *R. v. Kelly* [1998] 3 All E.R. 741, (purloining of preserved human body parts from Royal College of Surgeons' collection held to be theft, on the basis that skilled work done on them and hence not covered by human body exception). In the same case Rose L.J. left it open whether body parts might not be property even if no process had been applied to them, e.g. if required for transplanting or as an exhibit at a trial. (See [1998] 3 All E.R. at 750.)

4.—PERSON ENTITLED TO SUE

(a) *Generally*

For a recent case where a right to possession prevailed against an actual owner,   **13–51**
see *Indian Herbs (U.K.) Ltd v. Hadley & Ottoway Ltd* (unreported, January 21, 1999, CA) (seller under reservation of title clause repossessed before total price paid, but also before period of credit expired: liable to buyer in conversion.)

Right to possession where return illegal   **13–55**

See also *Slater v. Metropolitan Police Comm'r, The Times,* January 23, 1996 (police have no right to retain money unlawfully obtained by plaintiff).

(b) *Title by Mere Possession*

13–60   NOTE 92. Note that the Police (Property) Act 1897 has been amended by the
Police (Property) Act 1997. Previously the police had powers to sell unclaimed
property but not to retain it for their own use. This restriction is now abolished, and
a power conferred to make regulations whereby a police authority may, if they think
such property would be useful for their own purposes, by resolution cause title to
vest in themselves.

13–62   **Finders**
NOTE 96. Add: That this is so has now been confirmed in *Waverley B.C. v.
Fletcher* [1995] 4 All E.R. 756. The defendant, using a metal detector in a public
park, found a buried brooch. The Court of Appeal held that, whether or not his
excavations were lawful, he obtained no title as against the owners of the park.
Although the lack of a manifest intention in the owner to exercise control over his
land might prevent him being in possession of things found on it, items attached to
or under it were invariably regarded as being in his possession.

13–63   NOTE 96. *cf. Trachuk v. Olinek* [1996] 4 W.W.R. 137, a Canadian case holding a
finder of buried money entitled to it as against the freeholder. However, this case is
of little significance, since the land had been leased and the leaseholder, who on
orthodox principles would have been better entitled than anyone, was not before the
court.

13–65   The last sentence relating to treasure trove must now be read in the light of the
Treasure Act 1996, which replaces the ancient law of treasure trove with a modern
statutory code. The essential provision of the new Act is section 4(1), providing that
"treasure" when found shall, subject to any pre-existing rights, automatically vest
in the Crown. "Treasure" is defined for these purposes in section 1. It includes: (i)
any coin over 300 years old found as part of a hoard of 10 or more; (ii) any such
coin forming part of a hoard of two or more, if it contains at least 10 per cent gold
or silver by weight; (iii) any other artefact over 300 years old if it contains at least
10 per cent gold or silver by weight; and (iv) anything that would under the previous
law have counted as treasure trove. In addition, the Secretary of State has power
under section 2 of the Act to adjust this definition by removing certain descriptions
of property from it, or (conversely) adding to it any class of objects over 200 years
old which are considered to be of cultural importance.

In contrast to the old law, no distinction is drawn between property lost and
property hidden (see section 4(4)(b)). Furthermore, it is specifically enacted in section 4(4)(a) that the new code applies to "treasure" wherever found—thus pre-
empting any argument that it should be limited to buried items. The result is a
potentially very wide definition of objects covered by the provisions of the Act. For
example, a Carolean silver spoon inadvertently left behind in a house by a now
untraceable previous occupier will today apparently vest in the Crown as soon as
the new occupant comes across it.

The Crown's rights in treasure are, for the first time, expressly stated to take effect
subject to prior rights in the property concerned. This new provision was necessitated
by the abolition of the old common law limitation restricting the Crown's rights in
hidden property to cases where the owner was untraceable. Prior rights are defined
in section 4(2) as rights held when the property was placed in the position where it
was found (or, in the case of latent property which has since been moved, in the
position where it was before it was moved). As a result, it is always open to a
previous owner of lost or hidden treasure, or his successors in title to it, to prove a
title. The Act does not say what the position is if the previous owner had purported
to abandon his property when he dropped or deposited it. It is tentatively suggested
that in such a case his rights in it would be regarded as not having been extant at
the relevant time, and hence that title would vest indefeasibly in the Crown.

The Crown's rights of course prevail over those of the finder—as they did with treasure trove. The finder has to be content under section 10 of the Act with a discretion in the Secretary of State (though not a duty—section 10(6))—to compensate him and/or the owner or occupier of the land where the item was found with a sum up to, but not exceeding, the value of the item concerned. However, presumably as against anyone other than the Crown the old cases as to who is entitled to found property will continue to be relevant.

The Act is now in force as from March 13, 1997 (s.11) and September 24, 1997 (the rest of the Act). (See S.I. 1997 Nos 760 and 1977.) As regards previous findings, the old law of treasure trove remains in effect.

For title to sue by virtue of an interest in an undivided bulk, see also Gullifer **13–79** [1999] L.M. & C.L.Q. 93.

(c) *Title to Sue by Virtue of Immediate Right to Possession*

Equitable rights **13–80**
See too Tettenborn [1996] C.L.J. 36. The suggestion made there, and in the text, that mere equitable title cannot found title to sue in conversion, has now been vindicated. See *MCC Proceeds Inc v. Lehman Bros* [1998] 4 All E.R. 675 (A holds share certificates in its possession on bare trust for B: A pledges them to C, who take bona fide and later sells them: no action by B against C for conversion).

5.—POSITION OF DEFENDANT

(a) *Co-owners*

Co-owners under the Torts (Interference with Goods) Act 1977 **13–86**
Add a new paragraph as follows:

Special rule: co-ownership and buyers from a fixed bulk **13–86a**
Under sections 20A and 20B of the Sale of Goods Act 1979, inserted by the Sale of Goods (Amendment) Act 1995, where a buyer pays for a quantity of goods forming part of a larger bulk, he prima facie becomes a proportionate co-owner of the goods in that bulk together with the seller or the other buyers, as the case may be.

Where the total quantity of goods in the bulk is not enough to satisfy a number of buyers, the shares of each buyer are reduced *pari passu* (see section 20A(4)). This causes problems where one buyer obtains delivery of his full contractual allocation and thus prevents another buyer getting his own aliquot share. On principle the short-changed buyer could bring an action in conversion against both the seller (for delivering the excess) and the other buyer (for accepting it).

This liability is, however, heavily qualified. Section 20B(1)(a) protects the seller by deeming the buyer to have consented to any deliveries to other buyers up to their contractual entitlements; it should be noted that there seems to be no requirement of good faith or lack of knowledge in order for this immunity to be invoked. Moreover, the other buyer is also protected by section 20B(3)(a), providing that nothing in either section 20A or section 20B shall "impose an obligation on a buyer of goods out of a bulk to compensate any other buyer of goods out of that bulk for any shortfall in the goods received by that buyer". Note, however, that this latter protection is limited to actions for compensation: *quaere* whether it would apply to (a) an action against the other buyer for specific delivery of the excess if he still had it, or (b) a restitutionary action in respect of the price received for the excess if he had sold it.

It should be remembered that sections 20A and 20B are limited in their effect to property issues: it is specifically provided by sections 20B(3)(b) and 20B(3)(c) that contractual liability is to remain untouched.

119

13–103   NOTE 36: RSC, Ord. 15, r.10A and CCR, Ord 15, r.4 were abrogated on April 26, 1999. They were not preserved in the Schedules to the new Civil Procedure Rules, nor does there seem to be any equivalent provision elsewhere. this could cause difficulties. Section 8 of the 1977 Act allows the defendant to show, *in accordance with rules of court,* that a third party has a better title than the plaintiff. One hopes that the apparent lack of any extant rules of court will not be held to deprive section 8 of any effect.

NOTE 37: On RSC, Ord. 15, r.10A and CCR, Ord. 15, r.4, see the entry to Note 36 *supra.*

NOTE 39: On RSC, Ord. 15, r.10A and CCR, Ord. 15, r.4, see the entry to Note 36 *supra.*

13–109   NOTE 61: For proceedings started after April 26, 1999, RSC, Ord. 13, r.3 and Ord. 19, r.4 are replaced by CPR, r.12.4(1); RSC, Ord. 42, r.1A by CPR, § 10.14. Their county court equivalents are similarly superseded.

NOTE 64: For proceedings started after April 26, 1999, RSC, Ord. 42, r.1A and CCR, Ord. 22, r.4 are replaced by CPR, r.40.14.

8.—ORDERS FOR DELIVERY

(a) *Judgment for Specific Delivery*

13–110 **Judgment for specific delivery and consequential damages**

On the discretion to refuse an order of specific delivery, see too *Probert v. Society for the Welfare of Horses,* Pontypool County Court (H.H. Judge Evans), reported in the *Daily Telegraph* for February 1, 1997. The owner of a horse was convicted of mistreating it and fined; the animal was later removed and unlawfully kept by an animal charity. The judge declined to make an order for specific delivery against the charity, despite the owner's undisputed title.

13–111   NOTE 76: For proceedings started after April 26, 1999, RSC, Ord. 13, r.3 is replaced by CPR, r.12.4(1).

13–112   NOTE 78: For proceedings started after April 26, 1999, RSC Ord. 13, r.3 is replaced by CPR r.12.4(1).

13–113   NOTE 79: From April 26, 1999, RSC, Ord. 29, r.2 is replaced by CPR, r.25.1(1)(c) (orders for preservation, etc.) and r.25.1(1)(e) (interim delivery up).

13–114   In *Middle Temple v. Lloyds Bank plc* [1999] 1 All E.R. Comm. 193, a cheque was converted by two banks on two separate occasions. Although the issue did not arise, Rix J. opined, *obiter,* that in such a case one serial converter who paid damages in full might recover contribution from the others under the Civil Liability (Contribution) Act 1978. *Sed quaere.* If the two conversions took place on different occasions, were both defendants liable for the "same damage" as required by section 1(1) of the Act? It seems doubtful.

9.—DAMAGES

(a) *General Rule: Value of the Goods*

13–121 **Rise in value after conversion**

It has been held that while under the principle in *Sachs v. Miklos* [1948] 2 K.B. 23 a plaintiff who culpably fails to collect his goods from a bailee cannot take advantage of a subsequent rise in value when he sues for non-delivery, this does not apply if the plaintiff founds his case on a conversion by sale or destruction. In *Irving*

v. Keen (unreported, March 3, 1995) the plaintiff failed to collect his car when asked
to do so in 1984; in 1988 the defendant bailee converted it by disassembling it. The
plaintiff recovered its 1988 value, even though this was substantially more than the
1984 figure.

Decline in value after conversion   **13–122**
NOTE 16. See too *Trailways Transport v. Thomas* [1996] 2 N.Z.L.R. 443, following *Solloway v. McLaughlin* but showing some scepticism over *Brandeis God-
schmidt*.

On proof of the value of a converted article, see too *Williamson v. Phillips, Son &* **13–134**
Neale (unreported, July 29, 1998) (presumption in *Armory v. Delamirie* only applies,
if at all, where other evidence of value completely lacking).

On remoteness of consequential loss, see too *Saleslease Ltd v. Davis* [1999] 1 **13–136**
W.L.R. 1664 (MOT testing machine worth £5,000 converted: owner could have
made £13,000-odd by leasing it out: no claim for latter figure in absence of knowledge of potential loss on defendant's part).

(b) *Damages Beyond Value of Goods: Special Damages*

Loss of hire   **13–138**
The principle in *Strand Electric & Engineering Co. v. Brisford Entertainments*
[1952] 2 Q.B. 246, that the owner of a chattel wrongfully retained may recover a
reasonable hire value whatever he would in fact have got for it, has been endorsed
by the Privy Council in *Inverugie Investments v. Hackett* [1995] 1 W.L.R. 713.
Although that case concerned mesne profits in respect of land, Lord Lloyd at 845
specifically stated that a similar rule applied to chattels. See too *Ministry of Defence
v. Ashman* [1993] 2 E.G.L.R. 102 (another land case).

NOTES 74 and 77: For proceedings started after April 26, 1999, RSC, Ord. 42, **13–141**
r.1A and CCR, Ord. 22, r.4 are replaced by CPR, r.40.14.

On the apparent disappearance of RSC, Ord. 15, r.10A without replacement, see **13–142**
supra, Supplement, § 13–103.

On *Chinery v. Viall,* see too *Indian Herbs (U.K.) Ltd v. Hadley & Ottoway Ltd* **13–147**
(unreported, January 21, 1999, CA) (partly paid seller wrongfully retook goods in
misguided reliance on reservation of title clause: accepted, in conversion action by
buyer, that credit to be given for unpaid balance of price).

(d) *Return of Chattel*

Transaction equivalent to return   **13–151**
This paragraph must now be reads in the light of *Irving v. Keen* (unreported,
March 3, 1995), holding that where a chattel is returned in an entirely different form,
the right to recover its value at the time of a previous conversion remains. So a
defendant who wrongfully dismantled the plaintiff's car in 1988 and returned the
mouldering remnants in 1990 was nevertheless liable to pay its value in 1988.

(f) *Contributory Negligence*

NOTE 28. See too *Boma Mfg Co v. Canadian Imperial Bank of Commerce* (1997) **13–156**
140 D.L.R. (4th) 463, where the Supreme Court of Canada held the defence unavailable at common law.

On the effect of foreign limitation periods on actions for conversion, see *Gotha* **13–157**
(City of) v. Sotheby's, The Times, October 10, 1998.

11.—NEGLIGENCE RESULTING IN DAMAGE TO GOODS

13–165 NOTES 76 and 77: On the apparent disappearance of RSC, Ord. 15, r.10A without replacement, see *supra,* Supplement, § 13–103.

14.—REPLEVIN

13–170 NOTE 1: Remove reference to CCR, Ord. 50, r.9.

CHAPTER 14.—DECEIT

		PARA.
□1.	Introduction	14–01
□2.	Representation of fact	14–05
□3.	State of defendant's mind	14–20
□4.	Representation must be intended to be acted upon by plaintiff	14–29
■5.	Plaintiff must have been influenced by misrepresentation	14–34
□6.	Damage	14–39
□7.	Statutory liability under Misrepresentation Act 1967, s.2(1)	14–43
8.	Misrepresentation as to credit of third person	14–46
9.	Statutory liability for misstatement in a prospectus	14–49
10.	Trade descriptions and alternative relief	14–50

1.—INTRODUCTION

Fraud and illegal transactions   14–03

In the House of Lords' decision in *Tinsley v. Milligan* [1994] A.C. 340 (where the defendant claimed a beneficial share in a property, the title to which had been acquired in a course of illegal conduct) Lord Browne-Wilkinson and Lord Goff (the latter dissenting in the case itself) disapproved of the "public conscience" test (whereby the court would have regard to the extent to which the public conscience would be affronted by recognising rights acquired by illegal transactions) noted in *Saunders v. Edwards* [1987] 1 W.L.R. 116, CA.

2.—REPRESENTATION OF FACT

Continuing representations   14–07

Slough Estates plc v. Welwyn Hatfield DC [1996] 2 P.L.R. 50, May J. The defendants were liable when their representation became false and the plaintiffs were not informed.

3.—STATE OF DEFENDANT'S MIND

Ambiguous representations   14–27

The test set out in *Akerhielm v. De Mare* [1959] A.C. 789 was applied in *Henry Ansbacher and Coln v. Binks Stern, The Times*, June 26, 1997, CA.

4.—REPRESENTATION MUST BE INTENDED TO BE ACTED UPON BY PLAINTIFF

Who is within the defendant's intention?   14–31

NOTE 28. Add: Re negligent misrepresentation add *Possfund Custodian Trustee Ltd v. Diamond and Others* [1996] 1 W.L.R. 1351.

5.—PLAINTIFF MUST HAVE BEEN INFLUENCED BY THE MISREPRESENTATION

The plaintiff must have been influenced by the misrepresentation   14–34

The correct test for establishing causation discussed by Hobhouse L.J. in *Downs v. Chappell* [1997] 1 W.L.R. 426, CA.

14–36   Carelessness of plaintiff in not discovering the untruth no defence
Add; *Nationwide Building Society v. Thimbleby & Co.* [1999] Lloyd's Rep. RM
359, Blackburne J.

6.—DAMAGE

14–40   Measure of damages
Banque Bruxelles Lambert SA v. Eagle Star Insurance Co Ltd [1997] A.C. 191,
HL: the measure of damages for fraud is in a special category regulated by the
principles of *Doyle v. Olby (Ironmongers) Ltd* [1969] 2 Q.B. 158. See also the House
of Lords' decision in *Smith New Court Securities Ltd v. Scrimgeour Vickers (Asset
Management) Ltd* [1997] A.C. 254. This gives guidance on assessing the value of
shares for fraud damages (and generally on the principles to apply in assessing the
damages payable when the plaintiff has been induced by fraudulent misrepresentation to buy property). The plaintiff had bought shares in a public company, FIS, at
an inflated price because of the false representations of the defendant's broker. Due
to a fraud involving FIS the value of the shares slumped. The Court of Appeal had
held that the plaintiff's loss upon subsequently selling the shares was not foreseeable
and not recoverable. The House of Lords held, however, that the defendant was
liable for all losses directly flowing from the fraud, even if not foreseeable. Though
normally the damages would include the price paid by the plaintiff, less the market
value of the property on the date of purchase ("date of transaction rule"), that rule
was flexible. Here the plaintiff had become "locked into" the property because of
the fraud. Dicta of Hobhouse L.J. in *Downs v. Chappell* [1997] 1 W.L.R. 426, CA,
that the court should cross-check its quantification of recoverable loss by assessing
what the value of the business would have been if the misrepresentation had been
true, disapproved. House of Lords decision in *Smith New Court* discussed by Thomson, "Damages for Misrepresentation", 1997 S.L.T. 37, 301–303.
NOTE. 52. The Court of Appeal decision in *Smith New Court Securities Ltd v.
Scrimgeour Vickers (Asset Management) Ltd* has now been overturned by the House
of Lords: [1997] A.C. 254.

14–41   Consequential losses
Smith New Court Securities Ltd v. Scrimgeour Vickers (Asset Management) Ltd,
[1997] A.C. 254, HL. Following fraud, consequential losses could be recovered but
the plaintiff was obliged to reasonably mitigate their loss once they were aware of
the fraud. Lord Browne-Wilkinson: "once the fraud has been discovered, if the
plaintiff is not locked into the asset and the fraud has ceased to operate on his mind,
a failure to take reasonable steps to sell the property may constitute a failure to
mitigate his loss requiring him to bring the value of the property into account as at
the date when he discovered the fraud or shortly thereafter". (at 266).

7.—STATUTORY LIABILITY UNDER MISREPRESENTATION ACT 1967, s.2(1)

14–44   Measure of damages
The House of Lords in *Smith New Court Securities Ltd v. Scrimgeour Vickers
(Asset Management) Ltd*, [1997] A.C. 254 declined to express a view on the cor-
rectness of the Court of Appeal decision in *Royscott v. Rogerson* [1991] 2 Q.B. 297.
However, Lord Steyn noted (at 283) that there had been trenchant academic criticism
of the case: see Hooley (1991) 107 L.Q.R. 547.

CHAPTER 15.—MALICIOUS PROSECUTION, ETC.

		PARA.
□1.	Kinds of damage caused	15–01
□2.	Malicious prosecution	15–05
	(a) Prosecution	15–06
	(b) Determination of prosecution	15–18
	(c) Reasonable and probable cause	15–20
	(d) Malice	15–37
	(e) Courts-martial and foreign courts	15–40
□3.	Malicious proceedings in bankruptcy and liquidation	15–42
4.	Abuse of civil process	15–43
■5.	Vexatious use of process	15–50

The judgment of the House of Lords in *Martin v. Watson* [1995] 3 All E.R. 559, overruling the judgment of the Court of Appeal cited in the main text, has profound implications for the future development of the tort. Their Lordships found that an individual who falsely and maliciously gave information to the police desiring and intending that a prosecution of the plaintiff ensue can, if certain conditions are met, be liable for malicious prosecution. Lord Keith opined (at 568) that any alternative result "... would be to stultify completely the tort of malicious prosecution" and to deny the victim of baseless and malicious accusations against them any effective remedy. In *Gibbs v. Rea* [1998] 3 W.L.R. 72, the Privy Council endorsed the existence of an action for maliciously procuring a search warrant.

1.—KINDS OF DAMAGE CAUSED

Nature of damage thereby caused   15–02

Two recent judgments seek to limit the expansion of any wider tort of malicious abuse of process. In *Gregory v. Portsmouth City Council, The Times*, November 26, 1997, CA, the plaintiff, a local councillor, sought to sue the defendant council for maliciously instituting disciplinary proceedings against him. He contended that the disciplinary process caused such damage to his reputation, and put him to such charges and expenses, as to fall within the ambit of a general tort of abuse of process. The disciplinary process was akin to a criminal prosecution. His claim was struck out. The Court of Appeal held that there were no grounds to expand the remit of the tort of malicious prosecution beyond the existing categories of criminal proceedings, malicious winding up and bankruptcy.

In *Gizzonio v. Chief Constable of Derbyshire, The Times*, April 29, 1998, the Court of Appeal rejected an attempt to construct a tort of malicious refusal of bail. Note however, *Gibbs v. Rea, post* confirming the existence of a tort of maliciously procuring a search warrant.

2.—MALICIOUS PROSECUTION

Essentials of the tort of malicious prosecution   15–05

NOTE 11. Add: See *Dunlop v. Customs and Excise Commissioners, The Times*, March 17, 1998 (limitation period runs from acquittal).

(a) *Prosecution*

Search warrant   15–08

In *Gibbs v. Rea* [1998] 3 W.L.R. 72, the Privy Council endorsed the existence of a tort of maliciously procuring a search warrant: "That it is an actionable wrong to procure the issue of a search warrant without reasonable cause and with malice has long been recognised though seldom successfully prosecuted" (at 80). The tort is committed on proof of intent to use the process of obtaining a warrant for purposes other than lawful search. Damage will generally ensue from the execution of the warrant, but, exceptionally, it may be shown that the issue of the warrant itself caused harm.

15–10   Who is the prosecutor?
The House of Lords in *Martin v. Watson* [1995] 3 All E.R. 559 unanimously reversed the judgment of the Court of Appeal holding the defendant liable in malicious prosecution.

Their Lordships held merely giving information to the police, which resulted in a prosecution being brought, did not of itself render the informant a prosecutor. A complainant may however be regarded as a prosecutor and liable for malicious prosecution if the following conditions are met:

(1) He falsely and maliciously gave information about an alleged offence to a police officer, stating his willingness to testify against the plaintiff, and in a context where it could properly be inferred that he desired and intended that the plaintiff be prosecuted.

(2) The facts of the alleged offence are such that they are only within the knowledge of the defendant so that it is virtually impossible for the police officer to exercise any independent discretion or judgment. The conduct of the complainant must be such that he makes it virtually inevitable that a prosecution results from his complaint to the police.

15–14   Deceiving tribunal
See now *Martin v. Watson, supra*, Supplement § 15–10.

(c) *Reasonable and Probable Cause*

15–20   Reasonable and probable cause
In *Gibbs v. Rea* [1998] 3 W.L.R. 72, the Privy Council (Lords Goff and Hope vigorously dissenting) found that the silence of the defendant might afford some evidence of absence of reasonable and probable cause and malice.

15–21   Province of judge and jury
NOTE 70. Add: *Ward v. Chief Constable of West Midlands Police, The Times,* December 15, 1997, CA.

(d) *Malice*

15–38   The Prosecution of Offences Act 1985
See now *Martin v. Watson, supra*, Supplement § 15–10.

15–39   Conduct of prosecutions
In *Thacker v. Crown Prosecution Service, The Times,* December 9, 1997, the Court of Appeal directed that any action, purportedly for malicious prosecution, brought against employees of the Crown Prosecution Service should be carefully scrutinised. It must be shown that the relevant allegations amounted to more than mere claims of negligence or incompetence from which the Crown Prosecution Service is generally "immune" by virtue of the judgment in *Elguzouli-Daf v. Commissioners of Police for the Metropolis*. Incompetence cannot constitute malice.

3.—Malicious Proceedings in Bankruptcy and Liquidation

Malicious proceedings in bankruptcy and liquidation　　　　　**15–42**
Note 69. Add: *Partizan Ltd v. O.J. Kilkenny & Co. Ltd* [1998] 1 B.C.L.C. 157.

5.—Vexatious Use of Process

No civil action for perjury　　　　　**15–53**
See *Martin v. Watson* [1995] 3 All E.R. 559 at 569–570.

A series of judgments of the Court of Appeal address the scope of witness immunity establishing that that immunity operates in any claim for misfeasance in public office. A plaintiff alleging a malicious use of the legal process, but unable to establish all the requisite elements for the tort of malicious prosecution, cannot reframe his claim in the tort of misfeasance to circumvent the operation of witness immunity; *Silcott v. Commissioners of Police for the Metropolis* (1996) 8 Admin. L.R. 633, CA; *Docker v. Chief Constable of West Midlands Police, The Times*, April 29, 1998, CA; *Gizzonio v. Chief Constable of Derbyshire, The Times*, April 29, 1998.

The absolute immunity afforded to witnesses extends to the preparation, as well as the presentation, of evidence. Allegations of fabrication of evidence which cannot be brought in malicious prosecution, perhaps because there was reasonable and probable cause for the prosecution, cannot thus lie in the tort of misfeasance; *Silcott v. Commissioner of Police for the Metropolis supra; Docker v. Chief Constable of West Midlands Police, supra.*

Note 7. Add: *Mond v. Hyde* [1999] 2 W.L.R. 498, CA.

CHAPTER 16.—PUBLIC OFFICERS

		PARA.
□1.	Judicial acts	16–01
2.	Statutory protection of justices	16–19
3.	Ministerial acts	16–24
□4.	Execution of process	16–26
5.	Priority of claim for rent	16–82
■6.	Constables and their duties	16–89
■7.	Warrants	16–127
■8.	Misfeasance in public office	16–136

Note the steady rise in claims for misfeasance in public office: *post*, Supplement § 16–137.

1.—JUDICIAL ACTS

16–03 **Different kinds of courts**

In *Warren v. Warren* [1996] 3 W.L.R. 1129 at 1137, Lord Woolf M.R. acknowledged that Lord Denning's attempt in *Sirros v. Moore* to sweep away *all* distinctions between different kinds of courts was ineffective at least as far as justices were concerned. His Lordship did not address the position of other courts of limited jurisdiction. However the Court of Appeal held that any distinction between different kinds of courts was inapplicable in relation to the compellability of a judge to give evidence. *No* judge can be compelled to testify in relation to matters of which he became aware ". . . relating to and as a result of his judicial functions".

16–07 **Absence of jurisdiction**

Note the comments of Lord Woolf M.R. in *Warren v. Warren, supra*, at 1137.

4.—EXECUTION OF PROCESS

16–26 **Execution of process**

In *McLeod v. Butterwick* [1996] 1 W.L.R. 995 Judge Roger Cooke, reflecting on the extreme antiquity of the law of execution, made a plea that sooner rather than later the law of execution should attract the attention of the Law Commission. The complex judgment of the Court of Appeal in *Khazanchi v. Faircharm Investments Ltd*; *McLeod v. Butterwick* [1998] 2 All E.R. 901 testifies to the wisdom of His Honour's words.

16–33 **Right of entry**

See also *McLeod v. Butterwick, supra*; *Khazanchi v. Faircharm Investments Ltd, supra*.

16–37 **Forcible re-entry**

The Court of Appeal ruled in *Khazanchi v. Faircharm Investments Ltd* [1998] 2 All E.R. 901, that neither a bailiff levying distress for rent, nor a sheriff executing a writ of *fieri facias*, could exercise any right of forcible re-entry to premises, unless the tenant or debtor had deliberately excluded him from the premises, or, he had been expelled from the premises by force. What constitutes deliberate exclusion is a question of fact in each case. Evidence that the premises were locked is of itself insufficient when no notice of intention to re-enter has been given to the tenant or debtor. The first instance judgment in *McLeod v. Butterwick (supra)* was partially overruled, meeting the disquiet expressed by Judge Roger Cooke about the implications of rights to re-enter locked premises in an era when often all members of the household may be out at work during the day and the house locked against burglars.

The seizure

The sheriff may retain walking possession of goods even in the absence of a formal walking possession agreement. A walking possession agreement ". . . is always an extremely sensible thing to have if it can be had" but lack of such an agreement does not of itself destroy the sheriff's walking possession of goods seized; *McLeod v. Butterwick* [1996] 1 W.L.R. 995; affirmed in part: *Khazanchi v. Faircharm Investments Ltd, supra.*

NOTE 1. Add: *McLeod v. Butterwick, supra*; *Khazanchi v. Faircharm Investments Ltd, supra.*

Harassment of debtors

NOTE 45. Add: The words in section 40, "calculated to subject" the debtor, or members of his family, to alarm, distress or humiliation, mean likely to subject and not intended to subject. The offence created by section 40 is not limited to the case where the creditor expressly sets out to cause harm to the debtor: *Norweb plc v. Dixon* [1995] 1 W.L.R. 636.

6.—CONSTABLES AND THEIR DUTIES

Reasonable force

Where a constable has failed to inform the occupier why he is exercising a power of entry into property under section 17 of the Police and Criminal Evidence Act 1984, section 117 does not authorise the use of force to effect entry simply because the occupier refuses to allow the police to enter: *O'Loughlin v. Chief Constable of Essex* [1998] 1 W.L.R. 374, CA; see *post*, Supplement § 16–107.

Public order legislation

The Prevention of Terrorism (Additional Powers) Act 1996 confers on the police further powers to stop and search persons, to search goods and to impose police cordons.

Acting on reasonable suspicion

The discretion to arrest vests in the arresting officer personally not in any superior officer. Thus a mere order to arrest is insufficient to create reasonable grounds for suspicion to justify arrest. The arresting officer must himself be in possession of information generating reasonable suspicion: *O'Hara v. Chief Constable of the Royal Ulster Constabulary* [1997] 2 W.L.R. 1, HL; see *supra*, Supplement § 12–49.

Arrest: general power of arrest

A constable purported to arrest the accused for obstruction. No power of arrest without warrant for obstruction exists. Nor could it be argued that section 25 (granting a general power of arrest) could be relied on, where the arresting constable had not given his general power as a reason for the arrest; *Mullady DPP* [1997] C.O.D. 422.

Other statutory powers of arrest

Note that section 26 of the Police and Criminal Evidence Act 1984 repeals only those prior statutory provisions conferring powers of arrest exclusively on constables. Where, as in section 6 of the Vagrancy Act 1824, a general power of arrest is conferred exercisable by constables and private citizens that power of arrest survives the 1984 Act: *Gapper v. Chief Constable of Avon and Somerset Constabulary* [1998] 4 All E.R. 248, CA. *See, supra,* Supplement § 12–51.

16–106 **Duty when making an arrest**
NOTE 54. Add: *R. v. Chalkley* [1998] 2 All E.R. 155, CA.

16–107 **Entering premises**
A constable exercising a power of entry under section 17 must give his reasons for exercising that power unless those reasons are self-evident. The plaintiff and his wife had been engaged in a noisy public row. Just before going into the plaintiff's house, the wife had smashed the windscreen of a neighbour's car and the police were called. Arriving at the house, police officers demanded entry without informing the plaintiff that they were empowered to enter to arrest his wife by virtue of section 17(1)(b). On the plaintiff's refusal of entry, officers used force to break into the house. The plaintiff's claim in trespass succeeded. Officers are generally obliged to give reasons for entry and the failure to do so rendered their resort to forced entry unlawful: *O'Loughlin v. Chief Constable of Essex* [1998] 1 W.L.R. 374, CA.

The Prisoners (Return to Custody) Act 1995 amends section 17 of the Police and Criminal Evidence Act to empower a constable to enter premises without a warrant to arrest any child or young person remanded or committed to local authority accommodation under the Children and Young Persons Act 1969 and to recapture any prisoner unlawfully at large. The requirement of hot pursuit thus no longer applies to limit powers of entry to retake escaped or absconding prisoners.

NOTE 68. See *McLeod v. Commissioner of Police for the Metropolis* [1994] 4 All E.R. 553, CA (power of entry extends to private premises). And note now *McLeod v. United Kingdom* (1999) 27 E.H.R.R. 493, ECHR. See, *supra*, Supplement § 12–37.

16–110 **Powers to stop and search**
Note the new powers conferred by the Prevention of Terrorism (Additional Powers) Act 1996.

16–119 **Limitations on police detention: duration**
It has been confirmed by the Court of Appeal that a continuance of detention beyond the periods prescribed in the Police and Criminal Evidence Act 1984 would constitute false imprisonment even subsequent to the judgment of the Court of Appeal in *Oluto v. Home Office* [1997] 1 W.L.R. 328; see *supra*, Supplement § 12–20. In that judgment it was held that failure by the Crown Prosecution Service to comply with maximum periods of custody prescribed by the Prosecution of Offences (Custody: Time Limits) Regulations did not render the plaintiff's continued detention by the prison authorities unlawful. The prison governor had neither the duty nor the authority to release the plaintiff who remained in custody under the original warrant of commitment. In relation to detention under the 1984 Act, the situation is quite different. On the expiry of the prescribed period of detention, any authority to continue the detention of the arrested person ceases to exist and continued detention is unlawful. In *Roberts v. Chief Constable of Cheshire* [1999] 2 All E.R. 326, CA, it was held that failure to comply with mandatory provisions to review the plaintiff's detention rendered his continued detention in police custody unlawful and a false imprisonment. It was irrelevant that detention would have been lawful if the requisite review had been carried out, or that there were in fact grounds for continuing the plaintiff's detention.

16–124 **Other powers of constables**
NOTE 48. Add: *Kerr v. DPP* [1994] 158 J.P. 1048.

7.—WARRANTS

16–129 **Search warrants**
A search warrant issued under section 8 of the Police and Criminal Evidence Act 1984 authorises only search for, and seizure of, material within the description set out in the warrant and reasonably believed to be of value in the investigation of a

serious offence: *R. v. Chief Constable of the Warwickshire Constabulary* [1999] 1
W.L.R. 564, DC.

Note the new powers conferred by the Prevention of Terrorism (Additional
Powers) Act 1996.

Note that an application for a search warrant must specify which part of the
premises is to be searched where police are aware that the premises comprise a
number of individual dwellings: *R. v. South Western Magistrates' Courts, ex p. Cofie*
[1997] 1 W.L.R. 885, DC.

8.—MISFEASANCE IN PUBLIC OFFICE

Misfeasance   **16–137**

In *Three Rivers District Council v. Bank of England (No. 3)* [1996] 3 All E.R.
558 Clarke J. held that the tort of misfeasance in public office did indeed consist of
two alternative limbs. Either (1) the plaintiff must establish a deliberate intent on
the part of a public officer to cause injury to him or a class of persons to which he
belongs or (2) he must establish that the defendant acted knowing that he acted
unlawfully, or being reckless as to the legality of his action. However, the Court of
Appeal has now ruled, in *Three Rivers District Council v. Bank of England (No. 4),
The Times,* December 10, 1998, that courts must avoid too rigid a distinction
between the two supposed limbs of the tort. In every case it must be proven that the
defendant committed a deliberate and dishonest abuse of power knowing that, or
indifferent to the fact that the plaintiff would suffer loss or harm as a consequence
of his actions. To establish the tort of misfeasance in public office, the defendant
must necessarily be shown to have committed some unlawful act. When local council officials contacted the police to report their suspicions about the plaintiff's voluntary work in assisting people to make claims for benefit, the plaintiffs' claim in the
tort of misfeasance was struck out. The defendants had not been guilty of any misconduct, nor had they exceeded their powers. They had done no more than their
public duty in reporting their suspicions to the police: *Ealing L.B.C. v. Metha*, Trans.
Ref. CCRTL 96/014715, April 24, 1997, CA.

Note the judgment of Sir Richard Scott V.-C. in *Elliott v. Chief Constable of
Wiltshire, The Times,* December 5, 1996. A police officer who had been subjected
to an investigation by the plaintiff, a journalist on a local newspaper, used his position to gain access to the Police National Computer revealing the plaintiff's criminal
record. He passed on that information, together with some false allegations against
the plaintiff, to the editor of the paper and the plaintiff was dismissed. The Vice-
Chancellor refused to strike out the plaintiff's claim for misfeasance in public office.
There was the necessary connection between the police officer's public office and
his conduct. He obtained information about the plaintiff and if malice, or intention
to cause harm and damage, were established the tort of misfeasance in public offence
could be proven.

Neither the Crown Prosecution Service nor the police are afforded any general
immunity from suit against a claim for misfeasance in public office: *Bennett v.
Commissioner for the Metropolis, The Times,* October 24, 1997. However, the protection afforded by witness immunity to any claim in tort (save for malicious
prosecution) operates fully in any action for misfeasance. The scope of that immunity extends beyond the presentation of evidence in court to the preparation of evidence. Allegations of fabrication of evidence cannot then generally be litigated in the
tort of misfeasance. See *Silcott v. Commissioner of Police for the Metropolis* (1996)
8 Admin. L.R. 633, CA; *Docker v. Chief Constable of the West Midlands, The
Times,* April 29, 1998, CA. Nor can claims which in essence allege malicious prosecution be brought within the ambit of the tort of misfeasance of public office;
Gizzonio v. Chief Constable of Derbyshire, The Times, April 29, 1998, CA (see
supra, Supplement § 15–53).

The judgment of the Court of Appeal in *Toumia v. Evans, The Times,* April 1,
1999 leaves it open whether non-feasance might constitute a tort if the defendant's

conduct nonetheless met the other conditions for liability in misfeasance in public order. Prison officers refused to unlock the plaintiff's cell and disrupted meals in the course of illegal industrial action. The Court of Appeal refused to strike out the plaintiff's claims in false imprisonment and misfeasance in public office.

16–138 Public office

In *R. v. Bowden* [1996] 1 W.L.R. 98, the Court of Appeal held that the common law crime of misconduct in a public office could be committed by any person appointed to discharge a public duty and paid out of public funds. The maintenance manager of a local authority works department could thus rightly be convicted of the offence.

CHAPTER 17.—TRESPASS TO LAND AND DISPOSSESSION

		PARA.
■1.	The nature of trespass	17–01
■2.	Who may sue for trespass	17–09
3.	Trespass by relation	17–24
■4.	Offences of entering property	17–27
5.	The subject-matter of trespass	17–30
■6.	Justification of trespass	17–32
7.	Measure of damages	
	(a) General	17–59
	(b) Exemplary damages	17–67
	(c) Limitation for bringing trespass	17–68
□8.	Action for the recovery of land	17–69
■9.	Statutes of limitation	17–74
10.	Waste	17–95

One of the most sensitive contemporary issues involving the remedies for trespass **17–01** to land concerns the private wheel-clamping of wrongfully parked motor-vehicles. In what is apparently the first case on the matter to reach the Court of Appeal, *Arthur v. Anker*, the Court held that the owners of the vehicles in question had not been justified in forcefully removing the clamps, and that the prominent notices surrounding the land in question had made the owners of the vehicles *volenti* with respect to the practice of clamping and the imposition of a reasonable charge for the removal of the clamps. It seems unsatisfactory, however, that the precise extent of the legality of private wheel-clamping should be left to the vagaries of an uncertain area of the common law. There is an urgent need for statutory intervention to control the practice in the interests of all concerned: land-owners, drivers, and security companies. In *DPP v. Jones* a fundamental re-examination of the authorities governing use of the highway was undertaken by the House of Lords, when holding that a peaceful and non-obstructive assembly on the highway did *not* necessarily constitute a trespass so as to fall within section 14A of the Public Order Act 1986. Yet another aspect of the law relating to remedies for trespass, the action for mesne profits, was considered by the Privy Council in *Inverugie Investments v. Hackett*.

2.—WHO MAY SUE FOR TRESPASS

Exclusive possession
17–17

In *Gray v. Taylor, The Times,* April 24, 1998 the Court of Appeal, distinguishing *Street v. Mountford,* held that an occupant of a charitable almshouse, who paid rent and claimed to have been granted exclusive possession as a tenant, was a mere licensee since her occupation was a personal privilege as a beneficiary of the charity.

NOTE 98. Delete and substitute: See *Bruton v. London and Quadrant Housing Trust* [1993] 3 All E.R. 481, HL. See also *Family Housing Association v. Jones* [1990] 1 W.L.R. 779, CA. In *Aslan v. Murphy (No. 1) and (No. 2); Wynne v. Duke* [1990] 1 W.L.R. 766, the Court of Appeal gave guidance on the drawing of the distinction between licences and tenancies is the light of the recent authorities.

NOTE 2. Delete and substitute: *Westminster City Council v. Clarke* [1992] 2 A.C. 288, HL.

Licensees and third parties
17–18

In *Manchester Airport plc v. Dutton* [1999] 2 All E.R. 675 the Court of Appeal held, by a majority, that the court had jurisdiction to grant a licensee an order for possession against trespassers even *before* the licensee was in *de facto* possession, if such an order was necessary in order to give effect to the licensee's right to occupy under the contract with the licensor.

17–19   Guest at hotel
For an exceptional case where the long-term occupant of a hotel room had exclusive possession and was able to sue for trespass as a contractual licensee: see *Mehta v. Royal Bank of Scotland plc, The Times,* January 25, 1999.

17–23   Co-owners
For detailed provisions relating to party walls see the Party Wall, etc., Act 1996.

4.—OFFENCES OF ENTERING PROPERTY

17–28   Aggravated trespass and public order offences
The law relating to "trespassory assemblies" was considered at length by the House of Lords in *DPP v. Jones* [1999] 2 All E.R. 257, in which the principles governing lawful use of the highway were subjected to a fundamental re-examination. By a bare majority, the House of Lords (reversing the Divisional Court) held that peaceful and non-obstructive assemblies will not necessarily constitute a private law trespass against the owner of the land merely because they involve an activity other than, or incidental to, mere passage over the highway. (See, further, *post,* Supplement § 17–41). Accordingly, since the criminal liability under sections 14A–14C is predicted upon the existence of such a trespass, the appellants, who had participated in a peaceful demonstration near Stonehenge, were considered not to have been trespassers and hence to have been wrongly convicted.

6.—JUSTIFICATION OF TRESPASS

17–34   Modern statutes
For provisions relating to rights of entry in order to carry out work on party walls see the Party Wall, etc., Act 1996, s.8.

17–35   Entry for recaption of goods
NOTE 87. Add: In *Arthur v. Anker* [1996] 1 W.L.R. 602 the Court of Appeal held that the owners of motor vehicles which had been privately wheel-clamped following their wrongful parking were not entitled to remove the clamps and locks in order to free the vehicles. Notices surrounding the area in question had been sufficient to render the plaintiffs *volenti.* They were therefore taken to have impliedly consented to the consequences of their trespass, including the detention of their vehicles until a reasonable sum was paid for their release. The defendants' charges were considered to have been reasonable.

17–39   Justification under right of way
NOTE 11. Add: See also *Jobson v. Record* [1997] N.P.C. 56, CA.

17–41   Public way
The rights of the public in respect of a highway have undergone a significant extension as a result of the majority decision of the House of Lords in *DPP v. Jones* [1999] 2 W.L.R. 91, in which their Lordships held that it is not the case that a member of the public who uses the highway for a purpose other than that of passing and re passing, or a purpose ancillary thereto, will necessarily become a trespasser. Moreover, the broad proposition in the text that the public "have no right of holding public meetings in a public highway" can no longer be taken, at least not without major qualification, to be an accurate statement of the law. The defendants had been convicted of taking part in a "trespassory assembly" contrary to sections 14A–14C of the Public Order Act 1986 (see *supra,* Supplement § 17–28). Since liability under

the provision is predicated upon exceeding "the limits of the public's right of access" the conviction necessarily depended upon the assumption that the defendants, who had participated in a peaceful and non-obstructive demonstration upon a highway, had thereby committed the tort of trespass to land by using the highway for a purpose other than of passing and re passing. Lord Irvine of Lairg L.C., Lord Hutton and Lord Clyde, in the majority, denied the validity of that assumption while Lord Slynn and Lord Hope, dissenting, accepted it. All five of their Lordships delivered full speeches, in each of which the law relating to permissible use of the highway is carefully analysed along with the classic cases of *Harrison v. Duke of Rutland* [1893] 1 Q.B. 142 and *Hickman v. Maisey* [1900] 1 Q.B.752. Some care is, however, needed in interpreting the decision since the majority speeches reveal potentially significant differences of emphasis. Lord Irvine adopted the broadest approach. He refused to "accept that, to be lawful, activities on the highway must fall within a rubric incidental or ancillary to the exercise of the right of passage", and expressed himself as follows:

"I conclude therefore the law to be that the public highway is a public place which the public may enjoy for any reasonable purpose, provided the activity in question does not amount to a public or private nuisance and does not obstruct the highway by unreasonably impeding the primary right of the public to pass and repass; within these qualifications there is a public right of peaceful assembly on the highway." ([1999] 2 All E.R. 257 at 265).

His Lordship also added that "since the law confers this public right" he would "deprecate any attempt artificially to restrict its scope". Lord Clyde, however, while agreeing with Lord Irvine as to the result, expressed the view that the argument for the defendants "went further than it needed to go in suggesting that any reasonable use of the highway, provided that it was peaceful and not obstructive, was unlawful, and so a matter of public right". He continued:

"Such an approach opens a door of uncertain dimensions into an ill-defined area of uses which might erode the basic predominance of the essential use of a highway as a highway ... The test then is not one which can be defined in general terms but has to depend upon the circumstances as a matter of degree. It requires a careful assessment of the nature and extent of the activity in question. If the purpose of the activity becomes the prominent purpose of the occupation of the highway, or if the occupation becomes more than reasonably transitional in terms of either time or space, then it may come to exceed the right to use the highway." [1999] 2 All E.R. 257 at 287)

The third member of the majority, Lord Hutton, was anxious, like Lord Irvine, to assert that "the common law recognises that there is a right for members of the public to assemble together to express views on matters of public concern" and he considered "that the common law should now recognise that this right, which is one of the fundamental rights of citizens in a democracy, is unduly restricted unless it can be exercised in some circumstances on the public highway" ([1999] 2 All E.R. 257 at 292). At the same time, however, his Lordship said the following:

"I desire to emphasise that my opinion that this appeal should be allowed is based on the finding of the Crown Court that the assembly in which the defendants took place on this particular highway, the A344, at this particular time, constituted a reasonable use of the highway. I would not hold that a peaceful and non-obstructive public assembly on a highway is always a reasonable user and is therefore not a trespass ... If members of the public took part in an assembly on a highway but the highway was, for example, a small, quiet country road or was a bridleway or a footpath, and the assembly interfered with the landowner's enjoyment of the land across which the highway ran or which it bordered, I think it would be open to the justices to hold that, notwithstanding

135

the importance of the democratic right to hold a public assembly, nevertheless in the particular circumstances of the case the assembly was an unreasonable user of the highway and therefore constituted a trespass." [1999] 2 All E.R. 257 at 297–298)

It is therefore apparent that, even after the decision in *DPP v. Jones*, the question whether or not a particular use of the highway exceeded the public right will inevitably remain predominantly a question of fact. Moreover, even though the narrowest interpretation of the earlier authorities is clearly no longer tenable, it should be noted that there is no suggestion in *DPP v. Jones* that *Harrison v. Duke of Rutland* and *Hickman v. Maisey*, both of which resulted in findings of trespass, were wrongly decided. Rather closer to the facts of those cases, than to those of *DPP v. Jones* itself, is *Secretary of State for Defence v. Percy, The Times,* May 11, 1998, in which the High Court held that going onto a public footpath simply in order to remove notices constituted a trespass, notwithstanding that the notices were invalid and known to the landowner so to be.

8.—ACTION FOR THE RECOVERY OF LAND

17–73 **What mesne profits include**

In *Inverugie Investments Ltd v. Hackett* [1995] 1 W.L.R. 713 the plaintiff had been wrongfully dispossessed for many years of a block of hotel apartments in the Bahamas which he had acquired for investment purposes. In an action for mesne profits the question arose how a "reasonable rent", to which the plaintiff was entitled, should be calculated. The plaintiff claimed that he was entitled to a reasonable figure for each apartment for 365 days a year, regardless of whether the defendants had, or could in practice have, let all the apartments. The defendants contended for a much lower figure. They pointed out that it was not possible to achieve 100 per cent occupancy and argued that the block should be treated as a whole rather than as a collection of separate apartments. On that basis it was, in their submission, relevant that for much of the year the best that could be achieved was partial occupancy by tour operators at heavily discounted prices. The Judicial Committee of the Privy Council decided in favour of the plaintiff. Lord Lloyd of Berwick, delivering the judgment of the Board, said:

> "The plaintiff may not have suffered any *actual* loss by being deprived of the use of his property. But under the user principle he is entitled to recover a reasonable rent for the wrongful use of his property by the trespasser. Similarly, the trespasser may not have derived any *actual* benefit from the use of the property. But under the user principle he is obliged to pay a reasonable rent for the use which he has enjoyed. The principle need not be characterised as exclusively compensatory, or exclusively restitutionary; it combines elements of both ... If a man hires a concrete mixer, he must pay the daily hire, even though he may not in the event have been able to use the mixer because of rain. So also must a trespasser who takes the mixer without the owner's consent. He must pay the going rate, even though in the event he has derived no benefit from the use of the mixer. It makes no difference whether the trespasser is a professional builder or a do-it-yourself enthusiast." ([1995] 3 All E.R. at 845–846, italics in the original.)

9.—STATUTES OF LIMITATION

17–74 **Adverse possession and licensed possession**

For an unsuccessful attempt by a lessee to rely on an option to renew in order to defeat a trespasser's claim based on adverse possession see *Chung Ping Kwan v. Lam Island Development Co, The Times*, July 16, 1996, PC.

Licence a matter of fact 17–75
In *Smith v. Lawson* (1998) 75 P.&C.R. 466 the Court of Appeal held that a representation that no further rent would be collected gave rise to a promissory estoppel which would have prevented the owner from claiming possession for non-payment of rent. It followed that the occupant was effectively a licensee and could not establish adverse possession.

When right of action accrues 17–77
The nature of the conduct required in order to demonstrate the requisite intention to possess, so as to establish adverse possession, was considered by the court of Appeal in *Prudential Assurance Co. Ltd. v. Waterloo Real Estate Inc, The Times*, February 8, 1999 in which a claim to ownership of a wall, based upon adverse possession, was successful.
NOTE 96. Add: See also *Hounslow L.B.C. v. Minchinton* [1977] N.P.C. 44, CA.

Freeholder 17–81
NOTE 4. *Spectrum Investment Co. v. Holmes* was distinguished in *Central London Commercial Estates Ltd v. Kato Kagaku Ltd, The Times*, July 27, 1998.

CHAPTER 18.—NUISANCE

		PARA.
■1.	The nature of nuisance	18–01
□2.	Nuisance and the standard of duty	18–25
3.	Nuisance and trespass	18–38
□4.	Who can sue for nuisance	18–39
■5.	Who can be sued for nuisance	18–46
■6.	Defences to an action for nuisance	18–55
	(a) Inevitable accident	18–56
	(b) Act of a trespasser	18–57
	(c) Ignorance of the nuisance	18–59
	(d) Contributory negligence	18–62
	(e) Ineffectual defences	18–63
□7.	Nuisance to water rights	18–70
8.	Withdrawal of support	18–79
□9.	Nuisance to ancient lights	18–86
□10.	Obstruction of access to highway	18–93
□11.	Obstruction of highway	18–94
■12.	Prescriptive right to commit nuisance	18–113
□13.	Authorisation by statute	18–115

18–01   In *Hunter v. Canary Wharf Ltd*, which arose out of the redevelopment of London's docklands, the House of Lords handed down the most important and far-reaching decision on the law of nuisance for many years. The House held that occupiers with no formal interest in land could not sue in the tort, and considered how long-established principles should be applied to the analysis of claims for interference with television reception. In *Baxter v. Camden London Borough Council* the Court of Appeal held that the principle of caveat lessee is still good law and that a lessee is deemed to take the premises as they are. Accordingly, a landlord will not be liable in nuisance for interference with enjoyment of the tenant's premises due solely to a defect in their construction prior to the letting.

1.—THE NATURE OF NUISANCE

18–01   **Nuisance defined**
NOTE 1. Substitute: Buckley, *The Law of Nuisance* (2nd ed., 1996); Jenny Steele, "Private law and the environment: nuisance in context" (1995) 15 L.S. 236; Conor Gearty, "The Place of Private Nuisance in a Modern Law of Torts" (1989) 48 Camb. L.J. 214.

18–03   **Public nuisance**
The Noise Act 1996 contains measures concerned with noise, including a new criminal offence relating to the emission of noise at night, subject to a resolution by the local authority adopting the Act's provisions.
NOTE 12. Add: But an action for damages for breach of statutory duty is not available: *Issa v. Hackney LBC* [1997] 1 W.L.R. 956.

Examples
18–07   In *Hunter v. Canary Wharf Ltd* [1997] 2 W.L.R. 684, [1997] 2 All E.R. 426, in which the mere existence of the defendants' building was unsuccessfully alleged to have caused a nuisance, Lord Goff of Chievely said (at 432h): ". . . for an action in private nuisance to lie in respect of interference with the plaintiff's enjoyment of his land, it will generally arise from something *emanating* from the defendant's

land" (italics supplied). His Lordship regarded *Thompson-Schwab v. Costaki* [1956] 1 W.L.R. 335 (using a house for prostitution) and *Bank of New Zealand v. Green-wood* [1984] 1 N.Z.L.R. 525 (glass roof causing deflected sunlight to throw a daz-zling glare on neighbouring premises) as exceptional cases. *cf. per* Lord Lloyd of Berwick in *Hunter's* case at 445j–446a:

> "If further precision is needed in answering the question why the plaintiffs have no legal redress in nuisance, it could be, as my noble and learned friend Lord Goff has suggested, because there is nothing emanating from the defend-ants' land in the present case. The eminently sensible conclusion reached in *Bank of New Zealand v. Greenwood* might not be easy to reconcile with this approach. So that case may go to the limit of the law of nuisance. But the facts were most unusual . . ."

NOTE 30. Add: For statutory provisions see the Noise Act 1996.

Encroachment and physical damage
18–08

The distinction between physical damage to property, and mere inconvenience, was applied by the Court of Appeal in favour of a claimant for injurious affection, under section 10 of the Compulsory Purchase Act 1965, in *Clift v. Welsh Office, The Times,* August 24, 1998.

Interference with enjoyment
18–09

In *Murdoch v. Glacier Metal Co. Ltd, The Times*, January 21, 1998, CA., an action in nuisance for sleep disturbance caused by noise at night from the defend-ants' factory was unsuccessful in view of the character of the neighbourhood, which included a bypass close to the plaintiff's home, and the absence of any other com-plaints from local residents. Although the noise level from the factory was just above that at which, according to a report from the World Health Organisation, sleep could be adversely affected, that was insufficient in itself to constitute an actionable nuisance.

In *Baxter v. Camden London Borough Council* [1999] 1 All E.R. 237 the Court of Appeal affirmed that ordinary domestic use of premises cannot constitute a nuis-ance, even if it interferes with the enjoyment of neighbouring premises, if the inter-ference results solely from construction defects for which the defendant is not responsible.

Standard of comfort
18–10

NOTE 52a. Delete.

The question whether interference with television reception is capable of constitut-ing an actionable private nuisance was considered by the House of Lords in *Hunter v. Canary Wharf Ltd* [1997] 2 W.L.R. 684, which arose out of the construction of Canary Wharf Tower in London's docklands. The House held (unanimously upholding the Court of Appeal on this point) that where the cause of the interference was the erection of a large building, which blocked the path of the television signal, the plaintiff would be without a remedy. Lord Goff of Chieveley, Lord Lloyd of Berwick, Lord Hoffman, and Lord Hope of Craighead treated the situation as analog-ous to that of loss of a view or prospect, which had for centuries been accepted as giving rise to no cause of action (see, *e.g. Aldred's Case* (1610) 9 Co. Rep. 57b at 58b, *per* Wray C.J.). Lord Cooke of Thorndon preferred to base the decision on "the principle of reasonable user, of give and take", the erection of the tower being "a reasonable development in all the circumstances". His Lordship suspected that "only a lawyer" would suggest "that the amenity of television reception is fairly compar-able to a view of the surroundings". Lord Hoffman and Lord Hope, however, consid-ered the analogy to be appropriate because just as *uncertainty* as to the degree of protection required renders a right of prospect incapable of acquisition as an *ease-ment*, so not dissimilar factors applied in the present case:

139

"Radio and television signals ... come from various directions over a wide
area as they cross the developer's property ... Their passage from one point to
another is invisible. It would be difficult, if not impossible, for the developer
to become aware of their existence before he puts up the new building. If he
were to be restricted by an easement from putting up a building which interfered
with these signals, he might not be able to put up any substantial structures at
all. The interference with his freedom would be substantial. I do not think that
it would be consistent with principle for such a wide and novel restriction to
be recognised. If that is so for easements, then the same result must follow so
far as a remedy in nuisance is concerned". ([1997] 2 All E.R. 426 at 470, *per*
Lord Hope of Craighead)

This reasoning adopted by the House leaves open the possibility that interference
caused in other ways, such as by electronic devices (*cf. Bridlington Relay Ltd v.
Yorkshire Electricity Board* [1965] Ch. 436) might nowadays be held to be actionable. A majority of their Lordships (Lord Goff at 431, Lord Hoffman at 453, and
Lord Cooke at 463) do indeed appear to have taken the view, *obiter*, that a remedy
might be available in such circumstances. It is possible, however, that Lord Lloyd
of Berwick did not agree (see 445: ". . . interference with television reception is not
capable of constituting an actionable private nuisance").

18–11   **Character of neighbourhood**
The Court of Appeal in *Hunter v. Canary Wharf Ltd* [1996] 2 W.L.R. 684 considered the proposition that, by changing the character of the neighbourhood, planning
permission might indirectly render lawful what would otherwise have been an
actionable nuisance. On the assumption that this *can* occur, but only with respect to
large-scale developments, the Court refused to apply the principle in *Hunter's* case
despite the fact that the London Docklands Development Corporation had been given
wide delegated powers to ease planning restrictions within an area designated as an
"enterprise zone". The point was not pursued when *Hunter v. Canary Wharf Ltd*
reached the House of Lords (see [1997] 2 All E.R. 426). Lord Hoffman and Lord
Cooke of Thorndon did, however, confirm that "compliance with planning controls
is not in itself a defence to a nuisance action" (*per* Lord Cooke at 465j; see also,
per Lord Hoffman at 455d-e). Nevertheless both their Lordships also indicated their
agreement with the proposition that planning permission may be relevant indirectly.
Lord Cooke said that the principle that "although a planning consent could not
authorise a nuisance, it could change the character of the neighbourhood by which
the standard of reasonable user fell to be judged" appeared to him to be "sound"
(see 466f). Similarly Lord Hoffman observed, with reference to planning controls,
that "when your Lordships are invited to develop the common law by creating a
new right of action against an owner who erects a buiding on his land, it is relevant
to take into account the existence of *other* methods by which the interests of the
locality can be protected" (at 455g, italics supplied). Conversely, Lord Cooke suggested that *failure* to comply with planning restrictions might assist *plaintiffs*. He
said (at 465e):

"Although the primary responsibility for enforcement falls on the administering
authorities, I see no reason why neighbours prejudicially affected should not be
able to sue in nuisance if a building does exceed height, bulk or location restrictions. For then the developer is not making either a lawful or a reasonable use
of landowning rights. This is to treat planning measures not as creating rights
of action for breach of statutory duty but as denoting a standard of what is
acceptable in the community".

8–12   **Demolition and rebuilding**
The principle that harm caused by temporary building work is not actionable is
confined to mere inconvenience and does not extend to physical damage to property:
Clift v. Welsh Office, The Times, August 24, 1998, CA.

Temporary interference

In *Crown River Cruises Ltd v. Kimbolton Fireworks Ltd* [1996] 2 Lloyd's Rep.
533, Potter J. held that a firework display which lasted for only 15 or 20 minutes
could give rise to liability in nuisance, and rejected a submission that that was too
short a period to satisfy the requirements of the tort.

Acts done with the intention of annoying

In *Hunter v. Canary Wharf Ltd* [1997] 2 W.L.R. 684, [1997] 2 All E.R. 426 at
465f Lord Cooke of Thorndon said, *obiter*, that the "malicious erection of a structure
for the purpose of interfering with television reception should be actionable in nuisance" in circumstances in which such interference would not be actionable in the
absence of malice.

Natural nuisances

Leakey v. National Trust was applied in *Holbeck Hall Hotel Ltd v. Scarborough
Borough Council* [1997] 2 E.G.L.R. 213 (occupier of downhill land liable for failure
to take precautionary measures with respect to land slips of which it was aware and
which deprived the neighbouring uphill land of support).

Nuisance primarily a wrong to occupiers of land

The proposition that a private nuisance is primarily a wrong to the owner or
occupier of the land affected has been emphatically reaffirmed by the House of
Lords (Lord Cooke of Thorndon dissenting) in *Hunter v. Canary Wharf Ltd* [1997]
2 W.L.R. 684. In a fundamental review of the authorities the House upheld the
traditional test of possession or occupation as laid down by the Court of Appeal in
Malone v. Lasky [1907] 2 K.B. 141. Their Lordships accordingly refused to distinguish cases of direct physical damage to, or encroachment upon, a neighbour's land
from situations involving mere interference with enjoyment or utility. A plaintiff
had to have an interest in land in the latter category as well as in the former. Lord
Goff of Chieveley considered that "any . . . departure from the established law on
this subject" would cause uncertainty due to "the problem of defining the category
of persons who would have the right to sue" ([1997] 2 All E.R. 426 at 439). Even
legislative provisions relating to spouses, such as the Matrimonial Homes Act 1983,
would not be sufficient in themselves to confer a right to sue. In the words of Lord
Hoffman:

> "The effects of these provisions is that a spouse may, by virtue of an order of
> the court upon a break-up of the marriage, become entitled to exclusive posses-
> sion of the home. If so, she will become entitled to sue for nuisance. Until then,
> her interest is analogous to a contingent reversion. It cannot be affected by a
> nuisance which merely damages the amenity of the property while she has no
> right to possession". ([1997] 2 All E.R. 426 at 453)

In reaching its decision the House of Lords overruled the 1993 decision of a
majority of the Court of Appeal in *Khorasandjian v. Bush* [1993] Q.B. 727, and the
decision of the Court of Appeal in *Hunter v. Canary Wharf Ltd* itself, in both of
which residence in property as a "home", without any legally protected interest,
was held to be sufficient to confer a right to sue. This view was, however, supported
by Lord Cooke, in his dissenting speech in the House of Lords who considered it to
be "an acceptable criterion, consistent with traditional concern for the sanctity of
family life". ([1997] 2 All E.R. 426 at 462) For discussion see Kidner, "Nuisance
and Rights of Property" [1998] Conv. 267.

The proposition that the essence of nuisance is interference with the use or enjoyment of the plaintiff's *land* did not prevent liability from being imposed, in *Crown
River Cruises Ltd v. Kimbolton Fireworks Ltd* [1996] 2 Lloyd's Rep. 533 for damage
to a barge which was permanently attached to a mooring on a river-bed, the site of
which the plaintiffs enjoyed under a licence.

NOTE 86. The correctness of the decision in *Metropolitan Properties v. Jones*

[1939] 2 All E.R. 202 was questioned by Lord Hoffman in *Hunter v. Canary Wharf Ltd*: see [1997] 2 All E.R. 426 at 449–450.

NOTE 88. Add: See also *Delaware Mansions Ltd v. Westminster City Council, The Times*, August 25, 1999, CA, in which defendants who had refused to take remedial action is respect of tree-roots were held liable to the freehold owners of blocks of flats affected, notwithstanding that the claimants were not the owners of the freehold at the time when the physical damage caused by the tree-roots occurred.

Damages

18–23   In *Hunter v. Canary Wharf Ltd* [1997] 2 W.L.R. 684, [1997] 2 All E.R. 426 the House of Lords held that in cases involving interference with amenity and enjoyment of property the court must place a value on an intangible loss which "cannot be assessed mathematically" (*per* Lord Lloyd of Berwick at 442, citing *Ruxley Electronics and Construction Ltd v. Forsyth* [1996] A.C. 344; see also, *per* Lord Hoffman in *Hunter's* case, [1997] 2 All E.R. at 451, and, *per* Lord Cooke at 457). Observations in the Court of Appeal in *Bone v. Seale* [1975] 1 W.L.R. 797 at 803–804, to the effect that such damages may be assessed by analogy with damages for personal injury, were disapproved: see, *per* Lord Hoffmann in [1997] 2 All E.R. at 451g-j). Only the owner or the occupier with the right to exclusive possession is entitled to sue for such interference: accordingly, each member of a family does not have a separate cause of action and "the quantum of damages does not depend on the number of those enjoying the land in question" (see [1997] 2 All E.R. at 442–441 *per* Lord Lloyd of Berwick).

NOTE 4. Add: See also *Hunter v. Canary Wharf Ltd* [1997] 2 W.L.R. 684, [1997] 2 All E.R. 426 at 451–452, *per* Lord Hoffman.

NOTE 5. See *Hunter v. Canary Wharf Ltd* [1997] 2 W.L.R. 684, [1997] 2 All E.R. 426 at 438j, *per* Lord Goff of Chieveley:

> "I wish to draw attention to the fact that although, in the past, damages for personal injury have been recovered at least in actions of public nuisance, there is now developing a school of thought that the appropriate remedy for such claims as these should lie in our now fully developed law of negligence, and that personal injury claims should be altogether excluded from the domain of nuisance".

See also, *per* Lord Lloyd of Berwick in the same case (at 442d), but *cf. per* Lord Cooke of Thorndon, dissenting (at 462–463).

2.—NUISANCE AND THE SANDARD OF DUTY

18–29   **Unreasonable user and foreseeability**
An attempt to impose liability in nuisance for damage caused by floodwater failed in *Ellison v. Ministry of Defence* (1997) 81 B.L.R. 101: the defendants' had not been making an unreasonable use of their land and what had occurred had been unforeseeable.

4.—WHO CAN SUE FOR NUISANCE

18–39   **Occupiers and residents**
In *Hunter v. Canary Wharf Ltd* [1997] 2 W.L.R. 684, the House of Lords (Lord Cooke of Thorndon dissenting) overruled the decision of the Court of Appeal in *Khorasandjian v. Bush* [1993] Q.B. 727. Their Lordships perceived the basis underlying *Khorasandjian's* case as having been protection from *harassment* as such rather than relief from a private *nuisance* as traditionally conceived, and that in view of the subsequent passing of the Protection from Harassment Act 1997 it was no longer necessary, as Lord Hoffman saw it, to use the law of nuisance "merely as an

expedient to fill a gap". The House accordingly chose to reaffirm that a legally protected interest in the land affected remained an essential ingredient for a plaintiff to be able to sue in nuisance, Lord Goff of Chieveley considered, *inter alia*, that settlement of claims could become more difficult if "anybody who lived in the relevant property as a home had the right to sue": see [1997] 2 All E.R. 426 at 439f. (But *cf. per* Lord Cooke of Thorndon, dissenting, *ibid.* at 462g.)

5.—WHO CAN BE SUED FOR NUISANCE

Liability of actual wrongdoer   **18–46**
NOTE 85. After *Page Motors v. Epsom & Ewell BC*, add: see also *Lippiatt v. South Gloucestershire Council* [1999] 4 All E.R. 149, CA.

When landlord liable   **18–51**
Baxter v. Camden London Borough Council [1999] 1 All E.R. 237 the Court of Appeal held that a landlord is not liable for nuisance in circumstances in which the ordinary domestic use of the premises by one tenant causes a "nuisance" to another tenant merely as a result of defects in the construction of the property which existed *before* the letting to the claimant. Tuckey L.J. said that: "Such cases are decided on the principle of caveat lessee and the fact, albeit a fiction, that the lessee is deemed to take the premises as they are" ([1999] 1 All E.R. 237 at 246). In so holding the court applied the old principle that "there is no law against letting a tumble-down house" (see *Robbins v. Jones* (1863) 15 C.B.N.S. 221 at 240), and narrowly distinguished, on its own facts, the decision of the Court of Appeal in *Sampson v. Hodson-Pressinger* [1981] 3 All E.R. 710).

In *Habinteg Housing Association v. James* (1995) 27 H.L.R. 299 the Court of Appeal held that a housing association had an insufficient degree of control over an estate to render it liable to one of its tenants for an infestation of cockroaches, even assuming that the cockroaches had entered the tenant's property from other properties on the estate owned by the association.

Landlord's liability in other cases   **18–54**
In *Hussain v. Lancaster County Council* [1999] 4 All E.R. 125 the Court of Appeal (applying *Smith v. Scott* [1973] Ch. 314) struck out a claim in nuisance against the defendant landlord for failing to take action against its tenants who had subjected the plaintiff to racial harassment. Nevertheless a landlord can be liable in nuisance if he allows "troublemakers to occupy his land and to use it as a base for causing unlawful disturbance to his neighbours": *per* Evans L.J. in *Lippiatt v. South Gloucestershire Council* [1999] 4 All E.R. 149 at 157. In *Lippiatt's* case travellers, encamped on the defendants' land, which the latter failed to remove, committed nuisances against neighbouring farmers. The Court of Appeal, distinguishing *Hussain v. Lancaster City Council*, refused to strike out the claims against the defendants.

NOTE 27. Add: See also *Baxter v. Camden London Borough Council* [1999] 1 All E.R. 237 at 248, *per* Otton L.J.

6.—DEFENCES TO AN ACTION FOR NUISANCE

(c) *Ignorance of the Nuisance*

Trees   **18–60**
Noble v. Harrison was followed in *Chapman v. Barking and Dagenham L.B.C.* [1997] 11 C.L. 419, on similar facts (dangerous tree falling on to a vehicle on the highway); and in *Hurst v. Hampshire County Council* (1997) 96 L.G.R. 27, the Court of Appeal imposed liability upon a highway authority for reasonably foreseeable damage caused when a tree for which the authority was responsible collapsed

upon a house adjacent to the highway. In this case the Court of Appeal rejected a contention that a highway authority could only be liable for dangerous trees in circumstances which fell within the Highways Act 1980, s.96. The adoption or dedication of the highway was sufficient to give rise to liability on the authority in nuisance or negligence at common law.

18–67   Coming to the nuisance
In *Baxter v. Camden London Borough Council* [1999] 1 All E.R. 237 the Court of Appeal held that the principle that it is no defence that the plaintiff came to the nuisance has no application in cases of landlord and tenant, since in such cases the lessee is deemed to take the premises as they are: see [1999] 1 All E.R. at 246 (*per* Tuckey L.J.) and 250 (*per* Stuart-Smith L.J.).

7.—NUISANCE TO WATER RIGHTS

18–74   Pollution of stream
NOTE 16. Delete and substitute: *per* Lord Wilberforce in *Alphacell Ltd v. Woodward, supra,* at 835. See also *Empress Car Co. (Abertillery) Ltd v. National Rivers Authority* [1998] 1 All E.R. 481, HL (overruling *Impress Worcester Ltd v. Rees* [1971] 2 All E.R. 357).

9.—NUISANCE TO ANCIENT LIGHTS

18–92   Air and prospect
The continuing vitality of the old authorities denying that loss of a view or prospect is actionable in nuisance was reflected in the decision of the House of Lords in *Hunter v. Canary Wharf Ltd* [1997] 2 W.L.R. 684, [1997] 2 All E.R. 426, in which they were invoked by analogy to justify refusal of relief for interference with the path of television signals by the erection of a large building. Lord Lloyd of Berwick said (at 445):

> "The house owner who has a fine view of the South Downs may find that his neighbour has built so as to obscure his view. But there is no redress, unless, perchance, the neighbour's land was subject to a restrictive covenant in the house owner's favour. It would be a good example of what in law is called 'damnum absque injuria': a loss which the house owner has undoubtedly suffered, but which gives rise to no infringement of his legal rights. In the absence of a restrictive covenant, there is no legal right to a view".

10.—OBSTRUCTION OF ACCESS TO HIGHWAY

18–93   Right of access to highway
In *Great House at Sonning Ltd v. Berkshire County Council* [1996] R.T.R. 407 a majority of the Court of Appeal held that an alleged obstruction of the highway, caused by activities carried out pursuant to a statutory order, could only be challenged by judicial review to impugn the validity of the order and not by a private law nuisance action.

11.—OBSTRUCTION OF HIGHWAY

18–95   The proposition in *Thomas v. National Union of Mineworkers* [1986] Ch. 20 that an unreasonable interference, short of obstruction, with the use of the highway "might be described as a species of private nuisance" is no longer tenable after the decision of the House of Lords in *Hunter v. Canary Wharf Ltd* [1997] 2 W.L.R. 684 to the effect that an interest in land is necessary for a claim in the tort of private nuisance. The doubts expressed in the text, as to the correctness of the observations in *Thomas v. National Union of Mineworkers*, are therefore confirmed. It is possible, however, that activities similar to those engaged in in *Thomas'* case might now fall within the Protection from Harassment Act 1997.

Buildings adjoining highway   18–102
Where an occupier allows his land to interfere with visibility on the highway, it does not follow that the highway *authority* can itself be held liable in damages to a third party for failing to exercise powers available to it to compel removal of the interference: *Stovin v. Wise* [1996] 3 All E.R. 801, HL.

Standard of care   18–111
NOTE 96. Delete and substitute: *Haydon v. Kent C.C.* [1978] Q.B. 343, CA; *Cross v. Kirklees B.C.* [1998] 1 All E.R. 564, CA; Highways Act 1980, s.152.

12.—PRESCRIPTIVE RIGHT TO COMMIT NUISANCE

Prescriptive right to commit nuisance   18–113
In *Gardner v. Davis* [1999] E.H.L.R. 13 the Court of Appeal held that an easement which afforded share drainage into a septic tank did not constitute a defence to an action in nuisance by the owner of the servient tenement for the discharge of sewage into his garden. The easement could not have been intended to allow such escapes even though the owners of the dominant tenement contended that it was an inevitable consequence of their exercise of the easement.

NOTE 15. Add: See also *Hunter v. Canary Wharf Ltd* [1997] 2 W.L.R. 684, [1997] 2 All E.R. 426 at 469–470, *per* Lord Hope of Craighead.

13.—AUTHORISATION BY STATUTE

Allen v. Gulf Oil Refining Ltd   18–121
In *Hunter v. Canary Wharf Ltd* [1996] 1 All E.R. 582 Parliament had delegated extensive powers to a development authority to relax normal planning procedures, but the Court of Appeal held that those who obtained planning permission as a result nevertheless remained "well outside" the scope of the principle that statute can authorise a nuisance by necessary implication. Pill L.J. said:

> "The procedures do not . . . bring a permission obtained within the *Allen* principle. In permitting the establishment of a 'fast track' procedure for obtaining planning permission, Parliament cannot be said to have granted immunity to a particular structure built following such a permission . . . By conferring powers of a general, albeit extensive, nature, Parliament has not by necessary implication authorised a particular structure to enjoy an immunity from an action based on nuisance": *ibid.* at 491–492.

The decision of the Court of Appeal on this point was not challenged when *Hunter v. Canary Wharf Ltd* reached the House of Lords (see [1997] 2 All E.R. 426), but both Lord Hoffman and Lord Cooke of Thorndon indicated their agreement with the general proposition that it would "be wrong to allow the private rights of third parties to be taken away by a permission granted by the planning authority to the developer" (*per* Lord Hoffman at 455d; see also *per* Lord Cooke at 465j).

CHAPTER 19.—RYLANDS v. FLETCHER LIABILITY

		PARA.
■1.	The rule of strict liability	19–01
□2.	Exceptions to the rule of strict liability	19–18
□3.	Water	19–27
4.	Fire	19–44
5.	Gas	19–64
6.	Electricity	19–75
7.	Explosives	19–80
□8.	Poisonous waste and oil pollution	19–82
9.	Aircraft	19–86
■10.	Nuclear installations	19–90

19–01   The scope of the rule in *Rylands v. Fletcher* was considered, *obiter*, by the High Court in *Crown River Cruises Ltd v. Kimbolton Fireworks Ltd* in relation to a fire caused by the escape of fireworks from one moored vessel to another. It is significant, however, that although the court was not unsympathetic to the proposition that liability should be imposed on that basis, it preferred to decide the case on another ground in view of the perceived hostility towards any extension in the scope of the rule.

1.—The Rule of Strict Liability

19–07 **"Dangerous things"**
     Note 31. The decision in *Att.-Gen. v. Corke* was followed by the Court of Appeal in *Lippiatt v. South Gloucestershire Council* [1999] 4 All E.R. 149, which was decided on similar facts but on the basis of liability in nuisance rather than under the principle of *Rylands v. Fltecher*.

19–12 **Effect of Cambridge Water**
     In *Ellison v. Ministry of Defence* (1997) 81 B.L.R. 101, the carrying out of construction works on a disused airfield were considered to constitute an ordinary use of land and hence not to be within the concept of non-natural user for the purposes of the rule in *Rylands v. Fletcher*.

19–13 **Who is liable under the rule**
     In *Crown River Cruises Ltd v. Kimbolton Fireworks Ltd* [1996] 2 Lloyd's Rep. 533 Potter J. indicated, *obiter*, that since the rule in *Rylands v. Fletcher* had been applied to accumulations on the highway, which caused damage to the owners of property nearby, there were good reasons to extend it to cover accumulations on a vessel on a navigable river.

19–15 **Personal injuries**
     The doubts surrounding the recoverability of damages for personal injury under the rule in *Rylands v. Fletcher* are further reinforced by dicta in the House of Lords in *Hunter v. Canary Wharf Ltd* [1997] 2 W.L.R. 684 [1997] 2 All E.R. 426 to the effect that such damages should now be recoverable only in negligence: see, especially, *per* Lord Goff of Chieveley at 438j and see also, *per* Lord Lloyd of Berwick at 442d. But *cf* the contrary view expressed by Lord Cooke of Thorndon, dissenting, at 462–463.

19–16 **Remoteness of damage**
     Cambridge Water Co. Ltd v. Eastern Counties Leather plc [1994] 2 A.C. 264,

was applied in *Ellison v. Ministry of Defence* (1997) 81 B.L.R. 101, in which damage caused by escaping flood water was held, on the facts, to have been unforeseeable.

2.—Exceptions to the Rule of Strict Liability

Exceptions   19–18
The suggestion by Taylor J. in *Rigby v. Chief Constable of Northamptonshire* [1985] 1 W.L.R. 1242 that the rule in *Rylands v. Fletcher* is confined to accidental, as distinct from intentional, escapes—the latter being remediable in trespass—was questioned by Potter J. in *Crown River Cruises Ltd v. Kimbolton Fireworks Ltd* [1996] 2 Lloyd's Rep. 533. His lordship saw no good reason to limit the rule in that way, at least where the intentional release was not deliberately aimed at the plaintiff with the intention of causing damage to him.

3.—Water

Liability in respect of water   19–27
The authorities on liability for the escape of water were reviewed in *Ellison v. Ministry of Defence* (1997) 81 B.L.R. 101, in which, following a violent storm, an obstruction on the defendants' land caused rainwater to overflow onto the plaintiffs' property. The plaintiffs' claim failed: the floodwater was of natural origin and the obstruction on the defendants' land did not constitute non-natural user, moreover the damage which occurred had not been foreseeable.
NOTE 33. Add: *Gartner v. Kidman* was not applied in *Ellison v. Ministry of Defence* (1997) 81 B.L.R. 101.

8.—Poisonous Waste and Oil Pollution

Oil pollution   19–85
NOTE 27. For the Merchant Shipping Act 1974 substitute the Merchant Shipping Act 1995, ss.172–182.

10.—Nuclear Installations

Nuclear installations   19–90
NOTE 36. Delete and substitute: See, generally, Tromans and Fitzgerald, *The Law of Nuclear Installations and Radioactive Substances* (1997); Street and Frame, *Law Relating to Nuclear Energy* (1966).

Liability under the Act   19–93
Liability was imposed in *Blue Circle Industries plc v. Ministry of Defence* [1999] 2 W.L.R. 295 in respect of radioactive contamination of the plaintiffs' land, the topsoil of which had had to be removed before the property could be sold. The defendants contended that the very small amounts of radioactive material had not physically damaged the plaintiffs' property. But the Court of Appeal, distinguishing *Merlin v. British Nuclear Fuels* [1990] 2 Q.B. 557, held that the plaintiffs had suffered damage to property within section 7(1)(a).

CHAPTER 20.—ANIMALS

		PARA.
□1.	The Animals Act 1971	20–01
□2.	Strict liability for animals under section 2	20–02
■3.	Strict liability for dogs under section 3	20–09
4.	Strict liability for livestock under section 4	20–10
□5.	Liability for animals on the highway	20–14
■6.	Common law liabilities	20–16

1.—THE ANIMALS ACT 1971

20–01   Common law and statute

In *Jaundrill v. Gillett, The Times*, January 30, 1996, Russell L.J. in the Court of Appeal commented on the difficulty of dealing with some of the wording of the 1971 Animals Act, recalling that it had been the subject of adverse judicial comment. NOTE 9. Add: Also see Love, Mark, *Animals and the Law*.

2.—STRICT LIABILITY FOR ANIMALS UNDER SECTION 2

20–03   Liability for animals of a non-dangerous species

In *Jaundrill v. Gillett, The Times*, January 30, 1996, the plaintiff had been driving on a dark night when he saw in his headlights a number of riderless horses, belonging to the defendant, galloping towards his car which then collided with the horses. The plaintiff sued the defendant as their "keeper" under section 2(2) of the Animals Act for the damage, but the defendant denied liability. It was accepted by both parties that the horses had escaped from the field because a malicious intruder had opened a gate and driven the horses on to the road. The court at first instance had to decide whether the defendant was liable under section 2 on the ground that "the likelihood of the damage or of its being severe was due to characteristics of the horses which are not normally found in animals of the same species or are not normally so found except at particular times or in particular circumstances".

The Recorder in the county court held in favour of the plaintiff on the ground that evidence had been given by a veterinary surgeon that horses, when moved from their normal environment would tend to behave abnormally and that horses removed from their field on to the road in the dark would tend to panic and to gallop aimlessly. The Court of Appeal, however, doubted whether the horses in question had been displaying a "characteristic" within section 2. Also there had to be a causal link between the characteristic and the damage and in the view of Russell L.J., with whom Singer L.J. concurred, "the real and effective cause of the accident was the release of the animals on to the highway; the real cause of the damage the presence of the horses there at that time". The defendant's appeal was therefore allowed.

In the Scottish case of *Foskett v. McClymont* 1998 S.L.T. 892, the court considered whether a bull which had caused personal injury to the plaintiff fell within section 1 of the Animals (Scotland) Act 1987 so as to bring its owner within the category of strict liability. The court held that in assessing whether the bull was "an animal likely to cause severe injury" the common law preceding the Act was not relevant. Even though a bull was not an animal classifed in section 1(3) of the Act as "likely . . . to injure severely or kill persons or animals etc, the bull in question could still be deemed by the court to fulfil the criteria laid down in the statute.

20–05   For a recent application of section 2(2)(b) see *Jaundrill v. Gillett, The Times*, January 30, 1996 (see above § 20–03).

3. STRICT LIABILITY FOR DOGS UNDER SECTION 3

NOTE 47. Add: *Briscoe v. Shattock* [1999] 1 W.L.R. 432.   **20–09**

5.—LIABILITY FOR ANIMALS ON THE HIGHWAY

Animals straying on to the highway   **20–14**
   In *Jaundrill v. Gillett, The Times*, January 30, 1996 in the Court of Appeal, Russell
L.J. raised the possibility of liability under section 8 where the defendant's horses
had been released from a field by a malicious act of a third party, but the section
was not applied in that case, though it might presumably have been relevant if the
plaintiff could have shown that the defendant had failed to use reasonable care.

6.—COMMON LAW LIABILITIES

Common law liabilities   **20–16**
   NOTE 88. Add *Hall v. Dart Valley Light Railway* 1998 C.L.Y. 3933.
   NOTE 89. Add: *Fairlie v. Carruthers*, 1996 S.L.T. (Sh Ct) 56.

CHAPTER 21.—DEFAMATION

		PARA.
■1.	Generally	21–01
■2.	What is defamatory?	21–12
3.	Joint injury	21–27
4.	Slander	21–28
	(a) Imputing a criminal offence	21–29
	(b) Imputing disease	21–30
	(c) Imputing unchstity to a woman	21–31
	(d) Slander on a man in his calling or office	21–32
	(e) Slander causing special damage	21–38
■5.	Construction of language used	21–39
■6.	Defamatory matter within section 4 of the Defamation Act 1952—"unintentional defamation"	21–59
■7.	Publication	21–61
■8.	Defences	
	(a) Generally	21–74
	(b) Justification	21–76
	(c) Privilege	21–88
	(d) Fair comment and criticism	21–138
	(e) Reports	21–182
■9.	Malice	21–182
10.	Repetition	21–197
■11.	Damages	
	(a) In general	21–203
	(b) Special damage	21–121
	(c) Mitigation of damages	21–214
	(d) Excessive damages	21–225
	(e) Costs	21–230
	(f) Payment into court	21–231
■12.	Injunction	21–232

1.—GENERALLY

21–01 **Action of defamation**

The law of defamation continues to give rise to much litigation, expense and criticism. The case of *McDonalds Corporation v. Steel, The Times*, June 1997, which was the longest civil trial in English legal history, lasting for 313 days, demonstrates some of the quirks of libel litigation; the plaintiffs, the McDonald Corporation, sued the two defendants for libel in respect of leaflets which contained a number of accusations about the plaintiffs' fast food business. The plaintiffs succeeded in establishing libel in relation to the defendants' allegations that, *inter alia*, the company was responsible for environmental damage and for endangering its customers' health by serving unhealthy products. However the court did regard as justified the defendants' allegations that the company exploited its young work force and that animals were treated inhumanely in the process of being reared for meat production for the company. The two defendants, who represented themselves in the proceedings and had no financial means, appealed on no less than 63 counts, including wider issues relating to defamation, such as Article 10 of the European Convention on Human Rights and the right of a commercial company to sue in defamation. The defendants were partially successful in their appeal on the ground that the allegations in the offending leaflet, relating to employment conditions world-wide and to the health hazards of McDonalds' food if eaten sufficiently often, did constitute fair comment.

150

The damages awarded against them were accordingly reduced from £60,000 to £40,000.

The Defamation Act 1996 (see *post* Supplement § 21–03) introduced a number of reforms of the law of defamation which give effect to the recommendations of the Neill Committee's Report, the proposals of Hoffmann L.J. and the Lord Chancellor's consultation paper on *The Defence of Innocent Dissemination* (1990). The principal provisions of the Act are set out below (*post*, Supplement § 21–03). In order to reform some of the expense, delay and complexity of defamation litigation, a new statutory defence is provided for distributors who neither knew nor ought to have known that a publication was defamatory. This replaces the existing defence of "innocent dissemination". Section 4 of the Defamation Act is repealed and with it the unlamented provisions relating to "unintentional defamation". This is replaced with a new procedure for the making of an offer of amends by a defendant who is willing to pay compensation assessed by a judge, as well as to make the required correction and apology. The limitation period for defamation is reduced from three years to one year and a new summary procedure is introduced for the trial of defamation actions.

The Act makes an important change in the law and one which has constitutional implications. Under section 13, parliamentary privilege, as provided for in Article 9 of the Bill of Rights 1689, can now be waived by an M.P. in legal proceedings—a development which will profoundly affect such cases as *Allason v. Haines* and *Hamilton v. Guardian* (*post*, §§ 21–03 and 21–96). The Act also amends the law relating to privilege and to evidence of convictions in defamation actions; the rule that evidence of a conviction is conclusive proof that the person in question committed the offence shall apply only to plaintiffs in such actions. The rule in *Scott v. Sampson* has been retained.

The Human Rights Act 1998, gives effect in the courts of the United Kingdom to rights and freedoms guaranteed under the European Convention on Human Rights. The impact of the Act on the law of defamation is not clear as yet, but it may be predicted that there will be further issues raised under Article 6, Article 8 and Article 10 in relation to defamation. (see *post*, Supplement § 21–03). The Act is expected to come into force in the latter part of 2000. See also *Reynolds v. Times Newspapers* [1998] 3 All E.R. 961, HL.

In relation to statements published abroad but disseminated in England, see Chapter 6.

NOTE 3. Add: In *Malik v. BCCI, The Times*, June 13, 1997, the House of Lords held that an employee could, in principle, recover damages for the financial loss stemming from stigma and loss of reputation caused by the employer's breach of the implied obligation not to act in a way likely to destroy or seriously damage the trust between employer and employee. In *Fulton v. Globe & Mail*, (1997) 152 D.L.R. 4th 377, the Canadian Courts held that a claim for negligence should not be combined with a claim for defamation.

Complexity of defamation   **21–02**

In *McDonalds Corporation v. Steel, The Times*, June 1997 and in *Shanson v. Howard* [1997] 4 C.L. 237, the plaintiffs were litigants in person, and these cases demonstrate some of the hazards of litigation of this kind in a complex area such as defamation. In the former the proceedings were immensely long, in the latter the plaintiff was faced with the complications of meaning and innuendo. Brooke L.J. in the Court of Appeal expressed the court's concern for such litigants in saying "As the law gets more and more technical and the services of litigation solicitors and counsel get more and more expensive, it is incumbent on trial judges to do what they can to avoid shutting out litigants in person from saying what they want to say" (LEXIS transcript, January 30, 1997). Nonetheless the plaintiff's action failed on the grounds that the statements complained of were not susceptible to the meanings alleged by him.

The Defamation Act 1996 introduced new provisions which will simplify and reform the law of defamation. Although hardly radical, the provisions of the Act will meet some of the concerns expressed over the years by the judiciary in relation to defamation actions.

Add: See Carter-Ruck and Elliott, *Carter-Ruck on Libel and Slander*: Price, D., *Defamation: Law, Procedure and Practice*. Rampton, R., Sharp, V., Neill, Sir B.Q.C. *Duncan & Neill on Defamation* (4th ed.) Milmo, O., *Gatley on Libel and Slander* (9th ed., 1998).

21–03   Recent developments

The Defamation Act 1996 contains new provisions aimed at reforming and improving the law and practice of defamation. Its principal provisions are:

(a) A new statutory defence will now be available to distributors, printers and others provided that they neither knew nor had reason to believe that their acts contributed to the publication of defamatory material. See *post*, § 21–61.

(b) A new defence of offering to make amends replaces the present, unsatisfactory plea of "unintentional defamation" under section 4 of the Defamation Act 1952.

(c) The Act reduces the limitation period for defamation actions to one year.

(d) One of the most controversial provisions in the Act is contained in section 13 whereby the effect of Article 9 of the Bill of Rights is modified in so far as a member of either House of Parliament may waive the effect of Article 9 of the Bill of Rights in so far as it affects him or her and may therefore allow matters which have occurred in Parliamentary proceedings to be raised in court. This section will in future permit such actions as *Allason v. Haines*, [1995] E.M.L.R. 143, contrary to the previous principle laid down by the Privy Council in *TVNZ v. Prebble* (1994) 3 All E.R. 407 (*post*, Supplement, § 21–96)

(e) Sections 8 to 10 provide for a new summary procedure which will enable cases to be dealt with by a judge who can give relief, including damages up to a ceiling of £10,000. However the procedure will only apply if certain conditions are fulfilled.

(f) The Act provides that statutory privilege for contemporaneous reports of judicial proceedings is absolute and brings up to date and extends the list of communications covered by qualified privilege (*post*, §§ 21–179 and 21–180)

Further effects on defamation proceedings will result from the introduction in April 1999 of the Civil Procedure Rules 1998 and accompanying Practice Directions, as a result of the Woolf Report on civil justice. In addition to the provisions specifically concerned with defamation, namely Practice Direction 16, para. 8 and Sched. 1 and the amended RSC, Ord. 82, civil litigation, including defamation litigation, will be governed by the overriding objective of the Civil Procedure Rules, that is, of dealing with a case justly. This includes, so far as is practicable, ensuring that the parties are on an equal footing, saving expense, dealing with the case in ways which are proportionate to the amount of money involved, the importance of the case, the complexity of the issues and the financial position of the parties, ensuring that the case is dealt with expeditiously and fairly and allotting to it an appropriate share of the court's resources. In *McPhilemy v. Times Newspapers Ltd* [1999] 3 All E.R. 775, Lord Woolf in the Court of Appeal stressed that these principles might well affect the extent and complexity of defamation proceedings, e.g. in relation to pleas of justification.

In *Gilberthorpe v. Hawkins, The Times*, April 3, 1995, the courts acknowledged the difficulties of the lack of legal aid for defamation actions and took a sympathetic view of the plaintiff's delay since he had to raise the required funds for his litigation.

In *Joyce v. Sengupta* [1993] 1 W.L.R. 337 the Court of Appeal, in allowing the plaintiff to succeed in malicious falsehood, had accepted that one of the reasons for her proceeding in that tort rather than libel was the fact that legal aid was not available for defamation. It is not always advantageous, however, for the plaintiff to sue for malicious falsehood rather than defamation, even if both are potential causes of action. In *Allason v. Campbell, The Times*, May 8, 1996, the plaintiff sued in malicious falsehood rather than in libel in respect of allegations made by the defendant journalist, but failed since the court held that the plaintiff could not show actual damage. He recovered nominal damages (see *The Times*, July 31, 1998). (For malicious falsehood see *post*, Chapter 22.)

In July 1997 the Norwich Union Insurance Company was ordered by the High Court to pay £450,000 damages and costs and to issue an apology to the plaintiffs, Western Provident Association, for libelling WPA by electronic mail (e-mail). This is believed to be the first occasion in England where damages have been obtained for e-mail defamation.

In *Godfrey v. Demon Internet* [1999] 4 All E.R. 342, the plaintiff successfully **21-04** sued the defendant Internet service provider (ISP) for libel in respect of an article, defamatory of him, which had appeared on the Internet through the defendants' forum. This was the first English case of an action for defamatory material on the Internet.

The courts have continued to refer and to be referred to Article 10 of the European Convention on Human Rights. In *Tolstoy Miloslavsky v. United Kingdom* (1995) 20 E.H.R.R. 442, the applicant to the European Court of Human Rights claimed successfully that the £1.5 million awarded against him to Lord Aldington in a libel action were in breach of Article 10 as being an undue restraint on freedom of speech.

Article 10 was also discussed by the Court of Appeal in *John v. MGN* [1996] 2 All E.R. 35 but the Court concluded that the decision in that case could be reached without recourse to Article 10 since the common law provided a remedy (*per* Sir Thomas Bingham M.R. at 58). However, Article 10 will now, after the passage of the Human Rights Act 1998, be directly applied to defamation cases in English courts.

The Human Rights Act now makes it unlawful for "a public authority" to act in a way incompatible with one or more of the rights laid down in the Convention. "Public authorities" here will include courts and tribunals and, to the extent that they are exercising "public functions", companies responsible for areas of activity which were previously within the public sector. The approach of the Act is to provide those alleging a breach of the Convention with a remedy for that breach in the domestic courts of the United Kingdom. Sections 7 and 8 of the Act provide that persons who have been victims of such actions may bring proceedings in which the court may "grant such relief or remedy, including damages, as is just and appropriate". See further, *supra*, Supplement § 1–05A. Section 9 provides that proceedings in the case of judicial acts will be by way of appeal, judicial review (or in another forum as may be prescribed).

Article 6 of the Convention, which provides for the right to a fair trial, might be cited by parties in relation to defamation actions in future, *e.g.* by plaintiffs to challenge the striking out of their claims or by defendants to dispute the issue of injunctions. Further, on this ground, either party might dispute the denial of jury trial.

Article 8 which states that "Everyone has the right to respect for his private and family life, his home and his correspondence" may be used by the courts to build up a body of case law respecting privacy. It may be used to limit press "intrusion" and to add a further brake on press coverage of matters relating, *e.g.* to personal conduct of public figures. It is unlikely that the press will come within the Act, although the BBC may well do so. However, since the courts are included under "public authorities", individuals complaining of revelations about their private life may argue that the courts are in breach of the Act if they fail to protect the right to privacy under Article 8 of the Convention. (see P. Milmo Q.C., "Human Rights Privacy and the Press" 147 N.L.J. 1631–1632)

Article 10, enshrining the right to freedom of speech, has already been considered by the English courts (*e.g. Reynolds v. Times Newspapers* [1998] 3 All E.R. 961, HL). In applying it under the new legislation the courts may be called upon to reconcile this right with the right to privacy under Article 8, particularly in cases involving the media. However, the approach already adopted by the courts before the 1998 Act suggests that they are anxious to protect freedom of speech and will do so vigorously under the new Act.

NOTE 13. Add: T.P. Kennedy and Alan Reed, "The Europeanisation of Defamation" (1996) 5(2) JEL 201–225.

21–05   In *John v. MGN* [1996] 2 All E.R. 35, the court considered the impact of Article 10. The Human Rights Act 1998 now gives further effect to the rights provided for under the European Convention (see, *supra*, Supplement § 21–04) and *Tolstoy Miloslavsky v. United Kingdom* (1995) 20 E.H.R.R. 442.

The Defamation Act 1996, s.5 amends the Limitation Act so as to reduce the period of limitation in actions for libel and slander and malicious falsehood from three years to one year. The same section, however, does give the court discretion to override the time-limit where it would be equitable to do so. The same change is made under section 6 in relation to Northern Ireland by amending the Limitation (Northern Ireland) Order 1989.

In *C v. Mirror Newspapers* [1996] 4 All E.R. 511, the plaintiff sought to sue the defendants for an article in which they had reported defamatory allegations about her, made by her husband, after a trial in which he was in dispute with her over their children. The plaintiff believed that the paper was reporting what had been said in court in the course of proceedings but in 1993 she received a letter from the judge assuring her that the allegations had not been made in court. Seven months later she issued proceedings against the newspaper in libel and malicious falsehood. The Court held that her action in libel was statute barred, as being more than three years after the publication of which she complained and not within the exception. The plaintiff argued that she was within section 32A of the Limitation Act 1980 which provided that an action for libel or slander could be brought with leave at any time within one year from the earliest date at which she knew "all the facts relevant to that cause of action". Her appeal against this ruling was dismissed by the Court of Appeal which held that the phrase "the facts relevant to the cause of action" meant those facts which established the cause of action itself; the section did not cover facts which were relevant to possible defences. The plaintiff had believed that there was a defence of privilege to her action as she believed that the statements had been made in court. This misapprehension did not come within the relevant statutory provision and the plaintiff's action for libel was therefore statute barred.

The change in the law in s.13 of the Defamation Act 1996 and the cases of *Hamilton v. Guardian, The Times*, July 22, 1995, *Allason v. Haines* [1995] E.M.L.R. 143 and of *Aitken v. Preston* [1997] E.M.L.R. 415 have stimulated further discussion of the position of public figures in relation to defamation. An interesting comparison with New Zealand is the case of *Lange v. Atkinson Australia Consolidated Press* [1997] 2 N.Z.L.R. 22 (May 1998), N.Z., also *Lange v. Australian Broadcasting Corp.* (1997) 145 A.L.R. 91.

NOTE 16. Add: A. Sharland and I Loveland, "The Defamation Act and political libels", [1997] P.L. Spring, 113–124. Williams, K. "Only flattery is safe; political speech and the Defamation Act 1996" [1997] 60 M.L.R. 388–393. I. Loveland, "Political Libels and Qualified Privilege; a British Solution to a British Problem" [1997] P.L. 428–436. I. Loveland, "The Constitutionalisation of Political Libels in English Common Law" [1998] P.L. 633–646.

21–09   Motive immaterial

The defence of "unintentional defamation" provided by section 4 of the Defamation Act 1952 has been abolished and replaced by a new statutory procedure providing for an "offer of amends" to be made. The defence is dealt with in greater detail below (§§ 21–59 to 60).

2.—What is Defamatory?

"or be likely to affect a person adversely in the estimation of reasonable people   **21–12**
generally", *per* Neill L.J. in *Gillick v. BBC, The Times*, October 20, 1995.
   In *Berkoff v. Burchill* Neill L.J. in the Court of Appeal discussed the authorities as to the meaning of "defamatory", with reference to the traditional definitions and to additional meanings gleaned from decided cases: [1996] 4 All E.R. 1008, 1011–1017.

Defamatory nature   **21–13**
   In *Gillick v. BBC* [1996] E.M.L.R. 267, Neill L.J. referred to the guidance of the Master of the Rolls in *Skuse v. Granada Television* [1996] E.M.L.R. 278, CA, to the effect that the court should give to the material in question the natural and ordinary meaning which it would have conveyed to the ordinary reasonable viewer, bearing in mind that a television audience would not give the programme the analytical attention of a lawyer to the meaning of a document, an auditor to the interpretation of accounts or an academic to the content of a learned article. In *Mitchell v. Faber & Faber* [1998] E.M.L.R. 807 the plaintiff complained of a statement made in a book, published by the defendants, in which he claimed he was represented as being racist and intolerant in that he had made racist comments and used insulting terms to the guitarist Jimi Hendrix and other non-white colleagues. At first instance the court held that the conduct described in the book should be viewed in the light of the time at which they were allegedly made, namely the 1960s, when such comments were less unacceptable. On appeal, the plaintiff's claim was upheld by the Court of Appeal which accepted that the statements in the book were capable of defamatory meanings and that the judge had been wrong in holding that the surrounding context and the date of the events described were capable of "drawing the sting" of the allegations. In *Berkoff v. Burchill* [1996] 4 All E.R. 1008, the plaintiff, a film director, sued a journalist who described him as being "hideously ugly". The defendants sought a preliminary ruling that such an allegation was without substance and that therefore the action should be struck out. However the majority of the court held (Millett L.J. dissenting) that the question whether the statement was defamatory should be left to the jury.
   In *Shanson v Howard* [1997] 4 C.L. 237 the plaintiff, a freelance journalist, issued writs in two actions against the defendants, in respect of an article in *Jane's Defence Weekly* which, he alleged, damaged his reputation. On a preliminary issue as to the meaning of the material concerned, the Court of Appeal held that the statements were not capable of bearing the meaning of which the plaintiff complained.
   See *Awa v. Independent News Auckland* [1995] 3 N.Z.L.R. 701, where the description of the plaintiff as "body-snatching" was held not to be defamatory.
   Note 75. Add: *CBC v. Color Your World Corp.* (1998) 156 D.L.R. 4th 27.

   In *Aspro Travel v. Owners Abroad plc* [1996] 1 W.L.R. 132, the Court of Appeal   **21–14**
had to consider whether the expressions, used of the plaintiffs' small family travel company, that "they were going bust" and "they would be bankrupt in a few days" were capable of being defamatory. They decided that the words might be understood to mean that the company was insolvent and that the plaintiff directors permitted the company to trade knowing that it was insolvent, which could lower their standing in the community. In the Scottish case of *Quilty v. Windsor* 1999 S.L.T. 346, the court was of the opinion that an allegation of homosexuality would not be defamatory *per se*.
   In *Gillick v. BBC* [1996] E.M.L.R. 267, the plaintiff, a well-known campaigner against the provision of contraception to young girls, sued the BBC in respect of an

allegation, made on a television programme, which, she maintained, suggested that her campaign had led to girls committing suicide. The Court of Appeal refused to overrule the judge's initial decision that words used on the broadcast were capable of being defamatory of her. In deciding whether a statement is defamatory the words must be considered in the light of all the surrounding circumstances and the question is not merely whether the words in their natural and ordinary meaning are defamatory *per se*. Thus in *Berkoff v. Burchill* [1996] 4 All E.R. 1008, CA the Court of Appeal held that the judge at first instance had been correct in refusing to rule that a description of the plaintiff as "hideously ugly" was incapable of being defamatory. It was for a jury to decide whether the statement was libellous. In *Marks & Spencer v. Granada Television*, the plaintiff company sued for defamation arising out of the defendants' television programme which dealt with the exploitation of child labour in the manufacture of goods sold by the plaintiff company. The judge, Popplewell J., asked the jury in advance of the trial if they thought the programme conveyed the meaning to viewers that the plaintiffs knew that child labour was used in producing goods to be sold in their shops and that they deliberately misled their customers by knowingly selling goods made abroad under the label "made in the U.K.". The jury decided that such was, indeed, the meaning of the programme whereas the defendants had argued that the meaning of the programme was not that the defendants knew of the exploitation and deception but that they should have known. In the light of this the defendants settled, since they would have been unable to show that the company had the knowledge in question. (See *The Guardian*, March 4, 1998.) This was an unprecedented course for the judge to take in a defamation action. The jury would usually hear the evidence before it decides on matters of meaning. The approach of Popplewell J. in the *Marks and Spencer* case was endorsed by the Court of Appeal in *Shah v. Standard Chartered Bank* [1998] 3 W.L.R. 592, CA but does have disadvantages (see article by Patrick Milmo Q.C. (1997) 148 N.L.J. 655–656).

Section 7 of the Defamation Act 1996 provides that "In defamation proceedings the court shall not be asked to rule whether a statement is arguably capable, as opposed to capable, of bearing particular meaning or meanings attributed to it". The object of this provision seems to be to reduce the complexity and delay of defamation proceedings.

21–17   Ridicule

In *Berkoff v. Burchill* [1996] 4 All E.R. 1008 the defendants had applied to have the plaintiff's case struck out on the grounds that an allegation that the plaintiff was "hideously ugly" was not capable of being defamatory. The application was refused and they appealed against this decision. The Court of Appeal dismissed the appeal and held that it should be left to the jury to decide whether the statement which might be said to ridicule the plaintiff was defamatory. Millett L.J. dissented, on the grounds that the allegation was not capable of being defamatory. In *Norman v. Future Publishing*, February 1999, C.L. 175 the plaintiff, a world famous opera singer, complained of an anecdote, published by the defendants, which attributed a remark to her which referred humorously to her size. The judge ruled that the words quoted did not amount to defamation. She appealed but her appeal was dismissed on the grounds that the words in question were evidence that she was dignified and had a self-deprecating sense of humour which showed her in an attractive light. Overall the article was admiring. In so far as there was humour, she was not being held up to ridicule and *Berkoff v. Burchill* was distinguished on the ground that in that case the defendant showed a deliberate intention to ridicule the plaintiff.

It was held in *Prophit v. BBC*, 1997 S.L.T. 745, that it is not a defence to a defamatory statement that it was made as a joke.

21–18   Criminal association

In *Mapp v. News Group*, [1997] E.M.L.R. 397, the plaintiffs were police officers attached to a London police station. There had been a serious problem of drug offences and a suggestion of some police corruption or impropriety. The sergeant in charge of the investigation committed suicide and a report in the defendants' newspaper, the *News of the World*, stated that a number of officers had been moved to a different station. The plaintiffs claimed that the report complained of could be construed to imply guilt on the part of the officers concerned. They sought to distinguish their case from *Lewis v. Daily Telegraph* on the ground that the account of the police sergeant's suicide gave emphasis to the fact that they were under suspicion and, in the words of Lord Devlin a case where "loose talk about suspicion can very easily convey the impression that it is well founded". However the Court of Appeal refused to accept that the statement imputed guilt to the plaintiffs.

In *Bennett v. Guardian Newspapers, The Times*, February 27, 1997, the same five police officers sued the *Guardian* newspaper for libel in respect of a report which described the operation of an internal police inquiry into allegations by drugs offenders relating to police officers. The action failed as the jury found for the defendants.

Imputation of insolvency

21–22

In *Aspro Travel v. Owners Abroad plc* [1996] 1 W.L.R. 132, the Court of Appeal refused to rule that the statements "they are going bust" and "they will be bankrupt in a few days" were incapable of being defamatory of the plaintiff company directors. They could imply that the plaintiffs were prepared to trade knowing that the company was insolvent, which would lower their standing in the eyes of the community.

Corporations

21–25

The court held in *Goldsmith v. Bhoyrul* [1997] 4 All E.R. 268, [1997] E.M.L.R. 407, that a political party may not sue in defamation for damage to its reputation. The Referendum party was registered as a company, but a company whose sole purpose was to function as a political party. Referring to *Derbyshire County Council v. Times Newspapers* [1993] A.C. 534 Buckley J. ruled that it would be undesirable for a political party to be entitled to sue in defamation.

5.—CONSTRUCTION OF LANGUAGE USED

Language not defamatory on the face of it

21–39

NOTE 8. Add: See *Shanson v. Howard* [1997] 4 C.L. 237, CA.

Trial by jury

21–41

In *Kirby-Harris v. Baxter* [1995] E.M.L.R. 516, the plaintiff sued in respect of defamatory statements made by the defendants, who were five non-executive directors of a healthcare trust, of her performance as chairman of the trust. The judge at first instance had made an order for a preliminary issue to be tried to decide whether the defendants' statements were made bona fide for the purpose of executing the relevant legislation; if so they were protected from liability for their actions. The plaintiff succeeded in having the order discharged; the Court of Appeal held that the essential nature of inquiring into the bona fides of the defendants was equivalent to inquiring into malice. To allow this to be tried on a preliminary hearing would be to deprive the plaintiff of her constitutional right to trial by jury.

There have been many criticisms of trial by jury in defamation actions, but Parliament refused to overturn this right, still regarded as a vital issue of civil liberties. The Defamation Act 1996 does not directly affect the question of trial by jury for defamation cases but if the new offer of amends defence and the new summary procedure in defamation cases become popular, the number of trials by jury for libel and slander will inevitably fall.

(For parliamentary discussion of jury trials in defamation see *Hansard*, HL Deb. March 8, 1996, 592–595, 597–598.)

NOTE 20. Add: In the case where Jonathan Aitken, an ex-Cabinet Minister, sued the editor of *The Guardian* and Granada Television the trial was commenced without a jury. (*Aitken v. Preston; Aitken v. Granada TV* [1997] E.M.L.R. 415.)

21–42   Libel or no libel, Fox's Act
See *Kirby-Harris v. Baxter* (*supra*, § 21–41).

21–43   Under the Civil Procedure Rules, Practice Direction 16, para. 8(2), "Where in a claim for libel or slander the claimant alleges that the words or matters complained of were used in a defamatory sense other than their ordinary meaning, the particulars of claim must describe that defamatory sense."

NOTE 33a. Add: In relation to the decision in *Charleston v. News Group* [1995] 2 All E.R. 313, see Prescott [1995] M.L.R. 752 to the effect that the statement might surely have been defamatory even if read as a whole (might bring the plaintiff into disrepute). The *Charleston* case was also criticised in the Australian case of *Chakravarti v. Advertiser Newspapers* (1998) 72 A.L.J.R. 1115–1116.

21–45   Defamatory matter published as hearsay
In *Aspro Travel v. Owners Abroad plc* [1996] 1 W.L.R. 132 the defendants sought to justify statements to the effect that the plaintiffs company were "going bust" and "would be bankrupt in a few days" by showing that there was a rumour to that effect in the travel trade. The Court of Appeal held that although hearsay and rumour did not amount to justification for asserting that the rumour was well-founded, the existence of a rumour might entitle a person to repeat the rumour and it might be sufficient justification that the rumour(s) did really exist.

In *Stern v. Piper* [1996] 3 W.L.R. 715, CA, the plaintiff sued the defendants for libel, contained in their newspaper, to the effect that he was in financial trouble and was unable to pay large debts. The defendants sought to plead by way of justification that proceedings were pending in the High Court against the plaintiff and in doing so quoted allegations made against the plaintiff in an affirmation, sworn by a third party, for purposes of that litigation. The Court of Appeal held that the defence of justification would not apply here and that the "repetition rule", that a statement is not less actionable because it is stated as a matter of rumour, hearsay or repetition, would apply. In *Shah v. Standard Chartered Bank* [1998] 3 W.L.R. 592, the Court of Appeal considered the cases of *Aspro Travel v. Owners Abroad* [1996] 1 W.L.R. 132, and *Stern v. Piper* [1996] 3 W.L.R. 715, CA, in relation to statements made by an agent of the defendant to Bank of England representatives, to the effect that the plaintiffs company had been guilty of money laundering. The plaintiffs sued and the defendants alleged, *inter alia*, that they were merely repeating what had been rumoured. The Court of Appeal applied the repetition rule affirming that, in the words of Lord Devlin in *Lewis v. Daily Telegraph* [1964] A.C. 234, "for the purposes of the law of libel a hearsay statement is the same as a direct statement and that is all there is to it". It is therefore not enough to justify the existence of the rumour, but publication of the rumour would be justified only by showing objectively that there were reasonable grounds for such belief. The court preferred *Stern v. Piper* to the *Aspro* case which, in their view, should be confined to its own facts and should not be treated as laying down a general principle.

21–49   Judge to rule if words capable of defamatory meaning
RSC, Ord. 82, r.3A (1994) introduced in accordance with the Neill Committee's proposals, provides that at any stage in defamation proceedings, once the statement of claim has been served, either party may apply to a judge in chambers for an order determining whether or not the words complained of are capable of bearing a particular meaning or meanings attributed to them in the pleadings. In deciding that question, the court would reject meanings that could only emerge as a result of strained, forced or utterly unreasonable interpretation. See *Mapp v News Group* [1997] E.M.L.R. 397. In *Hinduja v. Asian T.V. Ltd* [1988] E.M.L.R. 524 the Court of Appeal held that, since the purpose of RSC Ord. 82, r.3A, is to provide a swift means by which a decision can be given in chambers whether words are capable of bearing the meaning advanced by the parties, appeals under it should not be encouraged. However, in *Geenty v. Channel Four T.V. Corp.* [1988] E.M.L.R. the Court of Appeal held that where the trial judge ruled that the words complained of by the

plaintiff were incapable of conveying a defamatory meaning, the Court of Appeal will not necessarily refrain from intervening. Although appeals under RSC, Ord. 82, r.3A, should be discouraged, and the Court of Appeal would be slow to intervene where the judge decided that the words in question were capable of a defamatory meaning, the same would not necessarily be true where the decision was that the words were incapable of such a meaning, and see comments of Brooke L.J. in *Cruise v. Express Newspapers* [1999] 1 W.L.R. 327, CA.

The Civil Procedure Rules 1998 retain this jurisdiction. RSC, Ord. 82, r.3A (CPR, Sched. 1) provides that "At any time after the service of the particulars of claim either party may apply to a judge sitting in private for an order determining whether or not the words complained of are capable of bearing a particular meaning or meanings attributed to them in the statements of case."

Section 7 of the Defamation Act 1996 provides that a court shall not be asked to rule whether a statement is "arguably capable" of bearing a particular meaning" as opposed to capable of bearing a particular meaning.

In *Aspro Travel v. Owners Abroad Group plc* [1996] 1 W.L.R. 132, the statements complained of by the plaintiffs, to the effect that their company was "going bust" and would be "bankrupt within a few days" were capable of a defamatory meaning, since the plaintiffs as company directors might have their reputation lowered in the community by the allegation that they traded knowing that the company was insolvent. **21–50**

In *Mapp v. News Group* [1997] E.M.L.R. 397, the plaintiff police officers complained that a statement to the effect that they had been moved from the police station where they had worked, coupled with an account of how one of their colleagues had committed suicide, after stating that there was police corruption involved in the drugs case, amounted to an allegation that they were guilty. The Court of Appeal refused to accept that this was a legitimate interpretation of the statement in question. See *Shah v. Standard Chartered Bank* [1998] 3 W.L.R. 592.

Section 7 of the Defamation Act 1996 expressly prevents the court being asked to rule whether a statement is "arguably" capable of bearing a particular meaning (as opposed to being capable of so doing). See above § 21–14. **21–51**

In *Mapp v. News Group Newspapers* [1997] E.M.L.R. 397, Hirst L.J. in the Court of Appeal described the role of the judge in applying RSC, Ord. 82, r.3A. Whereas before 1994, under RSC, Ord. 18, r.19 application could be made to strike out the plaintiff's case on the ground that the meaning contended for was clearly untenable, the new procedure after 1994 under RSC, Ord. 82, r.3A required the judge to "evaluate the words complained of and to delimit the range of meanings of which the words are reasonably capable, exercising his own judgment in the light of the principles laid down in *Slim v. Daily Telegraph* [1968] Q.B. 157, *Lewis v. Daily Telegraph* [1964] A.C. 234, *Jones v. Skelton* [1963] 1 W.L.R. 1362 and *Morgan v. Odhams Press Ltd* [1971] 1 W.L.R. 1239. This should be done "without any RSC Ord. 18, r.19 overtones." If he decides that any pleaded meaning falls outside the permissible range, it is his duty to rule accordingly.

It will still be possible for the plaintiff at trial to rely on lesser defamatory meanings but only within the permissible range. The object of the new procedure was to enable the court to fix in advance the permissible meanings, so as to assess damage to reputation and in order to evaluate possible defences such as justification or fair comment. In *McPhilemy v. Times Newspapers* [1999] 4 All E.R. 775; Lord Woolf discussed the implications of the Civil Procedure Rules 1998 for defamation litigation. Having observed that the exchange of witness statements should reduce the need for extensive pleadings, he added that the overriding requirements were of proportionality and greater equality between the parties.

Effect of alteration of the rules of pleading **21–55**

The Civil Procedure Rules 1998 brought into force in April 1999 to put into effect Lord Woolf's review of civil justice, constitute a radical new approach to civil litigation which will affect defamation as it affects all civil cases. The specific provisions relating to defamation are contained in Practice Direction 16, paras 8 and 9 and Sched. 1 and in RSC Ord. 82, as amended. In addition the overriding objective of the Rules will influence the way in which defamation cases are handled. It is the duty of the court to ensure that trials are justly dealt with; as far as is practicable parties should be on an equal footing; the case should be dealt with in ways proportionate to the money involved, the importance of the case, the complexity of the issues and the financial position of the parties and the case should be dealt with expeditiously and fairly and should absorb an appropriate share of the court's resources. The court may therefore take a stricter approach to complex and expensive pleadings in defamation (see the observations of Lord Woolf in *McPhilemy v. Times Newspapers* [1999] 4 All E.R. 775.)

In *Aspro Travel v. Owners Abroad plc* [1996] 1 W.L.R. 132, the court refused the defence's application under RSC, Ord. 82, r.3A for a declaration to the effect that the statements complained of by the plaintiff were not capable of a defamatory meaning.

In *Berkoff v. Burchill* [1996] 4 All E.R. 1008, the defendants sought to have the action dismissed on the grounds that the meaning of the words complained of was not capable of being defamatory. The Court of Appeal upheld the decision of Sir Maurice Drake and refused the defendants' appeal.

Also see *supra*, Supplement § 21–49.

6.—DEFAMATORY MATTER WITHIN SECTION 4 OF THE DEFAMATION ACT 1952—"UNINTENTIONAL DEFAMATION"

21–59   **Unintentional defamation**

Section 4 of the Defamation Act 1952 is repealed by the 1996 Defamation Act which abolishes the unsatisfactory defence of "unintentional defamation" and substitutes for it a new procedure where a statement has been published alleged to be defamatory of another and the person concerned comes within section 1 of the 1996 Act. Sections 2–4 of the 1996 Act provide as follows:

> "The offer of amends may be general or 'qualified'—*i.e.* in relation to a specific defamatory meaning. It must be in writing, must be expressed to be an offer for the purposes of this section and must state whether the offer is a qualified offer.
>
> The making of an offer consists of making a suitable correction and sufficient apology; the person making the statement must publish the correction and apology in a 'reasonable and practicable manner' and pay to the aggrieved party such compensation (if any) and costs as are agreed or determined to be payable.
>
> An offer may not be made by a person who has served a defence in relation to the statement complained of. An offer of amends under the section can be withdrawn before it is accepted.
>
> The aggrieved person cannot, after accepting the offer, bring or continue defamation proceedings against the maker(s) of the statement but he is entitled to enforce the offer and the court will enable him to do so."

Section 4 provides that if an offer is duly made and not accepted then the fact of the offer shall be a defence to defamation proceedings against the offeror by the person aggrieved. Importantly there is no defence available to the person who made the statement if that person

> "knew or had reason to believe that the statement complained of—
>
> (a) referred to the aggrieved party or was likely to be understood as referring to him, and
>
> (b) was both false and defamatory of that party".

The interesting aspect of the section is that section 4(3) states that it shall be presumed *until the contrary is shown* that he did not know and had no reason to believe that this was the case. The burden of proof is therefore on the person aggrieved to show that the maker of the statement was at fault in this way.

Even if the offer is not relied on as a defence it can be relied on in mitigation of damages.

<h2 align="center">7.—PUBLICATION</h2>

Publication

The Defamation Act 1996 introduced a new statutory defence available to a **21–61** person other than the author, editor or publisher of the statement complained of if such a person can show that he took reasonable care in relation to the publication of the statement and that he did not know and had no reason to believe that what he did caused or contributed to the publication of a defamatory statement.

The Act defines "author", "editor" and "publisher".

> " 'author' means the originator of the statement, but does not include a person who did not intend that his statement be published at all;
> 'editor' means a person having editorial or equivalent responsibility for the content of the statement or the decision to publish it; and
> 'publisher' means a commercial publisher, that is, a person whose business is issuing material to the public, or a section of the public, who issues material containing the statement in the course of that business.
>
> A person shall not be considered the author, editor or publisher of a statement if he is only involved—
>
> (a) in printing, producing, distributing or selling printed materials containing the statement;
> (b) in processing, making copies of, distributing, exhibiting or selling a film or sound recording (as defined in Part I of the Copyright, Designs and Patents Act 1988) containing the statement;
> (c) in processing, making copies of, distributing or selling any electronic medium in or on which the statement is recorded, or in operating or providing any equipment, system or service by means of which the statement is retrieved, copied, distributed or made available in electronic form;
> (d) as the broadcaster of a live programme containing the statement in circumstances in which he has no effective control over the maker of the statement;
> (e) as the operator of or provider of access to a communications system by means of which the statement is transmitted, or made available, by a person over whom he has no effective control.
>
> In a case not within paragraphs (a) to (e) the court may have regard to those provisions by way of analogy in deciding whether a person is to be considered the author, editor or publisher of a statement."

The statutory provisions therefore embrace those who distribute material on the Internet or who provide services enabling others to obtain access to it. In *Godfrey v. Demon Internet Ltd* [1999] 4 All E.R. 342 the defendant, an Internet provider, was sued for libel in respect of material distributed through its forum and sought to invoke the defence of unintentional defamation under the Defamation Act 1996, s.1. Morland J. in the High Court held that the defence was unavailable to the defendant since it did not fulfil the requirements of section 1(1)(b) and (c). The defendant had failed to remove the offending article from the Internet after its managing director had received a fax from the plaintiff complaining of the material in question. Hence it could not show that it had taken reasonable care in relation to the statement nor that it did not know and had no reason to believe that what it did caused or contributed to the publication of the defamatory statement. The defendant also sought to raise by way of defence that there had been no "publication" of the material complained of and that the defendant was merely the owner of an electronic device through which electronic "postings" were passed, but this was not accepted and this defence was also struck out. Section 1 (3)(d) provides a defence to broadcasters and section 1 (3)(e) to internet service providers but only if they fulfil the threefold requirement laid down in section 1. In order to show that to show that he is not to be considered to be the author, editor or publisher of the statement (section 1) the defendant must be able to show that he had "no effective control" over the maker of the statement. (See P. Carey, "Defamation, live broadcasts and the Internet" (1997) 147 N.L.J. 1633–1634)

In *Taylor v. SFO* [1997] 4 All E.R. 887 an SFO employee wrote to the Attorney-General of the Isle of Man, proposing that the plaintiff, T, a solicitor, should be interviewed. T was shown the document by a suspected person and sued the defendants for defamation. His claim was struck out and he appealed to the Court of Appeal which held, following *Mahon v. Rahn* [1997] 3 W.L.R. 1230, that where documents have been prepared as part of a criminal investigation, the person preparing them is entitled to immunity from suit and they cannot therefore be used to ground a civil action, *e.g.* a suit for defamation. However, in *P v. T Ltd* [1997] 1 W.L.R. 1309, an order was granted to the plaintiff directing disclosure of the identity of a complainant whose allegations had led to the plaintiff's dismissal from his employment. Sir Richard Scott V.-C. granted the order on the ground that the interests of justice required that the plaintiff should be able to discover if the tort of defamation had been committed against him.

21–65 **Publication by agent**

Section 1(4) of the Defamation Act 1996 provides, in relation to the statutory defence under section 1, that "Employees or agents of an author, editor or publisher are in the same position as their employer or principal to the extent that they are responsible for the content of the statement or the decision to publish it".

21–66 **Intention or negligence**

In relation to a person other than the author, editor or publisher of a publication who seeks to avail himself of the statutory defence under section 1 of the 1996 Defamation Act such a person must show that he took reasonable care and that he did not know, and had no reason to believe, that what he did caused or contributed to the publication of a defamatory statement: section 1(5) provides that:

> "(5) In determining for the purposes of this section whether a person took reasonable care, or had reason to believe that what he did caused or contributed to the publication of a defamatory statement, regard shall be had to—
>
> (a) the extent of his responsibility for the content of the statement or the decision to publish it,
> (b) the nature or circumstances of the publication, and
> (c) the previous conduct or character of the author, editor or publisher."

21–69 **Innocent dissemination**

The new statutory defence available under the 1996 Act to those responsible for publication places a lighter burden on the person concerned than the former defence of "innocent dissemination" (see *supra*, Supplement, § 21–59).

8.—DEFENCES

(a) *Generally*

21–75 **Defences**

Section 4 of the 1952 Defamation Act was repealed by the 1996 Defamation Act

(Schedule 2) and a new defence introduced for cases arising after the Act (see *supra*, Supplement § 21–59).

(b) *Justification*

Justification

In *Aspro Travel v. Owners Abroad plc* [1996] 1 W.L.R. 132, the defendants, who were business rivals of the plaintiffs' family company in the holiday travel business, told a number of hoteliers and travel agents in countries with which the plaintiffs dealt that the plaintiffs were "going bust" or would be "bankrupt in a few days". The company settled with the defendants but the plaintiff directors continued with their action for defamation. The defendants pleaded, *inter alia*, that their comments were justified as they meant that there were reasonable grounds to suspect the plaintiffs' financial soundness. They also claimed that they were entitled to make the statements on the basis of rumour. The Court of Appeal stressed the danger of allowing rumour as justification, but expressed the view that the existence of a rumour may entitle a person to repeat that rumour and that existence of the rumour might be sufficient justification. However, in *Stern v. Piper* [1997] Q.B. 123, the court held that the defence of justification did not apply where the defendants relied on allegations made against the plaintiff in an affirmation, sworn by a third party, for purposes of proceedings pending against the plaintiff in the High Court. This decision was approved and applied in *Shah v. Standard Chartered Bank* [1998] 4 All E.R. 155 where the Court of Appeal held that the defendants could not rely, by way of justification, on a hearsay statement that the plaintiffs were suspected of money laundering, but that "words must be interpreted, and the imputations they contained justified, by reference to the underlying allegations of fact and not merely by reliance upon some second hand report or assertion of them". The court preferred the decision in *Stern v. Piper* to that in the *Aspro Travel* case which they said should be confined to its own facts.

See *McDonalds v. Steel*, *The Times*, June 1997.

NOTE 90. *Loveless v. Earl, The Times* November 11, 1998.

Every material fact must be justified

Section 12 of the Defamation Act 1996 changes the law in relation to conclusiveness of convictions for purposes of defamation actions. It amends section 13 of the Civil Evidence Act 1968. Now the rule that a previous conviction is to be conclusive evidence of commission of the offence will apply only in relation to the plaintiff or plaintiffs and will not apply to other parties (see Civil Evidence Act 1968, s.2A, inserted by Defamation Act 1996, s.12(1)):

"Proof that any of the plaintiffs stands convicted of an offence shall be conclusive evidence that he committed that offence so far as that fact is relevant to any issue arising in relation to his cause of action or that of any other plaintiff".

In *Cruise v. Express Newspapers* [1999] 1 W.L.R. 327, the plaintiffs, two well-known film actors, sued in respect of articles in the defendants' newspaper which contained damaging allegations about their private life. The defendants pleaded justification but the Court of Appeal held that where the plaintiffs (claimants) sue in respect of an article containing two separate and distinct stings and the plaintiffs complained of one of the stings, the defendants could not by way of justification rely on pleas of fair comment and justification in relation to the other sting.

(c) *Privilege*

(1) *Absolute privilege*

21–91   **What are judicial proceedings?**

In *Waple v. Surrey County Council* [1998] 1 All E.R. 624, CA, the plaintiff and her husband had had problems with their adoptive son, aged 12 and the defendant council had placed the boy with foster parents. The council served notice on the plaintiff's husband, requiring him to contribute to the son's maintenance, whereupon the solicitor acting for the plaintiff and her husband wrote to the council, requesting information as to who had instigated the removal of the son to foster parents. He received the reply that the plaintiff had "threatened to lock [the son] in his room if he was not removed". The plaintiff issued proceedings against the council in defamation. On the council's application the writ and statement of claim were struck out by the trial judge, on the ground that the letter had been written on an occasion of absolute privilege, as the events following the service of the contribution notice were "legal proceedings of a sort". On appeal the Court of Appeal held that the letter was not covered by absolute privilege; the defence applies to statements made in the course of judicial or quasi judicial proceedings and documents connected with them and will only be extended where it is strictly necessary to do so, in order to protect those who participate in the proceedings from being sued themselves. Here it was not inevitable that legal proceedings would begin following the contribution notice and the letter did not have an immediate link with possible proceedings.

In *Daniels v. Griffith* [1998] E.M.L.R. 489, CA, the plaintiff, a prisoner, was seeking parole. He sued the defendant in respect of a statement made by her to the police for use by the parole board, which related to the existence or non-existence of her previous relationship with the plaintiff. The Court of Appeal rejected the defendant's claim of absolute privilege stating that there was no justification for extending the defence to such communications. The Parole Board is not a court of law.

In *S v. London Borough of Newham* [1998] 1 F.L.R. 1061 the plaintiff, a social worker employed by the defendant council, sued in respect of a letter sent by the Council to the Department of Health, questioning his suitability to deal with children. The Court of Appeal refused to rule that such a communication was covered by absolute privilege. Although the protection of children was vitally important, it was in the public interest that S should be allowed to bring his action to vindicate his reputation.

NOTE 66. Add: In the New Zealand case of *Tertiary Institutes Allied Staff Association v. Tahana* [1998] 1 N.Z.L.R. 41, it was held that a polytechnic council even though it had a duty to act judicially was not covered by absolute privilege. In *Mond v. Hyde* [1998] 3 All E.R. 833, CA, it was held by the Court of Appeal that an official receiver was immune from suit in respect of statements made by him in the course of bankruptcy proceedings. This immunity extended to statements made for the purpose of Court proceedings.

21–95   **Reports of judicial proceedings**

Section 3 of the Law of Libel Amendment Act 1888, as amended by the Defamation Act 1952 and the Contempt of Court Act 1981, was repealed by the 1996 Defamation Act. For the new provisions of the Act see, *post*, § 21–166 in relation to reports of judicial proceedings in section 14 of the Act. Also see, *post*, §§ 21–165 and 21–167 for qualified privilege in relation to records of other judicial proceedings.

21–96   **Parliamentary proceedings**

A controversial and important constitutional change has been effected by the Defamation Act 1996. Section 13 of the Act provides as follows:

"13. Evidence concerning proceedings in Parliament

(1) Where the conduct of a person in or in relation to proceedings in Parlia-

ment is in issue in defamation proceedings, he may waive for the purposes of those proceedings, so far as concerns him, the protection of any enactment or rule of law which prevents proceedings in Parliament being impeached or questioned in any court or place out of Parliament.

(2) Where a person waives that protection—

(a) any such enactment or rule of law shall not apply to prevent evidence being given, questions being asked or statements, submissions, comments or findings being made about his conduct, and

(b) none of those things shall be regarded as infringing the privilege of either House of Parliament.

(3) The waiver by one person of that protection does not affect its operation in relation to another person who has not waived it.

(4) Nothing in this section affects any enactment or rule of law so far as it protects a person (including a person who has waived the protection referred to above) from legal liability for words spoken or things done in the course of, or for the purposes of or incidental to, any proceedings in Parliament.

(5) Without prejudice to the generality of subsection (4), that subsection applies to—

(a) the giving of evidence before either House or a committee;

(b) the presentation or submission of a document to either House or a committee;

(c) the preparation of a document for the purposes of or incidental to the transacting of any such business;

(d) the formulation, making or publication of a document, including a report, by or pursuant to an order of either House or a committee; and

(e) any communication with the Parliamentary Commissioner for Standards or any person having functions in connection with the registration of members' interests.

In this subsection 'a committee' means a committee of either House or a joint committee of both Houses of Parliament."

This change in the law was controversial, effecting an important constitutional change. The effects of Article 9 of the Bill of Rights are lessened, in that a member of either House of Parliament can choose to waive Article 9 (contrary to the ruling of the Privy Council in *Prebble v. TVNZ* [1994] 3 All E.R. 407) so that proceedings in Parliament can be brought in evidence in Court. The incentive for the clause was provided in part by the cases of *Hamilton v. Guardian, The Times*, July 22, 1995 and *Allason v. Haines* [1995] E.M.L.R. 143 in each of which an M.P. sued a newspaper for libel and in each of which the defendants wished to plead justification by reference to things said or done by the plaintiffs in the course of Parliamentary proceedings. The actions were stayed by the court, since the defendant newspaper publishers would be jeopardised by being unable to raise matters which had occurred in Parliament. It was argued that it was unjust that the plaintiff M.P.s were thereby prevented from vindicating their reputations and that the purpose of Article 9 of the Bill of Rights had been to protect the freedom of speech in Parliament, not to prevent M.P.s from asserting their legal rights. Section 13 re-affirms the protection given by Article 9 to M.P.s in relation to words spoken or things done for the purposes of or incidental to any proceedings in Parliament and section 13(5) sets out some of the activities or functions of M.P.s which are to be regarded as being within that protection, see above.

In the event both Allason and Hamilton withdrew their libel actions. Sir Gordon Downey, the Parliamentary Commissioner for Standards has criticised this change in the law and suggested that it should be repealed (See *The Guardian*, April 29, 1998).

In *Hamilton v. Al-Fayed (No. 1)* [1999] 1 W.L.R. 1569 the plaintiff, a former MP, sued the defendant for libel in respect of the latter's allegations that he had given money to the plaintiff in return for his asking parliamentary questions. The plaintiff had begun a libel action against a newspaper which had made the same allegations but had withdrawn that action whereupon his conduct had been investigated by the Parliamentary Commissioner for Standards, who concluded that the plaintiff had accepted such payments. The Commissioner's report had been accepted by the House of Commons Committee on Standards and Privileges.

The defendant argued that the plaintiffs libel action against him should be struck out, on the grounds that to allow it to proceed would be contrary to Article 9 of the Bill of Rights, since a judgment for the plaintiff would amount to a collateral attack on the decision of Parliament, in that it would go against the findings of the House of Commons Committee.

In *Hamilton v. Al Fayed* (No. 1) [1999] 1 W.L.R. 1569, the Court of Appeal also held that the parliamentary proceedings could not be raised by the defence by way of justification of the allegation, nor could those proceedings be relied on as mitigating an award of damages, since they occurred after the publication of which the plaintiff complained.

The Court of Appeal held that to allow the plaintiff's action would not amount to an attack on the decision of the Parliamentary Commissioner or on Parliament. The court should not condemn what Parliament had concluded but provided that it exercised this self-denying policy, to allow the plaintiff's action was not a threat to Parliament's authority and the plaintiff could avail himself of section 13 of the Defamation Act 1996 notwithstanding the intervening parliamentary inquiry.

21–97 NOTE 79. Add: as in *Hamilton v. Guardian* and *Allason v. Haines* (*supra*, § 21–96).

21–98 **Official communications**
NOTE 87. But see *Multigroup Bulgaria Holdings v. Oxford Analytica Ltd* [1997] 7 C.L. 248.

(2) *Qualified privilege*

21–112 **Publication by agent**
NOTE 56. Add: *Watts v. Times Newspapers* [1997] Q.B. 650.

21–117 **Grounds of qualified privilege**
In *Aspro v. Owners Abroad plc* [1996] 1 W.L.R. 132 the Court of Appeal refused to strike out the defendant's plea of qualified privilege on the ground that the defendants, large and well established travel agents and ABTA members, had a sufficient interest in safeguarding their business and their industry. In *Reynolds v. Times Newspapers* [1998] 3 All E.R. 961, HL, the Court of Appeal considered the application of qualified privilege to newspaper reports relating to the reputation of a politician. The plaintiff, an Irish politician, sued the defendant newspaper for allegations relating to a political crisis in Ireland and to his resignation from the post of Taoiseach. Granting the plaintiff a new trial, on the ground of factual misdirection in the trial judge's summing-up to the jury, the Court of Appeal considered the claim that such statements in newspapers, relating to matters relating to the conduct of individuals in public life, should be covered by qualified privilege. The court accepted that the common welfare of British democracy was best served by "ample dissemination to the public of information concerning, and vigorous discussion of matters relating to the public life of the community and to those who participated in it", but stated that certain conditions must be fulfilled if a newspaper report of this kind is to attract qualified privilege, namely:

(1) that the newspaper must have a duty, legal moral or social, to the general
public to publish the material,

(2) that the public must have a corresponding interest to receive it and

(3) that the nature, status and source of the material and the circumstances of
its publication should be such as to warrant the protection of qualified
privilege.

The second of these conditions is to be more readily satisfied than in the past.
However, after hearing argument on Article 10, on the approach of the courts of the
United States (in Sullivan), of the Court of Human Rights and of the courts of
Australia and New Zealand, the Court of Appeal concluded that the defendants'
statements had not satisfied the test relating to the circumstances of publication and
were not covered by qualified privilege.

In the Scottish case of *Baigent v. McCullough* 1997 Rep. L.R. the defendant, a
nurse, speaking on television, criticised the level of care in a nursing home. It was
held that a defamatory statement made to the BBC by a defendant, albeit in the
public interest, was not protected by qualified privilege.

In the Canadian case of *BSOIW Local 97 v. Campbell* (1997) 152 D.L.R. 4th 547,
it was held that the defendant political party, its leader and the publisher of a press
release were entitled to the protection of qualified privilege in respect of a forthright
statement relating to the plaintiff union.

Interest of person to whom communication addressed 21–119

Chapman v. Lord Ellesmere was considered in *Friend v. Civil Aviation Authority*
[1998] I.R.L.R. 253. The plaintiff, F, had been dismissed by the defendants after a
disciplinary hearing. On appeal the Employment Appeal Tribunal upheld the dismissal, holding that the hearing had been procedurally flawed but that the plaintiff
had contributed 100 per cent to his dismissal. He then sued the defendants for defamation, which he alleged was contained in the memoranda prepared by senior
employees of the CAA. In relation to the original publication of the memoranda the
plaintiff was statute barred but he based his action on the re-publication of the matter
to the Employment Appeal Tribunal. The Court of Appeal held that F could not sue
the CAA in respect of the republication as he had consented to the procedure used
in the disciplinary proceedings.

In *Multigroup Bulgaria Holdings Ltd v. Oxford Analytica Ltd* 1997 7 C.L. 248, it
was held that where the defendants provided a daily brief to subscribers to its service, the allegation of corruption by the plaintiff reported on that service was not
covered by qualified privilege since the defendant's principal reason for providing
the information was commercial self-interest

In *Reynolds v Times Newspapers* [1998] 3 All E.R. 961, HL, the court held that,
subject to certain conditions, the public has a legitimate interest in receiving reports
and discussion of political and public matters.

Reciprocity essential 21–120

The Court of Appeal in *Reynolds v. Times Newspapers* [1998] 3 All E.R. 961,
HL, recognised a reciprocity of duty and interest in media reports, subject to certain
conditions being fulfilled (see *supra*, Supplement § 21–117).

Interest of person making the communication 21–131

In *Watts v. Times Newspapers* [1997] Q.B. 650, the defendants published an
article suggesting that the plaintiff writer had plagiarised a book for which he had
received an award. The article was accompanied by a photograph which was not
that of the plaintiff but of a property developer of the same name, who complained
via his solicitor and demanded an apology. The defendants published an apology
and at the behest of the property developer's solicitor included in the apology a
reference to the allegation of plagiarism contained in the original article. The plaintiff then sued the newspaper for the two libels contained in the article and the apology

respectively. The newspaper brought in the property developer's solicitors as third parties. The Court of Appeal held that the apology was defamatory of the plaintiff but that the solicitors had the defence of qualified privilege. In *Bhatt v. Chelsea & Westminster Healthcare NHS Trust*, [1988] C.L.Y. 172 the defendants had ceased to refer patients to the plaintiff's clinic and the plaintiff sued them in defamation in respect of press releases which they had prepared in relation to their conduct of the matter but had not released to the press. It was held that these press releases were covered by qualified privilege since they were prepared in reasonable expectation of an attack upon them, even though that attack was not by B himself but by the media or other bodies.

21–135 Public interest

The question of public interest was addressed by the Court of Appeal in *Reynolds v. Times Newspapers* [1998] 3 All E.R. 961, HL. The Court emphasised that the nature, status and source of the material and the circumstances of publication must be such that the publication should be protected in the public interest. In *Younger-wood v. Guardian* 1997 9 C.L. 230 the Court of Appeal held that there was no public interest in the newspaper promulgating untrue allegations of racism which had been made in regard to the plaintiff. A comprehensive discussion of the issues was given by the New Zealand Supreme Court in *Lange v. Atkinson* [1998] 3 N.Z.L.R. 424. See also *Lange v. Australian Broadcasting Corp.* (1997) 145 A.L.R. 91.

The idea of qualified privilege in pursuance of a moral duty—to support the dignity of tenants who were alleging improprieties by the management of their apartment block—was accepted in the Canadian case of *Silva v. Toronto Star Newspapers Ltd* (1999) 167 D.L.R. (4th) 554.

And see *Baigent v. McCullough* 1997 Rep. L.R. 107 (see *supra* , Supplement § 21–117).

(e) *Reports*

21–164 Reports

The Defamation Act 1996 extends absolute privilege to contemporaneous reports of judicial proceedings in public (see section 14 and *post*, Supplement § 21–166) and extends and rationalises the law relating to qualified privilege for other proceedings.

(1) *Of judicial proceedings*

21–166 The Defamation Act 1996 changes the law so as to give absolute privilege to reports of judicial proceedings. Section 14 extends absolute privilege to a fair and accurate report of proceedings in public before a court specified in section 14(3) namely:

"(a) any court in the United Kingdom
(b) the European Court of Justice or any court attached to that court
(c) the European Court of Human Rights, and
(d) any international criminal tribunal established by the Security Council of the United Nations or by an international agreement to which the United Kingdom is a party.

Such a report must be published contemporaneously (it will be treated as so published if publication is postponed by order of the court and it is published as soon as practicable after publication permitted)".

21–167 Newspapers and broadcasting

The Defamation Act 1996 repeals section 3 of the Law of Libel Amendment Act 1888, as amended by section 8 of the Defamation Act 1952 and the Contempt of Court Act 1981. Section 14 extends absolute privilege to contemporaneous reports of judicial proceedings (see *supra*, Supplement § 21–166).

In addition the first Schedule to the 1996 Act lists all the other reports which will be protected by qualified privilege. (Section 166(3) of the Broadcasting Act is repealed, as is section 9(2) of the Defamation Act 1952.) Under the new provisions the protection afforded to reports of various proceedings is not limited to newspaper and broadcast reports but applies to any other medium also.

(4) *Of other proceedings and meetings*

Reports of other proceedings and meetings   **21–175**
    The Defamation Act 1996 updates, rationalises and extends the categories of meetings and occasions which are covered by qualified privilege (see, *post*, § 21–179 to § 21–180).

Reports in newspapers and broadcast reports   **21–177**
    The Defamation Act 1996 brings up-to-date and makes more comprehensive the list of reports which are covered by qualified privilege. As in the previous legislation, such reports are divided into two categories—those having qualified privilege without explanation or contradiction (Schedule I, Part I) and those privileged subject to explanation or contradiction (Schedule I, Part II). The medium of publication is not specified and is not limited to newspapers, radio and television but will include other forms of broadcasting. Section 7 of the Defamation Act 1952 is repealed but section 15 of the 1996 Act retains the provision that there is no defence in relation to Part II reports:

> "if the plaintiff shows that the defendant
>
> (a) was requested by him to publish in a suitable manner a reasonable letter or statement by way of explanation or contradiction, and
> (b) refused or neglected to do so."

For this purpose "in a suitable manner" means in the same manner as the publication complained of or in a manner that is adequate and reasonable in the circumstances.

    The 1996 Act, like the previous legislation, states that section 15 giving qualified   **21–178**
privilege to certain statements does not apply to the publication to the public or a section of it of matter which is not of public concern and the publication of which is not for the public benefit (section 15(3)).
    In *Tsikata v. Newspaper Publishing plc* [1997] 1 All E.R. 655 the Court of Appeal held that the publication by the defendants of reports describing findings of a government inquiry conducted in the plaintiff's country and implicating him in a plot was not deprived of a prima facie defence of qualified privilege under section 7(3) of the Defamation Act 1952 on the grounds that it was "not of public concern . . . and not for the public benefit". This was a question of fact and the court held that there was legitimate public concern about human rights in the Commonwealth and public benefit in receiving information about the proceedings since the plaintiff was a politician and a public figure and there was an approaching election in his country.
    Like section 7 of the Defamation Act 1952, the 1996 Act in section 15(4) provides expressly that nothing in section 15 is to be construed as protecting the publication of matter the publication of which is prohibited by law or as limiting or abridging any privilege subsisting apart from this section. Note 56 will therefore presumably still apply.

Statements privileged without explanation or contradiction   **21–179**
    Part I of Schedule 1 to the Defamation Act 1996 specifies the following statements as having qualified privilege without explanation or contradiction:

> "1. A fair and accurate report of proceedings in public of a legislature anywhere in the world.

2. A fair and accurate report of proceedings in public before a court anywhere in the world.

3. A fair and accurate report of proceedings in public of a person appointed to hold a public inquiry by a government or legislature anywhere in the world.

4. A fair and accurate report of proceedings in public anywhere in the world of an international organisation or an international conference.

5. A fair and accurate copy of or extract from any register or other document required by law to be open to public inspection.

6. A notice or advertisement published by or on the authority of a court, or of a judge or officer of a court, anywhere in the world.

7. A fair and accurate copy of or extract from matter published by or on the authority of a government or legislature anywhere in the world.

8. A fair and accurate copy of or extract from matter published anywhere in the world by an international organisation or an international conference."

In *Tsikata v. Newspaper Publishing* [1997] 1 All E.R. 655, the plaintiff sued in respect of a report in the defendants' newspaper which stated that the plaintiff had been implicated by a special inquiry in Ghana, his native country, ten years earlier into the killing of several judges. The defendants pleaded qualified privilege under section 7(1) and paragraph 5 of the Schedule to the Defamation Act 1952 in that the report was "a fair and accurate report of . . . proceedings in public of a . . . person appointed to hold a public inquiry by the government or legislature" of Ghana. The plaintiff denied that the report was privileged on a number of grounds, namely that this was not a "report" within the relevant enactment since it was published ten years after the inquiry, that it was not "fair and accurate" since it did not refer to certain facts, especially that the plaintiff had not been prosecuted because of the lack of evidence against him, that the inquiry had not been a "proceeding in public" and that, because of the passage of time, the publication could no longer be said to be of public concern or for the public benefit. On the trial of a preliminary issue the judge held that the report was covered by qualified privilege and the plaintiff appealed. The Court of Appeal dismissed the appeal and upheld the finding that a prima facie defence of qualified privilege had been established. In relation to the report of the inquiry, the Court held that on a purposive interpretation of the term "report" did not have to be contemporary and that the inquiry had been a "proceeding in public". See also *supra*, Supplement § 21–178.

21–180 Statements privileged subject to explanation or contradiction

Part II of Schedule I of the 1996 Defamation Act specifies the following statements as having qualified privilege subject to explanation or contradiction:

"STATEMENTS PRIVILEGED SUBJECT TO EXPLANATION OR CONTRADICTION

9.—(1) A fair and accurate copy of or extract from a notice or other matter issued for the information of the public by or on behalf of—

(a) a legislature in any member State or the European Parliament;

(b) the government of any member State, or any authority performing governmental functions in any member State or part of a member State, or the European Commission;

(c) an international organisation or international conference.

(2) In this paragraph 'governmental functions' includes police functions.

10. A fair and accurate copy of or extract from a document made available by a court in any member State or the European Court of Justice (or any court attached to that court), or by a judge or officer of any such court.

11.—(1) A fair and accurate report of proceedings at any public meeting or sitting in the United Kingdom of—

(a) a local authority or local authority committee;

(b) a justice or justices of the peace acting otherwise than as a court exercising judicial authority;

(c) a commission, tribunal, committee or person appointed for the purposes of any inquiry by any statutory provision, by Her Majesty or by a Minister of the Crown or a Northern Ireland Department;

(d) a person appointed by a local authority to hold a local inquiry in pursuance of any statutory provision;

(e) any other tribunal, board, committee or body constituted by or under, and exercising functions under, any statutory provisions

(2) In sub-paragraph (1)(a)—
"local authority" means—

(a) in relation to England and Wales, a principal council within the meaning of the Local Government Act 1972, any body falling within any paragraph of section 100J(1) of that Act or an authority or body to which the Public Bodies (Admission to Meetings) Act 1960 applies,

(b) in relation to Scotland, a council constituted under section 2 of the Local Government etc. (Scotland) Act 1994 or an authority or body to which the Public Bodies (Admission to Meetings) Act 1960 applies,

(c) in relation to Northern Ireland, any authority or body to which sections 23 to 27 of the Local Government Act (Northern Ireland) 1972 apply; and

"local authority committee" means any committee of a local authority or of local authorities, and includes—

(a) any committee or sub-committee in relation to which sections 100A to 100D of the Local Government Act 1972 apply by virtue of section 100E of that Act (whether or not also by virtue of section 100J of that Act), and

(b) any committee or sub-committee in relation to which sections 50A to 50D of the Local Government (Scotland) Act 1973 apply by virtue of section 50E of that Act.

(3) A fair and accurate report of any corresponding proceedings in any of the Channel Islands or the Isle of Man or in another member State.

12.—(1) A fair and accurate report of proceedings at any public meeting held in a member State.

(2) In this paragraph a 'public meeting' means a meeting bona fide and lawfully held for a lawful purpose and for the furtherance or discussion of a matter of public concern, whether admission to the meeting is general or restricted.

13.—(1) A fair and accurate report of proceedings at a general meeting of a UK public company.

(2) A fair and accurate copy of or extract from any document circulated to members of a UK public company—

(a) by or with the authority of the board of directors of the company,

(b) by the auditors of the company, or

(c) by any member of the company in pursuance of a right conferred by any statutory provision.

(3) A fair and accurate copy of or extract from any document circulated to members of a UK public company which relates to the appointment, resignation, retirement or dismissal of directors of the company.

(4) In this paragraph "UK public company" means—

(a) a public company within the meaning of section 1(3) of the Companies Act 1985 or Article 12(3) of the Companies (Northern Ireland) Order 1986, or

(b) a body corporate incorporated by or registered under any other statutory provision, or by Royal Charter, or formed in pursuance of letters patent.

(5) A fair and accurate report of proceedings at any corresponding meeting of, or copy of or extract from any corresponding document circulated to members of, a public company formed under the law of any of the Channel Islands or the Isle of Man or of another member State.

14. A fair and accurate report of any finding or decision of any of the following descriptions of association, formed in the United Kingdom or another member State, or of any committee or governing body of such an association—

(a) an association formed for the purpose of promoting or encouraging the exercise of or interest in any art, science, religion or learning, and empowered by its constitution to exercise control over or adjudicate on matters of interest or concern to the association, or the actions or conduct of any person subject to such control or adjudication;

(b) an association formed for the purpose of promoting or safeguarding the interests of any trade, business, industry or profession, or of the persons carrying on or engaged in any trade, business, industry or profession, and empowered by its constitution to exercise control over or adjudicate upon matters connected with that trade, business, industry or profession, or the actions or conduct of those persons;

(c) an association formed for the purpose of promoting or safeguarding the interests of a game, sport or pastime to the playing or exercise of which members of the public are invited or admitted, and empowered by its constitution to exercise control over or adjudicate upon persons connected with or taking part in the game, sport or pastime;

(d) an association formed for the purpose of promoting charitable objects or other objects beneficial to the community and empowered by its constitution to exercise control over or to adjudicate on matters of interest or concern to the association, or the actions or conduct of any person subject to such control or adjudication.

15.—(1) A fair and accurate report of, or copy of or extract from, any adjudication, report, statement or notice issued by a body, officer or other person designated for the purposes of this paragraph—

(a) for England and Wales or Northern Ireland, by order of the Lord Chancellor, and

(b) for Scotland, by order of the Secretary of State.

(2) An order under this paragraph shall be made by statutory instrument which shall be subject to annulment in pursuance of a resolution of either House of Parliament."

In *McCartan Turkington & Brean v. Times Newspaper* [1998] W.I. 358 it was held that the presence of members of the public was not sufficient to render a press conference a "public meeting" for the purpose of the Northern Ireland Defamation Act 1955. The defendants' report of the event was not therefore covered by qualified privilege.

The list of statements subject to qualified privilege can be extended by the Lord Chancellor (or, for Scotland, by the Secretary of State).

9.—MALICE

21–182 Meaning of malice

The defence laid down by a United States court in *New York Times v. Sullivan* US 376 254 (1964), to the effect that a public figure cannot sue in libel without establishing malice, is not likely to be followed here, despite the favourable comments on it made by some commentators in this country. There are a number of objections to it, especially as the press or certain sections of it have been subject to strong criticism over the conduct of certain journalists and editors in relation to intrusions into the personal life of public figures. In *Bennett v. Guardian Newspapers, The Times*, December 28, 1995 the Court of Appeal refused to accept the defendants' submission that the plaintiff police officers as public figures should expect to be criticised and should not be allowed to sue unless they could show "actual malice" on the part of the defendant(s). Sir Michael Davis, sitting as a High Court judge, had refused to apply a "public figure" defence (a defence which would involve drastic judicial law-making), not least because of the profound differences between the culture of the United States and that of the United Kingdom.

It was held in *Kirby-Harris v. Baxter* [1995] E.M.L.R. 516 that where the defend- **21–183** ants sought to raise by way of defence a statutory justification for their actions the issue was essentially one of good faith and therefore involved an issue of malice; the court therefore refused to deny the plaintiff a jury trial.

In *Loveless v. Earl, The Times*, November 11, 1998, the Court of Appeal held that the question of malice cannot be decided at a preliminary hearing.

Strong language not always evidence of malice **21–189**

In the Canadian case of *Macarthur v. Meuser* (1997) 146 D.L.R. (4th) 125, where the chair of the medical education committee at a hospital addressed a memorandum to the head of a department accusing a physician in that department of "profanity, rudeness and failure to give proper supervision to interns" it was held that although the defendant's action was precipitate and injudicious, it did not amount to malice.

11.—Damages

(a) *In General*

Damages in general **21–203**

The size and unpreditability of awards of damages in defamation cases has been a frequent cause of comment by lawyers and lay people alike. Since the jury in such cases decide not only the issue of liability but also the amount of damages, there has been inconsistency between awards, since the jury could hitherto be given only the most general guidance by the judge on an appropriate amount (*e.g.* the cost of a new car, a holiday or some other purchasable item). Juries have tended to give large sums, especially when defendants such as newspapers are wealthy and unpopular in the public eye. There have also been suggestions that the unpredictability of damages awards constitutes a possible infringement of Article 10 of the European Convention on Human Rights (as discussed in *Rantzen v. Mirror Newspapers* [1993] 3 W.L.R. 953). This issue could be raised under the 1998 Human Rights Act.

The problem of excessive damages was to some extent overcome by the introduction of section 8 of the Courts and Legal Services Act and RSC, Ord. 59, r.11(4), which enables the Court of Appeal to alter awards of damages in defamation, but as was pointed out in *Rantzen v. Mirror Newspapers*, it will take a considerable time to set up precedents of Court of Appeal awards. To some extent the case of *John v. MGN* [1996] 2 All E.R. 35, has taken the English courts further along the road to predictability in awards for defamation. However as long as juries award damages there will be an element of unpredictability.

The Law Commission in its Consultation Paper No. 140 considered the question whether juries should continue to be used in defamation cases at all or whether they should be used to decide issues of liability only, leaving the judge to decide on the amount of damages. However they concluded that juries should continue to decide both issues (pp. 127–140, 163–164).

In *John v. MGN* [1996] 3 W.L.R. 593, the plaintiff, a well known popular singer and entertainer, sued the defendant newspaper for libel in respect of a report which described him as chewing his food and then spitting it out at a Hollywood party—a symptom of an eating disorder. It was well-known that the singer had in the past suffered from eating disorders and from alcohol and drug dependence which he had overcome. The court accepted that the report was defamatory and awarded the plaintiff £350,000, comprising £75,000 damages for the damage to his reputation and £275,000 exemplary damages. The Court of Appeal confirmed that the statement was defamatory but reduced the sums to £25,000 compensatory damages and £5,000 exemplary damages. The Court discussed at some length the principles on which damages in libel should be awarded and held that, contrary to its dictum in *Rantzen v. Mirror Newspapers* [1993] 3 W.L.R. 953, CA, it accepted, (as did the Australian High Court in *Carson v. John Fairfax & Sons Ltd* (1993) 113 A.L.R. 577), that it would no longer be inappropriate to refer the jury to awards in personal injuries cases—not as a precedent but to give the jury some sense of proportion as to the appropriateness of extremely high amounts of damages for defamation. Sir Thomas Bingham M.R., delivering the court's judgment, also stated that the trial judge should, in future, be able to indicate the level of award which would be appropriate.

21–204   The principles of damages awards in defamation were discussed in *John v. MGN* by the Master of the Rolls [1996] 1 All E.R. 35 at 47–55.

In *Quinn v. TVNZ* [1995] 3 N.Z.L.R. 216 the court stated that "the assessment of damages in libel cases—is more of a social function than a judicial function".

Damages must be proportionate to the loss suffered. See *Jones v. Pollard* 1997 where an award of £100,000 was reduced to £40,000 in accordance with the guidance of the Court of Appeal in *John v. MGN*; also *Brooks v. Lind, The Times*, March 26, 1997.

21–209   **Exemplary or punitive damages**

In *John v. MGN* the plaintiff at first instance recovered £275,000 exemplary damages. The Court of Appeal reduced that amount to £5,000 but confirmed the appropriateness of awarding exemplary damages in this case. Sir Thomas Bingham M.R., giving the judgment of the court discussed if and when exemplary damages should be awarded. Accepting the test laid down by the Court of Appeal in *Riches v. News Group Newspapers Ltd* [1985] 3 W.L.R. 43 [1985] 2 All E.R. 845 at 850, such damages should only be awarded where

(a) at the time of publication the defendant knew that he was committing a tort or was reckless as to whether it was tortious or not and decided to publish because the prospects of material advantage outweighed the prospects of material loss.

(b) the publisher acted in the hope or expectation of material gain. Mere publication for profit does not satisfy this test; there has to be an element of calculation, *e.g.* that the gain from the publication will exceed the potential disadvantages, especially if the plaintiff may not sue.

(c) exemplary damages should be awarded only when the sum of compensatory damages is insufficient to punish the defendant.

The defendants, in appealing against the awards of damages in the case as excessive, also argued by way of objection to exemplary damages that to award such damages is a breach of Article 10 of the European Convention, but the Master of the Rolls denied this, stating that the award of exemplary damages is not outside Article 10 if it is strictly necessary for the protection of reputation.

The court concluded that the conditions necessary for the award of exemplary damages were fulfilled in this case. The conduct of the defendant newspaper's staff amounted to recklessness, in that little attempt had been made to authenticate the story before publication. Secondly there had been that element of "calculation" whereby the defendants had profited from the publication and had, indeed, calculated that the plaintiff was very unlikely to sue. The Court refused to rule that the judge at first instance had misdirected the jury on the question of recklessness and calculation and on the award of exemplary or punitive damages generally. In *Thompson v.*

Commissioner of Police for the Metropolis [1997] 2 All E.R. 762; 3 W.L.R. 420, Lord Woolf discussed the principles governing exemplary damages (at pp. 770–771). See also *Clark v. Chief Constable of Cleveland Police, The Times*, May 13, 1999.

(c) *Mitigation of Damages*

Apology   21–218
An apology must not in itself be defamatory of a third party as was the case in *Watts v. Times Newspapers* [1966] 1 All E.R. 152.

Bad reputation of plaintiff   21–219
It was originally intended that the Defamation Bill, introduced in 1995, would abolish the rule in *Scott v. Sampson* but the clause to this effect was subsequently removed at the Committee stage in the House of Commons.

(d) *Excessive Damages*

The Court of Appeal in *John v. MGN* reduced the award of £350,000 damages, **21–225** consisting of £75,000 compensatory damages and £275,000 exemplary damages to £75,000 comprising £25,000 compensatory damages and £50,000 exemplary damages, the higher figure being excessive. The approach of the Court of Appeal in the case should help to make future awards by juries less high or less unpredictable.

In *Tolstoy v. Aldington* the respondent had recovered £1.5 million damages against **21–227** the appellant for a serious libel, alleging that, when acting as a senior British officer at the end of the Second World War, he had knowingly handed over a number of cossacks and white Russians to the Soviets, knowing that they would almost certainly be killed or persecuted. The respondent brought a case against the United Kingdom Government before the European Court of Human Rights on the grounds that the award of £1.5 million was so high that it amounted to an unauthorised breach of Article 10 of the Convention, providing for freedom of speech. The Court of Human Rights upheld the claim on these grounds. (*Tolstoy Miloslavsky v. United Kingdom* (1995) 20 E.H.R.R. 442.)

In *John v. MGN* the Court of Appeal again affirmed the consistency of English **21–228** law with Article 10 of the European Convention on Human Rights ([1996] 1 All E.R. 35, 58.) The Human Rights Act 1998 has now to some extinct rendered the European Convention on Human Rights enforceable in the English courts (see *supra*, Supplement §§ 1–105A–1–105G and § 21–04).

The Court of Appeal in *John v. MGN* [1996] 2 All E.R. 35 has approved the **21–229** giving of general guidance to a jury by the judge and has stated that, contrary to previous practice in the courts, it is now appropriate, in guiding juries before they assess amounts of damages in defamation, to refer to awards in personal injuries cases, as a means of giving the jury some sense of proportion about the amount of damages appropriate for damage to reputation. This should further enhance the building up of a corpus of awards referred to in *Rantzen v. Mirror Group Newspapers*.

12.—INJUNCTION

Self-justification   21–232
In *British Data Management plc v. Boxer Commercial Removals plc and another* [1996] 3 All E.R. 707 the Court of Appeal confirmed that a *quia timet* injunction may be issued to a plaintiff to restrain the publication of a threatened libel in a case where there is reasonable certainty as to the words of the publication. Normally this

will require the plaintiff to plead the actual word or words to the same effect; he is not required to set out verbatim the words complained of, provided that they are stated with reasonable certainty (which was lacking in the instant case).

In *Holley v. Smyth* [1998] Q.B. 726 the plaintiffs sought an interlocutory injunction to prevent the defendant from publishing statements accusing them of fraud in relation to dealings between them and a trust, established by him, which had lost money when a land deal failed. At first instance, following *Bonnard v. Perryman*, the injunction was granted. The court took the view that, although the plea of justification was not plainly untrue, the rule was founded on the right of free speech and did not protect a defendant whose motive was to extract money from the plaintiff as the price of not exercising it. On appeal the Court of Appeal, Staughton L.J. dissenting, reversed the decision on the ground that the defendant's motive was not relevant in deciding whether he was entitled to exercise his right of freedom of speech. Such an injunction should not readily be granted and should not be granted in this case.

CHAPTER 22.—MALICIOUS FALSEHOOD

		PARA.
□1.	Malicious falsehood	22–01
■2.	Essentials of the action	22–10
	(a) Published falsehoods	22–12
	(b) Malice	22–13
	(c) Damage	22–17
■3.	Rival traders	22–19

1.—MALICIOUS FALSEHOOD

The general principle
22–02

Samuels v. Coole & Haddock, May 22, 1997, CA, [1997] 9 C.L. 591. Defendants were a firm of solicitors who succesfully supported their application to strike out the plaintiff's third party proceedings against their clients by an affidavit, sworn by one of their partners. The plaintiff sought to sue the defendants on the basis of allegations made against him in that affidavit. Held, the affidavit came within the absolute privilege of witness immunity. There was no cause of action

Malicious falsehood and defamation compared
22–03

In *Vodafone plc v. Orange* [1997] F.S.R. 34 the parties agreed that in a claim for malicious falsehood the judge should apply, in determining the falsity of a statement, the "one meaning rule" in libel. However, note that the judge, Jacob J., expressed some doubt as to whether this rule should apply. He indicated that he might prefer to apply the "substantial number of people" test as in the tort of passing off.

As far as a claim under section 10(6) of the Trade Marks Act 1994 (which covers, *inter alia*, comparative advertising) there was no "one meaning rule" in the law of registered trade marks.

"Threats" actions in patents cases
22–05

In *Brain v. Ingledew Brown Bennison & Garrett* [1996] F.S.R. 341, CA the defendant was entitled to justify the threat while the patent was pending, provided the patent was granted before the action reached trial, section 70(2) of the Patents Act 1977. However, it is not clear what the position would be if the patent had not been granted by the time of trial. Aldous L.J. felt that the court could perhaps look at the published specification and decide, upon the balance of probabilities, whether the alleged acts would infringe the patent, when granted, and whether a valid patent would be granted. Hobhouse L.J., however, was not convinced that this would be a satisfactory approach or consistent with principle.

Threats actions in registered trade mark cases are covered by section 21 of the Trade Marks Act 1994. In *Prince plc v. Prince Sports Group Inc.* [1998] F.S.R. 21, Neuberger J. (Trade Marks Act 1994, s.21, threats action) held that subsequent communications could not alter the fact that the original communication constituted a threat. *Brain v. Ingledew Brown Bennison and Garrett* [1996] F.S.R. 341, CA, applied. See also *Trebor Basset Ltd v. The Football Association* [1997] F.S.R. 211 Rattee J. Summary judgment was given for the plaintiffs in a trade mark threats action; the defendants' cross-action for infringement was struck out as an abuse of process. The evidence was undisputed, the only issue was whether trade mark infringement arose from the plaintiffs' activities. The court was satisfied that no substantial defence existed to the plaintiffs' claim for a declaration of non-infringement.

Guidance on the law relating to threats is contained in the judgement of Laddie J. in *Brain v. Ingledew Brown Bennison and Garrett (No. 3)* [1997] F.S.R. 511.

Laddie J. The test whether a communication constituted a threat (at 521): "What is particularly important is the initial impression which the letters would have on a reasonable addressee . . . meticulous analysis is not what would happen in the real world and the court must guard against being led down a path of forensic analysis to a meaning which is narrower or broader than would occur to the ordinary recipient reading the letter . . . in the normal course of business". The concept of a "person aggrieved" requires that person to show a likely adverse effect on his commercial interests. At 520: "Where the threats are made against him directly . . . the court will infer such adverse effect. When the threats are made indirectly, he will need to demonstrate it. But I do not think the court should be astute to find that a complainant has not been affected in his commercial activities where it is clear that the purpose of the threat was to do so."

22–06   NOTE 21. Add: Re trade libel and interlocutory injunctions, add *Eastcare Inc. v. Bryan Lawrence & Co.* [1995] F.S.R. 597, Aldous J. (Patents Court). The normal principles applicable to interlocutory injunctions do not apply where the defendant contends that the alleged defamatory statements are true: this applies to trade libels. See *Bestobell Paints Ltd v. Bigg* [1975] F.S.R. 421. In *Macmillan Magazines Ltd v. RCN Publishing Co. Ltd* [1998] F.S.R. 9, Neuberger J. noted that the court should be mindful of the defendant's right of free speech.

2.—ESSENTIALS OF THE ACTION

(b) *Malice*

22–10   **Essential of the action**
Schulke & Mayr U.K. Ltd v. Alkapharm U.K. Ltd [1999} F.S.R. 161, Jacob J. (false statements about the defendants' own goods, *per se*, are not actionable as malicious falsehood).

22–13   **Malice and bona fide publication**
    Barker v. Statesman and Nation Publishing Co. Ltd, The Times, January 8, 1997, CA. Guidance given by the Court of Appeal on the timing of the submission of no case to answer on the issue of malice. The Court of Appeal granted the plaintiff leave to appeal against a decision to strike out his action for malicious falsehood. The trial judge had struck out the action without hearing any evidence from the plaintiff or his witnesses, even though the integrity of the defendants (including the BBC) was an issue for decision.

(c) *Damage*

22–18   **Where proof of special damage required**
    See *Allason v. Campbell, The Times*, 8 May, 1996. As the plaintiff was unable to show he had suffered pecuniary loss he was unable to succeed in malicious falsehood (Sir Maurice Drake, sitting as a judge of the Queen's Bench Division).

3.—RIVAL TRADERS

22–19   **Comparative advertising**
    Vodafone plc v. Orange [1997] F.S.R. 34, Jacob J. The plaintiffs complained that the comparison made between their service and the defendants' in the defendants' advertising campaign was so flawed as to be false. However, the court accepted the defendants' argument that the public would assess the comparison by making reasonable assumptions about the methods used for the comparison.
    In deciding upon the ordinary meaning of the words used, *De Beers Abrasive Products Ltd v. International General Electric Co of New York Ltd* [1975] 1 W.L.R. 972 was applied *viz* whether a reasonable man would take the claim being made as

one made seriously. Jacob J. noted of the facts of the case before him: "This is a case about advertising. The public are used to the ways of advertisers and expect a certain amount of hyperbole. In particular the public are used to advertisers claiming the good points of a product and ignoring others". The more precise the claim, the more likely the reasonable man would take the claim seriously—the more general or "fuzzy", the less so.

Macmillan Magazines Ltd v. RCN Publishing Co. Ltd [1998] F.S.R. 9, Neuberger J. The case involved rival publishers of trade magazines relating to the nursing services sector. "Where advertising is contained in a specialist magazine and addressed to a specialist group of people, namely advertisers, there must be a respectable argument for saying that one should judge the advertisement by the effect that it would have on such advertisers and not by the effect that it would have on the general public" (at 13).

Where registered trade marks are concerned, section 10(6) of the Trade Marks Act 1994 is relevant to comparative advertising deemed to be "not in accordance with honest practices in industrial or commercial matters". In *Cable & Wireless plc v. BT plc* [1998] F.S.R. 383 Jacob J. considered that the tort often added nothing to a claim based on section 10(6), though it increased costs. In *Emaco Ltd v. Dyson Appliances Ltd The Times*, February 8, 1999, Parker J, false claims in a publication about a competitor's product did not amount to the tort of malicious falsehood: though containing false representations and "thoroughly misleading", they were not published maliciously. However, they failed the ''honest practice'' test of section 10(6) of the Trade Marks Act 1994 and the use of the plaintiffs' trade mark in that publication was, therefore, an infringement of that trade mark.

CHAPTER 23. — ECONOMIC TORTS

		PARA.
■1.	General	23–01
■2.	Procuring a breach of contract	23–09
■3.	Intimidation	23–38
■4.	Unlawful interference	23–56
■5.	Conspiracy	23–76
■6.	Trade disputes	23–91

1.—GENERAL

23–01 The core economic torts

NOTE 1. See especially P. Cane, *Tort Law and Economic Interests* (2nd ed., 1996); H. Carty, "International Violation of Economic Interests" (1988) 104 L.Q.R. 250; also R.J. Smith (1977) 41 Conv. (N.S.) 318 (effects on real property); T Weir, *Economic Torts* (1997, selected aspects); R. Bagshaw (1998) 18 O.J.L.S. 729; K Oliphant (1999) 62 M.L.R. 320; P. Sales and D. Stilitz (1999) 115 L.Q.R. 411; J. Fleming, *Law Of Torts* (9th ed., 1998) 30; W. Rogers *Winfield and Jolowicz on Tort* (15th ed., 1998); *Street on Torts* (10th ed. 1999, eds M. Brazier, J. Murphy); W. van Gervern, J. Lever, P. Larouche, C. von Bar and G. Viney, *Tort Law: Scope of Protection* ("national, supranational and international", 1998, Chap. 6, comparative).

NOTE 3. For some Commonwealth developments: on Australian law see, Trinidad and Cane, *Law of Torts in Australia* (2nd ed., 1993); Mullany (1995) 111 L.Q.R. 44; and after the Australian Workplace Relations Act 1996 (Cth): B Creighton (1997) 10 A.J.L.L. 31; McCarry, *ibid*, 133 (industrial action); T McDermot (1998) 6 Can. Lab. E.L.J. 127–145. On New Zealand, Todd, Burrows, Chambers, Hawes, Beggwood, Beck, *Law of Torts in New Zealand* (2nd ed., 1997) and especially on the Employment Contracts Act 1991: Dannin, 16 Berkeley Jo. Emp. and Lab L. 1 (1995)

NOTE 4. Amend reference to read: Cornish, *Intellectual Property* (3rd ed., 1996).

Although it has been held that contributory negligence is not a defence to an intentional tort, and that the Law Reform (Contributory Negligence) Act 1945 does not therefore apply, and that the same principles apply by analogy to breach of fiduciary duty, some part or all of the damage in such cases may be rendered too remote having regard to the claimant's behaviour, so that the damages or compensation are for that reason reduced: *Nationwide Building Society v. Various Solicitors (No. 3), The Times*, March 1, 1999; see *post*, § 23–37, note 54c. Compare on contributory negligence and economic loss: T. Dugdale (1999) 62 M.L.R. 281.

NOTE 5. Replace note with following text: See, *e.g. Microdata Information Services Ltd v. Rivendale and Clyne* [1991] F.S.R. 681, CA: *Essex Electric (PTE) v. IPC Computers (U.K.)* [1991] F.S.R. 690. On the relationship to defamation and injunctions, see too: *Gulf Oil (Great Britain) Ltd v. Page* [1987] Ch. 327; *Femisbank (Anguilla) Ltd v. Lazar* [1991] Ch. 391; *Holley v. Smyth* [1998] Q.B. 726, CA. See too the uncertain boundaries of each species of the genus: *Credit Lyonnais Bank Nederland (now Generale Bank Nederland) v. Export Credit Guarantee Department* [1998] 1 Lloyd's Rep. 19 at 42–46, CA, upheld on other grounds [1999] 2 W.L.R. 540 HL (new principles of primary tortious liability should not be developed "purely in order to extend the vicarious liability of an employer", *per* Lord Woolf M.R. at 551). Contrast *Three Rivers District Council v. Governor and Company of Bank of England (No.4.), The Times*, December 10 1998, CA (extensions of liability for misfeasance in public office); and *Toumia v. Evans, The Times*, April 1, 1999, CA. *Indata Equipment Supplies Ltd v. ACL Ltd, The Times*, August 14, 1997, CA; defendant liable for tort of unlawful interference because of breach of equitable duties in "blatant disregard" of commercial ethics and practice in misuse of confidential information: *per* Otton L.J., citing *Lac Minerals v. International Corona* [1990] F.S.R. 441, SCC. And the courts' are willing to expose the disloyal employee: *Camelot Group plc v. Centaur Communications Ltd* [1998] I.R.L.R. 80, CA (not a "whistleblower" case, *per* Shiemann L.J. at 84). On protection of "whistleblowers", see the rather cumbersome provisions of the Public Interest Disclosure Act 1998.

NOTE 6. Add at end: *Secretary of State for Employment v. Mann* [1997] I.C.R. 209 at 351 CA.; Cases 178, 179 & 188/94 *Dillenkofer v Germany* (178/94) [1997] I.R.L.R. 60, ECJ. With the Human Rights Act 1988 about to come into force, introducing the European Convention on Human Rights, Canadian experience usefully illustrates how narrow the protections may be which are afforded in this area of law by a constitutional charter of rights: *e.g. UFCW Local 1518 v. K. Mart* (1997) 149 DLR (4th) 1, B.C. CA; *SGEU v. Saskatchewan* (1997) 149 D.L.R. 109, Sask. CA; *NTSU v. Att.-Gen. Nova Scotia* (1993) 102 D.L.R. (4th) 267, N.S.S.C.; *Re Public Service Employees Relations Act* (1987) 38 D.L.R. (4th) 161, SCC *Canadian Egg Marketing Agency v. Richardson* (1999) 166 D.L.R. (4th) 1 (SCC); D. Freedman [1999] C.L.J. 288 (breach of confidence may be regarded as a tort, breach of contract, a misuse of property or *sui generis*; that does not limit the court from granting an appropriate remedy: at 590–591, Binnie J.). On the right of association under the European Convention: T. Novitz on *Gustafsson v. Sweden* (1997) 26 I.L.J. 79; and (1998) 27 I.L.J. 169 (ILO).

NOTE 15. Amend reference to read: *Law Debenture Trust Corp. v. Ural Caspian Oil Corp.* [1995] Ch. 152, CA. **23–02**

NOTE 16. Amend reference to read: Cane, *Tort Law and Economic Interests* (2nd ed., 1996), Chaps 3, 10; Rogers (ed.), *Winfield and Jolowicz on Tort* (15th ed., 1998), Chap. 18; Fleming, *The Law of Torts* (9th ed., 1998) p. 766. Amend reference to read: *Salmond and Heuston on the Law of Torts* (21st ed., 1996) pp. 334–347.

NOTE 23. Add at end: The courts have recently insisted that there is no such tort **23–03**
as knowingly "assisting" the commission of a tort even though the criminal law goes further in prohibiting soliciting, aiding or abetting a criminal act; procuring a tort may make one a joint tortfeasor in pursuance of a common design, but not merely "facilitating" a tort: *Credit Lyonnais Bank Nederland (now Generale Bank Nederland) v. Export Credit Guarantee Department* [1999] 2 W.L.R. 540 at 549, HL, per Lord Woolf M.R. Compare *supra*, § 23–01, 5; *Jameson v. Central Electricity Generating Board* [1999] 2 W.L.R. 141 HL; *Brown v. Bennett, The Times*, January 3, 1998, Rattee J. (liability for knowing assistance of an actual breach of trust) and *Royal Brunei Airlines v. Tan* [1995] 2 A.C. 378, HL, *post*, § 23–23, note 1.

NOTE 24. Amend reference to read: *Law Debenture Trust Corp. v. Ural Caspian Oil Corp.* [1995] Ch. 152, CA.

NOTE 26. Amend reference to read: *Law Debenture Trust Corp. v. Ural Caspian Oil Corp.* [1995] Ch. 152, CA. **23–04**

NOTE 30. Amend to: Smith and Wood, *Industrial Law* (eds Smith and Thomas, 1996), Chap. 11.

NOTE 34. Add at end: But see *Credit Lyonnais Bank Nederland (now Generale Bank Nederland) v. Export Credit Guarantee Department* [1999] 2 W.L.R. 540, HL; *Yukong Line of Korea v. Rendsberg Investments Corp.(No. 2)* [1998] 1 W.L.R. 294, *per* Toulson J. at 314, holding that the act relied upon as unlawful means must be actionable at the suit of the plaintiff (the opposite view from that in the Court of Appeal decision *Associated British Ports v. TGWU* [1989] 1 W.L.R. 939, Stuart-Smith and Butler-Sloss L.J.J.), see also *post*, § 23–69, note 45. Compare *British Telecommunications plc v. One in a Million* [1998] 4 All E.R 476, CA.

NOTE 37. Add: The suggestion that there is a tort of "appropriating another's personality" has received little support (see B.M. Hylton and P. Goldson, "The New Tort of Appropriating Personality" [1996] C.L.J. 56, discussing *Robert Marley*

Foundation v. Dino Michelle (unreported, May 12, 1994, HCt Jamaica) and *Goold Estate v. Stoddart Publishing Co.* (1998) 161 D.L.R. (4th) 321, Ont. CA.

23–05 NOTE 38. Amend reference to read: *Martin v. Watson* [1996] 1 A.C. 74, HL.

23–06 NOTE 43. Add at end: See the suggestion of a wide tort of "discrimination" to fill the gaps in the Canadian constitutional charter: *Smith v. New Brunswick (Human Rights Commission)* (1996) 137 D.L.R. (4th) 76, 86–89, n.b. QBD.

23–07 NOTE 48. Add at end: see also *Normart Management Ltd v. West Hill Redevelopment Co.* (1998) 155 D.L.R. (4th) 627, Ont. CA; to add a conspiracy claim would have no impact on the success of the litigation. On joint tortfeasors, see *post*, § 23–83; and on joint tortfeasors and vicarious liability in intentional economic torts: *Credit Lyonnais Bank Nederland (now Generale Bank Nederland) v. Export Credit Guarantee Department* [1999] 2 W.L.R. 540, HL (where the employee committed acts within the course of his employment, not in themselves actionable, but with the intention to assist in the violation of a third party's rights, the employer was not vicariously liable; nor was there any new primary liability in tort. *Sed quaere*: whether such assistance could give rise to the tort of conspiracy: see at 548–549.

23–08 NOTE 57. Add at end: see the apparent lack of congruence between *Associated British Ports v. TGWU* [1989] 1 W.L.R. 939, CA (reversed on other grounds, *ibid.*, HL) and *Credit Lyonnais Bank Nederland (now Generale Bank Nederland) v. Export Credit Guarantee Department* [1998] 1 Lloyd's Rep. 19 at 32, CA, as understood in *Yukong Line of Korea v. Rendsberg Investments Corp. (No. 2)* [1998] 1 W.L.R. 294, now upheld on other grounds: [1999] 2 W.L.R. 540, HL.

NOTE 58. Add at end: The problems are not reduced by the emergence of "restitution" as a freelance category, distinct from liability in both contract and tort: *Kleinwort Benson Ltd v. Glasgow County Council* [1999] 1 A.C. 153 HL; *Banque Financiere de la Cite v. Park (Battersea)* [1999] 1 A.C. 221, HL (restitution and subrogation); also P. Cane, *Tort Law and Economic Interests* (2nd ed., 1996), pp. 295–300.

Add after note 58: Although the level of intention required is "far from settled",[58a] the tendency is for the courts to demand not a predominant intent to injure in such torts, but something deliberately and intentionally directed at the plaintiff. [58b]

NOTE 58a. *Per* Mason C.J., *Northern Territory v. Mengel* (1995) 185 C.L.R. 307, HCt.

NOTE 58b. *Northern Territory v. Mengel* (1995) 185 C.L.R. 307 at 340–345 (HCt), see *post*, Supplement, § 23–43, note 8; and see B. McDonald and J. Swanton (1995) 69 A.L.J. 868; N. Mullany (1995) 111 L.Q.R. 583; *Cheticamp Fisheries Co-op v. Canada* (1995) 123 D.L.R. (4th) 121, N.S. CA, especially *per* Chipman J.A. at 128–134; *Ontario v. Barleven Town Centre Inc.* (1995) 121 D.L.R. (4th) 748, Ont. Compare *Three Rivers District Council v. Bank of England (No. 3)* [1996] 3 All E.R. 558 at 579–583, 632, 633; "recklessness" is also sufficient in misfeasance in public office, applying *Mengel's* case above; and *Three Rivers District Council v. Bank of England (No. 4) The Times*, December 10 1998, CA; see too *Bennett v. Commissioner of Police for Metropolis, The Times*, October 24, 1997, Scott V-C (absence of a plea of malice); *Gibbs v. Rea* [1998] A.C. 786, PC (malice required for liability in procuring search warrant: Lords Goff and Hope dissenting). It is to be remembered that "an intentional wrongdoer is not entitled to the benefit of the foreseeability test of remoteness" *per* Lord Steyn, *Smith New Court Securities v. Scrimgeour Vickers* [1997] A.C. 254 at 281, HL; see *post*, § 23–57; but see also *supra*, n. 4: *Nationwide Building Society v. Various Solicitors (No.3), The Times*, March 1, 1999, for a rather different approach, allowing damages to be reduced where the behaviour of the claimant caused some part of the loss to be too remote (a doctrine applied to a breach of fiduciary duty which, *semble*, applies in tort also).

NOTE 59. Amend reference to read *Law Debenture Trust Corp. v. Ural Caspian Oil Corp.* [1995] Ch. 152 at 164–166, 170–172, CA.

2.—PROCURING BREACH OF CONTRACT

Knowingly and intentionally procuring a breach of contract   **23–09**
NOTE 62. Amend reference to read: *National Hockey League v. Pepsi Cola
Canada Ltd* (1995) 122 D.L.R. (4th) 412, B.C. CA; contrast the position in American
jurisdictions: Danforth, 81 Col. L.Rev. 1491 (1981); Vandevelde, 19 Hofstra L.R.
447 (1990).
NOTE 63. Amend reference to read: *Law Debenture Trust Corp. v. Ural Caspian
Oil Corp.* [1995] Ch. 152 at 164–166, 170–172, CA. After "Law of Property Act
1925)" insert: *McCausland v. Duncan Lawrie* [1997] 1 W.L.R. 38, CA (variation
of contract for disposition of land must comply with section 2).
NOTE 66. At end add: Nor is an act assisting or facilitating, even if intended to
help the wrongdoer: *Credit Lyonnais Bank Nederland (now Generale Bank
Nederland) v. Export Credit Guarantee Department* [1999] 2 W.L.R. 540 at 546,
548, 551, HL, Lord Woolf M.R.

Knowledge and intention   **23–10**
NOTE 69. Amend reference to read: *Stovin v. Wise* [1996] A.C. 923, HL.
NOTE 74. Amend reference to read: *Law Debenture Trust Corp. v. Ural Caspian
Oil Corp.* [1995] Ch. 152, CA.
After "See too" insert: *Meridian Global Funds Management Asia Ltd v. The
Securities Commissioners* [1995] 2 A.C. 500, PC (Lord Hoffmann: diverse attribu-
tions of persons' knowledge and intent to corporate bodies: and below § 23–26
insert: ; Grantham (1996) 59 M.L.R. 732).
NOTE 75. Amend reference to read: *Cheticamp Fisheries Co-op v. Canada* (1995)
123 D.L.R. (4th) 121, N.S. CA; *post*, § 23–57. But see *Timeplan Education Group
Ltd v. NUT* [1997] I.R.L.R. 257, CA.

NOTE 82. Add at end: *Timeplan Education Group Ltd v. NUT* [1997] I.R.L.R.   **23–11**
457.
NOTE 86. At end add: Rogers in *Winfield and Jolowicz on Tort* (15th ed., 1998),
p. 629 suggests a distinction between "targets" and "ricochet" victims, as in *Millar
v. Bassey* [1994] E.M.L.R. 44, CA, *per* Ralph Gibson LJ and Peter Gibson LJ
(dissenting).
NOTE 86/87. Amend reference to read: *Law Debenture Trust Corp. v. Ural Casp-
arian Oil Corp.* [1995] Ch. 152, CA.
NOTE 87, line 5. Amend to read: On incidental damage, see Cane, *Tort Law and
Economic Interests* (2nd ed., 1996) pp. 126–128, 130–133.
NOTE 87, line 15. After "Peter Gibson L.J. dissenting" insert, see D. Howarth,
Textbook on Tort (1995) pp. 479–484 (concluding that *Lumley v. Gye* was wrongly
decided, p. 484).
NOTE 87. Amend reference to: Cane, *Tort Law and Economic Interests* (2nd ed.,
1996) 127–133. Add: See Rogers in *Winfield and Jolowicz on Tort* (15th ed., 1998):
"The whole question clearly requires fuller examination than can be given in interlocutory proceedings" (pp. 629–630).
NOTE 90. Add at end: *Mercedes Benz v. Clydesdale Bank* 1997 S.L.T. 905, Ct of
Sess, Outer House (a further indication that Scottish courts retain a more classical
view of knowledge and intention in this tort; a bank refused to make payment as
instructed, but was not liable as there was no evidence of sufficient knowledge, nor
of any intention to induce the breach of the customer's contract with a third party
which was to be financed by the payment); see too, *The Nadezhda Krupskaya* [1997]
2 Lloyd's Rep. 35 (sufficient knowledge and intention in acts of interference with
charter party).
NOTE 92. Add at end: ; *Mercedes Benz v. Clydesdale Bank* 1997 S.L.T. 905, Ct
of Sess, Outer House. Compare also *Millar v. Bassey* [1994] E.M.L. R. 44, CA.

NOTE 97. Add at end: Compare *Mercedes Benz v. Clydesdale Bank* 1997 S.L.T.   **23–12**
905, Ct of Sess, Outer House.

23–13 **Breach of existing contract**

NOTE 1. Add to reference: *National Hockey League v. Pepsi Cola Canada Ltd* (1995) 122 D.L.R. (4th) 412, B.C. CA.

NOTE 8. Amend reference to read: *Law Debenture Trust Corp. v. Ural Caspian Oil Corp.* [1995] Ch. 152 at 170. Add: *Daishowa v. Friends of the Lubicon* (1998) 158 D.L.R. (4th) 699, Ont. CA.

23–14 NOTE 13. Add at end: On the effect of illegality on employment contacts: Jefferson [1996] 25 I.L.J. 234. Under the Contracts (Rights of Third Parties) Bill 1999, a third party is enabled to enforce a term in a contract for his benefit provided that is the intention of the parties, but certain types of term or contract are excluded (such as some terms against workers). The Bill, may be of greater importance in the tort of intimidation than in procuring breach of contract (see *post*, § 23–38).

23–15 NOTE 23. Amend reference to read: *Law Debenture Trust Corp. v. Ural Caspian Oil Corp.* [1995] Ch. 152, *per* Bingham M.R. at 165–166; Beldam L.J. at 169–170; Saville L.J. at 172. Add *Intelsec. v. Grech-Cini* [1999] 4 App. E.R. 11 (duty of Fidelity.)

NOTE 26. Amend references to read: (line 8) Treitel, *Law of Contract* (9th ed., 1995) pp 207–221; (line 14) Treitel, *op. cit.* pp. 227–259.

23–16 NOTE 33. Add at end: *Wandworth London Borough Council v. D'Silva* [1998 I.R.L.R. 193, CA (code about absences from work held unilaterally open to variation by the employer); contrast *Anderson v. Pringle of Scotland* [1998] I.R.L.R. 64, Ct of Sess, Outer House; Brodie (1998) 27 I.L.J. 37, where interdict was granted to maintain the provisions of a "Last In; First Out" arrangement incorporated into the employment of contracts. *Quaere* whether English courts would exercise such a discretionary remedy in personal contracts.

NOTE 34. At end add: On the interpretation of collective agreements, see *Ali v. Christian Salveson Food Services* [1997] I.C.R. 25, CA. Even if incorporated into the individual contract of employment, the collective agreement may on its proper construction permit the employer to amend the terms unilaterally: *Airlie v. Edinburgh City District Council* [1996] I.R.L.R. 516. *cf. Burke v. Royal Liverpool University Hospital NHS Trust* [1997] I.C.R. 730; *Whent v. T. Cartledge* [1997] I.R.L.R. 153; *Edinburgh Council v. Brown* [1999] I.R.L.R. 208.

23–17 NOTE 35. At end add: On the Convention see Novitz (1997) 26 I.L.J. 79. See now the Human Rights Act 1998.

23–18 NOTE 48. Amend reference to read: Smith and Wood, *Industrial Law* (6th ed., 1996) pp. 564–567.

NOTE 50. Delete final seven lines from "With one solitary . . . " to "Aus. J.L.L. 69". Replace with: Compare Canada: *R. v. TNT Canada Inc.* (1996) 131 D.L.R. (4th) 289, Ont. (employees on strike remain employees) and on Australia: see G. McGarry (1997) 10 Aus. J.L.L. 133.

Add at end: Industrial action in many other countries not in breach of employment contracts; interlocutory injunction refused: *Patrick Stevedores Operations v. ITWF* [1998] C.L.C. 1022, Thomas J.

New text: As between employers and unions, collective agreements in Britain have long been presumed to be intended not to be legally binding as between the parties.[51a] In the procedure introduced in the 1999 Act trade unions will be legally entitled in certain circumstances to negotiate with an employer in collective bargaining and the Central Arbitration Committee will have the competence to specify a "method" for collective bargaining which will operate as if it were a legally binding agreement.[51b] In such a case, it appears that the procurement of breach of such an agreement would appear to be tortious (though, if done in contemplation or furtherance of a trade dispute, it might attract protection from liability for the procurer).[51c] In fact, the remedy for breach of such an agreement imposed by the

Central Arbitration Committee ("specific performance") appears to be limited to breach of contract as such; [51d] (and to limitations inherent in the equitable remedy)[51dd] a tort action against a third party for inducing the breach of such an agreement would appear not to attract the limitation and might therefore have the added attraction of a variety of remedies, such as an interlocutory injunction or damages.[51e]

NOTE 51a. See now s. 179 of the Trade Union and Labour Relations (Consolidation) Act 1992 (TURCA). On incorporation into individual employment contracts, see *supra*, 23–16.

NOTE 51b. Employment Relations Act 1999, Sched. 1 (inserting Sched. A1 in TULRCA 1992, "Collective Bargaining: Recognition"), especially paras 31, 63, 168.

NOTE 51c. See *post*, §§ 23–91 and 23–134.

NOTE 51d. On the limitation of the remedy, see Employment Relations Act 1999 ("ERA 1999") Sched. 1 (now TULCRA 1992 Sched. A1), paras. 31(6), 63(5) (where the CAC specifies a binding method for bargaining between the parties, "specific performance shall be the only remedy available for breach of anything which is a legally enforceable agreement by virtue of this paragraph"). No limitation is imposed, however, upon the right of a party to the "agreement" to take action against someone who induces the other party to break the imposed "legally enforceable agreement" or interferes or threatens to interfere with its performance (*e.g.* a parent company instructing a subsidiary, or a union instructing an official for whose acts it is liable (see s. 20 TULCRA 1992) not to conform with the "method" of bargaining specified by the CAC which has "effect as if it were contained in a legally enforceable contract made by the parties": paras 31(3)(4), 63(3)(4)). On principle, liability would arise in tort from the unducement of breach or threat to induce breach, of the agreement, not "by virtue of this paragraph" (see *Rookes v. Barnard* [1964] A.C. 1129, HL). The limitation of remedies to "specific performance" does not appear to affect tort liability for inducing breach of contract (see *Torquay Hotel Co. Ltd v. Cousins* [1969] 2 Ch. 106, CA; tort liability, even though remedies for breach of contract emasculated). The power of the parties to vary the agreement, afforded by para. 31(5), cannot, it appears, exclude legally enforceable status altogether because the varied agreement "shall have effect as a legally enforceable contract" (*sed quaere*, for a different view see *Explanatory Notes: Employment Relations Act 1999* (DTI, HMSO 1999) p. 23.

INSERT new text: The remedy of specific performance is discretionary and subject to many limitations.[51dd]

NOTE 51dd. On the doctrine that a claimant for "specific performance" must come with "clean hands", see *Curust Financial Services v. Loewe-Lack-Werk Gmbh* [1994] 1 I.R. 450 (Barron J. and Sup. Ct); this doctrine requires "an element of turpitude", not merely a breach of contract. *Quaere* whether the High Court in enforcing "specific performance" for union recognition would apply this doctrine and whether it would thereby necessarily become embroiled in the legal and industrial questions in the case? And whether s. 236 Trade Union and Labour Relations (Consolidation) Act 1992 would prevent orders which compelled an employee to do work to secure that performance? Compare *Anderson v. Pringle* [1988] I.R.L.R. 64, Ct. S.

NOTE 51e. It seems that the limitation of the remedy to specific performance applies only where actual or prospective breach of the agreement made binding by the Schedule is shown and not to other actions, *e.g.* against third parties based upon tort even if the breach might be part of the cause of action (such as procurement or threat of breach, or interference by unlawful means). If a union which is not a party to the "agreement" is found to have induced one of the parties to it to act in breach of its obligations under the "method" laid down by the Central Arbitration Committee (*e.g.* if it causes an employer not to open talks with a union which is "entitled" to conduct negotiations with the employer because it won a sufficient majority in a ballot of the workforce at the employer's bargaining unit) the court would hardly confine claimants' remedies to specific performance for the tort — indeed the third party defendants would have no contractual obligations specifically to be enforced;

if Sched. 1, para. 31(6) were enforced here, common law liability would be destroyed by mere implications in the Schedule. It may be asked whether the Schedule chips away any existing rights in connection with union "recognition". It is true that the Employment Relations Act 1999 contains the right for one or more workers to apply for *derecognition* of a union, see Sched. 1, Part IV. But the Schedule does not appear to detract from workers' rights to take industrial action otherwise lawful in a trade dispute, merely because the pressure on the employer and the centre of the dispute is "union recognition"; s. 244 of TULRCA 1992 has not here been amended: see *post*, § 23–91 to 23–134; *cf.* 23–122, note 90.

23–19   **Bare interference without breach**
Note 63. Amend reference to read: *Law Debenture Trust Corp. v. Ural Caspian Oil Corp.* [1995] Ch. 152, CA, and *per* Baldam L.J. at 169–170.
Note 63a. Amend reference to read: *Law Debenture Trust* [1995] Ch. 152, CA and *per* Baldam L.J. at 169–170.

23–21   Note 71. Replace to read: *Salmond and Heuston on the Law of Torts* (16th ed., 1996), pp. 344–345. Add at end: see too, *McGregor on Damages* (16th ed. 1997), pp. 1252–1256.
Note 76. Amend to read: *National Hockey League v. Pepsi Cola Canada* (1995) 122 D.L.R. (4th) 412, B.C. CA.
Note 80. Add at end: ; see too, *National Hockey League v. Pepsi Cola Canada Ltd* (1995) 122 D.L.R. (4th) 412 B.C. CA: interference with the plaintiff's economic position under limited contractual rights was not actionable in the absence of interference causing breach, citing *RCA v. Pollard* [1983] Ch. 135 at 156; see above § 23–21, n. 73.

23–23   **Breach of other obligations**
In text, first line, amend to read: "So too, liability may attach to the inducement of a breach of an equitable obligation ... "
Insert in second paragraph, line 9 after "finally settled": Contrary to recent authority,[2a] it has been convincingly argued that "a person who has intentionally interfered with another's equitable rights should be liable" on the principle of *Lumley v. Gye*.[2b]
Note 89. Amend reference to read: *Law Debenture Trust Corp. v. Ural Caspian Oil Corp.* [1995] Ch. 152, CA.
Note 93. Amend reference to read: Cornish, *Intellectual Property* (3rd ed., 1996), Chap 8, pp. 263–293. See *Indata Equipment Supplies Ltd v. ACL Ltd, The Times*, August 14, 1997, CA (no fiduciary relationship between the parties, therefore liability could no be based upon a "core of duties of loyalty and fidelity"; but defendant was liable for tort of unlawful interference by reason of breach of equitable duties in regard to commercial ethics and misuse of confidential information: *per* Otton LJ: Simon Brown LJ concurring on liability, but doubting whether this was the tort of unlawful means).
Note 94. Delete and insert: Cornish, *Intellectual Property* (3rd ed., 1996), Chap. 8; Law Commission *Breach of Confidence* Report No. 110 (Cmnd. 8388, 1981); Competition Act 1998.
Note 95. At end amend reference to read: Cornish, *op. cit.* pp. 276–285. On the constituents of liability for breach of confidence: *Murray v. Yorkshire Fund Managers Ltd* [1998] 1 W.L.R. 951, CA; and *Indata Equipment Supplies Ltd v. ACL Ltd, The Times*, August 14, 1997, CA, (defendant liable for tort of unlawful interference because of his breach of equitable duties in "blatant disregard" of commercial ethics and practice by misuse of confidential information: *per* Otton L.J., citing *Lac Minerals v. International Corona* [1990] F.S.R. 441, SCC; *Coulthard v. Disco Mix Club* [1999] 2 All E.R. 457. See also *post*, § 23–62, notes 77–81.
Note 96. Delete "Cornish *op. cit.*, p. 232" Insert: Cornish, *Intellectual Property* (3rd ed., 1996) p. 280.
Note 99. Add at end: *Indata Equipment Supplies Ltd v. ACL Ltd, The Times*, August 14, 1997, CA (no duties of fidelity between the parties, but liability arose in

tort for unlawful interference by breaches of equitable duties, misuse of confidential information: *per* Otto L.J. citing *Lac Minerals v. International Corona* [1990] FSR 441, SCC; so too, Simon Brown L.J., *sed dubitante* whether this was the tort of unlawful means).

NOTE 1. *Metall und Rostoff AG v. Donaldson Lufkin & Jenrette Inc.* [1990] 1 Q.B. 391, CA (overruled on other matters: *Lonrho plc v. Fayed* [1992] 1 A.C. 448 at 481, HL: no justification for a new tort); but left open in *Crawley Borough Council v. Ure* [1996] Q.B. 13, CA. Compare liability for inducing a breach of personal equitable obligations, such as a duty to account: *Prudential Assurance Ltd v. Lorenz* (1971) 11 K.I.R. 78 (accepted by the Court of Appeal in *Associated British Ports v. TGWU* [1989] 1 W.L.R. 939; reversed on other grounds, *ibid.*) which might be thought to come close to treating interference with equitable duties, even of a trustee's duties as a tort, or treating breach of trust as unlawful means. In *Metall und Rostoff* (above) the Court of Appeal, commenting on the uncertainties in this area, especially on different forms of constructive trust, was willing (for the purposes of that case) to regard "in some circumstances . . . assertion of remedial constructive trust" (but not other types) as a claim founded on tort for the purposes of RSC, Ord. 11, r.1(1)(f) (at 473–480). On claims in contract or tort overlapping with fiduciary duties or breach of constructive trust: *Coulthard v. Disco Mix Club Ltd* [1999] 2 All E.R. 457 (contractual duty to account or honest breach of fiduciary duty equivalent to tort claims for limitation period); *Nationwide Building Society v. Various Solicitors (No. 3), The Times,* March 1, 1999 (equitable compensation for breach of fiduciary duties; analogies with tort); *Belmont Finance Ltd v. Williams (No. 2)* [1980] 1 All E.R. 383, CA; *Apotex Fermentation Inc. v. Novopharm* (1998) 162 D.L.R. (4th) 111, Man. C.A.; *Royal Brunei Airlines v. Tan* [1995] A.C. 278 (third party dishonestly procures breach of trust, liable for breach whether trustee dishonest or not); *Satnam Investments Ltd v. Dunlop Heywood Ltd* [1999] 3 All E.R. 652, CA ("the law relating to constructive trusts, confidential information and fiduciary obligations is in a state of continuous development": *per* Nourse L.J.); *Brown v. Bennet, The Times,* January 3, 1998; R. Grantham and C. Rickett (1998) 144 L.Q.R. 357 (interference in breach of trust). Also, *Soulos v. Korkontzilas* (1997) 146 D.L.R. (4th) 214, SCC (constructive trust "an ancient and eclective institution" to remedy unjust enrichment); Smith (1998) 114 L.Q.R. 14 (fiduciary duty and constructive trust); Cane, *Tort Law and Economic Interests* (2nd ed., 1996), pp. 283–295. On constructive trusts and restitution: Lord Millett (1998) 114 L.Q.R. 398; Tettenborn [1996] C.L.J. 36; Gardner (1996) 112 L.Q.R. 56; *Martindale Estates v. Martindale* (1998) 163 D.L.R. (4th) 475, B.C. CA; *Citadel General Assurance v. Lloyds Bank Canada* (1998) 152 D.L.R. (4th) 411, SCC (knowing receipt of trust funds); *James v. Williams, The Times,* April 13, 1999; *Dubai Aluminium v. Salaam* (1999) 1 Lloyd's Rep. 415 (partner as constructive trustee); *French v. Mason, The Times,* November 13, 1998 (property subject to a constructive trust arising from breach of fiduciary obligation).

NOTE 2. Amend to read: *Law Debenture Trust Corp. v. Ural Caspian Oil Corp.* [1995] Ch. 152, CA *per* Beldam L.J. at 167–168; *per* Saville L.J. at 172–173. Rejection of inducing a breach of trust or inducing a breach of fiduciary duty as unlawful means in tort frequently owes much to the need for "privity" to prevent third parties from enforcing such duties, especially fiduciary duties: *Stein v. Blake* [1998] 1 All E.R. 724, CA, *per* Millett L.J. at 727–730 (directors owe their fiduciary duties to the company but in certain circumstances also to the shareholders); *Yukong Line of Korea v. Rendsberg Investments Corp. (No. 2)* [1998] 1 W.L.R. 294 (no *locus standi* for individual creditor). Contrast the robust approach of the courts to breach of confidence: *Indata Equipment Supplies Ltd v. ACL Ltd, The Times,* August 14, 1997, CA ("blatant disregard" of commercial ethics in misuse of confidential information). On compensation for undue influence, *Mahoney v. Purnell* [1996] 3 All E.R. 61; see Heydon (1997) 113 L.Q.R. 8. The alleged deliberate breach of a fiduciary duty may be no more than the equitable counterpart of a claim at common law: *Coulthard v. Disco Mix Club* [1999] 2 All E.R. 457 at 477–479 and on equitable compensation generally, see Tjio and Yeo (1998) 114 L.Q.R. 181; *Swindle v. Harrison* [1997] 4

All E.R. 705, CA. On "accessory liability" see *Credit Lyonnais Bank Nederland (now Generale Bank Nederland) v. Export Credit Guarantee Department* [1981] 1 Lloyd's Rep. 19 (aff'd on other grounds: [1999] 2 W.L.R. 540, HL). The constituents of liability of breach of confidence are discussed in *Murray v. Yorkshire Fund Managers Ltd* [1998] 1 W.L.R. 951, CA; and *Indata Equipment Supplies Ltd v. ACL Ltd, The Times,* August 14, 1997, CA, see *supra* n. 95; *Lac Minerals v. International Corona* [1990] F.S.R 441, SCC.

NOTE 2a. *Royal Brunei Airlines v. Tan* [1995] 2 A.C. 378, PC (Lord Nicholls).On trusts and constructive trusts, see *United Mizrahi Bank Ltd v. Doherty* [1998] 1 W.L.R. 435; *Foskett v. McKeown* [1998] 2 W.L.R. 298, CA; *Soulos v. Korkontzilas* [1997] S.C.R. 217, SCC. On rights in confidential information: *Murray v. Yorkshire Fund Managers* [1998] 1 W.L.R. 951, CA.

NOTE 2b. (1853) 2 E. & B. 216; see A. Berg (1996) 59 M.L.R. 443 at 452, citing Lord Hoffman in P. Birks (ed.), *The Frontiers of Liability* (1994), p. 27; and see P. Birks (1996) L.M.C.L.Q. 1, 5.

NOTE 4. Amend to read: *Law Debenture Trust Corp. v. Ural Caspian Oil Corp.* [1995] Ch. 152, CA, *per* Beldam L.J. at 167–168; *per* Saville L.J. at 172–173. *Satnam Investments Ltd v. Dunlop Heywood, The Times,* December 31, 1998.

The wrongful procurement.
NOTE 17. Add at end: Where the officer of a company commits a tort within the course of his employment as a joint tortfeasor with a third party, the company will be liable; but it is not normally vicariously liable for his act within his employment which is not itself tortious (even if done with the intent to assist in the violation of the rights of a third party); and the company officer himself will not normally be liable for "assisting" or "facilitating" the commission of a tort as against participation as a joint tortfeasor in the common design: *Credit Lyonnais Bank Nederland (now Generale Bank Nederland) v. Export Credit Guarantee Department* [1999] 2 W.L.R. 540, HL. Nor, where he has entered into a transaction for the company, will the director be treated, in the absence of clear evidence, as the company's undisclosed principal: *Yukong Line Ltd v. Rendsburg Investments Corp.* [1998] 1 WLR 294 (nor will the "corporate veil" be lifted to that end: *per* Toulson J. at 300–310); *cf. Williams v. Natural Life Health Foods* [1998] 1 W.L.R. 830, HL (see Lord Steyn 835–837; directors will not be personally liable for acts done on behalf of the company unless they create a clear impression of personal liability or assume responsibility for what is to be done: R. Grantham and C. Ricket (1999) M.L.R. 133 and S. Griffin (1999) 115 L.Q.R. 36; a policy of support for their limited liability, J. Payne [1999] C.L.J. 456); see too, *AGDA Systems v. Valcom Ltd.* (1999) 168 D.L.R. (4th) 351, *per* Carthy J.A. 356–365 (Ont. CA).

23–26   NOTE 21. Add: But the "alter ego" test must be used with caution, as the knowledge of a diverse range of persons may be attributed to a corporate body for the purpose of different liabilities: *Meridian Global Funds Management Asia v. Securities Commission* [1995] 2 A.C. 500, PC; Robert-Tissot (1996) 17 Co. Law 99; and where statute imposes a strict duty, the test is irrelevant as there is no need to prove that the company's "directing mind or will" had knowledge of the defect: see *R v. Gateway Foodmarkets Ltd* [1997] I.C.R. 382, CA. The court refused to lift the veil even where a person had transferred funds to his own benefit as part of a fraudulent scheme in a breach of fiduciary obligations when he could be said to be the "alter ego" of the relevant company: *Yukong Line of Korea v. Rendsburg Investments Corp. (No 2.)* [1998] 1 W.L.R. 294, *per* Toulson J. at 302–311.

23–27   NOTE 27. At the end add: See too, *The Nadezhda Krupskaya* [1997] 2 Lloyd's Rep. 35.

23–28   NOTE 41. Amend to read: *National Hockey League v. Pepsi Cola Canada* (1995) 122 DLR (4th) 412, B.C. CA.
NOTE 45: Add at end: Acts which do no more than "facilitate" the wrongdoing

are not by themselves actionable: *Credit Lyonnais Bank (now Generale Bank Nederland) v. Export Credit Guarantee Department* [1999] 2 WLR 540, HL.

Inconsistent transactions
23–29

NOTE 4. At end add: The law of tort does not go as wide as the criminal law and rejects the liability for merely "facilitating" a tort: *Credit Lyonnais Bank Nederland (now Generale Bank Nederland) v. Export Credit Guarantee Department* [1999] 2 WLR 540 at 551 *per* Lord Woolf MR; *British Telecommunications plc v. One in a Million Ltd* [1998] 4 All ER 476 at 487.

NOTE 58. Amend to read: *Law Debenture Trust Corp. v. Ural Caspian Oil Corp.* [1995] Ch. 152, CA.

NOTES 61–62. Amend to read: *Law Debenture Trust Corp. v. Ural Caspian Oil Corp.* [1995] Ch. 152, CA.

NOTES 62. At end add: For provisions adding new exceptions to the doctrine of "privity of contract", see the Contracts (Rights of Third Parties) Bill 1999.

NOTE 66. Amend reference to read: Treitel, *Law of Contract* (9th ed., 1995), pp. 562–565.

NOTE 69. Amend to read: *Law Debenture Trust Corp. v. Ural Caspian Oil Corp.* [1995] Ch. 152, CA.

NOTE 71a. Amend to read: *Law Debenture Trust Corp. v. Ural Caspian Oil Corp.* [1995] Ch. 152, CA.

NOTE 71b. Amend to read: *Law Debenture Trust Corp. v. Ural Caspian Oil Corp.* [1995] Ch. 152 at 170 *per* Beldam LJ.

NOTE 77. After "trustees CA" add: ; and see *Crawley Borough Council v. Ure* **23–30** [1996] Ch. 13, CA (acts constituting breach of trust); and on liability as accessory to a breach of trust: *Royal Brunei Airlines v. Tan* [1995] 2 A.C. 378, PC; *Brinks Ltd v. Abu-Saleh (No. 3), The Times*, October 23, 1995; *Corporacion Nacional del Cobre de Chile v. Sogemin Metals Ltd* [1997] 1 W.L.R. 1396 (bribery); *Indata Equipment Supplies Ltd v. ACL Ltd, The Times*, August 14, 1997, CA (unlawful interference by breach of equitable obligations in "blatant disregard" of commercial ethics in misusing confidential information, Simon Brown L.J. agreeing on liability, *sed dubitante* whether this was a tort of unlawful means; *Credit Lyonnais Bank (now Generale Bank Nederland) v. Export Credit Guarantee Department* [1999] 2 W.L.R. 540, HL (no new primary tortious liability to extend vicarious liability of an employer); and see further *supra*, § 23–23, nn. 1 and 2. See *post*, § 23–62.

(2) *Other direct intervention.*

NOTE 81. Amend to read: *Law Debenture Trust Corp. v. Ural Caspian Oil Corp.* **23–31** [1995] Ch. 152, CA. *The Nadezhda Krupskaya* [1997] 2 Lloyd's Rep. 35 was, it is submitted, not a case of direct intervention by unlawful means, but a direct procurement by way of embargo, making the vessel unavailable: *per* Rix J, at 39.

(3) *Indirect procurement*

NOTE 83. Add at end: Compare *Indata Equipment Supplies Ltd v. ACL Ltd, The* **23–32** *Times*, August 14, 1997, CA, tort of unlawful interference because of breach of equitable duties in "blatant disregard" of commercial ethics in misuse of confidential information *per* Otton LJ, citing *Lac Minerals v. International Corona* [1990] F.S.R. 441, SCC.

NOTE 85. Amend and insert: *National Hockey League v. Pepsi Cola Canada* (1995) 122 D.L.R. (4th) 412, B.C. CA: no interference with limited contractual rights, per Carrothers J.A. at 419–421.

NOTE 88. Amend to read: *Law Debenture Trust Corp. v. Ural Caspian Oil Corp.* [1995] Ch. 152, CA.

23–34   NOTE 11. Amend reference to read: Private International Law (Miscellaneous Provisions) Act 1995, ss. 9–15.

NOTE 15. Add: But see now *McGregor on Damages* (16th ed., 1997), pp. 1254–1255 (why should damages for injured feelings be excluded from conspiracy claims, but permitted for injurious falsehood and procuring breach of contract?). Compare the new wave of liability in contract based on "mutual trust and confidence": *Mahmud v. Bank of Credit and Commerce International SA* [1998] A.C. 20, HL; *Johnson v. Unisys* [1999] I.R.L.R. 90 CA; *Hill v. General Accident* [1998] I.R.L.R. 641, (Court of Session, Outer House); *Wood Group etc v. Crossan* [1998] I.R.L.R. 680; *Brown v. Merchant Ferries* [1998] IRLR 682, N.I. CA. See too, D. Brodie (1998) 27 ILJ 79. After "loss; *cf.*" amend to *McGregor on Damages* (16th ed., 1997), pp. 143.

NOTE 16. Amend. "After § 2–02)" to *McGregor on Damages* (16th ed., 1997), pp. 143 and 1252–1256; *Lonrho v. Fayed (No/ 5)* [1993] 1 W.L.R. 1489, CA; *Joyce v. Sengupta* [1993] 1 W.L.R. 337, CA.

23–35   NOTE 24. Amend reference to read: *MacMillan Bloedel v. Simpson* (1997) 137 D.L.R. (4th) 637, SCC.

NOTE 27. Add Deakin and Morris, *Labour Law* (2nd ed., 1998), pp. 914–922).

23–37   Justification

NOTE 40. At end add: Treitel, *Law of Contract* (9th ed., 1995), pp. 245–254.

NOTE 44. At end add: *Timeplan Education Group v. NUT* [1997] I.R.L.R. 457, CA.

NOTE 52. At end add: ; *Knowles v. Fire Brigades Union* [1996] I.R.L.R. 617, CA.

NOTE 54. At end amend: Cane, *Tort Law and Economic Interests* (2nd ed.. 1996), pp. 111–127; and on statutory rights to interfere with interests of third parties; *R. v. City of London Corp. Ex parte Mystery of the Barbers of London, The Times*, June 28, 1996, Dyson J.

At end of text, after "independent role", insert text and notes: There are cases where a party can cure his breach of contract by reference to facts which come to his knowledge only after the initial breach (*e.g.*, where an employer wrongfully dismisses an employee and acquires knowledge of his misconduct at a later date justifying the dismissal); but this principal of justification does not apply to the tort of interference with contractual relations,[54a] "except perhaps in exceptional circumstances",[54b] The defence of contributory negligence is not available in this tort, at any rate where the defendant has engaged in dishonest means, such as bribery.[54c]

NOTE 54a. SOS *Kinderdorf International v. Bittaye* [1996] 1 W.L.R. 987, PC.

NOTE 54b. *ibid.*, at 994, PC (Lord Keith).

NOTE 54c. *Corporacion Nacional del Cobre de Chile v. Sogemin Metals Ltd* [1997] 1 W.L.R. 1396 (defendants' bribery excludes such defences both in law and equity); *Alliance and Leicester Building Society v. Edgestop Ltd* [1993] 1 W.L.R. 1463 (deceit). *Semble* the same is the case even where the defendant's inducement does not involve dishonesty, save where the plaintiff's conduct breaks the chain of causation. The claimant's behaviour may have the effect of reducing the compensation both in equity and at common law, because it renders some or all of it too remote: *Nationwide Building Society v. Various Solicitors (No. 3) The Times*, March 1, 1999, see *supra* § 23–01, 1.

3.—INTIMIDATION

23–38   The tort of intimidation

NOTE 55. Add at end: See the extraordinary decision in *DPP v. Fidler* [1992] 1 W.L.R. 91 (and the role of the DPP and Nolan L.J. at 98).

NOTE 58. Add after "intentional injury": The intent to injure is central to the tort of intimidation: *Cheticamp Fisheries Co-op v. Canada* (1995) 123 D.L.R. (4th) 121 at 137, *per* Chipman J.A.

NOTE 60. Amend reference to read: Cane, *Tort Law and Economic Interests* (2nd ed., 1996), pp. 118–119, 152.

The threat   23–39

NOTE 65. But for a statutory right to protect against threats, this must be clearly indicated by the statute: *Mennelll v. Newell and Wright* [1997] I.C.R. 1039, CA (employer requires subscription from workers for training, if necessary to be deducted from wages; not illegal under what are now Employment Rights Act 1996, ss. 13 and 104; threat insufficient to found liability; the assertion of statutory rights was an allegation falling within the statute (Employment Rights Act 1996, s. 104) but on the evidence was not here the reason for dismissal, even though the employer had plainly threatened the dismissed worker that he would make the unlawful deductions). *Quaere* whether such a threat could found an action for intimidation.

NOTE 70. Delete from "In such types of . . . " in line 4 to end of note ("1992,   23–40
CA"). Add after "205–206" in line 4: See now *post* § 23–42A.

NOTE 71. Amend to read: There is no need for the defendant and the victim to be in physical proximity: compare the criminal liabilities in *DPP v. Mills* [1996] 3 W.L.R. 1093, DC; *R. v. Ireland* [1998] AC 147, HL. On "harassment" and the Protection from Harassment Act 1997, see *post*, § 23–42A.

Unlawful act or means   23–41

NOTE 89. Add: Where a defendant has threatened to infringe the plaintiff's statutory rights, statute may provide for a remedy other than an action in tort: see *Mennell v. Newell and Wright* [1997] I.C.R. 1039 CA (action for threat of dismissal when employee refused to accept deductions from wages not valid under Wages Act 1986; action for infringement of statutory rights rejected on appeal: section 60A(1) of the Employment Protection (Consolidation) Act 1978, as amended, see now Employment Rights Act 1996, ss. 13 and 104).

There is little consistency in the decisions based on tort: see the contrast between *Associated British Ports v. TGWU* [1989] 1 WLR 939, CA and *Credit Lyonnais Bank Nederland (now General Bank Netherland) v. Export Credit Guarantee Dept* [1998] 1 Lloyd's Rep. 19, CA (upheld on other grounds [1999] 2 W.L.R. 540, HL); and *Yukong Line of Korea v. Rendsberg Investments Corp (No. 2)* [1998] 1 W.L.R. 294 at 314.

NOTE 96. *Crawley Borough Council v. Ure* [1996] Q.B. 13 at 23–25, *per*   23–42
Glidewell LJ.

NOTE 97. Add: See too on *James v. The Commonwealth* (1938) 62 C.L.R. 364, HCt, the discussion in *Northern Territory v. Mengel* (1995) 185 C.L.R. 307, HCt.

NOTE 98. Amend reference to read: Cornish, *Intellectual Property* (3rd ed., 1996), Chap. 8. On the constituents of liability for breach of confidence: see *Murray v. Yorkshire Fund Managers Ltd* [1998] 1 W.L.R. 951, CA; and for an enthusiastic use of breach of confidence for liability; *Indata Equipment Supplies Ltd v. ACL Ltd, The Times* August 14, 1997, CA, liability for misuse of confidential information: *per* Otton L.J. and Owen J. citing *Lac Minerals v. International Corona* [1990] F.S.R. 441, SCC; Simon Brown L.J. agreed on liability but questioned whether this was the tort of interference by unlawful means. The distinction between the tortious and equitable liability makes no sense "except in historical terms": P. Cane, *Tort Law and Economic Interests* (2nd ed., 1996), p. 75.

NOTE 99: At end insert: *Credit Lyonnais Bank Nederland v. Burch* [1997] 1 All E.R. 144, CA (undue influence: bank third party fixed with a constructive notice where employee manifestly at risk); contrast *Banco Exterior Internacional SA v. Thomas* [1997] 1 W.L.R. 221, CA; *supra* § 23–23.

Insert the following text and notes: It was for some time uncertain whether unreason-   23–42A
able "harassment" could be as such tortious, *e.g.* where a person "stalks" another or subjects them to persistent telephone calls.[1a] Outside the law of tort, the courts have

made use of the concept in extending such remedies as injunctions, not least in family law.[1b] The balance of authority, however, was to the effect that harassment or "ill treatment" short of physical coercion"[1c] were not in themselves tort.[1d] A wider view was taken of some criminal liabilities, such as harassment by telephone calls which were held to be a public nuisance,[1e] and calls which could amount to a criminal "assault" if psychological damage ensued creating fear of immediate violence.[1f]

In the law of tort some judges turned equally to liability for nuisance, as where pickets subjected workers who were using the highway to enter the workplace during a strike to unreasonable harassment[1g] and, by a creative extension of liability for private nuisance, where a defendant had harassed the plaintiff by unwanted telephone calls, thereby interfering with the reasonable enjoyment of the property by all those living in it.[1h] The House of Lords, however, disapproved of the extension of liability in nuisance to a new range of plaintiffs and, preferring to maintain the traditional character of the tort of nuisance as a wrong against property rather than extend the rights of ordinary persons, refused to diverge from the old principle that a person who had no legal interest in the land could not bring an action in tort for a private nuisance.[1i] That tort therefore can provide protection from harassment only for those who have an interest in the land in question or who are lawful users of the highway, though the common law has other principles on which liability for harassment might have been based.[1j]

In 1997, however, Parliament intervened. Under the statute a person commits an offence when he pursues a course of conduct (which includes speech) on at least two occasions, if he knows or ought as a reasonable person to know that it amounts to harassment of another person.[1k] It is a defence to show that the conduct was pursued for the prevention or detection of crime or under any enactment or rule of law or was in the circumstances reasonable. Civil proceedings may be brought by the victim against the person guilty of unlawful harassment on the same principles, and damages may be claimed for "anxiety caused" by it as well as for any financial loss.[1l] Where an injunction is granted and the victim considers the defendant has done anything prohibited in the order, he may apply for a warrant for the arrest of the defendant; and such an act done in breach of an injunction without reasonable cause is in itself an offence.[1m] Acts done on behalf of the Crown by a person specified by the Secretary of State do not give rise to liability where they relate to national security, prevention or detection of serious crime or "the economic well-being of the United Kingdom", a somewhat extended defence for officialdom against the tort of harassment.[1n]

NOTE 1a. See *supra* § 23–39 and *post,* § 23–123, on unreasonable acts done in course of picketing: *Thomas v. NUM (South Wales Area)* [1986] Ch. 20 at 63; but that liability was explained as based on nuisance by Stuart-Smith J. in *News Group Newspapers Ltd v. SOGAT (No. 2)* [1987] I.C.R. 181 at 205, an analysis which appears still to be good law even after *Hunter v. Canary Wharf Ltd* [1997] A.C. 655. HL, *post,* n. 1I, because the plaintiffs had *locus standi* to sue for nuisance as users of the highway.

NOTE 1b. *Burris v. Azdani* [1995] 1 WLR 1372 at 1377, *per* Bingham M.R.; *McCann v. Wright* [1995] 1 W.L.R. 1556, CA; *Johnson v. Walton* [1990] 1 F.L.R. 350, CA. In Australia "it is not acceptable (if it ever was) for a person in authority over another in a work place to harass, belittle or demean that other as a method of enforcing his authority or relieving his frustration", *per* Dodds J., *Carlile v. Council of Shire of Kilkivian and Brietkreutz*, December 2, 1995, Qnsld, noted M. Spry (1997) 10 A.J.L.L. 229, 231.

NOTE 1c. *Davey v. Chief Constable of RUC* [1988] N.I.L.R. 139; but physical coercion can amount to intimidation: *Godwin v. Uzoigwe, The Times*, June 18, 1992, CA.

NOTE 1d. See Waterhouse J., *Patel v. Patel* [1988] 2 F.L.R. 179 at 182, CA; Peter Gibson L.J. dissenting in *Khorasandijan v. Bush* [1993] Q.B. 727 CA, see *post* n. 1h; *Burnett v. George* [1992] 1 F.L.R. 525, CA ("molestation"); *Harrow LBC v Johnstone* [1997] 1 W.L.R. 459, HL (husband protected from "molestation" by wife, but wife able to assert her rights as a joint tenant); *Nicholls v. Nicholls* [1997] 1

W.L.R. 314, CA; J. Murphy (1996) 49 M.L.R. 845. It appears that the courts will be slow to allow the Act to impede mere protests or demonstrations: *Huntingdon Life Sciences Ltd v. Curtin, The Times*, December 11, 1997, Eady J.; also Gardner (1998) 114 L.Q.R. 33, especially after the liberal interpretation of trespass on the highway by the majority in *DPP v. Jones* [1999] 2 W.L.R. 625, HL (Lords Slynn and Hope dissenting), and thereby of Public Order Act 1986, ss.14A, 14B, as amended 1994; compare Case 265/95 *EC Commission v. France, The Times*, December 11, 1997, ECJ (*post*, §§ 23–123, 23–124).

NOTE 1e. *R v. Johnson* [1997] 1 W.L.R. 367, CA (obscene telephone calls to at least 13 women over five years, affected "the comfort and convenience of a section of the public").

NOTE 1f. *R v. Ireland* [1998] A.C. 147, HL (telephone calls followed by silence). See too, *Smith v. Chief Superintendent Woking Police* (1983) 76 Cr. Appr. R. 234; *Barton v. Armstrong* [1969] 2 N.S.W.R. 451 (civil assault by telephone); and *DPP v. Mills* [1997] Q.B. 300 (no need for physical proximity for criminal liability for "intimidation" of witnesses, etc., under (Criminal Justice and Public Order Act 1994, s.51); see *ibid*, s.154, inserting s.4A in Public Order Act 1986, introducing an offence of causing unreasonable "harassment, alarm or distress" by insulting or threatening words, behaviour or visible representation, otherwise than in a dwelling.

NOTE 1g. Stuart-Smith J. in *News Group Newspapers Ltd v. SOGAT (No. 2)* [1987] ICR 181 at 205; see also *supra*, n. 1a.

NOTE 1h. *Khorasandjian v. Bush* [1993] Q.B. 727, CA, Peter Gibson L.J. dissenting on this aspect overruled in *Hunter v. Canary Wharf Ltd* [1997] A.C. 655 HL, see next note.

NOTE 1i. *Hunter v. Canary Wharf Ltd* [1997] A.C. 655, HL, Lord Cooke dissenting, holding (i) interference of television signals by new building not capable of being a tortious nuisance, and (ii) the plaintiffs had no standing to sue for nuisance for deposits of dust from construction work. The Court of Appeal had held that occupation of a family home was sufficient, but in the House of Lords the majority relied in respect of the second action upon the old law stated in *Malone v. Laskey* [1907] 2 K.B. 141, CA (only a person with "exclusive possession" can sue for nuisance, see Lord Goff at 692–694, who found "no analysis" of the problem in academic commentary, when a "crumb of analysis is worth a loaf of opinion", at 694). For an understanding of the social problems inherent in the retention today of the principles of 1907 subjugating the interests of persons to those of property, see Lord Lloyd, at 695 and the analysis in the dissenting speech of Lord Cooke, at 711, 719–722, who was not prepared to retain the confinement of the tort of nuisance to "injury to land", as Lord Hoffman insisted it must be restricted at 706–709; J. Wightman (1998) 61 M.L.R. 870; J. O'Sullivan [1996] C.L.J. 184; on the *Hunter* decision, see P. Cane (1997) 113 L.Q.R. 515.

NOTE 1j. For example the principle in *Wilkinson v. Downton* [1897] 2 Q.B. 57 and *Janvier v. Sweeney* [1919] 2 K.B. 316, CA, (*supra* §§ 12–15, 12–16) provided the intentional harassment had caused injury or (possibly) distress; see Lord Hoffman in *Hunter v. Canary Wharf Ltd* [1997] A.C. 655, who alone appears to take note of this analysis and, thus far therefore, may approve of the actual decision in *Khorasandjian v. Bush* [1993] Q.B. 727, CA; but "it is unnecessary to consider how much the common law might have developed" because the 1997 legislation intervened.

NOTE 1k. Protection from Harassment Act 1997, sections 1, 2 and 7. It is also a separate offence to engage in a course of conduct on two or more occasions causing a fear of violence in another person, if a reasonable person would think that such a fear would result: s.4. Moreover, on conviction under s.2 or s.4, the court has power to restrain the defendant from doing anything described in the order: s.5. On the width of liabilities disclosed in the Act: Herring [1998] C.L.J. 10.

NOTE 1l. *ibid.*, s.3(1) (2). The Act would seem to encompass liability for racist conduct or other "hate-mail" and "hate-calls": compare the problems of a human rights "charter" on these matters: *Canada (Human Rights Commission) v. Canadian Liberty Net* (1998) 157 D.L.R. (4th) 385, SCC. So, too, there appears to be an overlap between the Act and the common law principle of intentional harm in *Wilkinson v. Downton* [1897] 2 Q.B. 57, *supra*, n. 1j.

NOTE 1m. *ibid.* s.3(6). Where a person is punished under these provisions, he is not guilty of contempt: s.3(7). But if he is punished for contempt, the conduct is not punishable further under subs. (6): see s.3(7).

NOTE 1n. See *ibid.*, s.12. Similar provisions apply to Scotland (*ibid.*, ss.8–11) and to Northern Ireland by Order: 1997 No. 1180 (NI9).

23–43   NOTE 2. Amend to read: *Law Debenture Trust Corp. v. Ural Caspian Oil Corp.* [1995] Ch. 152, CA; *Royal Brunei Airlines v. Tan* [1995] 2 A.C. 378, PC, see *supra* § 23–23 n.1. Gardner (1996) 112 L.Q.R. 56. On constructive trustees, see *Brown v. Bennett, The Times*, January 3, 1998; *Re Polly Peck International plc (No. 4), The Times*, May 18, 1998; *Coulthard v. Disco Mix Club*, [1999] 2 All E.R. 457; *French v. Mason, The Times*, November 13, 1998; *Soulas v. Korkontzilas* [1997] S.C.R. 217, SCC (constructive trust an "ancient and eclectic institution" to remedy unjust enrichment and uphold rights to property "in good conscience", at 213–230; see too rejection of inducing breach of trust or breach of fiduciary duty as unlawful means in tort in part rests upon notions of privity disallowing third parties from enforcing a breach: L. Smith (1998) 114 LQR 14: *Stein v. Blake* [1998] 1 All E.R. 724, 727, CA; *Yukong Line of Korea v. Rendsberg Investments Corp. (No. 2)* [1998] 1 W.L.R. 294, *per* Toulson J. (*no locus standi* for creditor). A relaxation allowing third parties to enforce provisions in some contracts for their benefit is to be enacted in the Contracts (Rights of Third Parties) Bill 1999. Contrast the robust approach of the courts to breach of confidence: *Indata Equipment Supplies Ltd v. ACL Ltd, The Times*, August 14, 1997, CA (no fiduciary relationship between the parties; defendant liable for tort of unlawful interference because of "blatant disregard" of commercial ethics in misuse of confidential information; *sed dubitante per* Simon Brown L.J. whether this was the tort of unlawful means; compare *Boulting v. ACTT* [1963] 2 Q.B. 606). See further on the authorities on interfering with fiduciary duties, or trustee's obligations, see *supra*, § 23–28, n. 2 and *post*, § 23–62.

NOTE 6. Amend reference to read: Treitel, *Law of Contract* (9th ed., 1995), pp. 404–405.

NOTE 7. Add: See *Mid Kent Holdings plc v. General Utilities plc* [1997] 1 W.L.R. 14 (no private cause of action under Fair Trading Act 1973, s.93); *post* § 23–67 nn. 67, 68; Competition Act 1998.

NOTE 8: Delete from "On recent . . . " to end; and insert: The wider liability suggested by *Beaudesert Shire Council v. Smith* (1996) 120 C.L.R. 145 has now been rejected in *Northern Territory v. Mengel* (1995) 185 C.L.R. 307, HCt (the *Beaudesert Shire* decision is "no longer good law"; approving *Kitano v. Commonwealth* (1974) 129 C.L.R. 151); and see B. McDonald and J. Swanton (1995) 69 A.L.J. 868; but for a lament at the death of the wider liability: N. Mullany (1995) 111 L.Q.R. 583. It has been said that misuse of statutory powers is enough (*Cheticamp Fisheries Co-op v. Canada* (1995) 123 D.L.R. (4th) 121 (N.S. CA), but in such a case liability would seem more appropriately measured by the wrong of misfeasance in public office: see *supra* § 16–139; *Three Rivers District Council v. Bank of England (No. 3)* [1996] 3 All E.R. 558; *Three Rivers District Council (No. 4) The Times*, December 10, 1998, CA, (misfeasance in public office, need for deliberate intention or recklessness; Auld L.J. dissenting).

23–44   NOTE 12. The Attorney-General has a right, also, to begin proceedings in the civil courts where this is necessary in the public interest to prevent the consequences of criminal activity: *Att.-Gen. v. Blake* [1997] Ch. 84. In a sense this may be seen as a mirror image of the civil action in *Springhead Spinning Co v. Riley* (1868) L.R. 6 Eq. 551 (if it still exists), see *post*, § 23–47, note 54 and § 23–65, note 10

NOTE 13. Add: But the court has jurisdiction in civil proceedings to grant injunctive relief to restrain the dissemination of an instrument of fraud: *British Telecommunications plc v. One In a Million* [1998] 4 All E.R. 476, CA (Internet domain names).

NOTE 14. Add: See for other examples of the "construction" principle: *R. v. Northavon District Council ex p Palmer, The Times*, August 1, 1995, CA; *R. v. Portsmouth City Council, ex p. Bonaco Builders* (unreported June 6, 1995), see S. Arrowsmith (1996) 3 P.P.L.R. CS90 (breach of compulsory competitive tendering rules under Local Government, Planning and Land Act 1980 does not afford an action in tort): compare the statutory civil right of action in the Public Works Contracts 1991, SI 1991 No. 2680 (implementing what is now EC Directive 93/36); compare *Great House at Sonning Ltd (The) v. Berkshire County Council* [1996] R.T.R. 407, CA (validity of order open to challenge only by way of judicial review, not private rights; Saville L.J. dissenting, whose judgment is to be preferred after *Boddington v. British Transport Police* [1998] 2 W.L.R. 639, HL); *Issa v. Hackney LBC* [1997] 1 W.L.R. 956, CA; *Bermuda Cablevision v. Colica Trust* [1997] I.R.L.R. 346.

NOTE 17. Amend to read: *Macmillian Bloedel Ltd v. Simpson* (1997) 137 D.L.R. (4th) 637, SCC. The defendant may challenge the validity of the legislation, *e.g.* Orders or byelaws, see *e.g. Boddington v. British Transport Police* [1998] 2 W.L.R. 639; but the courts have sometimes treated welfare or regulatory legislation from which groups of individuals benefit as legislation not passed for their advantage as a class, but passed for the "benefit of society in general": *O'Rourke v. Camden L.B.C.* [1998] A.C. 188, HL (approving Lord Browne-Wilkinson in *X (Minors) v. Bedfordshire County Council* [1995] 2 A.C. 633 at 731–732), thereby limiting their right to launch a civil action. See *K.A. Feakins v. Dover Harbour Board, The Times*, September 9, 1998 (no right of action for exporters of animals against harbour board bound to keep harbour, dock and pier "open to all persons"), but compare *Blue Circle Industries plc v. Ministry of Defence* [1999] 2 W.L.R. 295, CA (damage from overflowing radioactive pond; statutory duties permit damages for economic loss).

NOTE 23. Amend to read: *Law Debenture Trust Corp. v. Ural Caspian Oil Corp.* [1995] Ch. 152, CA.   **23–46**

NOTE 54. Amend to read: *MacMillan Bloedel Ltd v. Simpson* (1997) 137 D.L.R. (4th) 637, SCC.   **23–47**

NOTE 56. Add at the end: But remarkably Stuart-Smith L.J. subsequently held in *Credit Lyonnais Bank Nederland (now Generale Bank Nederland) v. Export Credit Guarantee Department* [1998] 1 Lloyd's Rep. 19 at 32, CA (upheld on other grounds [1999] 2 W.L.R. 540, HL), that the unlawful means in conspiracy must be actionable by the plaintiff, the classical principle followed in *Yukong Line of Korea v. Rendsberg Investments Corp (No. 2)* [1998] 1 W.L.R. 294 at 314; see § 23–61, n.76 and § 23–81. Contrast *Associated British Ports v. TGWU* [1989] 1 W.L.R. 939 (reversed on other grounds; *ibid*, HL).   **23–48**

NOTE 63. Amend to read: *Law Debenture Trust Corp. v. Ural Caspian Oil Corp.* [1995] Ch. 152, CA.   **23–50**

NOTE 64. On privity of contract see the Law Commission Report No. 242 (Cm. 3329); N. Adams, D. Beyleveld, R. Brownswood (1997) 60 M.L.R. 230; Reynolds (1997) 113 L.Q.R. 53; Contracts (Rights of Third Parties) Bill 1999.

NOTE 72. At end add: It is instructive that comparative scholars have understood the House of Lords' decision in *Rookes v. Barnard* [1964] A.C. 1129, HL, to put English law into the rather odd posture whereby "threats to commit breaches of contract undoubtedly constitute unlawful means" but, by contrast, "so far as actual breaches of contract are concerned, it would seem that the English law doctrine of privity of contract precludes A from suing B because B's breach of contract with C has caused loss to A, even if that was B's intention": W. van Gerven *et al, Tort Law, Scope of Protection* (1998) p. 257; *supra*, § 23–01 n. 1, and see *post*, § 23–72, § 23–84.

NOTE 74. Add: But a demand for an increased price not permitted by a contract,   **23–51** may not even be a repudiation of the contract especially where it involves a genuinely held but erroneous view as to the effect of the contract, though subsequent conduct may evince an intention not to be bound: *Vaswani v. Italian Motors* [1996] 1 W.L.R. 270 at 276–277, PC (Lord Woolf); but intimidation was not argued in that case and there appears to have been no coercive threat.

23–52   Note 88. Amend to read: *MacMillan Bloedel Ltd v. Simpson* (1997) 137 D.L.R. (4th) 637, SCC.

23–55   Note 16. Add at end: ; see the discussion in *Ranger Uranium Mines v. Federation Miscellaneous Workers Union* [1987] 54 N.T.R. 6 (1988) I.L.L.R. 429 (justification pleaded despite unlawful means).

4.—Unlawful Interference

23–57   **Unlawful interference with economic and other interests**
Note 32. Add: The interference must be "directed at the plaintiff" but no doctrine of "constructive intent to injure" is appropriate in this tort: *Cheticamp Fisheries Co-op v. Canada* (1995) 123 D.L.R. 121, 132, N.S. CA.
Note 36. Add: ; and see D Howarth, *Textbook on Tort* (1995), pp. 479–484.
Note 38. Add: ; and see *Cheticamp Fisheries Co-op v. Canada* (1995) 123 D.L.R. 121, N.S. CA: "intent to injure is the essence of unlawful interference".

23–59   **Unlawful means**
Note 45. Add at end: Compare the powers of the Attorney-General in *R. v. Blake* [1997] 1 W.L.R. 1167.
Note 46. Add at end: *Chapman v. Honig* [1963] 2 Q.B. 502 was approved by the House of Lords in *Harrow LBC v. Johnstone* [1997] 1 W.L.R. 459 (see especially Lord Hoffman at 471); but the approach of Lord Denning MR to contempt in *Att.-Gen. v. Butterworth* [1963] 1 Q.B. 696, 719, was approved in *Connolly v. Dale* [1996] Q.B. 120 at 125, DC; *Harrow LBC v. Johnstone* [1997] 1 W.L.R. 459, HL (no contempt where wife and council arrange for tenancy not to be renewed; not a molestation of husband); compare *Brown v. Durham Region Police* (1996) 134 D.L.R. (4th) 177, Ont.
Note 47. Amend to read: *Law Debenture Trust Corp. v. Ural Caspian Oil Corp.* [1995] Ch. 152, CA.
Note 52. Amend to read: *Re. Supply of Ready Mixed Concrete* [1995] I.C.R. 25, HL.

23–60   Note 55. Add at end: On the other hand, an unlawful purpose is not actionable where it is unconnected with a relevant act or threat: see *Brown v. Durham Regional Police Force* (1996) 134 D.L.R. (4th) 177, Ont.
Note 56. Add after "81–267": and now *Northern Territory of Australia v. Mengel* (1995) 185 C.L.R. 307, HCt. Delete from "compare" to end and insert: and on the overruling of the *Beaudesert* case in *Northern Territory v. Mengel* (1995) 185 C.L.R. 307, HCt.

23–61   Note 74. Add: Compare *Bogajewicz v. Sony of Canada* (1996) 128 D.L.R. (4th) 530, Queb. SC: use of photographs an interference with fundamental right to dignity and reputation: constitutional Charter, s.4; and see R. St M. Hylton and P. Goldson, "The New Tort of Appropriation of Personality" [1996] C.L.J. 56, on Commonwealth extensions of the tort of passing off: especially *Robert Marley Foundation v. Dino Michelle Ltd* (unreported May 12, 1994); but see *Goold Estate v. Stoddart Publishing Co* (1998) 161 D.L.R. (4th) 321, Ont CA, and contrast *Harrods Ltd v. Harrodian School, The Times*, April 3, 1996, CA (link between names insufficient to establish passing off).
Note 75. Add at end: *Ernst and Young v. Butte Mining* [1996] 1 WLR 1605.

After "488" in line 4, insert: *Bennett v. Commissioner of Police of the Metropolis, The Times*, October 24, 1997, (Scott V.-C., misfeasance in public office not made out).

NOTE 76. Add at end: But the courts have come to regard breach of fiduciary duty to a company as insufficient, see *Stein v. Blake* [1998] 1 All E.R. 724, CA; *Yukong Line Ltd v. Investments Corp (No. 2)* [1998] 1 W.L.R. 294 (a director in breach of his fiduciary duty owed to the company does not owe a parallel duty to third parties, such as creditors). But contrast the approach in *Coulthard v. Disco Mix Club Ltd* [1999] 2 All E.R. 457; *Apotex Fermentation Inc. v. Novopharm Ltd* (1998) 162 D.L.R. (4th) 111, Man. CA.

NOTE 77. Insert after "above § 23–43, n.2 ": See *Crawley BC v. Ure* [1996] Q.B. **23–62** 13 at 23–25, CA (leaving open the question whether there is no tort of procuring breach of fiduciary duty as held in *Metall und Rohstoff AG v. Donaldson Lufkin & Jenrette* [1990] 1 Q.B. 392 at 481, *per* Slade L.J.). On the need for dishonesty *and* knowledge in a third party to be liable as an "accessory" to breach of trust, see *Royal Brunei Airlines v. Tan* [1995] 2 A.C. 378, PC *per* Lord Nicholls at 382, and *Brinks Ltd v. Abu-Saleh (No. 3), The Times*, October 23, 1995; S. Gardner (1996) 112 L.Q.R. 56; and *supra* § 23–23, n.1.

Add at end: On liability as a constructive trustee, see *Brown v. Bennett, The Times*, January 3, 1998, Rattee J., on secondary liability: actual breach and knowing assistance for liability as a constructive trustee, applying *Royal Brunei Airlines v. Tan* [1995] 2 A.C. 378 at 382; *Soulos v. Korkontzilas* (1997) 146 D.L.R. (4th) 214, SCC (constructive trust, an "ancient and eclectic institution" to remedy unjust enrichment and retention of property persons should not have "in good conscience", see *per* La Forest J. *et al.* at 221–230; *Citadel General Assurance v. Lloyds Bank Canada* (1998). 152 D.L.R. (4th) 411, SCC (knowing receipt of trust funds; "assisting" a breach not enough); *Toronto Dominion Bank v. Carotenuto* (1968) 154 D.L.R. (4th) 627, B.C. CA. *Dubai Aluminium v. Salaam* [1999] 1 Lloyd's Rep. 415 (vicarious liability of partner as a constructive trustee), *French v. Mason, The Times*, November 13 1998; *Satnam Investments v. Dunlop Heywood* [1993] 3 All E.R. 652, CA (mere knowledge of breach of fiduciary duty not making recipient constructive trustee; "commercial good sense" without dishonesty). Rejection of inducing breach of trust or a breach of fiduciary duty as unlawful means in tort often owes much to the need to prevent third parties not within the bounds of privity from enforcing such duties: *Stein v. Blake* [1998] 1 All E.R. 724 at 727, CA (company the only plaintiff); *Yukong Line of Korea v. Rendsberg Investments Corp. (No. 2)* [1998] 1 W.L.R. 294, *per* Toulson J, (no *locus standi* for creditor complaining about a breach of fiduary duty, see *post*). It is not always clear why this should be so compared with the robust approach of the courts to breach of confidence: see *Indata Equipment Supplies Ltd v. ACL Ltd, The Times*, August 14, 1997, CA (misuse of confidential information as unlawful means). On liability for breach of confidence: *Murray v. Yorkshire Fund Managers Ltd* [1998] 1 W.L.R. 951, CA, see *post*, § 23–62. On compensation in equity for breach of fiduciary duty: *Nationwide Building Society v. Various Solicitors (No. 3), The Times*, March 1, 1999. On rejection of "privity" where the alleged unlawfulness is a breach of contract, see *post Rookes v. Barnard* [1965] A.C. 1129, HL, § 23–72.

NOTE 78. Amend to: Law *Debenture Trust Corp. v. Ural Caspian Oil Corp.* [1995] Ch. 152, CA.

NOTE 79. Add at end: Actions for breach of confidence can be met with a public interest defence: *Hellewell v. Chief Constable of Derbyshire* [1995] 1 W.L.R. 804. No action for breach of confidence will lie unless the information has a confidential quality, was imparted in circumstances where a confidential obligation existed and its use was unauthorised: *Maudsely v. Palumbo, The Times*, December 19, 1995.

NOTE 81. Add: See too P. Cane (1966) 112 L.Q.R. 13, 16 (on *X v. Bedfordshire County Council* [1995] 2 A.C. 633, HL). So too *Associated British Ports v. TGWU* [1989] 1 W.L.R. 939, CA and HL, especially *per* Stuart-Smith L.J. at 964–966, Butler-Sloss L.J. at 959–962. But see the Court of Appeal in *Credit Lyonnais Bank*

*Nederland (now Generale Bank Nederland NV) v. Export Credit Guarantee Depart-
ment* [1988] 1 Lloyd's Rep 19 at 32, CA (upheld on different grounds: [1999] 2
W.L.R. 540, HL) where Stuart-Smith L.J. has been understood to say that the unlawful means must be actionable *in itself* by the plaintiff, despite his judgment to the
opposite effect in *Associated British Ports v. TGWU* [1989] 1 W.L.R. at 939, 965–
966, see *Yukong Line of Korea v. Rendsberg Investments Corp. (No. 2)* [1988] 1
WLR 294, *per* Toulson J. at 314: "the law on this point is as stated by Stuart-Smith
L.J. in *Generale Bank Nederland NV v. Export Credits Guarantee Dept* [1998] 1
Lloyd's Rep 19, 32 that in an unlawful act conspiracy, the act relied upon must be
actionable at the suit of the plaintiff". *Quaere* whether a trustee whose liability is
excluded short of actual fraud (as in *Armitage v. Nurse* [1998] Ch. 241, CA), may
be treated as guilty of "unlawful means" parallel to a party to a contract who is
protected only by a *force majeure* clause (*e.g. Torquay Hotel v. Cousins* [1969] 2
Ch. 106, CA as interpreted in *Associated British Ports v. TGWU* [1989] 1 W.L.R.
939, CA).

NOTE 82. Delete from "Heydon" to end, and insert: *Northern Territory v. Mengel*
(1995) 185 C.L.R. 307, HCt, overruled the *Beaudesert Shire* decision (*supra*, § 23–
43, n. 8). The objections of N. Mullany (1995) 111 L.Q.R. 583 would create an
unduly wide liability.

23–63   NOTE 85. Amend to read: *West Wiltshire District Council v. Garland* [1995] Ch.
297, CA.

NOTE 88. Add at end: But see now *Mid-Kent Holdings plc v. General Utilities
plc* [1997] 1 WLR 14; see *supra*, § 23–43, n. 7 and § 23–44. But acts which are
ultra vires by reason of a statute rendering them void are not unlawful means:
Sanders v. Snell (1998) 72 A.L.J.R. 1507, HCt; McCarry (1999) 12 A.J.L.L. 56.

NOTE 91. Add at end: *Northern Territory v. Mengel* (1995) 185 C.L.R. 307, HCt.

NOTE 92. Add: Case C-178/94 *Dillenkofer v. Germany* [1997] I.R.L.R. 60, ECJ.

23–64   NOTE 95. Add at end: That case was however decided before *Lonrho Ltd v. Shell
Petroleum (No. 2)* [1982] A.C. 173, HL.

NOTE 96. Add at end: See reliance on breach of statutory duty, Barrett (1998) 27
I.L.J. 59. Although it is now open to judges to consult the debates in Parliament, in
many such areas of life as safety at work, in order to seek the intention of Parliament,
they "do not have to go to Hansard to ascertain this": Lord Johnstone *Littlejohn v.
Wood and Davidson* 1997 S.L.T. 1353 at 1355, Court of Sess, Outer House; compare
Alcock v. Chief Constable of South Yorkshire Police [1992] 1 A.C. 310, HL; *Young
v. Charles Church (Southern) Ltd, The Times*, May 1, 1997, CA (breach of regulations preventing electrocution at work; psychiatric illness actionable after seeing
colleague electrocuted). Where delegated legislation or byelaws are the alleged
ground of illegality, it is open to the defendant in the action to prove that they are
ultra vires and illegal: *Boddington v. British Transport Police* [1998] 2 W.L.R. 639
HL; but compare *Secretary of Defence v. Percy* [1999] 1 All E.R. 732.

NOTE 98. Add at end: *Mid-Kent Holdings plc v. General Holdings plc* [1997] 1
W.L.R. 14.

NOTE 99. Add: ; and see on the "policy" of the statute, *Stovin v. Wise* [1996] AC
923, HL.

NOTE 2. Add: See now: *R. v. Northavon District Council, ex p. Palmer, The
Times*, August 1, 1995, CA; *R. v. Portsmouth City Council, ex p. Bonaco Builders*
(unreported June 6, 1995); S. Arrowsmith (1996) 3 P.P.L.R. CS90 (breach of compulsory competitive tendering rules under Local Government Planning and Land Act
1980 does not afford an action in tort); compare *Great House at Sonning Ltd (The)
v. Berkshire County Council,* [1996] R.T.R. 407, CA (validity of order under Act
open to challenge only by judicial review; Saville L.J. dissenting, *supra*, § 23–44, n
14).

23–65   NOTE 5. Amend to read: *West Wiltshire District Council v. Garland* [1995] Ch.
297, CA.

NOTE 6. Add at end: See *Credit Lyonnais Bank Nederland (now General Bank Nederland) v. Export Credit Guarantee Department* [1999] 2 W.L.R. 540, HL at 549–551, *per* Lord Woolf M.R. (for liability as a joint tortfeasor; assisting a tort is not enough).

NOTE 8. Add at end: The House of Lords appears to have accepted that the unlawful act must not only be more than "facilitating" the tort, but must be actionable *per se* by the plaintiff: *Credit Lyonnais Bank Nederland (now Generale Bank Nederland) v. Export Credit Guarantee Department* [1999] 2 W.L.R. 540: upholding on different grounds the Court of Appeal [1998] 1 Lloyd's Rep. 19, see especially Stuart-Smith LJ at 32, ; and *Yukong Line of Korea v. Rendsberg Investments Corp (No. 2)* [1998] 1 W.L.R. 294, *per* Toulson J. at 312–314.

NOTE 10. Amend to read: *MacMillan Bloedel Ltd v. Simpson* (1997) 137 D.L.R. (4th) 637, SCC.   **23–66**

NOTE 19. Add at end: So too, *per* Knox J., *Mid-Kent Holdings plc v. General Holdings plc* [1997] 1 W.L.R. 1428–1437; but it is significant that no argument appears to have been advanced here based on the reasoning of the Court of Appeal in *Associated British Ports v. TGWU* [1989] 1 WLR 939, especially at 958–966, see *post* § 23–69.

NOTE 23. Add at end: *O'Rourke v. Camden LBC* [1998] A.C. 188 HL, approving Lord Browne-Wilkinson in *X (Minors) v. Bedfordshire County Council* [1995] 2 A.C. 633 at 731–732; although welfare legislation does in fact provide protection to those individuals particularly affected by that activity, the legislation is to be treated as being passed not necessarily for the benefit of those individuals as a class but for the benefit of society in general.

NOTE 24. Add: For other examples of the "construction test" see *supra*, § 23–44, nn.13–15; *Olotu v. Home Office* [1997] 1 W.L.R. 328 CA (no civil action under Prosecution of Offences Act 1985); *Mid Kent Holdings plc v. General Utilities plc* [1997] 1 W.L.R. 14 (enactment must disclose an intention to provide "a civil remedy for the particular wrong which the plaintiff will or may suffer", *per* Knox J, 37) *Blue Circle Inds v. Ministry of Defence* [1999] 2 W.L.R. 295, CA. Compare *supra*, § 23–48; but see also *post*, § 23–69.   **23–68**

NOTE 28. Amend reference to *MacMillan Bloedel Ltd v. Simpson* (1997) 138 D.L.R. (4th) 637 (SCC).

NOTE 43. Amend to read: *Law Debenture Trust Corp. v. Ural Caspian Oil Corp.* [1995] Ch. 152, CA.   **23–69**

NOTE 44. Add at end: *KA Feakins Ltd v. Dover Harbour Board, The Times*, September 9, 1998 (general administrative function with discretion).

NOTE 45. Amend to read: *Law Debenture Trust Corp. v. Ural Caspian Oil Corp.* [1995] Ch. 152, CA. Moreover, Stuart-Smith L.J. himself held that the unlawful means must be in itself actionable by the plaintiff; *Credit Lyonnais Bank Nederland (now Generale Bank Nederland) v. Export Credit Guarantee Department* [1998] 1 Lloyd's Rep. 19, CA at 32, followed in *Yukong Line of Korea v. Rendsberg Investments Corp (No. 2)* [1998] 1 W.L.R. 294, *per* Toulson J. at 314, (liability for conspiracy by unlawful means requires that the illegality must be actionable at the suit of the plaintiff); the point was not expressly dealt with in the House of Lords, [1999] 2 W.L.R. 540, HL.

In *Wilson v. Housing Corporation* [1997] I.R.L.R. 346 (where the plaintiff's claim was for "inducing unfair dismissal") Dyson J. appears *per incuriam* to overlook the arresting reasoning of Butler-Sloss and Stuart-Smith L.J.J. in the dock strike case by which liability for unlawful means can arise even if the breach of statutory duty is not actionable (959–965, see *supra* nn. 35–40) when he insists that the breach of statutory duty must be "actionable in the courts" before it can be unlawful means. On the need for codification of liabilities stemming from breach of statutory duties: Bennion (1996) 17 Stat. L.R. 192.

23–70   NOTE 49. Amend to read: *Crawley Borough Council v. Ure* [1996] Q.B. 13 at 23–25, CA. On the refusal to treat breach of trust of fiduciary duty as unlawful means generally, primarily by reason of such duties being owed to particular beneficiaries, see *supra*, § 23–23. Contrast breach of confidence: *Indata Equipment Supplies Ltd v. ACL Ltd, The Times*, August 14, 1997, CA: breach of equitable duties in misuse of confidential information as unlawful means: *per* Otton L.J., citing *Lac Minerals v. International Corona* [1990] F.S.R. 441, SCC; but compare the doubts on the basis of liability, Simon Brown L.J.; *Satnam Investments Ltd v. Dunlop Heywood Ltd* [1999] 3 All E.R. 652, CA.

NOTE 51. Amend to read: *Gower's Principles of Modern Company Law* (1997, P. Davies ed.) pp. 263–280; *Apotex Fermentation Inc v Novopharm Ltd* (1998) 162 D.L.R. (4th), Man. CA.

NOTE 52. Add at end: *Credit Lyonnais Bank Nederland (now General Bank Nederland) v. Export Credit Guarantee Department* [1999] 2 W.L.R. 540, HL.

23–71   NOTE 62. Add at end: But a defendant may challenge the legality of delegated legislation, thereby overcoming the alleged unlawful means inherent in his breach of it: *Boddington v. British Transport Police* [1998] 2 W.L.R. 639, HL.

NOTE 64. Delete from after "but see now" to end, and insert: The *Beaudesert* doctrine has now been overruled in *Northern Territory v. Mengel* (1995) 185 C.L.R. 307, HCt, see N. Mullany (1995) 111 L.Q.R. 583 for objections to this judgment; and *supra* § 23–43, n. 8. In line 9, after ". . . 742–745" add: ; *UFCW Local 1518 v. K Mart Canada* (1997) 149 DLR (4th) 1, B.C. CA; *RWDSU v. Pepsi Cola* (1999) 167 D.L.R.; (4th) 412 (Sask. CA): secondary picketing not *per se* unlawful).

NOTE 66. Add: ; and see *Great House at Sonning Ltd (The) v. Berkshire County Council,* [1996] R.T.R. 407, CA; but note the dissenting judgment of Saville L.J. who upholds private rights under the statute: *supra*, § 23–44, n. 4. His judgment is now to be preferred in the light of *Boddington v. British Transport Police* [1998] 2 W.L.R. 639, HL; but see *Secretary of Defence v. Percy* [1999] 1 All E.R. 732.

NOTE 67. At end add: *R v. Chief Constable of Sussex, ex p. International Trader's Ferry Ltd* [1998] 3 W.L.R. 1260, HL (effect of Arts 34 and 36 of the Treaty of Rome); but pet.all. [1997] 1 W.L.R. 1092, HL. Compare Case C-46/93 *Commission v. France*, December 9, 1997, ECJ, post, § 23–124, note 9a.

NOTE 68. Add at end: "See too, *Brasserie du Pêcheur v. Germany* (178/94) [1996] 1 E.C.R. 1029, ECJ; Craig (1997) 113 L.Q.R. 67.

NOTE 70. At end add: Case 178/94 *Dillenkofer v. Germany* (46/93) [1997] I.R.L.R. 60, ECJ.

23–73   NOTE 79. Insert in line 3 after "703": *Salmond and Heuston on the Law of Torts* (21st ed., 1996), pp. 346, 362–363; Barrow, *Industrial Relations Law* (1997), pp. 290–295; Cane, *Tort Law and Economic Interests* (2nd ed., 1996), p. 130.

Insert in line 5 after "189": See too for partial, but significant recognition of the problem: W van Gerven *et al, Tort Law: Scope of Protection (1998)*, p. 257, *supra* § 23–01, n. 1; T. Weir, *Economic Torts* (1997), pp. 66–67.

23–76   NOTE 1. Add at end: also *R v. Secretary of State for Home Department ex p Gilmore* [1998] 2 W.L.R. 6 at 18.

5.—CONSPIRACY

23–77   NOTE 6. At end add: On pleading conspiracy to defraud along with deceit and breach of trust: *Paragon Finance plc v. Thakerar* [1999] 1 All E.R. 400; *supra*, § 23–07.

23–78   **The combination**

NOTE 22. Add at end: But see now *Yukong Line of Korea v. Rendsberg Investments Corp (No. 2)* [1998] 1 W.L.R. 294, *post*, § 23–83, n. 88.

NOTE 23. Amend to read: *Meridian Global Funds Management Asia v. Securities*

Commission [1995] 2 A.C. 500; compare *R. v. Gateway Foodmarkets* [1997] I.C.R. 382, CA; *Williams v. Natural Life Health Food Ltd* [1998] 1 W.L.R. 830, HL; R. Grantham and C. Rickett (1999) 62 M.L.R. 133.

NOTE 27. Add at end: ; see *Yukong Life of Korea v. Rendsberg Investments Corp (No. 2)* [1998] 1 W.L.R. 294, *per* Toulson J. at 314, relying on Stuart-Smith L.J. in *Credit Lyonnais Bank Nederland (now Generale Bank Nederland) v. Export Credits Guarantee Department* ([1998] 1 Lloyd's Rep. 19 at 32: in unlawful act conspiracy, the act relied upon "must be actionable at the suit of the plaintiff" (upheld on other grounds [1999] 2 W.L.R. 540, HL).

NOTE 32. Add at end: For an equivalence between being a joint tortfeasor and party to a conspiracy, see *Credit Lyonnais Bank Nederland (now General Bank Nederland) v. Export Credit Guarantee Department* [1999] 2 W.L.R., 540, HL (where no claim rested on conspiracy: Lord Woolf M.R. at 548–549); *British Telecommunications v. One in a Million* [1998] 4 All E.R. 476 at 486–487, CA, *per* Aldous L.J.   **23–79**

NOTE 33. After "140, CA" insert: See the analysis by Hobhouse L.J., *Credit Lyonnais Bank Nederland (now General Bank Nederland) v. Export Credit Guarantee Department* [1998] 1 Lloyd's Rep. 19, CA, especially Hobhouse L.J. at 42–46; *Mahoney v. Kruschich* (1984) 156 C.L.R. 522, HCt.

NOTE 39. Amend and insert after "but see": *Crawley Borough Council v. Ure* [1996] Ch. 13, CA; *Royal Brunei Airlines v. Tan* [1995] 2 A.C. 378, PC; and see *Brinks Ltd v. Abu Saleh (No. 3), The Times*, October 23, 1995 (*supra*, § 23–23, nn. 1,2. Add at end: See on constructive trusts: *Re Polly Peck International plc (No. 4), The Times*, May 18, 1998; *United Mizrahi Bank Ltd v. Doherty* [1998] 1 W.L.R. 435; *Soulos v. Korkontzilas* [1997] S.C.R. at 217, 221, S.C.C., an "ancient and eclectic institution" to remedy unjust enrichment and prevent person retaining property they should give up "in good conscience", *per* La Forest J. Smith (1998) 114 L.Q.R. 14; and Grantham and Rickett (1998) 114 L.Q.R. 357 (an especially helpful note). The courts' dislike of inducing breach of trust or breach of fiduciary duty as unlawful means in tort points to the parallel concept of privity whereby third parties cannot enforce fiduciary duties: *Stein v. Blake* [1998] 1 All E.R. 724 at 727, 730 , CA; *Yukong Line of Korea v. Rendsberg Investments Corp (No. 2)* [1998] 1 W.L.R. 294, *Satnam Investments v. Dunlop Heywood Ltd* [1999] 3 All E.R. 652, CA; (no *locus standi* for creditor); compare *Credit Lyonnais Bank Nederland (now General Bank Nederland) v. Export Credit Guarantee Department* [1998] 1 Lloyd's Rep. 19, CA, Hobhouse L.J. at 42–46 upheld on other grounds, [1999] 2 W.L.R. 540, HL. Contrast the broader approach to breach of confidence: *Indata Equipment Supplies Ltd v. ACL Ltd, The Times*, August 14, 1997, CA (misuse of confidential information; but *per* Simon Brown L.J., although wrongful this may not be the tort of use of unlawful means). On constructive trusts see too: *Satnam Investments Ltd v. Dunlop Heywood Ltd, The Times*, December 31, 1998, CA; *Re Polly Peck International (No. 4), The Times*, May 18 1998; *French v. Mason, The Times*, November 13, 1998; and fiduciary duties: *Nationwide Building Society v. Various Solicitors (No. 3), The Times*, March 1, 1999; *Citadel General Assurance v. Lloyd's Bank Canada* (1998) 152 DLR (4th) 411, SCC (whether bank liable for knowingly receiving funds, whether or not "assisted" in breach of trust). On the constituents of liability for breach of confidence: *Murray v. Yorkshire Fund Managers Ltd* [1998] 1 W.L.R. 951, CA; *supra*, § 23–23 and § 23–62.   **23–80**

NOTE 40. Add at end: *Silcott v. Commissioner of Police of the Metropolis, The Times*, July 9, 1996, CA.

NOTE 46. Add at end: But Stuart-Smith L.J. himself has been taken to reject this possibility, at least for liability in conspiracy: *Credit Lyonnais Bank Nederland (now General Bank Nederland) v. Export Credit Guarantee Department* [1998] 1 Lloyd's Rep. 19, CA, at 32, followed in *Yukong Line v. Rendsburg Investments Corp. of Korea (No. 2)* [1998] 1 W.L.R. 294 (no fiduciary duty to creditor).

23–81   NOTE 47. Add at end: See too now the opposite view in *Credit Lyonnais Bank Nederland (now General Bank Nederland) v. Export Credit Guarantee Deptartment* [1998] 1 Lloyd's Rep 19 at 32, CA (upheld on other grounds *ibid* [1999] 2 W.L.R. 540, HL) applied in *Yukong Line of Korea v. Rendsberg Investments Corp (No. 2)* [1998] 1 W.L.R. 294, *per* Toulson J. at 314: "the law on this point is as stated by Stuart-Smith L.J. in *General Bank Nederland NV v. Export Credits Guarantee Dept* ([1998] 1 Lloyd's Rep 19, 32) that in an unlawful act conspiracy the act relied upon must be actionable at the suit of the plaintiff" (Stuart-Smith L.J. relied on part of the sentence of the text in *post*, § 23–80, but not on what followed).

NOTE 49. Add at end: In an actionable conspiracy based upon unlawful means there must be more than recklessness: S. Todd *et al., Law of Torts in New Zealand* (2nd ed. 1997), pp. 715–716, citing *N.Z. Jet Boat River Racing Inc v. N.Z. Seamen's Union* [1990] 1 N.Z.I.L.R. 529, and *Van Camp Chocolates v. Aulsebrooks* [1984] 1 N.Z.L.R. 354.

NOTE 59. Add: ; *Beaudesert Shire* has now been overruled in *Northern Territory v. Mengel* (1995) 185 C.L.R. 307, HCt, *supra*, § 23–43, n. 8.

NOTE 62. Add at end: But see the opposite view in *Credit Lyonnais Bank Nederland (now Generale Bank Nederland) v. Export Credit Guarantee Department* [1998] 1 Lloyd's Rep. 19, CA (aff'd by H.L. [1999] 2 W.L.R. 540).

23–82   NOTE 67. Add: On the "construction test" see *supra*, §§ 23–44, 23–64; *Olatu v. Home Office* [1997] 1 W.L.R. 328, CA (no civil action under Prosecution of Offenders Act 1985); *Mid Kent Holdings plc v. General Utilities plc* [1997] 1 W.L.R. 14 (enactment must disclose an intention "to provide a civil remedy for the particular wrong which the plaintiff will or may suffer", *per* Knox J. at 37).

NOTE 81. Amend to read: *Law Debenture Trust Corp. v. Ural Caspian Oil Corp.* [1995] Ch. 152, CA.

NOTE 84. At end add: *Meehan v. Tremblett* (1996) 133 D.L.R. (4th) 738, N.B. CA (alleged conspiracy to falsify records).

NOTE 85. Insert after "wrongdoing)": See now the formulations on "intention" by Mason CJ in *Northern Territory v. Mengel* (1995) 1.8.5. CLR 307, HCt.

NOTE 86. Add: On breach of confidence, see *Maudsley v. Palumbo, The Times*, December 19, 1995, Knox J.; and *Indata Equipment Supplies Ltd v. ACL The Times*, August 14, 1997, CA: disregard of commercial ethics in misuse of confidential information: *per* Otton L.J., citing *Lac Minerals v. International Corona* [1990] F.S.R. 441, SCC.

NOTE 87. Amend to read: *per* Glidewell L.J. in *Crawley Borough Council v. Ure* [1996] Q.B. 13 at 23–25.

NOTE 88. No defence of contributory negligence is available in such cases: *Corporacion Nacional del Cobre de Chile v. Sogemin Metals Ltd* [1997] 1 W.L.R. 1396, [1997] 2 All E.R. 917(bribery), *per* Carnwath J. at 920–926. But see *Nationwide Building Society v. Various Solicitors (No. 3), The Times* March 1, 1999 (claimant's behaviour may make damage too remote). Breach of director's fiduciary duty, however, may not be unlawful means. In *Yukong Line of Korea v. Rendsberg Investments Corp. (No. 2)* [1998] 1 W.L.R. 294, a shipowner sued various defendants including Y for repudiation of a charterparty signed for the brokers of X Corporation, by its director Y. The market having fallen, Y later repudiated the charterparty on behalf of the brokers. His predominant purpose was to shelter the assets of X by passing them to L, and to remove the funds for his own benefit, part of a scheme in breach of his fiduciary duty owed to X Corporation. Although he owed a fiduciary duty to X as an insolvent company, and thereby a duty to consider the interests of the creditors, he owed the duty to no individual creditor as a conspiracy to use unlawful means. Unless there is a special rule for conspiracy, this reasoning may be thought to be contrary to that of the Court of Appeal in *Associated British Ports v. TGWU* [1989] 1 W.L.R. 939 (reversed on other grounds, *ibid.*, HL).

23–83   NOTE 93. Add: *Mid-Kent Holdings plc v. General Utilities plc* [1997] 1 WLR 14.

NOTE 95. After "merges in the tort)" at line 5, insert; *Normart Management Ltd v. West Hill Redevelopment Co.* (1998) 155 D.L.R. (4th) 527, Ont CA (a conspiracy to use unlawful means does not necessarily merge into other torts, but it will do so if it adds nothing to the causes of action).

NOTE 96. At the end add: For a reluctance to accept defendants as joint tortfeasors, see Lord Steyn, *Williams v. Natural Health Foods Ltd* [1998] 1 W.L.R. 830 at 838–839, HL (though the point was not properly pleaded); *AGDA Systems v. Valcom Ltd* (1999) 168 D.L.R. (4th) 351, 356–368 (Ont. CA); see too *Credit Lyonnais Bank Nederland (now Generale Bank Nederland) v. Export Credit Guarantee Department* [1998] 1 Lloyd's Rep. 19, CA ("even knowing assistance does not suffice to make the secondary party jointly liable as a joint tortfeasor with the primary party", at 46, *per* Hobhouse L.J.); so too, Lord Woolf M.R., *ibid.* [1999] 2 W.L.R. 540 at 545–547, HL (conspiracy was not relied upon on appeal to HL); compare Gardner [1998] C.L.J. 259 and [1997] C.L.J. 259; *Yukong Line of Korea v. Rendsberg Investments Corp (No. 2)* [1998] 1 W.L.R. 294. For an analysis of joint tortfeasors and vicarious liability in intentional torts, and the different scope in crime, see Hobhouse L.J. *Credit Lyonnais Bank Nederland (now Generale Bank Nederland) v. Export Credit Guarantee Department* [1998] 1 Lloyd's Rep. 41–47; on "assisting crime" Law Commission Paper No. 131, *Assisting and Encouraging Crime* (1993). On joint tortfeasors, see too *British Telecommunications v. One In A Million* [1998] 4 All E.R. 476 CA at 486–487, *per* Aldous L.J.

NOTE 99. Amend reference to: Cane, *Tort Law and Economic Interests* (2nd ed., 1996). Last line, after "*Salmond and Heuston on the Law of Torts*", insert: (21st ed., 1996) pp. 346, 353, 362–363.

NOTE 10. Add at end: See now *Credit Lyonnais Bank Nederland (now General Bank Nederland) v. Export Credit Guarantee Department* [1998] 1 Lloyd's Rep. 19, CA (unlawful means must be in itself actionable by the plaintiff) upheld on other grounds: [1999] 2 W.L.R. 540, HL, followed in *Yukong Line of Korea v. Rendsberg Investments Corp (No. 2)* [1998] 1 W.L.R. 294 at 312–313: *supra*, § 23–6, note 81; and on secondary liability in tort and in crime, *ibid.*, Hobhouse L.J. 42–46.

NOTE 13. Add at end: *Daishowa Inc. v. Friends of the Lubicon* (1998) 158 D.L.R. (4th) 699, Ont. Ct.

NOTE 19. At end add: *Mid Kent Holdings plc v. General Utilities plc* [1997] 1 W.L.R. 14. See now Competition Act 1998. **23–86**

NOTES 63 and 64. Amend reference to: Smith and Wood, *Industrial Law* (6th ed., 1996)

NOTE 48. The doctrine has its origins in the criminal law, where the net is thrown more widely than in the law of tort; see *R v. Macklin* (1838) 168 E.R. 1136, and the analysis by Hobhouse L.J. in *Credit Lyonnais Bank Nederland (now Generale Bank Nederland) v. Export Credit Guarantee Department* [1998] 1 Lloyd's Rep 19 at 42–46, CA, and by Lord Woolf M.R., *ibid.* [1999] 2 W.L.R. 540 at 551. *Quaere* whether the principle as stated by Lord Evershed M.R. above is applicable today to all forms of conspiracy to use unlawful means. Both tortfeasors, where they are joint, "are responsible for the tortious conduct as a whole": *per* Lord Woolf M.R. at 547. **23–88**

NOTE 59. On line 2, amend text to: *McGregor on Damages* (16th ed., 1998), p. 1253. Add at end; see *McGregor on Damages*, Chap. 38. **23–90**

NOTE 60. Add at end: See *McGregor on Damages* (16th ed., 1998), pp. 1251–1255.

6.—TRADE DISPUTES

Trade disputes and economic torts **23–91**

NOTE 63. Amend to read: Smith and Wood, *Industrial Law* (6th ed., 1996, Smith and Thomas eds). Add: Deakin and Morris, *Labour and Law* (2nd ed., 1998); Hepple (1995) 24 I.L.J. 303. Add at end: Barrow, *Industrial Relations Law* (1997).

NOTE 64. Add at end: Despite criticism from international sources (see the annual reports by the Committee of Experts of the ILO, Reports Part 4A, III); compare S. Gibbons, *International Labour Rights* (1998); Wedderburn *Labour Law and Freedom* (1995), the U.K. Government in 1997 made it clear that it planned to repeal very little of the legislation concerning trade disputes which was passed between 1980 and 1993, most of it consolidated in the Trade Union and Labour Relations (Consolidation) Act 1992 "TULRCA". See now Employment Relations Act 1999 ("ERA").

NOTE 65. Add at end: Compare Millett L.J. in *London Underground v. NURMT* [1995] I.R.L.R. 636 at 640: the requirement for a secret ballot (*post*, § 23–112) "has not been imposed for the protection of the employer or the public, but for the protection of the union's own members". *Sed quaere* TULRCA 1992, in ss.226A, 231, 234A, where the interests of the relevant employers appear to be the primary subjects for protection. Moreover, it is respectfully submitted that the section which primarily and expressly protects workers' interests as union members in ensuring that there is a proper ballot before industrial action is called by the union, is s.62 of TULRCA1992 (member entitled to order from the court if union members are proceeding to industrial action without a ballot); see *post*, § 23–112, and § 23–120.

23–95   NOTE 9. Add at end: For difficulties in the "balance of convenience" where both sides claim equally to be at risk of "irreparable harm": *Hogan v. Newfoundland* (1997) 149 D.L.R. (4th) 468, Nfd SC.

23–96   Trade disputes and procuring breach of contract
NOTE 27. Add: This provision "first conferred by Parliament in 1906 . . . is today recognised as encompassing a fundamental human right": *London Underground Ltd v. NURMT* [1995] I.R.L.R. 636 at 641, *per* Millett L.J.

23–100   NOTE 66. Line 5, replace to read: Goff and Jones, *Law of Restitution* (5th ed., 1998 ed. G. Jones), pp. 327–321."
NOTE 67. At end add: See too the impact of undue influence on employment relationships: *Credit Lyonnais Bank Nederland v. Burch* [1997] 1All E.R. 144, CA; and Brodie (1996) 25 I.L.J. 121.

23–103   NOTE 2. At end add: See too now Health and Safety (Consultation with Employees) Regulations 1996, S.I. 1996 No 1513 (consultation obligatory directly or through elected representatives where there are no union safety representatives under the 1974 Act).

23–104   NOTE 8. At end amend to: [1995] 2 A.C. 454, HL.
NOTE 9. Add at end: The 1978 Act is now consolidated in the Employment Rights Act 1996.
NOTE 15. Amend reference to: Smith and Wood, *Industrial Law* (6th ed., 1996).

23–105   NOTE 17. Add: In *Tracey v. Crosville Wales Ltd* [1997] I.C.R. 862, HL, the view of the Court of Appeal was upheld: in a decision on unfair dismissal of employees participating in industrial action who were selectively dismissed or re-engaged (so that the jurisdiction of the employment tribunal was restored: TULRCA 1992, s.238) participation by the workers in the industrial action cannot by itself amount to "contributory fault" (see Employment Rights Act 1996, ss.122(2), 123(6)) so as to reduce the compensation awarded, although there must be situations where "individual blameworthy conduct in addition to 'mere participation' in the industrial action must be capable of amounting to "contributory fault": *per* Lord Nolan at 880 (overruling in part *TNT Express (UK) Ltd v. Downes* [1994] I.C.R. 1, EATP.
NOTE 25. Amend to: Employment Rights Act 1996, s.44(1)(d), (e) and s.100(1)(d), (e).

NOTE 63. At end add: But see now the opposite view, *Credit Lyonnais Bank* **23–110**
Nederland (now General Bank Nederland) v. Export Credit Guarantee Department
[1998] 1 Lloyd's Rep. 19, CA, *per* Stuart-Smith L.J. at 32 (aff'd on other grounds
[1999] 2 W.L.R. 540, HL).

Trade disputes and ballots **23–112**
NOTE 88. Add: Millett L.J. put great emphasis in his judgment in *London Under-
ground v. NURMT* [1995] I.R.L.R. 636 at 639–640, on the fact that the ballot was
required for the "collective" industrial action and did not limit the basic protection
in s.219 for inducing an individual to join in.
NOTE 90. After "para. 24" (line 3) insert: (see now s.216 of the Employment
Rights Act 1996)
Add: Applying the definition of "strike" in s.246 the Court of Appeal found that
an overtime ban and a ban on rest-day working are "strike" action: *Connex South
Eastern Ltd v. NURMT* [1999] I.R.L.R. 249, CA. There may be "a divergence
between the popular understanding and the statutory definition of the term
'strike' . . . ": *per* Hutchison L.J. at 252. But the Employment Relations Act 1999,
defines, for the purpose of ballots, an overtime ban and a call-out ban as "industrial
action *short* of a strike": Schedule 3. para. 6(2), new s.229(2) TULRCA 1992)
(reversing the *Connex* case, and excepting these two practices from the normal
definition of "strike' in s.246, *i.e.* "any concerted stoppage of work"). The same
Schedule revises the statement which must accompany the voting paper to members
(see s.229(4) TULRCA: in addition to stating that the industrial action may be a
breach of the contract of employment, it must inform the employee that dismissal
by reason of taking part in a strike or other industrial action fewer than eight weeks
after the start of it, will be unfair and may be unfair in some circumstances later
(this is part of the new law on dismissal *by reason of* strike action in s.238A
TULRCA, ERA 1999, Sched. 5 para. 3).
NOTE 91. Add: Millet L.J. in *London Underground v. NURMT* [1995] I.R.L.R.
636 at 640 held that the requirement for a secret ballot "has not been imposed for
the protection of the employer or the public, but for the protection of the union's own
members" and even "to strengthen industrial democracy". *Sed quaere*: whether, in
TULRCA 1992, ss.226A, 231, 231A, 234A, are not the interests of the relevant
employer the target of the protection in the procedures required in a ballot, *e.g.*
under section 234A and ERA Sched. 3, para. 11, the union must give seven days'
notice to the employer with details of the intended stoppage (*e.g.* continuous or
discontinuous action) and details in the union's possession describing the persons to
be induced to take part (at least their number, category or workplaces) so as to "help
the employer to make plans" and to inform the employees. But the union's notice
is not invalidated by a failure to send the names of those employees (new section
234A (5A)). Parallel obligations are imposed on the union's giving notice of a ballot
and sample ballot paper which it is previously obliged to send to the employer (s.
226A(3)(3A)(3B) TULRCA 1992, Sched. 3 para. 3 ERA 1999). An applicant for
relief may be refused if he fails to cross-reference various documents supplied to
him: *R J B Mining (U.K.) Ltd v. NUM* [1997] I.R.L.R. 621, 624.

NOTE 92. Add: On the revised *Code of Practice on Industrial Action Ballots and
Notices to Employers*, see B. Simpsons (1995) 24 I.L.J. 337.
Insert text at end of paragraph after "at that time[3]" and add additional notes: But **23–114**
this suggestion was rejected by the Court of Appeal in 1995.[3a] In calling upon newly
recruited members to take part in industrial action after a successful ballot of members at an earlier time had afforded the necessary support to that industrial action, a
trade union does not lose the fundamental protection from liability in section 219(1)
for inducing the new members to break their employment contracts, even if the new
members are significant in their numbers and important to the likely success of the
industrial action.[3b] The same applies where the newly recruited persons after the
ballot are non-members. The union can still rely upon the basic protection for inducing breach of contracts of employment in section 219, because the requirement of

"support by a ballot" applies to the industrial action, which is a collective phenomenon, and once that industrial action has the support of a ballot of members envisaged at the time to be those likely to take part in the action, the union is later free to call upon new members or non-members individually to "take part in" the *same* industrial action.[3c] "There is simply no objection to a small union, which has the support of its own members, seeking to attract support from non-members."[3d] On the other hand, where the union has formed a view as to which members are likely to be called out, it is acting in contravention of the Act if it fails to include a significant number of those members in the balloting process and, equally, if it includes members who had not been within the chosen constituency as members who would be likely to be called out. The union would not be asked for "100 per cent perfection" (see *British Railways Board v. NUR* [1989] I.R.L.R. 349, CA), but it could not rely upon difficulties caused by its own organisation (*e.g.* its federal structure) to excuse a breach of section 227.[3e] The Employment Relations Act 1999 will affect such areas of the 1992 Act.[3f]

NOTE 2. Delete from "But the court . . ." to ". . . M.R. 865". Insert at end: See too, ss. 227 (as amended ERA 1999, Sched. 3 para. 4).

NOTE 3a. *London Underground Ltd v. NURMT* [1995] I.R.L.R. 636, CA, disapproving Lord Donaldson M.R. in *Post Office v. UCW* [1990] I.C.R. 258 at 267–268.

NOTE 3b. *London Underground Ltd v. NURMT* [1995] I.R.L.R. 636 at 638–639, *per* Millett L.J., with whom other members of the Court of Appeal agreed.

NOTE 3c. *ibid.* 639–641: contrasting ss. 219 and 220, with the formulations in ss. 226–235. If the new members had been recruited *before* the ballot, and would have been expected to join in the action if the ballot turned out to be supportive, the union would have been obliged to include them in the ballot: at 641.

NOTE 3d. *ibid.*, 641 *per* Millett L.J. This result, whereby a union with only a few members can, after a successful ballot of those members, lawfully call upon thousands of other workers to join their union's industrial action (at any rate where they can be parties to the dispute with their employer: see *post*, § 23–130) is likely to surprise the authors of the legislation, especially in view of the amendments to the Trade Union Act 1984 made by the Employment Act 1988, s. 17 and Sched. 3, para. 5, the Employment Act 1990, s.7 and Sched. 2 (see the exchanges between the Secretary of State Mr Howard and Tony Blair M.P., Committee May 17, 1990, cols 1041 *et seq*), and the Trade Union Reform and Employment Rights Act 1993, ss.17–21.

The analysis of Millet L.J. that the strike ballot provisions are for the protection of the union members, to sustain "industrial democracy", may derive some support if ss.226A and 234A as amended by ERA, Sched. 3, paras 3 and 11, are regarded as separate from the general balloting requirements. The union is obliged to give notice *only* to the employer of the specimen ballot paper and details about the impending strikers (s.226A) and notice of the nature of the industrial action (s.234A) and if it fails to do that, it loses its protection *only* against the employer (see s.226(3A) added by ERA, Sched. 3, para. 2(3). The general conditions necessary to sustain the support of a ballot do not now include s.231A, demanding notification of the result to the relevant employer (ERA 1999, Sched. 3 para. 2(2) amending s.226 (2)(a)(ii) TULRCA). That brings this provision into accord with s.62 (2)(a)(ii) (conditions required before a member can apply to the court). Parliament would appear to have intended protection for member under s.62, rather than ss.226A and 234A.

NOTE 3e. *RJB Mining (U.K.) Ltd v. NUM* [1997] I.R.L.R. 621. This decision may be distinguished from that of Millett L.J. in the *NURMT* decision in 1995, *supra*; here the NUM never reached first base, *i.e.* a valid ballot, whereas the RMT had achieved an adequate ballot which could "support the industrial action", into which it could then invite others who could pursue the trade dispute with them. It is submitted, however, that the new participants must be acting in furtherance or contemplation of the trade dispute with the same employer (s.244 TULRCA).

NOTE 3f. The Employment Relations Act 1999, provides that the ballot shall not be effective where a member is induced to take part in the action but was not accorded entitlement to vote (Sched. 3 para. 8) but that where a failure to conduct the ballot arises in respect of entitlement to vote or some other defects (such as failure of voting papers to arrive by post), the ballot will be effective if the failure is accidental and on a scale which is unlikely to affect the result of the ballot (Sched. 3, para. 8): new ss.232A and 232B TULRCA 1992.

DELETE para. 23–115 and notes 4 to 9. Insert text and note: The 1999 ERA **23–115** retains the principle of TULRCA 1992 that there should be a separate ballot in each workplace if the relevant members do not all have the same workplace (see s.238 TULRCA, ERA Sched. 3, para. 5). But the ERA amendments have greatly widened the exceptions from that rule (new s.238A(2) to (5)) to avoid difficulties in collective bargaining. So, a single aggregate ballot may be held where (i) a worker at the workplace is a union member "*affected* by a dispute": this includes members directly affected by a decision which the union reasonably believes the employer has made or will make, concerning a matter set out in TULRCA 1992, s.244(1)(a)(b) or (c) (employment matters within the definition of a trade dispute, below §23–131) and to which the dispute (wholly or partly) relates. The same applies where the dispute relates to a matter within subsection (1)(d)("discipline"); and where it relates to (1)(e), the members are those whose membership or non-membership is in dispute; and if the dispute concerns a matter within (1) (f), "affected members" are the union officials to whom use of the facilities applies. (ii) A further exception applies where the union reasonably believes all the members entitled to vote have a common occupation or occupations of particular kinds and are employed by an employer in dispute with the union (s.238A (3)); and (iii) the last exception arises where members entitled to vote are all employed by the employer or employers with whom the union is in dispute (s.238A(4)). A "workplace" is the premises where the work is performed (or the most closely connected premises: s.228(4)). There may still be difficulty regarding cases where a few members do not take part in the industrial action in some workplaces, e.g. to provide safety cover.[10]

NOTE 34. Add at end: Dissemination of false information to members (albeit **23–118** innocently) might be interference or constraint prohibited by TULRCA 1992, ss.230(1)(a): *RJB Mining v. NUM* [1997] I.R.L.R. 621 at 623 per Kay J..

NOTE 46. Amend to read: Smith and Wood *Industrial Law* (6th ed., 1996, Smith **23–119** and Thomas eds), p. 563.

NOTE 50. Delete. After ERA 1999, Sched. 3, para. 2(2) the conditions in s.62(2)(a) **23–120** and s.226(2)(a)(ii) are now parallel.

NOTE 57. Insert after "date of the ballot, s. 236": The period of four weeks ends **23–121** at the stroke of midnight on the last day of the fourth week: *RJB Mining v. NUM* [1995] I.R.L.R. 566, CA (that is the "use by date": Henry L.J. at 566).

Picketing and trade disputes **23–123**
NOTE 77. Add at end: But see the wide interpretation of the right to pass and repass on the highway in *DPP v. Jones* [1999] 2 W.L.R. 625, HL (Lords Slynn and Hope dissenting); V. Pickford (1999) N.L.J. 927. (trespassory assembly; Public Order Act 1986, s.14A, inserted by Criminal Justice and Public Order Act 1994, s.70); a peaceful non-obstructive assembly is within the right to pass and repass on the highway; this accords with Art. 11 on freedom of assembly, in the European Convention on Human Rights.
NOTE 90. Delete from "tortious" to end. Insert: But see *DPP v. Fidler* 1 W.L.R. 91, DC (reinterpreting s.7 of the 1875 Act, changing its meaning remarkably as from 1906 when the original proviso making attendance for the purpose of information was repealed by s.2 of the Trade Disputes Act 1906, now s.241 of TULRCA 1992). On harassment as a tort, now under the Protection from Harassment Act 1997, see *supra*, § 23–42A.

NOTE 91. Add: See too *Ontario Attorney-General v. Dielman* (1994) 117 D.L.R. (4th) 449, Ont.

Add the following text and notes at end: Workers in national States mounting a successful picket or demonstration, which avoids interlocutory injunctions and other immediate sanctions within the principles of their national labour law, may nevertheless discover that European law affords employers or other plaintiffs remedies on different grounds, both against the State itself and possibly against them. Where, *e.g.* demonstrating French farmers were obstructing the passage of goods along the roads as part of a demonstration about their livelihood, the public authorities were held to have contravened Articles 30–36 of the Treaty of Rome, now Articles 28–30, E.C. Treaty (of which the main aim is to ensure that no restrictions are imposed on the passage of exports and imports across the frontiers of Member States) and the European Court of Justice found that the French Government had not taken adequate and proportionate steps to ensure "free movement" for the passage of goods.[9a] The European Court habitually takes some two years to reach its decisions; but the importance of this judgment lies not only in the legal procedures available in the Court, but in the support which the Commission has drawn from it in pursuit of proposals for a Decision or Regulation which would lay down obligatory norms enforceable in national courts, with powers to impose "provisional measures" (injunctions) to implement "necessary and proportionate measures" in order to safeguard free movement of goods.[9b]

23–124   NOTE 96. On the liability for "harassment" at common law and now under the Protection from Harassment Act 1997, which might be relevant to tortious liabilities in picketing, see *supra*, § 23–42A. See too now the crime of trespassory assembly (Public Order Act 1986, s.14A, as inserted by s.70 of the Criminal Justice and Public Order Act 1994): *DPP v. Jones* [1999] 2 W.L.R. 625, HL.

NOTE 2. At end insert: See too *DPP v. Jones* [1999] 2 W.L.R. 625, HL; a peaceful assembly on the highway is lawful as a reasonable and usual activity, there being no unreasonable obstruction; nor did it constitute a trespassory assembly as such within s.14A of the 1986 Act (Lords Slynn and Hope dissenting). *Per* Lord Irvine of Lairg L.C: "Unless the common law recognises that assembly on the public highway *may* be lawful, the right contained in article 11(1) of the [European Convention on European Human Rights] is denied" (at 634); and *supra*, § 23–123, note 77 and § 17–41).

NOTE 9a. *E.C. Commission v. France, C-265/95, The Times,* December 11, 1997, ECJ. See too *R. v. Chief Constable of Sussex, ex p. International Trader's Ferry Ltd* [1998] 3 WLR 1260, HL (discretion of Chief Constable in using resources to prevent obstructions), *supra*, § 23–71, note 67.

NOTE 9b. E.C. Commission *Explanatory Memorandum*, November 26, 1997. The Commission asserts that a Community instrument would apply to "unjustified obstacles to the free movement of goods" — a prescription which could readily apply to pickets — but that "fundamental rights" of workers would be maintained. It is not clear what interpretation would be put upon "fundamental rights" to picket or to take industrial action in Britain.

23–130   NOTE 59. At end add: An NHS Trust wished to arrange for unidentified private companies to build and run a new hospital. Some of the Trust's employees would be transferred to the work. The union (U) opposed the scheme on principle but asked the Trust to enter into a 30–year agreement guaranteeing that transferred employees and all future subcontracted employees would receive equivalent terms and conditions. When the Trust refused to agree U called for strike action which was supported in a ballot. The judge granted an interlocutory injunction until trial of the action, holding that the dispute was mainly related to U's political objectives. The Court of Appeal held that it was unlikely that the main motivation of U would be proved to relate to political objectives. But such a dispute about the terms and conditions of employees of future employers not yet known, or even a dispute about the additional security which existing employees would feel if future employers were guaranteed by the Trust to be so bound over the 30-year period, cound not be a trade dispute within s.244 of TULRCA 1992: *University College London Hospitals NHS Trust v. Unison* [1999] I.C.R. 204, CA.

NOTE 66. Insert after "as" (line 2): amended by Trade Union Reform and Employment Rights Act 1993, s.33; see now *Betts v. Brintel Helicopters Ltd* [1997] I.R.L.R. 361, CA; *Süzen v. Zehnacker Gebäudereinigung GmbH* (13/95) [1997] I.R.L.R. 225 ECJ; and now *Cornwall County Care v. Brightman* [1998] I.R.L.R. 228, EAT; *Jules Dethier Équipment SA v. Dassy and Sovram* [1998] IRLR 266 ECJ; *ECM (Vehicle Delivery Service) Ltd v. Cox* [1998] I.C.R. 631; *Frankling v. BPS Public Sector* [1999] I.R.L.R. 212.

NOTE 74. Amend to: ss.44 and 100 of the Employment Rights Act 1996.   **23–131**

NOTE 90. At end add: See too *University College London Hospitals NHS Trust v. UNISON* [1999] I.C.R. 204, CA.   **23–132**

CHAPTER 24.—STATUTORY INTELLECTUAL PROPERTY RIGHTS

		PARA.
□1.	Introduction	24–01
■2.	Copyright and related rights	24–03
□3.	Infringement of copyright	24–17
■4.	Remedies for infringement of copyright	24–26
□5.	Moral rights	24–35
□6.	Competition and control of licensing	24–40
■7.	Performers' rights	24–41
■8.	Design rights	24–44
□9.	Registered designs	24–51
■10.	Registered trade marks	24–61
■11.	Patents	24–76

1.—INTRODUCTION

24–01   Intellectual property

Add to end of second paragraph: "respectively": *Kitechnology BV v. Unicor GmbH Plastmachinen* [1995] F.S.R. 765.

Add: In *Fort Dodge Ltd v. Akzo Nobel NV* [1998] F.S.R. 222 (patent and *Pearce (Gareth) v. Ove Arup Partnership Ltd* [1999] F.S.R. 525 (copyright), the Court of Appeal gave guidance as to the circumstances in which the owner of a foreign intellectual property right may bring proceedings in the English courts under the Brussels Convention for infringement of the Foreign right.

2.—COPYRIGHT AND RELATED RIGHTS

24–07   Literary and dramatic works

NOTE 25. A dramatic work must be capable of being physically performed: *Norowzian v. Arks Ltd* [1999] F.S.R. 79.

NOTE 26. Add: Anything which is appreciated simply with the eye is excluded from the scope of literary copyright. Thus a circuit diagram may not attract protection as a literary compilation: *Electronic Techniques (Anglia) Ltd v. Critchley Components Ltd* [1997] F.S.R. 401. The representation of a circuit diagram could be entitled to copyright as an artistic work but a circuit produced from a circuit diagram would only reproduce that diagram if it bore some visual similarity thereto in terms of layout of the circuit board: *Aubrey Max Sandman v. Panasonic U.K. Ltd* [1998] F.S.R. 651. That case casts doubt on the correctness of the approach taken in *Electronic Techniques* as to protection of circuit diagrams as literary works.

NOTE 30. Replace with: For existing copyright works, and works made or first qualifying for protection on or after January 1, 1996, the period is now 70 years. It runs from either the end of the calendar year in which the author dies or, if the work is of unknown authorship, from the end of the calendar year in which the work was made or first made available to the public, whichever is the later: CDPA 1988, s.12 as amended by reg. 5 of S.I. 1995 No. 3297 (Duration of Copyright and Rights in Performances Regulations 1995). For works which are computer generated, the period is 50 years from the end of the calendar year when the work was first made.

NOTE 32. Add: or reproducing the work in three dimensions. See *e.g. Autospin (Oil Seals) Ltd v. Beehive Spinning* [1995] R.P.C. 683.

Musical works and artistic works   **24–08**
NOTE 42. Replace with: The period is now 70 years: see *supra*, n. 30.

Sound recordings and films   **24–09**
Add at beginning of paragraph: A sound recording is defined as a recording of sounds, or the whole or any part of a literary, dramatic or musical work, from which the sounds or the sounds reproducing the work or any part may be produced. (CDPA 1988, s.5A (as amended by S.I. 1995 No. 3297, reg. 9(1) reg. 9(1). Copies of previous sound recordings are excluded).

NOTE 46. Replace with: CDPA 1988, s.13A (as amended by S.I. 1995 No. 3297, reg. 6(1)). "Release" consists of first publication, playing in public, broadcasting or inclusion in a cable programme service.

NOTE 48. Replace with: *ibid.* s.5B (as amended by S.I. 1995 No. 3297, reg. 9(1)). The definition includes the sound track accompanying the film but excludes copies of previous films. References to copyright in a film include any copyright as a dramatic work or in photographs forming part of the film.

Delete "The period of copyright is as for sound recordings". Add: For existing copyright works, and works made or first qualifying for protection on or after January 1, 1996, the period of copyright is now 70 years from the end of the calendar year in which the death occurs of the last to die of the principal director, screenplay author, dialogue author or film music composer; or if the work is of unknown authorship, from the end of the calendar year in which the film was made or first made available to the public, whichever is the later: CDPA 1988, s.13B (as amended by S.I. 1995 No. 3297, reg. 6(1)).

Add at end of paragraph: Such acts are not infringing if done at a time when, or in pursuance of arrangements made when, the identity of the director, author or composer cannot be ascertained by reasonable inquiry and it is reasonable to assume that either the last of them died at least 70 years before the year in which the act is done or arrangements made, or copyright has expired: CDPA 1988 s.66A (as amended by S.I. 1995 No. 3297, reg. 6(2)).

Broadcasts and cable programmes   **24–10**
NOTE 52. Add: (as amended by S.I. 1995 No. 3297, reg. 7(1)). No copyright arises in respect of a repeat broadcast or programme after copyright in the original has expired.

Authorship   **24–13**
NOTE 59. Add: *Robin Ray v. Classic F.M. plc*, [1998] F.S.R. 622 April 8, 1998, Lightman J. To establish joint authorship for s.10 of the CDPA 1988, it is necessary to show that each of the alleged authors had direct responsibility for what actually appeared on paper. Simply contributing ideas to the author was not sufficient. Something approximated to "penmanship" was necessary (*Cala Homes (South) Ltd v. Alfred McAlpine Homes East Ltd* [1995] F.S.R. 818, Laddie J. referred to). See also *Fylde Microsystems Ltd v. Key Radio Systems Ltd*, *The Times*, February 18, 1998, Laddie J. Testing and debugging software did not result in joint authorship.

Originality   **24–12**
NOTE 56. Add after *James Arnold & Co.*: *Autospin (Oil Seals) Ltd v. Beehive Spinning*, above.

Ownership of copyright   **24–14**
NOTE 60. Add: For effect on ownership of extended and revived copyright see S.I. 1995 No. 3297, regs 18–20.

Assignment and disposition of copyright   **24–15**
NOTE 65. Add: Extended and revived copyright can be assigned by a prospective owner: see reg. 20 of S.I. 1995 No. 3297.

3.—INFRINGEMENT OF COPYRIGHT

24-17   **Infringement of copyright**
NOTE 70. Add: As to infringement of revived copyright, see S.I. 1995 No. 3297, reg. 23.

24-20   **Causal derivation and substantial similarity-copying a substantial part**
Add: The concept of infringement by taking small but regular amounts is problematic. For an analysis, see: *Electronic Techniques (Anglia) Ltd v. Critchley Components Ltd* [1997] F.S.R. 401. Although the copying of an unoriginal shape may not amount to the copying of a substantial part of a copyright work, it is likely to do so where the amount copied includes the context in which the shape is portrayed. When considering whether there has been infringement, the court must take into account all that has been copied, whether or not it was itself copied by the author, but should keep in mind what it was that made the drawing an original work: *Biotrading & Financing OY v. Biohit Ltd* [1998] F.S.R. 109, CA.

24-24   NOTES 11 and 12. Add: Note that "criticism or review" and "reporting current events" are expressions of wide and indefinite scope which should be interpreted liberally. The subjective intentions of the defendant are of limited importance in assessing whether the use of the work were for those purposes: *Pro Sieben Media AG v. Carlton UK Television Ltd* [1999] 1 W.L.R. 605, CA. In *Hyde Park Residence Ltd v. Yelland* [1999] R.P.C. 655, Jacob J. upheld a "public interest" defence to infringement of copyright.

4.—REMEDIES FOR INFRINGEMENT OF COPYRIGHT

24-29   **Damages or account of profits**
NOTE 55. Add: The plaintiff is entitled to sufficient information to make an informed choice between damages and profits: *Island Records Inc. v. Tring International plc* [1995] F.S.R. 560. For practice, see: *Brugger v. Medicaid* [1996] F.S.R. 362.
NOTE 60. Add: *Redrow Homes Ltd v. Betts Brothers plc* [1998] F.S.R. 345, HL. Plaintiff sought account of profits and additional statutory damages (s.97 (2) of the 1988 Act). Held additional damages could not be claimed when plaintiff had elected for an account of profits; and *Claydon Architectural Metalwork Ltd v. D.J. Higgins & Sons Ltd* [1997] F.S.R. 475, Martin Mann Q.C. Action for infringement of copyright and/or design right. Compensatory damages sought for loss of profits and secondary losses (the expense of repairing consequential damage to cash flow). Held; the tort test of remoteness applied to copyright infringement.

5.—MORAL RIGHTS

24-35   **The nature of moral rights**
Add at end of paragraph: Moral rights are exercisable in relation to revived copyright. Any prior waiver or assertion of moral rights shall continue to apply. See reg. 22 of S.I. 1995 No. 3297.

24-38   NOTE 9. Add: To establish the tort of false attribution of authorship it is not necessary for the plaintiff to be a professional author or to have any goodwill or reputation as an author to protect. The tort is actionable *per se*. In deciding whether the work in question contained a false attribution the court must determine what was the single meaning conveyed by it to the notional reasonable reader: *Clark v. Associated Newspapers Ltd* [1998] R.P.C. 261 (action for false attribution and for passing off succeeded in respect of parody diaries where the plaintiff was well known as a diarist).

212

6.—COMPETITION AND CONTROL OF LICENSING

The Copyright Tribunal—control of licensing   24–40
   Add at end of first paragraph: For effect of extended copyright on existing licences
see S.I. 1995 No. 3297, regs. 21, 24, 25.

7.—PERFORMERS' RIGHTS

Rights in performances   24–41
   Add after "The rights subsist for 50 years.": from the end of the calendar year in
which the performance takes place, or if during that period a recording of the performance is released, from the end of the calendar year in which it is released.
   NOTE 32. Add: *Bassey v. Icon Entertainment plc* [1995] E.M.L.R. 596.
   NOTE 38. Should read *ibid.* s.191. Add: (as amended by S.I. 1995 No. 3297, reg.
10). "Release" consists of first publication, playing or showing in public, broadcasting or inclusion in a cable programme service. No account is to be taken of an
unauthorised act.

Recording rights   24–42
   NOTE 48. Replace with: see § 24–41 and n. 38 above.

8.—DESIGN RIGHTS

Design right   24–46
   Add: In *Ocular Sciences Ltd v. Aspect Vision Care Ltd* [1997] R.P.C. 289, Laddie
J. gave guidance as to the following matters. *First*, the meaning of "design" in the
design right provisions of the Copyright, Designs and Patents Act 1988. That Act
gives design right protection to wholly functional designs (compare registered
designs, where protection only extends to features which are judged by and appeal
to the eye). *Secondly*, the meaning of "commonplace". A design is likely to be
commonplace which is trite, trivial, common or garden, hackneyed or of the type
which would excite no peculiar attention in those in the relevant art. But a design
made up of features which, individually, are commonplace is not itself necessarily
commonplace. To attract protection, the combination must not be commonplace.
Thirdly, the application of the "must fit" criteria in section 213(b)(i). That section
is widely drafted so as to exclude protection to articles which must fit any object
including things such as parts of the human body (in that case, the human eye). Any
feature of shape and configuration which meets the interface criteria of the section
is excluded from being considered as part of the design right even if it performs
some other purpose, for example, it is attractive. In *Farmers Build v. Carrier Ltd*
[1999] R.P.C. 461 the Court of Appeal gave further guidance as to the meaning of
"commonplace", stating that if there were aspects of the plaintiff's design which
are not to be found in any other design in the field in question and those aspects are
found in the defendant's design, the court would be entitled to conclude that the
design in question was not "commonplace".

   See Design right infringement—remedies.   24–47
   NOTE 78. Add: *Mark Wilkinson Furniture Ltd v. Woodcraft Designs (Radcliffe)
Ltd* [1998] F.S.R. 63, Jonathan Parker J. Copying a surface decoration on an original
design was not an infringement under section 226 as surface decoration was
excluded from the definition of a design under CDPA 1988, s.51(3) and s.213 (2)
(c).

9.—REGISTERED DESIGNS

24–51   Registered designs

NOTE 94. Add: Protection can be given to the shape as a whole, even though the design includes features dictated by function: *Valeo Vision SA v. Flexible Lamps Ltd* [1995] R.P.C. 205.

24–54   Registration

NOTE 2. Add: For "article" see *Ford Motor Co. Ltd's Design Applications* [1995] R.P.C. 167.

24–56   Infringement of registered design rights

NOTE 12. Add: Although a case on pleadings, *Lone Star Toys Ltd v. JM Enterprises of Wetherby Ltd* [1996] F.S.R. 857 is helpful in indicating the use of prior art in limiting the scope of a registered design as well as affecting its validity.

10.—REGISTERED TRADE MARKS

24–62   Trade Marks Act 1994

NOTE 25. Add after *Conseil National: Wagamama Ltd v. City Centre Restaurants plc* [1995] F.S.R. 713 (not relying on minutes). It is inappropriate to rely upon *Hansard* when construing the Act: *British Sugar plc v. James Robertson & Son Ltd* [1996] R.P.C. 281.

NOTE 34. Add: See on "distinctive" *British Sugar plc v. James Robertson & Sons Ltd* [1996] R.P.C. 281.

24–65   Registration of trade marks and applications for registration of trade marks

NOTE 40. Add: On effect of disclaimers see *Paton Calvert Cordon Bleu Trade Mark* [1996] R.P.C. 94.

24–68   Revocation and invalidity of registration

NOTE 44. Add: See, *e.g. ORIENT EXPRESS Trade Mark* [1996] R.P.C. 25.

24–70   Infringement of registered trade mark

NOTE 60. Add: See on infringement: *British Sugar v. Robertson* above. Add: See on the meaning of "use in relation to goods", *Trebor Bassett Ltd v. The Football Association* [1997] F.S.R. 211.

NOTE 62. Add: The question of similarity of goods under s.10(2) was considered in *British Sugar v. Robertson* above where a list of relevant factors was set out.

NOTE 62. Add: The likelihood of confusion must be appreciated globally, taking account of all factors relevant to the circumstances of the case. That global appreciation of the visual, aural or conceptual similarity of the marks in question must be based on the overall impression given by the marks, bearing in mind in particular their distinctive and dominant components: Case C-251/95 *Sabel BV v. Puma AG* [1998] R.P.C. 199, ECJ; *The European Ltd v. The Economist Newspaper Ltd* [1998] F.S.R. 283, CA. In assessing the likelihood of confusion, there is some interdependence between the similarity of the marks and the similarity of the goods or services. In assessing whether the similarity of goods or services is sufficient to give rise to a likelihood of confusion, the reputation of the registered trade mark is relevant: Case C-39/97 *Canon Kabushiki Kaisha v. Metro-Goldwyn-Mayer Inc.* [1998] F.S.R. 332, ECJ.

NOTE 63. Add: It has been suggested, *obiter*, by Aldous L.J. that, in an action based on s.10(3), it is not necessary to prove that the use complained of be trade mark use nor that it be confusing use. It was held to be an infringement under that section to register Internet domain names incorporating the trade marks of famous companies and threaten to use them or sell them to others. Such conduct is also actionable as passing off: *British Telecommunications plc v. One in Million* [1999] F.S.R. 1, CA.

Limitations on the effect of a registered trade mark   **24–71**

NOTE 65. Add: In *Barclays Bank plc v. RBS Advanta* [1996] R.P.C. 307 the court held that the test was objective and depended on whether the use would be considered honest by members of a reasonable audience.

NOTE 66. Add: The use must either give some advantage to the defendant or inflict some harm on the character or repute of the registered mark so as to be above the level of *de minimis: Barclays Bank v. RBS* above. There are several decisions on the application of s.10(6) to comparative advertising. Their effect is summarised by Jacob J. in *Cable & Wireless plc v. British Telecommunications plc* [1998] F.S.R. 383. As long as the use of the competitor's mark is honest, there is nothing wrong in telling the public of the relative merits of competing goods or services and using registered trade marks to identify them. The test is objective: would a reasonable reader be likely to say, upon being given the full facts, that the advertisement is not honest? An advertisement which is significantly misleading (considered as a whole and without minute textual examination) is not honest for the purpose of s.10(6). The court will not grant an interlocutory injunction in a comparative advertising case where the defendant has an arguable case and to do so would interfere with its right to free speech: *Macmillan Magazines Ltd v. RCN Publishing Co. Ltd* [1998] F.S.R. 9.

NOTE 69. Add: See for a review of the principles of EEA exhaustion of trade mark rights: *Bristol Myers Squibb v. Paranova* Cases C-427/93, C-429/93 and C-436/93 [1997] F.S.R. 102. The European Court of Justice has held that the registered trade mark owner's rights are not exhausted by placing goods on the market under the mark *outside* the EEA: Case C-355/96, *Silhouette International Schmied GmbH & Co. KG v. Handelsgesellschaft mbH*, [1998] F.S.R. 729; Opinion of Advocate General Jacobs [1998] F.S.R. 474. Damage done to the reputation of a trade mark can be a legitimate reason for objecting to further commercialisation of the goods within the meaning of s.12 of the Act. However, where a proprietor uses a trade mark for bringing the public's attention to the further commercialisation of the goods, the proprietor must show that the use of the trade mark for this purpose seriously damages the reputation of the trade mark: *Parfums Christian Dior SA v. Evora BV* [1998] R.P.C. 166, ECJ. *Silhouette* and *Christian Dior* were considered in *Zino Davidoff SA v. A&G Imports Ltd* [1999] R.P.C. 631 refusing summary judgment in respect of goods originally placed on the market outside the Community. Questions concerning (i) the circumstances in which a trade mark proprietor is to be taken to have consented to goods, marked with the trade mark and originally sold outside the EC, being re-sold in the EC and (ii) the circumstances in which a proprietor may object to further commercialisation of the goods, were referred to the ECJ by Laddie J. on June 24, 1999.

NOTE 75. Add: See on the extent to which the merits may be taken into account: *Series 5 Software Ltd v. Philip Clarke* [1996] F.S.R. 225.

NOTE 81. The test of whether a particular communication constitutes a threat is   **24–75** whether it would have been read by the ordinary reader in the position of the plaintiff as constituting a threat. A person wishing to raise the possibility of infringement proceedings is required to take care in expressing himself and it is incumbent on him to indicate in terms if he wishes to rely on one of the expecting paragraphs of s.21(1) of the Act: *Prince v. Prince Sports Group Inc.* [1998] F.S.R. 21. Implied threats are actionable: *Scandecor Development AB v. Scandecor Marketing AB* [1999] F.S.R. 26, CA.

11.—PATENTS

Ownership, entitlement, licensing and employee inventions   **24–81**

NOTE 85. Add after second sentence: Commission Regulation 240/96 on Technology Transfer Agreements [1996] F.S.R. 397 which covers patent and know-how licences is particularly relevant.

24–82 The specification—description and claims
NOTE 2. Add: The Court of Appeal is bound to apply the *Catnic* test when considering the ambit of a patent claim under the 1977 Act: *Kastner v. Rizla Ltd* [1995] R.P.C. 585. "Variants on the claimed invention" is at § 24–90.

24–83 Validity

Novelty
NOTE 4. Add to reference to *Merrell Dow Pharmaceuticals Inc. v. H.N. Norton & Co*. The appeal to the House of Lords was dismissed [1996] R.P.C. 76.

Not obvious
NOTE 5. Add: See also *Beloit Technologies Inc. v. Valmet Paper Machinery Inc.* [1995] R.P.C. 705.

Capable of industrial application
NOTE 6. Add: See *Chiron Corporation v. Murex Diagnostics* [1996] F.S.R. 153.

Not specifically excluded.
NOTE 7. Add: As to the patentability of a computer programmed to perform a particular task, see *Fujitsu Limited's Application* [1997] R.P.C. 610.
In the light of recent decisions of the EPO, the Patent Office has indicated a more liberal approach to allowing claims for programs for computers: [1999] R.P.C. 563.

24–84 Other grounds on which patent may be revoked

Insufficiency
In *Biogen Inc v. Medeva plc* [1997] R.P.C. 1 HL, Lord Hoffmann gave general guidance on the scope for a challenge to a patent on the grounds of insufficiency where the claims of the patent exceeded the technical contribution to the art.

Added matter
NOTE 12. Add after *Molnlycke AB v. Procter and Gamble; Richardson-Vicks Inc.'s Patent* [1995] R.P.C. 568.

Infringement
24–88   Add: For meaning of "directly" under section 60(1)(c) see *Pioneer Electronics Capital Inc. and Anr v. Warner Music Manufacturing Europe GmbH and Anr.* [1995] R.P.C. 487.

24–90 Variants on the claimed invention
NOTE 45. Add: When determining whether a variant falls within the scope of the patent, the court has regard to the context of the dispute including the prior art and the alleged infringement: *Kastner v. Rizla Ltd* [1995] R.P.C. 585.
Add: Although the *Improver* questions provide helpful guidance, an over-rigid application of any cannons of construction is not appropriate: *Brugger v. Medic-Aid Ltd* [1996] R.P.C. 635.

Defences
24–92   NOTE 51. Add: See also *Roussel Uclaf SA v. Hockley International Ltd* [1996] R.P.C. 441.
NOTE 57. Add: See now *Lubrizol Corporation v. Esso Petroleum Corporation Co. Ltd* [1997] R.P.C. 195.
NOTE 59. Add at end of note: (appeal dismissed) [1996] F.S.R. 153 CA. The mere fact of securing the benefit of an exclusive right to prevent others from manufactur-

ing or selling without the patentee's consent could not be an abuse of dominant position. Nor is it an abuse to refuse to licence such a right. The exercise of an exclusive right may be prohibited if it gave rise to abusive conduct on the part of an undertaking such as for example the arbitrary refusal to supply repairers: *Philips Electronics NV v. Ingman Ltd* [1999] F.S.R. 112 (Art. 86 defences struck out and Art. 85 claims stayed to be tried separately).

Relief and remedies 24–93
NOTE 53. Add: See for a comprehensive review of exhaustion of patent rights: Cases C-267/95 and C-268/95 *Merck & Co Inc v. Primecrown Ltd* [1997] F.S.R. 237 ECJ.

NOTE 60: Add. There is no cause of action for unjust enrichment to supplement the statutory remedies for patent infringement: *Union Carbide Corp. v. BP Chemicals Ltd* [1998] F.S.R. 1.

NOTE 63: Add: In *Coflexip SA v. Stolt Comex Seaway MS Ltd* [1999] F.S.R. 473, an injunction in the form "restraining the defendant from infringing the patent" was refused. The injunction was limited to the acts of infringement proved, with liberty to apply for wider relief.

NOTE 65. Add: The merits of the claim can be considered in an appropriate case: *Series 5 Software Ltd v. Philip Clarke* [1996] F.S.R. 273.

NOTE 67. Add: now reported at [1995] R.P.C. 383.

Action to restrain unjustified threats of infringement proceedings 24–97
NOTE 88. Delete final sentence of note and add: On scope of s.70(4) see *Cavity Trays Ltd v. RMC Panel Products Ltd* [1996] R.P.C. 361.

Add: A system of plant variety rights also exists at E.C. level under Council Regulation 2100/94, O.J. L227/1, 1.1.94 [1995] F.S.R. 396. This provides an alternative to national plant variety or patent rights and does not allow cumulative protection. **24–98**

CHAPTER 25.—PASSING OFF

25–01   **General principles**
   Chocosuisse Union des Fabricants Suisses de Chocolate v. Cadbury Ltd, The Times, March 15, 1999, CA. A trade association, the membership of which included the majority of Swiss-based chocolate manufacturers but which did not itself sell chocolate, lacked *locus standi* (whether in its own right or as a representative) to sue in passing off since it lacked a legitimate business interest to sue.
   NOTE 8. Add: *Matthew Gloag & Sons Ltd v. Welsh Distilleries Ltd,* [1988] F.S.R. 718, Laddie J. Inverse passing off could amount to the tort.

25–06   **Non-traders**
   NOTE 27. Add: *Law Society of England and Wales v. Society of Lawyers* [1996] F.S.R. 701.

25–07   **Misrepresentations actionable as passing off**
   Waterford Wedgewood plc v. David Nagli Ltd [1998] F.S.R. 92: no misrepresentations were made to the public by the defendants but they were liable for the misrepresentations made by them to the representatives of companies to whom they had supplied counterfeit goods.

25–09   **Trade marks and trade names**
   NOTE 35. Add: *British Telecommunications plc v. One in a Million* [1999] F.S.R. 1, CA. The defendants by registering the plaintiffs' company names as domain names as part of a scam to gain money from the legitimate owners, were held liable in passing off, threatened passing off and under the doctrine of instruments of deception. Aldous L.J. commented that Lord Diplock's test in *Advocaat* did not confine the cause of action forever "as to do so would prevent the common law evolving to meet changes in methods of trade and communication as it had in the past".

25–14   **Proof of deception and confusion**
   NOTE 66. Add: *Harrods Ltd v. Harrodian School Ltd* [1996] R.P.C. 697, where the Court of Appeal held that the misrepresentation must be of a connection which would lead the public to think that the defendant had "made itself responsible for the quality of the plaintiff's goods or services".
   Add: The test on the issue of deception or confusion was whether on the balance of probabilities a substantial number of members of the public would be misled into purchasing the defendants' product in the belief that it was the plaintiff's: *Neutrogena Corporation v. Golden Ltd* [1996] R.P.C. 473.

CHAPTER 26.—BREACH OF CONFIDENCE

		PARA.
▪1.	Where an obligation of confidence arises	26–01
▪2.	The nature of confidential information	26–10
3.	The parties	26–12
☐4.	Defences	26–16
▪5.	Remedies	26–20

1.—WHERE AN OBLIGATION OF CONFIDENCE ARISES

General principles   26–01
NOTE 1. *Kitechnology* is reported at [1995] F.S.R. 765. Breach of confidence may amount to unlawful means for the purposes of an action for unlawful interference with business interests (as to which see § 23–56 of the main work): *Indata Equipment Supplies Ltd v. ACL Ltd* [1998] F.S.R. 248, CA, where both causes of action succeeded.

As to the position of co-owners of confidential information, see *Drummond Murray v. Yorkshire Fund Managers Ltd* [1998] F.S.R. 372 (confidential information ceased to be the plaintiff's once the relationship had dissolved).

Add: It is not necessary for there to be a pre-existing relationship between the   26–03
parties for an obligation of confidence to arise. Thus, *e.g.*, interlocutory injunctions based, *inter alia*, on breach of confidence have been granted in cases where the defendant threatened to publish confidential details of film set and record cover designs: *Shelley Films Ltd v. Rex Features Ltd* [1994] E.M.L.R. 134; *Creation Records Ltd v. News Group Newspapers Ltd* [1997] F.S.R. 444.

NOTE 9. Add: A claim in breach of confidence can arise in confidential market   26–04
reports: *PCR Ltd v. Dow Jones Telerate Ltd* [1998] F.S.R. 170 (the confidence case failed on the facts but a parallel copyright claim succeeded).

Family and personal matters   26–07
NOTE 39. Add: See also *Michael Barrymore v. News Group Newspapers Ltd* [1997] F.S.R. 600, (merely disclosing fact of relationship may have added nothing new but defendant went into details not in the public domain injunction granted).

Professional relationships   26–08
NOTE 46. Add: For the position of police photographers, see *Hellewell v. Chief Constable of Derbyshire* [1995] 1 W.L.R. 804 (duty of confidence could arise but unanswerable public interest defence on the facts).

2.—THE NATURE OF CONFIDENTIAL INFORMATION

NOTE 64. Add: see also *CMI-Centres for Medical Innovation GmbH v. Phyto-*   26–10
pharm plc [1999] F.S.R. 235.

4.—DEFENCES

Public interest   26–19
NOTE 2. Add: See also *Hellewell v. Chief Constable of Derbyshire* [1995] 1

W.L.R. 804 (public interest in dissemination of confidential photograph reasonably directed to the prevention of crime).

5.—REMEDIES

26–20   Injunction

NOTE 4. Add: It is not a universal principle that an injunction will be granted to prevent a party availing himself in any manner of a breach of confidence. Whether the use of a derived product should be treated as a use of the confidential information used in its creation has to be determined by the particular facts of the case. Further, an injunction may be refused if it would be oppressive: *Ocular Sciences Ltd v. Aspect Vision Care Ltd* [1997] R.P.C. 289.

Add: Where an interlocutory injunction is sought to restrain breach of confidence the court will be wary of granting relief where no attempt is made to disentangle material which is confidential from that which is not: *CMI-Centers for Medical Innovation GmbH v. Phytopharm plc* [1999] F.S.R. 235, also emphasising the importance of identifying that which is alleged to be confidential and why.

CHAPTER 27.—DAMAGES

		PARA.
1.	Introduction	27–01
□2.	General principles	27–02
■3.	Damages for personal injuries	27–09
■4.	Death: survival of causes of action	27–30
■5.	Death as a cause of action	27–38
6.	Destruction of or damage to goods	27–57
□7.	Recovery of costs of action	27–63
□8.	Equitable damages	27–64
□9.	Exemplary damages	27–66
■10.	Restitutionary damages	27–73
□11.	Appeals on quantum of damages	27–74

2.—GENERAL PRINCIPLES

(f) Certainty   27–07

NOTE 72. Add: In *Allied Maples Group Ltd v. Simmons & Simmons* [1995] 1 W.L.R. 1602, the Court of Appeal held that where the plaintiff's loss resulting from the defendant's negligence depended on the hypothetical action of a third party, the issue fell within the sphere of quantification of damages dependent upon the evaluation of the chance that the third party would have taken the action which would have enabled the loss to be avoided rather than the sphere of causation, where the plaintiff could only succeed if he showed on the balance of probability that the third party would have taken that action. Hence, the plaintiff was entitled to succeed provided he showed that there was a substantial, and not merely a speculative, chance that the third party would have taken the action to confer the benefit or avoid the risk to the plaintiff. See also *Stovold v. Barlows, The Times*, October 30, 1995 where the Court of Appeal took a similar approach. Both cases concerned solicitors' negligence but the principles are of general application. See also *Doyle v. Wallace* [1998] P.I.Q.R. Q146. For a useful general summary of the English law, see Hogg, "Lost Chances in Contract and Delict" 1997 S.L.T. 71.

3.—DAMAGES FOR PERSONAL INJURIES

Itemisation of award   27–09

NOTE 87. Add: In *John v. MGN Ltd* [1996] 3 W.L.R. 593, the Court of Appeal laid down that in defamation cases the scale of awards for non-pecuniary loss in personal injury cases can be drawn to the attention of juries and that the level of an appropriate award can be indicated by a judge. See also § 21–203, *ante*, and § 27–74, *post*. In *Thompson v. Commissioner of Police for the Metropolis* [1997] 2 All E.R. 762, it was held that a similar approach of giving juries guidance on the level of awards should apply in false imprisonment and malicious prosecution cases as was laid down for defamation cases in the *John* case. Indeed the Court of Appeal went on to lay down the appropriate starting figures (and some "ceiling figures") for compensatory (including aggravated) and exemplary damages in such cases of actions against the police: see §§ 27–68 and 27–74, *post*.

Medical and other expenses   27–10

In the second sentence substitute 3 per cent for 2 per cent.

NOTES 7–8. The cases referred to in these notes must now be read subject to *Wells v. Wells* [1998] 3 W.L.R. 329, HL, which has laid down, *inter alia*, that the discount

rate used in calculating the cost of the capital, for the purposes of applying *Roberts
v. Johnstone*, is the interest rate on index-linked government stock (ILGS), which
was for the time being treated as being 3 per cent.

NOTE 14. Add: In *Kroeker v. Jansen* (1995) 123 D.L.R. (4th) 652, the plaintiff's
injuries rendered her less able to perform household tasks involving bending and
lifting. After the accident, she married and the household tasks were shared with her
husband who performed the heavier work. The majority of the British Columbia
Court of Appeal, citing *Daly v. General Steam Navigation* as authority for awards
for partial loss of housekeeping capacity, accepted that the plaintiff would be "disabled from some of her housework beyond the level that her husband ought reasonably to do for her" to the extent of 130 hours per year and awarded $7,000 com-
pensation calculated on the basis of $10 per hour. The minority distinguished *Daly*
on the ground that there it was reasonable for the wife to engage outside household
help whilst in *Kroeker* no outside help was required because the tasks were such
that the husband might be expected to share. He did not "do those tasks *for his wife*,
as might be the case were personal or nursing care involved, but does them for the
benefit of the household they share. It is work he would do if he lived on his own."
The minority concluded that compensation for loss of domestic self-sufficiency
should form part of the plaintiff's non-pecuniary award.

27–11 Plaintiff's needs supplied by a third party

NOTE 24. Add: In *Fairhurst v. St Helens and Knowsley Health Authority* [1995]
4 P.I.Q.R. Q1, the High Court assessed the costs of the care provided by a mother
for her child, born severely disabled due to the defendant's negligence, on the basis
of three-quarters of the crossroad rate for home helps accepted by the local authority.
This was considered to be the proper basis for the award as the mother had no firm
plans to return to work after the birth.

NOTE 25. See also *Dimond v. Lovell* [1999] 3 W.L.R. 561, CA (provision of a
car). The High Court of Australia in *Kars v. Kars* (1996) 71 A.J.L.R. 107 has refused
to follow *Hunt v. Severs* [1994] 2 W.L.R. 602, preferring the approach in *Donnelly
v. Joyce* [1974] Q.B. 454.

27–12 Loss of earnings

NOTE 26. Add: *West v. Versil Ltd, The Times*, August 31, 1996, CA; *Longden v.
British Coal Corp.* [1997] 3 W.L.R. 1336, HL.

NOTE 28. Add: See *Kent v. British Railways Board* [1995] 4 P.I.Q.R. Q42, where
the claim was for loss of business profits. The plaintiff and her husband ran the
business, splitting the profits 40/60 for tax purposes. The Court of Appeal held that
the presumption of equal partnership prevailed over the tax split and the plaintiff
was entitled to 50 per cent of the loss of profits suffered by the whole business as a
result of its being scaled down after her accident. The husband had no claim as he
was owed no duty of care by the defendant. In *Ward v. Newalls Insulation Co. Ltd*
[1998] 2 All E.R. 690, the Court of Appeal awarded the plaintiff, as damages for
loss of earnings, 50 percent of the lost business profits, even though he was in
partnership with three other partners and, prior to his illness, had been treated, for
taxation purposes, as taking only 25 percent of the partnership's profits. The reality
was that he was in partnership with one other; the other two partners (their wives)
contributed nothing to the business (in contrast to the factual position in the *Kent*
case).

NOTE 45. Add: *Wells v. Wells* [1998] 3 W.L.R. 329, HL, has confirmed that
Hodgson v. Trapp [1998] A.C. 807, remains good law in laying down that higher
rate tax, payable on the income from investing the damages for future pecuniary
loss, should normally be ignored.

27–14 Future inflation

All this must now be read subject to the important decision of the House of Lords
in *Wells v. Wells* [1998] 3 W.L.R. 329. It was there laid down that the appropriate
discount rate for calculating future pecuniary loss in personal injury cases is the rate

of return on index-linked government stock (ILGS). At present this was taken to be 3 per cent (net of basic rate tax) which contrasts with the traditional basing of multipliers on $4\frac{1}{2}$ per cent interest (which is the rate of return to be expected from investing in equities and gilts). Their Lordships' preference for the ILGS rate was based on three main strands of reasoning.

First, and most importantly, personal injury victims are not to be regarded as being in the same position as ordinary prudent investors. This is because they have to rely on the investment fund to pay for their everyday needs. Therefore where the fund has fallen in value the personal injury victim cannot choose to leave it largely untouched in the expectation that its value will recover over time. Lord Lloyd of Berwick said, at 335–336:

> "While . . . I agree with the Court of Appeal that, in calculating the lump sum, courts are entitled to assume that the plaintiff will behave prudently I do not agree that what is prudent for the ordinary investor is necessarily prudent for the plaintiff. Indeed the opposite may be the case. What the prudent plaintiff needs is an investment which will buy him the income he requires without the risks inherent in the equity market; which brings us back to ILGS."

Secondly, although at present there is no ILGS maturing later than 2030, ILGS is the most accurate means of calculating future loss precisely because it is inflation-proof. As Lord Lloyd said, at 336, "[T]he court now has at its disposal a tool for calculating damages which enables it to assume a stable currency until at least 2030."

Thirdly, even if true (which was contradicted by research carried out by the Law Commission), it is irrelevant that the majority of plaintiffs (or the particular plaintiff) are likely to invest the damages in equities or gilts. The important question is rather whether the plaintiff is entitled to have his damages calculated on the basis that he will not take the risk of investing in equities and gilts.

Their Lordships further pointed out that the views of the Ogden Working Party, (*Actuarial Tables for Use in Personal Injury and Fatal Accident Cases* (3rd ed., 1998, HMSO)), the Law Commission and of David Kemp Q.C., who have all favoured the ILGS rate, are entitled to great weight.

It should be noted that section 1(1) of the Damages Act 1996 provides that:

> "in determining the return to be expected from the investment of a sum awarded as damages for future pecuniary loss . . . the court shall . . . take into account such rate of return (if any) as may from time to time be prescribed by an order made by the Lord Chancellor."

The Lord Chancellor said that, in deciding whether to make an order under this section, he would await the outcome of the *Wells v. Wells* case. It remains to be seen what, if anything, he will now do.

The decision in *Wells* is also important because of their Lordships' willingness to apply the Ogden Working tables as giving the appropriate multiplier for a particular rate of discount. In Lord Lloyd's words, at 347, "I do not suggest that the judge should be a slave to the tables. There may well be special factors in particular cases. But the tables should now be regarded as the starting-point, rather than a check. A judge should be slow to depart from the relevant actuarial multiplier on impressionistic grounds, or by reference to 'a spread of multipliers in comparable cases' especially when the multipliers were fixed before actuarial tables were widely used."

Loss of earning capacity   **27–15**

NOTE 71. Add: But see *Dhaliwal v. Personal Representatives of Hunt* [1995] 4 P.I.Q.R. Q56, where the Court of Appeal in the context of assessing damages for a five-year-old for handicap on the labour market, commented that it might be equally appropriate to apply the multiplier approach as the lump sum approach. Both were equally speculative where it was impossible to say what the plaintiff could have done but for the accident.

27–16   Effect of plaintiff's liability to tax

NOTE 74. Add to the second sentence: Dawes, "Tax and Damages" (1998) 148
N.L.J. 337.

NOTE 81. Add: *Deeny v. Gooda Walker Ltd (No. 2)* [1996] 1 W.L.R. 426, provides
a recent example of damages being subject to tax. The House of Lords held that an
award of damages to Lloyd's names against their agents constituted a receipt of the
names' underwriting business and was taxable in their hands as arising out of trade.
Lord Hoffmann stated that for a receipt to arise out of trade, it did not need to
become payable by virtue of some pre-existing trade relationship and hence, compensation for tortious damage to the trade was taxable.

27–17   Receipts of social security benefits

This must be read subject to the Social Security (Recovery of Benefits) Act 1997.
See the deatailed article by Andrew Dismore, "Social Security (Recovery of
Benefits) Acts 1997 and Regulations" [1998] J.P.I.L. 14. This Act replaces the
Social Security Administration Act 1992, Pt IV. The essential change made by the
new Act is to protect damages awarded for pain, suffering and loss of amenity
against recoupment of social security benefits. That is, by section 8 and Schedule 2
of the new Act recoupment shall only be against compensation for loss of earnings,
cost of care and loss of mobility, and then only "like for like". So, while the defendant remains liable to the Secretary of State for an amount equal to the total amount
of the recoverable benefits paid to the victim, payment of that amount will not
discharge a liability of the defendant to pay damages for pain, suffering and loss of
amenity to the victim. In effect, therefore, the 1997 Act imposes a new additional
liability on defendants for the (unrecoupable) loss suffered by the DSS in providing
social security benefits to plaintiffs injured by a tort (or other wrong).

Under the 1997 Act, there is no automatic exclusion for "small payments" (of
£2,500 or less) but Part II of Schedule 1 enables regulations to be made for the
disregarding of small payments. Section 2(1) (and the linked sub-sections (1A), (3)
and (6)) of the Law Reform (Personal Injuries) Act 1948, which applied a half-
deduction for five years of social security benefits, where damages were £2,500 or
less, is repealed.

In the 1992 Act, there was a specific provision (section 103) to the effect that, in
assessing the amount of interest payable on damages, the relevant sum of damages
was to be reduced by the amount of the recoupable social security benefits. This
was in line with principle in ensuring that the claimant was awarded interest only in
respect of his loss (or put another way, in respect of those damages which he had
been kept out of). But that specific provision was not re-enacted in the 1997 Act
and this led the Court of Appeal in *Wadey v. Surrey County Council* [1999] 2 All
E.R. 334 to decide that interest should be payable on the whole amount of damages
irrespective of the recoupable social security benefits. Reliance was placed on the
decision to the same effect of the Scottish Court of Session (Inner House) in *Wisely
v. John Fulton (Plumbers) Ltd* 1998 S.L.T. 1026.

In the 1992 Act there was a provision specifically excluding Fatal Accident Act
claims from the recoupment scheme. The 1997 Act has no such specific provision
but it would appear that the listed social security benefits to be recouped do not
include those that would be paid to dependants consequent on another's death.

In *McCafferey v. Datta* [1997] 1 W.L.R. 870 it was held that, in determining
whether an award of damages exceeds a payment in, it was irrelevant that some or
all of the damages were to be paid by the defendant to the Compensation Recovery
Unit, rather than to the plaintiff. On the facts, therefore, a payment in of £2,500 did
not beat an award of £22,373.33 the whole of which was payable to the CRU.

Hassall v. Secretary of State for Social Security was considered in *Hunter v.
Butler* [1996] R.T.R. 396, CA; and, following the solution suggested in *Hassall*,
damages for loss of the social security benefits that the plaintiff was receiving prior
to the accident were awarded in *Neal v. Bingle* [1998] 2 W.L.R. 57, CA.

27–20   Receipts of other benefits

NOTE 26. Add: In *Longden v. British Coal Corp.* [1997] 3 W.L.R. 1336, the House of Lords followed *Parry v. Cleaver* in deciding that the plaintiff was entitled to damages for his net loss of pension after normal retirement age (*i.e.* one should deduct from the retirement pension he would have received after normal retirement age the disability pension that he would now receive after normal retirement age). The defendants' argument that, in calculating the loss of pension, one should also deduct the disability pension received prior to normal retirement age was rejected as inconsistent with *Parry v. Cleaver*. The defendants conceded that, applying *Parry v. Cleaver*, the disability pension must be ignored in calculating damages for loss of earnings. See also *West v. Versil Ltd, The Times*, August 31, 1996, CA.

NOTE 27. Add: But in *Longden v. British Coal Corp.* [1997] 3 W.L.R. 1336, Lord Hope, with whom the other Law Lords agreed, regarded it as irrelevant whether the incapacity pension was or was not derived from the same scheme as the retirement pension.

NOTE 35. Add: See also *Page v. Sheerness Steel plc* [1996] 5 P.I.Q.R. Q26, in which it was held that the plaintiff's permanent health benefits under his employer's pension scheme were deductible from his claim for loss of earnings because the employer and not the plaintiff had paid the premiums and hence the benefits corresponded to wages in the sense of sick pay. Dyson J. stated that it was an essential requirement of the insurance exception that the cost of the insurance be borne at least in part by the plaintiff.

Non-pecuniary loss generally 27–21

See generally the Law Commission's Report, *Damages for Personal Injury: Non-Pecuniary Loss* (Law Com No. 257, 1999).

NOTE 48. Add: In *Andrews v. Grand & Toy Alberta Ltd* (1978) 83 D.L.R. (3d) 452, Dickson J., giving the judgment of the Supreme Court of Canada, adopted a "functional approach" under which the purpose of the award is seen as providing solace to the plaintiff, *e.g.* by enabling him to purchase substitute pleasures, rather than the traditional "diminution of value" approach under which the purpose is to compensate him for what he has lost. The Law Commission Report No. 257, *Damages for Personal Injury: Non-pecuniary Loss* (1999), discussed both approaches and came to the conclusion that the "diminution of value" approach was to be preferred.

NOTE 49. Add: In *Dureau v. Evans* [1995] 5 P.I.Q.R. Q18, the Court of Appeal suggested in the case of non-pecuniary loss for multiple injuries, that the figures given in the Judicial Studies Board guidelines might not be much help because of the need to take an overview of the injuries and offset losses. The preferable approach might be to take the most serious injury, find a comparable award and add to that elements for the other injuries.

Pain and suffering 27–22

NOTE 51. Add: See also *Bryan v. Philips New Zealand Ltd* [1995] 1 N.Z.L.R. 632, where compensation for cancerphobia was awarded.

Interest on damages 27–25

The third paragraph on interest on damages for non-pecuniary loss must now be read subject to *Wells v. Wells* [1998] 3 W.L.R. 329. Although the rate for awarding interest was not in issue, it is strongly arguable that the preference for the ILGS rate, as the most accurate indicator of the rate of interest on a low-risk investment, means that 3 per cent, rather than 2 per cent, should now be the rate of interest applied on damages for pain, suffering and loss of amenity.

Interim payments 27–27

NOTE 19. An interim payment order can now be made against the Motor Insurers' Bureau: *Sharp v. Pereira* [1999] 1 W.L.R. 195 (*Powney v. Coxage, The Times*, March 8, 1988 having been reversed by changes in the Rules of the Supreme Court).

27–28 **Provisional damages**

Add to end of paragraph: Section 3 of the Damages Act 1996 provides that where a plaintiff dies of his injuries after receiving a provisional award, his dependants will not be precluded from claiming for loss of dependency but that such part of the provisional damages or further damages awarded before the plaintiff's death "as was intended to compensate him for pecuniary loss in a period which in the event falls after his death shall be taken into account in assessing the amount of any loss of support" suffered by dependents.

27–29 **Structured settlements**

Add to end of paragraph: The Damages Act 1996 which came into force on September 24, 1996, gives effect to the principal recommendations of the Law Commission report *Structured Settlements and Interim and Provisional Damages* (1994) No 224. Section 2 provides that a court awarding damages may with the consent of the parties, order such damages to take the form of periodical payments. This ensures that the possibility of structuring the damages is not precluded in those few, but often more serious cases, where a court hearing takes place. Section 4 provides the plaintiff with complete protection under the Policyholders Protection scheme if an insurer backing a structured settlement goes bankrupt. Section 6 provides analogous protection for public sector structured settlements by allowing the Crown to provide a guarantee so that the plaintiff will be protected if the public sector body backing the settlement, for example an NHS trust, were to cease to exist. It should be noted that section 142 of the Finance Act 1995 implemented the Commission's recommendation that a liability insurer should be able to assign the benefit of the annuity to the plaintiff so that he can receive payments free of tax directly from the life office.

4.—DEATH: SURVIVAL OF CAUSES OF ACTION

27–36 **Provisional damages**

See *supra*, § 27–28.

5.—DEATH AS A CAUSE OF ACTION

27–40 **Dependants**

Add note 90a at end of phrase "and had been so living for two years before the death;" in line 9:

Add to the end of the paragraph: These criticisms have now been reflected in the Court of Appeal judgment in *Shepherd v. The Post Office*[94a] where it was said that a simpler approach would have been to enact a provision that any person who could show a relationship of dependence on the deceased should be entitled to make a claim.

NOTE 90a. See *Pounder v. London Underground Ltd* [1995] P.I.Q.R. P217, in which it was held that a brief absence from the home during the two-year period prior to death did not give rise to a break in continuity in the context of a ten-year relationship.

NOTE 94a. *The Times*, June 15, 1995.

27–41 **Nature of action under Fatal Accidents Act**

NOTE 3. See now s.3 of the Damages Act 1996, *supra,* § 27–28.

NOTE 4. In *Jameson v. Central Electricity Generating Board* [1999] 2 W.L.R. 141, HL, a settlement, satisfying a claim against one joint and several tortfeasor, on its true interpretation extinguished the cause of action against the other joint and several tortfeasor.

Bereavement damages
NOTE 16. Add: In *Navaei v. Navaei* (unreported, 1995), the court rejected a father's argument that he was entitled to the full award as the child's death was caused by the mother's negligence. It was said that the statutory scheme was intended to ensure that there was just one claim. Hence, the father had to claim for the mother as well. As there could be no award from the mother for the mother, the father's claim was limited to half the full award.

Loss of pecuniary benefit
NOTE 19. Add: See also *Hunter v. Butler* [1996] R.T.R. 396 where the Court of Appeal rejected the plaintiff's claim to an expectation of benefit from her husband's part-time earnings which he had fraudulently failed to disclose when claiming social security benefits. It was held that the proceeds of illegal concealed earnings could not be treated as a valid head of recovery. But loss of dependency can include a loss of, or reduction in, state benefits because of the death: *Cox v. Hockenhull* [1999] 3 All E.R. 577, CA.

NOTE 26. Add: See also *Johnson v. British Midland Airways Ltd* [1996] 5 P.I.Q.R.
Q8, where a father successfully claimed the costs of journeys home from work abroad to support his son, and for the cost of extra tuition to compensate for the deceased mother's support for the child's school-work.

NOTE 2a. Add: See also *Cox v. Hockenhull* [1999] 3 All E.R. 577, CA.

Pecuniary gains
Stanley v. Saddique [1992] Q.B. 1 was followed in *R. v. Criminal Injuries Compensation Board, ex p. K.* [1999] 2 W.L.R. 948. In the latter case, the question was what compensation should be payable to children under the old Criminal Injuries Compensation Scheme where their mother had been murdered but the children had been well looked after by their uncle and aunt. On a judicial review application, the Divisional Court held that, following *Stanley v. Saddique,* the gratuitous services of the uncle and aunt should be disregarded under section 4 of the 1976 Act. The children's compensation should not therefore have been reduced from £35,000 to £9,000. *Hayden v. Hayden* [1992] 1 W.L.R. 986 was distinguished as a case on its special facts, namely that the provider of the gratuitous services was the tortfeasor and indeed was carrying out his parental duty.

Carriage by Air Act 1961
NOTE 8. Add: *Herd v. Clyde Helicopters Ltd* [1997] 2 W.L.R. 380, HL (Sc).

7.—RECOVERY OF COSTS OF ACTION

NOTES 84 and 86. Add: *British Racing Drivers' Club Ltd v. Hextall Erskine & Co*
[1996] 3 All E.R. 667.

8.—EQUITABLE DAMAGES

Jurisdiction to award damages
NOTE 91. Add: For the different remedy of equitable compensation awarded for, for example, breach of trust, see *Target Holdings Ltd v. Redferns* [1995] 3 W.L.R. 352, HL.

NOTE 93. Add: Note that in *Mahoney v. Purnell* [1996] 3 All E.R. 61, May J. held that the court has a wider jurisdiction to award compensation in equity where the normal equitable remedy of setting aside an agreement and taking of an account would not do practical justice between the parties. The case concerned undue influence but the principle is equally applicable to other forms of breach of fiduciary duty. As such situations may also give rise to liability in tort, it is possible that "fair

equitable" compensation may be an alternative to common law compensation in
some cases. Whether this is likely to make a difference is more questionable. In
Mahoney May J. adopted a similar approach to calculating the equitable damages
against the relative with the undue influence and to the common law damages against
the solicitor who failed to warn of the need for independent advice.

9.—EXEMPLARY DAMAGES

See, generally, *Exemplary, Aggravated and Restitutionary Damages*, Law Com.
No. 247 (1997).

27–66   Distinguished from aggravated damages
Add: This has now been recommended by the Law Commission in its Report,
Aggravated, Exemplary and Restitutionary Damages, Law Com. No. 247 (1997),
para. 2.42 and Draft Bill, clause 13.

See on the distinction between aggravated and exemplary damages, *John v. MGN
Ltd* [1996] 3 W.L.R. 593 and *Thompson v. Commissioner of Police for the Metropolis* [1997] 3 W.L.R. 403.

NOTE 18. Add: See also *Appleton v. Garrett* [1996] 5 P.I.Q.R. P1, where aggravated damages were awarded against a dentist who deliberately withheld from patients
the information that the treatment was unnecessary.

27–67   Scope of exemplary damages
NOTE 28. Add to the end of the penultimate sentence: *Cala Homes (South) Ltd v.
Alfred McAlpine Homes East Ltd (No. 2)* [1996] F.S.R. 36. But the decision of
Laddie J. was expressly not applied by the Court of Session in *Redrow Homes Ltd
v. Bett Brothers plc*, 1997 S.C. 142. The question in each case was whether additional damages under s.97(2) of the Copyright, Designs and Patents Act 1988 could
be awarded where the plaintiff had elected for an account of profits rather than
compensatory damages. Laddie J. in the former case thought that as "additional
damages" were equivalent to exemplary damages they could be so added. In the
latter case, the Court of Session considered that as additional damages were compensatory, they could not be added to an account of profits. It should be emphasised,
however, that Scottish law has no concept of exemplary damages. In Scotland, therefore, there is a particularly strong reason for not construing s.97(2) as empowering
the award of exemplary damages. On appeal, the House of Lords [1998] 2 W.L.R.
198, overruled the *Cala Homes* case and, in upholding the Court of Session, decided
that, as a matter of statutory interpretation, additional damages could not be added
to an account of profits under s.97(2) of the 1988 Act. While not deciding the point,
Lord Clyde at 205, said that damages under s.97(2) were, more probably, aggravated
rather than exemplary.

27–68   The categories
NOTE 40. Add: In *Thompson v. Commissioner of Police for the Metropolis* [1997]
3 W.L.R. 403, the Court of Appeal laid down guideline figures for juries on *quantum*
(including exemplary damages) in false imprisonment and malicious prosecution
actions against the police. The starting figure for basic compensatory damages in a
case of false imprisonment should be £500 for the first hour of "imprisonment" and
£3,000 for 24 hours. (*c.f. R. v. Governor of Brockhill Prison, ex p. Evans (No. 2)*
[1999] 2 W.L.R. 103 where, in a very different type of case, a global figure of
£5,000 was awarded for 59 extra days of imprisonment). The starting figure in a
case of malicious prosecution should be £2,000 and for prosecution continuing for
as long as two years and going to the Crown Court, an award of £10,000 could be
appropriate. Aggravated damages might then be added which would not be likely to
be less than £1,000 but unlikely to be more than double the basic compensatory
damages. If exemplary damages are awarded they should not be less than £500 but

not more than £50,000; and it would be unusual for exemplary damages to be more
than three times the sum of (basic and aggravated) compensatory damages. All these
figures would need to be adjusted in the future to take account of inflation. See also
post, § 27–74.
Note 46. Add: *John v. MGN Ltd* [1996] 3 W.L.R. 593.

No exemplary damages prior to Rookes v. Barnard
27–69
Note 58. Add: See also *R. v. Secretary of State for Transport, ex p. Factortame
Ltd (No. 5), The Times,* September 11, 1997, QBD.
Note 61. Add: One might have also thought that *AB v. South West Water Services
Ltd* [1993] Q.B. 507, dictates that exemplary damages cannot be awarded for unlawful eviction under ss.27–28 of the Housing Act 1988. But in *Francis v. Brown* (1998)
30 H.L.R. 143, CA, there was no mention of *AB v. South Water Services* as barring
exemplary damages under the Housing Act 1988, although they were in any event
denied because one of the joint defendants did not merit punishment (see *supra*, §
27–71). See also on European Community law wrongs, *R. v. Secretary of State for
Transport, ex p. Factortame Ltd (No. 5), The Times,* September 11, 1997, QBD.

Considerations in awarding exemplary damages
27–70
Add: In *Lancashire County Council v. Municipal Mutual Insurance Ltd* [1996] 3
W.L.R. 493, it was held that, at least where exemplary damages are being awarded
against a defendant on the basis of vicarious liability for another's wrong (here
against a county council or police chief constable for false imprisonment and malicious prosecution by police constables), there is no public policy prohibiting insurance against a liability to pay exemplary damages. It was also held that the insurance
policy in question, although phrased in terms of indemnifying against a liability to
pay compensation, could be and should be construed as indemnifying against a
liability to pay exemplary damages.
Note 65. Add: *John v. MGN Ltd* [1996] 3 W.L.R. 593.
Note 66. Add: In *Gray v. Motor Accident Commission* (1978) 73 A.L.J.R. 45 it
was held by the High Court of Australia that, where a defendant had been imprisoned
for the conduct in question (deliberately injuring the claimant by driving a car at
him), there was an automatic bar against the claimant being awarded exemplary
damages in an action for negligence.

Joint defendants
27–71
This paragraph was cited with approval by the Court of Appeal in *Francis v.
Brown* (1998) 30 H.L.R. 143.

10.—Restitutionary Damages

See, generally, the Law Commission's Report, *Aggravated, Exemplary and Restitutionary Damages,* Law Com. No. 247 (1997).
Note 71. Insert after the *Potton* case: *Island Records Ltd v. Tring International
plc* [1995] 3 All E.R. 444.
27–73
Note 73. Add: See also *Inverugie Investments Ltd v. Hackett* [1995] 1 W.L.R.
713, where Lord Lloyd giving the judgment of the Privy Council, held that a person
who let out goods on hire or the landlord of a residential property was entitled to
recover damages from a trespasser who wrongfully used his property irrespective of
whether he could show that he would have let the property to anybody else and
whether or not he would have used the property himself. On the facts, the plaintiff
was held entitled to recover a reasonable rent for the wrongful use of his property
by the trespasser although the plaintiff might not have suffered any actual loss by
being deprived of the property.

11.—Appeals on Quantum of Damages

27-74   **Appeals from jury**

Add: In *John v. MGN Ltd* [1996] 3 W.L.R. 593 the Court of Appeal laid down that in defamation cases the scale of awards for non-pecuniary loss in personal injury cases could be drawn to the attention of juries and that the level of an appropriate award could be indicated by the judge. (This was in line with the majority of the High Court of Australia in *Carson v. John Fairfax & Sons Ltd* (1993) 178 C.L.R. 44.) Nevertheless Sir Thomas Bingham M.R. said, at 615. "The jury must of course make up their own mind and must be directed to do so. They will not be bound by the submission of counsel or the indication of the judge. If the jury make an award outside the upper or lower bounds of any bracket indicated and such award is the subject of appeal, real weight must be given to the possibility that their judgment is to be preferred to that of the judge". The Court of Appeal substituted a figure of £35,000 compensatory damages for the "excessive" £75,000 damages awarded by the jury. The Court of Appeal also substituted a figure of £50,000 exemplary damages for the "manifestly excessive" £275,000 awarded by the jury. In *Thompson v. Commissioner of Police for the Metropolis*—see *supra*, § 27–68—the Court of Appeal substituted £15,000 exemplary damages for the £200,000 awarded to Mr Hsu.

CHAPTER 28.—INJUNCTIONS

		PARA.
■1.	Introduction	28–01
2.	Prohibitory injunctions	28–04
3.	Mandatory injunctions	28–08
4.	Action *quia timet*	28–10
■5.	Interlocutory injunctions	28–13
6.	Injunctions and declarations against the Crown	28–35

1.—INTRODUCTION

Torts of all kinds may be restrained by injunction where "just or convenient"   28–02

In *Burris v. Azadani* [1995] 1 W.L.R. 1372 the Court of Appeal upheld the legality of an injunction effectively imposing an "exclusion zone" on the defendant to prevent him repeating his harassment of the plaintiff. The court acknowledged that the effect of the order was to forbid certain lawful actions on the part of the defendant namely, his free and lawful use of the highway. Nonetheless the defendant had engaged in clearly tortious conduct and the order was necessary to protect the interests of the plaintiff who had an interest in her health and personal safety ". . . which the court must be astute to protect". Such orders should not be made readily and only with good reason. No restraint should be imposed on a defendant which is not necessary to protect the plaintiff.

In *Coflexip SA v. Scott Comex Seaway MS Ltd* [1999] 2 All E.R. 593 Laddie J. held that an injunction in wide standard form ("to restrain the defendant from infringing" the patent in question) went beyond what was necessary to protect the claimant and was unfair to the defendant. A narrow form injunction, limited to the particular types of infringement threatened, with liberty to apply to extend the injunction, was more appropriate.

Discretion of the court   28–03

The importance in relation to the grant of any injunction of the exercise of discretion, and the role to be played by public policy considerations, is re-inforced by the judgment in *Department of Social Security v. Butler* [1995] 1 W.L.R. 1528, CA.

5.—INTERLOCUTORY INJUNCTIONS

Interlocutory injunctions   28–13

Note the judgment in *Burris v. Azadani* [1995] 1 W.L.R. 1372, *supra* at § 28–02. In *Series 5 Software Ltd v. Clarke* [1996] 1 All E.R. 853 Laddie J. held that in determining whether or not to grant an interlocutory injunction the court was not precluded from considering the strength of the parties' respective cases albeit no attempt should be made at that stage to resolve any complex issues fact or law. In assessing the balance of convenience in relation to the plaintiffs' application, a key factor leading to the refusal of the application in that case was that to grant the application would effectively deprive the defendants of their livelihood. The plaintiffs' claim of immediate damage was poorly substantiated, and the status quo too, favoured refusal of an injunction.

NOTE 77. Add: *Hodge Clemco Ltd v. Airblast Ltd* [1995] F.S.R. 806.

NOTE 96. Add: *R. v. Ministry of Agriculture, Fisheries and Food, ex p. Monsanto plc, The Times,* October 12, 1998.

NOTE 98. Add to the list of cases in the first sentence: *Holley v. Smyth* [1998] 2 W.L.R. 742, CA.

28–21   Undertaking as to damages

NOTE 12. Add: For the approach to striking out, for want of prosecution, proceedings to enforce a cross-undertaking in damages, see *Barratt Manchester Ltd v. Bolton Metropolitan Borough Council* [1998] 1 W.L.R. 1003.

28–22   *Anton Piller* orders

Under the new Civil Procedure Rules 1998, an *Anton Piller* order is to be known as a "search order": see CPR, r.25.1(1)(h).

Anton Piller orders (within England and Wales) were put on a firm statutory footing by section 7 of the Civil Procedure Act 1997 which came into force on April 27, 1997.

All references in the footnotes to the *Practice Direction (New Forms for Mareva and Anton Piller Orders)* [1994] 4 All E.R. 52 ("the 1994 Practice Direction") should now be read subject to the new Practice Direction on Interim Injunctions in the Civil Procedure Rules: see CPR, Pt 25, see *White Book*, paras 25PD–003 to 25PD–007.

On line 15 of 28–25, insert "basically" between "This" and "provides".

NOTE 18. Add to the penultimate sentence: Copper, "The Duties of a Plaintiff with an Anton Piller Order" (1998) 49 N.I.L.Q. 210.

NOTE 39. Add: In *Cobra Gulf Ltd v. Rata* [1997] 2 All E.R. 150 Rimer J. held that the removal of the privilege against self-incrimination extends to civil contempt proceedings as "proceedings . . . for the recovery of a . . . penalty".

NOTE 53: Add: *cf. Cobra Gulf Ltd v. Rata* [1997] 2 All E.R. 150.

28–28   *Mareva* injunction

Under the new Civil Procedure Rules, a *Mareva* injunction is to be known as a "freezing order": see CPR, r.25.1(1)(f). All references in the footnotes to the *Practice Direction (New Forms for Mareva and Anton Piller Orders)* [1994] 4 All E.R. 52 (the "1994 Practice Direction") should now be read subject to the new Practice Direction on Interim Injunctions in the Civil Procedure Rules: see CPR, Pt. 25, *White Book,* paras 25PD–003 to 25PD–007.

NOTE 68. Add: Capper, "The Trans-Jurisdictional Effects of Mareva Injunctions" (1996) C.J.Q. 211; "Further Trans-Jurisdictional Effects of Mareva Injunctions" (1998) C.J.Q 35.

NOTE 82. Insert after the third sentence: Applying section 25, a world-wide *Mareva* and associated disclosure order was granted, in aid of substantive proceedings in Switzerland, in *Crédit Suisse Fides Trust SA v. Cuoghi* [1997] 3 W.L.R. 871, CA. The Civil Jurisdiction and Judgments Act 1982 (Interim Relief) Order 1997, S.I. 1977 No. 302, which came into force on April 1, 1997, extends the effect of section 25 of the 1982 Act to proceedings commenced, or to be commenced, otherwise than in a Brusssels or Lugano Contracting State and to proceedings outside the scope of the Brussels Convention. Add: Applying *The Siskina* [1979] A.C. 210, and not following *X v. Y* [1990] 1 Q.B. 220, the Privy Council (Lord Nicholls dissenting) held in *Mercedes Benz AG v. Leiduck* [1996] 1 A.C. 284 that RSC Ord. 11, r.1(1) does not permit the service out of the jurisdiction of a writ claiming *Mareva* relief alone (albeit in respect of assets within the jurisdiction). In *Morris v. Murjani* [1996] 2 All E.R. 384, the Court of Appeal distinguished *The Siskina* in deciding that an interlocutory injunction restraining the jurisdiction from leaving the jurisdiction can be granted to a trustee in bankruptcy in aid of the public duty owed to the trustee by the bankrupt under section 333 of the Insolvency Act 1986 to supply to the trustee such information as he might require for the purpose of carrying out his statutory functions.

NOTE 88. Add: In *Department of Social Security v. Butler* [1995] 1 W.L.R. 1528 the Court of Appeal refused to grant a *Mareva* injunction against a father who had failed to make maintenance payments under the Child Support Act. The Department of Social Security sought such an order, pending obtaining a liability order from the magistrates' court, an order to prevent the defendant from reducing the funds held by his solicitors as part of his share of the proceeds of the matrimonial home. The court held that while the court may well have jurisdiction to grant a *Mareva* injunction in support of the jurisdiction of the magistrates' courts, no such injunction should be granted in the case because (1) applying the judgment *Veracruz Transportation Inc. v. VC Shipping Co. Inc.* a conditional *Mareva* injunction will not be granted when the cause of action on which the plaintiff relies has not arisen at the date of the application and (2) the grant of a *Mareva* injunction is always discretionary. Compelling reasons of policy indicated no injunction be granted because it ". . . cannot have been the intention of Parliament, nor is it desirable for the courts, that the statutory proceedings in the magistrates' courts should be duplicated and shadowed by "ancillary proceedings in the High Court" (at 1537, *per* Evans L.J.). In *Re Q's Estate* (1999) N.L.J. 442 it was held that (i) a court can grant a *Mareva* in respect of a dispute that is to be referred to arbitration; and that (ii) a *Mareva* can be granted prior to the accrual of a cause of action with its operation suspended until accrual.

NOTE 99. Add: *Camdex International Ltd v. Bank of Zambia (No. 2)* [1997] 1 W.L.R. 632, CA (post-judgment *Mareva* varied to enable defendant bank to export from England unissued bank notes that had been issued in England); *Customs and Excise Commissioners v. Anchor Foods Ltd* [1993] 3 All E.R. 268.

NOTE 5. It was clarified in *United Mizrahi Bank Ltd v. Doherty* [1998] 1 W.L.R. 435, that the expenses proviso does not give the defendant (or third parties, *e.g.* solicitors, receiving the expenses from the defendant) immunity from liability for breach of trust, or knowing receipt, by paying or receiving those expenses.

NOTE 15. Add: In *Baltic Shipping Co v. Translink Shipping Ltd* [1995] 1 Lloyd's Rep. a further proviso (going beyond that in *Derby & Co Ltd v. Weldon (No. 3 & No. 4)* [1990] Ch. 65 which applies only to those who are not subject to the jurisdiction of the English courts) was inserted in to a *Mareva* to protect a bank from being in contempt of the English courts where it complies with what it reasonably believes to be its legal obligations in the state where the assets are situated.

NOTE 16: Add: In *Bird v. Hadkinson, The Times,* April 7, 1999 it was held that a disclosure order contained in a *Mareva* injunction required the defendant not merely to tell the truth but also to take reasonable steps to investigate the truth or otherwise of the answer.

NOTE 28. Add: *Comdel Commodities Ltd v. Siporex Trade SA* [1997] 1 Lloyd's Rep. 424, CA.

CHAPTER 29.—SELF-HELP

		PARA.
1.	Introduction	29–01
□2.	Defence of the person	29–02
□3.	Defence of property	29–05
4.	Protection of property against damage by domestic animals	29–12
5.	Justifiable advance means of protection	29–15
6.	Protection of property against the forces of nature	29–18
□7.	Abatement of nuisances	29–22
□8.	Distress damage feasant	29–29
9.	Distress for rent	29–37

2.—DEFENCE OF THE PERSON

29–02 **Defence of the person**
The Court of Appeal in *Revill v. Newberry* [1996] 2 W.L.R. 239 upheld a judgment at first instance that firing a shotgun not knowing if it would cause injury to person and so shooting a burglar in the arm, where the latter had entered an allotment shed and displayed no violent intent, was a disproportionate response to the threat perceived by the defendant. A plea of self-defence therefore failed.

3.—DEFENCE OF PROPERTY

29–06 **Violent trespass**
The main text must now be read in the light of *Revill v. Newberry, post,* § 29–08.

29–08 **Limits of use of force in defending property**
The judgment of the Court of Appeal in *Revill v. Newberry* [1996] 2 W.L.R. 239 re-inforces the limits placed by the law on the use of force to defend property. Trespassers are owed a duty of care, either under the Occupiers Liability Act 1984 or via the common duty of humanity. The defendant, who fired his shotgun taking insufficient account of whether it caused serious injury to the plaintiff burglar and in fact shooting him in the arm, was found liable in negligence, albeit damages were reduced by two-thirds to take account of the plaintiff's own fault in embarking on his crime. The shot was held to be clearly more than a warning shot but rather one likely to cause injury. The impact of *Revill v. Newberry* appears to suggest that some form of warning or alternative attempt to repel an intruder is now required before resorting to any action likely to do significant injury to an intruder who is not posing any threat to the person or of irreversible damage to property.

7.—ABATEMENT OF NUISANCES

29–22 **Private Nuisances**
NOTE 2. Add: *Co-operative Wholesale Society Ltd v. British Railways Board, The Times*, December 20, 1995.

8.—DISTRESS DAMAGE FEASANT

29–29 **Right of distress damage feasant**
The Court of Appeal in *Arthur v. Anker* [1996] 2 W.L.R. 602 (Hirst L.J.

dissenting) sought to limit the availability of the ancient remedy of distress damage feasant. Landowners only enjoy a right to distrain trespassing chattels in order to ensure that they have a security to ensure compensation for damage actually caused to their land by that trespass. Wheel-clamping vehicles parked without authorisation on private land could not thus *normally* be justified by distress damage feasant. No damage was caused to the land. In appropriate circumstances, wheel-clamping might well be justified by a more appropriate defence of *volenti*, see *supra*, § 3–34. The language of the majority judgment in *Arthur v. Anker* (at 609–611, 615) suggests judicial reluctance to allow any liberal resort to a medieval remedy originally designed to deal with the depredations of marauding animals!

Actual damage   29–33
The presence of an unauthorised vehicle on land which has caused no damage to that land does not therefore justify distraining that vehicle; *Arthur v. Anker, supra*.

CHAPTER 30.—DISCHARGE OF TORTS

		PARA.
1.	Introduction	30–01
□2.	Waiver: election	30–02
3.	Accord and satisfaction	30–06
4.	Release	30–12
□5.	Judgment recovered	30–14
■6.	*Res judicata*	30–25
7.	Joint wrongdoers	30–36
8.	Joint plaintiff	30–38

2.—WAIVER: ELECTION

30–03 **Waiver by election**

In *Island Records Ltd v. Tring International plc* [1995] 3 All E.R. 444, where the alternative remedies in question were an account of profits and damages for copyright infringement, Lightman J. held that a party should in general not be required to elect between remedies unless and until he was able to make an informed choice. On the other hand, the exercise of the right of election should not be unreasonably delayed to the prejudice of the defendant. To achieve these competing aims, the court would direct the defendants to furnish within two months an audited schedule detailing the figures sought and direct the plaintiff to elect between the two remedies (an account of profits or damages) within seven days thereafter.

A very clear analysis of the law on alternative (inconsistent) remedies was made by Lord Nicholls giving the Privy Council's judgment in *Tang Min Sit v. Capacious Investments Ltd* [1996] 2 W.L.R. 192 (a breach of trust case). He said, at 196–197, "The law frequently affords an injured person more than one remedy for the wrong he has suffered. Sometimes the two remedies are alternative and inconsistent. The classic example, indeed, is (1) an account of the profits made by a defendant in breach of his fiduciary obligation and (2) damages for the loss suffered by the plaintiff by reason of the same breach. The former is measured by the wrongdoer's gain, the latter by the injured party's loss . . . Faced with alternative and inconsistent remedies a plaintiff must choose, or elect, between them. He cannot have both. The basic principle governing when a plaintiff must make his choice is simple and clear. He is required to choose when, but not before, judgment is given in his favour and the judge is asked to make orders against the defendant".

5.—JUDGMENT RECOVERED

30–20 **Different rights infringed by same wrongful act**

In *C (A Minor) v. Hackney London Borough Council* [1996] 1 W.L.R. 789, CA the defendants sought to strike out a claim brought by the plaintiff, a minor and a Downs' Syndrome child, suing through her next friend, her stepfather. C brought an action in negligence and breach of statutory duty arising out of illness which she alleged derived from the disrepair and dampness affecting the council house in which she lived with her family. The defendants attempt to strike out her claim rested on the settlement of an earlier action brought by the girl's mother, whereby they agreed to carry out repairs on the house and to pay £15,000 compensation to C's mother. Hackney contended that the sums paid to the mother included compensation to C and so allowing C's claim would represent double recovery. It was argued that C's mental state meant that C and her mother should effectively be regarded as the same party to the two actions. The Court of Appeal refused to strike

236

out C's claim. The judgment in *Talbot v. Berkshire County Council* that an
unlitigated monetary claim is barred, if it could have been advanced in earlier proceedings, cannot apply to those not themselves parties to the earlier proceedings.
Their Lordships could not accept the argument that C's disability and dependence
created such a nexus with her mother that the two be regarded as single legal entity.

6.—Res Judicata

Principle of res judicata   30–25
NOTE 7. Add: After the last case reference, *Desert Sun Loan Corp. v. Hill* [1996]
2 All E.R. 847, CA; *Buehler AG v. Chrones Richardson Ltd* [1998] 2 All E.R. 960,
CA. For discussion of recent cases, see Gordon (1998) N.L.J. 1394 and (1999) N.L.J.
348.
NOTE 9. *Barrow v. Bankside Agency Ltd* [1996] 1 W.L.R. 257; add: *C (A Minor)
v. Hackney London Borough Council*, [1996] 1 W.L.R. 789, CA.

CHAPTER 31.—LIMITATION

PARA.
- ■1. Introduction 31–01
- ■2. Limitation of actions for damages for personal injuries and death 31–23
- ■3. Limitation of actions for latent damage (other than personal injury) in the tort of negligence 31–38
- □4. Other special periods of limitation 31–41

1.—INTRODUCTION

See, generally, Law Commission Consultation Paper No. 151, *Limitation of Actions* (1998).

31–01 **Periods of Limitation**

NOTE 10. Add: *International Bulk Shipping and Services Ltd v. Minerals and Metals Trading Corp. of India* [1996] 1 All E.R. 1017, CA; *J.F.S. (U.K.) Ltd v. Cymru Cyf* [1999] 1 W.L.R. 231, CA. It was held in *Yorkshire Regional Health Authority v. Fairclough Building* [1996] 1 W.L.R. 210 that the power to substitute a party under RSC Ord.15, r.7 (which deals with where in the course of proceedings the interests of the original plaintiff devolve upon another party) is unaffected by the limitation period. Here leave was given to amend the writ and statement of claim by substituting Bradford Hospitals National Health Service Trust for Yorkshire Regional Health Authority.

31–03 **Burden of proof**

NOTE 25. In *Crocker v. British Coal Corporation* (1995) 29 B.M.L.R. 159, Mance J. held that the legal burden of proof on limitation rests on the plaintiff, whether the issue is when the cause of action accrued or when the plaintiff first had knowledge of the facts. See also *Arab Monetary Fund v. Hashim* [1996] 1 Lloyd's Rep. 589, in which § 31–03 is cited. But in *Parry v. Clwyd Health Authority* [1997] P.I.Q.R. P1 Colman J. said at P14, "The burden of proof of constructive knowledge is on the defendant".

31–09 **When time begins to run**

Although concerning the date from which interest is payable, rather than limitation, the leading case on the accrual of the cause of action for negligent valuation is now *Nykredit Mortgage Bank plc v. Edward Erdman Group Ltd (No. 2)* [1997] 3 W.L.R. 1627. Lord Nicholls, giving the leading speech, first dealt with what he regarded as a simple case: "A purchaser buys a house which has been negligently overvalued or which is subject to a local land charge not noticed by the purchaser's solicitor. Had he known the true position the purchaser would not have bought. In such a case, the purchaser's cause of action in tort accrues when he completes the purchase. He suffers actual damage by parting with his money and receiving in exchange property worth less than the price he paid". He then went on to the more difficult case where, as a result of negligent advice, property is acquired as security for a loan. The measure of damages in such a case was dealt with by the House of Lords in *Banque Bruxelles Lambert SA v. Eagle Star Insurance Co. Ltd* [1997] A.C. 191. In this situation, it was a matter of fact when legally relevant loss was first suffered. One could not rigidly say that this was when the loan transaction was completed because, as the borrower might not default, the lender might not suffer any loss (even though it entered into a bad bargain and, in that sense, suffered detriment as soon as the loan transaction was completed). Nor could one rigidly say that it only ever accrues when the lender realises his deficient security or becomes entitled to have recourse to that security: the lender might become aware of the deficiency before those dates and wish to commence proceedings. On the facts of this particular case, it was held that the cause of action accrued at the date of the loan transaction (March 1990): this is because the borrower defaulted at once and the amount lent at all times exceeded the true value of the property. Interest was held to be payable from December 1990, when the lender had sustained its full allowable loss.

In *Invercargill City Council v. Hamlin* [1996] A.C. 624 the Privy Council considered a New Zealand case in which the local courts had declined to follow *Pirelli* on the question of when the cause of action accrues in the case of a defective property. They had held that until the damage is reasonably discoverable, the plaintiff suffers no loss, since he can sell the property for full value; thus, the cause of action accrues only when the damage is reasonably discoverable. The Privy Council held that this interpretation was open to the New Zealand courts, it being a matter of policy to be determined according to local conditions. Thus, the idea of a deliberately created inconsistency between different parts of the Common Law world was accepted. The question whether *Pirelli* remains good law in the United Kingdom did not directly arise and was expressly left open by the Privy Council.

NOTE 58. Add: *Byrne v. Hall Pain & Foster* [1999] 2 All E.R. 400.

Persons under disability   31–13
For an account of the deficiencies of the rules relating to disability and limitation see Jones (1995) 15 C.J.Q. 258.

2.—LIMITATION OF ACTIONS FOR DAMAGES FOR PERSONAL INJURIES AND DEATH

General
Walkin v. S. Manchester H.A. [1995] 1 W.L.R. 1543: an action for wrongful birth   31–23
brought by a plaintiff who has become pregnant after a failed sterilisation operation is an action for personal injuries within the meaning of section 11 of the Limitation Act 1980. See also *Das v. Ganju* (1998) 42 B.M.L.R. 28.

In *S v. W* [1995] 1 F.L.R. 862, *Stubbings v. Webb* was considered and distinguished. In that case P had been sexually abused during childhood (her father was imprisoned for the abuse in 1985). She sued her mother for failing to protect her from the abuse. It was held that this was not an action for trespass to the person, since no trespass was alleged against the mother. However, it clearly was an action for damages for personal injuries, so that the three-year limitation period of section 11 of the 1980 Act applied. *Stubbings v. Webb* was therefore distinguishable. The Court of Appeal pointed out that the Report of the Tucker Committee, used by the House of Lords in *Stubbings v. Webb* to justify its decision, had also recommended that the three-year period for non-intentional trespass to the person should be extendable at the discretion of the court, but not beyond six years. This recommendation was not taken up. The court added that the obvious anomaly revealed by these two cases merited the attention of the Law Commission.

An application by the victim in *Stubbings v. Webb* [1992] Q.B. 197 was made to the European Court of Human Rights claiming that there had been a breach of Articles 6, 8 and 14 of the European Convention on Human Rights: Case 36–37 *Stubbings v. United Kingdom, The Times*, October 24, 1996. The Court held that there had been no violation of the Convention.

NOTE 24. Add: In *Bennett v. Greenland Houchen & Co.* [1998] P.N.L.R. 458 the Court of Appeal decided that a claim for solicitors' negligence, which included a claim for damages for distress and depression, fell within s.11 (and was therefore time-barred) as being a claim which included damages in respect of personal injuries to the claimant.

NOTE 25. Add to the articles criticising the House of Lords in *Stubbings v. Webb*, Allinson, "Limitation of Actions in Child Abuse Cases" [1996] JPIL 19; Mullis, "Compounding the Abuse? The House of Lords, Childhood Sexual Abuse and Limitation Periods" (1997) Med.L.R. 22.

31–26   The knowledge of the plaintiff; Constructive knowledge

In *Forbes v. Wandsworth Health Authority* [1996] 3 W.L.R. 1108, the plaintiff's leg had been amputated in 1982 after two unsuccessful operations on it. The plaintiff alleged medical negligence, in that had the second operation been carried out on the same day as the first, the leg might have been saved. In 1991 the plaintiff consulted a solicitor through whom in 1992 a vascular surgeon's report was obtained suggesting possible negligence. The Court of Appeal held that the claim was time-barred. While the plaintiff was held not to have actual knowledge that the amputation might have been attributable to an omission of the defendant until 1992, he had constructive knowledge from about 12 to 18 months after the operation. That is, a reasonable man would have made a decision to consider a claim, and hence to take advice, within that period of time. Doubt was cast on whether the plaintiff's intelligence and character are relevant factors to take into account (*cf.* § 31–30 n. 46) given that the test for constructive knowledge under section 14(3) is an objective one. Nor did the Court of Appeal think that the discretion under section 33 should be exercised in the plaintiff's favour. Colman J. in *Parry v. Clwyd Health Authority* [1997] P.I.Q.R. P1 favoured the exclusively objective interpretation of section 14(3) preferred in the *Forbes* case. He held that a plaintiff born with cerebral palsy in 1966 did not have actual or constructive knowledge for the purposes of section 14 until 1990 when she saw a television programme about cerebral palsy being caused by breech delivery.

The Court of Appeal in *Spargo v. North Essex District Health Authority* [1997] P.I.Q.R. P235 made clear that the level of knowledge for the purposes of actual knowledge under section 14(1) is a low one albeit subjectively assessed. Brooke L.J. said, "[T]he policy of Parliament . . . is to give a plaintiff who has the requisite low level of knowledge three years in which to establish by inquiry whether the identified injury was indeed probably caused by the identified omission and whether the omission (identified initially in broad terms) amounted to actionable negligence". In construing section 14(1)(b), Brooke L.J. considered that the following principles could be derived from the decisions:

"(1) The knowledge required to satisfy s.14(1)(b) is a broad knowledge of the essence of the causally relevant act or omission to which the injury is attributable;

(2) 'Attributable' in this context means 'capable of being attributed to', in the sense of being a real possibility;

(3) A plaintiff has the requisite knowledge when she knows enough to make it reasonable for her to begin to investigate whether or not she has a case against the defendant. Another way of putting this is to say that she will have such knowledge if she so firmly believes that her condition is capable of being attributed to an act or omission which she can identify (in broad terms) that she goes to a solicitor to seek advice about making a claim for compensation;

(4) On the other hand she will not have the requisite knowledge if she thinks she knows the acts or omissions she should investigate but in fact is barking up the wrong tree: or if her knowledge of what the defendant did or did not do is so vague or general that she cannot fairly be expected to know what she should investigate; or if her state of mind is such that she thinks her condition is capable of being attributed to the act or omission alleged to constitute negligence, but she is not sure about this, and would need to check with an expert before she could be properly said to know that it was."

Applying these principles the Court of Appeal held that the plaintiff had actually knowledge more than three years before the issue of the writ so that her claim was time-barred. Given that decision the court did not need to decide the difficult question on constructive knowledge of how the proviso to section 14(3) should be construed where the plaintiff had sought the advice of a solicitor who had then delayed in seeking medical advice. (*cf.* Collins J.'s decision at first instance [1996] 7 Med. L.R. 219 that the plaintiff should not be penalised by the delay of the expert he has consulted: that is, if the plaintiff has acted reasonably in consulting a solicitor, but has been let down, he does not have constructive knowledge).

NOTE 41. Add: *Saxby v. Morgan* [1997] P.I.Q.R. P531. For a useful discussion of *Dobbie v. Medway HA* [1994] 1 W.L.R. 1234 and some subsequent cases see Meakin, "The Role of 'Knowledge' Under the Limitation Act 1980" [1996] J.P.I.L. 12.

Constructive knowledge   31–30

NOTE 48. Add to the end of the second sentence: In *Henderson v. Temple Pier Co. Ltd* [1998] 3 W.L.R. 1540, it was held by the Court of Appeal that, even if a solicitor can be an appropriate expert within s.14(3)(b), the identity of the defendants (the owners of a ship on which the claimant had been injured) was not "a fact ascertainable only with the help of expert advice" within that subsection.

The discretion of the court   31–31

NOTE 53. Add: In *Coad v. Cornwall Health Authority* [1997] 1 W.L.R. 189 the Court of Appeal emphasised that, in respect of s.33(3)(a), it was legitimate to take into account that the reason for delay on the plaintiff's behalf was her lack of knowledge of her legal rights. It was irrelevant that that lack of knowledge was unreasonable because s.33(3)(a) imported a subjective, and not an objective, test.

The impact of the discretion on the court's power of strike out an action for want of prosecution   31–32

In *Grovit v. Doctor* [1997] 1 W.L.R. 640, the House of Lords laid down that, in addition to the *Birkett v. James* principles, a claim could be dismissed for abuse of process (as opposed to want of prosecution) where the plaintiff had commenced litigation which he had no intention to bring to a conclusion. Striking out for abuse of process does not depend on the need to show prejudice to the defendant. It was explained by Lord Woolf M.R., giving the judgment of the Court of Appeal in *Arbuthnot Latham Bank Ltd v. Trafalgar Holdings Ltd* [1998] 2 All E.R. 181, that the fact that the limitation period has not expired is not as important a factor where the proceedings which are being struck out constitute an abuse of process, as opposed to being struck out for want of prosecution; and that a court should assume that, unless a special reason is identified to the contrary, a second action should be struck out for abuse of process where a first action had been so struck out.

NOTE 60. Add: As laid down in *Arbuthnott Latham Bank Ltd v. Trafalgar Holdings Ltd* [1998] 2 All E.R. 181, the fact that the plaintiff has a non-time-barred different cause of action is irrelevant to deciding whether, applying *Birkett v. James*, the particular cause of action should be dismissed for want of prosecution.

The exercise of the discretion   31–33

NOTE 73. Add: See also *Forward v. Hendricks* [1997] 2 All E.R. 395. CA.

3.—LIMITATION OF ACTIONS FOR LATENT DAMAGE (OTHER THAN PERSONAL INJURY) IN THE TORT OF NEGLIGENCE

Latent Damage Act 1986, ss.1–2   31–38

NOTE 35. Add: *Hamlin v. Edwin Evans, The Times*, July 15, 1996. In *HF Pension Trustees Ltd v. Ellison* (unreported, 8 February 1999), the defendant solicitors advised the claimant trustee that it could transfer surplus funds of an occupational pension scheme to a similar scheme. That advice was incorrect. It was held by

Parker J. that, under s.14A, the claimant acquired knowledge of the relevant facts —
knowledge of the law being irrelevant under s.14A(9) — as soon as it acted to its
detriment in reliance on the incorrect advice.

4.—OTHER SPECIAL PERIODS OF LIMITATION

31–42   Carriage by Air Act
NOTE 44. Add: See analogously the Merchant Shipping Act 1995, section 183 and
Sched. 6 (dealing with personal injuries or damage to baggage suffered by passen-
gers at sea) to which s.33 does not apply: *Higham v. Stena Sealink Ltd* [1996] 1
W.L.R. 1107.

Defamation
31–43   The law on limitation periods for defamation and malicious falsehood has been
reformed by the Defamation Act 1996. This repeals the Administration of Justice
Act 1985, s.57 and inserts new sections 4A and 32A into the Limitation Act 1980
which lay down a limitation period of one year from the accrual of the cause of
action, subject to the court having a discretion to disapply that limit. The factors
that the courts must take into account in exercising its discretion are: the length of,
and the reasons, for the delay on the part of the plaintiff (section 32A(2)(a)); the
date at which the plaintiff became aware of the facts relevant to the cause of action
and the extent to which he acted promptly and reasonably once he knew whether or
not the facts in question might be capable of giving rise to an action (section
32A(2)(b)); and the extent to which relevant evidence is likely to be unavailable or
less cogent than would have been the case if the action had been brought within the
limitation period set by section 4A (section 32A(2)(c)). These factors correspond to
sections 33(3)(a) (b) and (e) of the Limitation Act 1980 in relation to personal injury
claims. (The other factors in section 33(3)(c), (d) and (f) were presumably thought
irrelevant or insufficiently important to defamation as opposed to personal injury
actions.) The limitation provisions came into force on September 4, 1996.

For cases on the old law under section 57 of the Administration of Justice Act
1985 see, *e.g. Oyston v. Blaker* [1996] 1 W.L.R. 1326; *C v. Mirror Group Newspapers* [1997] 1 W.L.R. 131.

APPENDIX

Human Rights Act 1998

(1998, c.42)

ARRANGEMENT OF SECTIONS

Introduction

SECTION
1. The Convention Rights.
2. Interpretation of Convention rights.

Legislation
3. Interpretation of legislation.
4. Declaration of incompatibility.
5. Right of Crown to intervene.

Public authorities
6. Acts of public authorities.
7. Proceedings.
8. Judicial remedies.
9. Judicial acts.

Remedial action
10. Power to take remedial action.

Other rights and proceedings
11. Safeguard for existing human rights.
12. Freedom of expression.
13. Freedom of thought, conscience and religion.

Derogations and reservations
14. Derogations.
15. Reservations.
16. Period for which designated derogations have effect.
17. Periodic review of designated reservations.

Judges of the European Court of Human Rights
18. Appointment to European Court of Human Rights

Parliamentary procedure
19. Statements of compatibility

Supplemental

20. Orders etc. under this Act.
21. Interpretation, etc.
22. Short title, commencement, application and extent.

SCHEDULES
　　Schedule I — The Articles.
　　Part I — The Convention.
　　Part II — The First Protocol.
　　Part III — The Sixth Protocol.

An Act to give further effect to rights and freedoms guaranteed under the European Convention on Human Rights; to make provision with respect to holders of certain judicial offices who become judges of the European Court of Human Rights; and for connected purposes.

[9th November 1998]

BE IT ENACTED by the Queen's most Excellent Majesty, by and with the advice and consent of the Lords Spiritual and Temporal, and Commons, in this present Parliament assembled, and by the authority of the same, as follows:

Introduction

The Convention Rights

1. — (1) In this Act "the Convention rights" means the rights and fundamental freedoms set out in—
　　(a) Articles 2 to 12 and 14 of the Convention,
　　(b) Articles 1 to 3 of the First Protocol, and
　　(c) Articles 1 and 2 of the Sixth Protocol,

as read with Articles 16 to 18 of the Convention.

(2) Those Articles are to have effect for the purposes of this Act subject to any designated derogation or reservation (as to which see sections 14 and 15).

(3) The Articles are set out in Schedule 1.

(4) The Secretary of State may by order make such amendments to this Act as he considers appropriate to reflect the effect, in relation to the United Kingdom, of a protocol.

(5) In subsection (4) "protocol" means a protocol to the Convention—
　　(a) which the United Kingdom has ratified; or
　　(b) which the United Kingdom has signed with a view to ratification.

(6) No amendment may be made by an order under subsection (4) so as to come into force before the protocol concerned is in force in relation to the United Kingdom.

Interpretation of Convention rights

2. — (1) A court or tribunal determining a question which has arisen in connection with a Convention right must take into account any—
　　(a) judgment, decision, declaration or advisory opinion of the European Court of Human Rights,
　　(b) opinion of the Commission given in a report adopted under Article 31 of the Convention,
　　(c) decision of the Commission in connection with Article 26 or 27(2) of the Convention, or

(d) decision of the Committee of Ministers taken under Article 46 of the Convention,

whenever made or given, so far as, in the opinion of the court or tribunal, it is relevant to the proceedings in which that question has arisen.

(2) Evidence of any judgment, decision, declaration or opinion of which account may have to be taken under this section is to be given in proceedings before any court or tribunal in such manner as may be provided by the rules.

(3) In this section "rules" means rules of court or, in the case of proceedings before a tribunal, rules made for the purposes of this section—

(a) by the Lord Chancellor or the Secretary of State, in relation to any proceedings outside Scotland;

(b) by the Secretary of State, in relation to proceedings in Scotland; or

(c) by a Northern Ireland department, in relation to proceedings before a tribunal in Northern Ireland—

(i) which deals with transferred matters; and

(ii) for which no rules made under paragraph (a) are in force.

Legislation

Interpretation of legislation

3. — (1) So far as it is possible to do so, primary legislation and subordinate legislation must be read and given effect in a way which is compatible with the Convention rights.

(2) This section—

(a) applies to primary legislation and subordinate legislation whenever enacted;

(b) does not affect the validity, continuing operation or enforcement of any incompatible primary legislation; and

(c) does not affect the validity, continuing operation or enforcement of any incompatible subordinate legislation if (disregarding any possibility of revocation) primary legislation prevents removal of the incompatibility.

Declaration of incompatibility

4. — (1) Subsection (2) applies in any proceedings in which a court determines whether a provision of primary legislation is compatible with a Convention right.

(2) If the court is satisfied that the provision is incompatible with a Convention right, it may make a declaration of that incompatibility.

(3) Subsection (4) applies in any proceedings in which a court determines whether a provision of subordinate legislation, made in the exercise of a power conferred by primary legislation, is compatible with a Convention right.

(4) If the court is satisfied—

(a) that the provision is incompatible with a Convention right, and

(b) that (disregarding any possibility of revocation) the primary legislation concerned prevents removal of the incompatibility,

it may make a declaration of that incompatibility.

(5) In this section "court" means—

(1) the House of Lords;

(b) the Judicial Committee of the Privy Council;

(c) the Courts-Martial Appeal Court;

(d) in Scotland, the High Court of Judiciary sitting otherwise than as a trial court or the Court of Session;

(e) in England and Wales or Northern Ireland, the High Court or the Court of Appeal.

(6) A declaration under this section ("a declaration of incompatibility")—

    (a) does not affect the validity, continuing operation or enforcement of the
        provision in respect of which it is given; and

    (b) is not binding on the parties to the proceedings in which it is made.

Right of Crown to intervene

5. — (1) Where a court is considering whether to make a declaration of incompatibility, the Crown is entitled to notice in accordance with rules of court.

    (2) In any case to which subsection (1) applies—

    (a) a Minister of the Crown (or a person nominated by him),

    (b) a member of the Scottish Executive,

    (c) a Northern Ireland Minister,

    (d) a Northern Ireland department,

is entitled, on giving notice in accordance with rules of court, to be joined as a party
to the proceedings.

    (3) Notice under subsection (2) may be given at any time during the proceedings.

    (4) A person who has been made a party to criminal proceedings (other than in
Scotland) as the result of a notice under subsection (2) may, with leave, appeal to the
House of Lords against any declaration of incompatibility made in the proceedings.

    (5) In subsection (4)—

        "criminal proceedings" includes all proceedings before the Courts-
        Martial Appeal Court; and

        "leave" means leave granted by the court making the declaration of
        incompatibility or by the House of Lords.

Public authorities

Acts of public authorities

6. — (1) It is unlawful for a public authority to act in a way which is incompatible
with a Convention right.

    (2) Subsection (1) does not apply to an act if—

    (a) as the result of one or more provisions of primary legislation, the authority
        could not have acted differently; or

    (b) in the case of one or more provisions of, or made under, primary legislation
        which cannot be read or given effect in a way which is compatible with
        the Convention rights, the authority was acting so as to give effect to or
        enforce those provisions.

    (3) In this section "public authority" includes—

    (a) a court or tribunal, and

    (b) any person certain of whose functions are functions of a public nature,

but does not include either House of Parliament or a person exercising functions in
connection with proceedings in Parliament.

    (4) In subsection (3) "Parliament" does not include the House of Lords in its
judicial capacity.

    (5) In relation to a particular act, a person is not a public authority by virtue only
of subsection (3)(b) if the nature of the act is private.

    (6) "An act" includes a failure to act but does not include a failure to—

    (a) introduce in, or lay before, Parliament a proposal for legislation; or

    (b) make any primary legislation or remedial order.

Proceedings

7. — (1) A person who claims that a public authority has acted (or proposes to
act) in a way which is made unlawful by section 6(1) may—

(a) bring proceedings against the authority under this Act in the appropriate court of tribunal, or

(b) rely on the Convention right or rights concerned in any legal proceedings,

but only if he is (or would be) a victim of the unlawful act.

(2) In subsection (1)(a) "appropriate court or tribunal" means such court or tribunal as may be determined in accordance with rules; and proceedings against an authority include a counterclaim or similar proceeding.

(3) If the proceedings are brought on an application for judicial review, the applicant is to be taken to have a sufficient interest in relation to the unlawful act only if he is, or would be, a victim of that act.

(4) If the proceedings are made by way of a petition for judicial review in Scotland, the applicant shall be taken to have title and interest to sue in relation to the unlawful act only if he is, or would be, a victim of that act.

(5) Proceedings under subsection (1)(a) must be brought before the end of—

(a) the period of one year beginning with the date on which the act complained of took place; or

(b) such longer period as the court or tribunal considers equitable having regard to all the circumstances,

but that is subject to any rule imposing a stricter time limit in relation to the procedure in question.

(6) In subsection (1)(b) "legal proceedings" includes—

(a) proceedings brought by or at the instigation of a public authority; and

(b) an appeal against the decision of a court or tribunal.

(7) For the purposes of this section, a person is a victim of an unlawful act only if he would be a victim for the purposes of Article 34 of the Convention if proceedings were brought in the European Court of Human Rights in respect of that act.

(8) Nothing in this Act creates a criminal offence.

(9) In this section "rules" means—

(a) in relation to proceedings before a court or tribunal outside Scotland, rules made by the Lord Chancellor or the Secretary of State for the purposes of this section or rules of court,

(b) in relation to proceedings before a court or tribunal in Scotland, rules made by the Secretary of State for those purposes,

(c) in relation to proceedings before a tribunal in Northern Ireland—

   (i) which deals with transferred matters; and

   (ii) for which no rules made under paragraph (a) are in force,

   rules made by a Northern Ireland department for those purposes,

and includes provision made by order under section 1 of the Courts and Legal Services Act 1990.

(10) In making rules, regard must be had to section 9.

(11) The Minister who has power to make rules in relation to a particular tribunal may, to the extent he considers it necessary to ensure that the tribunal can provide an appropriate remedy in relation to an act (or proposed act) of a public authority which is (or would be) unlawful as a result of section 6(1), by order add to—

(a) the relief or remedies which the tribunal may grant; or

(b) the grounds on which it may grant any of them.

(12) An order made under subsection (11) may contain such incidental, supplemental, consequential or transitional provision as the Minister making it considers appropriate.

(13) "The Minister" includes the Northern Ireland department concerned.

Judicial remedies

8. — (1) In relation to any act (or proposed act) of a public authority which the court finds is (or would be) unlawful, it may grant such relief or remedy, or make such order, within its powers as it considers just and appropriate.

(2) But damages may be awarded only by a court which has power to award damages, or to order the payment of compensation, in civil proceedings.

(3) No award of damages is to be made unless, taking account of all the circumstances of the case, including—

    (a) any other relief or remedy granted, or order made, in relation to the act in question (by that or any other court), and

    (b) the consequences of any decision (of that or any other court) in respect of that act,

the court is satisfied that the award is necessary to afford just satisfaction to the person in whose favour it is made.

(4) In determining—

    (a) whether to award damages, or

    (b) the amount of an award,

the court must take into account the principles applied by the European Court of Human Rights in relation to the award of compensation under Article 41 of the Convention.

(5) A public authority against which damages are awarded is to be treated—

    (a) in Scotland, for the purposes of section 3 of the Law Reform (Miscellaneous Provisions) (Scotland) Act 1940 as if the award were made in an action of damages in which the authority has been found liable in respect of loss or damage to the person to whom the award is made;

    (b) for the purposes of the Civil Liability (Contribution) Act 1978 as liable in respect of damage suffered by the person to whom the award is made.

(6) In this section—

"court" includes a tribunal;

"damages" means damages for an unlawful act of a public authority; and

"unlawful" means unlawful under section 6(1).

Judicial acts

9. — (1) Proceedings under section 7(1)(a) in respect of a judicial act may be brought only—

    (a) by exercising a right of appeal;

    (b) on an application (in Scotland a petition) for judicial review; or

    (c) in such other forum as may be prescribed by rules.

(2) That does not affect any rule of law which prevents a court from being the subject of judicial review.

(3) In proceedings under this Act in respect of a judicial act done in good faith, damages may not be awarded otherwise than to compensate a person to the extent required by Article 5(5) of the Convention.

(4) An award of damages permitted by subsection (3) is to be made against the Crown; but no award may be made unless the appropriate person, if not a party to the proceedings, is joined.

(5) In this section—

"appropriate person" means the Minister responsible for the court concerned, or a person or government department nominated by him;

"court" includes a tribunal;

"judge" includes a member of a tribunal, a justice of the peace and a clerk or other officer entitled to exercise the jurisdiction of a court;

"judicial act" means a judicial act of a court and includes an act done on the instructions, or on behalf, of a judge; and

"rules" has the same meaning as in section 7(9).

Remedial action

Power to take remedial action

10. — (1) This section applies if—
    (a) a provision of legislation has been declared under section 4 to be incompatible with a Convention right and, if an appeal lies—
        (i) all persons who may appeal have stated in writing that they do not intend to do so,
       (ii) the time for bringing an appeal has expired and no appeal has been brought within that time; or
      (iii) an appeal brought within that time has been determined or abandoned; or
    (b) it appears to a Minister of the Crown or Her Majesty in Council that, having regard to a finding of the European Court of Human Rights made after the coming into force of this section in proceedings against the United Kingdom, a provision of legislation is incompatible with an obligation of the United Kingdom arising from the Convention.

(2) If a Minister of the Crown considers that there are compelling reasons for proceeding under this section, he may by order make such amendments to the legislation as he considers necessary to remove the incompatibility.

(3) If, in the case of subordinate legislation, a Minister of the Crown considers—
    (a) that it is necessary to amend the primary legislation under which the subordinate legislation in question was made, in order to enable the incompatibility to be removed, and
    (b) that there are compelling reasons for proceeding under this section,

he may by order made such amendments to the primary legislation as he considers necessary.

(4) This section also applies where the provision in question is in subordinate legislation and has been quashed, or declared invalid, by reason of incompatibility with a Convention right and the Minister proposes to proceed under paragraph 2(b) of Schedule 2.

(5) If the legislation is an Order in Council, the power conferred by subsection (2) or (3) is exercisable by Her Majesty in Council.

(6) In this section "legislation" does not include a Measure of the Church Assembly or of the General Synod of the Church of England.

(7) Schedule 2 makes further provision about remedial orders.

Other rights and proceedings

Safeguard for existing human rights

11. — A person's reliance on a Convention right does not restrict—
    (a) any other right or freedom conferred on him by or under any law having effect in any part of the United Kingdom; or
    (b) his right to make any claim or bring any proceedings which he could make or bring apart from sections 7 to 9.

Freedom of expression

12. — (1) This section applies if a court is considering whether to grant any relief which, if granted, might affect the exercise of the Convention right to freedom of expression.

(2) If the person against whom the application for relief is made ("the respondent") is neither present nor represented, no such relief is to be granted unless the court is satisfied—
    (a) that the applicant has taken all practicable steps to notify the respondent; or

(b) that there are compelling reasons why the respondent should not be notified.

(3) No such relief is to be granted so as to restrain publication before trial unless the court is satisfied that the applicant is likely to establish that publication should not be allowed.

(4) The court must have particular regard to the importance of the Convention right to freedom of expression and, where the proceedings relate to material which the respondent claims, or which appears to the court, to be journalistic, literary or artistic material (or to conduct connected with such material), to—
    (a) the extent to which—
        (i) the material has, or is about to, become available to the public; or
        (ii) it is, or would be, in the public interest for the material to be published;
    (b) any relevant privacy code.

(5) In this section—
    "court" includes a tribunal; and
    "relief" includes any remedy or order (other than in criminal proceedings).

Freedom of thought, conscience and religion

13. — (1) If a court's determination of any question arising under this Act might affect the exercise by a religious organisation (itself or its members collectively) of the Convention right to freedom of thought, conscience and religion, it must have particular regard to the importance of that right.

(2) In this section "court" includes a tribunal.

Derogations and reservations

Derogations
14. — (1) In this Act "designated derogation" means—
    (a) the United Kingdom's derogation from Article 5(3) of the Convention; and
    (b) any derogation by the United Kingdom from an Article of the Convention, or of any protocol to the Convention, which is designated for the purposes of this Act in an order made by the Secretary of State.

(2) The derogation referred to in subsection (1)(a) is set out in Part I of Schedule 3.

(3) If a designated derogation is amended or replaced it ceases to be a designated derogation.

(4) But subsection (3) does not prevent the Secretary of State from exercising his power under subsection (1)(b) to make a fresh designation order in respect of the Article concerned.

(5) The Secretary of State must by order make such amendments to Schedule 3 as he considers appropriate to reflect—
    (a) any designation order; or
    (b) the effect of subsection (3).

(6) A designation order may be made in anticipation f the making by the United Kingdom of a proposed derogation.

Reservations
15. — (1) In this Act "designated reservation" means—
    (a) the United Kingdom's reservation to Article 2 of the First Protocol to the Convention; and
    (b) any other reservation by the United Kingdom to an Article of the Convention, or of any protocol to the Convention, which is designated for the purposes of this Act in an order made by the Secretary of State.

(2) The text of the reservation referred to in subsection (1)(a) is set out in Part II of Schedule 3.

(3) If a designated reservation is withdrawn wholly or in part it ceases to be a designated reservation.

(4) But subsection (3) does not prevent the Secretary of State from exercising his power under subsection (1)(b) to make a fresh designation order in respect of the Article concerned.

(5) The Secretary of State must by order make such amendments to this Act as he considers appropriate to reflect—
   (a) any designation order; or
   (b) the effect of subsection (3).

Period for which designated derogations have effect

16. — (1) If it has not already been withdrawn by the United Kingdom, a designated derogation ceases to have effect for the purposes of this Act—
   (a) in the case of the derogation referred to in section 14(1)(a), at the end of the period of five years beginning with the date on which section 1(2) came into force;
   (b) in the case of any other derogation, at the end of the period of five years beginning with the date on which the order designating it was made.

(2) At any time before the period—
   (a) fixed by subsection (1)(a) or (b), or
   (b) extended by an order under this subsection,

comes to an end, the Secretary of State may by order extend it by a further period of five years.

(3) An order under section 14(1)(b) ceases to have effect at the end of the period for consideration, unless a resolution has been passed by each House approving the order.

(4) Subsection (3) does not affect—
   (a) anything done in reliance on the order; or
   (b) the power to make a fresh order under section 14(1)(b).

(5) In subsection (3) "period for consideration" means the period of forty days beginning with the day on which the order was made.

(6) In calculating the period for consideration, no account is to be taken of any time during which—
   (a) Parliament is dissolved or prorogued; or
   (b) both Houses are adjourned for more than four days.

(7) If a designated derogation is withdrawn by the United Kingdom, the Secretary of State must by order make such amendments to this Act as he considers are required to reflect that withdrawal.

Periodic review of designated reservations

17. — (1) The appropriate Minister must review the designated reservation referred to in section 15(1)(a)—
   (a) before the end of the period of five years beginning with the date on which section 1(2) came into force; and
   (b) if that designation is still in force, before the end of the period of five years beginning with the date on which the last report relating to it was laid under subsection (3).

(2) The appropriate Minister must review each of the other designated reservations (if any)—

251

(a) before the end of the period of five years beginning with the date on which the order designating the reservation first came into force; and

(b) if the designation is still in force, before the end of the period of five years beginning with the date on which the last report relating to it was laid under subsection (3).

(3) The Minister conducting a review under this section must prepare a report on the result of the review and lay a copy of it before each House of Parliament.

Judges of the European Court of Human Rights

Appointment to European Court of Humans Rights

18. — (1) In this section "judicial review" means the office of—

(a) Lord Justice of Appeal, Justice of the High Court or Circuit Judge, in England and Wales;

(b) judge of the Court of Session or sheriff, in Scotland;

(c) Lord Justice of Appeal, judge of the High Court or county court judge, in Northern Ireland.

(2) The holder of a judicial office may become a judge of the European Court of Human Rights ("the Court") without being required to relinquish his office.

(3) But he is not required to perform the duties of his judicial office while he is a judge of the Court.

(4) In respect of any period during which he is a judge of the Court—

(a) a Lord Justice of Appeal or Justice of the High Court is not to count as a judge of the relevant court for the purposes of section 2(1) or 4(1) of the Supreme Court Act 1981 (maximum number of judges) nor as a judge of the Supreme Court for the purposes of section 12(1) to (6) of that Act (salaries etc.);

(b) a judge of the Court of Session is not to count as a judge of that court for the purposes of section 1(1) of the Court of Session Act 1988 (maximum number of judges) or of section 9(1)(c) of the Administration of Justice Act 1973 ("the 1973 Act") (salaries etc.);

(c) a Lord Justice of Appeal or judge of the High Court in Northern Ireland is not to count as a judge of the relevant court for the purposes of section 2(1) or 3(1) of the Judicature (Northern Ireland) Act 1978 (maximum number of judges) nor as a judge of the Supreme Court of Northern Ireland for the purposes of section 9(1)(d) of the 1973 Act (salaries etc.);

(d) a Circuit judge is not to count as such for the purposes of section 18 of the Courts Act 1971 (salaries etc.);

(e) a sheriff is not to count as such for the purposes of section 14 of the Sheriff Courts (Scotland) Act 1907 (salaries etc.);

(f) a county court judge of Northern Ireland is not to count as such for the purposes of section 106 of the County Courts Act Northern Ireland) 1959 (salaries etc.).

(5) If a sheriff principal is appointed a judge of the Court, section 11(1) of the Sheriff Courts (Scotland) Act 1971 (temporary appointment of sheriff principal) applies, while he holds that appointment, as if his office is vacant.

(6) Schedule 4 makes provision about judicial pensions in relation to the holder of a judicial office who serves as a judge of the Court.

(7) The Lord Chancellor or the Secretary of State may by order make such transitional provision (including, in particular, provision for a temporary increase in the maximum number of judges) as he considers appropriate in relation to any holder of a judicial office who has completed his service as a judge of the Court.

Parliamentary procedure

Statements of compatibility

19. — (1) A Minister of the Crown in charge of a Bill in either House of Parliament must, before Second Reading of the Bill—

(a) make a statement to the effect that in his view the provisions of the Bill are compatible with the Convention rights ("a statement of compatibility"); or

(b) make a statement to the effect that although he is unable to make a statement of compatibility the government nevertheless wishes the House to proceed with the Bill.

(2) The statement must be in writing and be published in such manner as the Minister making it considers appropriate.

Supplemental

Orders etc. under this Act

20. — (1) Any power of a Minister of the Crown to make an order under this Act is exercisable by statutory instrument.

(2) The power of the Lord Chancellor or the Secretary of State to make rules (other than rules of court) under section 2(3) or 7(9) is exercisable by statutory instrument.

(3) Any statutory instrument made under section 14, 15 or 16(7) must be laid before Parliament.

(4) No order may be made by the Lord Chancellor or the Secretary of State under section 1(4), 7(11) or 16(2) unless a draft of the order has been laid before, and approved by, each House of Parliament.

(5) Any statutory instrument made under section 18(7) or Schedule 4, or to which subsection (2) applies, shall be subject to annulment in pursuance of a resolution of either House of Parliament.

(6) The power of a Northern Ireland department to make—

(a) rules under section 2(3)(c) or 7(9)(c), or

(b) an order under section 7(11),

is exercisable by statutory rule for the purposes of the Statutory Rules (Northern Ireland) Order 1979.

(7) Any rules made under section 2(3)(c) or 7(9)(c) shall be subject to negative resolution; and section 41(6) of the Interpretation Act Northern Ireland) 1954 (meaning of "subject to negative resolution") shall apply as if the power to make the rules were conferred by an Act of the Northern Ireland Assembly.

(8) No order may be made by a Northern Ireland department under section 7(11) unless a draft of the order has been laid before, and approved by, the Northern Ireland Assembly.

Interpretation, etc.

21. — (1) In this Act—

"amend" includes repeal and apply (with or without modifications);

"the appropriate Minister" means the Minister of the Crown having charge of the appropriate authorised government department (within the meaning of the Crown Proceedings Act 1947);

"the Commission" means the European Commission of Human Rights;

"the Convention" means the Convention for the Protection of Human Rights and Fundamental Freedoms, agreed by the Council of Europe at Rome on 4th November 1950 as it has effect for the time being in relation to the United Kingdom;

"declaration of incompatibility" means a declaration under section 4;

"Minister of the Crown" has the same meaning as in the Ministers of the Crown Act 1975;

"Northern Ireland Minister" includes the First Minister and the deputy First Minister in Northern Ireland;

"primary legislation" means any—

(a) public general Act;

(b) local and personal Act;

(c) private Act;

(d) Measure of the Church Assembly;

(e) Measure of the General Synod of the Church of England;

(f) Order in Council—

(i) made in exercise of Her Majesty's Royal Prerogative;

(ii) made under section 38(1)(a) of the Northern Ireland Constitution Act 1973 or the corresponding provision of the Northern Ireland Act 1998; or

(iii) amending an Act of a kind mentioned in paragraph (a), (b) or (c);

and includes an order or other instrument made under primary legislation (otherwise than by the National Assembly for Wales, a member of the Scottish Executive, a Northern Ireland Minister or a Northern Ireland department) to the extent to which it operates to bring one or more provisions of that legislation into force or amends any primary legislation;

"the First Protocol" means the protocol to the Convention agreed at Parish on 20th March 1952;

"the Sixth Protocol" means the protocol to the Convention agreed at Strasbourg on 28th April 1983;

"the Eleventh Protocol" means the protocol to the Convention (restructuring the control machinery established by the Convention) agreed at Strasbourg on 11th May 1994;

"remedial order" means an order under section 10;

"subordinate legislation" means any—

(a) Order in Council other than one—

(i) made in exercise of Her Majesty's Royal Prerogative;

(ii) made under section 38(1)(a) of the Northern Ireland Constitution Act 1973 or the corresponding provision of the Northern Ireland Act 1998; or

(iii) amending an Act of a kind mentioned in the definition of primary legislation;

(b) Act of the Scottish Parliament;

(c) Act of the Parliament of Northern Ireland;

(d) Measure of the Assembly established under section 1 of the Northern Ireland Assembly Act 1973;

(e) Act of the Northern Ireland Assembly;

(f) order, rules, regulations, scheme, warrant, byelaw or other instrument made under primary legislation (except to the extent to which it operates to bring one or more provisions of that legislation into force or amends any primary legislation);

(g) order, rules, regulations, scheme, warrant, byelaw or other instrument made under legislation mentioned in paragraph (b), (c), (d) or (e) or made under an Order in Council applying only to Northern Ireland;

(h) order, rules, regulations, scheme, warrant, byelaw or other instrument made by a member of the Scottish Executive, a Northern Ireland Minister or a Northern Ireland department in exercise of prerogative or other executive functions of Her Majesty which are exercisable by such a person on behalf of Her Majesty;

"transferred matters" has the same meaning as in the Northern Ireland Act 1998; and

"tribunal" means any tribunal in which legal proceedings may be brought.

(2) The references in paragraphs (b) and (c) of section 2(1) to Articles are to

Articles of the Convention as they had effect immediately before the coming into force of the Eleventh Protocol.

(3) The reference in paragraph (d) of section 2(1) to Article 46 includes a reference to Articles 32 and 54 of the Convention as they had effect immediately before the coming into force of the Eleventh Protocol.

(4) The references in section 2(1) to a report or decision of the Committee or a decision of the Committee of Ministers include references to a report or decision made as provided by paragraphs 3, 4 and 6 of Article 5 of the Eleventh Protocol (transitional provisions).

(5) Any liability under the Army Act 1955, the Air Force Act 1955 or the Naval Discipline Act 1957 to suffer death for an offence is replaced by a liability to imprisonment for life or any less punishment authorised by those Acts; and those Acts shall accordingly have effect with the necessary modifications.

Short title, commencement, application and extent

22. — (1) This Act may be cited as the Human Rights Act 1998.

(2) Sections 18, 20 and 21(5) and this section come into force on the passing of this Act.

(3) The other provisions of this Act come into force on such day as the Secretary of State may by order appoint; and different days may be appointed for different purposes.

(4) Paragraph (b) of subsection (1) of section 7 applies to proceedings brought by or at the instigation of a public authority whenever the act in question took place; but otherwise that subsection does not apply to an act taking place before the coming into force of that section.

(5) This Act binds the Crown.

(6) This Act extends to Northern Ireland.

(7) Section 21(5), so far as it relates to any provision contained in the Army act 1955, the Air Force Act 1955 or the Naval Discipline Act 1957, extends to any place to which that provision extends.

SCHEDULE 1

THE ARTICLES

PART I

THE CONVENTION

RIGHTS AND FREEDOMS

Article 2

Right to Life

1. Everyone's right to life shall be protected by law. No one shall be deprived of his life intentionally save in the execution of a sentence of a court following his conviction of a crime for which this penalty is provided by law.

2. Deprivation of life shall not be regarded as inflicted in contravention of this Article when it results from the use of force which is no more than absolutely necessary:

    (a) in defence of any person from unlawful violence;
    (b) in order to effect a lawful arrest or to prevent the escape of a person lawfully detained;
    (c) in action lawfully taken for the purpose of quelling a riot or insurrection.

Article 3

Prohibition of Torture

No one shall be subject to torture or to inhuman or degrading treatment or punishment.

Article 4

Prohibition of Slavery and Forced Labour

1. No one shall be held in slavery or servitude.

2. No one shall be required to perform forced or compulsory labour.

3. For the purpose of this Article the term "forced or compulsory labour" shall not include:

    (a) any work required to be done in the ordinary course of detention imposed according to the provisions of Article 5 of this Convention or during conditional release from such detention;
    (b) any service of a military character or, in case of conscientious objectors in countries where they are recognised, service exacted instead of compulsory military service;
    (c) any service exacted in case of an emergency or calamity threatening the life or well-being of the community;
    (d) any work or service which forms part of normal civic obligations.

Article 5

Right to Liberty and Security

1. Everyone has the right to liberty and security of person. No one shall be deprived of his liberty save in the following cases and in accordance with a procedure prescribed by law:

    (a) the lawful detention of a person after conviction by a competent court;

(b) the lawful arrest or detention of a person for non-compliance with the lawful order of a court or in order to secure the fulfilment of any obligations prescribed by law;

(c) the lawful arrest or detention of a person effected for the purpose of bringing him before the competent legal authority on reasonable suspicion of having committed an offence or when it is reasonably considered necessary to prevent his committing an offence or fleeing after having done so;

(d) the detention of a minor by lawful order for the purpose of educational supervision or his lawful detention for the purpose of bringing him before the competent legal authority;

(e) the lawful detention of persons for the prevention of the spreading of infectious diseases, of persons of unsound mind, alcoholics or drug addicts or vagrants;

(f) the lawful arrest or detention of a person to prevent his effecting an unauthorised entry into the country or of a person against whom action is being taken with a view to deportation or extradition.

2. Everyone who is arrested shall be informed promptly, in a language which he understands, of the reasons for his arrest and of any charge against him.

3. Everyone arrested or detained in accordance with the provisions of paragraph 1(c) of this Article shall be brought promptly before a judge or other officer authorised by law to exercise judicial power and shall be entitled to trial within a reasonable time or to release pending trial. Release may be conditioned by guarantees to appear for trial.

4. Everyone who is deprived of his liberty by arrest or detention shall be entitled to take proceedings by which the lawfulness of his detention shall be decided speedily by a court and his release ordered if the detention is not lawful.

5. Everyone who has been the victim of arrest or detention in contravention of the provisions of this Article shall have an enforceable right to compensation.

Article 6

Right to a Fair Trial

1. In the determination of his civil rights and obligations or of any criminal charge against him, everyone is entitled to a fair and public hearing within a reasonable time by an independent and impartial tribunal established by law. Judgment shall be pronounced publicly but the press and public may be excluded from all or part of the trial in the interest of morals, public order or national security in a democratic society, where the interests of juveniles or the protection of the private life of the parties so require, or to the extent strictly necessary in the opinion of the court in special circumstances where publicity would prejudice the interests of justice.

2. Everyone charged with a criminal offence shall be presumed innocent until proved guilty according to law.

3. Everyone charged with a criminal offence has the following minimum rights:

(a) to be informed promptly, in a language which he understands and in detail, of the nature and cause of the accusation against him;

(b) to have adequate time and facilities for the preparation of his defence;

(c) to defend himself in person or through legal assistance of his own choosing or, if he has not sufficient means to pay for legal assistance, to be given it free when the interests of justice so require;

(d) to examine or have examined witnesses against him and to obtain the attendance and examination of witnesses on his behalf under the same conditions as witnesses against him;

(e) to have the free assistance of an interpreter if he cannot understand or speak the language used in court.

Article 7

No Punishment without Law

1. No one shall be held guilty of any criminal offence on account of any act or omission which did not constitute a criminal offence under national or international law at the time when it was committed. Nor shall a heavier penalty be imposed than the one that was applicable at the time the criminal offence was committed.

2. This Article shall not prejudice the trial and punishment of any person for any act or omission which, at the time when it was committed, was criminal according to the general principles of law recognised by civilised nations.

Article 8

Right to Respect for Private and Family Life

1. Everyone has the right to respect for his private and family life, his home and his correspondence.

2. There shall be no interference by a public authority with the exercise of this right except such as is in accordance with the law and is necessary in a democratic society in the interests of national security, public safety or the economic well-being of the country, for the prevention of disorder or crime, for the protection of health or morals, or for the protection of the rights and freedoms of others.

Article 9

Freedom of Thought, Conscience and Religion

1. Everyone has the right to freedom of thought, conscience and religion; this right includes freedom to change his religion or belief and freedom, either alone or in community with others and in public or private, to manifest his religion or belief, in worship, teaching, practice and observance.

2. Freedom to manifest one's religion or beliefs shall be subject only to such limitations as are prescribed by law and are necessary in a democratic society in the interests of public safety, for the protection of public order, health or morals, or for the protection of the rights and freedoms of others.

Article 10

Freedom of Expression

1. Everyone has the right to freedom of expression. This right shall include freedom to hold opinions and to receive and impart information and ideas without interference by public authority and regardless of frontiers. This Article shall not prevent States from requiring the licensing of broadcasting, television or cinema enterprises.

2. The exercise of these freedoms, since it carries with it duties and responsibilities, may be subject to such formalities, conditions, restrictions or penalties as are prescribed by law and are necessary in a democratic society, in the interests of national security, territorial integrity or public safety, for the prevention of disorder or crime, for the protection of health or morals, for the protection of the reputation or rights of others, for preventing the disclosure of information received in confidence, or for maintaining the authority and impartiality of the judiciary.

Article 11

Freedom of Assembly and Association

1. Everyone has the right to freedom of peaceful assembly and to freedom of association with others, including the right to form and to join trade unions for the protection of his interests.

2. No restrictions shall be placed on the exercise of these rights other than such as are prescribed by law and are necessary in a democratic society in the interests of national security or public safety, for the prevention of disorder or crime, for the protection of health or morals or for the protection of the rights and freedoms of others. This Article shall not prevent the imposition of lawful restrictions on the exercise of these rights by members of the armed forces, of the police or of the administration of the State.

Article 12

Right to Marry

Men and women of marriageable age have the right to marry and to found a family, according to the national laws governing the exercise of this right.

Article 14

Prohibtion of Discrimination

The enjoyment of the rights and freedoms set forth in this Convention shall be secured without discrimination on any ground such as sex, race, colour, language, religion, political or other opinion, national or social origin, association with a national minority, property, birth or other status.

Article 16

Restrictions on Political Activity of Aliens

Nothing in Articles 10, 11 and 14 shall be regarded as preventing the High Contracting Parties from imposing restrictions on the political activity of aliens.

Article 17

Prohibition of Abuse of Rights

Nothing in this Convention may be interpreted as implying for any State, group or person any right to engage in any activity or perform any act aimed at the destruction of any of the rights and freedoms set forth herein or at their limitation to a greater extent than is provided for in the Convention.

Article 18

Limitation on use of Restrictions on Rights

The restrictions permitted under this Convention to the said rights and freedoms shall not be applied for any purpose other than those for which they have been prescribed.

PART II

The First Protocol

Article 1

Protection of Property

Every natural or legal person is entitled to the peaceful enjoyment of his possessions. No one shall be deprived of his possessions except in the public interest and subject to the conditions provided for by law and by the general principles of international law.

The preceding provisions shall not, however, in any way impair the right of a

State to enforce such laws as it deems necessary to control the use of property in accordance with the general interest or to secure the payment of taxes or other contributions or penalties.

Article 2

Right to Education

No person shall be denied the right to education. In the exercise of any functions which it assumes in relation to education and to teaching, the State shall respect the right of parents to ensure such education and teaching in conformity with their own religious and philosophical convictions.

Article 3

Right to Free Elections

The High Contracting Parties undertake to hold free elections at reasonable intervals by secret ballot, under conditions which will ensure the free expression of the opinion of the people in the choice of the legislature.

PART III

The Sixth Protocol

Article 1

Abolition of the Death Penalty

The death penalty shall be abolished. No one shall be condemned to such penalty or executed.

Article 2

Death Penalty in Time of War

A State may make provision in its law for the death penalty in respect of acts committed in time of war or of imminent threat of war; such penalty shall be applied only in the instances laid down in the law and in accordance with its provisions. The State shall communicate to the Secretary General of the Council of Europe the relevant provisions of that law.